Psychological Problems, Social Issues, and Law

Second Edition

Murray Levine
State University of New York at Buffalo

Leah Wallach
West London Mental Health
National Health Service Trust

David Levine
University of California,
Hastings College of the Law

PEARSON

Boston • New York • San Francisco • Mexico City • Montreal
Toronto • London • Madrid • Munich • Paris • Hong Kong
Singapore • Tokyo • Cape Town • Sydney

Editor in Chief: Susan Hartman	Manufacturing Buyer: JoAnne Sweeney
Marketing Manager: Karen Natale	Electronic Composition: WestWords, Inc.
Production Supervisor: Karen Mason	Photo Researcher: Annie Pickert/Naomi Rudov
Editorial Production Service: WestWords, Inc.	Cover Administrator: Elena Sidorova
Composition Buyer: Linda Cox	

For related titles and support materials, visit our online catalog at www.ablongman.com.

Between the time website information is gathered and then published, it is not unusual for
some sites to have closed. Also, the transcription of URLs can result in typographical errors.
The publisher would appreciate notification where these errors occur so that they may be corrected in subsequent editions.

Library of Congress Cataloging-in-Publication Data

Levine, Murray,
    Psychological problems, social issues, and the law / Murray Levine, Leah Wallach,
  David I. Levine.
      p.   cm.
    ISBN 0-205-47454-3
    1. , Forensic Psychology. 2. Law—Psychological aspects. 3. Insanity—Jurisprudence—
United States. 4. Psychologists—Legal status, laws, etc.—United States. I. Wallach, Leah, II.
Levine, David I. III. Title.

KF8965.L48 2006
349.73—dc22

                                                                    2006050133

Printed in the United States of America

10 9 8 7 6 5 4 3 2 1   11 10   09   08   07   06

To the memory of my mother, my father and my sister Elayne, all of whom were good people who had harder lives than they deserved.

—ML

To Michael, with thanks for his sometimes impatient, never inconstant, always loving support.

—LW

To Joanna, Arie, Howard, Jayme, Liora, Paul and Tama: I couldn't do it without you.

—DL

Contents

2 Social Science and Psychological Influences in Law 25

3 Prediction, Bail, and the *Tarasoff* Duty 51

8   The Death Penalty   216

9   Juvenile Court and the Legal Processing of Children and Adolescents   248

10   Protecting Children: Child Protection Proceedings   *283*

11   Children and the Criminal Process   *313*

12   Intimate Partner Violence   *341*

13   Child Custody   *377*

16   Psychological Tests and Discrimination in Education and in Employment   *473*

Preface

This second edition follows much the same format as the first edition. We have made some changes in response to the helpful comments made by the users of the text. We especially wanted to revise the text to enhance its readability. We have made other changes to keep the text current, despite the rapidly changing nature of the field. Perhaps a third of the references are new. The student is urged to keep up with reading the daily newspapers because there are frequently articles of relevance for this text. In order to illustrate the generality and variations of the issues, we have included some items describing responses in the United Kingdom, where Leah Wallach currently resides, to problems we discuss in the American context. David Levine, our new co-author, is professor of law at the University of California, Hastings College of the Law. He has brought to this task his knowledge of the field and his editorial skills. We look forward to your comments on this new edition to help us keep it relevant for students.

 Introduction

Law is a human invention. It is designed to solve the problem of how we can live together while preserving individual liberties. We have to give up some freedom in order to live together peacefully and to have the benefits that come from living in an orderly society that protects us and creates opportunities for our development, and happiness.

The Preamble to the Constitution expresses these aims very well:

> We the People of the United States, in Order to form a more perfect Union, establish Justice, insure domestic Tranquility, provide for the common defence, promote the general Welfare, and secure the Blessings of Liberty to ourselves and our Posterity, do ordain and establish this Constitution for the United States of America.

Because we live in a complex society and in a multidimensional world, conflicts inevitably emerge between the desire for individual freedom and the necessity for social limitations on freedom, between competing social values, and between the interests of different groups and different individuals. Law provides both the methods and the substantive rules for resolving such conflicts fairly. Laws tell us how we should live collectively; either explicitly or implicitly, laws also tell us why we should live that way for the common good.

Laws are intended to control or to guide human behavior, and reflect implicit psychological assumptions about human behavior. Those assumptions can be analyzed using the tools of psychology and other social sciences. Also, we can examine how legal concepts, set down as abstractions, are implemented in social contexts through various formal and informal social agencies. In order to understand whether the law's purposes are fulfilled or not, we have to examine how law works itself out in action. The empirical examination of the legal system cannot be accomplished through the lens of any single discipline. Universities are typically subdivided into various disciplines, including law, psychology, sociology, history, philosophy, political science, anthropology, and economics, but the problems in the world are not broken up in the same way. It is essential to use the diverse tools of different disciplines to help us to understand the effects of law on human behavior and to appreciate the assumptions law makes about human behavior.

In writing *Psychological Problems, Social Issues, and Law*, we express our fundamental belief that the understanding of law in society requires multidisciplinary perspectives. In each chapter, we present something of the history of a problem, something about the underlying human issues, the legal doctrines and procedures, and the empirical research bearing on the problem and on the legal doctrine. We did not seek to be comprehensive in our review either of legal doctrine or the body of social science research. We intended to state fundamental propositions accurately, and to describe fundamental research findings. We often review the intended and unintended consequences of law or doctrine as implemented, and try to develop an appreciation of the social forces that may be involved.

We will not present a chapter-by-chapter précis here as there is a detailed table of contents. Rather, we will outline the organization of this text.

Organizing Principles

Each chapter includes the following sections:

- A brief history of the problem that is the subject of the chapter and of the policies intended to address the problem. Here we illustrate how historical developments create new social and legal problems or lead people to frame in new ways the problems that are always prevalent in society.

- A discussion of the legal issues involved in the societal response to the problem, including a history of how relevant legal policy developed. We present the background law in accord with our contention that psychological research needs to be relevant to the legal issues if it is to influence policy and decision making.

- A summary of psychological research bearing on the problem. Psychologists derive their authority as experts, consultants, or advisors from several different kinds of research: clinical forensic work, which focuses on assessment, classification, and treatment of individuals; experimental work, which examines factors influencing behavior in legal contexts through controlled study; and evaluation research, which assesses the outcome of changes in the law or in legal procedures. These in turn have built on more basic research. We include some examples of each kind of research and note the strengths and limitations of different methodologies. We illustrate good research by describing some characteristics of well-designed studies.

- A discussion of professional responsibility. We consider the ethical and professional obligations of psychologists who bring their knowledge of the problem into the legal arena.

Content

The content of the book is shaped by our interest in social problems, public policy, and law as it is implemented and experienced in people's daily lives. In keeping with these interests, we have given somewhat more space to family and civil law issues than has been traditional in psychology and law textbooks. Our goal is to provide a broad perspective from which readers can view the work of social scientists and jurists, clinicians and judges in the larger context of the social and historical systems of which they are a part.

Just as each chapter opens by presenting the historical and legal background of the problem under discussion, so the first two chapters of the book set the legal and historical stage for the chapters that follow.

Chapter 1 describes the U.S. legal system in general. We include this brief review so that the "forest" of the legal system is in the student's mind when we examine the "trees" of each topic.

Chapter 2 looks at the history of the interaction between social science and the legal system, and introduces two themes that recur throughout the book: (1) how differences in the way law and social science conceptualize and study a problem affect the dialogue between them; and (2) when there is sufficient scientific knowledge in a given area to justify expert testimony or heed the recommendations of social and clinical scientists.

In Chapter 3, we introduce the problem of predicting "dangerousness." We discuss both the inherent limitations of predictive science and the moral issues raised by identifying high risk individuals. We refer back to the methodology described in this chapter later when we consider prediction in the context of juvenile justice, custody evaluations, and psychological testing.

In Chapters 4 through 8, we deal with issues important in the criminal justice system and especially in jury trials. We concentrate on the criminal justice system because of the large body of research in this area. However, we discuss some issues in civil law in Chapter 4 on competencies and in Chapter 5 on the jury trial. Chapters 5 and 6, on the jury trial and on eyewitness testimony respectively, discuss highlights of the rich body of research bearing on the trial process and on pretrial procedures, and consider some applications of research. Chapters 7, 8, and 9 address three controversial aspects of the justice system's response to crime: the insanity defense (Chapter 7), the death penalty (Chapter 8), and the juvenile justice system (Chapter 9).

Chapters 10 through 16 discuss social problems in the context of the legal system. We have selected problems for discussion that affect the lives of large numbers of people each year: child protection (Chapter 10), children as witnesses (Chapter 11), domestic violence (Chapter 12), custody disputes (Chapter 13), abortion (Chapter 14), sexual harassment (Chapter 15), and psychological tests (Chapter 16).

In Chapter 17, we examine the legal and ethical regulation or social control of the professions. All who will enter professions or who are the clients or patients of professionals are affected by such regulation. Yet few students have any detailed knowledge about its origins or purposes. We also consider malpractice suits and the repressed memory controversy in this chapter because of the effects of the controversy on the climate within which many mental health professionals and researchers operate.

Social and clinical scientists have conducted a great deal of research in all the areas discussed in the book In doing so, they have helped greatly to delineate the issues for the legal system. Courts often frame the adjudicative and political issues in therapeutic terms and use, for better or worse, clinical recommendations and studies by scholars and researchers.

We have attempted to develop the critical value and legal arguments bearing on each topic, many of which are highly controversial and elicit strong opinions. We have tried to maintain a balance when dealing with social controversy. We try to present several sides of arguments and to allow students with strong opinions to test their views. We don't intend to change opinions; we do intend to make the arguments explicit, and to point to relevant data where they are available. We have made a conscious effort to present materials to avoid the "political correctness" of the left or of the right that would get in the way of grappling intellectually with difficult problems.

 Audience

Psychological Problems, Social Issues, and Law has profited from the insightful and helpful comments and suggestions of undergraduates who have used earlier versions of the book over many years. We look forward to enlisting our students as critics and research assistants as we continue to develop the text. This book is directed toward upper-division undergraduate students and to first-year students in graduate and professional programs. It focuses on psychology, but we believe the book is appropriate for students in social work, in counseling, in sociology, and in some policy or government programs. It might also be useful in a prelaw curriculum, and some law schools might find it useful as an introductory text on psychology and law. General readers may also find this text of interest.

We don't believe that extensive prerequisites are necessary to understand the material in the book. Nevertheless, it will help if a student has had courses on basic research methods and abnormal psychology, and some introduction to statistical and psychometric concepts.

We hope our readers come away with an appreciation of the intimate interrelationships between the fields of psychology and law and with an approach to thinking about problems at the interface of the two fields. We would like to provide the reader as citizen with a better basis for understanding events that appear in the news on a daily basis and to encourage the reader as student to go on to become a professional contributor to this complex and exciting field.

Learning Aids

We have tried to write in as straightforward a way as we could while remaining faithful to the complexity of the ideas. To illustrate the human importance of the legal and empirical problems, we include cases and examples in every chapter, either in the text or in boxes. Each chapter after the first two includes a boxed feature, "A Legal Case in Point." To make the book more accessible, the chapters are broken up visually with photographs.

Each chapter includes an introduction, a summary, discussion questions, and a list of key terms designed to help students organize and retain the material as they read. The chapters contain cross-references to related material elsewhere in the text. Legal terms are highlighted in the text, and a glossary of those legal terms can be found at the end of the text. For qualified instructors, a bank of test questions and teaching suggestions has been prepared.

Acknowledgments

We would like to thank the following reviewers for this edition, provided by the publisher, for their excellent critiques:

John Lemmon, San Francisco State University
Gary McCullough, The University of Texas of the Permian Basin
Judith Rauenzahn, Kutztown University
Virginia Ryan, The Sage Colleges
Stefan Schulenberg, University of Mississippi

We are also thankful for the reviews and comments offered by previous edition reviewers:

George L. Blau, University of Wyoming
Bette L. Bottoms, University of Illinois at Chicago
Susan Clayton, The College of Wooster
James V. Couch, James Madison University
Jennifer L. Devenport, California State University, Fullerton
Carol Diener, University of Illinois
Robert E. Emery, University of Virginia
Dennis Fox, University of Illinois at Springfield
Thomas J. Guilmette, Providence College
Charles R. Honts, Boise State University
Kristine M. Jacquin, The Union Institute
Norman E. Kinney, Southeast Missouri State University
Margaret Bull Kovera, Florida International University
Daniel Linz, University of California, Santa Barbara
Sharon Portwood, University of Missouri–Kansas City
Diana L. D. Punzo, Earlham College
Beth Schwartz-Kenney, Randolph-Macon Woman's College
Jerry I. Shaw, California State University, Northridge
Paul Skolnick, California State University, Northridge
Mark Small, Southern Illinois University
Gregory J. Van Rybroek, University of Wisconsin–Madison
and Mendota Mental Health Institute
Bruce J. Winick, University of Miami School of Law

The book's final form owes much to the guidance and good work of our editor in chief, Susan Hartman, and her talented editorial staff.

CHAPTER **1**

The American Legal System

If social science research and practice are to be relevant to legal problems—'on point,' as our legal colleagues say—the student of psychology and law needs to understand the context of legal decision making and the powers and limitations of legal actors. In this chapter, we will set the legal stage by briefly describing

- the philosophical and historical background of our legal system;
- the federal system (federalism) that makes us the United States;
- the separation of legislative, executive, and judicial powers into independent branches of government;
- the concept of 'due process of law';
- the federal and state judicial systems;
- civil law and criminal law;
- case law and common law;
- constitutional law.

The material presented here will provide important background for understanding psychology and law problems. We will be emphasizing those features of our system most closely related to the social problems we discuss in the subsequent chapters. We will not be dealing with commercial matters, defense, the military, immigration, or a myriad of other topics related to the work of government.

Historical Roots

Our system of law follows traditions inherited from England by the 13 original colonies and is based on the political philosophy of the English rationalist and French Enlightenment philosophers. From these writers, our founders adapted a belief in natural rights—the rights to life, liberty, and pursuit of happiness asserted in our Declaration of Independence—and the idea of a **social contract**. To secure the benefits of society, individuals cede the right to regulate specified aspects of their behavior to a government whose rule they are then obligated to accept. In return, the government is obligated to promote the common welfare and to settle disputes in consonance with the community's sense of right and justice. When we broke away from the English king, we justified the action by explaining in the Declaration of Independence that the English government had failed to hold up its end of the social bargain.

Elements of eighteenth-century thinking remain fundamental to our system of government and our understanding of law.

- Our system is based on the belief that people should have the freedom to pursue their own legitimate interests, though within limits necessary for us to function as a society. The U.S. Constitution (see Figure 1.1) explicitly limits the power of government and specifies conditions (e.g., due process—see below) that the government must follow when it proposes to restrict individual liberty.
- Our government is organized as a contract between the people and the government. The nation is defined by this system of government, not by shared genes and historic territory. In the federal and state constitutions, citizens grant powers to the government to pursue specific ends, for example, to keep order, regulate disputes, punish wrongdoers, and promote commerce.

- We believe in rule by law, not individuals, and believe laws should be an expression of common values.

The question of how best to balance individual liberties with the need to restrain individual interests for the greater social good is central to many of the legal and social controversies we will discuss in this book.

Federalism

The **U.S. Constitution** is a compact among the original 13 states to form a federation, or union. The states agreed to yield some of their **sovereign power** (supreme, independent authority) to the central government, a system known as **federalism**. They established the Constitution and the laws made under its authority as "the Supreme law of the land" (U.S. Constitution, Article VI) in order "to establish Justice, insure domestic Tranquillity, provide for the common defense, promote the general Welfare, and secure the Blessings of Liberty to ourselves and our Posterity" (Preamble to the Constitution). Since 1787, 37 new states have been accepted into the Union, and each new state has agreed to the terms of the compact.

Limits of Federal Power

The Constitution limits the power of the federal government to ensure that local self-government and individual rights will be preserved. Article I (Section 8) lists what Congress can do, its **enumerated powers;** Section 9 lists constraints on congressional power. However, citizens who feared abuses of federal power did not consider these safeguards sufficient. In 1791, the states **ratified** (i.e., approved by vote of their legislatures) the first ten amendments to the Constitution. They were called the **Bill of Rights** because they enumerated fundamental rights that citizens had won in the American Revolution and wished to preserve against encroachment by a central government. Hyman and Tarrant (1975) described these amendments as: "a bill of wrongs which the national government was not to commit, more than a decalog of positive rights" (p. 31). As interpreted by the U.S. Supreme Court, the Bill of Rights also constrains the power of state governments to interfere with individual liberties and rights; the post–Civil War amendments (the Thirteenth Amendment, prohibiting involuntary servitude; the Fourteenth, providing for equal protection and due process; and the Fifteenth, providing for voting rights, intended to protect the newly freed slaves) do so explicitly.

State Sovereignty

Each state has its own constitution. Provisions vary greatly from state to state. State constitutions must be consistent with the U.S. Constitution. However, state governments yielded all **sovereignty** (supreme authority) to the federal government only over specified matters. In other areas of government, the states remain sovereign and, within constitutional restraints, act independently (e.g., the Tenth Amendment provided that powers not delegated to the federal government are reserved to the states or the people). The states retain broad authority to govern family, commercial, and contractual relationships, to resolve most problems and disputes; and to provide services in many of

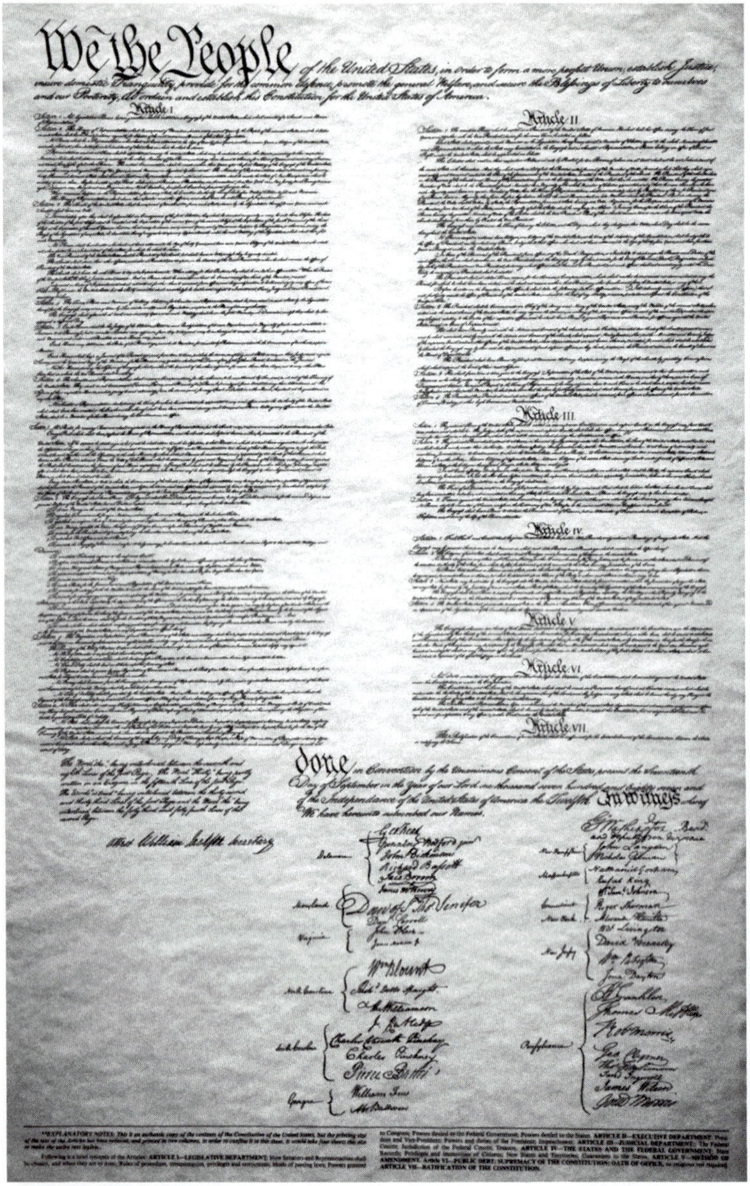

Figure 1.1

The U.S. Constitution

The U.S. Constitution is the "supreme law of the Land." Congress adopted the Constitution in 1787 and it was ratified by the states in that year and the next. The Bill of Rights was added as the first ten amendments in 1791.

the areas of special interest to the social and clinical sciences, including health, education, welfare, safety, and crime control.

Types of powers. Government powers are divided into two broad classes, **police power** and *parens patriae* (parent of the nation) **powers.** The state's police power gives it the authority to make laws designed to protect the health and safety of the population. The criminal laws are examples of the exercise of the police power. *Parens patriae* powers are derived from the conception of the state as a higher "parent," responsible for the welfare of all of its citizens. The provision of hospital care by state or local government, or welfare payments to persons in need, are examples of the state's exercise of its *parens patriae* power. Sometimes the distinction between welfare and policing is not all that clear. The involuntary hospitalization of a person diagnosed as mentally ill is partially an exercise of police power, designed to protect the ill person or society from harm. However, to the degree that treatment is provided to help the hospitalized person, the state is exercising its *parens patriae* power as well.

Congress and the states. Congress's authority to impose legislation on the states in their areas of sovereignty is limited. However, Congress can strongly influence state policy without directly mandating specific policies. In the areas of education, welfare, and health, Congress typically provides funding to states that establish recommended programs. Congress made federal highway funds to states contingent on states raising the drinking age to 21. This does not mean, however, that states have no discretion as to how federal law will be applied. Even when states pass legislation to enable them to participate in a federally sponsored health or welfare program, such as Medicare or Medicaid, they still retain the power to develop their own programs within federal guidelines. That means the details of implementation may differ from state to state. The state may accept none of the money and go without the program, or create a program of its own using state money only. But if the state wants the federal funds, it must pass state legislation that meets the requirements of the federal act. For example, many states objected to the tests required by the federal No Child Left Behind Act. In 2005, Utah Governor Jon Huntsman signed state legislation specifying the use of the Utah Performance Assessment System rather than federally required tests under the No Child Left Behind Act. Utah claimed it was already doing well in improving educational performance; it had aligned its curriculum to its own state tests and test scores had been rising. Because Utah would not be conforming with federal law, Secretary of Education Margaret Spelling threatened to withhold $76 million in federal aid from Utah (Associated Press, 2005a). These cases are usually settled by compromise, by waiver granted by the administrative agency, as in the case of Utah; or sometimes by lawsuits. As another example, a number of law school faculties prohibited giving military recruiters access to law students because the miliary discriminated against gays. In response, Congress required the Department of Defense to deny federal funding to institutions that denied access to the military for recruitment. The law schools, arguing the provision violated their First Amendment rights to free speech and association, took the case all the way to the U.S. Supreme Court, where they lost. The Court said that funds could be denied and that the law schools had other ways to express their views of discrimination in the military against gays (*Rumsfeld v. Forum, 2006*).

Laws can be different in different states. One important result of our federalism is that the laws about some issues are different in different states. For example, prior to the passage of the Nineteenth Amendment, women could vote in some states, but not in others. Today, whether or not a teacher can administer corporal punishment in a school, when an assault is a **felony** (a serious crime punishable by more than a year in prison) and when it is a **misdemeanor** (a lesser crime), and most of the other laws that most directly affect people's ordinary lives (e.g., divorce) are purely matters of state law. Sometimes nongovernmental organizations, such as the American Law Institute, write **uniform or model legislation** in areas where interstate consistency and cooperation would be especially useful. State legislatures look to these model codes when writing their own laws. States may adopt all, some, or none of the model legislation, making for some uniformity in the law in different states. An example is the Uniform Commercial Code governing a large variety of business transactions. The provisions of the commercial codes are similar from state to state, but not identical. As another example, the American Law Institute (2000) has promulgated a set of "principles" of family dissolution law with recommendations for legislation, including (in appendices) model language for the recommended changes in state laws. State legislatures may look to these statements if they consider revisions of their family law statutes.

Uniformity of law or states' rights? In the last century, some conservative thinkers have supported interpretations of federalism that provide support for states' authority, while liberals and progressives have tended to support a more active and influential federal government. Before the civil rights legislation of the 1960s, the term *states' rights* was often understood as a code meaning that states should be allowed to practice racial segregation. Ever since 1968 under President Richard Nixon, Congress has often provided funds to states with fewer specifications and strings attached so that states can have more room to implement the laws in their own way. Welfare reform is a good example. In 1996, Congress permitted states to experiment with their own welfare-to-work programs so that different models emerged in different states. Although some believe that greater uniformity in law is fairer and more desirable, others argue that the ability of the states to experiment as the "laboratories of democracy," and to tailor approaches to the particular needs of their communities, will lead to more effective solutions to social problems. Libertarianism is an emerging philosophical and political position that essentially decries all forms of federal or state government regulation. Proponents prefer that conflicts be resolved by market forces. Members of this group may oppose state licensing laws as restrictive, and rent control or zoning or environmental protection regulation as unreasonable infringements on property rights and therefore unconstitutional (Rosen, 2005).

Refereeing the Balance

The Supreme Court of the United States is the ultimate arbiter of the legal relationship between the state and federal governments. The Supreme Court may void a state law it determines is not compatible with the U.S. Constitution or a federal law it determines encroaches on powers the Constitution reserves for the states. It may also void a federal law if it finds the Constitution does not grant the federal government the authority to act. The federal Brady gun-control law is an example. James Brady was President Ronald Reagan's press secretary. He was shot and seriously injured in the assassination attempt on President Reagan in 1981. The Brady Law required local police to conduct background checks on persons who applied to purchase guns. The Supreme Court declared this provision unconstitutional. They ruled that the Congress did not have the specific authority to tell state officials what to do in this area (*Printz v. United States,*

1997). In still another case, *United States v. Lopez* (1995), the U.S. Supreme Court held that Congress did not have the power to ban guns near public schools. It also held in *United States v. Morrison* (2000) that the Congress had no authority to create a civil remedy for money damages for rape under the Violence against Women Act. In these latter two cases, the U.S. Supreme Court ruled that the Congress' powers to act under the Commerce Clause did not extend to these circumstances. California law allows people to grow marijuana for personal medical use on a physician's recommendation. U.S. law makes no exceptions to prosecution for possession under the federal Controlled Substances Act. A group of plaintiffs sought to prevent the federal government from enforcing federal law for persons in California who meet the requirements of California's Compassionate Use Act. They argued that in this instance, state law could override provisions of a federal law. The U.S. Supreme Court (*Gonzales v. Raich*, 2005) decided that federal law trumped state law in this instance, and that federal authorities can prosecute those who use or distribute marijuana for medical purposes even if they follow provisions of California law. In *Gonzales v. Oregon* (2006), however, the U.S. Supreme Court ruled that the attorney general could not override Oregon state law and prohibit doctors from prescribing regulated drugs in physician-assisted suicides. The rules do not seem to be completely consistent.

⊠ The Separation of Powers

The Constitution establishes three separate branches of government: the legislative, the executive, and the judicial, giving each different powers. Article I gives "All **legislative Powers**" to the Congress, which consists of the House of Representatives and the Senate. Article II gives the "**executive Power**" to the president, who is charged with carrying out (executing) the laws passed by Congress. Article III vests the "**judicial Power**" in "one supreme Court, and in such inferior Courts as the Congress may from time to time ordain and establish." The judicial power extends to all "cases and controversies arising under the Constitution, the Laws of the United States and Treaties."

Checks and Balances

The **separation of powers** was intended to allow each branch of government the benifits of the **checks and balances system,** which is to balance the others and to provide checks against arbitrary actions by any one branch. The president can veto legislation by Congress. The Congress can override a presidential veto with a two-thirds vote. The president appoints all federal judges, but the nominations must be confirmed ("advice and consent") by the Senate. The president and federal judges may be impeached in a formal process by the Congress, but they cannot be dismissed merely because of an unpopular decision.

The authority of the judiciary was augmented early in our history by the Supreme Court under Chief Justice John Marshall. In *Marbury v. Madison* (1803), Marshall delivered an opinion establishing that the judicial branch had the power to rule on the constitutionality of laws passed by Congress, a power not explicitly granted to the courts in the Constitution. Since then, when the constitutionality of actions by the other federal branches is challenged, the judiciary decides whether the other branches are acting within their proper authority. In 2006, the U.S. Supreme Court held the President had no congressionally approved authority to use a military tribunal to try an 'enemy combatant' held in Guantanomo Bay (*Hamdan v. Rumsfeld,* 2006).

Overlap between the powers. The separation of powers is not as sharp in practice as it is on paper. The Constitution is the supreme law of the land, but it consists of relatively few words and must be interpreted. Legislation often sets out only very general policies. Even when they are detailed, statutes can never be detailed enough to cover every situation that might arise. Because statutes and constitutional provisions cannot cover every eventuality, the other branches of government sometimes act as "lawmakers" by how they interpet and implement the law.

Administrative law. Congress frequently gives the executive branch explicit authority to develop regulations that specify how a more general statute is to be implemented. For example, Congress wrote laws establishing federal agencies such as the Social Security Administration, the Veterans Administration, and the Federal Trade Commission. It charged these agencies with developing regulations to implement programs described in broader terms in the legislation. Important examples for our purposes include the regulations governing the granting of disability under the Social Security Act; regulations governing payments under Medicare and Medicaid; regulations affecting employment discrimination, sexual harassment, and welfare; and regulations affecting the education of handicapped children. Regulations promulgated by executive agencies following a grant of congressional authority have the same force as any other law.

The branch of law dealing with administrative agencies and regulations is called **administrative law.** The practices of administrative law are governed by the federal Administrative Procedures Act (5 U.S.C. Secs. 551 et seq.). As part of the process of developing new regulations, agencies must publish drafts of the proposed rules for review and comment by interested parties before they publish final regulations. By commenting, advocates have the opportunity to influence the final regulations. For example, the Education for All Handicapped Children Act required states that accepted federal money to provide a "free, appropriate public education" for all children with disabilities. Advocates had an opportunity to comment on the regulations proposed by the secretary of health and human services. The secretary then issued final regulations saying what states should provide for these children. The final regulations in part reflected comments that advocates had submitted (see Box 1.1).

Administrative appeals. Disputes about the meaning and applicability of the regulations are adjudicated initially through an administrative process, which often has

---

Box 1.1

Regulations Governing Education of the Handicapped

Amy Rowley's family argued that, to give their deaf child an "appropriate" education, the local school board must provide her with a sign language interpreter in the classroom. The local school board refused. The school board said that the law did not require this specific (and expensive) form of support. The family appealed through administrative appeals procedures, and through the federal courts. The case was finally settled in the U.S. Supreme Court. The Court ruled that the law did not require schools to provide individual sign language interpreters for every deaf child, clarifying the limits of "appropriate" (Board of Education v. Rowley, 1982).

several levels of appeal. If the person with a complaint exhausts the administrative appeals procedures, he or she can go to court and ask a judge to review the agency's decision. The courts will decide whether the administrative ruling at issue is consistent with the regulations, and the intent of the original statute, and, at times, whether the regulations themselves are legitimate. In this way, the courts sometimes refine the meaning of statutes.

Proponents of the libertarian view believe such administrative regulation of economic enterprises, contracts, and personal liberties is unconstitutional. This group seeks to restore what it believes was the original intention of the framers of the Constitution, and to undo much of the administrative state that has grown since 1937 under the Franklin D. Roosevelt administration (Rosen, 2005).

Interplay among the Branches

When the three branches of government don't agree, they can use their particular powers to promote their own policies. The abortion controversy presents a good example of how the separation of powers and the political process interact in shaping policies about a controversial issue. In *Roe v. Wade* (1973) and subsequent decisions (*Webster v. Reproductive Health Services* (1989); *Planned Parenthood of SE Pa. v. Casey* (1992), the U.S. Supreme Court ruled that state governments could not prohibit abortion but could regulate it. Under the first President Bush, the secretary of health and human services initiated regulations prohibiting physicians in clinics that received federal money from discussing abortion with their patients. The policy drew strong opposition from pro-choice advocates, from the medical establishment, and from other citizens who did not like the idea of government interfering with doctor–patient relationships. An abortion provider who was affected by the regulation challenged it in the courts. The U.S. Supreme Court, more conservative in 1991 than the Court that decided *Roe v. Wade,* held that the rule prohibiting discussion of abortion with patients was not an unconstitutional restriction on free speech nor on the right to obtain an abortion (*Rust v. Sullivan,* 1991). Some clinics consequently refused federal funds rather than limit the information doctors could give patients; others changed their policies to get the funding. Congress, the legislative branch, then passed a law clarifying their legislative intentions by prohibiting restrictions on discussions between doctors and their patients in federally funded clinics. President George H. W. Bush vetoed the law. However, in response to intense criticism from advocacy groups, President Bush issued an executive order in effect watering down the application of the rule. When President Bill Clinton took office, he rescinded the regulation by an executive order. In turn, one of President George W. Bush's first acts in office was to issue an executive order to prevent organizations either here or abroad that advocated, promoted, or provided abortions from receiving federal funds (Turner, 2001). Each branch of government acted within its realm of power to advocate and modify policies.

Separation of Powers within State Government

The states also separate their governmental powers. The legislatures make laws, and the executive branch—the governor and members of the governor's cabinet—carry them out. Like Congress, the state legislatures often use the device of giving administrative agencies the power to implement legislation by developing administrative regulations. Each state also has a multilevel judiciary with the jurisdiction to interpret state laws and the state constitution.

⊠ The Special Role of the Judiciary

Those interested in the field of law and psychology must pay special attention to court decisions. The working meaning of laws is determined through court cases involving controversies about the application of law. The written records of judicial decisions provide source material for our understanding of what law means in practice and what factors enter into determining the meaning of law. The judiciary also has ultimate responsibility to protect individual rights. When the interests of the state and the rights of an individual conflict, the courts establish the limits of governmental action. In doing so, they are guided by a concept called *"due process of law."* It is the special role of the courts to define and defend this complex principle through their actions.

Due Process of Law

The Constitution prohibits state and federal governments from restricting individual liberties, broadly defined, except through due process of the law. **Due process** means, first of all, that governments and government agents cannot act arbitrarily. Governments, like citizens, must obey the law. In general, government cannot take action without first providing those affected with notice and an opportunity to be heard. On a deeper level, due process refers to the value we assign to individual rights and dignity. When the courts say that a government action violates due process, it is another way of saying that the action violates our fundamental values.

Legal scholars distinguish between *procedural due process* and *substantive due process.*

Procedural due process. **Procedural due process** refers to the manner in which the government undertakes an action that interferes with individual liberty. It means following the rules. A statute is enacted with due process when a legislature properly passes a law within its powers and the executive signs it into law. It violates due process if the executive acts without having the requisite authority. The term *due process* also applies to the manner in which the executive branch, including the police, implements the law and to the way in which the judiciary conducts trials. When an individual believes the government has taken an action against him or her without due process, the person can petition the courts to order the government to restore his or her rights, to refrain from the unlawful actions, or to compensate the person for the harms done. For example, in the Miranda ruling (*Miranda v. Arizona,* 1966), the Supreme Court decided that it was unfair—and a violation of the suspect's rights under the Fifth Amendment—to question suspects without telling them that they had a right to have a lawyer present (procedure); if the police got information this way, they couldn't use it in court. A state law that fails to give a consumer adequate notice and a hearing before a company can seize property purchased under an installment sales contract was held to be a violation of due process (*Fuentes v. Shevin,* 1972). In *Hamdi v. Rumsfeld* (2004), the U.S. Supreme Court ruled that a person detained in an American-run prison in Guantánamo Bay, Cuba, after having been captured in Afghanistan allegedly fighting against American troops, was entitled as a matter of due process to have access to a lawyer and to a judicial review of his detention. The Court acted to preserve fundamental rights even in a very difficult political atmosphere (see Box 1.2).

Box 1.2

11

The Special
Role of the
Judiciary

Due Process for "Enemy Combatants."

Yaser Esam Hamdi is an American citizen because he was born in Baton Rouge, Louisiana in 1980. His father, Esam Faoud Hamdi, was working there as a petroleum engineer. Shortly after Yaser's birth, the family moved back to Saudi Arabia. Yaser, a 20 year old college student, went to Afghanistan in July or August 2001 (before 9/11) to do relief work. He was captured in an active combat zone by the Northern Alliance who were fighting the Taliban. Yaser was turned over to American forces, interrogated in Afghanistan and then sent to the detention center for Al Qaeda fighters in Guantanomo Bay in Cuba. When authorities learned he was an American citizen, he was transferred to a naval brig in Norfolk, Virginia. All this time he had been held as an "enemy combatant" in solitary confinement and had had no access to a lawyer. Through his father's efforts, a law suit was brought challenging Yaser's confinement. He was being held, but had never been charged with a specific crime. Hamdi claimed he had not been fighting but had been traveling in Afghanistan and had been seized by the Northern Alliance. The case eventually reached the U.S. Supreme Court.

The government asserted that under the powers given it by a congressional resolution to use force in Afghanistan, it had the power to designate persons as enemy combatants and to hold them indefinitely without other charges. The Court did not challenge the power to designate persons as "enemy combatants." However, the Court said that the government's interests in an enemy combatant designation did not override a citizen's basic due process rights to challenge the government's case against him and to be heard by an impartial judge. (Hamdi v. Rumsfeld, 2004). Shortly after the decision was anounced, Hamdi reached an agreement with the government that he would give up his American citizenship and return to Saudi Arabia.

Hamdi's case confirmed that government could not ride roughshod over a citizen's fundamental rights to due process.

Criminal cases where charges are dismissed because they are based on illegal searches, confessions obtained without the Miranda warning, or other violations of constitutional rights are intrinsically dramatic, the stuff that movies and television crime stories are made of. But due process rights are important in the ordinary administration of government services as well. They obligate government to behave fairly in its day-to-day activities and provide citizens with a recourse when they believe the government has not been fair. (See *Hamdan v. Rumsfeld*, 2006).

Substantive due process. **Substantive due process** has to do with how our laws, interpreted through our courts, define liberty and justice. Substantive due process deals with the substance of the behavior subject to regulation by law. Courts have defined some basic elements of the rights guaranteed by the Constitution; these are called *liberty interests.* Generally, these are rights guaranteed in the Bill of Rights and those interpreted by the Court to be included under the concept of a liberty interest in the Fourteenth Amendment. Barring exceptional need, we believe governments have no business regulating behavior that involves a liberty interest, even if they follow the proper procedures for issuing and enforcing laws. For example, in *Pierce v. Society of Sisters* (1925), the Supreme Court established that parents have a liberty interest in directing the education and upbringing of their children. The *Pierce* Court overturned an Oregon law that made it a misdemeanor for parents to send their children to private and parochial schools. The Oregon legislature had followed the proper procedures in passing the law, but the Supreme Court said the content of the law represented an unconstitutional restriction on parents' rights. In *Griswold v. Connecticut* (1965), the Court struck down a Connecticut law forbidding physicians to give married couples contraceptive devices and information. The Court said the government had no business interfering in private reproductive choices. The U.S. Supreme Court decision in *Lawrence v. Texas* (2003), barring criminal prosecution of gays for engaging in consensual sexual acts, is another example of a decision based on substantive due process. The U.S. Supreme Court said that the state had no business barring consensual sexual relationships among adults.

Limiting rights. No right is absolute. Even basic rights may be restricted by law under some circumstances. When a **liberty interest** or basic right is limited by a governmental action, the people whose interests are affected are entitled to more procedural protections than when a less fundamental interest is at stake. Courts scrutinize laws restricting liberty interests more closely to ensure that the governmental restraint on liberty (1) is justified by compelling reasons, and (2) limited in scope to what is necessary to accomplish the state's legitimate purpose. For example, we have a liberty interest in being free from arbitrary search and seizure under the Fourth Amendment. If, to discourage drunk driving, state governments wished to stop cars on New Year's Eve without indication that the driver was breaking any law, they would have to persuade a court that the state's interest in preventing drunk driving justified stopping and testing drivers without specific grounds for suspecting they were drunk. Delaware argued that drunk driving was a serious public safety problem, and that stopping drivers for a brief check was a minimal restriction on Fourth Amendment rights (*Delaware v. Prowse*, 1979).

The judiciary, like the executive and legislative branches, is subject to due process constraints. Courts must act fairly and within the established rules. For the most part, the judiciary is its own watchdog. The basic corrective control over the courts is the appeals process.

The Federal and State Judicial Systems

Trial Courts

We have a multilevel judiciary. The first level consists of **trial courts,** where almost all cases are heard initially by one judge. Cases are brought by **parties with standing** (people who have a part in the controversy and a stake in its outcome). Parties need not be individuals: the state, various state agencies, corporations, institutions, as well as individuals can be parties in a case. The court's job is to resolve the question in dispute. In a criminal case, did the defendant commit the crime with which he or she is charged? In a civil case, is the defendant responsible for harm done to the plaintiff? The decision may be made either by a judge alone **(bench trial)** or by a jury **(jury trial).** Sometimes, the parties agree on the facts, and the issue is a matter of law. Given these facts, is there a legal theory under which the complaint may be sustained? The judge may decide in a **summary judgment** after hearing the initial presentation of a case that the plaintiff has no legal grounds for bringing the claim, or that the defense is not a valid legal defense. The judge's decision is subject to appeal. When facts are in dispute and the issue is decided in a trial based on evidence of what happened, we call the judge or the jury the **"finder of fact."**

In the federal system, the trial-level courts are the **U.S. District Courts.** There are 94 districts with 679 judges, one or more in each state and U.S. territory. The district courts have **jurisdiction** (the legal right to exercise authority) over all disputes arising under federal laws or the Constitution, including civil rights infringements, habeas corpus petitions (petitions to require an official to bring a party, often a prisoner, before a court), federal crimes like trafficking or manufacturing illegal drugs, and claims for federal entitlements (e.g., appeal of denial of a Medicare claim for nursing home care). In addition to **subject matter jurisdiction,** the courts also have **geographic limitations.** They can only adjudicate cases that are sufficiently related to their defined districts or the state in which they sit. In 2004, the district courts dealt with 281,338 civil cases and 71,022 criminal cases (Mecham, 2004).

State Court Systems

All the states have trial courts of general jurisdiction that hear a large variety of cases. Judges in the various state courts may be appointed, but often they are elected directly by the people. The systems can be very complex and vary from state to state, as do the names of the courts. (See Figure 1.2.)

A great deal of interest for the field of law and psychology is governed by state law, as interpreted by state courts. The vast majority of cases in the United States are heard by state courts and decided under state law, including most criminal cases and cases involving personal injury, malpractice, divorce, child protection, juvenile delinquency, or involuntary commitment of mental patients. States also have specialized courts that have jurisdiction over specific kinds of cases. Family and juvenile courts, for example, have been established by legislators in most states to hear cases involving problems like juvenile delinquency, child abuse and neglect, the termination of parental rights, and adoption. Other examples of specialized courts are traffic courts, probate courts, housing courts, mental illness courts, drug courts, and integrated domestic violence courts (Eaton and Kaufman, 2005). Many states are also using teen courts, in which adolescents set "sentences" for minor offenses by juveniles who pleaded guilty (see Chapter 9).

Appellate Courts

Any party to a proceeding in a court, including administrative hearings and cases brought to family and juvenile courts, usually has the right to appeal the decision at least once. (The most prominent exception is for *double jeopardy.* The state can't appeal a "not guilty" verdict in a criminal case.) Appeals are heard by separate courts usually designated as courts of appeals.

The federal system and many state systems have an intermediary level of appeal courts between the trial courts and the highest court. The **appellate courts** in the federal system are the 12 **U.S. Circuit Courts of Appeals** that hear appeals from the trial-level district courts within their geographic area, or circuit, and a Court of Appeals for the Federal Circuit with national jurisdiction over certain claims. In 2004, the circuit courts dealt with 68,762 cases (Mecham, 2004). Although about 20 percent of federal

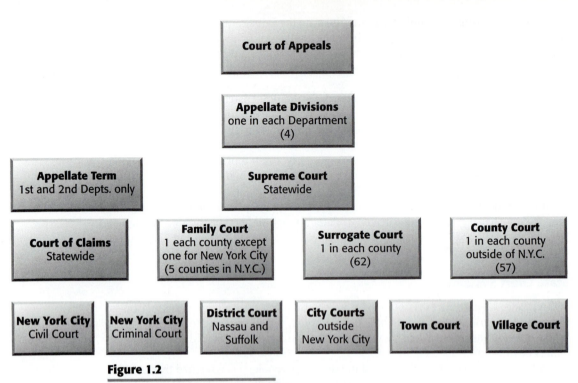

Figure 1.2

The New York State Court System
The diagram illustrates the complexity of the court system in New York. Each state has a court system with courts with different jurisdictions (geographic area, type of legal action, amount in controversy) and different lines of appeal. The Court of Appeals in New York is the state court of last resort. In most other states, the state court of last resort is usually called the Supreme Court.

judges are women, women are not well represented on the circuit courts (appellate courts just below the U.S. Supreme Court). Only 54 women have served on the U.S. Court of Appeals (Gender Gap, 2004).

Many states also have middle-level appellate courts. Some smaller states have a two-level system with only one high court reviewing all the trial courts. The appellate courts have different names in different states. In New York they are called the Appellate Division of the Supreme Court, and in California the Court of Appeal.

Appeal courts don't redo trials. The **appellant** (someone bringing an appeal) claims the trial court made a legal or procedural error. Attorneys present briefs and oral arguments to appeals courts, but the judges, usually working in a group of three, make their decisions based on the paper record established in the lower court. Appeals are about matters of law and legal procedure. For example, the appellant may claim that the trial court judge admitted evidence that should have been excluded, or excluded evidence that should have been admitted (e.g., see Boxes 2.4 and 2.6 in Chapter 2); that the trial court judge misinterpreted the law when he or she explained it to the jury (see the *Tarasoff* case in Chapter 3); that the law under which the case was decided was inconsistent with constitutional law; or that the lower court erred in deciding which legal principles applied in the case.

The federal circuit courts may differ in their interpretations of the same statute. In the absence of a ruling on a point of law from the U.S. Supreme Court, the interpretation of law made by one federal circuit court is **"binding precedent"** for the federal trial courts within that circuit. That means lower courts must decide similar cases using the legal principle established by the appeals court. The trial courts cannot decide an established legal principle for themselves. The U.S. Supreme Court often takes cases for decision when two or more circuit courts have interpreted a law differently.

Court of Last Resort

The **court of last resort** is the highest court in the state or federal system. It is usually the last stop in the appeals process. The exception is that losing litigants in some state high court cases may seek review in the **U.S. Supreme Court** if federal legal issues are involved. In the federal judicial system, of course, the nine-justice U.S. Supreme Court is the court of last resort. Decisions by the U.S. Supreme Court are binding on all state and federal courts.

Under most circumstances, parties don't have a right to have their appeal heard by the Supreme Court. Instead, they petition for a **writ of certiorari** asking the Court to review their case after all the lower courts have acted. The nine justices read the petitions with the help of law clerks on their staffs and by a vote of four justices choose which cases the Court will review. The Court can also choose to review decisions of state high courts when these are related to the federal Constitution or to federal laws. The U.S. Supreme Court agrees to a full review of only a small percentage of the petitions it receives. In recent years, the U.S. Supreme Court has had over 7,000 cases on its docket (new petitions for review, held-over cases, and so on). Of these, about 100 are granted review and scheduled for oral arguments each term; about 80 written opinions are delivered each year (Supreme Court of the United States, 2005).

Often the justices choose to hear a case when there is a conflict of interpretation of law between two or more circuit courts, or when lack of clarity or consensus about a legal or constitutional principle is interfering with the development of effective social or economic policies or with the conduct of government. For example, it was not **settled law** (no previous definitive decisions) whether a civil law suit brought against the president of the United States should be postponed until he left office. The issue, which involved the separation of powers and the need to have an effective executive, became important when Paula Jones brought a civil suit against then-President Clinton for events that were alleged to have happened before he became president. In *Clinton v. Jones* (1997), the U.S. Supreme Court said the president was accountable in a civil court of law, just like any other person.

All states have a court at the top of the legal pyramid, comparable to the U.S. Supreme Court. Again, the nomenclature is different in different states. In most states, the high court is called the Supreme Court. These courts have from five to nine judges all sitting together. State high courts spend most of their time interpreting state law in cases they have determined as being particularly important. These interpretations are definitive and must be followed by state court judges as well as by federal courts applying the law of that state. State high courts may also interpret federal statutory or constitutional issues, but such interpretations do not have the same precedential value (see discussion of case law and common law, below) as interpretations of the Constitution by federal courts.

⌧ Criminal Law and Civil Law

Courts in our system do not initiate cases on their own. Trial courts hear cases that are brought to them by parties with a legal claim. Once the plaintiff brings the case to the court, the other party or parties is required to respond. Cases are named for the participants. The aggrieved party who brings the case is named first. In general, the party who brings the case, who wants to change the status quo (the state of things now), bears the **burden of proof,** the burden of proving the charges are true.

Criminal Law

Criminal laws are those written into the state's criminal code. Crimes are actions that harm society directly, even though an individual is the victim. The punishment for crimes consists usually of prison terms or monetary penalties. The state brings charges and prosecutes an individual, the defendant, for a violation of the written criminal law. Because the state, as the representative of the people, is the "party" bringing the charge, criminal cases are consequently named *People* (or *State*) *v. Smith.*

Criminal cases usually begin when a police officer arrests a suspect. A citizen can also request that the state prosecute someone by filing a criminal complaint with the local prosecutor (often called a district attorney, or DA). The prosecutor has a great deal of discretion to decide whether to pursue the complaint (see Chapter 12).

Criminal defendants are entitled by the Constitution to a high degree of procedural protection, and to a jury trial under the Sixth Amendment for most crimes. In a jury trial, the jury decides the facts, then acquits the defendant or finds the defendant guilty. The judge acts as the umpire between the state as prosecutor and the defendant. The judge is responsible for seeing that the trial is conducted as the law requires, and provides interpretations of law when questions arise. After the jury has brought a guilty verdict, the judge sentences the defendant following legislative guidelines (see Chapter 5).

The defendant may waive the right to a jury trial and have a bench trial. In a bench trial, the judge decides whether or not the defendant is guilty. Defendants also waive their right to a jury trial when they accept a **plea bargain,** in which the defendant agrees to plead guilty in return for conviction of a lesser crime or fewer counts of a crime and a reduced sentence. They make the agreed-upon plea before the judge, who generally orders the agreed-upon sentence. Over 90 percent of criminal cases in this country are resolved by plea bargaining (Administrative Office of the U.S. Courts, 1999; Hoge et al., 1997).

Civil Law

Civil law governs disputes between private parties. The **plaintiff** is the aggrieved party who is bringing the case. The **defendant** (or the **respondent,** depending on the type of civil case) is the one accused of violating the rights of the plaintiff. Civil complaints can be brought, for example, by one individual against another, an individual against a corporation, a corporation against another, or individuals or corporations against the government. The cases are named for the parties, for example, *Smith v. Big Corporation.* When the plaintiff is suing the government, an official representing the agency (e.g., Secretary of Health and Human Services Mike Leavitt) may be named as the defendant.

Civil cases include a wide variety of disputes, including family law and administrative regulations, disputes about contracts, and **tort** (personal injury) cases. In many cases, the plaintiff, alleging injuries caused by the defendant's actions, seeks money damages to compensate for the injury. In civil cases, a plaintiff may also seek other forms of relief, such as asking the court to order (enjoin, or issue an injunction) the other party to stop doing something, or to do something (see Levine et al., 2006).

The Seventh Amendment of the Constitution preserves the right to a jury trial in many types of civil suits in federal courts involving money damages. Many state constitutions have similar provisions. Parties may waive their right to a jury trial and have a judge decide the case. If the plaintiff is not seeking money damages, depending on the type of case, there may not be a jury trial.

In civil suits in which there is no jury trial, the judge is both the fact finder and the interpreter of the applicable law. Judges also have the power to develop, tailor, and administer complex orders to effect a fair solution to a civil dispute involving something other than money damages (see Levine et al., 2006). For example, after *Brown v. Board of Education* (1954), federal judges issued and oversaw complex orders to school districts to desegregate their schools. Most of those orders have been fulfilled by now, but quite a few are still being supervised by a judge many years later.

Most civil cases are never tried. Instead, the parties settle privately "out of court." In 2002, the civil jury trial rate was only 0.6 percent of filings in state courts, and 1.2 percent in federal courts (Galanter, 2004; National Center for State Courts, 2005). Only 10 percent of medical malpractice claims go to trial (Vidmar, 1997). When you settle an automobile accident claim with the insurance company, you are essentially settling a potential lawsuit out of court. States encourage settlement and the use of mediation, arbitration, and other forms of alternative dispute resolution to minimize the hazards of the adversary model.

Making law through civil cases. The uses of tort law, which began in medieval England as a way of compensating victims of accidents, have expanded greatly (for more detailed discussion of tort and malpractice cases, see the *Tarasoff* section of Chapter 3). Many of the cases in which the judiciary has appeared to be changing the law, or developing new law through its interpretations, involve personal injury cases (e.g., a plaintiff alleges that a drug is insufficiently safe and causes injuries or fetal malformations). The prospect of a lawsuit may also have a deterrent effect. People may act more cautiously in order to avoid liability and the payment of money damages. Whether tort law has a deterrent effect is an interesting psychological problem related to the psychology of punishment and the anticipation of punishment (Shuman, 1993).

Advocates sometimes initiate **institutional reform suits** (Sandler and Schoenbrod, 2003) explicitly to alter government policies or practices. In these civil actions, plaintiffs allege unconstitutional treatment by institutions and agencies. If the court finds that the plaintiffs have been deprived of rights or services to which they were entitled or have suffered harms as a result, it may use its broad powers in equity to provide remedies for wrongs. For example, the judge in *Wuori v. Zitnay* (1978) signed an order requiring the State of Maine to improve a substandard institution and to provide group homes for the community care of individuals with retardation. The court monitored the state's progress in complying with the order (Levine, 1986). The order continues in effect (see *Consumer Advisory Board v. Glover,* 1993). Other successful suits have led to institutional change in institutions for the retarded, mental hospitals, prisons, and state departments of social services.

Institutional reform suits are often class actions. In **class action suits,** a small group of people make a complaint on behalf of a larger group that claims the same wrongs. Plaintiffs may be certified as a class when the same set of facts and the same considerations of law affect them all. For example, Chinese children in San Francisco were denied access to schools of their choice because of an existing school desegregation plan designed to preserve racial and ethnic balance in the schools. Admission standards to elite schools were set higher for Chinese than for students of all other races and ethnicities in order to maintain ethnic balance. A small group of Chinese school children brought a class action suit and successfully challenged the school desegregation plan on behalf of all San Francisco Chinese pupils (D. I. Levine, 2000, 2003). As a result, the school board could no longer use race as the basis for assignment to schools and they had to work out another plan.

Institutional reform suits are controversial. When courts correct an inequity by imposing a new requirement on a state agency, or monitor its implementation and enforce compliance the courts are accused of violating the separation of powers. They are said to be exercising "executive powers" when they order state or agency administrators to take action to correct the inadequacies, or when they require agencies to spend money normally authorized by the state legislature. Federal courts are accused of violating principles of federalism when federal judges order state officials to do or stop doing something (Sandler and Schoenbrod, 2003). On the other hand, in many of these cases, state agencies and officials were responsible for creating or tolerating unconscionable conditions in the first place. The courts were the only real source of relief (Feeley and Rubin, 1998).

Civil and Criminal Due Process

Criminal acts can be punished by loss of liberty, or even life. Because a criminal defendant may be deprived of the most basic liberties, the defendant is entitled by the U.S. Constitution to strict procedural protections. These protections have the side effect of making it harder to punish some who are truly guilty. But they are designed to prevent wrongful convictions. To quote a famous adage, our system assumes it is better for nine guilty persons to go free than for one innocent person to be imprisoned or executed.

Courts adjudicating civil claims are concerned with private interests and obligations. The state's interest in civil matters is to see that a dispute between private parties is settled fairly and peacefully. The burden of proof (**preponderance of the evidence,** sometimes defined as the greater weight of the evidence) is less than in a criminal trial, in which we require proof beyond a reasonable doubt. Another important difference is that, in a criminal trial, the defendant has a Fifth Amendment right to remain silent, and no inference can be drawn from the defendant's decision not to testify. In a civil case, a defendant's refusal to testify will be accepted as evidence against him or her. As discussed in Chapter 5, O. J. Simpson did not have to testify in his criminal trial for murder, but he couldn't avoid testifying in the civil trial for money damages for wrongful death.

Sometimes victims who receive no satisfaction in a criminal trial, because the charges could not be proven beyond a reasonable doubt, bring a suit for damages in a civil court in which it might be easier to prove the case. Of course, it is of little use to win a civil suit and an award of money damages if the defendant is **judgment proof** (has no assets). Double jeopardy does not apply because the criminal and civil suits involve different legal interests.

Case Law and Common Law

Courts interpret either statutory law (laws created by the legislature) or constitutional provisions. As judges interpret statutory law, they also create **case law,** the body of interpretations giving meaning to specific statutes. **Common law** refers to principles that courts have developed over the years to resolve disputes, especially where there is no binding statute or constitutional provision. These principles and precedents are found in case reports and in treatises on law. Common law principles are followed when positive law (e.g., a statute) is unclear or doesn't cover the case at hand. The common law reflects common usage, customs, and laws going as far back as English courts in pre-revolutionary days, and sometimes going back to ancient or Roman times.

When new cases arise, all courts try to follow case law, the precedents or principles established in past similar case. This is the principle of **stare decisis** ("stand by decided matters" or abide by decided cases). Moreover, appellate judges, and for some purposes trial court judges, are required to explain the reasoning behind their rulings in written opinions. The written opinion is a constraint over arbitrariness. The decision has to be justified by reference to precedents and accepted principles of law. Together, stare decisis and the requirement of a written decision help ensure legal consistency, protect against arbitrariness, and provide people and their lawyers with a means of understanding the law so they can conform their behavior to it.

The reliance on precedent is conservative in that it encourages continuity with past decisions and traditions and discourages abrupt change. Even when courts seem to make new law in resolving a case, judges are careful to find justification in past rulings. A court can make a decision based on an observation that times have changed, but when it does so, it builds on past cases to bolster the new rule (Levi, 1949).

Both federal and state judges adhere to binding precedents within their own respective jurisdictions. These precedents may differ and so the interpretation of law can differ from one jurisdiction to another.

Constitutional Law

When legislatures do not agree with the interpretations courts have made of a statute, they may pass new legislation to clarify their intent. The situation is different when a constitutional interpretation is involved. The Supreme Court of the United States has the final say about constitutional issues. As Supreme Court Justice Robert Jackson once said, "We are not final because we are infallible. We are infallible because we are final" (*Brown v. Allen,* 1953).

Once the Supreme Court establishes a constitutional interpretation, it is binding on all courts. Neither Congress nor a state legislature can reverse the interpretation with a new statute. If it is to be undone, either the Court must reverse itself or the Constitution must be **amended** (changed). Both are relatively rare events. However, our understanding of the Constitution may change to accommodate new contexts. This idea is not free from controversy. Supreme Court Justice Antonin Scalia, for one, believes that changing the meaning of the Constitution in response to changing conditions merely allows justices to "legislate" their personal views and preferences into the law. Other justices believe that good law is responsive to social needs. In practice, the judicial system has enough responsiveness and flexibility to respond to changing times and political shifts, while trying to preserve fundamental values.

One example of when the U.S. Supreme Court reversed itself is the famous school desegregation case, *Brown v. Board of Education* (1954). The *Brown* court overruled the separate but equal interpretation of the Fourteenth Amendment established in *Plessy v. Ferguson* (1896). It did so in part by questioning the factual assumptions of the earlier decision. The justices looked for a way to see the law differently because our views of racial justice were changing. Their reinterpretation of the constitutionality of segregation in turn accelerated the process of social change.

Brown was an unusual case. Because of stare decisis, the Supreme Court is generally reluctant to reverse itself. The justices, like other judges, decide new cases by applying principles enunciated in past rulings. However, they exercise selectivity in their choice of precedents and how they apply them to the case on hand. The Court uses this selectivity to subtly or not so subtly modify or expand its own interpretations. The modifications are sometimes motivated by the need to accommodate historical, political, and social changes. Sometimes shifts in legal and political philosophy follow changes in the composition of the Court as new justices are appointed by elected presidents and confirmed by elected senators.

In *Roe v. Wade* (1973), the U.S. Supreme Court followed the precedents of other cases that had developed the right to privacy in reproductive matters. Presidents Reagan and Bush, who opposed abortion, both appointed justices to fill Supreme Court vacancies. The more conservative court, headed by Chief Justice William Rehnquist, modified the constitutional interpretation of the right to privacy in reproductive matters to allow the states to impose greater restrictions on access to abortions (*Webster v. Reproductive Health Services*, 1989; *Planned Parenthood v. Casey*, 1992). However, because of the doctrine of stare decisis, the justices, including some of the Reagan and Bush appointees, stopped short of completely overruling *Roe v. Wade* (*Planned Parenthood v. Casey*, 1992). Now that the second President Bush has succeeded with the advice and consent of the Senate in appointing two new justices, Chief Justice John Roberts and Associate Justice Samuel Alito (to replace former Chief Justice William Rehnquist, who died, and Justice Sandra Day O'Connor, who resigned), it remains to be seen whether the Court will continue to uphold *Roe v. Wade,* overrule it, or allow many more restrictions.

After *Roe v. Wade,* and again after the Court refused to overturn the ruling that there was a constitutional right to abortion, opponents of abortion began talking about obtaining a right-to-life amendment to the Constitution. Similarly, after the Supreme Court ruled that flag burning was protected by the First Amendment right to political expression (*Texas v. Johnson,* 1989), citizens who were deeply affronted by this insult to a national symbol wanted an amendment prohibiting flag burning. Amending the Constitution is a difficult, highly political process (see Article V of the Constitution) unlikely to succeed without a broad consensus.

Legislative–Judicial Interplay

The executive branch and the legislative branch can't change the Supreme Court's rulings. However, they can use their powers to try to modify the impact of a ruling or to influence the Court's decisions. Presidents Reagan, Bush Sr., Clinton, and Bush Jr. used their power of appointment to try to fill the Court with justices more likely to be sympathetic to their positions. While the president nominates the justices, under its constitutional authority, the U.S. Senate must confirm the nominees. Only general judicial philosophy is ostensibly under scrutiny in the "advise and consent" process, but the prospective justice's possible vote on specific issues such as abortion, school prayer, and the extent of powers of the federal government is of critical concern to the president and the senators.

Legislators can get around decisions rejecting state laws by modifying statutes to meet the constitutional objections. For example, in *Furman v. Georgia* (1972), the U.S. Supreme Court ruled that all state statutes authorizing capital punishment were unconstitutional because they were unfair or discriminatory. Subsequently, states passed new laws with different procedures for imposing the death penalty that took into account constitutional objections. The new laws survived legal challenges, and states have executed convicted criminals under them (see Chapter 8). The abortion controversy followed the same pattern as states passed laws to test what the Supreme Court would say "unduly burdens" access to abortion (e.g., waiting periods, parental consent, and "partial birth" abortion restrictions). Legislators can also revise a statute to undo a judicial interpretation of the statute. When the U.S. Supreme Court insisted on conditions that made it more difficult to bring suits under the federal Civil Rights Act, the Congress passed a new statute effectively undoing the obstacles the Court had introduced. (See Chapter 16).

Politics and the Supreme Court

Supreme Court justices, as guardians of our highest law, are supposed to be wise, compassionate, and learned. Unlike political representatives, they are supposed to be insulated from the political process by lifetime appointment and by the fragile tradition of appointing only highly respected men and women to the court. They are supposed to guard our system and our liberties for all the people. However, they are not completely insulated from the political process. They are nominated by an elected president and confirmed by the elected U.S. Senate, a political process that has consequences that are not always predictable. Their wisdom is necessarily limited by the limitations of their experience. Until 1967, all the Supreme Court justices were white males. Since 1967, only two African Americans (Thurgood Marshall and Clarence Thomas) and only two women (Sandra Day O'Connor and Ruth Bader Ginsburg) have sat on the Court. No Asians, no Latinos, and no Native Americans have been appointed Supreme Court justices. (Women and minority group members are also underrepresented in the rest of the judiciary.)

Whatever their personal or political backgrounds, justices do try to be faithful to the language and meaning of the Constitution, to the principle of stare decisis, to the structure of government, and to our traditions. The interpretive principles they use cannot be precise, and there is much room for disagreement. The independence of the decision-making process from political considerations was widely questioned after *Bush v. Gore* (2000). In effect the U.S. Supreme Court, by a 5–4 decision, blocked further recounts of ballots in Florida. Their action guaranteed that George W. Bush would be elected the forty-third U.S. president over his opponent, Albert Gore Jr.

Much is made of the politics of these disagreements, of the politicization of the Supreme Court and of the differences between "liberal" and "conservative," and between **activists** (those who are interpretive, to create new principles) and **strict constructionists** (those who stay closely to the text of the Constitution). Critics have argued that the interpretation of the words of the Constitution necessarily reflects judicial philosophy and personal values. These interpretations, critics say, are related to the distribution of power in our society. But the Court itself is in the business of constructing, not deconstructing, meanings. We don't think it is overly idealistic, despite divisions on the Court and, on occasion, political acrimony surrounding appointments to the federal bench, to assert that judges and most citizens share the belief that there is a common set of values embedded in our Constitution, implicit in our history, and reflected in written law, precedents, traditions, and understandings about how we should live together. Ultimately, it is these values that the justices of the U.S. Supreme Court use or try to use to decide cases and accommodate new developments. The legal issues of importance in this book are about what we should do when the values that we endorse conflict with one another. The psychological and social sciences may contribute facts and theory to help illuminate and articulate the dimensions of these conflicts, but the resolutions lie in the political and judicial realms.

Summary

The United States is a federation of 50 states. The Constitution is an agreement between the states and their citizens to cede some power to a central government to achieve many goals, particularly to promote the common welfare. The Constitution imposes limits and obligations on the central government in order to protect individual rights and prevent the arbitrary use of power. The federal system also limits the power of the central government. The states, which have their own constitutions, retain power to prosecute crimes within their boundaries and to provide for the health, education, welfare, and safety of their citizens. However, the federal government can also address issues of crime and public welfare at the national level. The federal government can also influence state policies indirectly, but powerfully, by providing funds to states that establish programs that follow federal guidelines. Details of the implementation of these programs, like other state laws, can vary from state to state.

Within the federal government, the power of each of the three branches—the legislative, the executive, and the judicial—checks and balances the powers of the others. All three branches have a "lawmaking" function: the Congress by passing legislation, the executive branch by developing administrative regulations when authorized to do so by Congress, and the judicial by making decisions that determine what the law, including the Constitution, means in practice.

Court decisions are important for the fields of psychology and law because they let us see what the rules are and the reasoning behind the rules, which often contain psychological assumptions. The courts, through their decisions in specific cases, decide how laws can be applied in keeping with legislative purpose and due process. *Due process* refers to the obligations of government to follow lawful procedures and to refrain from impinging on basic liberties, except when there is a compelling reason (and then as little as possible).

The federal government and the states have multilevel court systems. Matters of fact—who did what to whom—are decided in trial courts. A large majority of trials take place in state courts under state law. Defendants in criminal cases, and both parties in most cases in which monetary compensation is at stake, have a right to a trial by jury. People may and often do waive the right to a jury trial. Instead they ask for a bench trial, plea-bargain in criminal cases, or settle out of court in civil cases.

Trials of defendants accused of crimes, violations of the law that can be punished by criminal penalties, follow rules governing criminal procedures. Procedural requirements are strict in criminal cases because of the prospect of losing liberty or even life. In criminal cases, the accused cannot be required to testify against him- or herself. In contrast, in civil cases the defendant's failure to testify is taken as an admission of the allegations in the complaint. The criminal defendant's guilt must be proven beyond a reasonable doubt. In most civil cases, the plaintiff need only establish the case by a preponderance of the evidence. Judges hearing certain types of civil cases in which the request is not for money damages, but for change in a harmful condition, have broad powers to impose a plan to remedy the complained-of situation. Advocates sometimes bring suits against government agencies to invite the court to use its power to order the agency to change the harmful situation, or to fulfill duties it has neglected.

In both state and federal courts, the defendant in a criminal trial and both parties in a civil trial can appeal to a higher court, an appellate court, to review the case for error. Appeals courts don't hold new trials to reweigh the evidence in a case. They review the record when the appellant (person bringing the appeal) asks the appeals court to dismiss the case, order a new trial, or modify a judgment on the grounds that the court in the first trial violated due process or made some other legal error. Appeals are helpful because they are the corrective for error in the trial courts, and often appellate decisions say more fully what legal principle will govern similar cases in the future.

All states have at least one appellate court. Most states and the federal government have a middle-level appeals court that reviews cases within a designated geographic area, and a high court that reviews selected decisions of the mid-level appellate court. Some trial courts and all appellate courts issue written opinions in which they explain their rulings in terms of legal principles and precedents established by courts in previous cases under the principle of stare decisis.

The U.S. Supreme Court is the highest court in the federal system and can hear appeals from state high courts when federal constitutional questions are at issue. There is no appeal from the U.S. Supreme Court's rulings on federal constitutional questions. However, legislatures can rewrite laws to accommodate Supreme Court rulings. The Supreme Court occasionally, but rarely, overturns its own rulings. It does extend and modify its rulings over time to take into account political and social change as it hears related cases. Ultimately, the justices of the U.S. Supreme Court are guided by values embedded in our Constitution, implicit in our history, in legal precedents, and in a common understanding of how we should live together.

Discussion Questions

1. What does the idea of a natural right mean? Do you believe people have natural rights? Would it be worthwhile to conduct a survey to determine people's beliefs about which natural rights exist? If yes, why? If no, why not?
2. Our system of government uses checks and balances to limit power. Why don't we rely solely on electing honest, public-spirited citizens to lead us and to expect them to do the right thing? What do we know from personality theory or social psychology about the motive to obtain and exercise power?
3. How can we tell if institutional reform suits are a good way to bring about social change? Why might advocates use the courts rather than the legislature to achieve reform?
4. What do plea bargaining and settling out of court have in common? What would be the advantages and disadvantages of requiring that all cases go to trial? What outcomes and attitudes could we examine to shed light on the question?
5. Could we have written laws (codes) to cover every conceivable situation? If not, we must rely on interpretation. How does case law relate to interpretation (judgments of similarities and differences of sets of complex "facts")? When is it preferable to legislate, and when is it better to let the common law take the lead in solving problems?

Key Terms

activist
administrative law
appellant
appellate courts
bench trial
Bill of Rights
binding precedent
burden of proof
case law
checks and balances
civil law
class action suits
common law
courts of last resort
criminal law
defendant
due process
enumerated powers
executive power
federalism

felony
finder of fact
geographic jurisdiction
institutional reform suits
judgment proof
judicial power
jurisdiction
jury trial
legislative power
liberty interest
misdemeanor
parens patriae powers
parties with standing
plaintiff
plea bargain
police power
preponderance of the
   evidence
procedural due process
ratify

respondent
separation of powers
settled law
social contract
sovereign power
stare decisis
strict constructionist
substantive due process
summary judgment
tort
trial court
uniform or model
   legislation
U.S. Circuit Courts of
   Appeals
U.S. Constitution
U.S. District Courts
U.S. Supreme Court
writ of certiorari

CHAPTER **2**

Social Science and Psychological Influences in Law

26

CHAPTER 2
Social Science
and
Psychological
Influences in
Law

In this chapter, we will trace the interplay between law and social science and discuss some of the problems and possibilities created by their interaction. The chapter will discuss the following:

- two U.S. Supreme Court cases that introduced the use of social science research by policy-making courts, *Muller v. Oregon* (1908) and *Brown v. Board of Education* (1954);

- developments in jurisprudence (the philosophy of law) and psychology from the late nineteenth century to the present day that have encouraged dialogue between the two fields;

- different ways in which psychologists and other social scientists participate as experts in the legal process;

- how courts can decide if scientific research or specialized knowledge in a given area is sound enough to provide a firm basis for expert testimony;

- some of the differences in psychological and legal ways of thinking about problems;

- how involvement with the legal system has affected the discipline of psychology; and

- ethical issues presented by psychology's interactions with the law.

From *Muller* to *Brown*

In 1903, Oregon enacted a law limiting the workday of women in factories and laundries to ten hours. A laundry owner named Curt Muller was convicted of violating the law. He maintained on appeal that the state had no right to interfere with his employment contracts, private economic arrangements he made with employees. The case, *Muller v. Oregon,* went to the Supreme Court in 1908.

Future U.S. Supreme Court Justice Louis Brandeis was counsel for the State of Oregon. Florence Kelley, an activist social worker with the Hull House settlement, had recruited him to participate in the case (Faigman, 2004). Hull House and social scientists and psychologists at the University of Chicago had long been interested in approaching social problems through the application of social science research (Faigman, 2004). Brandeis argued that the State of Oregon had a legitimate interest in maintaining the health of its female citizens, that a body of research and expert opinion established that women's health was impaired if they worked long hours, and that, consequently, the state was justified in limiting the number of hours women could work. To support his contention that working long hours harmed women, he appended summaries of 90 studies and reports to his brief. (A **brief** is a written document filed with a court summarizing the issues in the case and making arguments about relevant facts and interpretations of statutes and previous cases. Each side files a brief.)

The Supreme Court upheld the Oregon law. Justice David Brewer summarized the 90 studies in a footnote to the Court's opinion. He noted that, although the studies were not, "technically speaking, authorities," he would "take judicial cognizance of all matters of general knowledge" (*Muller v. Oregon*, 1908, pp. 420–421). He was saying the studies and reports were relevant to the constitutional issue of whether there was a valid reason for the restrictions Oregon's law placed on the freedom of individuals to enter into contracts.

Less than 50 years after *Muller*, in *Brown v. Board of Education* (1954), the U.S. Supreme Court cited social science data when it ordered the end of segregation in public schools (see Box 2.1). The *Brown* decision overturned the 1896 Supreme Court ruling in *Plessy v. Ferguson* that separate facilities and schools for the races did not violate the Fourteenth Amendment guarantee of equal protection if the segregated facilities were equal. In *Plessy*, the Court had declared, "We consider the underlying fallacy of the plaintiff's argument to consist in the assumption that the enforced separation of the two races stamps the colored race with a badge of inferiority" (*Plessy v. Ferguson*, 1896).

In their brief in *Brown* and the four companion cases heard with it, the National Association for the Advancement of Colored People (NAACP) argued that negative psychological effects of segregation were real and inevitable. The NAACP legal team, under the leadership of Thurgood Marshall (later to become the first African American Supreme Court justice; see Figure 2.1), had been challenging segregation in education for many years (Kluger, 2004). The NAACP relied heavily for support of its argument against segregation on facts provided by social science research. These facts had been introduced into testimony by expert witnesses at the trial phase. The experts' testimony was preserved in the record that came up on appeal. The research was also described in briefs to the trial courts and to the Supreme Court. This time, the Court unanimously ruled that segregated schools were inherently unequal. Although it was not the only reason, the opinion explicitly stated that the decision was based in part on the psychological knowledge presented by the plaintiff. In the opinion, Chief Justice Earl Warren wrote that separating black children solely on the basis of race "generates a feeling of inferiority as to their status in the community that may affect their hearts and minds in a way unlikely to ever be undone. . . . Whatever may have been the extent of psychological knowledge at the time of *Plessy v. Ferguson*, this finding is amply supported by modern authority" (*Brown v. Board of Education*, 1954, p. 494). In a now famous Footnote 11, the chief justice cited research by a number of social scientists, including Kenneth B. Clark, an African American psychologist who later became president of the American Psychological Association (APA; see Figure 2.2 for photos of Kenneth and Mamie Clark).

In the decades since *Brown*, social science has penetrated deeply into legal culture (Levine and Howe, 1985; Saltzman and Proch, 1990). It has become common for courts to discuss social science research in the body of their opinions alongside discussion of legal cases. Private litigants as well as public interest and nonprofit groups seeking to influence policy through the judiciary often present courts with economic, social, or psychological findings along with analyses of law. It is debatable whether courts are using social science data properly or whether studies are used selectively simply to bolster a justice's opinion (Faigman, 1989, 1991, 2005), but it is clear that courts use such information more than ever before.

28

CHAPTER 2
Social Science
and
Psychological
Influences in
Law

BOX 2.1

Dolls and *Brown v. Board of Education*

Kenneth and Mamie Clark's study of racial identification was one of the most famous studies included in the plaintiff's brief to the Supreme Court hearing (*Brown v. Board of Education,* 1954). The Clarks' subjects were 253 African American nursery and elementary school children. Of these, 134 attended segregated schools in Arkansas and 119 attended racially mixed schools in Massachusetts. The children were presented with four dolls, all wearing only white diapers and in the same position. Two were brown with black hair and two were white with yellow hair. Half the subjects were presented with dolls in the order white, colored, white, colored; for the other half, the order was reversed. The children were asked to choose a doll in response to each of the following instructions:

1. Give me the doll that you like to play with the best.
2. Give me the doll that is a nice doll.
3. Give me the doll that looks bad.
4. Give me the doll that is a nice color.

The following table summarizes the results:

Choices of Subjects in Northern (Mixed Schools) and Southern Segregated Schools Groups (Requests 1 through 4)*—Percent Choosing the Doll

Choice	North (%)	South (%)
Request 1 (play with)		
colored doll	28	37
white doll	72	62
Request 2 (nice doll)		
colored doll	30	46
white doll	68	52
Request 3 (looks bad)		
colored doll	71	49
white doll	17	16
Request 4 (nice color)		
colored doll	37	40
white doll	63	57

*Individual failing to make either choice not included, hence some percentages add up to less than 100.

As the reader can see, the results do not provide straightforward support for the assertion that segregated schools are more psychologically deleterious than integrated ones. All the children tended to prefer the white doll, but the children in the northern mixed school showed a stronger preference for the white doll than the children in segregated Southern schools. The Clarks argued that the Southern children were more adjusted to feeling they were not as good as whites. Thurgood Marshall debated whether or not to use the study. He finally decided that the findings on the whole demonstrated that segregation was hurting African American children and entered the study into evidence. Reports of the study may have gained support for the integration movement. Among the public, the details of the study were less important than the disturbing discovery that black children rejected a doll because it looked like them. (*Source*: Kluger, 2004).

29

The
Beginnings:
Pragmatic
Jurisprudence
and the New
Social Sciences

FIGURE 2.1

U.S. Supreme Court Justice Thurgood Marshall
Thurgood Marshall (1908–1993) was legal director of the NAACP dur-
ing the years the organization brought lawsuits challenging racially
segregated schools. A prime advocate of the use of social science data
in school desegregation suits, he argued Brown v. Board of Education
(1954) before the U.S. Supreme Court. President Lyndon B. Johnson
appointed him to the U.S. Supreme Court in 1967. He was the first
African American U.S. Supreme Court justice. He served until he retired
in 1991.

The Beginnings: Pragmatic Jurisprudence and the New Social Sciences

The progress of social science from a bit part in *Muller* to a central role in *Brown* reflected both the growing sophistication of the new human sciences and the rise of a legal culture conscious of social context and deliberate in its use of law to achieve desired social ends (Faigman, 2004).

Traditional Jurisprudence

In traditional U.S. **jurisprudence** (philosophy or science of law), specific laws were thought of as derivatives of a natural universal law as discussed by scholars and classical philosophers and found in the Bible. In the late nineteenth century Christopher Columbus Langdell, dean of the Harvard Law School, articulated and modernized this view of law (Auerbach, 1976). Langdell believed that the job of the good judge and lawyer was to identify the underlying legal principles that applied to the case at hand, just as a mathematician solves a geometry problem by analyzing the shapes and applying the appropriate geometric theorems. Under this view, judges didn't make law; they "found" it in the unchanging realm of natural law. Langdell developed the case method of study to hone students' skills at this kind of analytical and deductive reasoning (logical reasoning from first principles).

30

CHAPTER 2
Social Science
and
Psychological
Influences in
Law

FIGURE 2.2

Kenneth B. Clark and Mamie Clark

Professor Kenneth Clark and Dr. Mamie Clark conducted the doll experiments (see Box 2.1) that were cited by the U.S. Supreme Court in Brown v. Board of Education *(1954). Dr. Clark, a distinguished social psychologist, later served as president of the American Psychological Association. He and his wife were very active in antipoverty programs and organizations throughout the years. Professor Clark died in 2005 at the age of 90. Dr. Mamie Clark died in 1983.*

Experience, Not Logic

Social science and historical data were not relevant to Langdell's approach, which tried to treat law as a closed logical system. However, other legal theorists contemporary with Langdell rejected the existence of immutable and universal natural law. Oliver Wendell Holmes Jr. and Louis Brandeis saw law as a way of establishing social policies. Though they believed there were common values, they rejected the idea of abstract universal law. They thought that law should be approached pragmatically, as a means to an end. Inductive reasoning (reasoning from the particular to the general) should be used to learn from experience. Through observation of the world, judges and scholars could determine what rules led to what outcomes. They maintained that good solutions to legal problems could and should vary according to the social context and the goals of social policy. Holmes wrote,

> The life of the law has not been logic: it has been experience. The felt necessities of the time, the prevalent moral and political theories, intuitions of public policy, avowed or unconscious, even the prejudices judges share with their fellow-men, have had a

good deal more to do than the syllogism in determining the rules by which men should be governed. (From Oliver Wendell Holmes Jr., *The Common Law*, 1881; excerpted in Monahan and Walker, 2006, p. 2)

Roscoe Pound's **sociological jurisprudence** went further. Pound, who had a doctorate in botany before going to law school, believed that law should proceed on the basis of "social facts." Law students should study the law in action, the actual social effects of legal institutions and doctrines (Pound, 1906, 1908, 1910). Another influential jurist, New York Court of Appeals Judge and later U.S. Supreme Court Justice Benjamin Cardozo, wrote a well-received monograph discussing psychological and sociological influences on judicial reasoning and decision making (Cardozo, 1921). The writings of Pound and Cardozo encouraged judges to rethink precedents and to review more carefully the psychological and sociological premises for their decisions.

These different views of jurisprudence altered the way law is understood in the United States. Most U.S. students of law now accept that the law on the books and the law in action (to use Pound's famous aphorism; Pound, 1910) are two different matters. Legal scholars and judges continue to value precedents, legal procedures, and formal reasoning from principles, but many are now responsive to information and ideas from the social sciences as well. Faigman (2005) contends that greater attention to science and the social sciences in law is inevitable: "If the Constitution is to 'endure forever,' its guardians will have to read it in light of the science of today and be prepared to incorporate the discoveries of tomorrow" (p. 364).

Developments in Psychology

At the time that Holmes, Brandeis, and Pound were developing their ideas about law, the social sciences were still relatively new disciplines. The German Wilhelm Wundt, working in the second half of the nineteenth century, was one of the first experimental psychologists. In 1892, a student of Wundt's named Hugo Muensterberg came to Harvard where he became a vigorous and articulate proponent of the "new psychology." In *On the Witness Stand* ([1908] 1923), Muensterberg argued that this new science had much to offer the legal world. He discussed memory and perception related to eyewitness testimony, suggestibility and untrue confessions, applications of the physiology of emotion to lie detection, hypnotism and hypnotic treatment for criminal impulses, and other methods of crime prevention or treatment (Muensterberg, [1908] 1923). Muensterberg's work had limited influence, but it is worth mentioning as a historical note.

Muensterberg complained that lawyers and judges, unreasonably in his view, refused to accept his contributions. In a law review article, John Wigmore (1909), the most prominent scholar of the law of evidence, replied that the research Muensterberg was touting was too tentative and general to be of much use to the courts. However, at the end of the article in which he handily dismissed Muensterberg's work, Wigmore affirmed the potential value of a partnership between law and social science.

Legal Realism

In the 1930s and 1940s, an informal school of jurisprudence called **legal realism** took Brandeis's and Pound's pragmatic approach to law further. To the legal realists, Pound's law in action was the real law (Melton, 1990). The legal realists were willing

32

CHAPTER 2
Social Science
and
Psychological
Influences in
Law

to subject traditional legal values to a radical empirical reexamination (Minda, 1995). For this school of thought, what is (social reality) was as important as what ought to be (normative values). They understood law as a vehicle for advancing social goals, a means of policy making. **Policy** refers to the general course, methods, or principles adopted by a government or legislature to guide its development of legislation or management of public affairs (Black, 2004; Webster's, 2003). To illustrate the concept: at one time, Congress encouraged states to develop welfare policies that would enable single mothers to stay home with their children; now, states have changed their welfare policies to encourage and even require single mothers to enter the workplace. If Congress followed natural law principles, they might have said mothers should stay home with their children because, from time immemorial, mothers have taken care of children. Policies, unlike hypothesized immutable principles of universal law, change with time and are developed in complex cultural and political contexts.

During this period, research in psychology and law was becoming more sophisticated. By 1942, Poffenberger (1942) was able to devote four chapters of an applied psychology textbook to psychology and law research, including careful experiments on perception, memory, and language related to legal topics. The legal realists pursued working relationships with psychologists to help in the examination of "social reality" (Schlegel, 1979, 1980), and there were some valiant but short-lived attempts at joint empirical research.

The direct impact of legal realism should not be exaggerated. The movement more or less died out by the 1950s (Schlegel, 1979, 1980). Nonetheless, the idea that knowledge based on experience (empiricism) should replace formal logic in arriving at legal conclusions took a large step forward. Understanding of law had to go beyond reading cases and statutes (Faigman, 2004), but jurisprudence had to go beyond examining descriptive statistics. One cannot derive what "ought to be" from "what is." Most subsequent jurisprudence accepts, however, at least in part, the realists' premise that legal process takes social context and social facts into account in decision-making (Monahan and Walker, 2006).

Law and Social Science since *Brown*

Law and Psychology after World War II

During World War II, the armed forces used social scientists and psychologists to help assign and train soldiers, to maintain morale, to understand and communicate with citizens of allied and occupied countries, to treat war trauma, and to help soldiers readjust to civilian life. The partnership of the social sciences with government continued after the war. Social scientists helped design and implement President John F. Kennedy's New Frontier and President Lyndon Johnson's Great Society social programs.

New schools of jurisprudence developed in the postwar period as well. The legal process movement, acknowledging that values and beliefs about good policy may elude consensus, stressed the importance of procedural due process and fairness (see Chapter 1). Other movements give prominence to social science research (Minda, 1995; Slobogin, 1995). The law and economics movement, a distant, more politically conservative cousin of legal realism, undertakes to analyze and evaluate legal problems in terms of their economic implications. Judge (and Professor) Richard Posner, associated with this school, advocates legal and governmental pragmatism: an emphasis on consequences in decision making rather than on formal principle and on the balancing of interests (Posner, 2003). The social science and law movement applies knowledge and techniques from all the social sciences to resolving legal issues. Critical legal studies, feminist legal studies, and critical race theory are additional schools of thought that examine law as a social institution mediating control of various resources (Minda, 1995). Adherents of these new movements, many with homes in prestigious law schools, are receptive to research and empirical observation to further their analyses and to persuade others of the correctness of their views.

Today, psychologists, social workers, psychiatrists, sociologists, anthropologists, and other social scientists participate both directly and indirectly in all three branches of government and influence policy at every level (Saltzman and Proch, 1990). Clinical **forensic** ("belonging to courts of justice"; Black's, 2004) practice in general, and subspecialties in criminal and family law, have expanded greatly as well. Mental health professionals now contribute to the day-to-day administration of justice. They serve the courts as expert witnesses, and provide psychological services to the police and correctional systems. Family and juvenile courts work routinely with allied social service agencies. Clinical, cognitive, developmental, and social psychologists do the basic research on which expert opinion is grounded. Research by cognitive and social psychologists into issues such as the reliability of eyewitness testimony, false confession, juror biases, and juror decision making also influences the trial process, directly through expert testimony, and indirectly by suggesting ways judges and legislators may develop better procedures. Social scientists and legal scholars now quickly examine the legal implications of new developments in psychology and other social sciences.

Growth of a New Field

The expanded use of psychological research and mental health professionals by the courts and legislatures has stimulated the growth of the new field of law–psychology. Law–psychology is becoming a recognized subspecialty within psychology supported by a substantial infrastructure of training courses, journals, associations, and credentialing bodies (Levine and Howe, 1985). The American Psychology–Law Society, founded in 1969 with 101 members, has become the Psychology and Law Division (Division 41) of the APA (Grisso, 1991) and has about 4,000 members. The American Psychology–Law Society has a web page that describes educational and vocational opportunities in this field including a number of joint-degree (JD, Ph.D.) programs. Graduate schools of social work are also providing training in law and social science. There are now a very large number of joint MSW and JD programs all over the country offered through schools of social work in partnership with law schools. The National Association of Social Workers has a legal fund to promote interest in legal issues and legal education in social work.

A comparable infrastructure has developed within the field of law. Legal scholars write law review articles about social science and legal issues (Hafemeister, 1992). Basic law school courses on the laws of evidence use texts that devote large sections to social science, psychological, and clinical research as it applies to law (Faigman et al., 2005; Moenssens et al., 1995). Many law schools offer separate courses in law and social science using **casebooks** (textbooks that teach a field of law through the presentation and discussion of court cases and related materials). Some law courses

34

CHAPTER 2
Social Science
and
Psychological
Influences in
Law

provide technical introductions to statistical and research methods so that some future lawyers may be equipped to evaluate the strength of social science studies (Barnes and Conley, 1986). The Supreme Court's *Daubert* decision (*Daubert v. Merrell Dow Pharmaceuticals*, 1993; see below) has increased the need for scientifically literate judges and lawyers. The decision requires judges to decide what science is sound enough to be admitted as evidence in lawsuits, and to shut the gate on "junk science." To influence the judge's decisions, practicing lawyers will have to be prepared to argue the scientific validity or worthlessness of expert evidence (Levine, 1999).

Problem-Solving Judges and Therapeutic Jurisprudence

The increase in the last 25 years in the number of legal cases involving problems related to substance abuse, child abuse, family violence, juvenile crime, and crimes by the mentally ill has led judges, legal scholars, and social science research workers to consider the practical implications of recognizing social facts and social context. In some areas of law, the focus has shifted from the immediate disposition of cases to planning what will happen to participants after the case is decided (Rothman and Casey, 1999). Many courts are adopting a problem-solving approach to law in action and to that end are seeking to collaborate with community organizations. In 1990, the Commission on Trial Court Performance Standards of the U.S. Department of Justice proposed that courts should adjust their operations to meet new conditions and should maintain good relationships with the community (Rothman and Casey, 1999). In some jurisdictions, legislators have instituted legal system reforms or created new courts, such as drug courts, mental health courts, housing courts for the homeless, and integrated domestic violence courts, with the goal of holding defendants accountable while coordinating legal, social, psychological, and medical services to produce a therapeutic effect (Eaton and Kaufman, 2005). The last two decades have also seen an increasing emphasis on expanding the use of nonadversarial forms of dispute resolution, both traditional procedures like mediation and newer procedures like family conferencing, where parties to a conflict are brought together and empowered to resolve the conflict themselves. Advocates of alternative forms of dispute resolution argue that they are especially valuable in conflicts such as custody disputes, where a swift resolution is in everyone's interests, and in dealing with offenses, like juvenile crime, where society has a special stake in a swift reintegration of the offender into the community. Together, these approaches, courts, and procedures are sometimes described as an *alternative justice system*, one that emphasizes collaboration of parties, future planning and prevention, and reconciliation of needs and interests.

These developments have found conceptual and empirical support from a school of thought called **therapeutic jurisprudence.** Developed in the 1990s by David Wexler and Bruce Winick, therapeutic jurisprudence proposes to study how legal rules and actions affect the mental health of participants and how knowledge about mental health can shape the law (Wexler, 1990; Wexler and Winick, 1991, 1996a, 1996b; Winick, 1997). The movement attempts to combine a proactive helping perspective with a traditional "rights" perspective. Its adherents believe that, within the important constraints of due process and justice values, laws, legal procedures, and legal actors should attempt to maximize the therapeutic effects of law and minimize the untherapeutic effects.

The legal system uses information provided by social science in a number of different ways. Monahan and Walker (2006) developed a distinction between adjudicative and legislative facts, first proposed by administrative law scholar Kenneth Culp Davis. Davis (1960) suggested that evidence presented by social scientists about the issues in contention in a trial be referred to as *adjudicative facts.* Monahan and Walker call this testimony about **social facts.** They called general social science findings, which are used by courts in deciding questions of law or policy, **social authority (legislative) facts.** Monahan and Walker noted that testimony by social scientists is also used in a third way, to provide the jury or judge with general information that will help them evaluate and understand evidence introduced at trial. Monahan and Walker (2006) call this **social framework** testimony. This tripartite classification of psychological evidence nicely parallels different ways psychologists and social scientists can participate in the legal process.

Providing Social (Adjudicative) Facts

The most familiar use of professionals in court is to testify to **social (adjudicative) facts.** These are facts pertinent to the dispute that will be a basis for the adjudication (the outcome of a trial). Once qualified as an "expert" by virtue of training and experience with the subject matter, the mental health professional or social scientist testifies about a factual question in contention. The testimony may be based on a clinical examination, tests, or observations of a defendant, plaintiff, or victim; on past research; or even on an experiment designed to test a point at issue in the trial. In a civil suit for negligence, for example, a neuropsychologist might testify that a plaintiff has an intellectual deficit following a head injury attributable to the alleged negligence of the defendant (Matarazzo, 1990). The presence or absence of intellectual deficits is an adjudicative fact. In an insanity defense case, one of the adjudicative facts at issue is whether the defendant has a mental disease or defect. A clinical psychologist might testify about this question. In a case where an eyewitness account supports the contention that an event took place, an experimental psychologist might testify in rebuttal that a witness could not have seen what he or she claimed to have seen given the conditions of illumination, the distance, and the speed of a moving object.

Sometimes an experiment may be crafted specifically to provide adjudicative facts for a case. For example, in a trademark case, the fact at issue in the trial may be whether the defendant has infringed on the plaintiff's trademark by using one that is too similar. Social or cognitive psychologists could be hired to design experiments to see if consumers confuse the trademark owned by the plaintiff with the one used by the defendant. If the field experiments demonstrate that consumers don't distinguish the two very well, the plaintiff's case is strengthened (see Monahan and Walker, 2006, pp. 92–123).

Social scientists and mental health professionals only testify before courts; they do not make decisions. The decision is up to the ultimate fact-finder: a judge in a bench trial, the jury in a jury trial, and a review board in an administrative hearing. The fact-finders decide whether they believe what the social scientist or mental health expert says and how to weigh the expert evidence. Jurors are instructed that they are free to use expert evidence or to disregard it if they don't value it.

36

CHAPTER 2
Social Science
and
Psychological
Influences in
Law

Providing Social Frameworks

Sometimes an expert witness is not asked about any of the specific facts in contention at the trial. Instead, he or she provides the fact-finders (the jury or judge) with general background information that may help them evaluate and make judgments about the facts (Monahan and Walker, 2006; Walker and Monahan, 1987). This is social framework testimony. Its function is to educate the judge or jury. Social framework testimony may be especially useful when judges and juries are dealing with unusual or unfamiliar social or psychological phenomena (e.g., why children sometimes delay in reporting sex abuse or why some battered women don't leave their batterers; see Box 2.2). The testimony may help them to suspend prejudices or question intuitive beliefs and commonsense assumptions that may be wrong.

Social framework testimony can be used in the same kinds of cases where adjudicative testimony is used. An example should clarify the distinction. Suppose there is a hearing to decide which of two divorcing parents will get custody of a child. The husband argues that it is in the best interest of the child to live with him because his wife has come out as a lesbian. A mental health professional is asked to evaluate both the child and parents. Based on testing, interviewing, and observation (see Chapter 13), the expert expresses a professional judgment on whether the child is developing normally. He or she is providing testimony relevant to an adjudicative fact: whether or not *this* child is harmed by being in the custody of either parent.

Alternatively, the expert may be asked to summarize research about children raised by homosexual parents. The expert testifies that the research shows that the children of lesbian mothers as a group are not more disturbed or sexually confused than other children. The expert is offering **social framework** testimony, general information only, but information the judge may consider very important.

There is controversy about the best way to present social framework testimony. Some argue that the expert should not be called by the prosecution or the defense to testify about scientific findings; instead, the expert should provide a balanced summary of the research to the judge. The judge would then give the relevant information to the jury as an instruction. Others argue that the adversary process is the best

---

BOX 2.2

Social Framework Testimony: Part of an Effective Defense

As social science gained in social influence, the public has become increasingly sensitive to the way context, culture, and point of view influence people's judgment and behavior. In at least one case, a court ruled that social framework testimony was critical to a full understanding of the defendant. Valoree Jean Day's conviction on charges of killing her battering boyfriend was overturned by a California appellate court. Her lawyer failed to introduce expert testimony on the battered woman syndrome in her defense. The court called it ineffective assistance of counsel (*People v. Day*, 1993). The California appeals court evidently thought that hearing the testimony might have helped the judge and jury understand why the defendant did not leave her long-time live-in boyfriend despite being beaten. (As we will see in Chapter 12, the validity of a distinct battered woman syndrome has been questioned, but the usefulness of information about psychological responses to abuse has not.)

way of presenting any kind of information and that cross-examination is the best way to insure accuracy. We will encounter this debate again when we consider the insanity defense.

Presenting Social Authority (Legislative) Facts

When social scientists provide information that helps illuminate a policy decision or contributes to the formulation of new laws, they are providing social authority or legislative facts.

Informing legislators. Social scientists influence policy by working for executive agencies like state education and welfare agencies or the National Institutes of Health. They may act on legislative mandates to research public health and behavioral problems or help develop programs to implement legislative goals. Legislators frequently review relevant social science research when considering social problem legislation (e.g., sexual predator laws that permit civil commitment of repeated sex offenders after they have served their sentences). Individual legislators may have professionals on their own staff who prepare research summaries. Congress may invite professionals to sit on special commissions to review research and to make recommendations. Congressional committees can request reports from government research agencies and can ask professionals to testify at committee hearings. Government agencies like the National Institute of Justice and the Department of Education fund academic research and employ social science researchers directly to help them develop programs and initiatives and to evaluate program and policy effectiveness.

To illustrate the diversity of topics, in the past, psychologist Leonard Jason testified at a hearing held by the congressional committee considering legislation to regulate the tobacco industry. He based his testimony and his recommendations for legislation on his research on the effectiveneess of "sting" operations in curbing tobacco sales to minors. In 2004, psychologists Sandra Brown and Roger Weisberg testified on substance abuse and prevention services for adolescents to a U.S. Senate Subcommittee on Substance Abuse and Mental Health Services. Jeff McIntyre testified on media violence and children to the U.S. House Subcommittee on the Courts, and Cheryl King testified on suicide prevention before a U.S. Senate Committee on Education, Labor and Pensions.

Lobbying. Lobbyists and advocacy groups (e.g., the National Alliance for the Mentally Ill and the Association of Retarded Citizens) bring social science studies to the attention of legislators when the findings support policy choices beneficial to the groups they represent. To be effective, advocates can't just say they want something; they must also argue that their position represents good policy, not merely their "special interests." Citing research justifying their support or opposition to policies helps them to accomplish their goals.

Psychologists and other mental health professionals lobby Congress themselves to promote their own "guild" or professional interests, to advocate for their clients, and to disseminate research they believe has important policy implications. The APA employs professional lobbyists. They try to make legislators aware of research showing their practices are effective, socially useful, or necessary. The American Psychology–Law Society has provided informal luncheon briefings on various subjects to congressional staffers.

38

CHAPTER 2
Social Science
and
Psychological
Influences in
Law

No. 89-478

IN THE

Supreme Court of the United States

OCTOBER TERM, 1989

STATE OF MARYLAND,
> *Petitioner,*

v.

SANDRA ANN CRAIG,
> *Respondent.*

On Writ of Certiorari to the
Court of Appeals of Maryland

MOTION FOR LEAVE TO FILE BRIEF AMICUS CURIAE
AND BRIEF FOR AMICUS CURIAE
AMERICAN PSYCHOLOGICAL ASSOCIATION
IN SUPPORT OF NEITHER PARTY

DAVID W. OGDEN *
JENNER & BLOCK
21 Dupont Circle, N.W.
Washington, D.C. 20036
(202) 223-4400
Attorney for Amicus Curiae

March 2, 1990   * Counsel of Record

WILSON - EPES PRINTING CO., INC. - 789-0096 - WASHINGTON, D.C. 20001

FIGURE 2.3

The APA Amicus Brief to the Supreme Court Reviewing *Maryland v. Craig* (1990)
*The brief presented psychological evidence supporting the position that child witnesses
in sex abuse cases should testify using closed-circuit video to enhance the completeness
and accuracy of their testimony. The brief was successful in the sense that it was cited in
the majority opinion as part of the rationale for the Court's majority opinion. See Chapter 11 for a discussion of this case.*

Amicus briefs. Social scientists may also influence policy making by the judiciary. Appeals courts make policy in deciding cases when they specify the governing rule of law.

One of the ways social scientists can bring research to the attention of the appellate courts is by filing amicus curiae briefs. **Amicus curiae** means "friend of the court." Amicus curiae briefs are briefs submitted by a person or a group that is not a party to the case but that would like to inform the court of its ideas or knowledge about the issues being argued. The APA, the National Association of Social Workers, and the American Psychiatric Association have submitted many such briefs to bring research to the attention of courts, including the U.S. Supreme Court. The briefs may be filed in support of one of the parties to the case or may be submitted to be helpful to the court without supporting either side.

Social science and mental health organizations file *amicus briefs* for a number of reasons: out of public interest; when they feel the research may help a court to come to a more informed decision about an important issue; to protect the interests of a client or subject group, for example, children or the mentally retarded; or to protect professional guild interests, for example, to argue that neuropsychologists are qualified to testify as to causation of a head injury (*Landers v. Chrysler Corporation*, 1997). The organizations call on members with expertise to prepare the briefs in cooperation with legal counsel. The briefs summarize and evaluate pertinent research, and explain how the research bears on a legal point at issue in the case.

Are amicus briefs effective? Observers disagree about how much social science research has actually influenced court decisions, Supreme Court decisions in particular. There are few barriers to submitting amicus briefs to the U.S. Supreme Court. Whether they are read is another matter. Briefs submitted by prestigious organizations such as the APA may garner more judicial attention than others. The APA has a reputation for submitting well-written arguments containing relevant research information. Sometimes (e.g., *Maryland v. Craig*, 1990), the briefs are cited in court decisions, showing they are not without influence (see Box 2.3). Faigman (2005) observed that the results are mixed. He noted that the U.S. Supreme Court sometimes (1) conformed its conclusions to

---

BOX 2.3

Social Scientists as Friends of the Court

Nineteen children testified that Margaret Kelly Michaels, a teacher's aid in the Wee Care day care center, had performed various bizarre forms of child abuse, including some that were impossible (turning a child into a mouse) and some that were highly improbable (making a "poop-cake" that children ate before eating their regular lunch). Michaels was convicted in a jury trial. She appealed. Among her points for appeal were that the trial court permitted prejudicial expert testimony based on inappropriate procedures for interviewing children. The Committee of Concerned Social Scientists submitted an amicus brief for the case, *State of New Jersey v. Michaels* (1994). In the brief, Bruck and Ceci (1995) summarized research that addressed the issue of children's suggestibility and how it can be manipulated. Michaels's conviction was reversed on the grounds that expert testimony and closed-circuit television procedures used to interview the children had been misused. She was released. The State of New Jersey decided not to try her again.

40

CHAPTER 2
Social Science
and
Psychological
Influences in
Law

empirical findings, (2) misapplied the findings in coming to its conclusions, (3) found the research inconclusive, or (4) dismissed the relevance of a particular finding for its conclusions. Nonetheless, Faigman argues that social science research has changed the judicial process. When the justices have to deal with research, they can't base their decisions on assumed facts unsupported by investigation. The value premises underlying their arguments must be clarified. If they decide to disregard research data, they will not be persuasive unless they do so explicitly and explain their reasons.

When Are the Findings of Social Science and Psychology Sufficient to Be Admitted into Evidence in a Legal Proceeding?

To be admitted, **expert testimony** has to meet two criteria: it has to help prove a fact at issue (**probative value**), and the probative value has to outweigh any prejudicial or misleading effects the information might have. Of course, the testimony also has to be "expert." Most witnesses testify to what they have seen or heard directly. With some exceptions, they can't just give their own opinions. Experts are allowed to express opinions. Expert opinions are not considered mere conjecture because they are based on some special knowledge or skill. The testimony should provide something beyond common information known to most jurors. It is up to the courts to decide whether or not to admit testimony by a given witness as "expert."

Traditionally, someone was considered an expert, qualified to give testimony, if he or she had the appropriate credentials or experience. But as science and technology advanced early in the twentieth century and fads and false starts began proliferating, courts became concerned about the introduction of junk science into evidence. What standards should courts use to decide if scientific evidence was reliable enough to present to a jury that might be overly influenced by an expert's credentials, jargon, or use of fancy instruments? In 1923, a federal appeals court in Washington, D.C., proposed a standard for expert testimony that was subsequently adopted in most other jurisdictions (*Frye v. United States,* 1923).

The *Frye* Standard

Frye, a defendant in a murder case, appealed his conviction on the grounds that the trial court erred in refusing to admit scientific evidence that might have exonerated him. The evidence was a polygraph test, which he had passed. The trial court judge had denied his attorney's request to allow testimony about the test or to have it repeated in court. The federal appeals court affirmed the lower court ruling on the ground that the lie detector test had not gained general acceptance among psychologists and physiologists. After this decision, the standard used in federal courts and in many state courts to determine whether to admit scientifically based testimony (known as the *Frye* **standard**) was whether the expert's opinion was developed using methods generally accepted in the relevant professional community. (See the contrasting summaries of the evidence on the validity of polygraph tests in Faigman et al., 2005, by Raskin, Honts, and Kircher, 2005; and Iacono and Lykken, 2005.) When a lawyer wished to introduce scientific testimony, the judge held a hearing to determine if the testimony met the *Frye* standard.

The *Frye* standard posed difficulties. The main problem was that it confused quality with consensus. If a technique or theory was widely used, it was admitted even if there was little or no data supporting its validity. On the other hand, the standard could be used to exclude some testimony based on cutting-edge science, because the work was not yet disseminated or generally accepted. In 1975, the Federal Rules of Evidence were amended to make the procedures used in federal trial courts for admitting expert testimony easier and to clarify the basis of expertise.

The *Daubert* Decision and Social Science

The U.S. Supreme Court reviewed the issue of scientific testimony again in *Daubert v. Merrell Dow Pharmaceuticals* (1993). The appeal, described in Box 2.4, raised the question of when scientific evidence resulting from the use of new techniques should be considered valid.

Justice Harry Blackmun, writing the opinion of the Court, said that, although the 1975 Federal Rules of Evidence were meant to encourage flexibility, not everything was admissible. Before exposing the jury to an expert's opinion, the trial judge must decide whether the opinion has a valid scientific basis. To make the decision, he or she should examine the relevance and reliability of the proffered testimony carefully in an adversary

41

When Are the Findings of Social Science and Psychology Sufficient to Be Admitted into Evidence in a Legal Proceeding?

BOX 2.4

A Legal Case in Point: *Daubert v. Merrell Dow Pharmaceuticals,* 1993

Two children born with birth defects and their mothers sued the Merrell Dow Pharmaceutical Company. They claimed that their birth defects were caused by Bendectin, a drug prescribed to control morning sickness in pregnant women. Both sides acknowledged that the mother had taken the drug. The question was whether the drug caused the birth defects. Merrell Dow introduced experts who reviewed thirty published epidemiological studies involving 130,000 patients. They testified that there was no relationship between taking Bendectin and human birth defects.

The plaintiffs tried to introduce expert testimony by eight equally qualified experts who concluded that Bendectin did cause birth defects. The plaintiffs' experts' opinions were based on in vitro (test tube) studies of the organic effects of the drug, animal studies, and pharmacological studies showing a link between the chemical structure of Bendectin and other teratogens (agents that cause fetal deformity). They also wanted to introduce a meta-analysis of the epidemiological studies, which was undertaken specifically for the litigation. Meta-analysis is a statistical method, relatively new at the time, that is used to pool the results of a large number of studies.

The trial judge refused to allow the plaintiffs' experts to testify. The trial court ruled that the methods the plaintiffs' experts used to establish that Bendectin causes the defects (an adjudicative fact) did not have general acceptance in the field (*Frye* standard). The judge said that the generally acceptable approach for establishing causality was through human epidemiological studies, not animal or in vitro studies. He would not admit the meta-analysis because it had not been carried out for an independent scientific purpose and had not been reviewed and commented on by other scientists (for example published in a journal where articles are reviewed for methodological soundness by other experts before acceptance, or discussed at a conference). Because the plaintiffs had no way to prove Bendectin had caused the birth defects without their experts' testimony, the case was dismissed.

The plaintiffs carried their appeal to the U.S. Supreme Court. The Supreme Court's decision set forth new criteria for judges to apply in deciding whether an expert was basing an opinion on reliable or dubious science. On **remand** (return to a lower court for reconsideration), the Ninth Circuit Court of Appeals again sustained the trial court's decision, and the Dauberts finally lost the case.

42

CHAPTER 2
Social Science
and
Psychological
Influences in
Law

hearing without the jury present. The aim of the hearing, the opinion explained, should be to assess the "scientific validity" of the underlying principles and research that form the basis for the expert opinion.

To establish criteria for scientific validity or solid scientific knowledge, the Court turned to epistemology and to the philosophy of science. The opinion defined knowledge not as certainty, but as facts or ideas that are accepted as truth on good grounds (warrants for knowledge). Good grounds meant that the knowledge was derived from use of the "scientific method." The opinion specified several criteria that judges might use to determine whether testimony could be considered scientific knowledge:

- Are the ideas capable of being tested, that is, "falsified" (disproved)?
- Have the methodologies and ideas been subject to peer review through publication or other means?
- Is there general acceptance of the methods used in the appropriate scientific community? Do experts in the field reasonably rely on the method?
- Is there a known or potential rate of error in the use of a technique, measurement, or classification procedure? (See, for example, discussions of error rates in prediction of dangerousness in Edens et al., 2005; Miller, Amentia, and Conroy, 2005.)
- Are there professionally accepted standards for the correct application of the technique?

The Court noted that scientific testimony did not necessarily have to meet every one of these criteria to be admitted; rather, the criteria were intended to provide some guidance for the trial judge in deciding the admissibility of scientific testimony.

In subsequent cases, the U.S. Supreme Court made it clear that judges may also exclude evidence when they believe that the underlying methodology is sound but "there is simply too great an analytical gap between the data and the opinion proffered" (*General Electric Co. v. Joiner,* 1997). An expert witness' testimony about the reason for a tire failure was not admissible because the underlying method of determining the tire's propensity to fail was not deemed valid for that purpose (*Kumho Tire Co. v. Carmichael,* 1999).

***Daubert's* impact.** *Daubert* may have important effects on the admissibility of psychological and social science evidence in the federal courts and in the many states that use the Federal Rules of Evidence. The meaning and impact of the decision are determined by how it is applied in specific cases, and it is being applied (Faigman et al., 2005; see Studebaker and Goodman-Delahunty, 2002).

The *Daubert* **standards** make judges the gatekeepers who admit or exclude expert testimony from the trial after hearing pro and con arguments at a preliminary adversary hearing. This adversary hearing is the first crucial step in determining whether the evidence will ever reach the fact-finder. In most cases it will also be the last step. In *General Electric Co. v. Joiner* (1997), the Supreme Court ruled that *Daubert* decisions on admissibility of scientific evidence will be reversed only if the judge abuses his or her discretion. The Court reaffirmed this ruling in *Kumho Tire Co. v. Carmichael* (1999). The **abuse of discretion standard** means that, unless the trial judge's decision is almost completely without foundation in the evidence presented at the hearing, an appellate court will sustain the ruling. In *Weisgram v. Marley* (2000), the U.S. Supreme Court went further and held that if an appellate court found the underlying science insufficient or too speculative, the appellate court could even dismiss the case on its own without having to remand the case to the trial court for yet another hearing. Thus, in cases in which either side seeks to admit scientific testimony, lawyers and judges will have to take the admissiblity of scientific evidence very seriously.

Most judges have little training in scientific method, scientific practices, and technical language. Given time pressures, they may not be interested in delving deeply into the questions that occupy the attention of methodologists and philosophers of science. At present, despite *Daubert,* they are not exercising the gatekeeping function by excluding expert testimony based on unreliable social science data. Almost all courts seem to have adopted very liberal standards of admission, relying on the adversary process and cross-examination to expose weaknesses in the science underlying expert opinions and leaving it to the fact-finder to weigh the expert's testimony or reject it (Blanck and Berven, 1999; Lipton, 1999; Shuman and Sales, 1999; Studebaker and Goodman-Delahunty, 2002). However, judges may use their gatekeeping powers more actively in the future.

For judges to evaluate expert testimony actively and well, they will need some understanding of scientific methods and reasoning. At present, at least as reflected in the result of a simulation study, judges, especially those without scientific training, are relatively insensitive to good research design in the social sciences (Kovera and McAuliff, 2000a, 2000b; Kovera, Russano, and McAuliff, 2002). Lawyers will also have to be more aware of the underlying scientific issues to effectively present, defend, or challenge expert testimony. Pretrial briefs supporting or challenging expert evidence are already more common. Lawyers and psychologists will have to learn to understand and use each other's language (Levine, 1999). Treatises such as Faigman et al. (2005) that evaluate the status of the science underlying areas of commonly offered expert testimony may be consulted and used by judges and lawyers regularly.

Expert panels. Judges may also make more use of their authority to appoint independent experts to help them evaluate complex evidence (Rule 706, Federal Rules of Evidence). Supreme Court Justice Stephen Breyer supported the use of court-appointed experts in *General Electric Co. v. Joiner* (1997). Some members of the American Association for the Advancement of Science (AAAS) and the APA have also supported the use of neutral panels. However, lawyers have argued that even independent researchers may have biases and prejudices or simply be wrong. They believe cross-examination will lead to the fairest decisions (Monastersky, 1998). It is also not clear how judges would go about choosing "impartial" experts for a panel. Despite these questions, judges are beginning to appoint panels of experts in highly technical cases (Kolata, 1998). Perhaps we may see the development of something like a "science court," in which two sides will exchange position papers on an issue to determine areas of agreement and areas of disagreement. The disagreement can be subject to further exchanges, and eventually to an adversary hearing on a much narrowed issue (Task Force Presidential Advisory Group on Anticipated Advances in Science and Technology, 1976).

Technical or other specialized knowledge. Some areas of research psychology and many areas of applied psychology do not yet have a strong scientific research base. The complexity of the phenomena may make applications of the experimental method unfeasible or of limited utility. Does a person's knowledge need to be based on rigorous science to be accepted as "knowledge"? The U.S. Supreme Court, in *Kumho Tire Co. v. Carmichael* (1999), accepted testimony based on "experience." But Justice Breyer's opinion in *Kumho* unequivocally said that the trial judge should act as a gatekeeper in cases in which the expert offers testimony on the basis of "experience," just as the judge would if the expert were offering to testify on scientific grounds. Evidence

43

When Are the Findings of Social Science and Psychology Sufficient to Be Admitted into Evidence in a Legal Proceeding?

44

CHAPTER 2
Social Science
and
Psychological
Influences in
Law

that is too "speculative" may not be admissible (*Weisgram v. Marley*, 2000). A *Daubert* hearing and analysis are appropriate to scrutinize the underlying basis of technical or specialized knowledge and its fit to the facts of the case.

So far, clinical experts are rarely, if ever, barred from testifying because of limitations in the underlying science (Slobogin, 1999). The *Kumho* opinion should encourage judges to engage in greater scrutiny of the scientific research underlying testimony by practicing clinicians about such issues as diagnoses of mental illness, the prediction of dangerousness, custody decisions (Kraus and Sales, 1999), battered woman syndrome, rape trauma syndrome, or the child sex abuse accommodation syndrome, which includes delayed disclosure and retraction of disclosure of abuse. Traditionally, judges have been reluctant to admit expert testimony on the reliability of eyewitness evidence and on coerced confessions (see Chapter 6), but, paradoxically, the *Daubert* standards may result in changes in admissibility in those areas as the research base enlarges and methods become more sophisticated. However, in the future, clinical experts may have to become more knowledgeable about the scientific basis for their expertise, and be able to defend it against challenge, especially as new knowledge develops and as lawyers and judges become more sophisticated about the scientific issues.

Differences between Law and Social Science

Law and social science share some important characteristics. At a basic level, both are concerned with human social behavior and its regulation. Both law and social science change as society changes and as knowledge increases (Levi, 1949). However, the two fields have very different social functions, perform different kinds of tasks, and, when they address the same issues, do so in fundamentally different ways.

Social science is a participant–observer in social processes. As partial outsiders whose goal is new knowledge, social scientists try to be skeptical, exploratory, iconoclastic, and open to change of ideas based on new information. In psychology, every conclusion and every theory are subjected to criticism and challenge through attempts to replicate studies, through peer review before publication, and through published criticism by other scientists of published work. Law's fundamental role in society is conservative. Change in the legal system is necessarily gradual because one of the functions of law is to ensure social stability and to help maintain shared conceptions of justice. The system of law also has a role in maintaining a sense of cultural identity and continuity while slowly incorporating cultural innovation and changing values.

The willingness of social scientists to experiment and to throw out or radically alter their hypotheses can be problematic when professionals interact with courts. For social scientists and mental health professionals, being wrong is part of the trial-and-error process of learning. To judges and lawyers, this learning process may seem like mere unreliability. Trial courts seek to find out the truth about past events that are the subject of a specific dispute, then make a specific decision relatively quickly with whatever knowledge they have. When the legal process arrives at an erroneous conclusion, an injustice may be done. Justice Blackmun, writing in *Daubert*, characterized the difference in these terms:

> Scientific conclusions are subject to perpetual revision. Law, on the other hand, must resolve disputes finally and quickly. The scientific project is advanced by broad and wide-ranging consideration of a multitude of hypotheses, for those that are incorrect will eventually be shown to be so, and that in itself is an advance. Conjectures that are

probably wrong are of little use, however, in the project of reaching a quick, final and binding legal judgment—often of great consequence—about a particular set of events in the past. (*Daubert*, 1993, pp. 596–597)

Another difference has to do with the ways law and psychology evaluate behavior. Psychologists tend to see the behaviors, abilities, and responsibilities of different people as varying along a continuum and as varying in the same person with different situations. They generally present conclusions in probabilistic terms, not as absolutes. The legal system often requires that people or behaviors be placed in distinct categories: insane or not, dangerous or not, negligent or not, guilty or not.

Psychologists and judges may also approach issues differently at the legislative (policy) level. Differences in the way they conceptualize a policy problem may lead to misunderstanding between the two groups—and often disappointment for social scientists who sometimes feel that courts don't give their work the weight it deserves.

One of the functions of social scientists as scientists is to test conventional assumptions about human nature empirically. For example, existing research suggests that gay couples can be good parents. In the context of controversy about gay marriage, this finding runs counter to some fervently held "commonsense" beliefs. Policy makers are not always interested in or willing to credit research questioning commonsense or community beliefs (Redding, 1999). They may feel it is a community's right to implement policies that reflect its deeply held beliefs.

Judges have a complex job. Part of their job is to uphold or express the symbols of society's basic values (Faigman, 1991). Even when they are interested in empirical research bearing on a decision, data about the assumptions or outcomes of a policy will comprise only one of their considerations and often not the central one. Judges must take into account legal rights and duties, the fairness of procedures, the appropriate assignment of power and authority, and the role of legal precedent. Their reasoning about these kinds of problems and other legal values determines the conclusions they draw or don't draw from research facts or even whether they consider the research relevant at all.

How Involvement in the Legal System Has Affected the Discipline of Psychology

The involvement of psychology in the legal system serves several professional purposes. Researchers receive funding to pursue work illuminating issues of interest to the legal profession and to policy makers. Research workers may derive satisfaction from knowing that their work has meaning beyond the bounds of universities and research institutes. Some researchers actively seek to present their work so that it can potentially influence the legal system (see Melton, 1987a). Psychologists testifying at trials contribute to settling cases and often receive generous financial remuneration for their contribution. Attention and recognition by the courts, legislative bodies, and high administration officials enhance the status of the discipline.

Research, Pretrial Hearings, and Cross-Examination

Controversy about the knowledge base of the social and clinical sciences is sometimes discouraging to psychologists, but has also stimulated progress and has sharpened thinking about methodological, psychological, and legal problems. Because psychologists who testify in court are subject to cross-examination, the quality of research in the pertinent

46

CHAPTER 2
Social Science
and
Psychological
Influences in
Law

field and the clinical experience on which they base their assertions matter (Matarazzo, 1990). In response to these pressures, experts have learned to be better prepared, to be more careful about basic science and clinical conceptualization, and to state limitations of research. They also pay more attention to the relevance of their work to real social behaviors and to legal issues. The specter of *Daubert* pretrial hearings, conducted before the trial begins to review scientific evidence, or to assess the knowledge base of proffered expertise should stimulate researchers to be more attentive to both the rigor and the breadth of their work and to undertake further research to meet objections to admissibility (Levine, 1999).

Internal and External Validity

Psychological research often takes place in the isolated setting of the university laboratory with readily available student subjects. Some of this work seems contrived and artificial. Researchers ignored social context in pursuit of what they hoped would be basic principles of behavior. The artificiality allowed them to increase **internal validity** by increasing their control over confounding variables. An experiment is internally valid to the extent that the design, method, and analysis allow the researchers to attribute the results (changes in the dependent variable) to the independent variables they have been varying and not to other factors.

When academic psychologists entered the legal arena, **external** or **ecological validity,** the degree to which experimental findings can be generalized to real-life situations, became an issue (see *Lockhart v. McCree,* 1986). Psychologists who wish to influence the legal system have to be able to answer the following questions: do people actually behave in real-life situations the same way they behave when they are subjects in an experiment? Do they behave the way they say they would behave on a questionnaire? Do the variables the psychologist studies really reflect the legal issues the studies are meant to illuminate? As our legal colleagues say, "Are the studies **on point**?" That is, are they specifically relevant to an issue in the case at hand?

New Areas of Investigation

Legal problems have posed new research questions for clinical, social, developmental, and cognitive psychologists. For example, lawsuits around the recovery of **repressed memory** invigorated research on memory and traumatic events (American Psychological Association Working Group on Investigation of Memories of Childhood Abuse, 1998; Freyd, 1996; see also Chapter 17). Research on eyewitness accuracy, coerced confessions, psychological testing, the prediction of dangerousness, children's testimony, and adolescent competence to make an abortion decision, among other topics, has been influenced by legal issues. Research on the phenomenon of stalking increased rapidly after stalking was made a crime (Brody, 1998). Moreover, involvement with the legal system has influenced the specific questions researchers ask about each of these topics. Examining the way courts discounted research in cases like *Lockhart v. McCree* (1986), *McCleskey v. Kemp* (1987), and *Hodgson v. Minnesota* (1990), psychologists realized that studies need to be directly on point for the legal issues they are designed to illuminate if courts are to be influenced (Bersoff, 1987).

Finally, contact with the legal system has made psychologists sensitive to the real-life consequences of applying their work. Studying child maltreatment or children's adjustment to divorce is a very different matter emotionally from advising a court about a decision that will profoundly affect a real parent and a real child's life.

Almost every aspect of psychology's interactions with the legal system presents ethical dilemmas. These are just a sampling of issues that arise in clinical forensic work, in research, and in advocacy efforts to influence public policy:

- How do psychologists decide when they think they have sufficient scientific basis for testifying about an issue (regardless of what the judge thinks about the admissibility of the testimony)?
- What are the psychologist's responsibilities to his or her profession, to the client, to the attorney who solicits the testimony, and to the court?
- Can psychologists ethically agree to undertake work like custody evaluations and assessments of dangerousness when the knowledge base in these areas is limited? If they testify, are they obligated to communicate uncertainty to the court?
- What are the ethics of participating in jury selection using social science methods to try to select favorable jurors, or, more likely, exclude jurors with views unfavorable to the side using the jury consultant? In this context, is it fair that psychologists sell their services to the highest bidder?
- Can psychologists be "objective" when they are paid by one side only, even if they try? Can they be objective if they are independent and paid by the court?

Ethical Standards and Codes

None of these questions are easy ones. The APA's code of ethics (2003) contains general ethical guidelines, but these do not provide clear guidance about how to handle ethical issues specific to the law and psychology interactions. Standards have been developed specifically for custody cases (APA, 1994), and the organization has developed specialty guidelines to set practice and ethical standards for forensic psychology generally (American Psychological Association—Committee on Ethical Guidelines for Forensic Psychologists, 1991). The British Psychological Society has promulgated guidelines in a variety of practice fields related to forensic issues (British Psychological Society, 2002). The Psychological Society of Ireland has promulgated guidelines for specialty training in forensic psychology (Psychological Society of Ireland, 2005). In addition, to help psychologists struggling to apply the guidelines in complex real-life contexts, the APA is building a body of "case law" on ethical issues (Koocher and Keith-Spiegel, 1998).

Objectivity and Values: Controversy about Amicus Briefs

Psychologists have also been debating basic moral questions about whether and how psychology should attempt to influence policy at the legislative level. The ethical problems and the broader value issues are highlighted when the profession attempts to influence or bring psychological data to the attention of appellate courts or to the U.S. Supreme Court, whose decisions can strongly affect social policies.

The amicus curiae briefs submitted by the APA that do not directly involve psychologists' professional interests have often been the subject of controversy within the organization. The public policy briefs lend themselves to controversy because often they lean to one side. Often the controversy cannot be aired before the brief is written. The brief is written by experts in a field selected by the APA committee that commisions the briefs.

48

CHAPTER 2
Social Science
and
Psychological
Influences in
Law

The brief must be presented to the courts within a short period of time after the court indicates it has accepted the case for review. After the case has been resolved, there is sometimes heated discussion within the profession about whether the brief summarized the research fairly and whether there was sufficient good research to justify policy recommendations on scientific grounds.

Two important questions underlie the debates about the amicus briefs. When is a body of knowledge sufficiently well developed to be brought to the attention of a court in an amicus brief with the potential to affect sweeping policy changes? Behind this question is a larger one: what are and what should be the values of psychology?

Psychology's claim to social authority stems largely from a promise to provide scientific knowledge that is **objective,** that is, without interference from personal feelings, prejudices, or values. However, no one thinks psychology is or should be value-free. The traditional view is that psychologists should be as objective and dispassionate as researchers or scientists, but passionately ethical in their treatment of subjects and patients and in overseeing the application of their findings. This view is explicit in the APA's 2002 code of ethics. Members of the organization subscribe to the principles of respect for the rights, dignity, and worth of all people; are aware of cultural, individual, and role differences; and "encourage the development of law and social policy that serve the interests of their patients and clients and the public" (APA, 2002). Psychological research has not been insulated from these liberal and meliorist values. A cover story in the *Monitor,* the APA's newspaper (Azur, 1997), discussed a tendency in the field to avoid research questions that might threaten politically correct beliefs (for example, studies of racial and gender differences; see also Haney, 1993). Also, many journals reject or set higher thresholds of acceptability for research that calls into question liberal beliefs (Azur, 1997; Redding, 2001). Wright and Cummings (2005) collected a number of somewhat polemical essays critiquing aspects of psychology's overly liberal bias in a number of fields. These are instances in which psychologists' values, properly or improperly, are affecting their choices as "objective" researchers.

Prominent thinkers in law and psychology disagree about the proper social role of psychology. For example, Grisso and Saks (1991) argue that psychologists have no special claim to wisdom about legal and policy issues and, consequently, should not make policy recommendations. They maintain that psychology's social influence stems from its scientific credibility, and its credibility is compromised when it takes positions about issues whose resolution involves considerations beyond the scientific. Grisso and Saks believe, as does Faigman (2004), that the public is served when pertinent psychological research is presented to the Court, but that the research should be presented without supporting either side. Gary Melton, on the other hand, believes strongly that psychologists should use their knowledge to actively seek to improve society through the legal system (Melton, 1987a, 1990, 1994). In his view, when good research is behind them, psychologists have a duty to take sides. Haney (1993) also believes in a socially activist psychology. However, he has expressed concerns that, when researchers start working within the legal system, they will lose their critical outside perspective.

Looking at the APA's amicus curiae briefs makes the charge of pursuing a liberal agenda understandable, if not persuasive. Since 1972, the APA has submitted amicus curiae briefs in over 125 cases. About a third of the briefs primarily concerned interests of the profession (e.g., whether outpatient services provided by a psychologist should be considered "medical treatment" for billing purposes) or patient rights (e.g., confidentiality, privilege, and the right of institutionalized patients to refuse medication). These can be considered "guild" briefs. There was no systematic procedure for choosing to produce briefs in the remaining cases. Basically, a researcher who felt strongly about the issue suggested producing a brief and, on consideration through its committee and governance structure, the APA agreed. Many of these briefs argued for decisions supportive of civil rights and tolerance of homosexuals (e.g., *Boy Scouts of America, National Capital Area Council v. Pool*, 2002, and *Lawrence v. Texas*, 2003). A number argued against restrictions on access to abortion (e.g., *Planned Parenthood v. Casey*, 1992). Some argued for affirmative action at the college and professional school level (e.g., *Grutter v. Bollinger*, 2003; *Gratz v. Bolllinger*, 2003). APA argued against the death penalty for the mentally retarded in *Penry v. Lynaugh* (1989), and *Atkins v. Virginia* (2002), and against the death penalty for youth who committed their crime before they were 18 in *Roper v. Simmons* (2005). In many of the nonguild briefs, the APA took what is considered a liberal position on social issues about which the country is very divided. While there was a research basis for the specific contentions in the briefs, and the implicit values were consonant with the APA code of ethics, it is easy to see how conservatives might perceive a political agenda at work simply by the choice of cases and the positions that the APA took. The full text of most of the APA briefs can be retrieved at http://www.apa.org/psyclaw/issues.html (APA, 2006). They are worth studying to see how research undergirds the policy position the briefs take.

We are not suggesting here that any of the APA amicus curiae briefs were inappropriate. We do believe that discussions about the briefs are a good thing. While the issues raised here probably cannot be fully resolved, ongoing dialogue will help psychologists continue to address social issues with seriousness and integrity.

Summary

The modern use of psychological and social science research by the legal system is generally thought to have begun with *Brown v. Board of Education* (1954). Since *Brown*, interactions between law and psychology and law and other social sciences have increased dramatically. Psychologists and other social scientists are employed by the government to help plan and execute social service and justice programs and to deliver services directly. They influence the outcome of trials by testifying as expert witnesses about the facts of the case or by providing background information that will help the jury or judge interpret the facts. They also influence policy decisions by the courts, by testifying as witnesses for (or submitting amicus briefs to) courts deciding questions of law and by testifying to legislatures.

The increased use of psychological, social science, and medical testimony has led to new questions about what standards should be used to determine when testimony is "expert" and how to distinguish junk science from sound science. After the *Frye* decision, courts looked to the expert's peers for guidance, admitting evidence obtained by professionally accepted methods. In *Daubert*, the Supreme Court introduced a new standard, giving trial judges the responsibility of assessing the soundness of methodology on which evidence was based. Another question the courts must resolve is how to evaluate knowledge based on specialized training and experience but lacking the broad and rigorous experimental support required to meet the standard of scientific knowledge.

The relationship between law and psychology has not always been comfortable. Differences in the way the two fields think about problems and in the kind of work they do can lead to misunderstandings and, not infrequently, to frustration on the part of social scientists and psychologists. Nonetheless, the increased association with the legal system has brought greater social power to the psychological, clinical, and social sciences, and new sources of income and increased prestige to researchers and practitioners. With increased power has come a new appreciation of the importance of social context in determining behavior, and a renewed emphasis on sound methodology in general and on developing ecological valid research designs in particular. The increased social power that has followed

50

CHAPTER 2
Social Science
and
Psychological
Influences in
Law

psychology's involvement with the legal system has also created new ethical dilemmas for social scientists and mental health professionals, and added urgency to discussions about what it means to use psychological and social science knowledge responsibly and ethically.

We have entered an exciting era in which the importance of social science to everyday practical affairs is growing. The social sciences may also have a potentially far-ranging influence on society by influencing legislation and court decisions. It is more important than ever before for budding professionals and for intelligent citizens to be aware of their growing impact and potential to influence our lives.

Discussion Questions

1. Do you think law should be built on immutable principles or should respond to the social context? Why?
2. In the late 1990s, federal and state governments changed welfare laws by limiting the time people could remain on welfare and requiring that welfare recipients seek work or attend training. Can you think of two testable empirical assumptions the legislators made when they passed these laws? What are value-based arguments in support of the new laws?
3. Monahan and Walker (2006) made a distinction between adjudicative or social facts, social framework testimony, and social authority or legislative facts. Should the same criteria for sound scientific testimony be applied to each kind of testimony?
4. Would you as a citizen like to see social science groups submit amicus briefs more often or less often? Why? Would you as a future professional like to see social science groups submit amicus briefs more often or less often? Why?
5. What scientific concepts would a judge have to understand in order to decide whether the science in a given area was sufficiently valid to be admitted as testimony?
6. Do you think psychologists' and other social scientists' research is influenced by their political or social values? Similarly, do you think judges' political values influence the weight they give to social science testimony in coming to a decision? How could you test your hypotheses?

Key Terms

abuse of discretion standard	*Frye* standard	probative value
amicus curiae	internal validity	remand
brief	jurisprudence	social (adjudicative) facts
casebook	legal realism	social authority (legislative)
Daubert standard	meta-analysis	facts
expert testimony	objective	social framework
external or ecological	on point	sociological jurisprudence
validity	policy	therapeutic jurisprudence
forensic	pretrial hearings	

CHAPTER **3**

Prediction, Bail, and the *Tarasoff* Duty

This chapter introduces a subject that appears in different contexts throughout this book: the problems—methodological, practical, and ethical—of predicting behavior.

Social science and mental health professionals are frequently asked to make predictions as part of legal proceedings, for example, whether or not a formerly addicted person in treatment will relapse if he or she attends therapy once a week instead of three times a week; in whose home the children of divorcing parents will best adjust to the new family dynamic; or whether a police officer involved in a terrifying incident will be able to perform appropriately if allowed to return to patrol.

Among the most common tasks mental health professionals perform in court is to make **assessments** of dangerousness, also called **risk assessment.** In the legal context, **dangerous** means likely to be physically violent toward others in the future. The word may include suicidal behaviors as well. Legal determinations of dangerousness are usually made by a judge in a hearing, although in the penalty phase of a death penalty trial, the jury may have to make such a determination. However, the reports and recommendations of a mental health professional are often weighed heavily in the decision, and, in some contexts, virtually rubber-stamped. Assessments of dangerousness may have profound consequences for the person evaluated (see Box 3.1). Dangerousness, along with mental illness or a "mental abnormality," is a legal reason for restricting a person's liberty (*Kansas v. Hendricks,* 1997).

BOX 3.1

53

Prediction,
Bail, and the
Tarasoff Duty

Dangerous: A Dangerous Label

Decisions that may be made in whole or in part on the basis of an assessment of potential for violence include:

*   whether a suspect is released on bail or detained in jail;
*   whether a convicted person is imprisoned or placed on probation;
*   whether he or she serves the maximum sentence or is paroled;
*   whether a mentally ill person is involuntarily committed to a mental hospital, or allowed to make his or her own choices about hospitalization;
*   when a person will be released from mental hospital (even if the original admission was voluntary);
*   whether or not an abusive parent is allowed to keep custody of his or her child while receiving treatment;
*   whether or not a parent can retain his or her parental rights;
*   whether a young person charged with a crime is tried as a juvenile or an adult (Monahan, 1981).

An assessment of dangerousness may also contribute to a jury's decision about whether or not a convicted murderer should be executed (see Chapter 8, The Death Penalty).

Psychologists, psychiatrists, and social workers think of themselves as healers or helpers, but they also have a policing function. As agents of social control, they have a responsibility to protect the safety of the public. When they are asked to make an assessment of dangerousness, they sometimes experience a conflict between their different roles. The freedom of a person to whom they owe a duty of care depends on their very fallible judgment about whether that person is a potential risk to the safety of others.

The social and medical sciences can make accurate statements about the **probability** or likelihood of various future outcomes in a population based on information about what happened in the past. A **population** is defined as a group of people with common characteristics from which researchers draw samples: males, Latinos, all those released from a mental hospital the previous year, and so on. Social scientists may be able to say that 30 of 100 people in group A will engage in a certain behavior in the future but only 10 of 100 people in group B. Consequently, they can say that a member of A is more likely to engage in the behavior than a member of B. However, they will not be very good at identifying which specific individuals in either group will exhibit the behavior in the future. Crystal balls, fortunately or unfortunately, are not in the arsenal of the human sciences.

In this chapter we will look at the techniques of prediction social scientists use and at the ethical and practical problems, costs, and consequences of applying these techniques in a legal context. The chapter is divided into three sections. In the first, which relies heavily on the work of Paul Meehl (1954), Meehl and Albert Rosen (1955), and John Monahan (1981, 1982, 1997), we discuss the methodology of prediction, using dangerousness as an example. Topics discussed include the following:

*   The statistical principles underlying predictions
*   What inaccurate prediction means

- The special problems of using quantitative methods to assign individuals to groups at high, medium, and low risk of engaging in a violent act in the future
- Assessment of dangerousness among the mentally ill
- Accuracy of assessments of dangerousness
- Ethical problems in the use of assessments of dangerousness

In the next two sections, we will examine the application of risk assessment techniques in two real-world contexts: one involving the criminal justice system, and the other in the civil law context involving the patient–therapist relationship.

The second section looks at bail setting. Decisions about bail explicitly or implicitly involve predictions about the risks of two kinds of behavior: dangerousness (committing a crime while released after arrest but before trial), and running away or failure to appear in court. In this section, we will explain the following:

- A defendant's right to bail and the limits on those rights
- Different ways of making decisions about bail
- How the bail system functions in practice
- How predictive techniques have been applied to improve the bail system
- Bail bonds and bounty hunters

In the final section, we look at the effects of the famous *Tarasoff* decision (*Tarasoff v. Regents of the University of California,* 1974, 1976), which, under civil law, obligated therapists to assess the dangerousness of their patients. Here we will discuss the following:

- How courts decide whether to impose **liability** in a personal injury (tort) case
- The *Tarasoff* case and the imposition of a new liability (legal obligation) on therapists
- Therapists' concerns about the impact of the ruling
- Risk assessment issues raised by the *Tarasoff* duty
- Effects of the *Tarasoff* duty on therapists' attitudes, behavior, and decisions
- Effects on clients and potential victims
- Juror biases and their potential impact on *Tarasoff* tort cases

---

SECTION I
PREDICTION: METHODS AND DILEMMAS

⊠ Clinical versus Statistical Predictions

Psychologists distinguish two kinds of predictions: clinical and statistical (actuarial). **Clinical predictions** are predictions about the likelihood that a particular person will behave in a certain way in the future based on the judgment of an expert or professional. The expert uses an **idiographic** approach, focusing on the distinctive qualities of the individual he or she is assessing. When a psychiatrist in the emergency room interviews a patient who has threatened suicide, and decides that the patient needs to be hospitalized because the threat is serious, the doctor is making a clinical judgment.

When making clinical judgments, clinicians usually focus on the individual's personal characteristics and on observations of behavior and reactions in interviews, or on the results of psychological tests. Cognitive-behavioral therapists also look at the person's circumstances and at situational triggers for a client's unwanted behavior. These therapists estimate risk partly by estimating how likely it is that the person will be exposed to a triggering situation (for example, an urge to use drugs may be experienced by a recovering patient when upset or when socializing at a party). In making a prediction, the clinician tries to take into account "all the facts and circumstances" and whatever is known about the behavior of people with a certain kind of personality. Flexibly taking into account everything one can, rather than mechanically weighing a few quantitative "predictors," seems to make sense. However, we shall see that this very flexibility is a weakness for predictive purposes.

Statistical predictions, in contrast, are quantitative predictions based on **statistical** (or **actuarial**) formulas. The expert takes a **nomothetic** approach, looking at the regular and normative behavior and characteristics of populations rather than individuals. The prediction is made by assessing the individual in terms of a small number of characteristics known to be more common among people who exhibit the behavior in question (e.g., performing acts of violence) than among people who do not. The more characteristics the person shares with the group that exhibits the behavior, the more likely it is that he or she will also exhibit the behavior.

Courts and Clinical Prediction

Courts turning to mental health experts for predictions of dangerousness seek the experts' clinical assessments. Courts assume the experts will take into account the best knowledge in their field in making the assessment. In practice, neither courts nor experts routinely follow up cases to find out whether the predictions made in particular cases were right or wrong. The follow-up is left to the occasional research study.

Clinical assessments may appear more attractive to courts than assessments based on statistical formulas because they appear to take account of all of the complexities of individual character and circumstances. The task of the court, after all, is to make a judgment about the individual in the case at bar. Moreover, it seems unfair to base a judicial decision on group membership, which is basically what statistical assessments do. However, research has consistently demonstrated that statistical methods of prediction are more **accurate** than clinical methods. Over a series of cases, the overall percentage of correct predictions is actually higher when actuarial or statistical methods are used than when the expert relies on his or her own judgment on a case-by-case basis (Grove and Meehl, 1996; Meehl, 1954).

The Psychometrics of Statistical Predictions

Statistical prediction studies use a well-understood psychometric framework. (**Psychometrics** refers to psychologically relevant measurements.) The researcher begins by choosing one or more **criterion** variables; these are measures of the behavior the researcher wants to predict. Most past studies of violence have used arrest, conviction, or subsequent involuntary hospitalization rates as criterion measures of dangerousness. Sometimes a study will use self-report or the report of spouses or relatives as the criterion measure. Researchers track subjects' performance on the criterion behavior for a set period of time (e.g., six months, one year, five years, etc). The researcher then looks for **predictor variables,** variables that correlate with the criterion variable among a sample population. (The population might be all the mentally ill who were released from a hospital within the last year, all former sex offenders released from prison in a state, or other specific categories.) The predictors may be variables that are measured in the present (e.g., IQ scores). They may be variables determined from past history (e.g., number of prior arrests or personal history of child abuse). They may be **demographic variables** such as age, sex, socioeconomic status, marital status, or race. They may be behavioral variables the researchers thought might be related to the criterion and tracked along with it. Finally, the researcher uses a statistical formula to combine the predictor variables. Each variable is assigned a weight based on how strongly it correlates statistically with the criterion. The researcher uses the formula to produce a risk estimate for each individual, for example, classifying them as high, medium, or low risk of engaging in the criterion behavior. The formula is then retested with new samples.

The statistical method selects the variables with the best correlations, without respect to theoretical relationships between the predictor and the criterion variable. One problem is that the statistical procedures tend to weight the variables to maximize the relationship between the predictor and the criterion variable. The high-powered statistical formulas may take advantage of every bit of chance variation in a data set. For example, Steadman et al. (2002) note that two of the predictors that emerged in their statistical analysis contradicted findings from other research. In previous research, the two predictors had correlated positively with violence. In their study, the same two predictors correlated negatively with violence. The statistical result is also subject to *shrinkage.* That is, the empirically determined formula may not predict as well in another sample, or in other circumstances. For that reason, studies of predictors should be *cross-validated,* that is, tested for efficiency of prediction in a new sample. Few studies attempt cross-validation (Steadman et al., 2000).

Why Statistical Predictions Are More Accurate than Clinical Predictions

Clinicians using qualitative approaches may take into account the same variables included in statistical formulas. They consider other variables in their assessments as well. These may be based on "experience" with similar cases, on theory that has not yet been validated by research, on hunches or intuitions, or sometimes even on subconscious prejudices. To the degree that they use variables whose statistical relationship to the criterion is unknown or even invalid, and to the degree they weight known predictors differently in each case, their **error rate** increases. Moreover, many experienced clinicians don't systematically check back on a series of cases to see how they have done, so they have no idea if the factors they consider in their decision making are truly predictive. Some clinicians may become victims of **illusory correlation,** remembering cases that fit and forgetting those where they made errors. For these reasons, mechanical, statistical approaches to prediction produce fewer prediction errors.

Cutoff Scores, Hits, and Misses

When mental health professionals make an assessment of dangerousness, they produce an estimate of the likelihood that the individual will be violent. They determine that the person is at higher or lower risk (probability) of hurting someone. However, the

BOX 3.2

False Positives

Monahan (1981) describes a number of studies to illustrate the false positive problem. A study by Kozol, Boucher, and Garafolo (1972) was typical. The researchers looked at offenders who had been convicted of violent sex crimes. A team of mental health workers evaluated the prisoners when they became eligible for parole. The court followed the team's recommendation to release some of the offenders. The court also released some offenders that the team had recommended be retained. Both groups were followed in the community for five years.

The team didn't do badly. The rate of false negatives was low: only 8 percent of the 386 offenders whose release was recommended by the team committed a violent act. However, 34.7 percent of the 49 released by the court against the team's advice committed a violent act (true positives), but 65.2 percent had still not committed a violent act five years after release. Had the court followed all of the team's recommendations, the 65.2 percent who did not commit a violent act in the next five years would have remained in prison.

mental health professional working in a legal context is required to classify, or help the judge classify, the person being evaluated into a distinct category. The legal system usually needs to know if a person is dangerous or not. Because serious consequences can flow from the categorical placement, the law finds it unhelpful to have someone assessed as just "a little dangerous."

Statistical techniques can be used to place people into categorical groups by choosing cutoff scores as predictors (see Box 3.2). Everyone who scores above a certain cutoff will be considered at high risk and put in the dangerous box. When cutoff scores are used to classify individuals into two groups, there are four possible outcomes: two ways of being in error and two ways of being right. Using our dangerousness example, we would get the following:

1. *True positives:* individuals who are predicted to be violent and, according to the criterion measure, prove, in fact, to be violent
2. *True negatives:* individuals who are predicted not to be violent and, according to the criterion measure, prove not to be violent
3. *False positives:* individuals who are predicted to be violent but, according to the criterion measure, prove not to be violent
4. *False negatives:* individuals who are predicted not to be violent and, according to the criterion measure, prove to be violent

Cases that fall into categories (1) and (2) are *hits:* the predictions were correct. Correct predictions provide accurate information to decision makers. The accuracy rate is the total percentage of hits, whether the correct predictions are **true positives** or **true negatives.** Cases that fall into categories (3) and (4) are *misses,* errors of prediction. The two kinds of errors have different costs associated with them. When we make a **false positive error** about dangerousness, we may detain a person, depriving him or her of liberty unnecessarily. When we make a **false negative error,** we may fail to constrain a person who will then harm someone else.

We can set our cutoff scores higher to increase the likelihood of labeling as *dangerous* only people who will be violent. That approach will also increase the false negatives because we will be "predicting" that more people won't act out violently. We can set our cutoff lower, to be sure of detecting more of the people who will be violent, but, by lowering the cutoff, we will be creating more false positives because we will be "predicting" that more people will be violent.

Base Rates

The proportion of different kinds of errors is also affected by the base rate of a problem's occurrence. **Base rate** refers to the percentage of people in the entire population of interest who exhibit a given behavior over a specified period of time. When we have a low base rate, when a behavior is infrequent, the rate of false positives will be high even if the prediction technique is very accurate (Meehl and Rosen, 1955). If the base rate in a population is low, say 1 percent, if we predict no one will be violent, we will be right 99 percent of the time, and wrong only 1 percent of the time. If we use a risk assessment instrument for this low base rate behavior that classifies some people as likely to be violent and some as unlikely to be violent, it will "overpredict" violence. Most of the errors will be false positives ones, though it will make some false negative errors as well (i.e., it will miss some cases who will prove to be violent).

Attempted assassination is an example of a very low base rate behavior. In the last 50 years, only 83 people have attacked or tried to attack a U.S. political figure or major celebrity. The Secret Service carefully studied all these cases in an attempt to develop a profile of a typical assassin in order to predict in advance who might become an assassin. But no useful profile emerged. The traits that characterized the majority of the 83 assassins were shared by, literally, millions of other U.S. citizens: the "typical" assassins were white, adult, and male, and had some kind of contact with the mental health system (Fein and Vosskuil, 1998). Finding potential assassins in this group would indeed be trying to find a needle in a haystack. And no one would think of detaining hundreds of thousands, if not millions, of people over a 50-year period to prevent 83 individuals from perpetrating an assassination or an assassination attempt. In general, the odds of detecting the individuals who will be violent are better if we narrow the pool to include only people who have actually made a threat; but, even then, the vast majority of people who make threats don't carry them out (Harmon, Rosner, and Owens, 1998). Profiling persons to predict who is a terrorist getting on an airplane is another example of trying to identify a rare occurrence.

Accuracy of Predictions of Dangerousness

High Error Rates

In 1997, Monahan reviewed studies of the validity of predictions of violence among mentally ill people treated in psychiatric hospitals and mentally ill people charged with a crime and treated in a forensic hospital. Both clinical and statistical methods were evaluated. The professionals using the predictive techniques classified subjects more accurately than they would have done by assigning them by a flip of a coin (by chance). The methods for predicting violence have some validity. However, the majority of the individuals the professionals rated high risk did not commit any violent acts during the period of follow-up. The results of a study by Steadman et al. (2000) using very sophisticated statistical techniques are similar to the results of the large number of studies reviewed by Monahan (1997).

Steadman et al. (2000) tested a model predicting violence in discharged psychiatric patients after 20 weeks in the community. In that sample, about 19 percent committed an act of violence within the 20 weeks after release into the community. Based on their initial statistical analysis, they identified cutoff scores that assigned a low probability of risk to some cases, and a high probability of risk to other cases. In the *high probability of violence* group, 44 percent proved violent (true positives), but 56 percent of the cases in that group were not violent (false positives). In the *low probability of violence* group, 96 percent did not commit an act of violence in the 20 weeks (true negatives), but 4 percent did (false negatives). A third group could not be classifed into either the high- or low-probability groups. Of these, 21 percent were violent, close to the overall base rate. The actuarial method certainly did much better than chance in identifying violent cases, but it still made substantial numbers of false positive errors, partly because the base rate was relatively low (19 percent), and it made some false negative errors as well. The high error rates raise questions about the degree to which we can rely on predictions when the life or liberty of an individual is at stake.

Can Accuracy Be Improved?

Validity of Predictors

Recall that *validity* refers to the degree to which a predictor predicts a criterion measure. The choice and number of the predictor variables can improve or weaken validity. Risk assessment studies have tended to look at a few static (unchanging) variables such as diagnosis of mental illness, past history of violence, and demographic characteristics (e.g., age, gender, race, and ethnicity). Predictions might be improved by taking account of socioeconomic status, employment stability, intelligence, and the use of drugs and alcohol, all of which are related to arrests for violent crime (Silver, Mulvey, and Monahan, 1999).

Predictive accuracy might also be improved by including dynamic factors among the variables. In contrast to **static variables,** which do not change over time, **dynamic variables** are characteristics of people and situations that change. Characteristics that wax or wane over time, such as employment status or degree of anger, are dynamic factors.

Greater attention to possible dynamic factors, such as the active or quiescent status of the patient's psychosis (Link and Stueve, 1994), and situational variables might improve prediction techniques. Very few studies have analyzed situations in the community likely to trigger violent behavior in different individuals and calculated the likelihood that the individual would be exposed to these situations (Monahan, 1984, 1988). Even if dynamic characteristics or situations are better predictors, they are difficult to ascertain in time to prevent violent acts (Dedman, 1998; Fein and Vosskuil, 1998).

We now have sophisticated statistical methods for comparing the accuracy of different methods of prediction. One such method is the receiver operating curve (ROC), which provides an estimate of the probability that a violent person is correctly classified by the predictive method compared to a nonviolent person (Sjostedt and Grann, 2002). The same predictor may yield different levels of accuracy, depending on the criterion measure. Sjostedt and Grann (2002) compared actuarial risk assessement devices for sex offenders against several criteria. The predictions worked well for any sexual reoffending, and worked well for "imminent and less severe reoffending." However, they were less accurate in predicting "repeated and injurious sexual reoffenses," and the predictive formula had no value at all in predicting intrafamilial recidivism. The findings lead to the question of which criterion measure is the most important.

Williams and Houghton (2004) studied domestic violence reoffending in 1,465 male domestic violence offenders. They used a 12-item scale as the predictor (e.g., prior non–domestic violence conviction, prior assault, and harassing) and had an 18-month follow-up. Based on official records as the criterion, they were able to predict reoffending at a statistically significant level above chance, but the predictive accuracy was modest. They also used, as criterion measures, victim reports six months after the offender was sentenced. Here they developed measures of three forms of abusive behavior: (1) an index of control (using her income, stopping her from going someplace, pressuring her into sex, etc.), (2) an index of threats, and (3) an index of severe threats, including physically violent behavior. Their predictor, using ROC analyses, showed different levels of predictive accuracy for the several criteria. Predictions were not signficantly more accurate than chance for controlling behaviors, and for less threatening behaviors. Predictions were significantly greater than chance for severe threatening behaviors and for severe physical violence. While these predictions were significantly more accurate than chance, overall accuracy was only modest. Giving someone a longer sentence based solely on a prediction that the person has a level of probability of being violent is not consistent with constitutional due process rights, except perhaps for those convicted of sex offenses (see *State v. Halgren*, 1999). Are we willing to incarcerate all those with relatively high scores on the predictor scale when the level of accuracy is only modest?

Faulty Criterion Measures

The choice of criterion measures will also affect validity. The strength of a prediction depends not only on how well the variables predict the criterion, but also on how well the criterion assesses the broader behaviors it is intended to measure. Criteria are not interchangeable (Mulvey and Lidz, 1993). First, not everyone who commits an act of violence is detected. If arrest records are used, we will not gather data about people who commit violent acts but are not arrested. Family members are the targets in about half the incidents of violence, but may be more reluctant than strangers to call the police or request arrest. Consequently, many episodes of within-family violence won't be reflected in arrest records. If we use convictions, we will miss cases where a violent individual escapes conviction. Second, for some purposes it might be important to count milder forms of violence in which there is no grievous injury and the police are not called. About two-thirds of all violent acts take place in the home or another residence (Steadman et al., 1998). Milder forms of violence (shouting, pushing, menacing, gesticulating wildly, and impulsive damage to property) can be distressing. Neighbors may or may not be aware of and upset by these episodes. Their responses may differ from responses of family members or from arrest records. Which is the best criterion measure depends on our purposes in trying to make predictions.

Another problem is choosing the time period during which the criterion behavior is monitored. The follow-up period is different in different studies, making them hard to compare. Predictions about imminent dangerousness (in the next few days or weeks) might prove more accurate than predictions of behavior over the next five years or over a lifetime (Monahan, 1984, 1988).

Still another problem is specifying the circumstances under which risk is assessed. If the measure is a defendant's behavior on death row under tightly controlled conditions, one result might obtain (Death Penalty Information Center, 2005). If the measure is the person's behavior in an ordinary community, a different result might follow. A person may have a different likelihood of committing a dangerous act when he or she lives in a densely populated anonymous urban community where neighbors don't know each other than when he or she lives in a sparsely populated rural community. Predictors correlate with these criterion measures differently. Which criterion do we use for validation purposes, and which predictor of which criterion should we use for practical decision making?

Risk Management

Risk management is an alternative strategy to using a predictor to decide who to incarcerate and who to release. We can use a predictor to decide who needs to be most closely supervised upon release into the community. We can make reassessments during the supervision contacts. Heilbrun (1997) calls this approach a management model of risk assessment. Where prediction models aim at determining the relative probability of a person being violent, risk management aims at getting the information needed to reduce the risk and using the information in an ongoing way (Heilbrun et al., 1998). Risk management implies a context of ongoing monitoring, frequent reassessments, the availability of interventions, and an emphasis on dynamic risk factors that can be altered by supervision, intervention, and, perhaps, continuing treatment or support.

New laws mandating notification of a community that a previously convicted, high-risk sex offender lives in the neighborhood are based on risk management of a different kind. Persons who are at risk of reoffending are identified and, in theory, are "supervised" by parents, neighbors, school officials, and police who try to keep the known offender away from children. The method has its own advantages, but also its own difficulties (e.g., vigilante actions against the offender). Interventions sometimes have unpredictible negative consequences, including possible effects on property values in neighborhoods where there are known sex offenders. One known sex offender moved into a new real estate development. The police, following their responsibilities under the law in that state, distributed flyers informing the neighbors that a sex offender lived in their midst. As a result of that revelation, new buyers stopped buying homes in that development. The developer went to court to try to oust the sex offender from the neighborhood. He alleged that the sex offender offered to move, if the developer would give him $250,000 (Associated Press, 2005b).

Practical Considerations in Developing Risk Assessment Instruments

The most statistically sophisticated risk assessment instruments, which require potentially time-consuming mathematical weighting of each item, are difficult to use in police stations or emergency rooms where quick judgments are required. Consequently, researchers and clinicians sometimes prefer to develop structured instruments and questionnaires for risk assessment. Instruments of this kind predict about as well as more complex measures. Gottfredson and Snyder (2005) compared the validity of instruments derived from the same data set using several different statistical methods. The simpler measures had about as much predictive validity as the more sophisticated measures.

Because of their friendliness and comprehensibility, simple instruments are much used in practical settings and in multidisciplinary mental health settings (Webster et al., 1997). The simple instruments have disadvantages, however. They do not provide any information about interrelationships among variables. Consequently, statistically more complex instruments are more valuable in research for validating constructs and for generating hypotheses about the causes of violent acts.

Costs and Benefits of Risk Assessment

The methods of prediction will always be imperfect. We therefore have to consider the social costs and benefits of imperfect predictions and the justification for acting on them.

The courts agree that the state can legitimately use its power to protect society from individuals who might act in a dangerous manner (see *United States v. Salerno,* 1987; *Kansas v. Hendricks,* 1997). However, the state cannot do so aribitrarily; officials must follow lawful procedures. The required procedures usually involve a determination of dangerousness by a judge or, in some cases, a jury. For example, in death penalty cases in several states, including Texas and Oregon, in the penalty phase jurors will hear testimony from expert witnesses about the defendant's dangerousness when deciding whether to sentence a convicted defendant to death or life without parole. The experts will base their judgments on risk factors for reoffending in the community. But if not executed, these defendants would remain in prison, where different risk factors might operate. Few exhibit dangerous behavior, even though all have been convicted of murder (Death Penalty Information Center, 2005).

Despite professional questions about the validity of predictions of dangerousness and the scientific basis for such predictions, we should not expect much change from the courts in the foreseeable future. Under *Daubert* standards, the admissibility of expert testimony on predictions of dangerousness could be challenged. But in deciding what expert testimony is admissible, state trial judges are not concerned with detailed analyses of research, especially in a traditional area of testimony such as experts making predictions of dangerousness. Judges may lean toward admitting the expert opinion, and leave it to cross-examination to detect weaknesses in an expert's testimony and opinions (Dahir et al., 2005).

Mental health professionals and social scientists have debated the ethics of making and using imperfect predictions about dangerousness (Otto, 1994). Even if detaining someone to prevent future acts of violence is justified in limited circumstances for public safety, the justification becomes more dubious if the prediction of dangerousness on which it is based is flawed. Knowledgeable mental health professionals doing risk assessments know that their assessments of dangerous persons may be wrong more often than they will be right (false positives). In fact, the percentage of mistakes is so high that some argue that mental health professionals are ethically obligated to refuse to make predictions about dangerousness on the grounds that it is outside their competence to do so (Grisso and Applebaum, 1992; Mathiesen, 1998; Ogloff, 1998; Webster, 1998). The pragmatic value of risk assessment could also be questioned: is the gain to public safety from detaining some dangerous people great enough to justify the public dollar expense and unwanted human costs of detaining many people who are not dangerous? Participation in risk management, in contrast to making predictions that may result in someone's loss of freedom or even death, is less ethically troubling. Under risk assessment, the person's freedom is not completely limited, and the mental health professional may have a therapeutic role as well as a supervisory role.

On the other hand, the accuracy of prediction must be evaluated against some alternative (Monahan, 1984). Judges and jurors can only make some decisions by considering, among other factors, how they believe an individual might behave in the future. The important question, many professionals believe, is whether, over time, the imperfect but statistically valid predictions of mental health professionals improve court decision making overall or aid in treatment planning and relapse prevention (Heilbrun, 1997).

Relative Inaccuracy Is Ethically Tolerable

While relative inaccuracy should give us pause for concern, it is not, in and of itself, sufficient justification for abandoning the attempt to make reasoned predictions (Morris and Miller, 1987). We can be less concerned about inaccuracy and false positives when restrictions on liberty are slight. We impose slight restrictions on individual liberty even when expected risks are very low. We use metal detectors at airports even though hardly anyone will be detected carrying a weapon. In a sense, everyone without a weapon going through the detector is a false positive.

Unfairness is also less of an issue when there is no longer a presumption of innocence. A person who has been convicted of a crime and is considered for probation or parole is legitimately subject to the state's power to punish or restrain. Even if the state uses imperfect predictions about such a person's dangerousness to decide what sentence to impose or whether to consider early release from prison, it is acting within its authority. The state's use of predictions to make decisions about detaining a person who is only accused of a crime, or who has threatened but not carried out a violent act, is more morally problematic.

Prediction and Discrimination

Morris and Miller (1987) argue that, when carefully tested statistical tools are available, ethical considerations require using them rather than relying on less accurate, less consistent, unguided intuitive clinical predictions. However, statistical methods for predicting some behaviors, violence among them, may be discriminatory. For example, although the vast majority of each group doesn't commit acts of violence, a relatively small number of younger men and African American men are more likely to commit acts of violence than others are. Race, age, and gender are valid, if imperfect, predictors because using them in a large number of cases will improve overall predictions. But, if these predictors are used, young men, and especially young African American men, will make up a disproportionate number of the false positives, the people who will be unnecessarily detained. That is the problem with *racial profiling*. In research, the problem can be controlled to some extent by appropriate statistical methods, which take race into account but allow the development of a fairer, race-free instrument (Gottfredson and Snyder, 2005).

To take another example, Silver, Mulvey, and Monahan (1999) used data from the MacArthur Foundation's Risk Assessment study to investigate the effects of neighborhood environment on rates of violence among patients discharged from psychiatric hospitals. They characterized neighborhoods with poverty rates of 30 percent or higher as neighborhoods of "concentrated poverty" (although individual *socioeconomic status [SES]* still varied widely within these neighborhoods). Even when individual risk factors were controlled, the odds of committing a violent act increased by a factor of 2.7 in neighborhoods with concentrated poverty. These neighborhoods are also high in victims who need protection. Should we detain everyone living in such a neighborhood? As with race, the idea of making legal decisions regarding someone's liberty partly on the basis of his or her place of residence is not a comfortable one. In the end, a political and social choice must be made about the appropriateness of using predictions in each context (Grisso and Appelbaum, 1992).

Many social scientists believe that if predictions are to be made, the fairest way to make them is to use the best scientific methods available. Over time, decisions as a whole will be better than if judges and professionals just followed their instincts in the courtroom (Ennis and Litwack, 1974). This may be difficult to achieve in the real world. Unfortunately, the media have little interest in the science of prediction. Members of the media may be intent on publicizing an egregious violent act by a false negative case (someone who had been in contact with the mental health professions and released) rather than in educating the public about the statistical problems of prediction.

Sometimes research does have an influence in changing policy. For a long time, judges did rely primarily on their instincts and on rough guidelines in making decisions about setting or granting bail. Social scientists were able to demonstrate that the use of scientifically developed prediction methods could improve the bail system overall and make the system at least somewhat fairer for poorer people.

SECTION II
BAIL: A SYSTEMS REFORM

The Eighth Amendment to the U.S. Constitution mentions bail. **Bail** refers to the release of someone charged with an offense in return for a guarantee that he or she will remain within the court's jurisdiction and return at the appointed time for hearings and for trial. The word *bail* also refers to money or property that is given as a guarantee that the person will make the promised court appearances. (If he or she doesn't, the court keeps the money for the state.)

Bail is a social invention for fairly balancing the rights of the accused and society's need for peace and security during the period between arrest and trial. Justice benefits when there is a period of time between charge and trial to allow momentary passions against the accused to dissipate and to allow the defense and the prosecution to prepare their cases.

The practice of setting bail goes back at least to twelfth-century England. At that time, the king's judges rode a circuit from town to town to hear criminal cases. An arrested person had to wait, sometimes for months, until the judge reached the community where he or she lived (Green, 1985). In the interim, the defendant would be released to someone who would agree to produce him or her at trial. The custodian who failed to produce the defendant at the appropriate time could be tried for the crime in his or her place. By the thirteenth century, defendants could put up money or property as a bond that would be forfeited to the government if they failed to appear for trial.

Bail entails psychological assumptions and predictions about two behaviors. In setting bail, the court assumes that defendants will be motivated to leave the court's jurisdiction before trial if not restrained, and that a money bond will provide sufficient motivation for the accused person to appear in court when required. The judge decides what kind and how great a guarantee to require partly on the basis of implicit predictions about the defendant's behavior if set free. The court makes another prediction when it considers the likelihood the person will commit a crime if released on bail. In this section, we will see how social scientists empirically examined the assumptions underlying bail and how their findings led to a system-level reform.

Between Arrest and Trial

Bail is set when a suspect is charged with a crime. This is not the same thing as being arrested. The police can only hold a suspect 48 hours after arrest (*Riverside County v. McLaughlin,* 1991), after which they must release him or her, or the prosecutor's office must formally charge the person with a crime. The formal charge is made at an initial hearing before a judge called an **arraignment.** The arraignment brings the arrested person under the court's authority. The judge informs the suspect of the charges and of his or her rights, including the right to an attorney, and hears the prosecution's and defense's recommendations about bail. The defendant, if represented by an attorney, will usually plead "not guilty" at this point. If the defendant is not represented by counsel, the judge will grant a delay until the person can obtain representation. The judge then decides whether to detain the defendant while he or she awaits trial, release the person on his or her own recognizance, or release him or her on bail.

If the judge decides to release the defendant on bail, the judge sets the amount after a brief discussion with prosecutor and defense counsel. Additional conditions may also be imposed. For example, when John Gotti Jr., son of a Mafia boss, was charged with extorting payments from a nightclub, he was released on bail under strict conditions. He was confined to virtual house arrest. Authorities monitored his phone calls, his visitors were screened, and a 24-hour guard was posted outside his door ("Strict Bail Conditions," 1998). Mr. Gotti had to pay $24,000 a month for round-the-clock security guards, a condition of his bail. Mr. Gotti was convicted and served a seven-year term (Fitzgerald, 1999). If the judge denies bail at the initial appearance, the defense may appeal the decision. Once bail is set, it may be continued after trial pending sentencing or an appeal.

Juveniles brought into juvenile detention or family court are not eligible for bail. The issue of preventive detention of juveniles is discussed in Chapter 9.

Bail Options

A variety of bail devices are available today. A person can post the bond in cash. The cash bond will be returned if the person returns for all required appearances. A person may pledge property in place of the bail, with the knowledge that the property will be forfeited if the defendant fails to appear. The use of a **bail bond** is a common practice. The bondsperson functions like an agent for a surety company, pledging to pay the full bond to the court if the defendant fails to appear. In return, the defendant pays the bondsperson a percentage of the value of the bond as a flat fee. In effect, the defendant is taking a loan from the bondsperson. That means that, if the defendant obtains a $25,000 bond, he or she will be out the fee (for example, 10 percent or $2,500) whatever the outcome of the trial. Paying the bondsperson's fee can be a significant hardship to a poor person and his or her family. However, the bondsperson also has a financial stake in whether the defendant makes required court appearances.

In the last 30 years, the practice of releasing defendants on their **own recognizance** (promise to return with no financial stake) has become more common. Courts are also more willing to allow release without bond, but with the imposition of other conditions. For example, the defendant may be ordered to stay away from the person who brought the complaint or ordered not to travel outside the court's jurisdiction. In each type of bail, the defendant has a somewhat different economic stake and economic incentive to appear when required. It is an interesting question as to whether the differing economic stakes have an effect on the rate of failure to appear (see below, and see Helland and Tabarrok, 2002).

Defendants' Rights

The Eighth Amendment and Excessive Bail

The Eighth Amendment to the U.S. Constitution provides in pertinent part, "Excessive bail shall not be required."

What makes bail excessive? The primary legal objective of bail is to ensure that an individual will return for court appearances. Thus, bail should be proportional to the motivation to flee to avoid punishment. The motivation to flee should be higher for a more severe crime with a more severe penalty than for a lesser crime. It makes sense, then, that severity of the crime is a factor in setting bail. If the prosecutor requests a level of bail much higher than is normal for a given offense, the prosecutor must justify the request during the bail hearing. If the judge sets an unusually high bail, the decision is subject to appeal on the grounds that the amount is excessive. Bail should not be used to satisfy public prejudices or to manipulate public opinion (*Stack v. Boyle*, 1951).

In theory, *excessive* should also be defined in terms of the defendant's individual circumstances. The judge should individualize by choosing an amount that reflects (1) how much the person can raise, and (2) how much the person could afford to lose if he or she absconded. Ten thousand dollars may be "excessive" to a poor person, but not to a rich one. In practice, other factors such as ties to the community, or other risks of flight such as the person's previous history of failing to make court appeareances factor into the decision.

Denial of Bail

The Eighth Amendment prohibition on excessive bail does not establish a right to bail. But the policy of providing bail is related to important values and established rights: (1) an accused person is innocent until proven guilty, (2) a person should not be kept in jail on a mere accusation, (3) the accused person should be unhampered in preparing a defense, and (4) a person should not be subject to punishment before conviction. In recognition of these values, the states have established a right to bail in their constitutions or through statutes. Few rights are absolute. Bail may be denied, but the government must be able to show there is a compelling reason why the individual should not be released.

One reason to deny bail is a concern that the individual may abscond. Bail is not usually granted in capital cases (cases involving crimes for which the death penalty may be imposed) because the motivation to flee in such cases is presumed to be very great.

A second reason for denying bail is to protect the community against the release of allegedly dangerous individuals (**preventive detention**). In the 1970s, when the public became more concerned about law and order, some courts read a "public safety" exception into bail statutes to allow them to deny bail altogether to defendants thought likely to commit crimes if released while awaiting trial. Many states and the federal government (Bail Reform Act of 1984) modified their laws to permit the preventive detention of people accused of a crime and considered dangerous (U.S. Bureau of Criminal Justice Statistics, 1988).

Because defendants are presumed innocent of charges and their future crimes are hypothetical, preventive detention laws appear to violate the prohibition against punishing someone without due process. They force us to consider which we value more: protecting the community against a potential crime (a prediction), or protecting individual liberties and rights. In each decision to release a person on bail, the court is making a prediction that the individual will not commit a dangerous act. In *United States v. Salerno* (1987), the Supreme Court upheld the community's safety against the individual's right. The government may hold an individual in preventive detention without bail if the person presents a demonstrable danger to the community.

The Law in Action

Judges have considerable discretion in setting bail. In theory, they take into account (1) the amount of bail set for similar offenses, (2) the nature and circumstances of the charged offense, (3) the weight of evidence against the accused, (4) the defendant's financial ability to post bail, (5) the defendant's character, (6) any history of convictions, and (7) the defendant's ties to the community (family, job, etc.). In practice, judges tend to set bail on the basis of the nature of the offense, the prosecutor's recommendation, and their own sense of the likelihood of the defendant's guilt, with little or no consideration of the other factors that, in theory, should make a difference (Kadish and Paulsen, 1975, pp. 1101–1103). Time constraints may contribute to the tendency of judges to reduce the number of factors they consider: bail decisions are usually made in a hearing lasting only a few minutes.

The amount of bail is correlated with the severity of the crime. A national survey of 88,000 jail inmates conducted by the Bureau of Justice found that, in 1990, the median bail set for defendants charged with violent offenses and drug offenses was $5,000, while the median bail set for defendants charged with property offenses was $2,500 (Reaves, 1992).

The amount of bail has consequences. Among felony defendants, as bail goes up, so does the proportion retained in jail because they cannot make bail. If bail was set at $20,000 or more, 69 percent were detained until disposition. If bail was under $2,500, only 31 percent were detained until disposition. Those who couldn't raise bail and were not released had, on average, twice the amount of bail as those who did obtain release (Reaves, 1992). A higher percent of those accused of violent crimes couldn't make their bail and were held (35 percent) or were denied bail (9 percent) compared to those charged with public order offenses (26 percent and 8 percent respectively). Thus, (1) people who are accused of more serious crimes with higher bail are more likely to be retained in jail, and (2) poorer defendants have a higher likelihood of being detained

BOX 3.3

The Bail System: Biased against the Poor?

The case of Jose Padro illustrates how the bail system may result in pretrial detentions that exceed the length of time a person would have received had he pleaded guilty.

Jose Padro, a 28-year-old Bronx man, was arrested in June 1997 after a quadriplegic man for whom he had worked as a home health aide accused him of sexual assault. Mr. Padro had been working for his accuser, Alberto Edwards, about three months. Mr. Padro is gay, but said he never discussed his sexuality with Mr. Edwards.

After his indictment for first-degree sodomy and first-degree sexual assault, Mr. Padro's bail was set at $20,000. The bail was reduced to $5,000 in September 1997, but he was still unable to raise the money. He was represented by a total of three Legal Aid lawyers; two left before his case went to trial in November 1998. By that time, he had been in jail about a year and a half.

The prosecutor said the case would have gone to trial sooner if the defense had been ready to proceed. The delay was charged to the defense because otherwise Mr. Padro would have been released; his right to a speedy trial had been violated. The chief lawyer at the Bronx Office of Legal Aid's criminal division denied that the change in lawyers caused major delays. He said the defense needed several months to investigate Mr. Edwards's background because their case hinged on putting his credibility in doubt.

If found guilty, Mr. Padro could have been sentenced to 5–25 years in prison. Early in the case, the district attorney (DA) offered Mr. Padro a plea bargain that would give him a sentence of one to three years. Mr. Padro refused the offer. Just before the trial, the DA offered him another plea, which carried a sentence of a year. Because he had already been in jail 18 months, he would have gone free. Mr. Padro refused this offer, too. He was worried he would have trouble getting a job if he pleaded guilty to a felony.

Mr. Padro, fearful that a jury might be prejudiced against him because he was gay, waived his right to a jury trial. The bench trial went on, with breaks, into January 1999. The defense produced records and other evidence showing that Mr. Edwards had complained to the agency about other aides and had made false accusations about other aides. In January 1999, the judge found Mr. Padro not guilty.

After his release, Mr. Padro reported feeling depressed and fearful of returning to work as a home aide. He sued the health care agency for failing to warn him about Mr. Edwards, but his action did not succeed. The New York appellate court held that his only remedies were against Mr. Edwards for the injuries or a claim through Worker's Compensation insurance because the incidents occured in the course of his employment.

Reported by Alan Finder in *The New York Times,* Metro section, Sunday, June 6, 1999. *Padro v. Visiting Nurses Service of New York,* 276 A.D.2d 352, 714 N.Y.S.2d 438 (2000).

than wealthier defendants accused of the same offense. Members of minority groups are more likely to be detained for financial inability to post bail, but also for many other reasons including a prior criminal history. (See Box 3.3).

Because of the judge's considerable discretion, bail setting can also reflect a judge's prejudices about certain crimes or the judge's values. As an extreme and unusual example, 21-year-old Yuriko Kawaguchi, arrested for a credit card scam, charged she was denied bail to prevent her from having an abortion ("Abortion Issue," 1998). The corrective for an unfair bail is an appeal of the decision to a higher court.

The Costs of Detainment

Social scientists have gathered data that can help policy makers measure the costs of detaining people who fail to make bail or who are denied bail. There are both dollar and human costs when a person is not released on bail.

Dollar costs. On any given day in 2003, there were approximately 760,000 inmates in city and county jails (Bureau of Justice Statistics, 2003). City and county governments spent $10.4 billion on correctional facilities, or about $55 a day per person (Maguire and Pastore, 1998, Table 1.6). Costs may be much higher in some communities. Aside from necessities—food, laundry, beds and bedding, and medical care, especially for those who are intoxicated with drugs or alcohol or who show signs of mental illness—inmates have to be escorted by jail personnel when shuttled back and forth from jail to the courthouse for court appearances. If we could identify all the defendants who, if released, would return to court for trial or other appearances, and would not commit further crimes in the interim, the state could save money. Instead of confining these defendants, the courts could lower their bail or simply release them on own recognizance.

Human costs of failing to make bail. There is also a human cost to pretrial detention and a cost to justice. **Jails** (pretrial holding centers) are often oppressive and punitive institutions (Fisher, 2000) where inmates may be subject to violent attacks by other inmates in the absence of tight management by jail officials (O'Connell and Straub, 1999). The suicide rate among jail inmates, particularly for young people, is high (Fox, 1981, p. 671). In 2003, there were about 389 suicides in jails. About 25 percent of the largest urban jurisdictions in the country had a jail under court order to limit the population because of serious overcrowding; 23 percent of those jails were also under court order to improve poor conditions (U.S. Bureau of Criminal Justice Statistics, 1990b). Detention in such overcrowded, unsafe, and substandard conditions would be considered cruel and unusual punishment for convicts, much less for people not yet convicted and who may be innocent. About a fifth of felony defendants who do not make bail and are held in oppressive facilities are acquitted (Reaves, 1992). Hardened criminals and innocent people may be mixed together in jail cells.

Detainment can have long-term consequences. Incarcerated people are at high risk of losing their jobs because of absence, and their apartments because they are not working and cannot pay the rent. Their families may suffer in consequence. Moreover, if a person who couldn't make bail and lost a job is found guilty, he or she may be less likely to be placed on probation than someone found guilty who did make bail and was working.

Likelihood of conviction. The likelihood of conviction is also correlated with whether or not a defendant makes bail. Among those felony defendants who did make bail, 56 percent were convicted; among those who did not make bail and were detained, 77 percent were convicted (Reaves, 1992). Bail may be set higher for defendants when the evidence of their guilt appears greater, thus accounting for the result. But there are

FIGURE 3.1

Overcrowding in a Jail

Jails are short-term lockups. They hold people just arrested awaiting a bail hearing, those awaiting trial who can't make bail, convicted prisoners awaiting transfer to a state prison, and prisoners serving very short sentences. Jails have been the subject of institutional reform suits because of terrible conditions in many of them. A person who can't make bail may be held in an inadequate facility for months while awaiting trial.

other, more disturbing hypotheses. Detainees tend to be poorer than those released and so may be more likely to have lawyers supplied by the state. State-appointed lawyers are often less experienced and more overburdened than privately hired lawyers. The higher conviction rate among those detained could also reflect the greater difficulty incarcerated defendants have in participating actively in their own defense.

The only advantage to not making bail is that the cases of those who are detained are adjudicated more rapidly. In 1990, the median number of days from arrest to adjudication among those who were released on bail was 125 days; among those detained, it was 37 days (Reaves, 1992). Those who can't make bail might feel pressure to plead guilty, accounting for the lesser stay in the jail.

Released on One's Own Recognizance

The bail system is based on the assumption that defendants who post a money bond will return to be tried because they fear losing the bail money. If this is true, then it follows that people who can afford to post bail or a bail bond are better risks to return for trial than people who cannot make bail. They have something to lose by not returning. But do people return to court just because of the fear of losing their bail money?

BOX 3.4

71

How Well Is
the Bail System
Functioning
Today?

The Vera Institute of Justice Manhattan Bail Project

In the early 1960s, New York City criminal courts agreed to cooperate in an experiment with the Vera Institute. The experiment tested whether defendants could be identified who could safely be released on their own recognizance.

Suspects who had been arrested for homicide, sex offenses, and most narcotic offenses were excluded from the study. All the other suspects were evaluated by law students to see if they had a record of prior arrests or convictions and to ascertain their ties to the community, assessed by a ten-minute interview with the suspect and verified, with the subject's permission, by calling a relative or an employer. Stable work history, supporting a family, having relatives in the area, receiving unemployment or welfare, and length of residence in the area were considered indicators of community roots. These factors are traditionally used by judges in deciding bail. Each case was rated on a point system, with points added for a stable history and subtracted for previous criminal history of any kind.

Project personnel wrote a report for each subject who was rated at or above a minimum cutoff score, recommending who should be released on his or her own recognizance. The project sent half the recommendations to the judge, the prosecutor, and the defense attorney. They wrote the report for the other half of the qualified subjects, the controls, but did not send the report to the court. The judges evidently paid attention to the recommendations; they released about 60 percent of those recommended for release on their own recognizance without bail, but only 14 percent of the control cases. The Vera project directors followed up 2,630 persons released on their own recognizance. Of these, only 24 cases, less than 1 percent, failed to return.

The assumption that people who can make bail are better risks to return (a prediction) than people who can't could be cast as an empirically testable proposition. One reform proposed and evaluated in the 1960s was to release indigent defendants without bail, on their own recognizance. In the early 1960s, the Vera Institute of Justice sponsored a project in New York City that tested and confirmed the hypothesis that many defendants accused of less serious crimes would return for trial even if they were not required to post bail. The **Vera Institute project,** described in Box 3.4, was influential in encouraging reform of the bail system. Every state now has a similar program (Helland and Tabarrok, 2002).

⊠ How Well Is the Bail System Functioning Today?

In 2000, 30 percent of all felony defendants were released on their own recognizance, conditionally, or on some other nonfinancially secured basis. Thirty-two (32 percent) were released on some form of money bail. Another 31 percent were granted bail, but were held because they couldn't make bail. Only 7 percent were denied bail (Sourcebook of Criminal Justice Statistics, Online, 2003, Table 5.55). In other words, 93 percent of defendants are granted bail, although many can't afford to arrange it. That is a far cry from when the Vera Program started. Then, only 48 percent of misdemeanor defendants were released on bail or on their own recognizance.

Table 3.1

Mean Failure to Appear (FTA), Fugitive Rates (FR), and Rearrest Rates (RR) by Type of Bail (% of cases)

Type of Bail	FTA (%)	FR (%)[1]	RR (%)	Recap within One Year (%)
Own recognizance	26	32	14.9	70
Deposit bond	21	33	13.3	60
Cash bond	20	40	14.0	50
Surety bond	17	21	12.0	90

Source: Helland and Tabarrok (2002).

[1]Of those who failed to appear—about 7 percent overall.

Court Appearance

Approximately 25 percent of all felony defendants released either on their own recognizance or on bail fail to appear when they should. Helland and Tabarrok (2002) compared the rates of failure to appear (FTA), fugitive rates (FR, or remaining uncaptured for a year or more—about 7 percent of all those who fail to appear), and rearrest rates (RR, or arrested again while on bail) for those who were released on some type of bail or on their own recognizance. They used a sophisticated statistical matching procedure that corrected for preexisting differences in characteristics of those who obtained the several types of releases. They had access to a very large sample using official data sources. Table 3.1 summarizes their major results.

It is clear that those released on a surety bond posted by a licensed bail bondsperson had lower rates of failure to appear, and if they failed to appear, many fewer remained in fugitive status (Table 3.1). Those who failed to appear also stayed in fugitive status for shorter periods when they had been released on a surety bond. About 90 percent of those released on surety bond were recaptured within a year, and most of those within a short time. In contrast, half of those released on a cash deposit, 60 percent of those released with a deposit bond, and 70 percent of those released on their own recognizance who absconded were recaptured within a year.

What accounts for these large differences in failing to appear and in remaining in fugitive status depending on the type of bail? Helland and Tabarrok (2002) analyzed a number of subgroups to rule out rival plausible hypotheses (e.g., differences in the characteristics of those who received the different types of release, and differences in counties of release). They argued that bail bondspersons who issued the bail bonds had a strong financial interest in seeing to it that those granted the bonds appeared and did not forfeit the bond. Bondspersons estimated that 95 percent of their customers have to appear if they are to make a profit. They engage in a form of *risk management.* They often require their "customers" to check in periodically, and they remind the defendants of court dates. They also remind any co-signers (those who agree to pay in place of the defendant if bail is forfeited) of pending court dates. They have incentive to encourage the defendant to appear for court dates. Moreover, bondspersons obtain a great deal of information in the application process that is helpful in tracking someone who disappears (e.g., social security numbers, public databases, and names of friends, relatives, children, and employers).

Bondspersons usually have a "grace" period to find the fleeing person, put him or her in custody, and return him or her to court. For this purpose they use **bounty hunters** who receive a fee for capturing and returning defendants. Because fleeing defendants have the legal status of "escaped prisoners," and those on bond have already been given over to the custody of the bondsperson, private bounty hunters have great leeway in the actions they can take to recapture the defendant. They can seize the defendant without a warrant; enter or break into his or her residence without a warrant; use force, including deadly force; cross state lines in pursuit; and take the person into custody (*Taylor v. Taintor,* 1873). In addition to having specialized tasks and incentives, bounty hunters are better able than overworked local police to track and find persons who may have warrants out against them for nonappearance.

The rate of failure to appear of those released on their own recognizance is higher than in the Vera Institute study. Since the time of the original study, the number of defendants in jails has risen sharply, and political and legal pressures to reduce overcrowding and poor conditions in jails have increased the pressure on courts and prosecutors to reduce the census of jails by releasing more defendants. As a larger number of defendants are released on their own recognizance, the failure to appear rate also increased. The "cutoff" score for release may be such that many more false negatives (defendants predicted to return who don't) occur. Defendants, perhaps aware that overworked local police cannot be too diligent in tracing them, may be more casual about meeting court dates. These findings suggest that social-ecological factors and system factors strongly affect the ability to predict behavior.

One concern about bail is whether those released will commit another crime when released. Overall, about 14 percent of those released on some form of bail will be rearrested before their appearance date. The rearrest rate is correlated with the length of time the defendant has to await trial. The longer the delay, the more likely the person is to be rearrested. Bureau of Criminal Justice statisticians found a relationship between the length of time a released defendant awaited trial and "misconduct," a rearrest, a failure to appear at a hearing or a trial, or a violation of a condition of release. The misconduct rate increased from 10 percent of those waiting 90 days or less, to 14 percent for those waiting between 90 and 180 days, to 17 percent for those waiting between 180 and 270 days (U.S. Bureau of Criminal Justice Statistics, 1988). The rates were higher among those initially arrested on a felony charge in big cities and released on bail: 52 percent were rearrested on another charge within one month of release (Reaves, 1992). Keeping in mind that an arrest is not a conviction, does that high a rearrest rate justify denying bail to those arrested for felonies?

Box 3.5 describes William Shrubshall, the kind of violent defendant the public fears.

Denying Bail to the Dangerous

If our main aim was to prevent arrests for subsequent crimes, we could simply detain everyone arrested. Such a policy would obviously violate our values and the law. The laws that allow judges to deny bail in consideration of dangerousness do require some persuasive reason for believing the defendant's release will endanger the community. One study suggests that dangerousness provisions are not being used extensively. Only 7 percent of felony arrestees were denied bail (Maguire and Pastore, 1998, Table 1.68). Even some defendants who were charged with committing a rape, a robbery, or another felony while on bail for a previous offense were released again on additional money bail after a hearing. Courts may be using the dangerousness laws sparingly because

BOX 3.5

William Shrubsall: A False Negative

William Shrubsall was raised by his mother in Niagara Falls, New York. When he was 17, he was convicted of battering his mother to death with a baseball bat on the night of his high school prom, allegedly because she had verbally abused him. He was to have given the valedictory address the next day. He was an attractive young man, with no previous criminal history, and a forensic psychologist said that he was not dangerous. He served a relatively short sentence for manslaughter.

After his release, Shrubsall was arrested several times more, served 60 days for a misdemeanor, and finally was charged with sexually abusing an inebriated 17-year-old at a party. An aunt, with whom he had been living, put up $20,000 in bail. His aunt's money didn't stop him from running. While on trial, Shrubsall left a note implying that he was going to jump into Niagara Falls, and disappeared. His aunt lost her money. Shrubsall surfaced two years later, charged with a series of violent attacks in Canada. He is now in a Canadian prison. In 2001, a Canadian court classified him as a *dangerous offender,* which means he cannot be released until a court is convinced he is no longer dangerous, in effect a life sentence.

Shrubsall is a good example of a "false negative" in risk assessment; he was mistakenly classified as at low risk for violence, and as likely to return to protect his aunt's money. He may have been misclassified because he is an atypical criminal. Matricide is a rare crime, and most criminals do not do well in school.

overcrowding of detention centers and court-ordered plans to improve jail conditions create a pressure to release defendants.

As we shall see in the next section, in the context of psychotherapy, prediction is equally problematic but has different potential costs.

SECTION III
THE *TARASOFF* DUTY

Most mental health professionals are familiar with the *Tarasoff* case. Prosenjit Poddar, a former client of the outpatient mental health clinic of the University of California, Berkeley, shot and killed Tatiana Tarasoff (see Box 3.6). Tatiana's parents sued the therapist, the clinic, the police, and the university for wrongful death. In their decision in *Tarasoff v. Regents of the University of California* (1974, 1976), the California Supreme Court made therapists responsible for assessing the dangerousness of patients and made them potentially liable civilly when one of their patients hurts someone; this is known as the *Tarasoff* **duty.** (See Ewing and McCann, 2006, ch. 5, for more details about this case.) The opinion was, in the words of one commentator, "one of the most significant developments in medico-legal jurisprudence of the past century" (Gutheil, 2001). The anxiety normally accompanying professional responsibility for caring for potentially dangerous patients was compounded after *Tarasoff* by the threat of a malpractice lawsuit stemming from the patient's later assault on a third party (Tolman, 2001).

BOX 3.6

75

SECTION III
The *Tarasoff*
Duty

A Legal Case in Point: The Tarasoff Case

During a therapy session, Prosenjit Poddar implied to Dr. Lawrence Moore that he intended to kill Tatiana Tarasoff, who had rejected him as a lover. Dr. Moore judged that Poddar was indeed dangerous (a prediction) and should be involuntarily committed on an emergency basis. He notified campus police. The police spoke to Poddar, decided there was no legal basis to hold him, and released him with a warning. The supervising psychiatrist in the campus clinic decided that no further efforts were to be made to commit Poddar. No one warned Tatiana or her family of the threat. Two months after terminating treatment, Poddar shot Tatiana with a pellet gun, and then stabbed her to death.

Poddar was found competent to stand trial. He was convicted of second-degree murder, but his conviction was reversed on appeal because the trial court judge had refused to give a diminished capacity charge (see People v. Poddar [1974]). The state decided not to retry the case, and Poddar was deported to India.

The Tarasoff family sued the therapists and other mental health professionals who had had contact with the case, the campus police, and the Board of Regents of the University of California for wrongful death. (The Regents were included on the theory that an employer is generally responsible for the acts of employees—respondeat superior, 'let the master answer'). The family claimed that Tatiana's loss had injured them, and that the loss was caused by the defendants' negligence because they failed in their duty to protect Tatiana. The suit implied that therapists were or should be responsible for making predictions about their patients' behavior and acting on them.

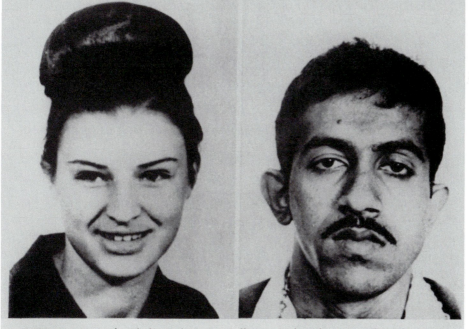

FIGURE 3.2 Murder victim Tatiana Tarasoff appears beside a mug shot of accused murderer Prosenjit Poddar.

⊠ *Tarasoff* and Tort Law

The *Tarasoff* case was a malpractice action, a **tort.** A tort is a civil wrong or injury for which the injured party (plaintiff) can seek money damages. Box 3.7 shows the legal structure of a malpractice suit.

Looking at Box 3.7, the reader will see that some aspects of the *Tarasoff* suit were unusual. Generally, a malpractice suit must be brought by someone who has a special relationship with the defendant (e.g., a professional mental health worker's patient), to whom the defendant owed a clear duty of care. The plaintiffs (the late Tatiana's mother

---

BOX 3.7

Malpractice Tort

Following are the elements of a malpractice suit:

There was a special relationship between the plaintiff and defendant, in which the defendant owed a duty of care to the plaintiff.

A professional accepts a duty to care for anyone to whom they agree to provide services. A therapist's duty of care includes making competent diagnoses, treating properly, and giving the patient adequate information for informed consent.

The defendant violated his or her duty.

Plaintiffs in a malpractice suit charge the professional with negligence: they claim that the professional failed to do something he or she should have done, or did something carelessly or inadequately. The standard of adequate care in a malpractice suit is defined by what comparable practitioners in that community would have done in similar circumstances. The standard is established by the testimony of other qualified professionals.

The plaintiff was injured.

A professional may be irresponsible or incompetent, but his or her clients cannot sue for money damages unless the professional's negligence has actually injured or damaged them. Death may be compensated as an injury to survivors. (A client who was not injured could seek redress, though not compensation, through an ethics or a licensing violation complaint. See Chapter 17.)

The failure to meet the duty of care was the "proximate" or legal cause of the plaintiff's injury.

Proximate cause means that, had the professional acted differently, the injury would not have occurred. The case for causation is clear when the injury is the result of a surgeon leaving a sponge in the patient after closing the incision. Causation is more difficult to establish when the link between the professional person's actions and the injury is less direct.

The remedy is money damages.

If a defendant is found liable, the jury or, in a bench trial, the judge may impose money damages after hearing evidence about the dollar value of the injury in terms of costs of medical care, lost wages, and, when appropriate, pain and suffering. In particularly egregious situations, on the theory that a high award may deter others from similar unconscionable actions, the jury may be permitted to impose punitive damages.

and father) in the *Tarasoff* case, however, did not have any relationship with the therapist they were suing. Nor did Tatiana. The only person to whom the therapist had a clear duty of care was his client Poddar. Tatiana's parents' claim of "proximate cause" was also notable. To claim compensation, they argued that their daughter would not have died if the therapist had warned her of a possible assault by Poddar.

The trial court, following existing legal standards, ruled that the mental health professionals had no duty of care to Tatiana. On appeal, the California Supreme Court ruled that there was indeed a duty of care toward a third party who was not in treatment. The Court said that when a threat against someone was made by a patient in therapy, the mental health professional was obligated (1) to make a risk assessment; and, (2) if he or she judged that the patient was dangerous and a potential victim was identifiable, to warn the intended victim. After this decision, if a patient communicated an intention to harm an identifiable person during a therapy session and later did harm that person, the therapist who failed to make an adequate assessment of dangerousness at the time of the threat and to warn the victim might be held liable for damages to the victim or victim's family.

The decision distressed the mental health community. Professional associations of psychiatrists, social workers, and psychologists petitioned the California Supreme Court to rehear the case. In an unusual move, the Court did reconsider and issued a decision modifying the original by giving therapists a little flexibility in how they respond to an assessment of dangerousness. The duty to warn became a duty to act reasonably to protect the third party (Felthous and Kachigian, 2001).

> When a therapist determines, or pursuant to the standards of his profession should determine, that his patient presents a serious danger of violence to another, he incurs an obligation to use reasonable care to *protect* the intended victim against such danger. The discharge of this duty may require the therapist to take one or more of various steps, depending on the nature of the case. Thus it may call for him to *warn* the intended victim of the danger, to notify the police, or to take whatever other steps are reasonably necessary under the circumstances. (*Tarasoff v. Regents of University of California*, 1976, p. 431)

After this decision, the case was settled out of court. No trial court actually determined whether the psychologist or other professionals in the clinic had actually breached the duty of care as defined in the *Tarasoff* decision. Despite the settlement of the *Tarasoff* case, the *Tarasoff* duty lives on.

⊠ Psychological and Professional Issues

The *Tarasoff* controversy illustrates some important differences in how social scientists and judges think about prediction.

Courts Balance Values

In arriving at a rule of law, a court weighs and balances values. The *Tarasoff* court said that the value of *attempting* to save a life outweighed other values and duties such as confidentiality. Therefore, therapists had to make an assessment of violence in conformity with *professional standards* (commonly used and widely accepted professional practices). The actual accuracy or inaccuracy of prediction methods and the actual positive and negative effects of the policy change were secondary considerations for the judges.

Social Scientists Evaluate Empirical Consequences

The social scientist is interested in evaluating real-world functioning by framing questions that can be answered by empirical observation. For mental health professionals, *Tarasoff*'s importance was not its symbolic meaning, but its practical consequences.

Possible consequences—the therapist. Many mental health professionals believed that in light of research on predictions of dangerousness, the *Tarasoff* decision imposed an unfair duty. Because of the low accuracy of predictions, a therapist could do everything "right" (according to professional standards) and harm could still result. The *Tarasoff* court confidently stated that "proof, aided by hindsight, that he or she judged wrongly is insufficient to establish negligence" (*Tarasoff*, 1976, p. 438). But therapists familiar with the powerful hindsight bias (Hawkins and Hastie, 1990; see below) feared that lay jurors, looking back, would be inclined to think the violence was more predictable (foreseeable) than it was.

Possible consequences—the victim. Therapists also had concerns about unintended consequences for potential victims. There was no evidence to support the assumption that warning potential victims, or taking any set of reasonable steps short of committing the patient, would actually prevent violence. The warning could potentially have negative effects on the potential victim's well-being and anxiety level. Gutheil (2001) discusses the hypothetical case of Dr. A., a forensic psychiatrist who was warned that a prisoner who Dr. A. had examined in the distant past bore him a grudge and threatened to kill Dr. A. upon his forthcoming release from prison. Dr. A. first called the police, who told him they could do nothing until the former patient showed up. Dr. A thought about hiring a bodyguard, but found the costs prohibitive. He thought about buying a handgun, but he thought the risk to his family in having a gun in the house was greater than the risk from the former client. He thought about changing his name and leaving town, but he had an established practice and a place in the community he could not give up lightly. Given that he could do nothing about the threat, would he have been better off not knowing about it (Gutheil, 2001)?

Possible consequences—the therapeutic relationship. Finally, therapists were concerned about how the *Tarasoff* duty might affect their practice. The requirement of informed consent meant they would have to tell prospective patients of the conditions under which the therapist would have to breach confidentiality. The obligation to warn potential victims conflicted with their obligation to keep patient or client confidences; it could conflict with the duty of care they owed their patients. A new problem has arisen. Some who have made warnings in keeping with the *Tarasoff* duty found themselves called to testify against the patient in a murder trial or in a trial for criminal stalking despite the therapist–patient privilege (Walcott, Cerundolo, and Beck, 2001). Ethics aside, therapists worried that the breach of confidentiality would weaken the alliance between therapists and patients, inhibit patients from revealing thoughts and fantasies in areas central to treatment, and cause patients to leave therapy (Stone, 1976; Wise, 1978). If treatment was used less, then it would reduce the potential of therapy to dissuade the perpetrator from violence. Moreover, therapists knew that breaches of confidentiality might also lead to charges of malpractice or professional misconduct.

The California Supreme Court noted therapists' legal concerns about confidentiality, but said that "the confidential character of patient-psychotherapist communications must yield to the extent to which disclosure is essential to avert danger to others"

(*Tarasoff*, 1976, p. 442). In other words, the court ruled that it was more important to take an action that has the possibility of saving a life than to preserve the value of confidential treatment.

⊠ Extension and Impact of *Tarasoff*

A number of other state courts, but not all, have adopted the *Tarasoff* duty. Some states wrote the *Tarasoff* duty into legislation, making the obligations more specific. In several states, professional organizations lobbied state legislatures to write statutes that limited and better defined therapist responsibility in *Tarasoff*-like situations. The threat of suits still exists, but both courts and legislatures acting in the 1990s have limited the circumstances in which liability could arise. In recent years, there have been fewer verdicts for plaintiffs in *Tarasoff*-like situations, and "duty to protect" cases are no longer among the most common causes of action in psychiatric malpractice suits (Walcott, Cerundolo, and Beck, 2001).

Despite relatively infrequent litigation and the fact that many jurisdictions have not established a duty to warn, the *Tarasoff* case has permanently altered therapeutic practice. The duty to protect, is, in effect, at present a national standard of practice, in spite of the fact that it is not the law in most jurisdictions, and in spite of the fact that the duty itself is subject to different interpretations by different courts (Beck, 1985a, p. 33; see also Perlin, 1992). All psychotherapists should practice as if the *Tarasoff* duty to protect is the law. Monahan (1993), based on his experience as an expert witness in *Tarasoff*-type cases, made suggestions to therapists about how to avoid litigation and what to do if litigation ensued. Many internship and residency training facilities now include some training on what the *Tarasoff* duty is in their states (Tolman, 2001).

⊠ Therapists' Responses to *Tarasoff*

In the first ten years after *Tarasoff*, three groups of researchers used mail surveys to question large samples of therapists about their reactions to the *Tarasoff* decision (Givelber, Bowers, and Blitch, 1984; Weil and Sanchez, 1983; Wise, 1978). The therapists' self-reports suggest that the *Tarasoff* decision had an impact on the behavior and attitudes of mental health professionals. The findings of all three studies of social workers, psychologists, and psychiatrists were consistent. However, the studies were not based on systematic observation of actual therapeutic practices.

Attitudes and Practice

A majority of therapists agreed that it was morally right to attempt to prevent harm to another, but they said they felt more anxious when the subject of dangerousness came up in treatment. Some said they were tempted to avoid probing into areas that might trigger the *Tarasoff* duty, while others said they directed the sessions toward dangerousness topics (see also Perlin, 1992). Many said that they had changed their record-keeping practices and consulted more frequently with colleagues to minimize their exposure to legal liability. They said that, since *Tarasoff*, they were more likely to take some action in regard to a potentially dangerous patient. About 15 percent of the psychiatrists in

Givelber, Bowers, and Blitch's 1984 study, as well as 13 percent of social workers and 5 percent of psychologists, said they had warned a potential victim. In recent years, about 48 percent of psychiatric residents said they had made a *Tarasoff* warning in the course of their training (Tolman, 2001). Although clinicians feel conflicted over violating confidentiality, most agree that it is morally correct to try to protect a third party against harm. Moreover, an intervention to prevent one's client from doing harm is also in the client's interests. It may keep the client out of prison, and may prevent the development of deep feelings of guilt about doing harm to another person.

Assessing Dangerousness

Fortunately for therapists, under *Tarasoff* they have a duty to meet professional standards, not to be accurate in their predictions. One consequence of *Tarasoff* is a sharp increase in research on predicting dangerousness, although there is still no standard protocol for assessing dangerousness in a *Tarasoff*-like situation (Borum and Reddy, 2001). Meeting professional standards means doing what other practitioners in the community would have done under the same circumstances. An important question, then, is whether or not there are general identifiable professional standards and practices for assessing dangerousness.

Most of the therapists in Givelber, Bowers, and Blitch's (1984, 1985) study thought that there were professional standards for assessing violence. They said that they could make assessments of potential violence, and believed that other therapists would agree with their assessments. Though they didn't refer to any standard interview or standard tests, they were able to list the predictors they used in making the assessments: a history of violent behavior; threats of violence; current hostile or aggressive behavior; possession of a weapon; violent fantasies or expressions of hostile feelings or anger; hostile, disturbed, or inadequate relationships; environmental stresses; and diagnosis (see Litwack, 1985). Gournic (1990) conducted a study that confirmed that clinicians can agree beyond chance levels on their assessment of a patient's potential for violence. The agreement among therapists and the consistency (reliability) of their predictions don't mean that their predictions about real cases would be accurate (validity). The therapists' assessments could all be consistent, and they could all be wrong.

Borum and Reddy (2001) state that methods of assessing dangerousness based on base rates, or on predictors derived from studies of whether a patient admitted to a hospital will be violent in the hospital, whether patients released from hospitals will act violently in the community, or whether sex offenders will reoffend, should not be ignored. But results from such studies may not provide useful guides in the immediate clinical situation. The concern is not about a patient or client potentially harming any third person, but is about *targeted violence,* danger to an identifiable third party. Predictors of violence to the specific individual cannot be known through population research.

Adapting methods used by the Secret Service to evaluate the risk of a political assassination, Borum and Reddy (2001) note that in the individual case that comes to a clinician's attention, there has already been a threat of violence; an individual who comes to the attention of the Secret Service has also voiced some kind of threat against a public figure. The problem is to inquire about factors that may indicate how far along the person is on a pathway to harm a specific other person. This type of evaluation seems analogous to a "lethality" assessment in a patient or client with suicidal thought.

Borum and Reddy sum up their views by saying,

> The central question in these cases is typically not whether the client has a certain sta-
> tistical probability of violence toward any given third party over a specified time
> period; rather it is whether the client's ideas and behaviors should give rise to a rea-
> sonable clinical concern about potential harm to a specific identifiable target, whether
> those indications suggest that the client is on a pathway toward a violent act, and, if
> so, what interventions have a reasonable likelihood of reducing the risk of harm.
> (Borum and Reddy, 2001, p. 394)

Just as the *Tarasoff* court was not concerned with the predictive validity of the
standard methods of assessing violence, so here we cannot ask for empirical verification that interviews using these principles will avoid harm. In the legal and in
the moral context, we can only ask the clinician to do what seems reasonable in light
of what we know. Violence will either happen or not happen in the individual case,
and the clinician who is responsible will have acted reasonably or not given the
circumstances. Acting reasonably means the professional's action makes sense to an
"objective" observer.

Reasonable Care

Tarasoff requires a therapist to take "reasonable care" to protect a potential specific victim of a patient assessed as dangerous. To see if there are widely shared beliefs about
reasonable care in specific cases, Gournic (1990) asked the psychologists and psychiatrists in her sample to select (from a list of alternatives) the actions they would have
taken given the facts in each of six case studies. Almost all therapists in all conditions
said they would discuss the problem with the patient and increase the amount of treatment or modify medications. Most said they would enter a note in the record, would
consult with colleagues, and would document the consultation in the record. More than
two-thirds said they would discuss the limits of confidentiality, and would offer the
client or patient concrete advice. When the probability of violence was high, therapists
agreed on more drastic measures such as notifying the family or the victim, or seeking
involuntary hospitalization. Givelber, Bowers, and Blitch (1985) reported very similar
results based on asking therapists what they had done in a recent actual case in which
a threat was present. These actions are consistent with Monahan's recommendations
for avoiding tort liability in *Tarasoff* situations (Monahan, 1993).

Protecting the Potential Victim

Givelber, Bowers, and Blitch (1985) asked the therapists they surveyed what had
happened in their last case involving a patient who might harm others. When therapists decided to warn the intended victim, the patient went on to attack the person in
28 percent of the cases. In 72 percent, no violence occurred. The false positive rate was
high. When they decided that a warning was not necessary, the patient went on to
attack someone in 29 percent of the cases. The false negative rate, therefore, was also
high.

Givelber, Bowers, and Blitch's (1985) findings suggest that even when dealing with
individuals who have made a specific threat, therapists' assessments of dangerousness
are wrong more often than they are right. As in studies of the prediction of violence in
other contexts, professionals' predictions may be consistent, and may exceed chance

levels, but are not highly accurate. Second, the findings suggest that there is a certain "base rate" of violence in the population of people who make threats of violence when in treatment. Treatment and warning do not appear to change that base rate. The study did not report the effects of false positive warnings on the people who were warned (see the case of Dr. A., above). We know of no research on this last point.

The Effects of the *Tarasoff* Duty on the Therapeutic Relationship

Perlin (1992) points out that trust is based on many things, so that it may be possible to maintain trust even if confidentiality is breached. Breaching confidentiality with the patient's knowledge to help establish self-control might be therapeutically beneficial. Beck (1985a) analyzed descriptions of 18 cases collected from colleagues in private practice. He concluded that carrying out the *Tarasoff* duty carefully and thoughtfully could result in an improved therapeutic relationship in some instances:

> Cases in which the clinician discusses the warning with the patient before giving it typically show no bad effects resulting from the warning. In some of these cases, especially when the therapist clearly sees the potential violence as a therapeutic issue (and correspondingly sees the duty to warn as having clinical relevance), the discussion of the warning appears to have a positive impact on the psychotherapeutic process, and on the development of the [therapeutic] alliance. Conversely, the cases in which the warning is not discussed ahead of time often turn out badly, and it is clear from the patient reports that patients resent warnings that are given without their knowledge. (Beck, 1985b, p. 80)

Some potentially violent patients who are paranoid, deluded, or suspicious and hostile may not have sufficient insight to ally with a therapist around issues of self-control. Nonetheless, at the very least, the dire predictions of routinely losing the patient or losing the therapeutic alliance when a warning is made have not been borne out in practice.

Impact on Therapists Who Are Sued

Many successful *Tarasoff* suits followed the release from an institution of a patient who subsequently injured someone. In consequence, the *Tarasoff* duty may affect policies and actions within institutions. Professionals within institutions may become demoralized or practice defensive therapy.

Poythress and Brodsky (1992) looked at the effects on a hospital staff of a successful liability suit brought against several staff members after a released patient killed a member of the plaintiff's family. Both defendant and nondefendant staff reported feeling emotionally distressed, but they denied that any change in risk assessment resulted from the suit. Hospital records, however, showed that, compared to before the suit, fewer patients were released during the civil trial and in the period immediately afterwards. It is not known if the reduced rates of discharge were appropriate or an unintended negative consequence of therapist anxiety and "defensive treatment." That question can be answered only with follow-up research.

Hindsight Bias and Liability

Hindsight bias is a well-established psychological phenomenon (Fischoff, 1975). Hindsight refers to the tendency for people to think, after an event has happened, that it could have been anticipated (Hawkins and Hastie, 1990). It is what gives us confidence as Monday morning quarterbacks. It's what makes us think, "I should have known," when something bad happens, whether or not there really was a way to have seen what was coming. The effect is so strong that subjects in experiments were not able to avoid the bias even when instructed to do so (Fischoff, 1975).

To bring a *Tarasoff*-type malpractice suit, the plaintiff or a relative of the plaintiff has to have been injured by a violent patient. Some researchers wondered whether the *hindsight* knowledge that the patient caused an injury would affect a jury's judgment about the adequacy of the therapist's assessment of dangerousness.

LaBine and LaBine (1996) tested the hindsight bias as a factor in judgments of *Tarasoff* liability with a vignette study. They found that mock jurors who were told that the patients in the vignettes had gone on to engage in serious violent actions rated the therapist more negatively on all the legally relevant dimensions than jurors who didn't know the outcome of the cases or who were told that the patient did not go on to engage in a violent act. Most important, the mock jurors who were told that the patient in the vignette acted violently were more likely to think that the therapist was negligent (see Box 3.8).

Fear of the Mentally Ill

Stereotyped fears of the mentally ill and the hindsight bias may reinforce each other. People tend to overestimate the rate of violence among the mentally ill (Monahan, 1993). This appeared to happen with LaBine and LaBine's (1996) subjects. Regardless of what information they were given about outcome, the majority of the mock jurors said they themselves would have predicted that the patient would be violent. This attitude about the propensity of mental patients to commit violent acts may place a therapist who makes a false negative error (predicting someone as nonviolent who is later violent) in legal jeopardy. The therapist may be blamed even if he or she used appropriate methods of assessing violence. Jurors may feel therapists should have "seen" more dangerousness in cases in which the facts showed a low probability of future violence.

These research results suggest the *Tarasoff* court was too optimistic in its judgment that jurors would not be affected by a hindsight bias, a problem that may be involved in other negligence cases.

Possible Legal Reforms

Psychological research, theory, and analysis suggest some practical recommendations for trial reform. Negligence trials can be **bifurcated** (divided into two phases: one to determine liability, and the second to determine the monetary award) to reduce bias. In a bifurcated trial, negligence would be established first with minimal attention to the plaintiff's injury; then, if the defendant was found negligent, damages are awarded in a separate trial. Poythress, Weiner, and Schumacher (1992) report that judges found the bifurcated trials were fairer than one-step trials and produced speedier outcomes.

BOX 3.8

Hindsight into Negligence

LaBine and LaBine (1996) conducted a vignette study to test the effects of hindsight on juror judgments of *Tarasoff* liability. They used six vignettes, each describing a case in which a therapist assessed a potentially violent patient and took action to prevent violence. The actions described in the vignettes had been judged appropriate for the case by at least half of the group of 90 psychologists and psychiatrists queried by Gournic (1990), and so were in conformity with professional standards.

The researchers used three versions of each of the six vignettes. One-third concluded with the description of the actions the therapist had taken but nothing more. In one-third, the subject was told that the patient did not become violent. In one-third, the subject was told that the patient engaged in a serious violent act.

LaBine and LaBine sent the experimental materials by mail to a random sample of 2,000 persons on the voting rolls of their local community. About 14 percent responded. Each subject received a description of the *Tarasoff* case, a definition of negligence, and one of the 18 vignettes (six cases × three outcome conditions). The subjects were asked to imagine they were jurors in a malpractice trial and to answer a questionnaire about their opinions.

Ninety-eight percent of the mock jurors in all the conditions agreed that the therapists had a duty to assess violence in the case; 91 percent also agreed that the therapist had a duty to protect the potential victim from harm. Appropriately, because the actions of all the therapists represented a consensus of professional opinion, a large majority of mock jurors in every condition did not think the therapist was negligent. However, the mock jurors rated the harm as significantly more foreseeable, and the therapists' actions significantly less reasonable and significantly less preventive of harm, when they had been told harm had followed, compared to the other two conditions. When asked directly whether the therapist was negligent or not, 6 percent said yes when a nonviolent outcome was specified, 9 percent said yes when no outcome was specified, but 24 percent said yes when a violent outcome was specified.

If liability was not found in the first phase, there was no need to spend courtroom time evaluating damages. If liability was separated from damages, would jurors be less favorable to plaintiffs? Or, to ask it another way, would jurors be inclined toward sympathy for the plaintiff when injuries are introduced, compared to the question of whether the defendant was liable for his or her actions? That is an interesting problem for research.

Summary

Social scientists and mental health professionals are asked by the courts to make predictions about individual behavior and about the effects of alternative dispositions of a case. Clinical predictions are subjective judgments based on the personal experience and knowledge of an expert. Statistical predictions are based on a formula derived from a mathematical relationship between "predictors" and a criterion. Statistical predictions are more accurate than clinical predictions. However, while statistical methods can distinguish well between groups of people at higher or lower risk for developing a problem, they are not as accurate at identifying which individuals will actually develop the problem.

One of the most common and controversial predictions psychologists are asked to make is risk assessment, or prediction of future violence. Research-based predictors and statistical formulas for predicting violence do show accuracy beyond chance levels. Psychologists and other mental health professionals do better at prediction than they would if they simply flipped coins. But, because violence is a low-base-rate behavior, predictions are incorrect more often than not. Professionals making predictions will make many false positive errors, and some false negative ones. In a legal context, the cost of errors in predictions of violence may be very great: false negatives may lead to the release of dangerous people who go on to hurt others, while false positives may lead to gross restrictions on the liberty of people who would hurt no one and to a huge cost of confinement to society.

Bail is an example of the use of research to improve decisions that bear on both individual liberty and public safety. Bail is used to ensure that an accused person will return for court appearances. The level of bail, in theory, is adjusted to achieve that end. The goal of preventive detention may also be served. Decisions to grant bail, and how much, involve weighing the value of an individual's right to be treated as innocent until proven guilty against the community's right to be protected against criminal predators. Making or not making bail has important consequences for the individual. Those denied bail, or who can't make bail, are deprived of freedom. Though not yet found guilty of any crime, they are detained under conditions that are often oppressive and deleterious, and are at a disadvantage when they come to trial. Critics of the bail system argued that money bail unfairly works against poorer defendants. Releasing certain defendants accused of minor crimes on their own recognizance was a reform based in part on research showing that most of those defendants did return for court appearances. By and large, the reforms have worked well. However, some defendants who are released either on bail or on their own recognizance do commit further crimes.

The *Tarasoff* decision under civil law imposed a duty on mental health professionals to assess the dangerousness of a client who threatened someone and to take steps to protect the potential victim. The case alarmed psychotherapists because it required that therapists make judgments of future dangerousness, something they knew they could do only very crudely. It created new legal vulnerabilities by making mental health professionals responsible for injuries to people who were not their clients. It created distress and role strain by requiring the professionals to breach client confidentiality to protect strangers. Initially, therapists predicted that the decision would have a strongly negative impact on psychotherapy, and would increase their exposure to liability without increasing public safety.

The dire predictions appear mistaken. There has not been much litigation involving the *Tarasoff* rule. The rule does not appear to have had profoundly negative effects on therapy. Contrary to clinicians' expectations, fulfillment of the duty sometimes had positive therapeutic effects if the warning and interventions were carried out with the patient's knowledge. However, the specific tactic of warning may not prevent harm to the identifiable victim. We don't know about the effects on potential victims of a false positive warning.

If a therapist is a defendant in a *Tarasoff* suit, even if the therapist makes a professionally appropriate assessment of the patient's potential violence, the hindsight bias may result in jurors holding therapists negligent simply because they know the victim has been harmed. Therapists may also be at a disadvantage because laypeople tend to believe that patients have a greater propensity for violence than the facts warrant.

We will deal with the issue of prediction again when we discuss juvenile delinquency, capital punishment, psychological testing, and child abuse. We will again encounter three of the themes introduced in this chapter: the limitations of the science of prediction, dilemmas created by the need to balance citizens' safety and their individual rights, and the role strain experienced by mental health professionals trying to manage the double role of healer and agent of social control.

Discussion Questions

1. Assume that college admission committees try to choose the applicants they think will (1) complete school and (2) achieve a grade point average of at least 3.0. Do you think the committees should rely on clinical or actuarial methods to predict which applicants will achieve these goals? Do you think the admission essay and interview increase predictive validity? Why?

2. What is a false positive? A false negative? Suppose you have developed a screening test for a potentially fatal disease. Under what conditions would you be more worried about false positives? About false negatives? Why? What factors would affect your decisions to use a test with a cutoff that yielded many false positives?

3. Why do you think the framers of the Constitution felt it was important to provide that excessive bail was prohibited?

4. Suppose you work in a psychiatric hospital. There are 25 patients in the psychiatric hospital who appear stable. You want to prepare them for discharge by giving them day passes to go to a day treatment program. In the late afternoon, when the program gets out, they are to return to the hospital. How would you develop a measure to assess which patients are most likely to return as they are supposed to?

5. Do you think the California Supreme Court made the right decision in *Tarasoff*? How does the decision illustrate differences in legal and psychological thinking?

6. How could you investigate the effects of warning potential victims of threats of violence on (1) the potential victim's safety and (2) the potential victim's general well-being?

Key Terms

accuracy	false negative error	psychometric
arraignment	false positive error	risk assessment
assessment	hindsight bias	risk management
bail	idiographic	sensitivity
bail bond	illusory correlation	specificity
base rate	jail	static variables
bifurcated	liability	statistical/actuarial predic-
bounty hunter	negligence	tions
clinical predictions	nomothetic	*Tarasoff* duty
criterion	own recognizance	tort
dangerousness	population	true negatives
demographic variables	predictor variables	true positives
dynamic variables	preventive detention	Vera Institute project
error rate	probability	

CHAPTER **4**

Competence to Stand Trial, and Other Competencies

Competence refers to the absence of incapacitating disabilities and the possession of those characteristics that make a person "legally fit" (Black's, 2004) to participate in a legal process. The disabilities and characteristics involved in legal competence are psychological. Adult competence is assumed unless challenged in court. Children's competence in different areas of legal activity is usually a matter of the child's age, established by law in each state.

Laws and rulings regarding competence are embedded in a complex social context. Many apparently contradictory rules seem so because we do not consider the multidimensional nature of the problem. For example, a state may require that a minor get parental **consent** (permission) to have her ears pierced, but permit the same minor to give consent herself for treatment of substance abuse or venereal disease or to seek an abortion without parental knowledge or consent, but with court approval, in states with parental notification or consent laws. The different standards involve different public policies as well as different assumptions about the minor's capacities.

In this chapter, we review several different competencies and discuss the methods psychologists use when asked to help a court make a competency determination. In the first section, we will discuss competence in the criminal justice system:

- The history and standards for competence to stand trial (the bread and butter of forensic practice)
- The consequences of finding a person competent or incompetent to stand trial
- The criteria for competence to stand trial
- How competence to stand trial is assessed and how evaluations have been and might be further improved

- Treatment to restore competence to stand trial
- Other criminal law activities requiring competence, including competence to plead guilty, to represent oneself, to refuse counsel, to be sentenced, and to refuse the insanity plea
- Competence to be executed (age and mental retardation)

(We will review juvenile competence to waive Miranda rights and to stand trial in Chapter 9.)

In the second section, we will discuss competence to carry out some of the activities regulated by civil law:

- Age and competence
- Competence to make a will
- Competence to manage one's financial affairs
- Competence to refuse or consent to medical treatment
- Competence to make treatment decisions and the mentally ill
- Competence of children to consent to medical treatment
- Competence to engage in consensual sexual activity, involving civil law when it relates to the ability to get married, and criminal law when it involves sex with an underage or impaired person

For each of the competencies, we will specify the legal standard, point out psychological issues, and review relevant research.

SECTION I
COMPETENCE AND CRIMINAL JUSTICE

Competence to Stand Trial

The assessment of competence to stand trial on a criminal charge (also called **adjudicative competence**) is the most frequent service that mental health professionals perform in the criminal justice system (Hoge et al., 1997). Its purpose is to protect the rights of individuals and the dignity of the justice system. In our legal system, with rare exceptions, individuals cannot be tried in absentia. The accused has a right to be there to defend him or herself. Our sense of justice demands this. We do not try a person who is mentally "absent" either, which is why, as a matter of fundamental fairness, we evaluate competence to stand trial. Individuals who are not mentally able to participate in their defense, who lack the capacity to understand the nature and object of the charges and proceedings, to consult with counsel, and to assist in preparing their defense (*Dusky v. U.S.*, 1960), are considered incompetent to stand trial.

Distinction between Competence to Stand Trial and the Insanity Defense

Although the insanity defense is probably better known, the question of a defendant's mental competence to stand trial arises far more frequently than the insanity defense.

The distinction between the two is important. The **not guilty by reason of insanity (NGRI)** plea has to do with the defendant's mental state *at the time of the alleged crime.* The person who enters an NGRI plea does not deny doing an illegal deed, but claims that, because of mental illness or disability, he or she did not appreciate at the time that he or she was doing something wrong (see Chapter 7).

A person may have his or her full mental faculties at the time *he or she is charged and tried* and still plead NGRI because of his or her state of mind at the time of the offense. For example, suppose that after accidentally eating poisonous mushrooms, a woman goes berserk, hallucinates, and attacks a fellow hiker who she thinks is a grizzly bear. By the time she is charged with assault, she has recovered from her mushroom-induced psychosis and is perfectly rational. She can still plead NGRI because of her mental state at the time of the attack. However, having recovered, she is competent to stand trial.

Incompetence to stand trial has to do with someone's state of mind *at the time of the trial,* in the period just before the trial when an evaluation may be ordered, or at any point in the trial thereafter up to and including sentencing. A defendant who is found incompetent is usually confined in a maximum security hospital and treated until competence is restored. He or she may then be returned to jail until trial. Thus, the incompetent defendant may spend additional time in custody because of incompetence rather than guilt; the trial is delayed until the person is deemed competent.

Historical and Legal Context

The requirement that a defendant be mentally able to participate in his or her defense is deeply rooted in the law. Sir William Blackstone, a highly influential English eighteenth-century legal scholar, said that

> if a man in his sound memory commits a capital offense, and before arraignment for it, he become mad, he ought not to be arraigned for it; because he is not able to plead to it with that advice and caution that he ought. And if after he has pleaded, the prisoner becomes mad, he shall not be tried: for how can he make his defense. (Quoted in American Bar Association [ABA], 1989, p. 160)

The requirement that a defendant be competent was introduced into U.S. law as early as 1835 (Winick, 1985). State and federal circuit courts developed standards to determine when a defendant lacked the capacity to participate in his or her legal defense. As mental health professionals became increasingly involved in the court system, judges began to turn to them for assistance with the determination. The problem shifted somewhat, from a question of what was fair to a question of the nature of the disorders and the disabilities that would render a person unable to defend him or herself.

Over the years, legal scholars have articulated at least four reasons why justice requires that the defendant be competent to stand trial:

1. If the defendant cannot give full cooperation during the trial, the accuracy of the trial may be compromised.
2. Procedural fairness requires that a defendant be fully able to exercise all of the rights accorded an accused, including the right to counsel, which may be compromised if the accused cannot assist his or her counsel in preparing a defense.

3. The dignity of the court and respect for judicial processes might be undermined by the public spectacle of trying an obviously disturbed individual.

4. The objectives of punishing and sentencing a defendant would not be achieved if the defendant didn't understand the nature of the punishment and why it was imposed (Weiner, 1985).

The U.S. Supreme Court specified some **standards (or criteria) for competence** in *Dusky v. U.S.* (1960) by instructing trial court judges to determine whether the defendant had sufficient present ability to consult with his or her lawyer with a reasonable degree of rational understanding, and whether he or she had a rational as well as factual understanding of the proceedings against him or her. This basic standard has not changed since.

Defendants' Rights

In *Pate v. Robinson* (1966), the Supreme Court held that trying an incompetent defendant violated his or her constitutionally based due process rights. The defendant in the case had killed his common-law wife and infant son. He had a history of frequent episodes of violent, if not bizarre, behavior, and had attempted suicide. The trial judge decided that the defendant was competent on the basis of his observation of the defendant in court without a specific competence hearing. The Illinois Supreme Court upheld the trial court judge's decision. The U.S. Supreme Court, however, said the trial judge should not have ignored the defendant's history. The Court placed a positive duty on trial judges to raise the issue and to hold a competence hearing if there was any reason to doubt a defendant's capacity to stand trial. The Court reaffirmed the obligation of trial court judges to respond to competence issues before or even during the trial in *Drope v. Missouri* (1974). Judges can order an evaluation when the issue of competence is raised by the defense or prosecution, or when the judge observes behavior or learns of evidence that raises questions about the defendant's mental capacities (Weiner, 1985). This duty continues even through sentencing (*United States v. Jones,* 2003).

Defendants do not have the right to refuse to participate in competence evaluations. If a defendant does refuse to participate in the evaluation, he or she may be confined for a period of time for observation. However, the defendant doesn't lose all rights. Information obtained in the competence evaluation is limited to the issue of competence to stand trial. It can't be used in violation of the defendant's **Fifth Amendment** right against self-incrimination. Moreover, mental health professionals who conduct competence evaluations have an ethical obligation to inform the defendant of the nature of the examination, the fact that its results are not held in confidence, and the likely uses of the information. A defendant who is found incompetent to stand trial should receive prompt treatment to restore competence (see ABA, 1989).

Scope of the Problem

Poythress et al. (2002) estimate that about 60,000 competency evaluations are conducted each year. Aubrey (1988) found that, in a community with a population of about 1,000,000, 6.7 percent of criminal defendants were referred for a competency evaluation. The percentage of criminal cases in which the defendant's competence is questioned increased sharply in the 1970s. The increase undoubtedly reflected deinstitutionalization, the then recent policy of releasing residents of mental hospitals to be treated in the community. Released mental patients sometimes do not receive adequate follow-up treatment or monitoring. They may stop taking medication, deteriorate, and begin to behave in bizarre or threatening ways, leading to their arrest (Teplin, 1983). When arrested, they are candidates for competency evaluations.

Strategic Uses of Competence Evaluations

Because it is relatively easy to obtain a court order for an evaluation of competence, the issue is sometimes raised by lawyers not simply to protect the defendant's rights, but also for strategic reasons. A defense attorney may request an evaluation when the attorney believes it is in the client's interest to be in treatment rather than stand trial, to delay a trial when a case is receiving publicity hurtful to the client, or to obtain information about the client's mental health that will be useful in his or her defense (ABA, 1989; Weiner, 1985). In the past, prosecutors sometimes used competency procedures to keep defendants in custody when the case against them was weak. Once the person was safely hospitalized, the prosecutor might use his or her discretion to drop the criminal charges.

The practice was challenged in *Jackson v. Indiana* (1972). Theon Jackson was a 27-year-old deaf mute who was probably mentally retarded. He was unable to read or write and could only communicate through the most rudimentary sign language. He was arrested twice, once for allegedly stealing $4.00, once for allegedly stealing $5.00. Jackson pled not guilty to both charges. The issue of his competence to stand trial was raised. He was examined by two psychiatrists who testified that he didn't understand the charges against him, could not communicate well enough to assist in his own defense, and was unlikely to learn to communicate sufficiently well to become competent. Another expert testified that the state had no facilities to teach communication skills to someone like Jackson. Jackson was found incompetent to stand trial and was ordered committed to the Indiana Department of Mental Health. He had not been found guilty of anything. Jackson was condemned to what was, in effect, permanent institutionalization without the state showing that he met criteria for civil commitment either as a mentally ill person or as a mentally deficient individual.

On review, the Supreme Court concluded that Indiana could not commit Jackson indefinitely just because he was incompetent to stand trial. The Court noted that many defendants who were committed before trial never went to trial, that their stay in institutions was often longer than the stay of those committed through ordinary civil procedures, and that treatment facilities to aid defendants to become competent were very poor. (Treatment facilities have probably improved since then because hospital care has improved due to institutional reform lawsuits and accrediation requirements affecting insurance reimbursement.) The Court ruled that a person found incompetent to stand trial could be held for treatment only so long as there was some promise that treatment would restore competence. If there was no possibility that competence would be restored in some reasonable time, the defendant must either be committed, using civil standards of commitment, or released.

The *Jackson* decision imposed a requirement on mental health professionals to assess whether those who are found incompetent can be restored to competence within a reasonable length of time. Thus, all evaluators who determine a defendant is incompetent are also asked to make a prediction about restoration to competence (Nicholson and McNulty, 1992).

Most referrals for competence evaluation made in recent years are appropriate. Aubrey (1988) found that defendants referred for competency evaluations were more likely to have histories of mental illness than other defendants. Fifty-five percent of those referred for a competency evaluation had a history of hospitalization for a psychiatric disorder; 20 percent had histories of outpatient treatment (Aubrey, 1987). Judges, whether acting on their own initiative or in response to a request by one of the lawyers, given defendant histories, appropriately referred the defendants for evaluation even though relatively few were later found incompetent. Attorneys suspected incompetence in a larger percent of cases than they referred for evaluation. They were not overusing the competency evaluation process (Poythress et al., 2002). Warren et al. (1991) found that defendants with less serious charges (e.g., trespassing or public disorder) were more likely to be found incompetent to stand trial than defendants charged with more serious offenses (e.g., robbery, homicide, or sex offenses). The results may reflect the fact that, when the deinstitutionalized mentally ill are arrested, it is often for minor charges like public disorder and trespassing. Mumley, Tillbrook, and Grisso (2003) indicated that a large number of defendants referred for competency evaluations do not meet civil commitment standards for "dangerousness." Even though many requests for evaluation are legitimate, some attorneys may feel their clients are in need of treatment even though the clients don't meet standards for involuntary hospitalization. They may use the competency route as a way of securing inpatient treatment.

Consequences of a Determination of Incompetence to Stand Trial

Of those referred for evaluation, the number who are found incompetent ranges between 10 and 30 percent (Poythress et al., 2002). Nicholson and McNulty (1992) studied 493 defendants admitted to a state hospital in Oklahoma for treatment following a determination of incompetence. The average hospitalization lasted 69 days; however, about five percent of the defendants were hospitalized more than six months. In 95 percent of the cases, the team recommended discharge because competence was restored. If competence is not restored, the defendant, usually suffering from severe and chronic mental illness or mental retardation, may be committed civilly for further treatment. Thus, some defendants found incompetent to stand trial are confined several months although they have not yet been found guilty. Some are later found not guilty or have charges dismissed when their competence is restored. If found guilty, the period of confinement may be credited against the sentence. When it is not, they may end up being confined longer than similar defendants who were able to plead guilty right away or to stand trial sooner (Winick, 1985).

Medication may be forcibly administered against the defendant's wishes to restore competence to stand trial under tightly limited circumstances. Refusal of treatment is a constitutionally protected interest. The government's interest in having a defendant fit to stand trial is also important, however. If the defendant is mentally ill and dangerous to himself or others, medication may be administered against his wishes to treat the mental illness and reduce symptoms. The restoration to competence may be a secondary consequence. A court considering approving forced medication must also consider whether the side effects of forced medication may interfere with a fair trial by interfering with the defendant's ability to consult with counsel, or affect the defendant's demeanor in a way adverse to his or her defense (see the Andrea Yates case in Chapter 7 on the insanity defense). An incompetent defendant may also have a guardian appointed, and the guardian may consent to treatment. If all other factors have been considered and there is no other reason to overrule the defendant's constitutional right to refuse antipsychotic medication, then in rare circumstances, the government may seek involuntary medication simply to restore competence to stand trial (*Sell v. U.S.*, 2003). (The American Psychological Association submitted an amicus brief in that case; APA, 2002.)

Given the negative consequences of being held for a competence evaluation, it may be better for incompetent defendants to allow the trial to proceed even without their full participation, with assistance of counsel and other supervision of the court to protect their interests (Winick, 1985; Bonnie, 1992). It would also save the taxpayer money. (A review of some of the costs to defendants in terms of time hospitalized and stigma, and of the dollar costs to society, may be found in Winick, 1985.) However, because competence is considered fundamental for due process, the system is unlikely to change.

Criteria for Competence: What Should Mental Health Professionals Evaluate?

When a defendant's competence is questioned, courts usually ask a mental health professional to assess the person. The evaluations may be done by psychiatrists, psychologists, or social workers; state laws establish the qualifications of an expert in this context (Weiner, 1985). The courts want information from mental health professionals bearing on the *legal* criteria for competence. The legal standards should set the parameters for the evaluation. The legal standards for competence enunciated in *Dusky* are not stated with precision: the defendant must have the ability to consult with a lawyer with "rational understanding," as well as a "rational understanding" of the proceedings. Other courts have offered more elaborate criteria. Nonetheless, legal scholars and critics continue to argue that legal standards are vague and contribute to a lack of uniformity of the assessment process (Mumley, Tillbrook, and Grisso, 2003).

Dusky did not require that the defendant have a mental disorder, defect, or illness. Most states wrote such a requirement into their laws (Weiner, 1985). However, a finding by a mental health professional that a defendant has a mental defect or mental illness does not in and of itself warrant a determination that he or she is not competent to stand trial. In a sample of jailed, but competent, inmates receiving psychiatric treatment, a quarter had a diagnosis of schizophrenia and 59 percent had an affective disorder (Poythress et al., 2002). In 1998, 16.2 percent of state prison inmates, 7.9 percent of federal prison inmates, 16.3 percent of the people serving short sentences in jails, and 16 percent of those on probation were mentally ill. All had been convicted of crimes, and many must have been mentally ill at the time of their trials (Bureau of Justice Statistics, 1999).

Criticisms of Standards

Most legal standards emphasize fairly elementary cognitive criteria, usually having to do with basic orientation to the courtroom and current knowledge of trial personnel and procedures. Some legal and health professionals (ABA, 1989; Nurcombe and Partlett, 1994) have recommended that evaluators assess more complex abilities in addition, for example, the ability to follow testimony for errors. Some propose that emotional as well as cognitive abilities be included, for example, the ability to trust and relate appropriately to an attorney, to tolerate the stress of a trial, and to behave appropriately in the courtroom. Zacarias Moussaoui, who confessed to intending to be a hijacker in the 9/11 attack, exhibited deficits in these abilities during his trial but was never found incompetent to stand trial or incompetent to defend himself (Lewis, 2002). Assuming more complex abilities are measurable, it is not clear how to weigh them in arriving at the competence-to-stand-trial decision.

The most important decision facing most defendants in the real world doesn't have to do with understanding and participating in trial proceedings; it is the decision whether to plead guilty and avoid a trial altogether. Close to 90 percent of the criminal cases in this country are resolved by **plea bargaining** (Hoge et al., 1997); the defendant pleads guilty to a lesser charge, and the case never goes to trial. Defendants who plea-bargain usually receive lighter sentences than those who go to trial. Because pleading guilty and standing trial seem to involve different kinds of abilities, some argued (ABA, 1989; Mumley, Tillbrook, and Grisso, 2003) that different tests of competence should be applied to the two tasks. However, in *Godinez v. Moran* (1993), the Supreme Court ruled that competence to stand trial and competence to plead guilty are the same.

Competence Determination in Practice

When the elements of participation in a defense are analyzed carefully, the task of determining competence is very complex. Judges generally follow the recommendations of the court-appointed mental health professional uncritically (McGarry et al., 1973; Roesch and Golding, 1980). Roesch and Golding (1980) found that the experts rarely testified at the hearings to determine competence. They were represented by reports. The typical hearing, in which no party objected to the examiner's report, lasted two or three minutes (see also ABA, 1989, p. 204 n. 1).

Because judges determining competence rely heavily on assessments of mental health professionals, fairness depends on well-done assessments. Researchers in the 1970s and 1980s identified and tried to address several serious problems with the assessment procedures.

One problem was that mental health professionals often made their recommendations about an individual's competence to stand trial on the basis of irrelevant medical criteria. Roesch and Golding (1980) found that once a mental health professional established that the defendant had a mental disorder, particularly a psychosis, they considered the defendant not competent to stand trial. The experts also tended to confuse the criteria for establishing nonresponsibility (insanity) with the criteria for establishing incompetence to stand trial. Judges sometimes contributed to the confusion by requesting, in the interests of efficiency, that the expert undertake to evaluate criminal responsibility and competence together.

A second problem was systemic: unnecessary hospital commitments. Whatever the criteria used by the evaluators, until fairly recently most defendants were committed to a hospital for competence evaluations. Only a small percentage of the patients hospitalized were actually found incompetent to stand trial. Defendants found incompetent to stand trial were often socially marginal men with some kind of mental illness. The majority of people found incompetent were male (88 percent), relatively poor, mostly unemployed (92 percent), and often living alone or in an institution (81 percent). On admission for evaluation, about 60 percent received a diagnosis of psychosis or some brain disorder (Nicholson and McNulty, 1992). Of 468 defendants sent to a secure medical facility for competency evaluation, 82 percent were found competent. The major factors discriminating between those found competent and those found incompetent were a psychotic diagnosis and employment history (Cooper and Zapf, 2003). These findings, suggesting that hospitalization was unnecessary in most instances, led to experiments with outpatient evaluations.

Outpatient Evaluation

Researchers and clinicians have made progress. Beginning in the late 1960s, researchers developed instruments that could provide objective, quantitative measures of defendants' *legally relevant* capacities. Such instruments were potentially a means of making efficient outpatient assessments and avoiding extended in-hospital evaluations. Conducting competence evaluations on an outpatient basis or in jails instead of in hospitals would benefit everyone. The majority of the defendants, who would be found competent, would avoid involuntary confinement in a mental hospital. They would be eligible for bail, making it easier for their attorneys to meet with them, improving trial preparation. The community would save money; the difference in costs between outpatient (or even jail) care and hospital care is huge.

Roesch and Golding (1980) trained eight professional mental health workers to use one of the early measures, the **Competence Assessment Instrument (CAI).** They found that conclusions based on the CAI were in 90 percent agreement with staff consensus based on a longer period of observation in the hospital. Roesch and Golding concluded that

> the high rate of agreement between the interviewers' and the hospital's
> determination of competence points to the facts that most decisions about
> competence are straightforward and that hospitalization is not necessary. Thus
> the amount of time spent in the hospital may not add to the decision-making
> ability of the evaluators. (p. 190)

Melton, Weithorn, and Slobogin (1985) developed and evaluated an outpatient model of forensic services for the Commonwealth of Virginia as an alternative to in-hospital competency evaluations. As it became clear that brief methods of examination were as effective as longer methods requiring hospitalization, the majority of states moved toward greater use of outpatient evaluation. Based on phone interviews with forensic mental health professionals and administrators in 50 states, Grisso et al. (1994) concluded that only 10 states still use inpatient institutions for two-thirds or more of their pretrial evaluations (for competence to stand trial and insanity). Research-based criticism of the existing practices and demonstration projects evaluating alternatives had been translated into formal policy change.

⊠ Improving Evaluations of Competence to Stand Trial

The key to improving competence evaluations is to sharpen the focus on issues bearing directly on legal standards (Nicholson, 1999). Another important step toward improved assessment is the development of psychometrically valid screening and evaluation instruments. Psychometrically valid instruments provide consistent measurements with a demonstrated relationship to the capacities or qualities the evaluator is trying to assess, However, the available instruments have different strengths in standardizing the competency evaluation process and in preparing reports for the court (Zapf and Viljoen, 2003). (The student should review basic concepts of reliability and validity in test construction. See Box 4.1, as well as Box 16.7 in Chapter 16.)

Assessment Instruments

There are now a number of assessment instruments developed to improve efficiency and ensure that an examination covers legally relevant issues. The main ones were reviewed by Nicholson (1999). Some have also been specifically developed to meet Canadian legal standards (Mumley, Tillbrook, and Grisso, 2003).

BOX 4.1

97

Improving
Evaluations of
Competence to
Stand Trial

Reliability and Validity

A valid instrument should have reliability (consistency of measurement) and validity (evidence that it measures what it claims to measure). There are different forms of reliability. One is *interexaminer reliability* (different people using the instrument should get the same results). Another is *internal consistency* (the items composing a scale should be measuring the same construct). It is usually evaluated by Cronbach's alpha. A third is *retest reliability,* the consistency of results when a test measuring a stable trait is administered at two different times.

Measures should also be valid. We speak of *criterion validity* when the measure correlates with another measure we accept as the "gold standard," if there is one, or the next best thing if there isn't. We speak of *construct validity* when the test correlates with another measure that purports to measure the essential trait or characteristic of interest. We speak of *face validity* when the items of the test seem clearly related to what we say the test is measuring. In the legal context, face validity is related to the fairness of making a decision using the instrument (Hoge et al., 1997). A good measure also has *discriminant validity*. The instrument should be able to distinguish groups of people with known differences in characteristics of interest but similar levels of related characteristics, e.g., disturbed people who have been found competent from disturbed people who have been found not competent.

A new instrument should produce the same classifications of competent and incompetent as traditionally accepted methods, but perhaps more efficiently. Note the difficulty. We are often bootstrapping. There is no "gold standard" of competence against which to judge a new instrument. Ideally a test used in a legal context should include some checks for response distortion related to malingering, suspiciousness, or defensiveness (Nicholson, 1999; Rogers, 1997). Scores should increase if a person improves after treatment.

McGarry et al. (1973) were pioneers who developed two instruments: the Competence Assessment Instrument (CAI) and the Competency Screening Test (CST). Initial tests of validity showed that CAI-based classifications, based on a one-hour, semi-structured interview, were in good agreement with competency determinations made by a judge (McGarry et al., 1973) and those made by hospital staff (Roesch and Golding, 1980).

The Competence Screening Test (CST) is a 22-item sentence-completion measure. Interrater reliability, using administrators trained with the scoring manual, is quite high; the test correlates well with other measures of competency (Nicholson, 1999). The CST has high rates of both false negatives and false positives (Roesch and Golding, 1980). The CST correlated significantly with a measure of verbal intelligence as well (Roesch and Golding, 1980). It may underestimate the competence of less verbally skilled defendants.

The **Georgia Court Competency Test (GCCT-MSH)** is another brief quantitative measure of adjudicative competence, and its revised version was developed at Mississippi State Hospital. The GCCT–MSH consists of 17 interview questions measuring understanding of courtroom procedure, understanding of the charge, and ability to communicate with an attorney. A scale to detect faking incompetence has been added

(Gothard et al., 1995). All measures are subject to some degree of *malingering,* or faking, which can be detected with varying degrees of efficiency (Rogers, 1997; Mumley, Tillbrook, and Grisso, 2003). The GCCT–MSH has good interrater reliability and internal consistency.

Nicholson et al. (1988) found that scores on the CST and the GCCT–MSH were highly correlated, suggesting that they are measuring the same construct **(construct validity)**. Using staff decisions made after a period of hospitalization as a criterion of competence, scores on the CST were 71 percent accurate, and scores on the GCCT–MSH were 82 percent accurate. The correlation of the tests with verbal IQ suggests that defendants with poor verbal skills (because of prior education or minority status) are probably at a disadvantage with these brief screening instruments. The Competence Assessment for Standing Trial for Defendants with Mental Retardation (CAST–MR; Everington and Luckasson, 1992, in Nicholson, 1999) was developed specifically to assess competence in defendants with mild to moderate mental retardation. Other tests have been criticized for not adequately assessing this population.

Although these instruments are in the process of development, their existence serves one important purpose. They enable clinical evaluators to systematize the information they seek, and focus attention on legally relevant variables over and beyond psychopathology.

The Mac SAC–CD: A New Research Instrument

Hoge et al. (1997) completed initial validation studies on a structured, standardized research measure called the **MacArthur Structured Assessment of the Competencies of Criminal Defendants (Mac SAC–CD).** (See also Poythress et al., 2002, for summations of the theory and research as well as some initial clinical norms.)

The research group based their newly developed instrument on Bonnie's theory of competence (1992, 1993). Bonnie, analyzing legal standards for competence, proposed that competence to stand trial has two dimensions: competence to assist counsel, and competence to make decisions. Bonnie argues that the ability and willingness to assist one's attorney are always crucial to ensuring a fair trial, but the ability to make decisions about specific strategies and choices may not be. The client does not necessarily have to understand the legal reasons for a motion to excuse a juror for cause, or why the attorney wishes to make a motion challenging the introduction of some piece of evidence. On the other hand, the client should be able to tell the attorney his story and to indicate when witnesses against him are not being truthful. Competence in both dimensions entails the capacity to understand the relevant information, to reason about the information and act appropriately, and to appreciate what the information means.

The Mac SAC–CD is a standardized test used to evaluate competence to assist counsel and decisional competence separately. The subjects read a story about a fight between Freddie and Reggie, who are playing pool at a bar. Freddie hits Reggie with a pool stick. Reggie falls and hits his head on the floor so hard he nearly dies. Freddie is arrested. The subjects are asked questions about this case. For example, to test subjects' ability to apply rational understanding to assist counsel, they are given six pairs of facts about the case and asked to choose which would be most important for Freddie's attorney to know (e.g., Reggie was bigger than Freddie, and Reggie pulled a knife on Freddie). Using a hypothetical case has the advantage of safeguarding the subject's right against self-incrimination (Nicholson, 1999). A section of the test refers to the defendant's own case in order to assess the defendant's appreciation of his personal situation. The defendant may be asked to describe the charge and to say who his lawyer is. Depending on his answer, the examiner may give him new information, such as the exact charges and his lawyer's name. The examiner will then ask what the lawyer does. Defendants' responses are assessed both before and after disclosure of new information in order to identify those who are ignorant about some aspects of the legal system but can learn and use new information. Administration and scoring are standardized.

Preliminary research demonstrated that the instrument showed adequate to good internal consistency and interrater reliability. The test discriminated a group of previously classified incompetent defendants from previously classified competent ones, thus showing validity and consistency with existing standards. The research design included some controls for mental illness and for status as a prisoner. There was some preliminary evidence that the instrument could differentiate competent from incompetent defendants among those in treatment because they were mentally ill and those in jail. The test was also sensitive to changes in status; when it was readministered to the hospitalized subjects after they had been restored to competence, their scores were significantly higher. (See also Poythress et al., 2002, for a summary of the research.)

The Mac SAC–CD takes a trained clinician about two hours to administer. It was designed for research rather than for practical use, but a 40-minute, 22-item clinical version (the Mac-CAT–CA) was developed. The short form measures the three elements of ability to relate to counsel: understanding, reasoning, and appreciation. The norming sample consisted of a group hospitalized for treatment for incompetence; a group of inmates who were in jail and considered competent, but who were being treated for some psychiatric disorder; and untreated jail inmates.

The hospitalized incompetent group showed lower scores on all three components of the Mac-CAT-CA scale than the other two groups. Using Mac-Cat-CA measures as predictors, the scale classifed 69.9 percent of the incompetent inmates correctly. Poythress et al. (2002) presented some norms and suggested cutoff scores for each of the measures, indicating *clinically significant impairment, mild impairment,* and *minimal or no impairment.*

Impairment scores discriminate between groups very well, but they are not the same as a judgment of legal incompetence. Given that there is no absolute gold standard of legal incompetence, one can ask whether someone who is impaired in one dimension, or mildly impaired in one dimension, is still competent. The issue came up in *United States v. Jones* (2003). The legal standard is that a defendant has "capacity to assist in his or her defense," and "comprehends the nature and possible consequences of a trial." The court can order a competency hearing if either prong is not met. The court-appointed psychologist used the Mac-CAT-CA scale to guide his evaluation of Donald Jones. He reported that Jones showed "clinically significant impairment" on the appreciation scale, and mild impairment in "understanding." He also said that the defendant possessed "some competence" in the area of cooperating with his attorney. On this basis, the appellate court concluded that there was sufficient doubt about Jones's competence to require the trial judge to hold a competence hearing. Note that the appellate court did not say that Jones was incompetent, just that the evidence raised sufficient doubt to require a competency hearing.

The *Jones* case highlights a problem in the difference between legal thinking and psychometric thinking. The law works with open definitions (*Dusky*'s verbal standards for competence) that set some loose boundaries around a construct and allows a decision maker to exercise discretion, taking into account all the facts and circumstances in arriving at a decision. Legal thinking is also categorical. One is either competetent

100

CHAPTER 4
Competence to
Stand Trial,
and Other
Competencies

or not. Psychometric thinking uses operationally defined measures that have reliablity, and that produce a continuum of scores. The cutoff along this continuum for "competence" is necessarily arbitrary. Under the law, it is possible that missing one item out of the 22 in the Mac-CAT-CA scale is grounds for declaring the defendant incompetent. We don't know how a judge would deal with a result showing competence in two of the factors, but incompetence in one. Having reliable quantitative measures may help, but it doesn't solve the problem that inheres in the distinction between the law's Aristotelian emphasis on classifying into discrete categories, and social science's Gallilean emphasis on quantification along a dimension.

⊠ Treatment for Defendants Incompetent to Stand Trial

The vast majority of adult defendants who are hospitalized as incompetent to stand trial are restored to competence and returned to jail to await trial (Nicholson and McNulty, 1992). As a general rule, juveniles are considered incompetent to proceed in juvenile court only if they have severe mental disorders or mental retardation. In almost all states, immaturity alone is not sufficient to raise questions of adjudicative competence (Mulford et al., 2004). Most juveniles (72 percent) treated for adjudicative incompetence complete treatment and are considered competent to procede in a delinquency hearing (Office of Program Policy Analysis and Government Accountability, 2000).

Miller (2003) notes that although disposition in the least restrictive alternative consistent with the defendant's needs and society's need for protection is a legal principle, outpatient treatment to restore competency occurs rather infrequently, in contrast to evaluation of competency. Many state laws require hospitalization for treatment to restore competency; other states permit outpatient treatment. However, in many states no outpatient treatment is used, and in others probably fewer than 5 percent of defendants are treated in the community to restore competence (Miller, 2003). How is competence restored?

Medication

Psychotic symptoms are generally treated with psychotropic medication, which stabilizes most patients. However, the medications may also interfere with a defendant's defense. For example, a defendant who is pleading not guilty by reason of insanity may be at a disadvantage if he or she appears calm and rational when the jury sees him or her (see the discussion of the Andrea Yates case in Chapter 7). Side effects of medication may make the person appear physically stiff and expressionless, sleepy and sedated, dull emotionally, and slow to respond. These effects on **demeanor** (appearance and behavior) may hurt his or her case. Moreover, some side effects, like drowsiness, may interfere with a defendant's ability to cooperate with his or her attorney, to stay alert, and to pay attention during the trial.

David Riggins, a defendant in a murder case, believed his medications were hurting his case, but he was not allowed to refuse them. He applied to the courts, claiming that he had a right to refuse medication. In *Riggins v. Nevada* (1992; see Box 4.2), the U.S. Supreme Court ruled that a competent defendant could be forced to take medication if there was sufficient evidence that the medication was medically appropriate. (See also *Sell v. U.S.,* 2003.)

BOX 4.2

101

Treatment for
Defendants
Incompetent to
Stand Trial

A Legal Case in Point: Riggins v. Nevada (1992)

While awaiting trial for murder, David Riggins couldn't sleep and began hearing voices. He was stabilized on Mellaril, a tranquilizer, and Dilantin, an anticonvulsant. Riggins asked to discontinue the Mellaril during his trial. He said when he was taking the drug he was less able to help his lawyer. Moreover, he believed the jurors would be more open to his insanity defense if they could see how he acted when he was ill. The judge refused to allow him to discontinue the medication. Riggins, who was convicted and sentenced to death, appealed the judge's decision. In 1992, the case reached the U.S. Supreme Court.

The Court ruled that forcing a defendant to take medication violated Sixth and Fourteenth Amendment due process rights. However, a court could order a defendant medicated against his or her will if certain conditions were met. The patient could be required to take medication if there was sufficient evidence that the treatment was medically appropriate, if medicating the patient served an essential state interest, including ensuring safety or ensuring a fair trial, and if no less intrusive means of furthering these ends was available. Maintaining competence was not an issue in Riggins's case. There was evidence in the record that Riggins would have been competent to stand trial even if he had stopped taking his medication (see *Sell v. U.S.,* 2003).

In its model code, the ABA (1989) recommends that the incompetent defendant with a mental disorder should not be permitted to refuse ordinary and reasonable treatment (e.g., antipsychotic medication), but should be entitled to refuse more drastic treatments that may have serious or irreversible side effects (e.g., electroshock or lobotomy). Under current legal standards, it is probably not too difficult to demonstrate that it is medically appropriate to treat an incompetent defendant. Moreover, new antipsychotic medications have been and are being developed that are less debilitating than those used in the past.

Psychological Treatment

There is not much research on whether incompetent defendants receive any treatment different from that given other patients. Grisso (1992) and Siegel and Elwork (1990) propose that narrowly tailored psychoeducational instruction about the legal system might be sufficient to restore cognitive competence or might restore it faster than general treatment for mental illness alone.

Siegel and Elwork (1990) conducted a treatment evaluation study that produced promising results. Forty-one patients who were ruled incompetent to stand trial were given the CAI as a pretreatment assessment measure. Half the patients were assigned to a nine-session psychoeducational treatment program in addition to receiving general mental health care. The program used videotapes from a real trial, a courtroom tour, training in legally related problem solving, and small-group discussion to enhance relevant cognitive capacities. At the end of the experiment, the CAI was administered a second time by examiners who had not been involved in the experiment. Those who received the program showed a sharp improvement in competence scores. There was virtually no change in CAI scores in the control group.

102

CHAPTER 4
Competence to
Stand Trial,
and Other
Competencies

Many of those who were exposed to the psychoeducational program retained the knowledge for at least a month and a half. Forty-five days after posttesting, the staff of the hospital reevaluated the 41 initially incompetent defendants who had participated in the experiment. The staff now found that 43 percent of the experimental group, but only 15 percent of the control group, were competent to stand trial. Staff judgments of competence were correlated with higher scores on the CAI. (Keep in mind that the patients all received other forms of treatment while in the hospital that may have enhanced their ability to respond to the competence-focused psychoeducational program.)

Siegel and Elwork (1990) concluded that focused treatment methods can serve the interests of justice. They protect patient rights by making more patients competent to stand trial, and they speed up the treatment process. The findings are limited because researchers did not follow the treated patients to see how they actually fared in court or how well they cooperated with their attorneys.

A Florida program restored to competence 72 percent of youth referred for treatment because they were considered incompetent to continue in a juvenile court proceeding. The treatment program, provided either in an institution or in the community, included "education, role-playing, watching videos, and game playing" (Office of Program Policy Analysis and Government Accountability, 2000, p. 4). Adjudicative competence training was more effective for those with a primary diagnosis of mental illness (91 percent restored) compared to those with a primary diagnosis of mental retardation (63 percent restored). Over half completed training within six months, and 93 percent within a year. The juvenile court judge concurred with the recommendation in over 95 percent of the cases (Office of Program Policy Analysis and Government Accountability, 2000). These results are comparable to those reported by Siegel and Elwork (1990).

Other Issues in Criminal Competence

The legal system frequently distinguishes issues that, on the surface, seem to be highly similar. Defendants can be competent to stand trial, but not competent to engage in other adjudicative activities, including waiving counsel and refusing to use the insanity defense. They can even lack the competence to be executed.

Representing Oneself

There seems to be a trend toward self-representation in a variety of cases, judging from the large number of websites offering help to those who act **pro se** (representing themselves). In Canada, for example, depending on the stage of the criminal proceeding and in different courts, the percent of accused who were unrepresented varied from 1 percent to 72 percent. More than half of the defendants in one study were convicted without benefit of legal representation. Moreover, prosecutors will not plea-bargain with an unrepresented client, who therefore cannot benefit from reduced or dropped charges (Hann et al., 2002).

When a defendant waives a fundamental right, the courts require the waiver to be knowing, voluntary, and intelligent. While the right to counsel is a fundamental right under the Sixth Amendment, so too is the right to represent oneself in a criminal trial (*Faretta v. California*, 1975). When a defendant requests the right to act pro se, the judge's duty is to ensure the waiver of counsel and the request for self-representation are knowing and voluntary. The judge's duty is to warn the defendant about what can be lost by self-representation. Lack of knowledge of the law is not a reason to deny self-representation (*Faretta v. California,* 1975). The judge will allow self-representation to go forward if the judge is convinced in a hearing that the defendant understood the warning. The adequacy with which the defendant conducts the defense is not a matter for appeal. Electing to represent oneself, a defendant can't complain on appeal of ineffective legal counsel (*United States v. Egwaoje,* 2003).

Mental illness alone does not necessarily render the defendant incompetent to represent him or herself. The competency standard for waiving counsel is the same as the standard to stand trial (*Godinez v. Moran,* 1993, p. 331). In practice, judges caution defendants strongly against representing themselves. Judges generally will allow defendants who are competent to stand trial and who request it to act pro se. The judge may appoint legal consultants to assist defendants who choose to represent themselves, but the defendants don't have to accept the consultant's advice. The legal consultant should be present in the court if the defendant wishes consultation, or if the judge has to terminate self-representation. A trial judge may terminate self-representation if the defendant "deliberately engages in serious obsructionist misconduct. . . . The right to self representation is not a license to abuse the dignity of the courtroom. Neither is it a license not to comply with relevant rules of procedural and substantive law" (*Faretta v. California,* 1975, p. 834).

Colin Ferguson, who randomly shot a number of people on a Long Island commuter train, represented himself. (See Ewing and McCann, 2006, Chapter 15, for further details about this case.) He was allegedly paranoid, and proved to be inept at defending himself; he was convicted. His case raised some public concern about whether he should have been allowed to represent himself. In capital cases, defendants who represent themselves rarely win. For example, Kenneth Dwayne Dunn, who was convicted of killing a bank teller during a robbery, was said to be delusional with fantasies of becoming a psychiatrist, a lawyer, or a king. He was found competent to represent himself. The jury deliberated only six minutes before finding him guilty of a capital offense. He was sentenced to death (Sengupta, 1998b). Dunn later appealed, claiming he was incompetent to waive his right to counsel. The appellate court said, "The level of competence required to waive counsel is the same as that required to stand trial. Dunn was competent to stand trial. It necessarily follows that he also was competent to waive the right to counsel" (*Dunn v. Johnson,* 1998, p. 308).

Competent does not equate with *wise.* Justice Harry Blackmun, in dissent in *Faretta,* said, "If there is any truth to the old proverb 'that one who is his own lawyer has a fool for a client,' the Court by its opinion today now bestows a constitutional right on one to make a fool of himself." Perhaps experience with self-representation in serious cases has proved Justice Blackmun a prophet.

Refusal to Plead Insanity

The insanity defense is a kind of not-guilty plea. Technically, it is the client, not the lawyer, who decides how to plead. However, when mentally ill clients reject their lawyer's recommendation that they plead not guilty by reason of insanity, their competence is sometimes challenged. Competence to waive the insanity defense is problematic. Some people with some serious mental disorders understand the trial process and exhibit good abstract reasoning skills outside the area of their delusions. Colin Ferguson rejected a "black rage" insanity defense and was ruled competent to represent himself (*People v. Ferguson,* 1998). Some do not realize that they have delusions or do not remember events that took place when they were psychotic. Should an obviously

104

CHAPTER 4
Competence to
Stand Trial,
and Other
Competencies

ill person be subject to criminal penalties because he or she refused to plead insanity? Even in such cases, the courts will generally accept the defendant's decision to reject the defense and to represent himself. Some argue that when the refusal to plead insanity is based on a delusional belief that some other defense can prevail (e.g., not believing the victim is dead), the defendant should be found incompetent to stand trial and efforts made to restore competence before imposing the defense against the defendant's wishes. Others maintain that the court protects the defendant's autonomy by not imposing a defense against the defendant's wishes (Litwack, 2003).

Defendants who have committed their crimes to further a political cause, rational or otherwise, may not wish to plead insanity. For example, Theodore Kaczynski, the Unabomber, sent package bombs through the mail to scientists and others to protest against the ravages of technological society. Despite a treatment history and much evidence of odd behavior, he refused to accept that he was mentally ill. He believed that an insanity plea would undercut the credibility of his views of the dangers to society of technology. He tried to fire his lawyers because they wanted to present an insanity defense. He was examined to establish his competency to stand trial because he wanted to conduct his own defense. He was found competent. In the end, he retained the lawyers but pled guilty without using an insanity defense. By pleading, he avoided a possible death sentence. He bargained for a life sentence, which he is currently serving.

In 1859, John Brown, the abolitionist, a fanatic convinced that he was God's instrument to destroy slavery, killed a number of people and raided a U.S. arsenal at Harper's Ferry, Virginia (now West Virginia), for guns to arm slaves and promote a slave insurrection. Many thought his rampage was an insane act, but Brown rejected a plea of not guilty by reason of insanity. He was hanged for treason. His acts contributed to the climate leading to the Civil War (Fine, 1999).

Competence to Be Executed

The U.S. Supreme Court has held that it violates the Eighth Amendment prohibition against cruel and unusual punishment to execute a convict who was "insane" at the time of execution (*Ford v. Wainright,* 1986). The problem arises when a prisoner on death row has a psychotic break. Although it may seem peculiar to worry about the sanity of one who is about to be executed, there is a very long tradition of protecting the dignity of the justice system by trying and punishing only those who understand what is happening to them. Some regard the execution of mentally ill persons as a moral outrage. The fairness of executing an incompetent person is also an issue. A competent person might come up with some fact that might support an appeal (Winick, 1992).

The role of the mental health evaluator. When a question arises about a convict's **competence to be executed,** the court may request an evaluation by a mental health expert. The standard is not very high. The prisoner needs only to know that he is about to be executed and the reason for it. Given the low standard, courts may even reject a request by a condemned prisoner for a competency-to-be-executed hearing. The U.S. Supreme Court's decision in *Atkins v. Virginia* (2002) barred the execution of those with mental retardation (Zarazua, 2005). However, the fact that a prisoner may have a mental disorder is not the same as a finding of incompetency to be executed (*Thompson v. Bell,* 2004).

Conducting an evaluation of competence to be executed comes uncomfortably close to participating in the execution process because the sole purpose of the evaluation is to determine the severity of the punishment. When a mental health professional is asked to provide treatment to an incompetent person facing execution, the dilemma

BOX 4.3

105

Other Issues
in Criminal
Competence

Horace E. Kelly

One hundred and seven defendants had been executed in California between 1950 and 1998. The issue of competence to be executed came up only once, in the case of Horace E. Kelly. Kelly sits in his own waste, goes for long periods without bathing, and has an IQ in the mentally deficient range (in the 60s). When he speaks at all, he speaks in sentence fragments and disconnected phrases. He told his lawyer that death row was a vocational school, and that he was going home as soon as he obtained his certification (Terry, 1998b). Kelly was found competent to be executed by a 9–3 vote of a California jury (Terry, 1998a). Kelly is still on death row in California. In a 2006 hearing, a trial judge ruled that Kelly's attorneys failed to prove he was retarded when he killed 3 people in 1984. Appeals are pending. (De Atley, 2006).

is even sharper. If treatment is unsuccessful, the convicted person will continue to live, either on death row or in an institution for the criminally insane. If the treatment is successful and the patient's competence is restored, the outcome is the patient's death. Many clinicians understandably balk at this treatment role.

Claude Maturana was a death row inmate who was declared incompetent to be executed and was moved to a state mental hospital. The hospital psychiatrist prescribed medication sufficient to decrease his symptoms, but the psychiatrist refused to give

106

CHAPTER 4
Competence to
Stand Trial,
and Other
Competencies

Maturana sufficient medication to restore competence. The state quickly found a second psychiatrist who believed Maturana was mentally ill but competent to be executed. Ethical codes may prohibit physicians from treating an inmate on death row simply to restore competence to be executed. Participating in a legally authorized execution makes the doctor "the hangman's accomplice." Some doctors justify participation in an actual execution if state laws place such activities outside of the practice of medicine. A doctor who is "not practicing medicine" is not subject to the ethical constraints on physicians (Freedman, 2001). Other doctors refuse to participate. In California, the execution of Michael Morales was postponed indefinitely when physicians withdrew from participation because of ethical concerns that the method of execution in use would cause serious pain (Rottman, 2006). In North Carolina, an inmate, Willie Brown Jr., was executed while a doctor and nurse watched a machine that monitored whether he was asleep before receiving the lethal injection from a prison staff member ("North Carolina," 2006). The issues of professional participation in executions are discussed at length by Brodsky (1990) and Bonnie (1990a, 1990b).

Bonnie (1990a) strongly endorsed the Supreme Court's *Ford v. Wainwright* (1986) ruling that an incompetent prisoner may not be executed. Even condemned prisoners, he says, should have the opportunity to make the few choices available to them

> to decide who should be present at his execution, what he will eat for his last meal, what if anything, he will utter for his last words, whether he will repent or go defiantly to his grave. A prisoner who does not understand the nature and purpose of the execution is not able to exercise the choices that remain to him. To execute him in this condition is an affront to his dignity as a person. (Bonnie, 1990a, p. 88)

How often? Although the debate is impassioned, the question of competence to be executed arises very infrequently. Death row prisoners typically don't feign mental illness in order to have their executions postponed (Radelet and Miller, 1992; Winick, 1992). More than 100 defendants have been executed in California since 1950. The issue of competence to be executed came up only once, in the case of Horace E. Kelly, described in Box 4.3. The handling of Kelly's case suggests that evaluating a convict's competence to be executed may be ritually undertaken to uphold the symbolic value of not executing an incompetent person. As a practical matter, much more often than not, the execution will go forward.

SECTION II
COMPETENCE IN CIVIL LAW

We speak about competence in civil law when a person's capacity to make personal decisions rationally is at issue. We call these *civil competencies* because they refer to ordinary transactions and ordinary freedoms, and do not involve the criminal law.

⊠ Age and Competence

When a statute draws a *bright line* (precise point) of age, it makes presumptions about a level of emotional and cognitive maturity sufficient to consent and to make decisions. Children under a certain age are classified by the legal term **minor.** Their rights and liberties are regulated in ways that adult rights and liberties are not because they are not considered competent to regulate themselves. They attain full adult rights and responsibilities when they reach the age of majority, established by the state legislatures. States have set 18 as the age of majority for most purposes. However, legislatures, acknowledging natural differences in the level of maturation required for different activities or responding to social needs or social conventions, set lower or higher ages for specific activities. For example, in New York State young people are allowed to get a driver's license at 16, to consent to consensual sex at 17, to vote at 18, and to purchase and possess alcohol at 21.

Status as a minor is a social construct. From a psychological perspective, there is no "bright line" of age. Individuals mature at different rates. If we had a psychological test for competence to make decisions, some minors would pass and some adults would fail. But, even if we had such tests, it is more convenient for most purposes to use these bright lines and to deal with the occasional exception.

Minors may be emancipated, that is, given adult status prior to the age of majority by a court under conditions established by state law (for example, on marriage, when in the armed forces, or when living apart from one's parents with parental consent and managing one's own financial affairs). In the absence of an agreement on child support in a divorce, the parent of an emancipated child may be relieved of child support responsibilities. An **emancipated minor** has many but not all of the rights of an adult (e.g., laws restricting drinking age or engaging in casino gambling still apply; Marnell and Schwartz, 2004). We will review the concept of a *mature minor* when considering competence to consent to medical treatment.

The competence of an adult can be challenged in a court hearing. An adult does not have to prove competence; it is up to the challenger to prove incompetence. The subjects of the challenges are most often the mentally ill, people with developmental disabilities or low functional intelligence, and elderly people exhibiting cognitive deficits. If a person is found incompetent, the court may appoint a guardian or conservator to manage the person's affairs or to make decisions for him or her.

The elderly constitute a growing percentage of our population. More and more people are living long enough to develop diseases of aging like Alzheimer's and other forms of senility that affect their mental ability. Competence determinations related to disabilities of old age, particularly competence to manage one's own financial affairs, may become more common as people live longer. A growing number of psychology graduate programs, clinical internships and postgraduate programs offer training in geropsychology. Psychologists may serve as evaluators and expert witnesses in guardianship cases. Psychologists working in Veterans Administration facilities where there are many aging patients do a lot of this work. World War II ended in 1945; many of those veterans are in their eighties. Those in private practice may find the field attractive and lucrative. The fees for competency evaluations of the elderly often come from private payers (e.g., relatives and attorneys), and the going rate is set by the market (Hartman-Stein, 1999).

Competence to Make a Will

When a person dies, the will is submitted to a special civil court, called **probate (or surrogate) court,** to be validated and to give the **executor** (person named in the will to carry out—execute—the terms of the will) the legal authority to act for the estate. A will can be contested after it is submitted to probate. The law has a strong policy

108

CHAPTER 4
Competence to
Stand Trial,
and Other
Competencies

favoring giving effect to a properly drawn will. However, the courts will entertain a challenge to the validity of a will if there is evidence that the deceased might have lacked the competence to make a will (**testamentary capacity**), or may have been unduly influenced. Experts may be asked to speculate about the competence of a dead person they have never examined. That problem is difficult because evidence of mental illness alone is not sufficient to establish incompetence to make a will.

The standards for testamentary capacity, which vary from state to state, are vague and not very high. Generally speaking, a **testator** (person making the will) is competent if he or she understands a will is being written, understands what property is being discussed and who the "natural objects of his or her bounty" are (e.g., spouse and children), and understands who will get the money or property. Evidence may be admitted regarding the deceased's inability to manage his or her affairs, physical disabilities, difficult and unusual behavior, and "unnatural provisions" (e.g., left money [devised] to a home for indigent canaries rather than to the decedent's children), but proof of any one of these points is not enough to invalidate a will (Brooks, 1974; Richie, Alford, and Effland, 1982). An **insane delusion** may be sufficient to invalidate a will. An insane delusion is one that is not based on fact, however slight, and is not removable by information to the contrary.

Thomas Szasz (1963), psychiatry's gadfly (Figure 4.1), questions whether a psychiatrist could ever "ferret out mental illness in persons he never saw and who are dead." In Szasz's view, testamentary (making a will) incompetence is a legal fiction. For Szasz, the real issue is who will inherit the property. Consider the case of Anna

FIGURE 4.1

Thomas Szasz

Thomas Szasz is an influential psychiatrist who is critical of testimony by mental health experts. He argues that mental health professionals have no knowledge that would enable them to judge the competence of a deceased person to make a will.

Nicole Smith, a beautiful young woman who married an 89-year-old man who died about a year after they were married. She claimed she married him for love. Her husband's death triggered a legal battle over his competence to give his estate to her in his will. An appeals court overturned a lower court decision favoring her, and she received only a relatively small award. Because of technical legal issues, in 2006, the U.S. Supreme Court ruled in her favor and sent her back to the lower courts for further consideration. If the terms of the deceased's will violate **social norms** (public sense of what is right), the court may be receptive to the idea that the person making the will was insane and therefore incompetent. But, as Szasz points out, in the absence of a will, a person's estate by law goes to his or her spouse and children, his or her natural heirs. If a person made out a will that disinherited his or her natural heirs, the person knew the rules of the game, and was in contact with reality. Brooks (1974) also thinks that the basis for findings of testamentary incompetence is that the judges disagreed with the values inherent in the choices the deceased made. Most wills are made out in accordance with normative beliefs about who should inherit (Johnson and Robbennolt, 1998).

Competence to Manage One's Affairs

The purpose of the statutes governing incompetence is to protect people and their property when they are unable to protect their interests themselves. Incompetence proceedings go back to the very earliest days in English law, perhaps as early as 1324, and in North America to colonial times. In England, the king became the guardian of the property and personal interests first of the mentally deficient, later of the mentally ill as well. The king delegated authority to a lord chancellor to hold a hearing, and, if it was determined the person was an "idiot" (mentally disabled from birth or an early age) or a "lunatic" (mental disability developed after a period of normalcy), a committee was appointed to supervise both the property and the person. The **court of equity** (justice based on fairness, involving a court order to change circumstances but not to pay money damages) supervised and controlled the committee. The guardianship was in place as long as the person remained incompetent.

Procedures for Declaring Someone Incompetent

In the United States, all the states have some procedure for declaring someone incompetent to manage his or her property or person. The process follows the basic lines laid out in medieval England. Depending on state law, a petition may be brought by a relative, a friend, a caseworker of a disabled person, or sometimes any interested person. Most petitioners are motivated by concern for the person, but sometimes control of assets is the issue.

The state itself sometimes uses the competence statute to protect an elderly person (Tatara, 1995). Almost all states have some version of a statute permitting or requiring reports of elder abuse or neglect, usually to an agency comparable to child protective services. **Elder abuse** includes neglect, mistreatment, emotional and physical abuse, and financial exploitation of an elderly person. If relatives or anyone else appear to be exploiting an elderly person financially or mistreating him or her, agency workers may initiate a petition for an adjudication of incompetence. In theory, the court will intervene to protect the elderly person's best interests.

Because basic liberties are at stake (loss of liberty and loss of control over property), the person whose competence is challenged is entitled to due process: to notice,

110

CHAPTER 4
Competence to
Stand Trial,
and Other
Competencies

to a hearing, and to legal representation. In the majority of states, jury trials may be requested. In practice, judges probably make most determinations. In most jurisdictions, the petitioner must prove the incompetence by *clear and convincing evidence,* the highest standard of proof in civil matters.

Role of Experts

Old age alone is insufficient to raise a question about a person's intellectual capacities to manage his or her own affairs. The petitioner must also show the person is "unable to manage" his or her property, or "will dissipate it" or become the "victim of designing persons" (Reisner, 1985). Establishing that the person has a disorder or a debilitating problem is not enough to establish incompetence; some mental disability must be demonstrated *and* shown to affect the ability to manage property. Often the court orders an examination of the person whose competence is at issue. Physicians, psychiatrists, or psychologists may be the expert examiners, depending on each state's law (Parry, 1985). There is little research and no validated, standardized instruments to help mental health professionals assess competence to manage one's affairs. Context may make a difference. If the estate is large, the examiner may want to be more certain about the quality of the elderly person's decision making. If the stakes are smaller, and the person is in a relatively protected situation (e.g., an elderly person living with adult children), the concerns may be fewer. Clinicians are left to their own judgment.

Competence is a complex concept. A person may be mentally disturbed in some areas, but quite competent in others. The award-winning film *The Aviator* (2005) was based on the life of multimillionaire Howard Hughes. (There are also numerous biographies of him.) Hughes was a film producer, an industrialist, a manufacturer of aircraft, an owner of a commercial airline, a test pilot who flew and contributed to the design of aircraft, and a controversial personality who was the lover of movie stars. Yet Hughes had some severe phobias about dirt, germs, or contaminated food; suffered from ideas of reference (believed without reason that people were looking at him or talking about him); and occasionally exhibited automatisms (uncontrollably repeating a word over and over). In one period of his life, he became extremely withdrawn and acted in a bizarre fashion, locking himself away nude. Yet he never lost control of his various enterprises and proved adept at defending himself against political attack.

If a person is found to be incompetent, the court appoints a guardian ad litem to protect his or her interests. The incompetent person becomes the guardian's **ward.** The guardian, under the supervision of the court, is responsible for managing and using the ward's assets for the ward's benefit. A guardian may also be appointed to make personal decisions for an incompetent person, for example, decisions about medical care or housing. If the ward is restored to competence, he can request another hearing to end the guardianship (Parry, 1985).

When someone's competence is challenged, it is often clear that the person can no longer manage his or her affairs. Elderly persons can develop Alzheimer's. As the disease progresses, they can lose their ability to care for themselves. For example, they may stop cleaning their home, or their utilities may be turned off because they forget to pay the bills. However, competence hearings may also be initiated in cases in which an elderly person is spending money in ways prospective heirs don't like. Comedian Richard Pryor suffered from multiple sclerosis and was disabled. His son unsuccessfully tried to intervene to have him declared incompetent because he claimed that his father was wasting his estate and was being unreasonably influenced by a former spouse in how he spent his money (Armstrong, 2000).

Competence to Make Medical Decisions

We place great importance in our legal tradition on voluntary agreements, including voluntary consent to treatment. **Voluntary** means more than being free of undue influence from others. It also implies making a decision on the basis of good understanding of relevant information.

Before beginning a treatment, doctors and therapists are obliged to obtain their patients' **informed consent** to the proposed procedures. The obligation was originally founded in the tort of battery. **Battery** is an offense to a person's dignity. It occurs when a person is intentionally touched by another without the person's consent. The requirement of consent obviously applies to surgical care. But the requirement extends to all medical treatment and, in recent years, to psychotherapy as well. The requirement protects a person's right to self-determination and protects against submission to authoritarian medical treatment (Mnookin and Weisberg, 2005). There are exceptions to rules requiring patient consent; for example, consent is not required in an emergency.

Consent must be given without coercion or pressure, and it must be adequately informed. Medical doctors are supposed to provide patients with the relevant information about treatment or examination: its risks, benefits, and costs, including side effects. They are also supposed to provide information about the availability of alternative procedures, and their risks and benefits (Wallach, 1993). The patient receiving the information must be competent to give consent. A **competent person** in this context is someone with sufficient mental capacity to understand the information, to weigh good and bad consequences of different actions, and to make and express a choice. (We will discuss the competence to agree to contraception or to sterilization below.)

Consent to Treatment and the Mentally Ill

Whether or when the mentally ill should be considered incompetent to make medical decisions is controversial. In practice, the controversy concerns the person's right to refuse treatment. The competence of patients who agree to follow their doctors' recommendations is rarely questioned, but it may be different for those who don't follow the doctor's recommendations for treatment. This is true for physical as well as mental illness. For example, in order to protect the potential child, sometimes maternal-fetal medicine facilities will seek court orders to support coercive treatment if a pregnant woman refuses treatment (Adams, Mahowald, and Gallagher, 2003).

The most invasive treatments of mental illness, electroconvulsive (shock) therapy and psychosurgery, are used relatively rarely today. We will limit our discussion here to the treatment most commonly at issue, psychotropic drugs. Psychotropic drugs are the first line of treatment for severe psychiatric symptoms. The question of competence to refuse medication comes up primarily, and it comes up frequently, with institutionalized patients; outpatients can simply stop taking drugs.

Patients' Rights

A person in a psychiatric ward or hospital is still a person with rights under the Fourteenth Amendment. Like anyone else, he or she is entitled to a presumption of competence until the presumption is rebutted in a due process hearing. A person who

112

CHAPTER 4
Competence to
Stand Trial,
and Other
Competencies

is hospitalized involuntarily has obviously lost the right to refuse hospitalization, but not all rights. In *Youngberg v. Romeo* (1982), the Supreme Court, while encouraging courts to defer to medical judgment in their decisions, ruled that involuntarily committed mental patients have some minimum basic rights. Many state courts have ruled that involuntarily hospitalized patients, like voluntarily hospitalized patients, are presumed competent to refuse treatment until proven otherwise (Applebaum and Grisso, 1995a; Schwartz, Vingiano, and Perez, 1990). Mentally ill convicts also have a right to refuse treatment under some conditions (see *Washington v. Harper,* 1990; *Riggins v. Nevada,* 1992; Box 4.2). Forced medication is permitted in emergencies and if a patient is considered dangerous to him or herself or others because of an illness and the treatment is appropriate for the illness (*Washington v. Harper,* 1990; *Sell v. United States,* 2003).

Even when it is not an emergency, the right to refuse medication is more symbolic than real. When doctors believe they need to treat a patient with psychotropic medications and the patient refuses, the hospital can go to court to have the patient declared incompetent or obtain court permission to forcibly medicate the resistant patient. Often, a judge will come to the hospital to hold a hearing. The courts probably go along with the doctor's professional judgment in most cases. Even lawyers assigned to represent patients refusing medication tend to treat their clients paternalistically. They often don't fight aggressively for their clients' wishes (Perlin and Dorfman, 1996). However, the assumption of competence to refuse treatment means that patients at least

---

BOX 4.4

John Du Pont and Vincent Gigante

Mental illness alone, even when it leads to hospitalization, does not in itself establish that a person is incompetent and needs a guardian. A case in point is John E. Du Pont, an heir of the Du Pont fortune. In 1996 Du Pont was charged with murder. He pleaded insanity. He was found incompetent to stand trial because of active symptoms related to mental illness, including delusions. He told his lawyer he was the Dalai Lama and referred to himself as the "Christ child." He also said he had been brainwashed by Buddhists, that he was the Fuehrer, and that his victim had been killed by Republicans because Du Pont had not contributed money to the party, among other delusional ideas. His lawyer said he had had no rational discussion with Du Pont since the defendant's arrest eight months earlier. He was committed to a state hospital for treatment. However, he was not declared incompetent to manage his property and continued to do so from the hospital. His competence to stand trial was restored and he was released and tried in 1997. The fact that he signed a fee agreement to pay his lawyers $300 an hour, that he didn't sign the agreement "Dalai Lama," and had been able to give sensible instructions regarding his property during his hospitalization was used as evidence that he wasn't insane. He was found Guilty but Mentally Ill under Pennsylvania law and is presently in prison for his crime. He will not lose control over his property just because he is in prison (Goldberg, 1996; New York Times, 1996).

Vincent "The Chin" Gigante, a Mafia boss called the Oddfather for his overtly "crazy" behavior, successfully put off prosecution from 1970 on by feigning incompetence to stand trial. He adopted incompetence as a life style. In 2003, he admitted that he had been faking and was convicted in a plea bargain that ended in a three year sentence (CBS News, 2003).

have an opportunity to have their cases reviewed. Adolescents who are in a mental hospital voluntarily may be able to consent to treatment, and by implication refuse it, depending on specific aspects of state law (Costello, 2003).

Dying with Their Rights On?

Many mental health professionals argue that the acute psychiatric symptoms that lead to hospitalization are almost always associated with severe impairments in judgment. Patients may deny having a disorder or have poor insight into its nature. They may be intensely suspicious of hospital staff or feel too hopeless or hostile to be interested in treatment. At worst, the mental health professionals argue, allowing severely mentally ill persons to refuse medication allows them to keep their civil rights at the cost of giving up their best hope of living a more normal life outside a mental hospital. Some have called this *dying with their rights on.* The presumption of competence, they say, wastes valuable time and money by imposing an additional burden on hospital staff. In non-emergency situations, staff members spend time preparing court cases to get judicial permission to medicate against the patient's will.

Schwartz and colleagues (Schwartz, Vingiano, and Perez, 1990) are among those who believe that most patients who refuse medication do so, not for rational reasons, but because of anger, paranoia, or disordered reasoning. They reason that, if patients were refusing medication for irrational reasons, they would feel differently about treatment after they recovered. To test this hypothesis, they studied 25 involuntarily hospitalized patients who were involuntarily treated at least once with psychotropic medication. On their discharge, 17 of the 25 reported some agreement with the statement "I know now that although I was given medication against my will here, it was necessary and important for my treatment."

Is Refusal Irrational?

Many patients probably do refuse drugs for irrational reasons. But how irrational? People who are not mentally ill do not always make medical decisions on rational grounds either, and many distrust the medical establishment. (Is a woman who refuses a recommended mastectomy because she can't bear the thought of losing a breast incompetent?) There are rational reasons for refusing psychotropic drugs. Some can have serious and debilitating side effects. Drugs that relieve psychotic symptoms do not necessarily make patients feel "normal." Some drugs may lower energy and dull sensation, emotion, and motivation. They may induce unpleasant physical sensations. In addition, patients with serious and persistent mental illness and with a history of repeated hospitalizations may well have experienced abuses of power by medical staff. They may have been overmedicated or inappropriately medicated, or simply had a bad drug reaction. Their distrust of the doctors' recommendations may be based on these experiences, not paranoia.

Assessing Competence to Refuse Treatment

Once courts recognized the right to refuse treatment, it became more important to have explicit standards for competence to refuse treatment, and some way of measuring patients' capacities against that standard. If there were agreed on standards and reliable means of assessing competence, we could tell whether all, most, some, or only a minority of hospitalized patients meet the standards of competence. This information

114

CHAPTER 4
Competence to
Stand Trial,
and Other
Competencies

could help policy makers develop procedures that balanced respect for individual autonomy with the need to care for people unable to care for themselves. Reliable means of assessing competence could also help clinicians make better individual evaluations. To these ends, the MacArthur Foundation funded a major study designed to develop instruments to assess competence among the mentally ill (Appelbaum and Grisso, 1995a, 1995b; Grisso et al., 1995; Winick, 1996).

The MacArthur Treatment Competence Study research team first identified four legal standards courts had used when they reviewed right-to-refuse treatment cases: (1) ability to understand relevant information, (2) ability to appreciate the situation and its likely consequences, (3) ability to manipulate information rationally, and (4) ability to communicate a choice (Appelbaum and Grisso, 1995a, 1995b). The research group then developed three measures for assessing competence by these standards (Appelbaum and Grisso, 1995a, 1995b; Grisso et al., 1995; Winick, 1996). The measures represented an attempt to **operationalize** (define in terms of observable and measurable behaviors) the relatively vague and abstract legal standards.

To measure *understanding,* subjects were given information about their condition and its treatment and were asked to paraphrase (say in their own words) what they were told. This format is similar to what clinicians do when obtaining informed consent from a patient. To measure *appreciation,* subjects were asked to acknowledge their illness and the potential value of treatment, not necessarily to accept treatment. Low scores were given to subjects who did not acknowledge their documented symptoms and to patients whose beliefs that treatment would not help were rigid. The procedure allowed the examiner to challenge the patient's illogical reasoning. The third element, *ability to manipulate information rationally,* was tested in a problem-solving format. Subjects were presented with a brief vignette describing a hypothetical person's mental illness or a medical illness. The subject was asked to give advice to the hypothetical patient in the vignette. The advice could be scored for its consistency with the information. The fourth element, *ability to communicate a choice,* was tested by asking subjects to select a treatment option in a task involving decision making.

The study was carried out in three different hospitals in three different states. The measures were given to 75 patients with schizophrenia, of whom half were voluntary and the other half involuntary admissions, and 92 voluntarily admitted patients with major depression. Patients whose doctors believed they were too disturbed to participate were not tested. One control group consisted of 82 patients with ischemic heart disease (inadequate circulation of blood in coronary arteries). Ischemic heart disease, like mental illness, tends to be chronic, is associated with multiple hospitalizations, and is treated with medication. This group was included to control for the effect of illness and hospitalization on decision-making capacities. Three groups of healthy controls were also studied. The patients were tested on admission and 14 days later to look at changes in their capacities over time.

The research team demonstrated that the interviews could be scored reliably by different raters. Forty-eighty percent of the schizophrenic group, 76.1 percent of the depression group, 87.8 percent of the heart disease group, and 96 percent of the control groups performed adequately on all three measures. In another study using the same instrument, a large majority (89–90 percent) of two patient groups were considered competent to make treatment decisions. Competencies in different areas are only poorly correlated. Only 29 percent and 40 percent of two groups with schizophrenia were considered to have both impaired treatment and impaired adjudicative competence (Poythress et al., 2002). A related issue concerns the competence to consent to participate in research, a federal requirement. Kovnick et al. (2003) used the MacCAT-

CR in a small sample of long-stay patients with schizophrenia who were resident in a state hospital research ward. Many showed poorer scores than a comparison group. Depending on the scale, between 33 percent and 48 percent of members of the schizophrenic group scored below the lowest score obtained by members of the comparison group. Kovnick et al. concluded that a "substantial proportion" of the patients with schizophrenia who may have been competent to give consent for medical treatment were impaired for giving consent to participate in research. That finding presents a problem for enlisting patients in clinical research that might be of benefit to them. It is another illustration that competence in one area doesn't necessarily correlate with competence in another area.

The most disturbed patients at the hospitals were not included in the studies. Consequently, these findings underestimate patient impairment. About half the patients with schizophrenia who could be tested exhibited deficits in decision-making abilities. The results strongly suggest that many, but far from all, mentally ill patients do have the capacity to make competent treatment decisions.

Is Consent Ever Fully Voluntary?

In practice, it is questionable whether consent can ever be given voluntarily by inpatients, most of whom realize that their release is related to cooperation with staff. This question applies to voluntary as well as involuntary patients. People who voluntarily choose admission often do so under pressure. Moreover, even though they admit themselves voluntarily, they are discouraged from leaving without the consent of staff. Staff can also request a court hearing to change a voluntary admission to an involuntary one (Lidz et al., 1993; Rogers, 1993). Certainly a large number of patients agree to take medication while in the hospital and stop immediately after they are released, suggesting that, in some cases at least, their initial consent did not reflect their real wishes.

This is a difficult area. We wish to respect basic rights of mental patients. Having a diagnosis does not in and of itself deprive persons of their fundamental rights. On the other hand, we do have some effective treatments, and there are people whose judgment, and capacity to conform sufficiently to social norms to live with others, are impaired by illness. The management of people who may not wish to be "managed" can be difficult and troublesome. Having a better analysis of the issues and a more precise way to judge capacity may be forms of control against arbitrary decision making by professionals, who are sometimes in an unchallenged position of power over the lives of others. The therapeutic jurisprudence perspective also asks us to look at the therapeutic benefits and costs to the recovery of the person of the governing legal rules (Schopp, 1996). Once again, we are faced with the problem of balancing important values without having an unambiguous scale on which to weigh them.

Children and Consent to Medical Treatment

Under the law, minor children lack the capacity to give consent or to make informed choices about medical care. Consistent with our belief that responsibility for child care belongs to parents and, with our respect for family autonomy, the right to consent to children's treatment belongs to their parents or legal guardians (Mnookin and Weisberg, 2005). Parental autonomy has limits. Because of its interest in the welfare of children,

116

CHAPTER 4
Competence to
Stand Trial,
and Other
Competencies

the state can and does impose obligations on parents to provide some basic health care; in some circumstances, a parent's refusal to provide recommended treatment can be considered medical neglect.

The appropriateness of parents making medical decisions on behalf of younger children is rarely questioned. The presumption that adolescents are not competent to make medical decisions is more controversial. Research suggests that many children 14 and older have some or all of the cognitive capacities needed for medical decision making (see Chapter 14). Adolescents concerned with privacy and independence, and who may be in conflict with parents, may be unwilling to share health problems with parents. Adolescents may be concerned about body image and the physical changes of puberty, with increased awareness of sexuality. Some experiment with drugs and alcohol, and may encounter more serious problems related to substance abuse. Many adolescents suffer from depression and suicidal thoughts. Genetic counseling to learn whether an adolescent is at risk for a genetic disorder may be a concern. Most states allow minors to consent to treatment independently for certain problems including alcohol, drug dependence, AIDS, and venereal disease. Many states recognize a *mature minor doctrine.* Generally, youth of 16 and 17 who have sufficient intelligence and understanding to appreciate what treatment and treatment options and their consequences entail are considered to have the legal capacity to consent to treatment even if it is not an emergency. In regard to mental health care, even though a minor might be considered legally capable of seeking treatment, the provider might be open to a lawsuit by the parent for violation of the parent's prerogatives. The outcome of the lawsuit would then hinge on the court's evaluation of whether the minor was sufficently mature to consent and whether consent was sufficiently informed (Gilmore, 2003).

The legal rules permitting these exceptions reflect the beliefs that (1) there is a strong public interest in treating these conditions, and (2) some minors who want treatment might not seek it if they knew their parents would be notified. Would recognition of the growing maturity of adolescents contribute to that maturity by permitting youth to seek treatment on their own? Would such a right serve public policy by increasing adolescent access to medical or psychological services? Would giving that option to adolescents further undercut parental authority and foster distance between adolescents and their families? These are questions about which we have little research.

The competence of adolescents to consent to treatment will be discussed further in Chapter 14.

Involuntary Psychiatric Hospitalization

Involuntary psychiatric hospitalization of adolescents is a special problem. Sometimes, children who did not need and would not benefit from hospitalization have been placed in mental hospitals by parents unable to handle them or by states unable to find a more appropriate placement.

In *Parham v. J.R.* (1979), the U.S. Supreme Court ruled that voluntary commitment to a mental hospital of minors by parents or guardians without the minor's consent was constitutional; formal adversary hearings were not required to protect the child's due process rights. The Court said that parents and the admitting physician, presumed to be a **neutral fact-finder,** would adequately ensure there was a need for hospitalization.

Some states have enacted legislation to provide court hearings to protect minors from inappropriate hospitalizations. But, in about half the states where the *Parham* rule applies, the sole control over arbitrariness in the admission of a minor is the admitting doctor, who may have a financial interest in hospitalizing the patient (Nurcombe and

Partlett, 1994). The trend, however, is to grant more due process rights to adolescents facing **involuntary hospitalization** (Reeves, 2004). Costello (2002) reported on the California statute that gives due process rights and a hearing to adolescents at risk of involuntary hospitalization. She believes that from a therapeutic jurisprudence perspective, there are psychological advantages to giving adolescents a voice in the decisions made about their lives, but it is not clear that outcomes are different under the different legal procedures. On the other side, Amaya and Burlingame (1990) report clinical observations that due process court hearings affect adolescents adversely when the judge rules against them, and make juveniles harder to manage in the institution.

The growth of private, for-profit psychiatric hospitals has capitalized on the lack of due process standards for the hospitalization of adolescents. Adolescents placed in private hospitals are much more likely to have diagnoses of conduct disorders or substance abuse than they are to have more serious psychotic disorders. Some claim that gay adolescents have been committed by their parents for treatment because of their sexual orientation. If admissions of these adolescents were subject to legal challenge, many would not qualify for **involuntary admission** (which is used for those mentally ill and dangerous to self or others; Weithorn, 1988). Among adolescents hospitalized because of alcohol abuse, a very large number met diagnostic criteria for personality disorders and affective disorders. Few received diagnoses of psychoses (Grilo et al., 1998).

Adolescents with serious behavioral and substance abuse problems may be difficult to live with, and may even be self-destructive or destructive of their futures. Parents seeking help with controlling unruly and defiant youth may seek involuntary hospitalization because they believe that hospitalization may make a stronger impression on their children than any other means of control. But many people question whether parents should be permitted to have an adolescent child detained for a coerced intervention that may not be medically necessary or even appropriate. Ironically, the only safeguards for adolescents in some jurisdictions may be those provided by insurance companies. Private mental hospitals have been accused of fraud and excessive billing, especially in cases involving adolescents (Kerr, 1991). Managed care companies have probably limited some abuses by instituting insurance reviews of the necessity for hospitalization in order to save money.

Managed care and related incentives may have contributed to the increase in discharges and a decline in length of stay in hospitals. From 1988 to 1995, the length of stay declined for children and adolescents hospitalized in private facilities covered by private insurance. However, the role of Medicaid (public insurance for poor people) insurance increased (Pottick, McAlpine, and Andelman, 2000). Reimbursement contracts for providers with incentives to reduce hospital care did reduce inpatient hospital care, but the use of residental treatment centers increased (Libby et al., 2002). Medicaid insurance was an important source of funding for psychiatric outpatient services as well as for inpatient services (Burns et al., 1997). We may be moving toward a two-tiered system in which adolescents from poorer families are sent to public mental hospitals and facilities, and those from wealthier families to residential treatment centers. In addition to clinical diagnosis, rules and laws governing reimbursement play a role in who gets treated and where the treatment is provided.

Competence to Consent to Sexual Relationships

We will include under this heading the competence to marry, involuntary sterilization of the mentally retarded, and the competence to consent to sexual relationships.

118

CHAPTER 4
Competence to
Stand Trial,
and Other
Competencies

Competence to Marry

The rules vary somewhat state by state, but those under a statutory age of consent cannot marry without the consent of a parent or guardian. However, while in most states those underage are by law considered incompetent to give consent to marriage, once married, they are presumed competent to give consent to sexual relationships. In an unusual case, Matthew Koso (age 22) was convicted of first degree sexual assault in Nebraska and sentenced to 18 to 30 months in prison after he married Crystal (age 14) with their parents' blessings (Ruethling, 2006). The couple, who live in Nebraska, married in Kansas, where persons as young as 12 may marry. Nebraska law defines statutory rape as intercourse between someone 19 and older and a person 16 or younger, even if the couple is married. The case was controversial in their community (Wilgoren, 2005).

Many states continue to have on their books laws restricting the rights of those with mental retardation to marry. Those who have been diagnosed with mental retardation and are of age may enter into a valid marriage if the participants understand the nature of a marriage contract and the duties and responsibilities of marriage. The standards are not very high. There is no premarital test of competence. The issue may arise only if for some reason someone challenges the validity of the marriage. Mental health professionals may testify as to the competence of the individual with a history of mental retardation (e.g., *Edwards v. Edwards,* 1980). There is very little research on which to base an assessment of the competence to marry of those who have had a diagnosis of mental retardation at some time in the past.

Involuntary Sterilization of the Mentally Retarded

In the past, especially when the eugenics movement was rampant, laws required or allowed the involuntary sterilization of those who would contaminate the gene pool: the "feeble-minded," the insane, the "criminalistic," epileptics, chronic alcoholics, those with certain diseases, the blind, the deaf, the deformed and chronically dependent, or children of paupers (Foote, Levy, and Sander, 1985, p. 547). In *Buck v. Bell* (1927), Justice Oliver Wendell Holmes, writing for the U.S. Supreme Court, upheld compulsory sterilization laws as reflecting the right of society to prevent "those who were manifestly unfit from continuing their kind." Justice Holmes also stated, "Three generations of imbeciles are enough" (p. 207; his statement of the facts in the case was not exactly accurate. Cary Buck was moderately retarded, and her out-of-wedlock baby was not retarded).

For a long time, 35 states had laws permitting, with the approval of an institution committeee, involuntary sterilization. Many thousands of inmates of institutions were involuntarily sterilized (Buckley, 2001). In those days, institutionalization was the treatment of choice for those with mental retardation. Today, many fewer of those with retardation are placed in institutions. In more recent times, with recognition of a constitutionally protected right to privacy and a right to reproduce, states have adopted legislation giving individuals due process rights before permitting involuntary sterilization. In 1977, Elizabeth Arnold-Lake, then 16 years old, was sterilized without her informed consent, and even without knowledge of what was done. Such persons were often told they were having an appendectomy or other surgery. Elizabeth later married Justin Lake. They discovered she was sterile only when she and her husband consulted a physician because they desired children. A federal appeals court permitted her to bring suit to recover damages against her guardians (*Lake v. Arnold,* 2000).

Parents are concerned about unwanted pregnancy, or sometimes about whether a daughter with retardation can manage menstruation. They may seek sterilization for the adolescent. Parents might also be concerned about controlling the sexual aggressiveness of a son with a mental disorder by involuntary medical treatment or sterilization (Realmuto and Ruble, 1999).

If the parents or guardians seek to have the adolescent sterilized today, the adolescent's rights are protected. Involuntary sterilization can only be carried out with a court order. The Delaware statute is probably typical. As used in the statute, *informed consent* means consent to be sterilized given by the person to be sterilized and given voluntarily and with an understanding of the nature and consequences of the procedure to be performed" (Section 5701, Title 16). Those in institutions or those for whom sterilization is requested by someone else (e.g., a parent or guardian) are presumed incapable of giving informed consent. The individual case must be heard by a court. Any petition for involuntary sterilization must include a statement from a licensed psychologist or psychiatrist to the effect that the person is "permanently incapable," or will be incapable for the foreseeable future, of giving informed consent to the procedure. The professional may also predict that the person is incapable of caring for a child. Sterilization can be requested if all other means of contraception are unsuitable or have failed. With appropriate findings, after a full evidentiary hearing, the judge may issue an order authorizing involuntary sterilization.

Competence to Consent to Sex

It is a crime—rape or assault—to touch another person sexually or perform sexual acts on another without his or her consent. Sexual intercourse with someone whose capacity to give consent has been impaired by drugs or intoxicants or with a person who is unconscious is legally defined as *sex without consent*. Laws also protect children from precocious sexual relationships by stipulating that people under a certain age are legally incapable of consenting to a sexual relationship. Having sexual relations with a person under the age of consent is **statutory rape** (rape under the law) even if the girl or boy says she or he wants relations and acts seductively. (In a very controversial decision, an Italian court recently said it made a difference in the severity of the crime and thus in the punishment if the minor was not a virgin; Reuters, 2006.) There is considerable variation among states in the age of legal consent. For example, in New York it is 17, it is 12 in Delaware and three other states, 16 in Michigan, and 18 in California and Oregon (Levesque, 2000). We have no developmental research that would enable us to say on what basis an adolescent has the maturity to truly consent to sexual relations.

Under many states' laws, the severity of the crime of statutory rape increases as the child's age decreases, and as the difference in age between the perpetrator and victim increases (Levesque, 2000). For example, in New York, if the younger person is older than 14, and the other person is *less* than five years older, proof of those ages will defeat a criminal charge. As a practical matter, then, adolescents who participate in consensual sexual activity with one another will not be subject to criminal prosecution. Instead, the underage adolescent may be charged as a status offender and be subject to a juvenile court's authority (see Chapter 9).

Mental limitations and competence to consent to sex.
Charges of statutory rape may be brought against someone who has sex with an adult of very low intelligence if that person is shown to be incompetent to consent. Under New York State law, for

120

CHAPTER 4
Competence to
Stand Trial,
and Other
Competencies

example, a person is deemed incapable of giving consent if he or she is "mentally defective." The statute does not define the degree of mental defect that would result in a lack of capacity to consent as a matter of law. In New Jersey, there is a legal presumption that a mentally retarded person is able to make up his or her own mind about having sex, though the presumption can be challenged. Once again, the law must reconcile two opposing values. On the one hand, we want to protect people less able to protect themselves from sexual exploitation. On the other hand, mentally retarded people are entitled to the equal protection of the laws, and should have the same right as others to engage in consensual sexual behavior (President's Commission on Mental Retardation, 1976). One program in New York provides those with mental retardation sex education and also coaches the participants in dating, romance, and physical intimacy (Gross, 2006). The problem is determining when someone who is mentally retarded is being exploited sexually.

Those with developmental disabilities living in institutions are vulnerable to sexual exploitation (McCartney and Campbell, 1998). The average age of those subject to sexual abuse in institutions was 30. Those living in institutions are especially vulnerable because they are encouraged to follow caregivers' instructions. They are dependent on caregivers, and often lack any sex education. They may be unaware they are being abused. All states have statutes or regulations governing institutions that forbid sexual contact between employees and residents independently of whether the victim can give consent. However, evidence of consent in a person who is legally capable of giving consent may help an employee avoid a rape charge.

It is not clear how often rape charges are brought in cases involving sexual relations with mentally deficient adults. Prosecutors may hesitate to prosecute because the victim might make a poor witness. A notorious New Jersey case illustrates the problem. The case, described below, certainly raises the question of how to determine whether an individual who is of legal age is capable of giving consent, and under what conditions juries will convict those who may be sexually exploiting the victim's cognitive limitations. We have neither clear standards nor research on this topic.

Gang rape or consensual sex? Four young men, former high school football players in a well-to-do New Jersey suburb, were charged with sexually assaulting a young woman whom they had known for years.[1] They had reputations for engaging in sexually harassing and predatory behaviors in high school. The female student, who was past New Jersey's legal age of consent, had been in classes for the learning impaired and for the educable mentally retarded. Promising her dates with popular boys, the former football players took her into a basement recreation room. She masturbated at the men's request, engaged in oral sex with the men, penetrated herself, and did not protest when they penetrated her with a broomstick, a baseball bat, and a stick. There were no charges that any of the defendants had used violence to coerce her.

A psychologist reported that the alleged victim had an IQ of 64, read at a second-grade level, and was susceptible, easily manipulated, eager to please, and eager to win friends. The prosecution argued that she was incapable of understanding and exercising her right to refuse sex, and that the men knew or should have known it. The

---

[1]This section is based on numerous reports that appeared in the *New York Times* during the trial—Hanley (March 17 and 21, 1993), Manegold (March 19, 1993), Nieves (December 15, 1992), and Quindlen (December 13, 1992)—and a book (Lefkowitz, 1997).

defense attorney maintained that the young woman was not mentally defective for purposes of consenting to sex. He contended that she initiated or eagerly joined in all the activities, depicting her as an oversexed aggressor. When she testified, she seemed ambivalent. She thought of the boys as her friends.

The jury deliberated for 12 days. The jurors had to wrestle with some difficult questions. Under New Jersey case law, mental deficiency need not be an impediment to the enjoyment of a reasonably normal life, including consensual sexual relationships. The defense emphasized that "boys will be boys." Questioned afterward, the jurors said that they agreed that the woman was mentally defective and unable to exercise her legal right to say no to sex. It took a number of days to decide whether the defendants knew or should have known that the young woman was mentally defective. In the end, the jury convicted three of the four defendants of two charges of sexually assaulting a mentally defective woman, and sexually assaulting her with a baseball bat and a broom handle. The three were sentenced to a maximum of fifteen years in prison, but were classified as *young adult offenders.* As young adult offenders and as first-time offenders, they received an indeterminate minimum term, which meant they could be released in approximately 2 years. The fourth defendant was acquitted of all charges except one count of conspiracy to commit aggravated sexual assault. He was sentenced to three years of probation and community service. None were convicted of the more serious charge of rape. Was justice served in this case? What could mental health professionals contribute to a better decision?

Standards for consenting to sex. Rape and consent to sex have been subject to intense conceptual analysis by legal philosophers who wish to establish the underlying basis for considering something a crime (Wertheimer, 2003). In analyzing consent, philosophers distinguish between positive autonomy (right to say yes) and negative autonomy (right to say no). A fully autonomous and therefore fully competent person should be able to exercise both rights. Consent is *transformative,* that is, consent can transform an illegal act into a legal act. Competence refers to an ability to understand the risks and benefits that follow from participation in sex. For both male and female adolescents, we can consider the risks of pregnancy, subsequent responsibility for a child, and sexually transmitted diseases as factors to take into account. We may consider the adolescent's understanding of and ability to use contraception. In a relationship, using contraception may include the ability to refuse to consent if a partner is unwilling to use contraception. Some females may experience a diminished sense of self and a loss of reputation after engaging in a sexual relationship. Should an appreciation of those potential harms be part of our evaluation of competence to give informed consent? Should we include in our measure of competence to consent possible failed expectations and potential emotional hurt in a relationship that doesn't work out? Can we evaluate the potential to say "no" when one may be overly compliant or so eager to please or so eager to have a relationship that desire overrides other concerns (e.g., the adolescent in the New Jersey case)? Should we also include an appreciation of the possible benefits of participation in sex: pleasure, intimacy, social standing, and having a relationship, even if temporarily? To protect potentially innocent partners who believed they were engaging in a consensual relationship, should we require something analogous to a driver's test or a licence to participate in consensual sex? If so, how would we measure the pertinent variables? We have measures of competence for the ability to stand trial. Can we apply the same psychometric approaches to evaluate competence to consent to sex? (See Gross, 2006.)

122

CHAPTER 4
Competence to
Stand Trial,
and Other
Competencies

Summary

Competence refers to possession of characteristics and capacities a person needs to participate intelligently and voluntarily in a legal process. The standards for competence are specific to the context: there are many kinds of competence, and a person can be competent for one task and not another. The abilities needed to be legally competent in any given area are multidimensional. Mental health evaluators asked to make competence evaluations face a challenging task because of the complex nature of the capacity they are asked to assess, and the lack of clear and precise legal standards.

The evaluation of competence to stand trial is one of the most frequent tasks assigned to forensic services. Competence to stand trial, which includes competence to plead guilty and to plea-bargain, has two major components: competence to assist counsel and competence to make decisions about issues related to the defense. The standards are vague. Mental illness is not sufficient to demonstrate incompetence.

Until well into the 1980s, patients whose competence was challenged were evaluated in mental hospitals, where they often spent many months. Research showed that most evaluations led to findings of competence. Long hospitalizations were not necessary to determine competence. Brief assessment instruments and techniques focusing on issues related to legal standards were tested and found to be effective. In consequence, the majority of states switched from using predominantly inpatient forensic services to a reliance on outpatient services. When a defendant is found incompetent, in most cases, competence is restored with treatment. More focused methods for treating incompetence to stand trial are being developed.

Evaluations of competence to be executed and treatment to restore competence to death row inmates create an ethical dilemma for mental health professionals. Treatment to restore competence is intended to enhance the dignity of the defendant, and the dignity of the justice system, but treatment also expedites a defendant's death. Mental health professionals working in the correctional system must confront the issues as citizens and moral beings rather than as scientists.

A person's competence to exercise various civil rights and participate in various civil processes may also be challenged. When a person dies, the validity of his or her will can be challenged. In this circumstance, the mental health professionals asked to provide testimony must assess the mental capacity of someone now dead at the time in the past when the will was made. It is questionable whether science can contribute to this task. Thomas Szasz and others have argued that what is really at issue in such cases is not the capacity of the person who made the will, but whether or not the property will be distributed in a socially approved manner. The same argument can be applied to cases in which a person's competence to manage his or her own affairs is challenged, though most such challenges are brought by relatives or caseworkers genuinely concerned about an elderly person suffering from diseases that cause cognitive impairment.

The right to make one's own medical decisions can also be challenged. Mentally ill patients, including those involuntarily committed, retain civil rights, and retain the right to give informed consent or to refuse medical treatment. Many patients do refuse psychotropic drugs even if the treatment can effectively relieve psychotic symptoms. When they do, their doctors routinely go to court to obtain permission to medicate them against their will. Lack of clear standards about what constitutes competence to consent to or refuse treatment makes it difficult to evaluate when it is appropriate to override a patient's autonomy. Research with new research instruments may at least clarify the issues.

Children are not considered competent to consent to or refuse treatment; the right to consent to their treatment belongs to their parents. However, because adolescents are sometimes confined in mental hospitals for behavioral problems rather than psychoses, some states enacted legislation to protect minors. In about half the states, minors have no formal due process protections from inappropriate hospitalization.

Children up to a certain age, established by law in each state, lack the legal capacity to consent to sexual relations. An adult who has sexual contact with a child under the age of consent is guilty of statutory rape or assault whether or not the child appears to "consent." Charges of statutory rape may also be brought against a person who has sexual relations with someone who is mentally defective. However, lack of a clear standard for capacity to consent to sexual activity and the limited capacity of the plaintiff or victim to help his or her own case may make such cases difficult to prosecute. Once again, as in other contexts when a civil competence comes into question, scientific issues may be secondary to questions about what behaviors are socially acceptable and when and how it is acceptable to suspend individual rights to manage socially unacceptable behavior.

Discussion Questions

1. Under the law, people can only engage in a legal process or activity if they are competent to do so. Why is competence so important in our understanding of justice?
2. How is incompetence to stand trial different from being mentally ill?
3. Courts have held that a person who is competent to stand trial is also competent to plead guilty in exchange for a plea bargain. Some psychologists have questioned this. Can you design a study to determine whether or not the two kinds of activity involve the same knowledge and decisional abilities?
4. How could you develop a measure to test the competence of elderly people with mild to moderate dementia to make their own medical decisions? What properties would you want your measure to have to make it psychometrically sound?
5. Do you think a lawyer asked to represent a mentally ill person who is refusing medication should represent the person's wishes less vigorously if he or she is obviously delusional (for example, if the individual says that someone important has told him or her that the doctors are aliens in disguise who want to use them for experiments)?
6. Suppose you are a lawmaker who must decide with your colleagues at what age teenagers are mature enough to consent to sexual relations. Assume that you are thinking about requiring adolescents to show a license saying they are qualified to engage in sexual relationships. What kind of empirical evidence, if any, could influence your decision?

Key Terms

adjudicative competence
battery
competence
competence assessment
   instrument (CAI)
competence to be executed
competent person
consent
construct validity
court of equity
criterion validity
demeanor
discriminant validity
elder abuse
emancipated minor
executor

face validity
Fifth Amendment
Georgia Court Competency
   Test (GCCT–MSH)
informed consent
insane delusion
interexaminer reliability
internal consistency
involuntary hospitalization
MacArthur Structured
   Assessment of the Com-
   petencies of Criminal
   Defendants (Mac
   SAC–CD)
minor
neutral fact-finder

not guilty by reason of
   insanity (NGRI)
plea bargaining
pro se
probate (or surrogate) court
reliability
retest reliability
social norms
standards (or criteria) of
   competence
statutory rape
testamentary capacity
testator
validity
ward

CHAPTER **5**

Trial by Jury

The right to trial by jury evolved over many centuries in England and in the United States. It is the right of an accused person to have a group of fellow citizens hear the evidence, decide what the "true" facts are, and deliver a verdict. It is basic to our system of justice.

Jury trials represent active democracy in one of its most dramatic forms. They hold a great fascination for the public and for students of law and psychology. Though social scientists have only recently begun to examine the characteristics of the jury trial, there is already an extensive body of jury studies (Hans and Vidmar, 1985; Hastie, Penrose, and Pennington, 1983; Kassin and Wrightsman, 1988). Most of the studies attempt to address legal and policy questions. Many researchers have also investigated the jury to ask questions about how ordinary people think about guilt, innocence, and responsibility or to test theories about small-group behavior.

As a general rule, scientists cannot observe real juries in deliberation. Much of the research is based on simulations using college students as *mock jurors*: The methods have varying degrees of ecological validity. Some work is based on field experiments, or postdeliberation interviews with jurors. The applicability of the research to the deliberations of real juries is open to question.

The extensive social science interest in jury research may be misleading in terms of the relative frequency of criminal and civil jury trials. Plea bargains, by far, account for most criminal convictions. Bench trials (i.e., trials in which the judge is the sole trier of fact) account for only 4.3 percent of felony dispositions, and jury trials for only 2.7 percent (Hannaford-Agor et al., 2002; and see Chapter 1 for definitions of plea bargaining and bench trials). Only 3 percent of civil cases actually go to trial. The parties and the courts resolve the issues before trial in 97 percent of the cases (Cohen and Smith, 2004). However, the concern about what a jury might do in the case is in the background of every motion, settlement negotiation, and plea bargain. Whether that will remain the case remains to be seen (Galanter, 2004).

In this chapter, we will look at how research has illuminated some questions and issues about juries and the jury system. We will discuss the following:

- The constitutional provisions that guarantee and structure the right to trial by jury
- The historical development of the right to trial by jury
- The issue of jury nullification
- The adversarial model
- Research on how juries function as small groups
- Methods of selecting juries and their validity
- The jury system in civil medical malpractice cases

⊠ Trial by Jury in the Constitution

The founders of this nation put the jury trial in the Constitution because they considered it an important counterbalance to arbitrary government authority. Article III of the Constitution, which authorizes the creation of a federal judiciary, states that in *federal* courts, "The trial of all Crimes except in Cases of Impeachment, shall be by Jury." The Bill of Rights provides further guarantees to the right to a jury trial. The Fifth and Sixth Amendments, which apply to the states as well as the federal government, elaborate and structure the right to a jury trial in criminal cases. The Seventh Amendment preserves the right of trial by jury in all federal civil "[s]uits at common law, where the value in controversy shall exceed twenty dollars." The Seventh Amendment does not apply to the states, but all have their own provisions guaranteeing the right to trial by jury in civil suits in their courts.

The Bill of Rights

Fifth Amendment. The **Fifth Amendment** contains three provisions to prevent government from using prosecutorial powers to harass or persecute citizens. One is indictment by a grand jury. A **grand jury** is a jury of inquiry. The grand jury represents the community at the **indictment** stage of a criminal proceeding, when a suspect is formally charged with a crime. The grand jury hears the state's evidence and decides if a trial is warranted. In theory, grand juries are supposed to prevent unwarranted prosecutions from going forward. In practice, grand juries are often regarded as the prosecutor's rubber stamp.

Another provision of the Fifth Amendment specifies that no "person be subject for the same offense to be twice put in jeopardy of life or limb." Because of this protection against **double jeopardy**, a jury bringing in a not guilty verdict has the last word; the state can't appeal and can't retry the person on the same charge. The Fifth Amendment also says that no one "shall be compelled in any criminal case to be a witness against himself." This provision protects defendants from torture or other forms of pressure to confess. Because a defendant can't be forced to testify against him or herself, the state has the burden of proving the charges with other evidence. Judges instruct juries in criminal cases to draw no inference about guilt when the defendant chooses not to testify. Whether jurors attend to the instruction is open to question. The presumption that a defendant is innocent until proven guilty (from the **Fourteenth Amendment**: "no person shall be deprived of life, liberty, or property, without due process of law") is another protection against the misuse of the state's power to prosecute.

Sixth Amendment. The **Sixth Amendment** guarantees "the right to a speedy and public trial, by an impartial jury of the state and district wherein the crime shall have been committed." Because the Constitution requires a *speedy* trial, an individual can't be held indefinitely without conviction. By providing that a criminal trial must take place in the "state and district" where the crime occurred, the Constitution implies that local community values are to be brought to bear in judgments.

The Sixth Amendment also gives the defendant the right *"to be informed of the nature and cause of the accusation; to be confronted with the witnesses against him;* to have **compulsory process** [enforceable subpoena to require a witness to appear in court] for obtaining witnesses in his favor, and to have the *Assistance of Counsel* for his defense" (emphasis added). These provisions support a fair adversarial trial. Because the defendant must be informed of the specific charges, he or she can prepare a defense in advance of the trial. The requirement of a specific accusation also limits the court to hearing only evidence relevant to proving the charges. The **right of confrontation** prevents secret accusations. It also reflects the traditional belief that it is more difficult for a witness to lie when face-to-face with a defendant. Confrontation includes the right to cross-examine witnesses as a basic safeguard. (See *Maryland v. Craig,* 1990, in Chapter 10 on child abuse; and *Crawford v. Washington,* 2004, in Chapter 12 on intimate partner violence). The right to **assistance of counsel** implies that there are sides in a trial. The prosecutor presents evidence in support of the charges, and the defendant presents a defense. The defendant can call witnesses, and they will be required to respond (compulsory process).

In a series of decisions, the Supreme Court has strengthened Sixth Amendment protections. These decisions affirmed that a defendant has a right to have a jury determine beyond a reasonable doubt not just whether the defendant is guilty, but also all facts legally essential to the sentence (*Apprendi v. New Jersey,* 2000; *United States v. Booker,* 2005).

The right to defend oneself before an impartial judge and jury in *public* view, including the view of the press, is a further constraint on arbitrary action by government. When a trial is open, the people can see whether the prosecution is justified. They can see if the trial is being conducted within the rules.

Citizen Participation

The jury system imposes an important citizenship duty and responsibility. The participation of the citizen juror guarantees that justice is done in accord with community values. Juries limit government power and ensure participatory democracy in the day-to-day administration of justice. But does the jury trial function as intended?

A Brief History

Precursors to the Jury

Trial by jury is an ancient right in our Anglo-Saxon system of jurisprudence.[1] Precursors to the jury include *compurgators,* or witnesses, who were called to offer evidence about property disputes in England before the Norman conquest of 1066. The compurgators

---

[1]The next several paragraphs rely heavily on Devlin (1966), Forsyth (1875), Green (1985), Hans and Vidmar (1985), Holdsworth (1931), and Hyman and Tarrant (1975).

were formed in groups of 12. They "testified" before a judge about a party's character, or about their personal knowledge of business transactions or ownership. Later, in some criminal cases, prominent citizens were called together somewhat as a grand jury to tell the king's representative what they knew of crimes in their area, and what they knew of accused persons. When there were no eyewitnesses to nonviolent offenses, 12 compurgators who were friends of the accused swore to the person's character. If the accused had a bad reputation, the accused was convicted unless 36 people swore to the person's innocence.

Judges in ancient times dealt with other criminal cases by ordering the accused to undergo a **trial by** *ordeal.* (Even today, one of the meanings of the word *trial* is "ordeal.") The accused might be made to carry a hot iron or stick one hand in a pot of boiling water. Judgments of guilt or innocence depended on how the wound healed. He or she might be tied up and thrown into a body of water: sinking was considered a sign of innocence (the bystanders then attempted a rescue). In another kind of ordeal, the accused would have to eat a piece of dry bread after having prayed that, if guilty, he would choke on the bread. These ordeals were carried out with prayer and religious ceremony on the theory that divine intervention would reveal the truth.

Trial by battle was introduced after the Norman conquest as a means of settling civil disputes among the nobility. Either the disputants or their "hired swords" would engage in battle. In some criminal cases, the accused could challenge the accuser to a fight. Again, the theory was that God would intervene on the side of right.

The system of justice changed as people developed reservations about trials by ordeal and by battle and as they recognized that compurgators frequently perjured themselves. At the Fourth Lateran Council in 1215, Pope Innocent III eliminated one ordeal by ordering priests not to bless the hot irons used in the ordeals by fire. By the end of the thirteenth century, trials by ordeal had been abandoned. Trial by combat also fell into disuse after the thirteenth century (it was not finally abolished legally in England until 1819). Other means of resolving conflict and administering justice developed.

The Jury Trial as Right

In 1215, King John of England responded to demands of the nobility by issuing the Magna Carta. The **Magna Carta** was an agreement between the king and the noblemen providing for the administration of justice and guaranteeing various rights. One provision was that a person of noble birth could only be tried by a jury composed of members of his own social rank. The idea that all citizens should be tried by an impartial jury of peers evolved from that right.

Jurors originally were more like witnesses or the old compurgators: They were asked to testify about their knowledge of the parties, of the matter in dispute, or of a crime. Later judges interrogated the defendant before a group of jurors selected from the community. The judge asked the jurors, using their own knowledge of the facts, the reputations of the parties, and their observations in court, to decide whether a guilty verdict was warranted. Jurors took an oath to find according to conscience (Green, 1985). Later, with population growth and anonymity of urban living, jurors were no longer expected to have personal knowledge of events. They were summoned to listen to evidence and to find facts.

The practice of challenging prospective trial jurors for bias grew. Jurors could be challenged because they were the defendant's accusers, had served on the indicting jury, or were personal enemies of the accused. However, defendants had little protection against the state or its representatives. The jurors were selected by the sheriff, who may have been inclined to select people favorable to the Crown's position. The judge could order a new trial with new jurors if he thought the jury's verdict was mistaken. And, until Bushel's case in 1671, jurors could be punished by the judge if they brought in a "wrong" verdict.

In Bushel's case, an English jury refused to convict William Penn, a Quaker leader, when he was tried for the crime of unlawful assembly and disturbance of the peace (see Figure 5.1). William Penn had broken the law by holding a Quaker prayer meeting in the street when the law allowed only Anglican church services. The jury didn't think it was a just law. Led by Edward Bushel, the jurors refused to convict. They were fined for contempt of court and jailed when they refused to pay. They appealed. The appeals court judges ruled that a juror could not be punished for a verdict. The balance of power for the control of rendering justice between the judiciary, representing formal law, and juries, representing local community sentiment, continues to this day. Judges instruct juries in the law. The jurors are supposed to follow the judge's legal instructions, but on occasion follow their own ideas inside the jury room of what is fair instead.

Figure 5.1

William Penn

William Penn was a Quaker leader tried because he violated a 1641 Act of Parliament that outlawed religious meetings not in conformity with Anglican Church services. The jury refused to convict him or his codefendant, William Mead. The judge wanted to punish jurors for bringing in an "incorrect" verdict. On appeal, Bushel's case (so called after jury member Edward Bushel) established the independence of juries.

Right to Jury Trial in the United States

The right to a trial by jury in the colonies was explicitly recognized in the original charter granted by King James to the Virginia Company (in 1607) and in all the colonies. As in England, county sheriffs selected the jurors, raising questions about fairness and the right to challenge prospective jurors. Jurors had to meet property qualifications to serve. Felony trials were short. The jury was locked up without amenities until it reached a verdict.

Legal issues related to free speech, treason, libel, diverse property rights, and commercial arrangements became the subject of conflicts between the colonists and the crown. The king's officers tried by various devices to maintain control over colonial juries, as they did over English juries. The colonists resisted royal control over juries, who represented the colonists' views of the law.

The jury's right to "interpret" the law and, thus, define it, as the English jury had done in Bushel's case, was central in the 1735 trial of John Peter Zenger. The trial set an important precedent for a free press. Zenger, a printer, published editorials critical of an unpopular royal governor of New York. He was charged with libel. Under then-existing laws, the prosecution needed to prove only that the accused had made the challenged statements to establish libel. It didn't matter whether the statements were true. If the jury found that the defendant had made the statements, the judge decided whether the statements were libelous on their face. A Philadelphia lawyer, Andrew Hamilton (no relation to Alexander Hamilton), told the jurors, over judicial objection, that regardless of the law if they found the statements were true, Zenger should not be criminally punished. The jury found Zenger not guilty, accepting Hamilton's view of the law. The belief that juries could decide the law as well as render verdicts gained widespread acceptance in colonial America and in the early days of the Republic. This was one way in which citizens participated directly in governance.

The first ten amendments to the Constitution (the Bill of Rights) were ratified by the states in 1791. The provision for jury trials in the Fifth, Sixth, and Seventh Amendments testifies to the founders' belief that a right to trial by a free and independent jury of one's peers was essential to the preservation of liberty.

Juries as Lawmakers

Jury Nullification

Today, jurors are regarded as **fact-finders,** not lawmakers. The jury's job is to say what the facts are, in other words, to determine what "really happened." Judges instruct the jurors about the law that is applicable to the case. Judges also act as "referees" during the trial to see that the procedural rules are followed. The jurors come to a verdict by deciding if the testimony they heard proves what the judge said needed to be proved.

In most criminal and civil cases, jurors accept the judge's statement of law as they are instructed to do. But sometimes juries decide an individual's fate by employing community rather than strictly legal standards, just as they did in John Peter Zenger's trial. **Jury nullification** refers to jurors voiding or canceling a law they are instructed to apply by rendering a verdict inconsistent with that law but consonant with their own sense of justice.

Juries do not have an explicit right to nullify a law in a particular case. However, a defendant in a criminal trial has the right to have the final decision about his guilt or innocence made by a jury, and juries have a freedom in decision making tantamount to a right to interpret law. Jurors cannot be questioned or punished for their verdicts (Bushel's case, above; see also *People v. Kriho*, 1997). They do not have to explain or justify their verdicts to anyone. If they want to nullify, they can. Thus, the power of the jury to decide the individual case allows jurors to represent community standards and values (see *Duncan v. Louisiana*, 1968).

Nullification and Civil Disobedience

Jurors struggling to come to a verdict "according to their conscience" face an especially difficult task when their sentiments and sense of justice conflict with the strict statement of the law (Green, 1985). The problem is most likely to arise in trials involving controversial moral or political issues. Defendants in "political" cases may have practiced **civil disobedience,** knowingly breaking laws they consider immoral. For example, some individuals and organizations have deliberately broken the law by aiding undocumented aliens. They believed they were saving people who were fleeing political persecution, but whose plights were not recognized by immigration authorities.

Individuals who are arrested for civil disobedience often see their trials as an opportunity to call attention to a wrong or an injustice. They want the jury and the public to judge them on the basis of the morality, not the legality, of their actions. Sometimes juries do that. For example, Dr. Jack Kevorkian, who assisted terminally ill persons to commit suicide, made a point of calling attention to his activities so he would be arrested. He was acquitted of criminal charges several times by juries. He was convicted when he went too far. He actually administered the substance that killed a terminally ill person himself, on television, in full view of the nation. He is serving a 25-year sentence. Partly as a result of Kevorkian's actions, "right to die" laws are debated nationally, a political outcome he probably would see as desirable (e.g., the Terri Schiavo case). The jury's power to nullify has not always been used in support of values or principles that are worthy of universal acclaim. Community values can be oppressive or intolerant. When the South was racially segregated, all-white juries frequently refused to convict whites accused of crimes against blacks despite overwhelming evidence of guilt. All-white juries also convicted black defendants on the basis of minimal evidence. These jury nullifications were a way of preserving white supremacy, a value nearly all people today think is despicable. Civil disobedience—a kind of bid for jury nullification—has been used by both sides of the abortion debate. Anti-abortion protesters, who sought to close down abortion clinics by illegal means, claim they are innocent of a crime because they were behaving morally. On the other side, a pro-choice Canadian physician who opened abortion clinics in a province where they were banned claimed he was innocent of a crime because he was acting morally in providing needed abortion services.

Juries may also nullify to protest methods used by the government when they are persuaded these methods are corrupt or overzealous. The jurors who acquitted the businessman and car designer John DeLorean of drug charges said they did so because they were appalled by the government's efforts to entrap the defendant. As one wit put it, the government failed to frame a guilty man (Ackerman, 2005).

Telling the Jury about Its Nullification Powers

Although it acknowledged the healthy role of the jury in responding to the law, the Supreme Court ruled against instructing federal juries about their nullification powers (*Sparf and Hansen v. United States*, 1895). The Court said that giving the instructions would affect the jury process in unpredictable ways (*United States v. Dougherty*, 1972). This produced an odd situation in federal courts. The law acknowledged the jury's right to nullify, but said they shouldn't be told about it (Horowitz, 1985).

There have been a handful of experiments on nullification involving mock juries that deliberated after being exposed to a trial scenario (video, written scripts, and so on). In one experimental condition, mock jurors were instructed about their power to nullify, and in another experimental condition, they were not. When juries were aware of their nullification powers, they acquitted more often. However, sometimes the instructions produced a "backlash." If the defense was inconsistent with general societal norms, and the facts about the defendant's guilt were clear, under nullification instructions, more would be found guilty. For example, Devine et al. (2001) found that jurors held the defendant more responsible for a death caused by his drunk driving than the law allowed.

In a series of four experiments, Niedermeier, Horowitz, and Kerr (1999) concluded that the results of juries deliberating with nullification instructions made sense. In the trial scenario, the medical director of a hospital, acting under emergency conditions, allowed the use of blood not screened for HIV. Under the law, he was absolutely obligated to screen all the blood for HIV before using it. Because it was an emergency, the medical director knowingly used some blood that had not been screened. Several years later, a patient who had received the unscreened blood as emergency treatment died of AIDS. The doctor was charged with a criminal violation. Jurors nullified when it appeared that conviction under the law would result in an injustice, exactly what nullification is supposed to accomplish.

We applaud a jury that nullifies the law to arrive at a decision based on values we personally approve, and decry a jury whose decision to nullify the law violates our personal values. What we need to ask, however, is whether we would be better off as a society if we had a jury system that insured that the law as written was applied in each case, or whether we are better off with a degree of flexibility that allows community sentiment to leaven the law.

Nullification is rare. Jurors usually follow the rules, even if they do not agree with them. An example is Jeff Kovelsky, a juror in one of Dr. Kevorkian's assisted suicide murder trials. By voting not guilty, he voted against his deep personal beliefs against suicide. He said, "There was a moment where I was very upset. . . . It was very hard for me to make this decision [not guilty]. We had to go by what the law said, not my beliefs. I took an oath and I had to throw those beliefs out the door" (Linsalata, Durfee, and Harmon, 1996).

Jury decision making and legal change

Jurors today may sometimes bring changing community sentiments to bear on legal controversies by their decisions in civil liability cases. Civil liability suits have become a means of regulating industries that in other eras have been regulated by the legislative and executive branch. If a jury finds a company liable for harms caused by its product or practices, and the industry changes its practices to avoid further lawsuits, the jury's decision has served a regulatory function. For example, when juries started to rule that tobacco companies were liable for smoking-related illnesses, they effectively made "new law."

Sometimes, there is a political backlash against liability litigation. Some suits seem to run counter to widely held beliefs about individual responsibility. For example, two New York teenagers sued McDonald's, claiming that eating its hamburgers made them obese. (*Pelman ex rel. Pelman v. McDonald's Corp.*, 2005). Many people thought it was ridiculous to hold restaurants responsible for knowledgeable people's eating choices or didn't like the idea of anyone but themselves deciding what they could and couldn't eat. Trade associations and the tabloid press promote the idea that greedy lawyers abuse the tort system for profit in cases such as this one. Industry lobbyists present information to lawmakers to try to persuade them that such suits are unfair, or that the damages they must pay are unreasonably large and will cripple their industry. They seek legislation to regulate and limit liability suits. Legislators may agree, perceiving the present system as unfair or as economically ruinous. They may introduce *tort reforms,* changing the rules to make it more difficult for jurors to find against defendants or limiting the size of damage awards (Finley, 2005). There are also strong defenders of the present tort system, who point out that it has been effective both in attaining compensation for individuals and in protecting consumers generally (e.g., see Bogus, 2001).

Critics on both sides of these arguments have also expressed concerns about the ability of the jurors to evaluate the evidence in liability suits, which sometimes involve quite complex technical, scientific, or contractual issues. The evidentiary rules developed in *Daubert* were designed to keep so-called junk-science from juries. Keeping out junk science would reduce the possiblity that suits will succeed when the evidence is not strong because of juror sympathy for injured persons (Edmond and Mercer, 2004). The efforts to control jury awards illustrate how much our legal system and the jury system are affected by complex processes in the larger society.

⊠ Juror Decision Making and Evidence

Juries use their power to decide cases responsibly. They do not tend to make decisions based on purely emotional reactions. They look carefully at the evidence. It is not unusual in transcripts of mock juries to find a juror saying, "Well, I really think he is guilty, but there isn't enough evidence in the case."

Weighing the Evidence

Studies of mock jury deliberation transcripts show that jurors spend most of the deliberation time reviewing and weighing the evidence (Hastie, Penrose, and Pennington, 1983). Each mock juror doesn't say something about each bit of evidence, but in the aggregate all the evidence is usually covered, though perhaps not systematically. When a juror misstates the evidence, others correct the person. Jurors refer to the evidence when explaining their positions to each other. They also spend time constructing a narrative, or a story that makes common sense of the evidence (Pennington and Hastie, 1991). The story is not just made up. It is anchored in the evidence.

Real jurors say that evidence is the most important factor influencing their individual votes. Research confirms that for mock jurors, the strength of evidence is critical. Over many mock jury studies, strength of evidence is strongly associated with verdicts of guilt in criminal trials or verdicts of liablity in civil trials (Devine et al., 2001). Extralegal factors (e.g., juror personality and attitudes, or witness appearance) account for just a little of the variance in votes of guilt or innocence (Visher, 1987). Unless the case materials are carefully balanced in any simulation, the strength of the evidence will outweigh the effects of any extralegal factors the psychologists are investigating. *Strength of evidence* has not been conceptualized to enable measurement of the persuasiveness of the evidence presented in simulations. Without a quantitative assessment measure, we have no way to directly compare the strength of evidence factor in scenarios with very different content. Still, the bulk of studies suggest that strength of evidence is the predominant factor in determining verdicts in mock jury studies, especially in criminal contexts (Devine et al., 2001).

Judges and Juries

Given that juries do focus primarily on the evidence, do they evaluate it appropriately? Kalven and Zeisel (1966) say yes. They surveyed a large number of judges who presided at both civil and criminal jury trials. The judge recorded the jury's verdict, and then said whether he or she agreed with it. The judge and jury agreed about 75 percent of the time. If the judge is accepted as the "gold standard of truth," juries' verdicts were "right" most of the time.

In the majority of cases, jurors try to follow the judge's instructions. However, instructions to ignore inadmissible evidence may not be very effective, if jurors think the inadmissible evidence may help them in arriving at a decision. Juries may pay more attention to procedural instructions and may use judicial instructions to help resolve disputes among themselves: "Remember, the judge said . . ." (We discuss judicial instructions with regard to the death penalty in Chapter 8.)

Jury "decisions are based on past experience in the form of scripts, schemas, stereotypes, and other cognitive mechanisms as well as personal beliefs and values about what is right, wrong, and fair" (Devine et al., 2001, p. 699). If jurors seem to be relying on their own sense of what is just (Finkel and Handel, 1989), the reasonably high rates of agreement between juries and judges found by Kalven and Zeisel (1966) may not be dependent on the jury's understanding of finer legal points. Judges and juries may agree because written legal standards and the community sense of justice are, for the most part, consistent.

Procedural Justice and the Adversarial Method

Jury trials take place within our adversarial system. In theory, truth emerges from the clash of adversaries. But there is no way of knowing with certainty what really happened in a case in dispute. In practice, trials provide a means for settling disputes peacefully. We might characterize our adversarial justice system as a set of rules for fact seeking that allows us to create a plausible "myth" about what happened in the past. On the basis of this assumed set of facts, we make decisions about resolving conflicts in the present.

The adversarial process evolved from trial by combat. Today, each side in the dispute, whether criminal or civil, presents its own best case and challenges the case made by the opposing side. In theory, the fact-finder will be persuaded by the strongest case, and "truth" will emerge from the battle of divergent stories.

Is the adversary system a fair way of resolving disputes? Legal proceedings are seen as fair if "it's a fair fight," that is, if the rules don't favor one or another party. When we feel the process has been fair, we can put the conflict behind us and get on with our lives with a feeling of satisfaction that the "system worked." The public's confidence that trials are fair helps maintain social cohesiveness. Riots broke out in black communities in Los Angeles after an all-white jury failed to convict white policemen who were seen brutally beating a black man named Rodney King on a nationally televised videotape. The trial seemed unfair.

Advocate Zealously

135

Procedural
Justice and
the Adversarial
Method

Lawyers have an ethical duty to "advocate zealously within the bounds of the law" for their clients. Some critics of the adversarial system argue that truth finding is undermined when each side "zealously" pursues its own interests. Each side wants to win, not to have the truth emerge, if it would be harmful to their case. In the adversarial model, truth is supposed to emerge when adversaries trying to win make competing presentations. But the model assumes both sides have equally able lawyers with equal resources. What if the sides are not equal? Will "truth" be purchasable? When William Kennedy Smith, a scion of the famous Kennedy family, was tried for the date rape of a woman he had met in a bar, Smith's family spent hundreds of thousands of dollars to mount a successful defense. The media raised questions about the fairness of the trial. However, a desired outcome can't always be bought. Wealthy and powerful executives of major corporations (e.g., Bernard Ebbers of WorldCom) are found guilty of financial manipulations by juries despite high-powered and expensive legal defenses.

The adversarial system encourages lawyers to use their special skills and training to get cases decided on the basis of technical and legal niceties rather than the issues of right and wrong. Lawyers may even work systematically, not just to manipulate the rules but also to tip the scales of justice a little by changing them. Galanter (1974) distinguishes between **repeat players,** institutions likely to be involved in many lawsuits (e.g., insurance companies, agencies of government, and industry representatives), and **one-time players** (e.g., the victims of automobile accidents). A one-time player is interested only in the outcome of that case. Repeat players, on the other hand, are interested in using their financial and legal resources to shape the rules for the long term. When their case is weak, repeat players will settle out of court so there is no recorded legal precedent (Vidmar, 1997). They will put their resources into fighting other cases in order to establish rules and precedents that will be favorable to them over the long run.

Is the adversarial model always appropriate? Lawyers for Roman Catholic dioceses around the country, defending churches against civil claims for money damages because of allegations of sexual abuse by priests, sometimes played "hard ball." They acted no differently than other lawyers in an adversarial system "zealously" defending clients. The lawyers subjected plaintiff-victims to days of grueling depositions, moved to reveal real names simply to humilate plaintiffs, and countersued plaintiffs, claiming parents were liable for endangering their child by allowing him to spend time with a priest in the face of warning signs. (Under the principle of comparative negligence, the amount of damages could be reduced by the "percent" parents were found to be responsible for the events entailing liability.) A bishop who addressed church lawyers recommended that certain documents be destroyed and that other documents be kept in a secret file to frustrate discovery (Liptak, 2002). The tactics infuriated parents and victims, and made the restoration of the church's reputation in the community that much more difficult (Dokecki, 2004). Since then, members of the church hierarchy have apologized to victims.

A Roman Catholic Church diocese, as a defendant in an adversarial process, is certainly entitled to a full legal defense. However, because the church is not "just another company making a bad product" but has a moral relationship to society, should its stance have been different? Should morality interact with legal ethics and duties in defining the limits of a "zealous" defense within the adversarial model? And, if true for one type of defendant, should the same questions of morality be raised in other suits— for example, those involving divorce or child custody—where moral issues are intertwined with the legal ones? Should a lawyer vigorously attack the victim's credibility in a rape trial when he knows or has strong reason to believe his client is guilty of the rape (see Dershowitz, 1994)?

Manipulating rules to gain advantages seems to undermine justice. But the problem, though real, is not unique to the adversarial system. Rules are necessary for fairness, and, if there are rules, opposing players will try to use them to their own advantage. No system of justice will be perfect. The risk of unfairness would be even greater in a system without rules, in which cases would be decided arbitrarily. Social perceptions are critically important. The questions are whether the adversarial system serves important social values and what procedures appear to participants and other citizens to be the fairest way of resolving disputes.

Do Participants Experience the Adversarial System as Fair?

Thibaut and Walker (1975) reported the results of an extensive series of controlled experiments that examined attitudes toward the adversary system. Students in the United States and in four other Western countries expressed greater satisfaction with the adversarial system than with the European inquisitorial procedure, in which the judge, and not the parties, takes the lead in investigating the case and then (often as part of a panel with other judges) decides a verdict.

Their studies suggested that, despite its problems, the **adversarial method** serves important social values. The opportunity to have a day in court, to control the presentation of evidence, and to be able to say what they wish to say is important in generating feelings of satisfaction in the process among the parties to a dispute. If both sides have their say, the procedure is usually viewed as fair. Paradoxically, the adversarial system of dispute resolution, which puts participants in "battle," may support the important purpose of promoting social cohesiveness because both sides are heard.

Thibaut and Walker (1975) did not test the perceived fairness of other areas of difference between the adversarial and inquisitorial systems (trial by one or more judges in active roles). For example, under the inquisitorial system, appeals courts review the trial evidence again, effectively trying the cases anew. The system permits frequent appeals. In the adversarial system as practiced in the United States, appeals are not allowed as frequently (Crombbag, 2003).

The steady decline since 1962 in the number of civil and criminal cases going to trial, and the increasing reliance on various other forms of case resolution—including plea bargaining, out-of-court settlements in civil matters, mediation, and alternative justice forums—suggest that despite the strong social and symbolic role of the trial in our culture, adversarial justice is now only one piece of a varied and complex justice system (Galanter, 2004).

The Jury as a Small Group

The adversarial process is played out in front of a jury. The jurors then come together to **deliberate** (collectively discuss the evidence and legal instructions carefully) under certain rules in order to reach a verdict, thus becoming a task-oriented group. Our knowledge of small-group process can illuminate how juries function.

A jury's task is to bring in a verdict. A **hung jury,** in which the jury cannot reach a unanimous decision, is usually considered a "failure," a "waste" of its members' efforts. After a hung jury, about a third of the cases are resolved by a plea bargain, about 22 percent are dismissed, and about a third are retried by another jury or a judge. (Hannaford-Agar *et al.*, 2002)

Like every task-oriented group, the jury faces two problems in successfully completing its task. The first is maintaining group cohesiveness. A working jury group needs to maintain a sense of solidarity (a *we-ness*) while managing the tensions that inevitably arise when people are thrown together. The second is responding to the task demands. The jury's task of arriving at a verdict has important consequences for other people's lives. For this reason, the task places great demands on jurors' emotions, personalities, interpersonal styles, and attitudes (Levine, Farrell, and Perrotta, 1981).

Despite the fact that a jury is a group of strangers, juries manage to form cohesive groups and complete their tasks most of the time. In criminal trials in California, the hung jury rate (averaged over three years) ranged from 8.0 percent to 29.1 percent in different counties. States that use a nonunanimity rule, or that permit juries of fewer than 12, have much lower hung jury rates. In trials in federal court, the hung jury rate falls between 1 and 2 percent of all jury verdicts. Civil juries are much less likely to hang. Six-person juries working with an easier standard of proof (*preponderance*) can resolve issues more readily than 12 people hearing criminal cases who must try to determine guilt beyond a reasonable doubt. Many jurisdictions do not keep track of hung juries because they occur so infrequently. Weakness of the evidence accounts for the bulk of hung juries (Hannaford-Agor et al., 2002).

Some juries may be unable to reach a verdict because of tensions that cause the group deliberative process to fail (see Box 5.1). Why do such splits happen relatively rarely? One reason is that the rules governing juries structure the jury's task and help it manage the problem of maintaining solidarity while doing the work of deliberation. The rules reflect evolution of the law on how juries are to deliberate. They are conveyed

---

BOX 5.1

A Legal Case in Point: A Hung Jury

The first trial of the Menendez brothers (Lyle, 24, and Erik, 21) is an example of a case in which the jury was unable to work as a group. The brothers admitted killing their wealthy parents by blasting them with shotguns as they sat in their living room watching TV. There was no question of their guilt; the only question was whether they should be found guilty of first-degree murder (a capital offense), second-degree murder, or manslaughter. As a defense, they tried to put their dead father on trial. They said they were in fear of their lives because they had threatened to reveal he had sexually abused them.

The brothers were tried together before separate juries. The juries for each brother heard almost all the same evidence, but deliberated separately. The jury for one of the brother was evenly divided between men and women. The six men argued for one verdict, and the six women for another. Both groups dug in their heels and refused to change their opinion. The result of this gender split was a hung jury. Interviewed afterward, the woman said they felt the men were domineering and didn't respect them.

The second jury also hung on the same question of which crime the defendants had committed. Because neither jury had been to reach a verdict, a second trial was conducted for each of the brothers. They were convicted of murder, but did not receive the death penalty. They are both serving life sentences. Erik and Lyle both married while in prison, Erik in 1999, and Lyle in 2003, to women with whom they had corresponded while in prison.

to the jury through the **charge,** the instructions the judge gives to the jury just before the deliberations begin. Jurors tend to follow procedural rules given by judges (Devine et al., 2001).

There are six basic precepts about the jury's role that are used in both criminal and civil trials. We will discuss these one by one, along with some relevant research findings.

Jury as Fact-Finder, Judge as Lawgiver

Jurors are told that the judge is the lawgiver and they are the fact-finders. The judge explains the applicable law in his or her charge to the jury just before deliberations begin. The jury decides what the evidence proves or doesn't prove given the requirements of law as the judge has explained it.

By giving the jury the law, the judge provides the interpretive and normative value framework for deliberation. For example, in a criminal case, the judge tells the jurors the elements of the crime that have to be proven. Jurors do not have to debate under what circumstances a killing is a murder or to decide whether murder is good or bad. The jurors have the task of deciding the "facts" (e.g., Did the defendant have a weapon? Did the defendant intend to kill the victim?) that meet the legal definition of *murder* as given in the judge's statement of the law. In theory, the judge's instructions define the group's task and eliminate value conflicts.

Value and personality conflicts, of course, still arise during jury deliberations. The instructions may not resolve all of these. The instructions are often long and complex, and cover many technical issues. Researchers have found that they are poorly understood.

Instructions can be presented in simplified language to improve juror comprehension, though experimentally validated, simplified instructions have not been widely adopted. Part of the problem is that an appeal can be based on an alleged error the judge made in the instructions to the jury. It is rare for a case to be appealed because the instructions were complicated or hard to follow (Diamond, 1993). Consequently, judges may be more concerned with the legal accuracy of their instructions than their comprehensibility to lay jurors. This concern may be alleviated now that the Judicial Council of California has completed an enormous project making its approved civil and criminal jury instructions more comprehensible to the average juror by using English that can be understood at a tenth-grade reading level. Other states may follow suit by adapting California's new comprehensive set of instructions.

Only Legally Acceptable Testimony Admitted into Evidence

In the distant past, jurors were chosen because they had personal information about a case. The opposite is true today. Jurors are instructed to base their decision only on the evidence the judge admitted into the trial. The rule that jurors use only the evidence they hear in court is intended to protect the defendant. The judge, in theory at least, will admit only reliable and relevant evidence. He or she is supposed to exclude testimony that is likely to be more **prejudicial** (to inflame feeling against the defendant) than **probative** (contributing to the proof of a "fact" at issue in the trial). The rule also enhances jury solidarity. All the jurors are on equal ground during deliberations because they have all received the same information. They can validate each other's recollections of the evidence and correct misunderstandings or misstatements (Saks and Marti, 1997).

Cognitive psychologists have found that people retain and use information better when they process it actively. On the theory that more active participation beyond sitting and listening is beneficial to juries, some courts and research workers are experimenting with variations in procedures. These include allowing jurors to take notes; giving them written material about the case and law; allowing jurors to ask questions of witnesses, usually filtered through the judge; giving jurors instructions both at the beginning of the trial and at the end, just before receiving the case for deliberation; and allowing discussion of the case before the jury finally receives the case for formal deliberation.

Dann and Hans (2004) found that jurors like to take and use notes. Jurors believe that taking notes improved their understanding and recall of the evidence. Some of their studies found that deliberations were more evidence oriented and focused when jurors took notes. No significant disadvantages of note taking emerged.

Some courts provide jurors with notebooks containing such items as glossaries of technical terms, blank paper, names of witnesses, copies of expert slides, and so on. Jurors rated such notebooks highly, and in studies using tests of comprehension, juries with notebooks performed very well (Dann and Hans, 2004).

Jurors appreciate the opportunity to ask questions. Jurors reported that questioning witnesses made them more confident that they had the information needed to decide a case. They seemed to use their questions to clarify testimony by both experts and other witnesses. The median number of questions jurors asked was about seven. Little new information seemed to emerge from juror questions, but neither attorneys nor judges felt the process was unfairly affected by juror questions (Dann and Hans, 2004).

Jurors also rated receiving the judge's instructions at the outset of the trial and again just before deliberation very positively. They reported that receiving the preliminary instructions helped them follow the evidence. Attorneys and judges also agreed that giving the instructions at the outset and again just before beginning deliberations was helpful in facilitating better juror understanding of the issues and the evidence (Dann and Hans, 2004; Devine et al., 2001).

It is a healthy feature of the American justice and the jury system that courts are willing to experiment. "The combined insights from pilot programs, field experiments, and laboratory research on jury trial innovations show the benefits that can derive from systematic evaluation of proposed trial reforms" (Dann and Hans, 2004, p. 19).

Voir dire and pretrial publicity. Various rules and procedures, from the voir dire to the final charge, are designed to ensure that jurors consider only the evidence introduced during the trial. At the **voir dire,** the procedure used to select jurors, lawyers and judges try to eliminate anyone from serving who has already developed strong opinions about the case based on exposure to pretrial publicity. When selected for a jury, jurors are asked to agree to disregard information they may have previously obtained and to rely exclusively on what they learn in court. A meta-analytic review of 44 studies of the effects of pretrial publicity showed that mock jurors exposed to negative pretrial publicity were significantly more likely to judge a defendant guilty than those not exposed to the publicity (Steblay et al., 1999; see Figure 5.2). However, the strength of the evidence in the case may override the effects of pretrial publicity (Devine et al., 2001). Once selected for a trial, jurors are admonished to avoid newspaper or TV accounts of the case and not to discuss it with anyone. During some trials, the jury is sequestered (e.g., required to stay in a hotel and not permitted to go

FIGURE 5.2

Pretrial Publicity and a Celebrity Trial

Actor Robert Blake, star of a popular crime show, Baretta, *was acquitted by a jury of charges of shooting his wife to death and soliciting someone to murder his wife. His wife was shot outside his favorite restaurant while he said he was inside retrieving his own gun. The case was delayed in coming to trial numerous times. The case received extensive publicity and was the target of frequent comment by late-night comedian Jay Leno. Leno made jokes implying Blake's guilt and implying Blake's story was not believable. The actual evidence against Blake was weak. The main witnesses against him lacked credibility, and Blake could not be tied to the weapon that killed his wife. There were no eyewitnesses, and no blood or DNA evidence to tie Blake to the crime. The jury deliberated nine days before acquitting him on two charges, and the jury hung 11–1 for acquittal on the third charge. The judge dismissed the third charge. This was a heavily publicized celebrity trial, with much public comment implying Blake was clearly guilty. However, the jury seemed to judge him on the evidence, not on the publicity. Blake was tried again in a civil suit, much as O. J. Simpson was. This time, Blake was found liable for his wife's death. The jury awarded $30 million to her heirs, who were the plaintiffs.*

home at night) to avoid "contamination" by information or opinions not presented at the trial.

How the evidence rule structures the jury's work. The rule that the jury must base its verdict only on evidence introduced in court structures its work. It tells jurors what they are to do—discuss the evidence. Only those arguments that flow from the evidence introduced in court and the judge's statement of the law are legitimate. If a juror were to say, "I don't like the defense lawyer's suit and therefore I will vote guilty," or were to make up facts, other jurors would challenge him or her. Jurors ask each other to justify their positions by referring to trial evidence.

Jurors can't help using personal experience, even though it is not evidence introduced at trial. Personal experience and common sense can appropriately provide a background against which jurors evaluate evidence. "My Aunt Minnie would throw him in jail in a minute" is not a legitimate argument. But "I know that police will sometimes stop a black teenager for no good reason because that has happened to me" is a legitimate use of personal experience to provide background for interpreting evidence. Jury selection procedures that enhance racial, ethnic, and gender diversity on juries are valuable because a diverse jury brings a broader range of experiences to the task of understanding the evidence.

Ignoring evidence struck from the record. Jurors are not simply asked to ignore evidence from sources other than the trial. Sometimes, they are asked to do something much trickier: to ignore information that is presented during the trial but is excluded by the court. The rules of evidence are intended to ensure that irrelevant, unreliable, or prejudicial evidence and testimony are not heard by the jury, but sometimes it is. When this happens, the opposing lawyer will (or should) object. If the judge agrees that the testimony should have been excluded, he or she orders it stricken from the record. The judge also instructs the jurors to disregard what they heard. But can jurors disregard what they heard? Can you unring a bell? Perhaps. There is very little research on whether deliberating jurors can or will pay attention to judicial instructions to disregard inadmissible evidence they have already heard (Devine et al., 2001).

Even though the little empirical evidence available suggests that instructing the jury to ignore objectionable evidence is not always effective, the fiction that errors can be corrected this way is useful. When inappropriate evidence reaches the jury, the judge has to do something in the interest of fairness. Declaring a mistrial every time an error occurs would be too inefficient. By instructing jurors to ignore testimony struck from the record, the judge can maintain an appearance of fairness for the appellate record should the case be reviewed by a higher court. The overall goal is a fair trial; a perfect trial is too ambitious a goal.

The appearance of fairness is important in legitimizing the system. So, of course, is real fairness. Judges do call mistrials when the effects of evidence introduced in error might be grievous. For example, if a confession had been excluded from evidence during a pretrial hearing on grounds that it was coerced, the prosecution may not introduce it. If the prosecution inadvertently introduces the confession, the error is considered weighty enough in its influence on a jury to warrant a mistrial. The evidence from simulations confirms what the courts have recognized on their own, that once a confession is introduced, mock jurors weight it very heavily regardless of instructions to disregard (Kassin and Wrightsman, 1985).

Jury Unanimity and Jury Size

Juries traditionally were composed of 12 citizens who came to a unanimous verdict. Some states have modified both **jury size** and **jury unanimity** requirements in order to improve efficiency.

The unanimity rule and the deliberation process. In *Johnson v. Louisiana* (1972) and in *Apodaca v. Oregon* (1972), the U.S. Supreme Court ruled that a state law authorizing a nonunanimous 9–3 verdict was constitutional. The justices said that a nonunanimous verdict would not interfere with either the deliberative process or the representativeness of the composition of juries.

Researchers suspected that the justices were wrong: they hypothesized that dropping the unanimity rule would change the jury process. The unanimity rule gives each juror's voice great weight. Just one person can hang a jury. In consequence, the jury group is motivated to listen to each individual member and to persuade everyone to agree. If the jury is not using a unanimity rule, jurors who are in the minority have less weight in the deliberations. There is less need to persuade them to change their minds.

Researchers investigated the question of the effect of the unanimity rule on deliberations by presenting mock jurors with evidence from a fictional trial. The mock jurors were then asked to deliberate until they reached a verdict. With nonunanimous decision rules, deliberations were shorter (Devine et al., 2001). If the requisite number of votes turned up in an early vote, the jurors reviewed the evidence less thoroughly than when deliberating with a unanimity rule. The deliberative process was the same in one important way. Mock jurors looking at the same evidence found the defendants guilty or not guilty at about the same rate under either rule (Hans and Vidmar, 1986; Saks and Marti, 1997).

Despite the fact that juries working with a unanimity rule took longer to reach a verdict and were more often hung, mock jurors expressed greater satisfaction with the unanimous than the nonunanimous condition. Perhaps jurors have a better sense of closure when all agree. We don't know how the general public feels about unanimous versus less than unanimous juries. Even if more efficient, trials decided on a less than unanimous basis might be perceived as less fair.

Effects of jury size. In the 1970s, the U.S. Supreme Court held that jury sizes smaller than 12 but larger than 5 did not violate due process except when the death penalty might be imposed on a guilty defendant (*Ballew v. Georgia,* 1978; *Colgrove v. Battin,* 1973; *Williams v. Florida,* 1970). The justices said that size mattered less than how juries functioned. Juries, they said, should be judged by "quality of deliberation, reliability of the jury's fact-finding, the verdict ratio [proportion of guilty verdicts], ability of dissenters on the jury to resist majority pressure to conform, and the jury's capacity to provide a fair cross-sectional representation of the community" (Saks and Marti, 1997, p. 451).

The Court's decisions encouraged investigators to study differences between 6-person and 12-person juries. Saks and Marti (1997) did a meta-analysis of 17 studies covering 2,016 juries and about 15,000 jurors. Ten of the studies were studies of mock juries in the laboratory; seven were field studies conducted in actual courts. The researchers analyzed findings related to the variables the U.S. Supreme Court identified as important (quality of deliberations, reliability of findings, verdict ratio, ability of dissenters to resist pressure, and representativeness of the jurors).

Smaller real juries were less likely to have one or more ethnic minority members than larger juries. This finding is consistent with statistical sampling theory. It is contrary to the Supreme Court's view that ethnic minority representation need not be affected by jury size.

In laboratory studies with mock juries using the unanimity rule, larger juries, on average, deliberated longer (70 minutes) than smaller juries (53 minutes). Trial testimony was discussed more fully and more accurately in larger compared to smaller juries.

There were no significant effects of jury size on verdicts. About as many small juries as large juries found defendants guilty (or liable). On these criteria, smaller juries meet the justices' requirements for good jury process.

It is only recently that research workers have turned their attention to civil rather than criminal juries. The rules for jury size in civil cases vary widely from state to state. Many states permit a 6-person jury, unless a 12-person jury is demanded by one side or the other. Many states do not require a unanimous decision in civil cases but use a two-thirds, three-quarters, or five-sixths rule (Cohen and Smith, 2004). These complexities may make it more difficult to develop experiments that speak to conditions in different states.

Efficiency versus fuller process. Juries of fewer than 12 do appear more efficient and less expensive. If fewer jurors are required and fewer citizens are called, there is a gain in efficiency. If deliberation time is reduced, and fewer juries hang, then costs are reduced. However, Saks and Marti's (1997) findings suggest that, by the Supreme Court's standards of quality of deliberation, the ability of dissenters to resist majority pressure, and the provision of a fair cross-sectional representation of the community, the traditional 12-person jury is better. Here is a clear conflict of values. Should a more deliberative process and better ethnic minority representation outweigh cost and efficiency? There is no information about the public's beliefs; we don't know if Americans accept juries of less than 12 as fair. There hasn't been any public protest on this issue.

No Time Limit Deliberation

In real trials, there is no minimum time the jury must deliberate and no maximum time limit on deliberations. The no time limit rule sets jury deliberation apart from most other activities and underscores the importance of the jury's work. It encourages debate and review of the evidence. Jurors can challenge each other as long as necessary to arrive at a verdict. Most real juries do arrive at verdicts (Hannaford-Agor et al., 2002). The rate of hung juries in simulations is higher, perhaps because of artificial restraints on deliberation time.

Two notorious trials of the 1990s illustrate the range of deliberation time. The O. J. Simpson criminal trial jury came back with a verdict of not guilty in four hours. In the first Menendez brothers' trial for killing their parents, the jurors deliberated for more than three weeks before the judge declared a mistrial. (Both young men were retried and convicted fairly quickly.)

In real trials, the jurors decide when they are hung. They tell the judge if they believe they will not be able to reach a verdict. Because there is no limit on deliberation time, when jurors tell the judge they are stuck, the judge can urge them to deliberate further to avoid a mistrial. The judge may appeal to their sense of fairness or use a so-called dynamite charge to pressure for a verdict and "blast" the deliberations open again. In the **dynamite charge,** the judge asks those in the minority position to be sure their doubts are reasonable (*Allen v. United States,* 1896).

Critics believe the dynamite charge does not serve justice. They fear it allows judges to use their authority to compel holdouts to change their vote even though their doubts were reasonable. Perhaps the juries hung because the evidence could support different inferences (Hannaford-Agor et al., 2002). Smith and Kassin (1993) tested the question. They used the dynamite charge with deadlocked mock jurors. The charge resulted in changes in votes by jurors who were in the minority, but they felt coerced. When the fairness of the dynamite charge was challenged, the Supreme Court upheld its use (*Lowenfield v. Phelps,* 1988).

Deliberate and Debate

In the charge given after the lawyers have presented all the evidence, the trial judge instructs the jurors to discuss the evidence in light of the substantive law and to debate the inferences that may be drawn from the evidence. This charge structures the group process.

Each juror tentatively arrives at a verdict as he or she listens to evidence and argument in a trial. To help ensure that they are open to discussion, the judge tells the jurors not to commit themselves publicly to a verdict before deliberations and not to discuss the case before deliberation with anyone, including other jurors. The law here is implicitly recognizing **cognitive dissonance.** Once a juror has stated a position in public, he or she may be less open to the views of the other jurors. In some recent experiments, jurors were allowed to discuss the case during breaks before formal deliberation began. Jurors did discuss the evidence among themselves, but there was little indication that jurors formed opinions prematurely or that they tried to influence each other before receiving the case for deliberation (Dann and Hans, 2004).

The instruction to discuss and debate the evidence may increase the likelihood of conflicts between jurors, but the normative framework and the rules for deliberating provide protections against group disintegration. Some judges offer suggestions for how the deliberations could be organized. Jurors found such instructions very helpful, especially since many had no previous experience serving on juries. Some courts provide written copies of the judge's instructions to the jurors. In pilot projects, judges, jurors, and attorneys agreed that the procedure was very helpful (Dann and Hans, 2004).

The judge's authority is always present symbolically in the jury room. Levine, Farrell, and Perrotta (1981) studied a videotape of mock jurors deliberating. The video was analyzed by methods used to code interaction in small groups. Conflict during deliberation among group members was often resolved when a member of the jury referred to the judge's instructions. The judge's authority was used to get over an impasse and to avoid disintegration of the group. For example, during a heated discussion of the responsibility of an adolescent girl for sexual abuse, one mock juror said to another, "The judge told us it didn't matter if the underage girl wanted to experiment with sex."

Vote Your Conscience

Jurors take an oath to vote according to conscience. Traditionally, this was the source of the jury's moral authority: "A verdict rendered according to conscience and reflecting the jury's conception of just deserts was divine in the sense that it was beyond judicial reproach" (Green, 1985, 20). The judge's instruction to each juror to vote according to conscience after deliberating openly emphasizes the juror's individuality and responsibility.

Juries often begin deliberations by holding an initial ballot. When there is a strong majority vote on the first ballot, most of the time the jury's final verdict is the one endorsed by the initial majority (Kalven and Zeisel, 1966; Devine et al., 2001). But the fact that the initial majority often prevails doesn't mean that jurors disregard their oath to vote according to conscience or to deliberate. The majority vote may reflect the strength of the evidence, and jurors in the minority position may be persuaded after listening to others. The majority doesn't always prevail. There are noteworthy examples of lone jurors swaying a group, or a lone holdout hanging a jury. The legal system presumes that the holdout is voting according to conscience.

Most jurors take their responsibility to decide a case according to their consciences seriously. Many go through difficult internal struggles while trying to decide what is just and right. The stress is exacerbated when there are conflicts among them. The process can be very painful. One juror in a death penalty case sobbed so uncontrollably when the verdict was announced that she nearly collapsed (Sengupta, 1998a). Some jurors report experiencing clinical symptoms of anxiety as a result of jury service.

Shuman, Hamilton, and Daley (1994) found that about 12 percent of jurors serving on traumatic trials suffered a diagnosable depression.

Jury Selection

The Sixth Amendment guarantees a defendant the right to an **impartial** (not favoring either party at the outset) trial in the state and district where the crime was committed. It does not mention a jury of peers, and it does not define *impartial.*

Trial juries are selected from panels of prospective jurors called for service in the locale in which the crime occurred, or, in a civil case, where the **cause of action** (event entitling a party to seek a judicial remedy) arose or where at least one defendant resides. The panels are chosen from the pool of people in the proper geographical area who are qualified to serve on a jury. The state establishes the qualifications for jury service within guidelines set by federal law. To ensure an impartial jury, both sides have an opportunity to challenge prospective jurors during the selection process. The right to **challenge** (object to) prospective jurors **for cause** (reasons the law recognizes as valid or important) goes back to the Middle Ages.

Representativeness

The idea that **impartiality** (lack of bias) is related to demographic representativeness is relatively new. For much of our history, little or no effort was made to ensure that the panels or pools of prospective jurors were representative of the community. In some courts, juries were selected haphazardly, sometimes from among people loafing around the courthouse. In others, distinguished community members submitted names of those who could be called for jury duty, leading to all of the discrimination inherent in an "old boys' network."

Until relatively recently, property, color, and gender qualifications were deliberately used to exclude large groups of Americans from jury service, including African Americans and women of any color. Overt discrimination against the right of African Americans to sit on juries was first attacked successfully in 1880 (*Strauder v. West Virginia,* 1880). However, states got around the ruling by setting up qualifications for jury service that did not explicitly mention race but had the effect of eliminating African Americans from the pool. Laws excluding or restricting women from jury service remained in place even after the passage in 1920 of the Nineteenth Amendment giving women the right to vote.

In the course of the twentieth century, the idea that jury pools should be roughly representative of the community gradually gained acceptance. In 1968, the U.S. Congress said that voter registration rolls should be used to call jurors. Voter rolls are not really representative, however. Younger people, poorer people, and minority group members are less likely to register to vote.

In the 1960s and 1970s, civil rights groups attacked discrimination in the jury system through court cases. They used statistical analysis to show that racial or ethnic groups were underrepresented on jury panels compared to their number in the population. The courts ruled that guilty verdicts could be set aside on appeal if the jury panel was drawn by biased methods of selection. These jury discrimination cases set important precedents for the use of statistical evidence in voting rights and employment discrimination cases (see Barnes and Conley, 1986).

In 1975, the U.S. Supreme Court struck down restrictions against women serving on juries (*Taylor v. Louisiana*). The Court interpreted the Sixth Amendment to require that a jury panel be selected from a "representative cross-section of the community," including women. The ruling did not require that every individual trial jury had to include a representative cross-section of the population. Rather, it required that the states use methods to call citizens for jury duty to ensure that the pools of prospective jurors from which panels of jurors were chosen would be reasonably representative. To ensure representativeness, states enlarged the ways of locating and calling people for jury service. Now occupational and other exemptions (such as being a mother) from being called for jury duty have been eliminated to enhance representativeness.

The Voir Dire

Though juries must now be selected from a representative pool of qualified jurors summoned to the courthouse, each jury does not have to be representative in a sampling sense. Each jury does have to be *impartial*. To ensure impartiality, prospective jurors may be excluded by the judge for *cause* or by lawyers using peremptory challenges.

Prospective jurors assemble in a large room where they await a call for service on a trial. This group is called a **venire** (from Latin, meaning "to come" or "appear"). They may be instructed in the juror role by hearing a talk or viewing a video explaining jurors' responsibilities. Members of the venire are assigned randomly to panels to be considered for service in particular cases. The randomly selected prospective jurors are brought into a courtroom for the *voir dire* (meaning "to see and say") in front of the judge and attorneys who will try the case. The prospective jurors are told of the general nature of the case, who the parties are, and the names of the prospective witnesses. Then they are questioned by the judge and the lawyers for both sides to determine their suitability to serve on that particular trial. The judge may dismiss prospective jurors for cause if they do not meet the standards of impartiality or competence.

In federal courts, judges conduct most of the voir dire. In state courts, where most cases are tried, the voir dire is usually conducted by lawyers; the judge supervises and may also ask questions of prospective jurors. In either case, the parties and their lawyers actively participate in the selection process through their right to ask the judge to dismiss certain prospective jurors.

Dismissal for cause. State and federal laws establish reasons that warrant dismissal for cause of prospective jurors for a case. The judge may dismiss jurors for cause if the juror doesn't meet legal qualifications (e.g., is underage or is not a resident of the county) or "has a state of mind that is likely to preclude him from rendering an impartial verdict based on the evidence adduced at trial" (New York Criminal Procedure Law § 270.20(b)). For example, jurors may be dismissed for cause if a previous relationship to one of the parties would undermine the juror's impartiality, if they had been a victim of a similar crime, or if they had a close relative accused of a similar crime. Culhane, Hosch, and Weaver (2004) found that jurors who said they had been a victim of a crime similar to the one depicted in a mock trial (e.g., burglary) or who knew a victim of a similar crime were significantly more likely to vote for guilt (65.8 percent) than those who had not been a victim of a similar crime (54.6 percent). These data support the rule dismissing for cause a juror who had been the victim of a similar crime. In a death penalty case, people with strong opinions against the death penalty may be dismissed for cause (see Chapter 8). Considerations for challenging a juror for cause are similar in civil cases. There is no limit on the number of jurors who may be challenged for cause for any of the reasons specified by law.

Peremptory challenges. Prospective jurors may also be dismissed as a result of **peremptory challenges**. The lawyer can request the judge to dismiss a prospective juror without explaining the reasons for the request. (This right is now subject to some limits, as we will see below.) In theory, peremptory challenges promote a sense of participation and fairness. Each side is given a limited number of peremptory challenges. Each side can dismiss jurors they feel may be biased against them. But lawyers don't necessarily want an impartial jury; they want a favorable one. The peremptory challenge is one of the tools lawyers use to attempt to select favorable juries. They can't choose the panel of prospective jurors, but they can exclude some prospective jurors they believe may be unfavorable to their side.

Each side has a limited number of peremptory challenges. The number varies in different states and by type of case. As an example, in criminal trials in New York, prosecution and defense can get 20 peremptories if the charge is a class A felony (more serious offense), 15 for class B or class C felonies, and 10 for all other cases (New York Criminal Procedure Law, § 270.25). In civil cases, each side may get three peremptory challenges, although the law may give the judge the discretion to add more (New York Civil Practice Laws and Rules § 4109).

Selecting favorable juries. A lawyer's first aim during the voir dire is to exclude prospective jurors who the lawyer thinks would be unfavorable. A lawyer decides if a juror is unfavorably disposed based on the juror's answers to questions posed during the voir dire and any additional information the lawyer may have obtained about the juror. If a lawyer thinks a prospective juror is unfavorable, the lawyer will try to get the juror to say something that will show a "state of mind that is likely to preclude him from rendering an impartial verdict." The judge then decides whether the prospective juror's statement meets the legal standard for dismissal for cause. If the judge doesn't dismiss for cause, the lawyer may exercise a peremptory challenge. Because these are limited in number, lawyers, in consultation with clients, must use such challenges carefully.

In most cases, the only background information that lawyers get about prospective jurors is their names, addresses, occupations, and prior history of jury service. Sometimes, in highly publicized cases, the prospective jurors are also given questionnaires to complete in advance to save time in the selection process in court. This information is supplemented by the jurors' answers to the questions the judge and lawyers pose in the courtroom. In the past, lawyers decided who to try to exclude on the basis of this information plus the hunches, intuitions, myths, prejudices, and generalizations about the characteristics of people in certain occupations or ethnic groups. These "theories" were never subject to systematic validation.

Now, when litigants have sufficient resources, they may employ trial consultants to help them with jury selection. Most consultants are social scientists. They use questionnaires and surveys to ascertain demographic, attitudinal, or background factors that may *predict* (correlate with) the prospective juror's sympathy for one side or another (Kressel and Kressel, 2002).

Prosecutors and public defenders, working with limited budgets, normally can't afford to use consultants for selecting jurors. In civil cases in which parties have significant resources or in which a lot of money is at stake, one or both sides may use consultants. The celebrated criminal trial of former Buffalo Bills star running back O. J. Simpson is a case in point. Simpson was charged with brutally murdering his wife,

BOX 5.2

Jury Selection Questionnaires

In a famous case of the 1990s, O. J. Simpson, former star running back with the Buffalo Bills, was charged with the murder of his estranged wife and an acquaintance who was escorting her that night. Simpson's defense team's consultants, and the prosecutors, developed a 300-item juror questionnaire that was very intrusive. The 300-item questionnaire was used as the basis for voir dire by both defense and prosecution.

In famous 2005 case, pop star Michael Jackson was accused of sexually molesting a minor. The jury questionnaire in his case was only 41 items. It centered on demographic information. It also asked about previous jury experience, previous experience with law suits, whether the prospective juror had friends in law enforcement, whether the prospective juror had been a victim of sex abuse. The jurors were also asked if they had worked for a children's rights advocacy group. One item asked whether the juror's experiences with people of a different race would affect the ability to serve as a fair and impartial juror. Personal questions and other attitudes measured in the O. J. Simpson questionnaire were not included. California law now restricts the questioning to material that might be a basis for a challenge for cause. Jury selection was completed rapidly in the Michael Jackson case. Jackson was also acquitted.

Nicole Brown Simpson, from whom he was separated, and her acquaintance Ron Goldman. Simpson was African American, and both victims were white. There was strong circumstantial (indirect) evidence against him. Some of the detective work was sloppy, which the defense claimed supported their theory that Simpson had been framed by racist police officers (see Figure 5.2).

Simpson's jury consultants concluded that African American women were the group least prone to convict. The defense lawyers consequently sought to exclude whites from the jury when possible. The prosecution made no attempt to exclude African American women despite the advice of their consultants to do so. (Although this was a rare case where the prosecutors hired consultants, the lead prosecutor, Marcia Clark, relied instead on her hunch that she had good rapport with African American female jurors.) The process generated a great deal of discussion about the fairness of excluding jurors on the basis of race and gender (see Box 5.2).

Science and Jury Selection

Jury consultants commonly use surveys and questionnaires to assist lawyers in jury selection, as they did in the O. J. Simpson case. The consultants may develop a case-specific questionnaire starting with items that past research or common sense suggests might be relevant in a case, including demographic (age, education and so on) variables and attitude variables. Attitudes may be assessed using attitude scales developed with mock jurors that measure traits such as *authoritarianism* or *conviction proneness*. The researchers then administer the scales along with criterion questions such as "Do you think O. J. Simpson is guilty?" to a local sampling survey of jury-eligible people. They analyze the results to find attitude and demographic variables that correlate with answers to criterion questions about the case (see Moran, Cutler, and De Lisa, 1994).

The method assumes that prospective jurors with the same characteristics or who answer items in the same way as those sampled will think about the case the same way and be inclined to vote the same way when serving as jurors.

Validity of scientific jury selection procedures. Is the assumption that one can predict juror behavior from pretrial information warranted? Jury consultants rarely, if ever, test their intuitive skills in a controlled study. We can raise questions on the validity of such predictions based on the general literature on the fallibility of predictions. The conditions under which the nonjuror sample responds to surveys or interviews are different than the conditions under which the prospective jurors called for jury duty will respond. Respondents asked to participate in a survey have no obvious motive to shade their answers. Prospective jurors may or may not wish to serve in a particular case, and shape their answers accordingly. If prospective jurors are not candid and accurate in their responses to voir dire questions, then the voir dire process has serious limitations for selecting jurors fairly.

There are other important differences. The survey respondents have no decision-making responsibilities, are not in the spotlight, and are not part of a group of jurors. But jury service puts an individual in the midst of a powerful social system. People's responses before they serve may not predict their responses later when they are in the role of a sworn juror and are part of a deliberating jury group. It is difficult to predict from individual difference measures how individuals will behave in a group because the correlations between individual difference measures and behavior in a group are usually low (Strier, 1999).

In one simulation of a rape trial, the only variable that showed even a weak correlation with individual juror votes was gender. In that trial, 29 percent of women jurors were willing to convict on the facts, and only 7 percent of men. The difference between men's and women's votes was statistically significant, but for the large majority of men and women, the evidence overrode any individual difference factor. The vast majority of jurors, both men and women, were willing to acquit given the facts of the case (Koski, 2002).

Juror behavior is very much situation specific and therefore hard to predict. There is no general tendency to convict or to acquit that can be recognized and used reliably to predict juror behavior during actual deliberations in criminal trials. In civil trials, surveys have suggested that, if anything, jurors start out with a bias against plaintiffs who seek money damages. Predicting how jurors will find liability and award damages may depend more on the nature of the plaintiff's injuries and the conduct of the defendants than on juror characteristics. Lawyers do no better in selection of sympathetic jurors than do consultants (Kressel and Kressel, 2002). Plaintiffs win more often and are awarded greater damages in bench than in jury trials (Cohen and Smith, 2004). (We have no scientific measures to predict the behavior of judges; in any event, the lawyers have very little say in who the judge trying their case will be.)

Moran, Cutler, and De Lisa (1994) argue that even a low correlation can improve prediction efficiency and is better grounds for selecting jurors than the lawyer's routine clinical judgment during voir dire (another example of pitting actuarial or statistical methods against clinical methods of prediction). They conducted four civil mock trials, and found that attitude measures correlated with judgments of liability about 0.21. That means the measures explained between 4 and 5 percent of the variability in subjects' scores on the criterion question of the defendant's liability for damages. Under some conditions, even a correlation of that magnitude can improve predictive effectiveness over using no valid predictor. The researchers believe the results of scientific jury selection based on attitude and demographic measures are likely to be better in real situations than in simulations, better when attitudes toward case-specific issues are measured, and better when the trial evidence is less clear-cut in favor of one side or the other. However, the advantage may be apparent only over a large series of cases. The single case matters to the client. The advantage of scientific jury consultation is difficult to demonstrate in the single case.

Social science techniques aren't the only techniques used by jury consultants. Consultants can sometimes help lawyers by thoroughly investigating the background of individual prospective jurors, rather than by applying scientific measurement techniques.

In addition to helping select jurors, consultants may conduct mock trials to test mock jurors' reactions to pieces of evidence or to lawyers' opening and closing arguments. They may also use focus groups for a similar purpose. These procedures help lawyers prepare their cases by giving them feedback about their own performance and about how their cases are perceived by laypeople similar to jurors (Kressel and Kressel, 2002). This is especially vital because many jurors may reach a strong tentative decision about the case after hearing the lawyers' opening statements but before any evidence is presented.

Despite the lack of substantial evidence demonstrating the validity of jury-consulting techniques, jury consultation is a $400 million industry with over 700 practitioners. Consultants charge from $75 to $300 an hour. Because they are so expensive, jury consultants are used more in high-stakes civil litigation than in the ordinary run of criminal cases (Strier, 1999; Kressel and Kressel, 2002).

Experienced jury consultants agree that in the final analysis, they rely on "intuition" in making their recommendations. The consultants may be able to provide lawyers with a language to help conceptualize the process of selecting a jury. They may also be useful for sharing responsibility (or blame) with lawyers if things go wrong. Kressel and Kressel (2002) conclude that "scientific jury selection can help attorneys manage their stress far more often than it helps them to capture a verdict" (Kressel and Kressel, 2002, p. 135).

Ethical issues. Jury consultation raises some ethical questions. One is the ethics of using scales and measures in the marketplace for purposes for which they have not been validated. The ethics of the entire endeavor can also be questioned. Assuming the techniques are effective, psychologists must ask whether deliberately manipulating the jury system in return for money, especially in cases in which the other side cannot afford similar services, is a socially responsible use of professional skills. The techniques of the consultants are largely employed out of sight of the public. But public awareness that expensive, private tools are available to one side only may tend to undermine confidence in the justice system.

Finally, we need to ask whether the jury-consulting techniques and indeed the voir dire itself inappropriately violate the privacy of prospective jurors. Citizens give up personal privacy when they are compelled to appear and to answer intrusive questions in public during a voir dire. The voir dire is supposed to serve the important public purpose of ensuring impartial justice, which in theory justifies the intrusion. For example, in California, the information that can be obtained from jurors is supposed to be used to help frame challenges for cause, not to select favorable jurors. But suppose the questions the prospective jurors must answer are invalid predictors or have only a tangential relationship to any statements that would constitute legally cognizable partiality? If peremptory challenges are meant to secure favorable, rather than

BOX 5.3

151

Racial
Composition
of Juries

An Investigation of a Prospective Juror by Consultants

Dr. Jack Kevorkian openly assisted terminally ill persons to commit suicide, which he believed should be their right, and was prosecuted several times for doing so.

In one of his trials, the defense managed to seat a minister named Donald Ott who had published about the right to die. The defense knew this as a result of a consultant's investigation of the man's background; the prosecution didn't know who he was. In a post-deliberation interview, Ott saw the trial as a political opportunity: "There is a major shift taking place in our country, and we found ourselves caught in that. It's a question of which way we were going to give it a nudge." Ott, a persuasive and urbane man, was probably a leader in the jury room and perhaps guided others to adopt his views (Linsalata, Durfee, and Harmon, 1996).

impartial, juries, they are arguably not serving the purpose of justice. And if the advantage in scientific selection is illusory, then the questions don't even serve the lawyer's purpose, but are simply a waste of time and unnecessarily intrusive. The argument could be made that peremptory challenges should be eliminated, the voir dire limited to the most directly relevant questions, and a jury selected at random from the jurors remaining after those obviously at risk of partiality were eliminated.

Random selection would enhance the dignity and authority of the justice system by protecting it from charges that juries are manipulated by unscrupulous lawyers who are only interested in winning. On the other hand, random selection might undermine the participants' sense of having some control over the process, and the public's perception that the process is fair.

Racial Composition of Juries

Lawyers and jury consultants sometimes attempt to exclude or include prospective jurors based on stereotypes about how women or members of ethnic groups think and behave (Rose, 1999). For example, one prosecutor made a training videotape for others in the office in which he asserted that blacks from poor neighborhoods were to be avoided on juries because they won't convict criminal defendants, but that older black men, particularly from the South, were desirable jurors because they tended to respect authority and were more prone to convict defendants (Kressel and Kressel, 2002). The U.S. Supreme Court prohibited prosecution and defense lawyers from using peremptory challenges to dismiss prospective jurors on the basis of race in criminal cases (*Batson v. Kentucky,* 1986; *Georgia v. McCollum,* 1992; *Powers v. Ohio,* 1991) and in civil cases (*Edmonson v. Leesville Concrete Co.,* 1991). The Supreme Court later extended the ban to peremptories based on gender (*J.E.B. ex rel T.B.,* 1994). Some courts and states have gone further and excluded challenges on the basis of religion and sexual orientation (e.g., California Code of Civil Procedure § 231.5).

These decisions may not have had much real-world effect. If a party suspects another side's lawyer is using peremptory challenges in a prohibited manner, the party can point out the suspicious pattern to the judge, who can ask the lawyer to explain. The lawyer must offer a nondiscriminatory reason for striking the jurors in question. The challenging party must try to show that the reason offered is just a pretext, and the judge must decide whether the reason is adequate or not. Because most lawyers anticipate the possibility of such a challenge to their exclusions of prospective jurors, they have little trouble coming up with nonprohibited reasons for dismissing the prospective jurors. In addition, the focus is on the plausibility of the reasons given, not their objective reasonableness (*Miller-El v. Dretke,* 2005). As a result, the process has limited value for eliminating racial or gender exclusion. Whether or not the attempts to eliminate biases in selection are effective, the symbolic value for the society as a whole of saying that racial discrimination in the courtroom is not acceptable is meaningful and important.

Juror Behavior and Race

The public fears that juror behavior may be influenced by race. Race loomed large in public discussion of two "high-profile" cases in the 1990s, the Rodney King case and the O. J. Simpson case. Many people believed the evidence pointed overwhelmingly to the guilt of the defendants in both cases, but in each, the defendants were acquitted. In one case, white policemen were accused of beating Rodney King, an African American man. A bystander had taken a video of the beating, which was broadcast on television and horrified the nation. The court found that community sentiment in Los Angeles, where the alleged crime took place, was so fiercely for conviction that the police officers could not get a fair trial. (Social science survey data can contribute to decisions about changing venues.) The case was transferred to an almost all-white community in which a large number of police officers lived. The all-white jury found the police defendants not guilty.

Similarly, many people believe prosecutors lost the O. J. Simpson criminal case when they elected to try it in downtown Los Angeles, where any jury panel would contain a high percentage of African Americans. Surveys showed that African Americans were strongly favorably disposed toward O. J. Simpson, while whites were strongly disposed to view him as guilty. Simpson's lawyers used the voir dire to favor the selection of African American women who consultants predicted were the group least likely to convict. The mostly African American jury deliberated only four hours before finding him not guilty.

After Simpson was acquitted in his criminal trial, the families of the two victims brought a suit against him in civil court seeking monetary damages for the wrongful death of their loved ones. The suit was brought in a more affluent and predominantly white area of Los Angeles County. Though lawyers on both sides during the voir dire appeared to be trying to reject jurors by race (Fleeman, 1996), they had relatively few peremptory challenges. However, because the jury pool contained a preponderance of whites, peremptory challenges would not have changed the final jury racial composition very much. Moreover, a nonunanimous verdict was acceptable in this California civil trial, so one or two holdouts would not have mattered. That jury unanimously found Simpson civilly liable for causing the deaths of his wife and her friend, and imposed both compensatory and punitive monetary damages (Fleeman, 1996). Simpson turned out to be "judgment proof," so very little of the judgments were ever paid. Most of his wealth was held in assets legally protected from being seized to pay the civil damages.

Though many believe the different outcomes of the criminal and civil trials of O. J. Simpson were a function of the racial composition of the juries, that may not be the case. The two trials differed in other, very important, ways as well. The two juries heard somewhat different evidence. The jury in the civil case was instructed to use a preponderance of the evidence rather than the more stringent *beyond a reasonable doubt* standard of proof required in the criminal case. Given these differences, we cannot conclude that racial composition alone accounted for the different verdicts.

Although there is some evidence that jurors act more favorably toward those who are like themselves, in most cases the evidence in the case reaching jurors and the circumstances of the case appear to override initial differences and biases among jurors (Devine et al., 2001). It would be a great blow to the integrity of the jury system if racial considerations interfered with the rational and careful evaluation of evidence. For the system to work as it should, individuals called to jury service must be able to put the role of juror and its duties ahead of other considerations.

The Jury and Medical Malpractice

Social science research on juries has concentrated on criminal trials. Recently, in response to criticisms of the way liability suits are resolved, researchers have paid more attention to civil juries (e.g., Bornstein and Rajki, 1994; Greene and Loftus, 1998; Hans, 2000; Hastie, Schkade, and Payne, 1998; Saks, 1992). We will focus here on medical malpractice suits.

Medical **malpractice** is a tort (see Chapter 3 on the *Tarasoff* case). If the doctor is found liable, the court will order the defendant to pay the plaintiff compensation for economic damages (e.g., medical expenses, and lost past and future income) and noneconomic damages (e.g., physical pain, emotional distress, and loss of consortium—companionship and services of a family member). A jury may also award **punitive damages** in dollars if it finds that the injury was intentional or malicious or if a defendant showed a reckless disregard for the plaintiff's right to proper care. Punitive damages punish a culpable defendant and set an example that, in theory, will deter others from similar conduct (Robbennolt and Studebaker, 1999; *State Farm Mutual Automobile Insurance Co. v. Campbell,* 2003).

Insurance companies and physicians have been seeking caps on the level of jury awards to plaintiffs in personal injury cases, claiming the awards are out of control (Robbennolt and Studebaker, 1999). The insurance industry and their political allies blame trial lawyers and juries willing to give excessive awards. Some physicians attribute the rapid rise in medical costs to the rise in the premiums for liability insurance for doctors, which in turn results from "litigation fever" and excessive awards. Scholarly analysis does not support the contention that there is a litigation explosion (Saks, 1992). The findings of a study of 15 leading insurance companies suggest that premiums increase for reasons other than excessive jury awards. Net claims paid out by insurance companies for medical malpractice did not rise over a five-year period, while net insurance premiums rose by 120 percent in the same period of time (Anderson, 2005). Nonetheless many members of the public believe that there is a civil litigation crisis (Hans and Lofquist, 1994). Whatever its empirical merits, the alleged "litigation crisis" is certainly a political issue.

Critics claim that lay jurors can't possibly judge the technical issues involved in medical care. They also claim that juries are biased toward compensating victims and against doctors, hospitals, and insurance companies. Moreover, they believe overgenerous jury awards have an effect beyond the case by raising out-of-court settlements in similar cases. Lawyers look to what juries do in similar cases to decide what a case might be worth when settling out of court. Critics usually do not object to reimbursement for direct losses, such as medical expenses or lost earnings, where wrongdoing is proved. Rather, they claim that excessive jury awards for intangible "pain and suffering" are responsible for the large settlements. They also claim, without presenting solid evidence, that damage awards have been increasing at a high rate, and that damage and punitive damage awards are capricious. We can look at some research to evaluate these charges.

Studies of Medical Malpractice Cases

Vidmar conducted comprehensive studies of jury awards in medical malpractice cases to examine the validity of the criticisms against them. His monograph (1997) is a model of the thoughtful integration of literature reviews, field studies, and laboratory studies.

Vidmar examined 95 percent of all medical malpractice cases filed in North Carolina courts over a three-year period ($N = 895$). Three years later, he examined another sample of 326 cases drawn from the 14 most populous counties in North Carolina. Medical insurers allowed him to look at a sample of 154 closed claim files. In addition, he observed medical malpractice trials and conducted posttrial interviews with jurors, plaintiffs, and lawyers on both sides. He also interviewed insurance company personnel.

Awards exaggerated. Vidmar examined sources of information about the claims that the dollar amount of malpractice awards was excessive. Criticism of jury awards was often based on newspaper stories. These were sometimes erroneous or misleading. Later researchers found that this is still the case. Tort reform advocacy groups run advertisements stating their position and provide press kits for reporters that promote the advocacy group's story line (Robbennolt and Studebaker, 2003). The media overreport medical malpractice cases compared to their actual number in the spectrum of litigation and tend to report such cases using vivid imagery (Robbennolt and Studebaker, 2003). Newspapers sometimes understate the grievousness of the injuries that resulted in the award while playing up the apparently absurd aspect of the case (e.g., burned by hot coffee). Cases with large punitive damage awards are also reported prominently. Stories calling attention to huge awards sometimes overstate them (Hans, 2000). The use of means or averages to describe the amount of awards rather than medians in itself distorts public perception. A small number of very large awards weigh very heavily in the calculation of a mean (see below). Some studies claiming that awards have increased over time have not adjusted their figures for inflation. Inflation has climbed more rapidly for the cost of medical care than for other prices. Newspaper reports often fail to note that judges or appeals courts have the power to reduce awards (Hans, 2000). In Texas, when the losing defendants in tort cases appeal, the awards are reduced by the appeals courts about 80 percent of the time (Glaberson, 1999b). The misreported cases are sometimes cited in political speeches and in articles by tort reformers. Information and beliefs about the size of awards may affect jury behavior, or the way legal cases are conducted. Media reports very likely influence perceptions of the state of the civil justice system, and potentially influence the thinking and actions of jurors and other participants in lawsuits (Robbennolt and Studebaker, 2003).

Defendants usually win. Vidmar found that, when medical malpractice cases went to trial, the defendant doctors won two-thirds of the time (Vidmar, 1997), suggesting that the juries weren't conviction prone. In one sample of cases, the defendant physicians or hospitals won four out of five times. When plaintiffs did win, they sometimes received large awards. However, even that finding is misleading when viewed out of context. Only a small percent (7 to 10 percent) of medical malpractice claims go to trial. The rest are settled out of court. Those that go to trial may involve more serious injuries or more emotionally horrifying injuries. These cases have the potential for greater awards.

Fifty percent of the original 895 North Carolina cases examined by Vidmar were settled out of court with the plaintiff receiving money damages. About 40 percent were withdrawn or dropped, or were terminated by a summary judgment. (In **summary judgment,** the judge considers the defendant's motion to dismiss on the grounds that there are no genuine issues of material fact to be determined by the jury and therefore the defendant is entitled to judgment as a matter of law.) Only 118 cases reached the trial stage, and of these only 84, or 9.4 percent, of the total cases initiated actually went to trial. Among these, there were five awards between $300,000 and $3.5 million dollars—but the lowest award was $4,000 and the median award was $36,500. (You can see how taking a mean of the awards would give a misleading picture.) Vidmar also found that out-of-court settlements sometimes exceeded the amounts won in court. Insurance companies try to settle cases out of court when the facts are clearly against them. They anticipate high jury awards because of the serious damages to the patient and the clearly erroneous practices by the doctor or the hospital. They wish to avoid bad publicity for the doctors and the hospital.

Later research has confirmed that juries continue to find for the defendant most of the time. Reviewing awards in trials in the 75 largest counties in the United States, Cohen and Smith (2004) found that plaintiffs won in only 27 percent of medical malpractice cases. The median award for economic and noneconomic damages combined was $422,000. About 30 percent of the cases received awards in excess of $1 million. Punitive damages were awarded in only 15 cases; the median award for punitive damages in medical malpractice cases was $187,000. Remember that these are the most egregious cases.

Jury decisions are rational. Based on interviews with jurors and observations of trials, Vidmar concluded that most juries, most of the time, arrived at rational, defensible decisions.

The issues involved in medical care are not always clear to doctors any more than to lay jurors. Doctors who are not in adversarial roles will disagree about the degree of negligence, if any, in different cases because the facts may be ambiguous (Vidmar, 1997). Nonetheless, in most cases Vidmar reviewed, there was little of such complexity that a lay jury couldn't understand the issues. Plaintiffs, defense lawyers, and experts generally made the facts clear. The jurors were aware of the adversary process, and weighed expert testimony accordingly.

In contrast, Hastie, Schkade, and Payne (1998) found that jury-eligible mock jurors did not understand the instructions regarding liability for *punitive* damages. Most of the mock juries decided that it was appropriate to consider punitive damages. In the actual cases on whose facts the mock trials were based, the judges had ruled that punitive damages were not warranted. The fault may be less with juries than with the way the law is presented to jurors.

Jurors are not biased against doctors. Vidmar concluded from the high percentage of verdicts in favor of the defense, and from his interviews, that jurors are not biased against doctors. On the contrary, he found that jurors were often skeptical about the plaintiff's injuries or motives in bringing suit. Hans (2000) found the same skepticism about plaintiffs who litigated against businesses. Vidmar also conducted simulations to test the hypothesis that laypeople are biased against doctors. His research team gave adults eligible for jury duty descriptions of two fictional cases. In one, the injury was due to medical negligence. In the other, the injury was due to negligent driving. The plaintiff's injury was the same in both scenarios. There was no statistically significant difference in the awards granted the victim in the medical malpractice and the motor vehicle negligence conditions. Vidmar concluded there was no evidence for the hypothesis that jurors were inclined to soak rich doctors with "deep pockets."

Does the System Work?

Vidmar's research strongly refutes critics of jury awards in medical malpractice. Greene and Loftus (1998) reviewed the literature on jury decisions in all kinds of liability cases, not just medical malpractice cases. Like Vidmar (1997) and Hans (2000), Greene and Loftus concluded that "jurors' decisions about damage awards are usually neither capricious nor irrational" (p. 51; see also Cohen and Smith, 2004). Given that the cases that go to trial likely have distressing facts, the jury awards do not seem to be on their face outrageous.

Despite these studies and others, in the 1980s and 1990s, legislatures in some states enacted laws limiting medical malpractice injury lawsuits and awards, especially awards for noneconomic and punitive damages. The laws were promoted by lobbyists for medical organizations and insurance companies. In those states that have put caps on awards, there has been no reduction in medical malpractice premiums. It appears likely caps on noneconomic damages will affect the monetary awards given to women, children, and the elderly disproportionately (Finley, 2005). Women have lower incomes than men. Most children have no income, and many elderly people are retired. For this reason, women and the elderly tend to get a higher percentage of their awards for noneconomic damages such as pain, suffering, and hedonic damages (lost enjoyment of life) and sometimes for punitive damages. The most frequent recipients of punitive damages awards in medical malpractice are female victims of sexual assault by a health care provider (Finley, 2005). Some researchers have used mock jury approaches to assess how juries award noneconomic damages. Given proper instructions, mock jurors seem to be able to distinguish the relative components of noneconomic damages (Poser, Bornstein, and McGorty, 2003).

Civil Juries and Democracy

The number of civil cases of all kinds in both federal and state courts has dropped. In 1962, 11.5 percent of the federal civil cases were resolved by trials; in 2002, the percentage was down to 1.8 percent (Galanter, 2004). Most of these cases are resolved in other ways. Are our society and our democracy helped or harmed by the change? Are we looking at alternative justice, or at bargaining instead of justice?

Vidmar concluded that the juries in medical malpractice cases for the most part are administering justice, and that they are serving our democracy in other ways as well. In his words,

> [C]ivil juries serve other societal functions. They provide a check against elitism and arbitrariness by professionals in the legal system. They help inject a measure of community values into the legal process. They help impart a sense of legitimacy to the legal process for the parties and the community as a whole. And, as Alexis de Tocqueville observed in his often quoted essay in *Democracy in America,* the civil jury institution also provides those who serve on it with some important civics lessons about rights and responsibilities. (Vidmar, 1997, p. 277)

These findings remind us that it is important to look at whatever facts we can find rather than to accept at face value emotionally charged arguments that are motivated by political, ideological, or economic interests.

Summary

Though only about 10 percent of criminal and civil cases ultimately go to juries, these trials have great symbolic importance to our society. The jury, as representative of the community, makes the ultimate decisions about guilt and innocence and brings closure to the conflict. There is no way of determining how often jury verdicts are correct without some independent way of assessing the truth in various cases. But the adversarial trial decided by a jury is widely regarded as a fair way of settling disputes.

Juries, whose decisions cannot be questioned, sometimes serve as lawmakers as well as fact-finders. They may nullify the law by delivering verdicts that are inconsistent with the definitions of the crime in the written law. These nullifications, on the one hand, undermine the power of the legislature and the principle of consistency of the rule by law. On the other hand, they give the system the flexibility to do justice in the exceptional case.

We have very little direct observational evidence of how real juries deliberate. However, our concepts of group process, supplemented by observations of mock jurors and postdeliberation interviews with real jurors, offer insights into how juries work. A substantial body of research suggests that juries use role and situational demands, the judge's instructions, and his or her implicit authority to cohere as a small group and complete the decision-making task. Psychologists have identified some extralegal factors that influence jurors' judgments in resolving cases. However, the strongest predictor of jury verdicts is the evidence.

Juries are selected from a panel called for service from the pool of potential jurors in the district. In the past, African Americans, women, and others were overtly or covertly excluded from jury service. A series of cases in the 1960s and 1970s established that the pool of potential jurors must be roughly representative of the community, though each individual jury selected need not be.

During the voir dire, the judge tries to eliminate prospective jurors who might not be impartial. The lawyers use peremptory challenges to eliminate individuals they feel will be unfavorable to their side. Psychologists are now offering lawyers their services as jury selection consultants, and in other capacities as well. Despite a lack of validation of its methods, jury consultation is a growth industry.

Jury awards in malpractice cases have been criticized as excessive. Research suggests, however, that juries in both criminal and civil trials generally make rational decisions based primarily on the evidence and on the law.

It is quite remarkable that small groups of ordinary people with nothing in common but geography can form working groups, take on challenging and sometimes stressful decision-making tasks, and deliver rationally arrived at verdicts. The jury is truly a pillar of democracy.

Discussion Questions

1. Why are juries important?
2. What are the pros and cons of the adversarial versus the inquisitorial trial?
3. When jury trials are held in France and Belgium, the judge sits in on the deliberations to act as legal adviser to the jury (Verkaik, 2000). How would this change the role of the jury in our system? Can you design an experiment to test whether jurors felt they did a better job deliberating alone or with a judge present? Do you think the kind of case would make a difference? How could you find out?
4. What are the pros and cons of allowing juries to decide cases by a 9 to 3 majority instead of requiring that they reach a unanimous verdict? Suppose you are given the transcripts of 25 mock juries deliberating under a unanimity rule and 25 juries deliberating the same case under a 9 to 3 rule. Can you think of ways you could analyze the transcripts to look for differences in the deliberation process between the two groups of juries?

5. A defendant of one race is accused of murdering a victim of another race; do you think a jury composed of citizens of only one of the two races can arrive at a just verdict?

6. Do you think jury consulting can be an ethical profession?

7. What are the advantages and limitations of studying jury deliberations by (1) interviewing or giving questionnaires to real jurors after a trial, and (2) conducting mock trials and taping deliberations of the mock juries?

8. Most tort cases are settled out of court before trial. What do you think motivates parties to agree to settle? How could you test your hypotheses?

9. Do you think medical malpractice awards are excessive? How could you design a study to decide whether this is true?

Key Terms

adversarial method	hung jury	probative
assistance of counsel	impartiality	punitive damages
challenge for cause	indictment	repeat players
civil disobedience	inquisitorial system	right of confrontation
cognitive dissonance	jury nullification	Seventh Amendment
compulsory process	jury size	Sixth Amendment
deliberate	jury unanimity	summary judgment
double jeopardy	Magna Carta	trial by ordeal
dynamite charge	malpractice	venire
fact-finder	one-time players	voir dire
Fifth Amendment	peremptory challenge	
grand jury	prejudicial	

CHAPTER **6**

Miscarriages of Justice: False Confessions and Eyewitness Error

160

CHAPTER 6
Miscarriages
of Justice: False
Confessions
and Eyewitness
Error

In this chapter, we will discuss two potential sources of miscarriage of justice: the problem of false confessions, and the problem of mistaken eyewitness testimony. We will examine what psychologists know about these problems and ways this knowledge has or might be used by the courts. We will concentrate on criminal cases because about 93 percent of the cases in which psychologists were asked to testify about these issues have been criminal matters (Kassin et. al. 2001). We will look at

- evidence that some people are wrongfully convicted based on making false confessions.
- the attitude of the courts to expert testimony about false confessions.
- evidence that some people are wrongfully convicted based on faulty eyewitness testimony.
- the importance of eyewitness testimony in our legal system.
- the attitude of the courts to expert testimony about eyewitness fallibility.
- basic research on the nature of perception and memory, and its implications for eyewitness accuracy.
- methods used by psychologists to study factors influencing eyewitness accuracy.
- selected research, including findings about the relationship between accuracy and eyewitness confidence and the effects of system variables (variables the justice system can control or modify) on accuracy.
- the degree of consensus among psychologists about the research findings.
- research on whether laypersons know what psychologists know about eyewitness fallibility.
- how information about eyewitness accuracy may be introduced in court.
- recommendations for changes in police procedures to minimize errors in eyewitness identification.

Miscarriages of Justice

Rates of Erroneous Convictions

Even though our system of justice is designed to guard against convictions of the innocent, **wrongful convictions** undoubtedly occur. Cutler and Penrod (1995) estimate that approximately 7,500 persons are wrongfully convicted each year. Research suggests that around half of wrongful convictions occur because of mistaken eyewitness identification. Surprisingly, another important reason for a wrongful conviction is a false confession.

Looking through databases, including books, court documents, and newspapers, Rattner (1988) identified 205 cases in which a person had been convicted of a felony, the conviction was overturned, and the errors were acknowledged officially. The convictions were overturned because the convicted person had not committed the crime, rather than because of "legal technicalities." About 90 percent of the wrongly convicted defendants had been imprisoned, over a third of these under life sentences, and about 10 percent had been sentenced to death. It was fortuitous that the twenty-one on death row were still alive when exonerated. More than half (52 percent) of Rattner's cases of wrongful convictions were accounted for by eyewitness misidentification. Coerced confessions were another important source of error. Perjury by witnesses, errors by prosecutors, "frameups," and forensic science errors accounted for the rest.

Wells (1993) cites literature describing 1,000 cases of wrongful conviction reported before 1986; half of these wrongful convictions were accounted for by eyewitness error. Some were due to false confessions. Costanzo (1997) estimates that about a dozen people a year are executed for crimes they did not commit; many of these cases involve faulty eyewitness identification. (See also Scheck, Neufeld, and Dwyer, 2000, for a discussion of eyewitness errors and other flaws in the criminal justice system that lead to wrongful convictions.)

DNA tests are increasingly used to exonerate wrongly convicted prisoners. Their use depends on the availability of appropriate biological samples (e.g., blood, semen, and skin scrapings). Wells et al. (1998) reported 40 cases of convicted persons who were exonerated later when DNA evidence showed conclusively that the defendant did not commit the crime. Of these 40 cases of wrongful conviction (most involving rape or some other sexual assault), 36 (or 90 percent) involved eyewitness identification. Most identifications were made by the victim, and sometimes more than one victim made the identification. In other cases, the defendant was incorrectly identified by non-victim witnesses, or a victim identification was confirmed by other eyewitnesses. Scheck, Neufeld, and Dwyer (2000) describe other defendants on death row who were convicted based on faulty eyewitness testimony and later were exonerated by DNA evidence. The eyewitnesses in these cases were sincere, but they were mistaken.

It is very difficult to estimate the rate of false confessions in a population of suspects who have confessed, because we can't reliably distinguish between false and true confessions (Drizin and Leo, 2004; Kassin, 2005; Kassin, Meissner, and Norwick, 2005). Nevertheless, researchers are certain that false confessions occur and lead to unjust convictions (Drizin and Leo, 2004; Kassin, 2005).

False Confessions

False confession is a common cause of miscarriage of justice. Kassin (2005) reported that 15 to 25 percent of those who were exonerated by DNA evidence had confessed before their trials. Drizin and Leo (2004) identified 125 cases where defendants who were factually innocent nevertheless confessed to a crime. In what follows, we rely on the accounts of these researchers. In these cases, there was indisputable evidence that the defendant who confessed was innocent: for example, he or she was in prison at the time the crime was committed, or, more commonly DNA evidence proved they could not have been the perpetrator.

Drizin and Leo (2004) cited several other studies of wrongful conviction. These were all persons who were convicted of crimes, but later proven innocent of the crime

162

CHAPTER 6
Miscarriages
of Justice: False
Confessions
and Eyewitness
Error

FIGURE 6.1

DNA "Fingerprints"

Noted criminologist Dr. Henry Lee is examining a DNA record that is in Connecticut's database of known criminals and that can be used to identify suspects in crimes when there is biological evidence.

to which they had confessed. In these samples, between 14 and 25 percent of the erroneous convictions were attributable to false confessions. Many of the false confessions were due to coercive interrogation techniques employed by the police. Drizin and Leo (2004) found that most who confessed falsely were interrogated for more than 6 hours. The median length of interrogation was 12 hours. In a few instances, several people confessed falsely to the same crime. Suspects falsely confessed to murder (81 percent of the false confessions were to murders), rape, and arson, all serious crimes, and all crimes that police are especially motivated to solve.

All who confessed falsely were detained for some period of time even when charges were dropped before trial. Of those who were convicted after confessing falsely (35 percent of their 125 cases), the median length of sentence was more than 20 years, and 20 percent were sentenced to death. Those convicted served a median of 6 to 10 years in prison. An additional consequence of a false confession is the implication that other innocent defendants were arrested and charged based on the false confession. Drizzin and Leo (2004) report a few instances where suspects confessed to murders that later proved to be the work of a serial killer, taking investigative attention away from the true perpetrator.

Interrogation Methods

Today's police interrogation techniques employ psychologically powerful manipulations, rather than physically coercive "third-degree" tactics. These psychological manipulations can induce people who have not been subject to physical torture to confess falsely to crimes they did not commit.

Kassin (1997, 2005) summarized evidence from his own studies and from studies of others about how police interrogation techniques work. Even before the formal interrogation, suspects are interviewed. During these interviews, police form strong impressions based on both verbal and nonverbal cues of the suspect's guilt. Based on laboratory studies, reliance on such cues is of questionable validity for detecting guilt or even lying. Nonetheless, whether the suspect is moved into the next stage of interrogation depends on the impressions police form in the preliminary stage (Kassin, 2005). Miranda rights (e.g., not to speak without an attorney present) offer questionable protection because most defendants waive their rights. That is especially true for juveniles or those with mental retardation. Strangely enough, based on laboratory studies, a higher percent of those who are "innocent" than those who are "guilty" waive their Miranda rights. Thus, a number of those who are innocent are interrogated by police (Kassin, 2005).

The police tend to presume defendants are guilty (Kassin, 2005). The first purpose of interrogation is to obtain a confession. Suspects are confronted by formidable authority figures in situations that "promote isolation, fear, powerlessness, and hopelessness" (Drizin and Leo, 2004, p. 910). Interrogators attack alibis and refuse to listen to denials. Suspects may be confronted with "evidence" that tends to incriminate them. The "evidence" may be true or false. Police interrogators are permitted by law to use deceptive or false information (e.g., "Your friend already confessed and said you did it," when the friend in actuality had made no statement) to encourage a defendant or suspect to confess. The police may also tell the suspect or defendant that he or she is really not morally culpable. "You didn't really mean to do it. It was an accident." Suspects may be given incentives to confess: "It will go easier for you if you confess" or "If you confess, you will feel better."

These interrogation techniques are designed to use social influence processes to "overcome a suspect's resistance, manipulate his perceptions and reasoning, and ultimately move him from denial (which is in his self-interest, whether he is guilty or innocent) to admission (which is always against his self-interest)" (Drizin and Leo, 2004, p. 911). Police have very little ability to detect false confessions (Kassin, 2005; Kassin, Meissner, and Norwick, 2005). The power of confessions is amplified by features of the criminal justice system. Confessions are weighted heavily by juries, and prosecutors are less inclined to plea-bargain. Defense attorneys, believing they are acting in their client's interests, may encourage the client to plead guilty to avoid a trial. Suspects who may be facing the death penalty may confess and plead guilty to a lesser offense to avoid the possiblity of a death sentence. Once convicted by his or her own words, the defendant faces an uphill battle to have mistakes rectified by the criminal justice system.

Groups Vulnerable to False Confessions

Drizin and Leo (2004) reported that juveniles, especially those under age 15, may be particularly susceptible to police pressure to make false confessions. Drizin and Leo identified 7 children under the age of 14 who confessed falsely. They describe the case of the Central Park jogger, who in 1989 was assaulted by several adolescents between the ages of 13 and 16. All confessed and were convicted (Kassin, 2005). A dozen years later, DNA evidence showed that another man committed the crime. The youths, who falsely confessed under interrogation by the police, were exonerated and released after having spent several years in prison. In addition to the Central Park jogger children, those with mental retardation were well represented in Drizen and Leo's population of cases (22 percent). About 10 percent of those who confessed falsely were mentally ill.

164

CHAPTER 6
Miscarriages
of Justice: False
Confessions
and Eyewitness
Error

Admissibility of Expert Testimony

A body of knowledge about false confessions has accumulated over a 100-year period using generally accepted scientific methods. The fact that false confessions occur has been established. (Drizin and Leo, 2004; Kassin, 2005; Kassin, Meissner, and Norwick, 2005).

The existence of a research base may make it possible for expert witnesses to be admitted to testify in trials where false or coerced confessions may be at issue. Some courts believe expert witnesses have much to offer (*United States v. Hall*, 1996). However, other courts are skeptical and have excluded expert testimony because the court believed the expert's testimony could not pass muster under *Daubert* standards (Pennsylvania Discovery and Evidence Reporter, 2004). In some cases, the expert may be limited to testifying about the defendant's mental capacity and its effect given the circumstances surrounding the confession. The expert may not be allowed to offer an opinion as to whether the confession is false because that is the province of the jury to decide (*Jackson v. Commonwealth of Virginia*, 2003). As the body of knowledge grows, more courts may be disposed to admit the expert testimony, especially if the court can be convinced that the expert will provide knowledge that goes beyond what a lay juror probably already knows.

Recommended Policy Changes

Police often start with "confirmation biases" (looking for information to confirm the belief they hold) and need to learn to suspend those biases. Once obtaining a confession, police cannot detect true from false confessions (Kassin, Meissner, and Norwick, 2005). Drizin and Leo (2004) also recommend that police be better educated about the risks of false confessions and trained to suspend their intuitive beliefs that a particular suspect must be guilty. They suggest that police should be taught to analyze what the suspect says to see whether the suspect's confession fits with the known details of the crime. Moreover, they should receive special training in interrogating juveniles and those who may suffer from mental retardation. Prosecutors and judges should receive similar training in understanding issues related to false confessions. Drizin and Leo (2004) also recommend procedural changes to protect against false convictions. They believe that the number of false confessions could be reduced if police were required to videotape the entire interrogation of suspects. (A number of states now require videotaped interrogations as does Great Britain.) They suggest that each confession should be thoroughly reviewed by an independent supervisor.

Eyewitness Testimony: The Legal Context

Eyewitness testimony, whether by victim or by bystanders, is of critical importance in the legal system. The statement "That's him—I am sure of it," can lead to the arrest, indictment, and conviction of the accused person. Mock jurors will vote guilty twice as often on the same facts when a credible eyewitness identifies the defendant than when there is no eyewitness testimony (Cutler and Penrod, 1995). Unfortunately, errors in perception or memory sometimes lead to mistaken identification and inaccurate **reconstruction of events**. The result can be a wrongful conviction.

Psychologists have studied memory and perception for over 100 years (e.g., see Muensterberg, 1923; Poffenberger, 1942; Whipple, 1909, 1918). This research has been the foundation for careful investigations into factors influencing the accuracy of eye-witness identifications. The courts have acknowledged the fallibility of eyewitnesses, but have been reluctant, historically, to admit expert testimony about the issue.

Potential Unreliability of a Single Eyewitness

The potential unreliability of a single eyewitness was recognized in the Old Testament: "A single witness may not validate against a person any guilt or blame for any offense that may be committed; a case can be valid only on the testimony of two witnesses or more" (Deuteronomy 19:15). In ancient times, the two-witness rule may have been followed primarily when death was the penalty for the offense. Under the U.S. Constitution, a conviction for treason also requires "the Testimony of two Witnesses to the same overt Act" (Article III, Section 3). With that exception, Anglo-American jurisprudence does not follow the two-witness rule because many crimes are solitary in nature. However, the courts have long recognized that eyewitness testimony may not always be accurate (see *United States v. Wade*, 1967). Our system relies on due process safeguards and cross-examination to protect defendants. It is the judge's job to ensure that the defendant receives fundamentally fair treatment (due process). One way judges ensure fair treatment is by excluding unreliable or prejudicial evidence. The courts have developed some standards to assess when an eyewitness identification may be unreliable. Judges may give jurors some instruction on aspects of eyewitness testimony. Courts are sometimes asked by parties to allow experts to testify to alert juries to the limitations of eyewitness testimony.

Excluding Eyewitnesses: The Totality of Circumstances

A mistaken eyewitness identification may be caused by limitations of the witness's perception and processing of information (Wells and Olson, 2003, call these **estimator variables**), or by factors under control of the justice system, including the police methods for obtaining identifications from witnesses (Wells and Olson, 2003, call these **system variables**). The courts have been reluctant to exclude evidence because of an "irreparable mistaken identification" unless the police procedures used with the witnesses to obtain an identification were "impermissibly suggestive." *Impermissively suggestive* is defined circularly as sufficiently biased to warrant overturning a conviction on appeal (*United States v. Wade*, 1967).

There is no list of impermissively suggestive procedures. Moreover, even if some possibly prejudicial or suggestive procedures are used, the trial judge may still decide to admit the testimony. Trial judges look to the "totality of circumstances" when deciding whether eyewitness identification is sufficiently reliable to go to a jury.

In **Neil v. Biggers** (1972), the Supreme Court summarized the factors to be considered by a judge as part of the "totality of the circumstances." The Court said factors to be considered in evaluating the likelihood of misidentification include

> the opportunity of the witness to view the criminal at the time of the crime, the witness' degree of attention, the accuracy of the witness' prior description of the criminal, the level of certainty demonstrated by the witness at the confrontation and the length of time between the crime and the confrontation.

The U.S. Supreme Court confirmed this standard in subsequent cases (e.g., *Manson v. Braithwaite*, 1977). Psychologists agree with the general criteria, except for one: research suggests that eyewitness's certainty is a modest index of accuracy.

166

CHAPTER 6
Miscarriages
of Justice: False
Confessions
and Eyewitness
Error

Excluding Expert Testimony about Eyewitness Accuracy

When prosecution eyewitness testimony is admitted (usually it is for the prosecution), it is up to the jury to decide how to weigh the testimony. The other party (usually the defendant) can raise the question of faulty identification during the trial. In addition to cross-examining eyewitnesses, defense lawyers sometimes ask psychologists to testify about eyewitness fallibility. Psychologists are rarely asked to testify for the prosecution (Kassin et al., 2001). However, just as the defense can argue that the judge should exclude the eyewitness's testimony, so the prosecution can ask the judge to exercise discretion (*People v. Lee,* 2001) and to refuse to allow an expert to testify about the unreliability of eyewitness identification. Judges frequently do so (Faigman et al., 2005). Judges have excluded the testimony because they believe it will not be useful to the jurors or will make the trial less fair. They make these decisions on the basis of criteria taken from the rules of evidence. The criteria used to make these decisions are reviewed in Box 6.1. Appeals courts have rarely overturned a trial court's decision to exclude expert testimony about eyewitness issues.

Sometimes expert testimony on eyewitness issues is permitted, however. Cutler and Penrod (1995) estimate that psychologist–experts have testified in hundreds of trials at the time they wrote. Psychologists may testify in cases when neither side objects. When the primary evidence against a defendant is eyewitness testimony supported by little else, courts are more open to receiving expert testimony despite the prosecution's objections (Faigman et al., 2005). For example, the trial judge in *People v. Radcliffe* (2003) admitted testimony about cross-racial bias in eyewitness identification. The New York court agreed there was a body of scientific evidence on point and cited Kassin et al.'s survey (2001) to the effect that there is general acceptance of eyewitness research on cross-racial bias. (Despite the expert's testimony, Radcliffe was convicted on the basis of the eyewitness identification; see *People v. Radcliffe,* 2005.)

In the next section, we will examine some of the substantive research on eyewitness testimony and explain why most psychologists believe that expert testimony in this area can be helpful to jurors. We will organize the material to address legal criteria for admissibility of expert testimony. You may want to refer back to Box 6.1 as you read.

⊠ Is There Sufficient Good Science to Support Eyewitness Testimony?

One of the questions courts ask in considering the admissibility of expert testimony is whether the testimony is based on sound science. Research into eyewitness testimony is grounded in basic theories about the mechanisms of memory and perception built on a body of "pure" laboratory research more than a century old. For example, Schacter (1999) discusses what he calls the "seven sins of memory," well-established psychological phenomena that can lead to false or distorted memories. The findings of some psychological experiments have been validated by neurophysiological studies. The techniques of functional magnetic resonance imaging (fMRI) and positron-emission tomography (PET) scans have revealed local changes in neural activity in the brain that correlate with some of these phenomena.

167

Is There
Sufficient
Good Science
to Support
Eyewitness
Testimony?

BOX 6.1

Criteria for Admissibility of Expert Testimony

Helpfulness

Rule 702 of the Federal Rules of Evidence allows for the admission of expert witness testimony, if it would be helpful to the fact-finder (jury). *Helpful* in this context means that the testimony will tell lay jurors something they do not already know that will contribute to their evaluation of the evidence.

Good Science

Under the *Daubert, Kumho Tire Co.,* and *Joiner* decisions, and Rule 702 of the Federal Rules of Evidence, federal judges, and judges in states that follow the Federal Rules of Evidence, are instructed to examine the underlying science carefully when considering whether to admit expert testimony. They are to consider the soundness of the research design, methods, and error rates with different procedures. The mission is to exclude "junk science" from the courts (see Chapter 2).

Consensus in the Field

In addition to examining the quality of the underlying science, following *Daubert* criteria, courts look to see if there is consensus in the expert's field on methods, theory, and findings in the area of the testimony.

Ecological Validity and "Fit"

The science has to be relevant as well as sound. Under *Daubert* and subsequent cases, courts look at how well the underlying research "fits" with the issues in the particular trial (*U.S. v. Downing,* 1985). For example, the court must decide if laboratory experiments are "ecologically valid," that is, whether they apply to real-world situations. Then they must look at the specifics. To what degree do the conditions in the eyewitness research (e.g., stressfulness of the experience, or length of time witness observed the perpetrator) on which the testimony would be based match the conditions under which the eyewitness made the identification in the case on trial?

Basic Science Underlying Research on Eyewitness Identifications

Basic concepts that have emerged from memory research and are relevant to considerations of eyewitness testimony include encoding and encoding errors, memory trace changes, effects of postevent questioning on memory traces, and memory as a reconstruction.

Encoding. If a perception is to be recalled, the perceiver must attend to the "stimulus" event or person and interpret or encode it appropriately (Schacter, 1999). Encoding involves recognition of key features. Laboratory experiments have demonstrated that, when subjects don't attend carefully to the stimulus, or when they are distracted and concentrate on something else, they perceive and encode less information about the stimulus (Schacter, 1999). Sometimes only fragments of the experience are encoded. For example, subjects will remember more letters if shown a field of same-size black letters than if shown the same field but with one large red letter in it. The red letter is a

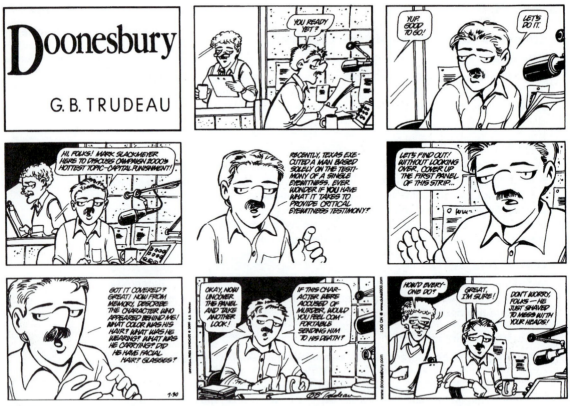

FIGURE 6.2

This Doonesbury *cartoon illustrates some problems in eyewitness identification.*

distracter. Eyewitness researchers have demonstrated that weapons have a powerful distracter effect (**weapon focus effect;** Steblay, 1992; Wells and Olson, 2003). If the perpetrator is holding a knife or gun, the witness's attention is drawn to the weapon and he or she encodes fewer details of the person's face.

Race can also affect encoding of information about people. If the perceiver is of one race, he or she is likely to attend to and encode fewer subtle facial features if the perpetrator is a member of a different race than if the perpetrator and victim are of the same race (Malpass and Kravitz, 1969). As a result, **cross-racial identification**s are 1.56 times more likely to be incorrect than within-race identifications. This relationship holds across many studies and many research procedures. The effect size is modest, but robust (Meissner and Brigham, 2001). It also held in studies conducted in England and in South Africa (Wright, Boyd, and Tredoux, 2001) (See Box 6.2).

Memories change with time and reconstruction. Encoded perceptions are stored in memory. Psychologists theorize that **stored memories** change over time. Some of what was stored may "fade" and be forgotten. The memories may also undergo transformations. Memories for events and for people can be strongly influenced by what happened between the time the event was encoded and the time the person was asked to retrieve or recall the memory (see Chapter 11).

Lay Knowledge of Research on Eyewitness Accuracy

Two women were walking to school one morning, one of them Asian and the other white. Suddenly, two men, one black and one white, jumped into their path and attempted to grab their purses. Later the women were shown photographs of known purse snatchers in the area. Which statement best describes the women's ability to identify the purse snatchers?

1. Both the Asian and the white woman will find the white man harder to identify than the black man.
2. The white woman will find the black man more difficult to identify than the white man.
3. The Asian woman will have an easier time than the white woman in making an accurate identification of both men.
4. The white woman will find the black man easier to identify than the white man.

   The correct answer is 2.

Source: Reprinted by permission of the publisher from *Eyewitness Testimony* by Elizabeth F. Loftus, Cambridge, Mass.: Harvard University Press, Copyright (c) 1979, 1996, by the President and Fellows of Harvard College.

They can also be changed in the course of the retrieval process itself. In fact, modern psychologists believe that memory is as much a matter of "reconstruction" as it is of faithful recall. Memories may consist of bits and pieces or strands of remembered experiences that are put together to make up a memory in a way that makes sense to the person remembering. The reconstruction may be affected by many factors, including the situation or conditions under which the memory is recalled. Loftus (1979), for example, has shown how information provided during **postevent questioning** can become part of the eyewitness's memory of an event.

Eyewitness Research Paradigms

Psychologists have been testing the applicability of these well-established principles of memory and perception to eyewitness accounts of crime for many years. Their assertion that they can offer expert testimony in court grounded in scientifically sound knowledge is based on this body of research.

Much of what psychologists know about eyewitness phenomena was learned from laboratory experiments that have used a consistent **research paradigm** since the 1930s (Poffenberger, 1942). The experimenters stage a "crime" in front of an audience of subjects. A favorite scenario is to have the culprit enter a room and "steal" something of value from a desk. Usually the eyewitnesses see the culprit for only a brief period of time. Shortly after the event is staged, or a few weeks later, the researchers ask the eyewitnesses to select the person who committed the crime from a photo array or, sometimes, from a lineup. Some experimenters use a film of a crime or a series of slides as the stimulus rather than a live enactment.

170

CHAPTER 6
Miscarriages
of Justice: False
Confessions
and Eyewitness
Error

The experiments are usually very carefully designed. The researchers often use a large number of subjects randomly assigned to experimental and control conditions. Most experiments have used college student subjects, but many have recruited jury-eligible subjects from the community.

This field has advanced because the paradigm is basically straightforward. The dependent variable, *accurate identification,* is simple and meaningful for the applied problem. Because the perpetrator is known in each case, there is a "gold standard" for accuracy.

Research using this paradigm has yielded some consistent results across experimental variations and over time (Cutler and Penrod, 1995; Wells and Olson, 2003). This consistency enhances the claim that expert testimony should be admitted in court. Two areas where research findings have been consistent are in the relationship of eyewitness accuracy to police lineup methods and to eyewitness confidence. This work has important implications for understanding the limits of eyewitness testimony and for improving the methods that law enforcement officials use to obtain eyewitness identifications.

 ## The Lineup

Researchers have studied the important question of how factors under control of the justice system (system variables), including the methods used by law enforcement officers and prosecutors, may affect memory construction and contribute to faulty identification.

One important system variable is how the police or other investigators elicit eyewitness identifications. They generally do this by asking the witness if he or she can find the perpetrator in a lineup or show up. In a **lineup,** the criminal suspect is placed among a group of other people to see if the witness can make the identification. The police may also use a lineup made up of photographs. (In a **show up,** the witness is exposed to only one suspect.) The lineup may or may not include the culprit. The witness may be told the suspect is present or maybe told that the suspect is not necessarily among the people being presented. The lineup may be simultaneous, or sequential. In a sequential lineup the witness sees one suspect at a time and selects the one he or she believes is the culprit). Experimenters have used these procedures in simulations. In experiments, the "culprit" is known. The simulated lineups may by design include or exclude him or her. The methods of obtaining the identification of the culprit are varied to see if they affect eyewitness accuracy.

Researchers have found that eyewitnesses have a tendency to pick out the person in a lineup who most resembles their own verbal description of the criminal. For example, if the witness previously said the crime was committed by a tall blond man and there is a tall blond man in the lineup, the eyewitness is more likely to identify him whether or not the identification is correct.

A lineup can consist of any number of people, usually 3–5 in addition to the suspect. The functional size of a lineup is the more important number, however; it is the number of foils who are reasonable choices (Wells and Olson, 2003). It is obviously unfair to put one blond man in a lineup with four dark-haired men if the eyewitness has said the perpetrator was a blond. The functional size would be 1 in that case. Standard police procedure is to use foils, all of whom fit the eyewitness's verbal description. But, even though the use of foils seems fair, in experiments the procedure results in a high rate of misidentifications, especially when the culprit is not present in the lineup.

Eyewitnesses appear to want to identify someone. Police instructions can intensify this impulse by seeming to imply that the situation demands an identification. When the "perpetrator" is present in the lineup and instructions are biased (subjects are told, or it is implied, that the suspect is present in the lineup), correct identifications vary from 40 percent to 75 percent in different studies. The eyewitnesses do much better than chance in identifying the culprit, but they still make many errors of identification.

Even when there is no "guilty" person in the lineup at all, eyewitnesses often identify someone. They may expect one of the persons in the lineup to be the criminal. The eyewitnesses may feel they must make an identification to please the police or to satisfy their desire to find the criminal. When the "perpetrator" is not present in the lineup, and instructions are biased toward selecting a culprit, the **false identification** rate varies from 37 percent to 90 percent (Cutler and Penrod, 1995; Wells and Seelau, 1995; Wells et al., 1998). In the *perpetrator absent* condition, with instructions saying the culprit may or may not be present, the average misidentification rate over a large set of studies is reduced from 60 percent to 35 percent. Accuracy of identification rate is not affected when the culprit is actually present (Steblay, 1997). Based on the research, the U.S. Department of Justice recommended using an instruction to the effect that the "culprit" may or may not be present to reduce mistaken identification rates when the culprit is not present (Wells and Olson, 2003).

Another system variable affecting the accuracy of eyewitness identification is whether the lineup is simultaneous, with all foils and the suspect presented together. In theory, the eyewitness then selects the person who looks most like the person the eyewitness believes he or she saw at the scene of the crime. The alternative is to present the lineup sequentially. The eyewitness is shown only one person at a time. This procedure requires the eyewitness to make an "absolute" judgment. Is this the person or not? If the eyewitness says, "No," he or she is shown the next picture. If the eyewitness says, "Yes," the procedure may end there.

Steblay et al. (2001) reported a meta-analysis of 23 studies comparing **simultaneous lineups** with **sequential lineups.** Some studies were unpublished. The aim of a meta-analysis is to include all data, including those studies called *file drawer studies* that were never published. In theory, file drawer studies may have not been published because they had weak or negative results. Omitting potentially negative results would bias the meta-analysis.

The meta-analysis permitted the investigators to compare accuracy in *simultaneous* and *sequential* lineups when the suspect was present and when the suspect was absent from the lineup. When the suspect was present, in the *simultaneous* lineup, the correct identification was made 50 percent of the time. The correct identification was made only 35 percent of the time in the *sequential* lineup with the suspect present. When the suspect is absent, the correct response is to reject all foils. In the *sequential* lineup, all the foils were correctly rejected 72 percent of the time. In the *simultaneous* lineup, the whole array was rejected only 49 percent of the time. Most important, the *sequential* lineup resulted in fewer false identifications (28 percent) compared to the *simultaneous* lineup, where the false identification rate was 51 percent. The authors conclude that in most situations, "sequential lineups are superior" (Steblay et al., 2001, p. 471). A large scale field study comparing sequential with simultaneous lineups failed to demonstrate the superiority of the sequential procedure (Zernike, 2006). Using a traditional lineup, witnesses chose a suspect 60 percent of the time, chose an known innocent person 3 percent of the time, and failed to make a choice 37 percent of the time. With the sequential, doubleblind lineup, the witness chose a suspect 45 percent of the time, chose a known

172

CHAPTER 6
Miscarriages
of Justice: False
Confessions
and Eyewitness
Error

innocent person 9 percent of the time, and made no choice 46 percent of the time. In traditional lineups, witnesses were more likely to choose a suspect, and less likely to choose an innocent person. Supporters of the sequential method say that the study was flawed because the officers in the traditional lineup were not blind to who was the suspect and could have influenced witnesses. However, the study raised questions about the degree to which we can generalize from laboratory studies to field situations.

Eyewitness Confidence

People believe that there is a strong relationship between an eyewitness's **confidence** in his or her identification and its accuracy. The U.S. Supreme Court in *Neil v. Biggers* (1972) said that "the level of certainty demonstrated by the witness at the confrontation" was one of the elements to be weighed by courts when deciding whether or not to admit eyewitness testimony. And when an eyewitness testifies confidently in court, jurors are more likely to find the testimony persuasive. The experimental evidence is fairly strong that mock jurors believe and will convict on the testimony of a confident eyewitness (Wells, Lindsay, and Ferguson, 1979).

Confidence Is Modestly Related to Accuracy

Researchers have used the eyewitness paradigm to study eyewitness confidence. Subjects asked to identify the person who committed a simulated crime are also asked how confident they are about the identification. Because the "culprit" is known, the researcher knows whether or not the identification is correct. The eyewitness–subject's confidence in an identification has a positive relationship to actual accuracy, but a modest one. Sporer et al.'s (1995) meta-analysis of 35 similar studies found an average correlation of 0.28 between a witness's statement of confidence in the identification and its accuracy. Using confidence as a "predictor" variable in a regression with the 0.28 coefficient yields a 67.5 percent rate of correct classification of accurate and inaccurate eyewitness identifications. That means that people who express a great deal of confidence are somewhat more likely to be right than those who don't express a great deal of confidence; nonetheless, they make many false identifications. The speed with which an eyewitness identifies a suspect may be a better predictor of accuracy than a witness' judgment of confidence in the identification (Wells and Olson, 2003).

Police are well aware that confident eyewitnesses sometimes select the wrong person; in fact, eyewitnesses sometimes identify a policeman included in the lineup as a foil as the criminal. From a practical point of view, a false identification of a nonsuspect is not a problem: the police know the eyewitness is wrong. However, if the eyewitness confidently identifies the person the police suspect, the prosecution is likely to proceed. A number of such confident identifications will be wrong and may result in wrongful convictions, especially when eyewitness identification is the primary evidence against the defendant.

The modest relationship between confidence and accuracy also means that eyewitness subjects who are less confident in their identifications are sometimes correct (Penrod and Cutler, 1995). However, police are less likely to follow up on uncertain identifications. Prosecutors are unlikely to ask eyewitnesses who are uncertain to testify, believing they will not make good witnesses.

Because confidence makes eyewitnesses more credible to jurors, it is important to ask if confidence can be manipulated (this makes it a system variable). Such a manipulation might destroy the modest degree of validity that confidence has as a predictor of accuracy. Wells and colleagues (1998) reviewed experimental studies of the malleability of eyewitness confidence. The research indicated that eyewitness confidence is highly malleable and that systems variables can affect it. For example, eyewitnesses may be asked to identify a suspect, especially one the police believe was the perpetrator, many times, and they will be asked repeated questions. Each time they make the identification, the witnesses may become more confident. By the time of trial, they may have become committed to the identification. They may assert confidence even more strongly in response to defense attorney challenges.

The reviewers concluded that "high confidence does not necessarily denote high accuracy and that high levels of confidence can come from external sources" (Wells et al., 1998, p. 626). It is important, then, for law enforcement to avoid using procedures with eyewitnesses that may bias the identification or increase the eyewitness's confidence in an incorrect identification (see Technical Working Group for Eyewitness Evidence, 1999).

Ecological Validity

Judges considering the admission of expert testimony need to determine whether the research underlying the testimony demonstrates **ecological validity.** In *Daubert* terms, is the proferred expert testimony a "fit" with the circumstances of the case? Will the research findings hold in real-life situations? It is not a far reach to go from the identification of the actor–perpetrator in an experiment to the perpetrator of a crime. The task is the same: to identify a person accurately. However, "real-life" circumstances could affect people's performance of the task. There are limits to how well simulations or field studies can recreate real-world experiences. For example, stress and level of emotional arousal can affect cognitive performance. Very high stress and very low stress are both related to poorer performance on laboratory tasks (according to the Yerkes–Dodson law, which holds that stress is related to performance in an inverted U function—moderate stress levels equal best performance, while high stress levels equal poorer performance). To add realism, to create high stress, and induce emotions in subject eyewitnesses, some researchers have used violent or bloody films of crimes as the stimulus. But the stressfulness of a film or any other experience in a laboratory can't readily be compared to the stressfulness of experiencing an actual crime. So far, cases on admissiblity do not seem to have turned on the issue of ecological validity.

Consensus in the Field

Consensus in the field is an important legal standard used by judges considering whether to admit an expert's testimony. Is there sufficient professional consensus about scientific findings related to eyewitness accuracy to meet the legal standard for admissibility?

174

CHAPTER 6
Miscarriages
of Justice: False
Confessions
and Eyewitness
Error

Leading eyewitness researchers (see Cutler and Penrod, 1995; Wells, 1993, 1997; Wells and Olson, 2003) point to the extensive peer-reviewed literature to support the argument that there is a body of robust scientific knowledge on which to base expert opinions. The research on eyewitness testimony is extensive, but not all of the findings are equally well established.

One way of determining consensus is to assess the degree to which researchers in the field accept specific findings. Assessments of this kind give a judge considering admissibility of eyewitness expert testimony a basis for evaluating the degree of consensus about findings relevant to the specific case (see *People v. Radcliffe*, 2003).

Kassin and colleagues (Kassin, Ellsworth, and Smith, 1989; Kassin, Hosch, and Memon, 2001) twice surveyed researchers and expert witnesses to determine what findings they believe have strong empirical support. This research was undertaken to bolster expert testimony, not because of a theoretical interest in the answers. Kassin and his colleagues found substantial agreement about the reliability of a number of findings, indicating that research in these areas is sufficiently strong to warrant confident expert testimony. On some phenomena that may be unfamiliar to lay jurors (e.g., the accuracy–confidence relationship) and on which experts agree, expert testimony can help jurors to come to better decisions. In *United States v. Lester* (2003), after a *Daubert* hearing on admissibility, the judge allowed an expert to testify about the limited relationship between accuracy of an eyewitness identification and the witness' confidence in making the identification (see Table 6.1 for a good overview of the types of issues psychologists have studied).

Judges tend to be skeptical about the admission of expert testimony on eyewitness identification. An expert may have to be prepared to answer detailed questions about the underlying research, its relevance to the facts in the case, and whether the effect of the factors in question reasonably can be quantified for the jury to evaluate (e.g., there is a 10 percent greater error rate in cross-racial identifications than in same-race identifications) (*United States v. Lester,* 2003).

Will Expert Testimony Be Helpful to Jurors?

Judges give juries standard pattern sets of instructions about evidentiary issues, including information on how to weigh eyewitness evidence. These instructions are theoretically based on an appreciation of what lay jurors know and understand (*United States v. Lester,* 2003). Many important psychological findings, including information about the confidence–accuracy relationship and the cross-race bias, are not generally included in these instructions. One of the parties, usually the defense, can ask the judge to permit an expert to testify on these or other issues.

The rules of evidence allow the judge to exclude expert testimony when he or she doesn't think it will be helpful to jurors. To be helpful, the expert must be able to give the jury information that goes beyond what the jurors as laypeople already know. Some judges have excluded expert testimony about eyewitness reliability because they believe that the research findings merely confirm the "commonsense" understanding that eyewitnesses can make mistakes. Decisions to exclude eyewitness experts have been upheld on appeal because this decision is a matter within the trial court's discretion. One court may be influenced by the fact that the proferred expert testimony addresses issues not usually covered in pattern sets of instructions that judges use to inform jurors

Table 6.1

Consensus Among Eyewitness Experts on whether Research Supports the Reliability of Findings

Topic	% Experts Agreeing on Reliability of Findings	
	1989 Survey	2001 Survey
Wording of questions (testimony affected by how questions are worded)	96.8	98
Lineup instructions (police instructions affect willingness or likelihood of witness to make an identification)	95.1	98
Postevent information (eyewitness testimony reflects what the witness learned after the event)	87.1	94
Accuracy and confidence (eyewitness confidence not a good predictor of accuracy of identification)	87.1	87
Attitudes and expectations (perception or memory for an event is affected by attitudes and expectations)	86.9	92
Exposure time (the less time to observe, the less well an event is remembered)	84.7	81
Unconscious transference (an eyewitness can identify as the culprit someone the eyewitness saw in a different place or context)	84.5	81
Show ups (one-person show up instead of full lineup increases chances of misidentification)	83.1	74
Forgetting curve (rate of forgetting greatest right after event, and levels off over time)	82.5	83
Cross-racial/white (white eyewitnesses identify other whites better than they identify blacks)	79.4	?
Lineup fairness (identification more likely accurate if more members of the lineup resemble the suspect)	77.2	70
Time estimation (duration of events tends to be overestimated)	74.5	?
Stress (very high levels of stress during the event impair eyewitness accuracy)	70.5	60
Hypnotic suggestibility (hypnosis increases suggestibility to leading and misleading questions)	68.5	91
Color perception (color judgments made under monochromatic light [e.g., orange streetlight] are highly unreliable)	65.7	63
Trained observers (police officers are no more accurate eyewitnesses than the average person)	58.7	61
Weapon focus (presence of a weapon impairs eyewitness's ability to accurately identify perpetrator's face)	56.5	87
Hypnotic retrieval (hypnosis does not facilitate retrieval of eyewitness's memory)	51.9	?

Continued to next page

176

CHAPTER 6
Miscarriages
of Justice: False
Confessions
and Eyewitness
Error

Table 6.1 (continued)

Consensus Among Eyewitness Experts on whether Research Supports the Reliability of Findings

Topic	% Experts Agreeing on Reliability of Findings	
	1989 Survey	2001 Survey
Cross-racial/black (black eyewitnesses are better at identifying other blacks than they are at identifying whites)	48.3	?
Event violence (eyewitnesses have more difficulty remembering violent than nonviolent events)	36.0	37
Sex differences (women are better than men at recognizing faces)	11.1	?
New Items Not Included in Earlier Survey		
Cross-race bias		83
Hypnotic accuracy		0
Alcohol intoxication		61.9
Mugshot-induced bias		79.4
Long-term repression		14.5
False childhood memories		46.9
Discriminability		4.7
Child accuracy		43.8
Child suggestiblity		76.6
Description matched lineup		40.3
Presentation format		64.5
Elderly witnesses		23.8
Identification speed		20.6

From S. M. Kassin, P. C. Ellsworth, and V. L. Smith, 1989 "The 'general acceptance' of psychological research on eyewitness testimony: A survey of the experts," *American Psychologist*, 44, 1089–1098; Table 4, adapted from 1094. Copyright © 1989 by the American Psychological Association. Adapted with permission. The second figure is from the 2001 survey as reported in Kassin et al., 2001, Table 5, 413. Items with a question mark were apparently not repeated in the later survey.

on how to weigh eyewitness evidence. Another court may assume that the years of judicial experience going into forming standard instructions to juries about evidentiary issues are based on an appreciation of what lay jurors know and understand (*United States v. Lester*, 2003), while another court might conclude that the expert testimony will help jurors in a particular case beyond what the instructions provide.

Presenting Research Findings in Court

Let's assume the judge agrees that the jury will make a better decision if it is given information about specific aspects of eyewitness fallibility. What kind of testimony should the expert offer?

It is the jury's job to decide whether to believe the identification of the defendant by the eyewitness. If an expert testifies directly that the eyewitness's identification is unreliable, the expert would be asserting a conclusion the jury should draw. To avoid intruding on the jury's job, the expert is permitted to testify only on certain restricted factors the judge has already agreed have a sufficient scientific basis and legal relevance to be relied upon in the case at hand. The expert's limited testimony provides a social framework that can help the jury to understand specific aspects of the evidence (see discussion of social framework testimony in Chapter 2). The expert may also discuss circumstances in the case that could have affected memory or perceptions of an eyewitness (Cutler, Penrod, and Dexter, 1989, p. 316). The expert might also describe relevant experiments (Leippe, 1995). An expert may also be asked to state the limits of the research in terms of how much a factor could have affected the eyewitness identification. Nevertheless, the expert does not express an opinion on the ultimate issue—whether or not a particular witness' testimony is reliable. The jury will have to reach a conclusion on that issue by itself.

An expert's testimony is subject to cross-examination, which, theoretically, should prevent the testimony from influencing the jury inappropriately (see Levett and Kovera, 2002). The cross-examination is used by the opposing side to cast doubt on the testimony. The answers an expert gives on cross-examination may provide additional facts or reveal information that will permit jurors to draw a different inference from the expert's testimony.

What Is the Effect of Expert Testimony?

Trial courts have sometimes excluded expert testimony because of the concern that hearing the experts' opinions will make the jury too skeptical of any eyewitness identification. Psychologists believe that testimony about the scientific research will make the jury appropriately skeptical of the identification.

Mock jurors are not good at distinguishing correct and incorrect eyewitness accounts. In the typical experiment, eyewitnesses to a staged crime are later asked to identify the culprit from a photo array or a lineup. Some eyewitnesses make a correct identification. Others make an incorrect identification. Still later, all the eyewitnesses testify to a mock jury. The mock jurors are asked to say whether the eyewitness identification is accurate or not. In most experiments, the mock jurors are unable to differentiate eyewitnesses who made accurate identifications from those who made inaccurate identifications (Cutler and Penrod, 1995; see also Chapter 11).

Psychologists have conducted studies to try to determine the actual effects of expert testimony on mock juror decision making. They have found that mock jurors exposed to expert testimony spend time discussing what the expert said. They may rate the prosecution's case as weaker or doubt the eyewitness more often than mock jurors not exposed to the expert testimony. Jurors exposed to expert testimony are also less likely to overvalue the testimony of confident eyewitnesses (see Box 6.3). Mock jurors who hear expert testimony vote to acquit more often on the same facts than those who don't hear from an expert.

We see from these experiments why defense attorneys would want to introduce experts on eyewitness identification. We can also see that lawyers who cross-examine expert witnesses need to know the eyewitness literature in order to be effective cross-examiners (see Loftus and Doyle, 1997). But not all eyewitness identifications are

178

CHAPTER 6
Miscarriages
of Justice: False
Confessions
and Eyewitness
Error

BOX 6.3

Judicial Instructions to Alert Jurors to Factors Affecting Eyewitness Identification

Are you convinced the witness had the capacity and an adequate opportunity to observe the offender?

Whether the witness had an adequate opportunity to observe the offender will be affected by such matters as how long or short a time was available, how far or close the witness was, how good the lighting conditions were, and whether the witness had occasion to see or know the person in the past.

Are you satisfied that the identification made by the witness subsequent to the offense was the product of his or her own recollection? You may take into account both the strength of the identification and the circumstances under which the identification was made.

You may also consider the length of time that lapsed between the occurrence of the crime and the next opportunity of the witness to see the defendant as a factor bearing on the reliability of the identification.

You may also take into account that an identification made by picking the defendant out of a group of similar individuals is generally more reliable than one that results from the presentation of the defendant alone to the witness.

You may take into account any occasions in which the witness failed to make an identification or made an identification that was inconsistent with his or her identification at trial (*U.S. v. Telfaire,* 1972).

wrong. None of the research has answered the fundamental question: are jurors exposed to expert testimony better able to distinguish accurate from inaccurate eyewitness identifications (Cutler and Penrod, 1995)?

Cutler, Penrod, and Dexter (1989) devised an elaborate study using a videotaped trial to assess the effects of expert testimony on mock jurors' ratings of eyewitness testimony. On average, the mock jurors found the defendant guilty as often when they heard an expert witness as when they didn't. Expert testimony appeared to be very important in some cases. However, the overall effects on the basic issue were not strong. For example, convictions were higher when the witnessing conditions were good than when they were poorer. The expert testimony might have helped in sensitizing mock jurors to what was important about the witnessing conditions but in this scenario might not have had too much effect.

Judicial Instructions

Assume that a judge decides not to admit expert testimony. The judge can decide instead to include **judicial instructions** to the jury on factors that might affect the accuracy of eyewitness testimony. When there is some doubt about the eyewitness identification (e.g., one eyewitness and no other corroborating evidence to show that the defendant is the guilty party), defense attorneys should ask the judge to alert the jurors to the circumstances in the case that might make an identification unreliable.

Judicial instructions alerting jurors to the limitations of eyewitness identifications give the appearance of fairness, at least to appellate courts that may review the trial court's instructions. They avoid the hazards of expert testimony and forestall the possibility of a costly and time-consuming "battle of the experts." Judges may believe that instructions suffice to call juror attention to potential errors of identification and that expert testimony would add nothing further.

Box 6.3 contains the instructions developed by a circuit court in *United States v. Telfaire* (1972) and used by many judges as a model. How effective are such judicial instructions in alerting jurors to the hazards of eyewitness identification? Courts assume that jurors pay careful attention to judicial instructions and understand them. This may not be the case. Psychologists have found that comprehension of many judicial instructions is poor. Greene (1988) developed a simpler version of the **Telfaire instructions.** However, most of a small sample of judges surveyed by Greene (1988) thought the modified instructions were biased toward the defense. A high percentage of the judges said they wouldn't use them.

Changing the System

As eyewitness research reaches the public through presentations in textbooks for psychology courses and through the popular media, the public's understanding of the nature of eyewitness identification may change. The views of judges, the police, and prosecutors may change also. Expert testimony may have effects beyond influencing individual verdicts. Challenges to police practices in court may lead the police to adopt fairer and less suggestive means of obtaining eyewitness identifications (Wells, 1986). In these ways, research can sometimes lead to "system"-level changes.

Publicity about people who were falsely convicted and exonerated has made the time ripe for the justice system to consider how research might be applied to improve the accuracy of eyewitness identifications (Wells et al., 1998). The U.S. Department of Justice asked a panel to develop recommendations for procedures for obtaining eyewitness identifications (see Box 6.4 and Figure 6.3). This official recognition may help when expert testimony on eyewitnesses is proferred to judges making decisions about admitting the testimony. Some states and some local prosecutors have referred to these guidelines in reforming their procedures for eliciting eyewitness identification.

Proposals for Research-Based Reforms

In 1998, the American Psychology–Law Society (Division 41 of the American Psychological Association) published a detailed scientific review paper on eyewitness research by Wells and colleagues (1998). This report was used by a U.S. Justice Department's technical panel. The authors concluded "that some lineup procedures lead to increased risk of false identification or inflated confidence" (Wells et al., 1998, p. 627). The report recommended four rules, based on research, for improving the lineup as a means of obtaining identifications.

Blinding lineup administrators. First, the group recommended that the lineup be conducted blindly. Regarding the **blind lineup,** Wells and colleagues (1998) recommended, "The person who conducts the lineup or the photospread should not be aware of which member of the lineup or the photospread is the suspect" (p. 627). Scientists

180

CHAPTER 6
Miscarriages
of Justice: False
Confessions
and Eyewitness
Error

BOX 6.4

Research Influences Law Enforcement Policy

U.S. Attorney General Janet Reno was concerned about cases in which DNA evidence conclusively showed that convictions based on eyewitness testimony were mistaken. She was also familiar with work by Gary Wells (1993) on how justice system procedures may stimulate or reinforce false identifications. She met with Wells in 1996 and subsequently created a national technical panel that included psychologists expert in eyewitness research along with prosecutors, defense attorneys, and law enforcement personnel. The panel was to recommend "best practices" for obtaining accurate eyewitness identifications.

In October 1999, the panel issued guidelines for obtaining eyewitness identifications. The list of recommended procedures directly reflects the conclusions of eyewitness research. Among the recommendations were using open-ended questions to avoid leading the witness, using lineups with foils who fit the general description the witness had given, and having only one suspect at a time in the lineup. The guidelines also recommend that the eyewitness be told that the suspect may not be in the lineup (Foxhall, 2000).

The guidelines can be found on the U.S. Department of Justice website at www.ncjrs.org/txtfiles1/nij/178240.txt.

FIGURE 6.3

Gary Wells

Professor Gary Wells of the University of Iowa is a leading research psychologist working on eyewitness testimony. He led the group of psychologists who worked with the U.S. Department of Justice to develop federal guidelines for obtaining eyewitness identifications.

have long known that a researcher's expectations can subtly or not so subtly affect the outcome of an experiment. To control for *experimenter effects,* researchers often keep people who actually administer the experiment and who are in direct contact with the participants in the experiment blind to the hypotheses of the study. The expectations of a policeman conducting a lineup would have similar effects, so using a "blind" officer would protect the integrity of the process.

Lowering perceived situational demand. Second, the researchers recommended,

> Eyewitnesses should be told explicitly that the person in question might not be in the lineup or photospread and therefore should not feel that they must make an identification. They should also be told that the person administering the lineup does not know which person is the suspect in the case. (Wells et al., 1998, p. 629)

This recommendation follows from research suggesting that suggestion or **situational demand** effects can influence choices, or may elevate eyewitness confidence about a tentative selection. Telling eyewitnesses they do not necessarily have to pick someone out—because the suspect may or may not be present—reduces the tendency to make a false identification. In experiments, instructions that the suspect may not be present result in a drastic reduction of false identifications when the culprit is not in the lineup, especially false identifications of someone who fits the verbal description of the perpetrator. These instructions do not seem to affect correct identifications when the culprit is present.

Another effective way to reduce system demands on witnesses to choose someone is to use sequential rather than simultaneous lineups. The sequential procedure is recommended because, in staged crime experiments conducted by Lindsay and colleagues (1991), it reduced the rate of false identification of innocent suspects. When sequential lineups were used the rate of rejection of the whole lineup when the criminal suspect was not in the lineup was higher than when simultaneous lineups were used. There was with little or no reduction in the correct identification rate (Lindsay and Bellinger, 1999; Lindsay et al., 1991; Lindsay and Wells, 1985; Steblay et al., 2001). The use of sequential lineups was challenged by the results of a field study which failed to support the results from laboratory studies (Zernike, 2006).

Use of distracters. Third, the researchers recommended,

> The suspect should not stand out in the lineup or the photospread as being different from the distracters based on the eyewitness's previous description of the culprit or based on other factors that would draw extra attention to the suspect. (Wells et al., 1998, p. 630)

The experimental data show that eyewitnesses tend to select the person who looks most like the description of the suspect (e.g., height, age, weight, race, and hair color), even if the person is innocent. The use of foils who all match the description reduces this tendency. This approach will also reduce the likelihood of making an innocent person stand out (e.g., one 6'4" person in a lineup of four others who were 5'7" tall). However, while the foils should all fit the verbal description of the subjects, they should not resemble each other too closely in other respects. (Think of trying to pick out the culprit from a lineup consisting of genetically identical quintuplets.)

182

CHAPTER 6
Miscarriages
of Justice: False
Confessions
and Eyewitness
Error

Initial assessment of confidence. Fourth, the researchers recommended,

> A clear statement should be taken from the eyewitness at the time of the identification
> and prior to any feedback as to his or her confidence that the identified person is the
> actual culprit. (Wells et al., 1998, p. 635)

Giving an eyewitness any information that verifies his or her identification can inflate the witness' confidence in the identification. It is difficult to control the flow of information to the eyewitness before his or her appearance in court. Assessing the eyewitness's confidence when the eyewitness first makes the identification can alleviate this problem.

It is helpful for the acceptance of the field of psychology and law when it can offer positive suggestions like these for improving the criminal justice system, rather than offering only findings that undermine confidence in the system. Officials are less likely to "behead" the messenger who brings bad and good news than the one who brings only bad news.

Summary

Miscarriages of justice can derive from many sources, including false confessions and incorrect eyewitness identification. False confessions were a frequent source of error in convictions that were later overturned because the convicted person was proven innocent despite the confession. Police may use social influence processes to induce confessions in vulnerable suspects who are isolated, fearful, and in powerless positions. Youth and those with mental retardation or mental illness may be particularly vulnerable. Confessions are also powerful evidence to juries and to prosecutors. Experts are sometimes allowed to testify in cases where false confession may be an issue. Videotaping confessions may help in reducing false confessions.

Eyewitness testimony is vital in the criminal justice system. It has great weight for jurors, especially when the eyewitness expresses strong confidence in the identification. Wrongful convictions resulting from faulty eyewitness testimony are a serious problem, however. Courts have long recognized the potential weaknesses of eyewitness testimony. The legal system relies on due process safeguards, cross-examination, and judicial instructions to provide jurors with information to evaluate eyewitness testimony.

Psychologists who have studied eyewitness testimony, especially in simulations in the laboratory, have developed an extensive body of data on factors affecting its accuracy. Eyewitness experts have been allowed to testify about these findings in criminal cases, but courts have also frequently rejected eyewitness expert testimony. Trial-level judges have great discretion in deciding whether or not to admit expert testimony. Appellate-level courts rarely overturn a trial court's decision regarding the admissibility of the testimony from a psychological expert.

Courts sometimes assert that psychologists cannot help jurors on those issues because most of what psychologists have to say is well-known to jurors. Psychologists believe the research reveals factors that are not known to jurors and that may unfairly influence their decisions. Psychologists also believe there is a large body of sound scientific evidence and agreed-on conclusions that support expert testimony on eyewitness issues. The underlying science is built on experiments testing hypotheses about eyewitness judgment as well as psychological work on memory and perception generally.

Knowledge about eyewitness testimony is based largely on simulations and laboratory experiments. A favored method is to stage a "crime" and then ask eyewitnesses sometime later to identify the culprit. Though this method of research is generally accepted in the field as having high internal validity, critics raise questions about the ecological validity of the research and about how well the experimental conditions "fit" the actual situation of real eyewitnesses.

When admitted as witnesses, experts offer social framework testimony rather than testimony about the credibility of the particular eyewitness. This general testimony is subject to cross-examination, and in any event is pitted against the vivid testimony of the eyewitness who asserts that the defendant is the culprit. Research suggests that expert testimony has some effect in sensitizing jurors to the importance of witnessing conditions and to the modest relationship of eyewitness confidence to the accuracy of the eyewitness's identification of the defendant. The issue of eyewitness confidence is particularly important. Jurors are influenced by eyewitness confidence, but a large body of research shows that confidence has only a modest relationship to accuracy. Moreover, research evidence suggests that an eyewitness's level of confidence in the identification is malleable and readily manipulated. If the level of confidence has been manipulated, the modest relationship to accuracy will be attenuated. Some courts alert jurors to the potential limitations of eyewitness testimony through judicial instructions. Their effectiveness remains to be demonstrated.

Psychologists are attempting to apply knowledge of memory and of factors that affect accuracy to improve eyewitness testimony. They have developed research-based recommendations for systems-based reforms, including restructuring lineups and photo array procedures to minimize faulty identification.

The research on eyewitness testimony may be helping to improve the criminal justice system. The development of DNA identification techniques has made legal professionals and laypeople alike aware that innocent people are sometimes found guilty. By presenting testimony in individual cases, and by educating lawyers, judges, police departments, and laypersons about their research findings, psychologists have been contributing to the effort to reduce faulty eyewitness identifications and the wrongful convictions that can result.

Discussion Questions

1. How might a requirement to videotape all confessions reduce the frequency of occurrence of false confessions?
2. Can police be trained to suspend their intuitive beliefs about a suspect's guilt or innocence?
3. Should suspects receive more information about their Miranda rights before being allowed to waive them?
4. Should strict time limits be imposed on the length of an interrogation session?
5. Suppose that an eyewitness's initial identification of the defendant was solicited in a way that might have been suggestive; what factors, if any, should a judge consider in deciding whether to allow the eyewitness's testimony?
6. How does psychologists' understanding of memory processes differ from commonsense understanding of memory?
7. What factors might limit the ecological validity of laboratory experiments in eyewitness accuracy?
8. Can you think of a "natural" experiment that would test the relationship between confidence and accurate memories of an emotion-laden event?
9. If you were asked to give expert testimony on eyewitness accuracy, what general information would you want to explain to the jury? What would you want to know about the specific case in order to make your testimony more relevant?
10. Are there any procedural reforms that would increase your confidence in the accuracy of eyewitness identifications?

184

CHAPTER 6
Miscarriages
of Justice: False
Confessions
and Eyewitness
Error

Key Terms

blind lineup
confidence
consensus
cross-racial identification
distracters
ecological validity
estimator variables
false confession
false identification

judicial instruction
limitations of the witness's
    perception and processing
lineup
Neil v. Biggers
postevent questioning
reconstruction of events
research paradigm
sequential lineup

show up
simultaneous lineup
situational demands
stored memory
system variables
Telfaire instructions
weapon focus effect
wrongful convictions

CHAPTER **7**

The Insanity Defense

Trom T he insanity defense is controversial. Several notorious cases illustrate why. Witnesses and physical evidence, including a refrigerator filled with body parts, established that Jeffrey Dahmer killed a number of young men, had sex with their bodies, and then cooked and ate some of their body parts. Andrew Goldstein, who had a long history of psychiatric hospitalizations, threw a woman he did not know in front of an oncoming subway train. When their cases came to trial, the defendants admitted committing the acts with which they were charged, but pleaded not guilty by reason of insanity (NGRI). To many people who are not legally trained, the defense didn't make sense. How could these men claim to be not guilty when they committed the act? Goldstein's criminal conviction was overturned by New York's high court on a procedural issue (*People v. Goldstein,* 2005). He will be retried. Dahmer was found guilty, and died while in prison. On the other hand, John Hinckley, who was televised while attempting to assassinate President Ronald Reagan in 1981, was found not guilty by reason of insanity.

The insanity defense appears to be stretched with additional diagnoses (e.g., posttraumatic stress disorder, or PTSD, and compulsive gambling) or acts that don't fit a stereotype of mental illness (e.g., a female school teacher who had sex several times with her middle school male student). Inconsistencies in the success of the defense also raise questions about its application. Andrea Yates, who killed five of her young children, was found guilty of murder when a Texas jury rejected her insanity defense. After a successful appeal, on retrial, a second Texas jury found her not guilty by reason of insanity. On the other hand, another Texas jury found Deanna Laney, who bashed in the skulls of two of her three young children, not guilty by reason of insanity. In each of these cases, experts testified on both sides. Even those who support the idea of the insanity defense may wonder how juries can fairly determine the mental status of a defendant when experts disagree in their assessments.

The not guilty by reason of insanity (NGRI) defense has survived criticism because it is tied in a very fundamental way to our understanding of guilt and of justice. In supporting the insanity defense, the National Mental Health Association (2004), an advocacy organization, has noted, "Society has long recognized the need for judges and juries to discern which defendants are 'criminally responsible' for their acts and which are not" (p. 1). In this chapter, we will look at how the insanity defense fits in with our beliefs about crime and punishment, at the real and perceived uses of the insanity defense, and at problems associated with testimony by mental health professionals. We will discuss

- the reasons for having an insanity defense.
- the history of the insanity defense.
- the legal standards and definitions of insanity.

- how jurors think about insanity.
- how the insanity defense is used in practice: the frequency and outcomes of insanity pleas.
- the role of expert witnesses in insanity trials.
- the guilty but mentally ill alternative.
- the effects of abolishing the insanity defense.

187

The Legal and
Historical
Context of
the Insanity
Defense

The Legal and Historical Context of the Insanity Defense

Responsibility, Blameworthiness, and Punishment

Mens rea. In our legal system, guilt is a quality associated with an individual, not with an act (Golding and Roesch, 1987). The principle is summarized in the doctrine *actus non facit reum, nisi mens sit rea*: the act does not make the doer guilty unless the mind is guilty. The **mens rea** doctrine reflects very basic concepts of responsibility and blameworthiness in English, U.S., and European law. *Mens* may also be translated as "intention, meaning, understanding, will," and *mens rea* as "a guilty mind; a guilty or wrongful purpose; a criminal intent. Guilty knowledge and willfulness" (Black's, 2004).

A central concept in our modern western understanding of guilt is the distinction between group and individual responsibility. In the ancient Mediterranean world, the family was the principal source of legitimate social power (Friedman, 1985). If someone killed one of its members, even if the killing was accidental, the family felt entitled to vengeance. Moreover, they didn't have to take revenge by killing the killer. Any member of the other family might do, to use today's language of vengeance, as "payback." Guilt was collective, not individual.

Over time, the Mediterranean world moved toward a system of individual responsibility. Some 4,000 years ago, the Code of Hammurabi specified remedies to be assessed against an individual who harmed another or who harmed another's property (Levine et al., 2006). Draco, the law scribe from whom the word *draconian* derives, outlawed the vendetta in ancient Greece (Robinson, 1980). Roman law provided that no one should be punished for crimes the person did not commit. A similar concept of people being held responsible for their own deeds is found in the Old Testament (Deuteronomy 24:16). Responsibility also came to mean conscious responsibility. Individuals were not held criminally responsible for actions they didn't intend. The Old Testament also described cities of refuge, where a person who had killed someone accidentally would be safe from an "avenger of blood" (Deuteronomy 19:3–7).The distinction between an involuntary or an unintentional misdeed and a misdeed committed intentionally was introduced into Anglo-Saxon secular law from ecclesiastical law as early as the tenth century. Thus, from its origins, criminal law in the West was predicated on the idea of a moral order in which only the guilty were punished, and guilt was a psychological and moral condition of a responsible and knowing individual.

Accidents: An example of nonculpability. The distinction between crimes and accidents provides a clear example of what we mean by a *guilty mind.* Consider a man coming home from his annual physical checkup, pleased that he has been given a clean bill of health. He is driving well within the speed limit in a recently inspected car. Suddenly he has a nonfatal heart attack and loses consciousness. Uncontrolled, his car hits and kills a mother and her child who are crossing the street following the direction of a walk sign at a green light.

His friends would tell the man, "It wasn't your fault; it was an accident." The law would say the same thing. Our legal system would not hold the man criminally responsible for the deaths caused by his car because he lacked a guilty mind: he did not intend to hurt anyone, nor was he *reckless*.

Degrees of culpability. Minds can be guilty to varying degrees. In general, the more specific the intent, the greater the premeditation and planning, the greater the blameworthiness, and, thus, the greater the degree of punishment (see Zaibert, 1997). A mens rea element is part of the definition of most crimes. The state must prove every element of a crime, including the mens rea.

The hierarchy of possible charges that can be brought against someone who kills someone else illustrates the importance of mens rea or state of mind in determining the potential punishment (New York Penal Law, Sections 120.10, 125.15, 125.20, 125.25, and 125.27). (The terminology and the definitions of different crimes will differ in different states.) If the state charges someone with **murder,** it must prove the defendant had intent to cause the death of a person. To win a conviction of *first-degree murder,* which carries the severest penalty the state imposes, the state must prove to the jury that the defendant acted with malice aforethought. The person who acts with **malice aforethought** acts with a "wanton disregard for human life." The late comedian Red Skelton played the character of a mischievous child who, before committing a bad act, conducted a dialogue with himself: "Should I dood it, or should I shouldn't? I dood it!" The essence of malice is in that internal dialogue.

A person is charged with the lesser crime of **manslaughter** if the state believes he or she intended to cause the victim serious injury but did not deliberately try to kill the victim. If the defendant was not trying to injure anyone but performed a "reckless" act that caused a death (for example, firing a gun into the air right over a crowd), he or she is charged with a lower degree of manslaughter, carrying a lesser penalty. If a death results when someone neglects to fulfill a duty with care (e.g., if a bus mechanic did not repair the brakes properly and there was an accident), the person may be charged with a still lesser offense, *criminally negligent homicide.* And, as we have seen, when someone kills someone else but there is no mental culpability, the death is considered an accident, not a crime.

Common experience and inference about mental states. We are in a fuzzy conceptual area when we try to characterize mental states (Faigman et al., 2005). The law presumes that people understand the nature and natural consequences of their actions. When someone is charged with a crime, the prosecution's case includes evidence about the circumstances of the act and what the defendant did and said. From that evidence, the finder of fact (the jury or, in a bench trial, the judge) infers the mens rea element of the crime. Thus, the law shares with psychology the technique of deducing internal states on the basis of observed behavior.

In the absence of a mental disorder, the inference of intention may be straightforward. But when defendants challenge the presumption that they perceive and reason as others do by raising the insanity defense, inferences from behavior become very difficult indeed. That was one of the issues in *Clark v. Arizona* (2006). The prosecutor wanted the jury to infer an intent to lure a policeman into an ambush from the defendant's act of driving around at 4 A.M. in a residential neighborhood with his stereo blasting away. The defense wanted an expert to testify that Clark was trying to drown out the sound of the "voices" in his head, but under Arizona law, the defense could not be introduced. The U.S. Supreme Court held that the expert testimony, did not have to be allowed at the trial.

189

The Legal and
Historical
Context of
the Insanity
Defense

Not guilty by reason of insanity. The capacity to understand the nature of one's actions and to make moral choices is a necessary prerequisite to mens rea, or criminal intent. Most states and countries provide that a person who doesn't have that capacity can't be held criminally responsible for a criminal act.

In our legal tradition and many others, children are presumed to lack the moral and mental capacity requisite for criminal guilt and punishment. Adults, unlike young children, are presumed to be morally responsible for their actions. However, adults whose mental functioning is severely limited or impaired are, like children, regarded as being incapable of forming criminal intent. Roman law exempted small children and those **non compos mentis** ("without power of mind") from criminal responsibility. The Jewish Talmud proscribed holding "deaf-mutes, idiots [including the mentally retarded and insane,] and minors" criminally responsible (Golding and Roesch, 1987). Even cultures without written legal codes distinguish the violent mentally ill and criminals (Murphy, 1976).

An adult who lacks the mental capacity to be criminally responsible is called *insane*. **Insanity** is a technical legal term, not a medical or psychological condition. When defendants plead not guilty by reason of insanity, they are denying mental culpability as a matter of law. They are challenging the prosecution to prove the mental element of the crime, the "guilty mind" (see Boxes 7.1 and 7.2 for examples of a mens rea defense).

Rather than a "loophole" to allow people to escape responsibility, theoretically the insanity defense is a reaffirmation of our belief that people are responsible for their own acts. By recognizing "a class of persons who fall outside the boundaries of blame," we emphasize that all others are responsible (Goldstein, 1967).

The History of Insanity Defense Standards

The specific standards for assessing criminal responsibility for purposes of the insanity defense are established legislatively. They vary somewhat among states and have varied over time. (See Petitioner's Opening Brief in *Clark v. Arizona*, 2006, for an overview of the insanity defense.) The modern history of the defense has been characterized by alternation between periods when legal standards and procedural rules for judging the criminally insane were liberalized and periods when they were tightened. We liberalize standards for insanity to accommodate more complex conceptions of mental illness and to embody more rehabilitative models of justice. A return to stricter standards has usually been precipitated by a particularly notorious trial, often a political assassination. The tightening of standards is intended to correct perceived misuses of the defense or to reduce perceived threats to public safety occasioned by its use.

BOX 7.1

Out of the Mouths of Babes: A *Mens Rea* Defense

Fifteen-month-old Eli started a game with his father. He climbed over a couch to reach a floor lamp standing behind it and shook it. He would look back to his father, who would gently but firmly tell him "no" and take him away from the lamp. The father explained to four-year-old big sister Ellen that he was gentle with Eli because Eli didn't know what he was doing. Shortly afterwards, big sister Ellen walked over to the lamp and shook it vigorously. When her father called to her in an angry voice, Ellen said coyly, "I didn't know what I was doing." She tried to invoke a *mens rea* defense.

BOX 7.2

Another Notorious Assassination Trial

The 1981 trial of John Hinckley, the unsuccessful assassin of President Reagan (see text), led to widespread criticism of the insanity defense as an easy way for criminals to escape justice. The trial of Charles Guiteau, who assassinated President James A. Garfield in 1881, ultimately had the opposite effect. Guiteau was hanged after a much publicized trial in which testimony that he was insane was rejected. Neurologists and psychiatrists believed that if he had killed someone less prominent, he would never have been convicted and hung (Rosenberg, 1968). An autopsy showed that he may well have had syphilitic paresis. The finding lent moral credibility to the insanity defense. (See the video *Asylum:* Stone Lantern Films, 1990.)

Mens rea always refers to a person's state of mind at the time the act was committed. All the standards refer to the defendant's mental capacities at the time of the unlawful act, not at the time of the trial. At the time of trial, the law is concerned with adjudicative competence (see Chapter 4), or the competence to participate in a legal proceding (e.g., to stand trial). A person who is not of sound mind at the time of trial may not be competent to be tried (see discussion of adjudicative incompetence in Chapter 4), but that is a different issue: a person lacking adjudicative competence might still have been capable of acting responsibly at the time of the crime. Conversely, a person who has full mental capacities at the time of the trial may have been insane at the time of the crime. In any trial where the insanity defense is at issue, the experts evaluating the defendant and, ultimately, the judge or jury have to make their determination about the person's state of mind in the past. This is obviously a difficult task at best. The brief review of the changing standards that follows relies heavily on Finkel (1988), Golding and Roesch (1987), and Robinson (1980).

Wild beasts. Until 1800, there was no separate verdict of *not guilty by reason of insanity* in English or U.S. law. A defendant found insane was simply found not guilty, meaning not criminally liable. (This didn't mean the community did not protect itself against the dangerous mentally ill; it did so in other ways. The person might be treated as a deranged individual and kept chained or caged.)

Early legal writers tended to define insanity by referring, as in Roman law, to the dumb and raving beast who lacked rationality. The courts also recognized that a psychotic person might not be insane all the time, but could have lucid intervals, or might behave crazily in one context and not in another. However, in the seventeenth and early eighteenth centuries, most jurists believed that partial insanity was not sufficient to remove criminal responsibility. In 1723 (*Rex v. Arnold*), an English judge articulated what became known as the **wild beast standard** for insanity:

> It must be a man that is totally deprived of his understanding and memory, and does not know what he is doing, no more than an infant, than a brute or a wild beast, such a one is never the object of punishment.

Morbid delusions. The issue of partial sanity arose again in 1800 when an otherwise unremarkable man named James Hadfield attempted to kill King George III (*Trial of James Hadfield*, 1800). Hadfield had sustained a head injury while fighting in the

British army. The day before the assassination attempt, a self-appointed prophet named Truelock (himself later confined to a mental hospital) persuaded Hadfield that Jesus wanted King George III killed before His imminent reappearance. Hadfield's barrister, Thomas Erskine, challenged the wild beast standard by pointing out that only a profoundly retarded person (*idiotus*) was totally deprived of reason. Erskine argued that it should be enough for the jury to decide whether Hadfield was insane when he performed the act. Further, Erskine contended that it should not be necessary to show that a defendant did not know the difference between right and wrong. It should be enough to show that, when the defendant's reason was under sway of a delusion, he believed the act was harmless or good. Because Hadfield tried to kill King George III in the belief that Jesus wished it, he could not be said to have intended or voluntarily caused evil (*Trial of James Hadfield,* 1800).

The nineteenth-century public was disturbed at the prospect that a man like Hadfield could be found not guilty because he lacked the requisite mens rea, and could then, because he was rational and seemingly coherent about matters that did not touch on his delusional system, be released like any other person who was acquitted. During the Hadfield trial, Parliament passed the Criminal Lunatics Act (1800), which established the special verdict of not guilty by reason of insanity (NGRI). The new law stipulated that an NGRI acquittee would be "kept in strict custody in such place and such manner as the court shall deem it, until His Majesty's pleasure be known" (Golding and Roesch, 1987). From its inception, then, the special NGRI verdict had a twofold function: to preserve the principle of moral responsibility by exempting the insane from criminal punishment, while, at the same time, protecting society by ensuring that the dangerously insane would be confined.

After medical experts testified that head wounds had damaged Hadfield's brain, the judge halted the proceeding, acquitted the defendant, and, under the new law, had him committed to a mental hospital to ensure the public safety (Freemon, 2001).

The use of the defense seemed well established in the United States when, in 1835, Richard Lawrence tried to shoot President Andrew Jackson. The jury found Lawrence NGRI, making this the first case of a successful insanity defense in the District of Columbia. (Frances Scott Key, composer of "The Star-Spangled Banner," was the prosecutor.) Perhaps because there were no mass media, there was no outcry from the public about the verdict (Johnston, 2003). We have no record of reform in reaction to this case.

Cognitive capacity: The *M'Naghten* rule. A new standard was articulated in the trial of Daniel M'Naghten in 1843. M'Naghten intended to shoot the Tory Prime Minister Robert Peel, but instead shot Peel's secretary, Edward Drummond. M'Naghten had followed his victim, stepped up behind him, put a pistol to the man's back, and shot him. After his arrest, M'Naghten made statements that mixed political motivation with delusional ideas that he was being persecuted by members of the Tory party.

No one thought M'Naghten was rational enough to be considered a criminal. The prosecutor conceded that M'Naghten was mentally ill, but relied on the wild beast test. He argued that M'Naghten's symptoms were insufficient to warrant an exemption from punishment. Nine expert witnesses testified that M'Naghten was insane. They said that, because M'Naghten was delusional and was reasoning from false premises, his judgment of right and wrong was the same as no judgment at all. This concept went well beyond the wild beast test but was nonetheless allowed partly because prominent psychiatrists of that day testified to the proposition.

By 1843, science was well established as a source of authority (Levine, 1981). Educated people were favorably disposed to expert testimony allegedly based on science. In that era, more so than today, lawyers and physicians, shared a common intellectual culture (Shapiro, 1983). Because there was no contrary evidence, the judge instructed the jury to find that M'Naghten was not guilty on grounds of insanity. M'Naghten was committed to a mental hospital.

The M'Naghten verdict distressed Queen Victoria, and aroused press and public opinion. At the queen's request, the House of Lords summoned 15 English judges and asked them to explain the ruling. The judges proposed what has come to be known as the **M'Naghten rule:**

> [T]o establish a defense on the ground of insanity, it must be clearly proved that, at the time of the committing of the act, the party accused was laboring under such a defect of reason, from disease of the mind, as not to know the nature and quality of the act he was doing; or if he did know it, that he did not know he was doing what was wrong. (*Queen v. M'Naghten,* 1843)

The judges in the M'Naghten inquiry had come up with a standard very like the one Hadfield's lawyer had suggested 40 years earlier.

Criticism of *M'Naghten*. The emphasis in the new standard on the defendant's **cognitive capacity,** or intellectual comprehension of moral issues, immediately drew criticism from the experts of the day. They argued that mental illness could affect volition (will) as well as cognition (thought); a person could know right from wrong but lack adequate self-control because of a mental disease (Ray, 1962). Psychiatrists who worked in the mental hospitals that had been created in the United States in the eighteenth century and earlier in England testified in insanity defense trials. Through their testimony, they introduced the idea of "moral insanity," the loss of voluntary powers over impulses, and the lack of apparent "ordinary" motivation for the criminal acts (Eigen, 1999). In 1869, the New Hampshire legislature promulgated an expansive standard: a person was not guilty by reason of insanity if the criminal act was the product of a mental disease or defect. Under the **product rule,** experts could testify to the presence of mental disease, and give their opinion on whether the act was a product of that disease. The jury assessed the expert's opinion in their deliberations.

The very open product rule was not adopted in other states. But, by the beginning of the twentieth century, a few states added a **volitional capacity** prong to their standard: a defendant was insane if he or she did not know what he or she was doing was wrong or if his or her act resulted from an **irresistible impulse.** The trend toward more liberal standards accelerated in the 1920s. Freud's influential theory of the mind emphasized that powerful unconscious forces found expression in behavior. The theory made the notion of "irresistible impulse" compelling (Goldstein, 1967). More states added a volitional test to the M'Naghten cognitive standard.

After World War II, psychiatry and law had something of a love affair. Greatly expanded funds for research and training, and the overdue reform of mental hospitals, brought psychiatry, psychology, and social work to favorable public attention. The law, never comfortable with the problems of the mentally ill, was willing to yield to mental health professionals (Levine, 1981). In this atmosphere, the old New Hampshire product rule ("The unlawful act was the product of a mental disease or defect"), a very flexible standard that implicitly relied on expert judgment, was adopted in the District of Columbia (*Durham v. United States,* 1954) and was briefly introduced in federal courts.

193

The Legal and
Historical
Context of
the Insanity
Defense

FIGURE 7.1

Charles Guiteau

The trial of Charles Guiteau, who assassinated President James A. Garfield in 1881, was an early example of a "show trial" with many expert witnesses. His insanity defense failed. He was found guilty of murder and hanged.

The American Law Institute Standard

By the 1960s, the movement toward more expansive definitions of the insanity defense peaked. The American Law Institute (ALI), a quasi-official group of leading lawyers, judges, and law professors, argued that the Durham product rule was too broad. It would lead to inconsistent verdicts, and would encourage jurors to relegate decision-making responsibilities to experts. The **Durham rule,** in fact, proved difficult to apply.

In 1962, the American Law Institute (1962) proposed a new insanity standard (the **ALI standard**). It was a modernized version of the two-prong cognitive incapacity/ inability to control one's action standard:

1. A person is not responsible for criminal conduct if at the time of such conduct, as a result of mental disease or defect, he lacks substantial capacity either to appreciate the criminality of his conduct or to conform his conduct to the requirements of law.

2. As used in this Article, the terms "mental disease or defect" do not include an abnormality manifested only by repeated criminal or otherwise antisocial conduct.

In *United States v. Brawner* (1972), a federal appellate court, dissatisfied with the Durham product rule, replaced it with the ALI standard. The ALI standard was adopted throughout the federal court system. Many states adopted it as well.

The ALI standard allowed testimony about modern psychiatric and psychological knowledge without turning the insanity determination into a purely clinical decision. Under the ALI standard, the *accused* must have a mental disease or defect to escape criminal responsibility. Psychiatric or psychological testimony is necessary for the diagnosis. However, the *trier of fact (jury, or judge in a bench trial)* must *independently* decide whether the defendant's mental disease or defect resulted in an inability to appreciate the criminality of the unlawful conduct, or to conform conduct to the requirements of law. A psychiatric diagnosis alone is not enough to meet the standard.

The requirement that the defendant "appreciate" the criminality of his or her conduct, rather than "know" the difference between right and wrong, permits testimony about the defendant's emotional as well as cognitive understanding. The phrase *conform his conduct to the requirements of law* is a rewording of the irresistible impulse concept. It opens the way for the discussion of modern psychological concepts such as ego strength, projection, and frustration tolerance.

Under the ALI standard, the defendant's mental disease or defect does not have to cause total impairment to release him or her from criminal responsibility. It is enough if, because of the "disease" or "defect," the person "lacks substantial capacity" to appreciate the criminality of the illegal acts or to conform his or her conduct to the law. Thus, someone like M'Naghten, who suffered from encapsulated delusions but did not appear irrational or unable to make judgments in most contexts, could plead insanity under this standard.

Many psychiatrists consider habitual criminal behavior since childhood to be a mental disorder in itself (Menninger, 1928). The American Psychiatric Association publishes a *Diagnostic and Statistical Manual of Mental Disorders* (*DSM*), which includes all the mental disorders accepted as valid by the profession according to diagnostic criteria. The diagnoses include *antisocial personality disorder,* "a pervasive pattern of disregard for, and violation of, the rights of others that begins in childhood or early adolescence and continues into adulthood" (American Psychiatric Association, 1994, p. 645). Nevertheless, the ALI standard prevented defendants with no symptoms of mental disorder other than habitual criminal behavior from using an NGRI plea. The exclusion of antisocial personality disorder from the legal understanding of "mental disorder or defect" in the context of the insanity defense reflected political and moral considerations, not scientific ones.

The ALI standard was more satisfying to many jurists than the older standards. However, the ALI standard did not resolve basic problems relating to the role of mental health experts in determinations of insanity, which we will discuss below.

Insanity Defense Reforms: The Aftermath of the *Hinckley* Trial

In 1981, John Hinckley attempted to assassinate President Ronald Reagan (Figure 7.2). Hinckley's lawyer claimed that Hinckley was obsessed with the actress Jodie Foster and with the movie *Taxi Driver*. He wanted to reenact the movie's climactic scene (see also Box 7.4) in order to impress her.

195

The Legal and
Historical
Context of
the Insanity
Defense

FIGURE 7.2

John Hinckley

*John Hinckley tried to assassinate President Ronald Reagan in 1981.
He was found NGRI of attempted murder, and committed to St. Elizabeth's Hospital in Washington, D.C., where he is still hospitalized. His
case led to a public outcry and reform of insanity defense legislation.*
See Ewing and McCann (2006, ch. 8, 91–101) for further details about this case.

Changing the law. After Hinckley was found NGRI (*United States v. Hinckley*, 1981),
polls confirmed that many people were dissatisfied with the insanity defense (Fulero
and Finkel, 1991; Roberts, Golding, and Fincham, 1987). Politicians made suggestions
for its reform (Morris, Bonnie, and Finer, 1986–1987; Steadman et al., 1993). Some
called for a return to stricter insanity standards to make acquittals more difficult. One
suggestion was to drop the volitional test (irresistible impulse). The cognitive impairment test (capacity to appreciate criminality, knowledge of right and wrong) seemed
more straightforward (see Bonnie, 1983; Ogloff, 1991).

Critics of the insanity defense also called for changes in the burden of proof. In
criminal trials, the prosecution has the burden of proving guilt, including the mens rea
element of a crime. At the time of the *Hinckley* trial, when a defendant raised the insanity plea, federal law placed the burden on the prosecution of proving the accused was
sane at the time of the crime as part of proving the mens rea element. Jurors in the
Hinckley trial said that they voted for NGRI because the prosecution failed to prove
that Hinckley was sane. Critics of the verdict argued that because proving sanity is a
difficult task, the defendant should bear the burden of proving insanity as an
affirmative defense.

In 1984, the U.S. Congress passed the **Insanity Defense Reform Act (IDRA),**
changing legal standards in federal jurisdictions to make insanity acquittals more difficult. IDRA eliminated the volitional prong and placed the burden on the defendant to
prove insanity to the jury. To ensure that decisions about guilt or innocence were made

by the jury, not by experts, IDRA prohibited expert witnesses in federal courts from giving their opinion about whether or not the defendant met the legal criteria for insanity. The experts could, of course, testify generally about the defendant's mental state or condition, but not draw legal conclusions. These reforms were adopted on theoretical grounds without any empirical evidence about their actual effects.

Subsequent to the *Hinckley* trial, 17 states changed their insanity defense statutes in order to reduce the frequency of NGRI acquittals. As of 1985, almost all the states used a cognitive standard for insanity (either the ALI or M'Naghten), and some used standards that included a volitional or irresistible impulse component as well (see Brakel, Parry, and Weiner, 1985, Table 12.5). Thirty-six jurisdictions placed the burden of proving insanity on the defendant, but 34 of these required only that he or she prove insanity by the lowest standard, a preponderance of the evidence. Twelve states instituted a new **guilty but mentally ill (GBMI)** verdict, while making insanity acquittal more difficult. Three states abolished a separate insanity defense distinct from mens rea defenses. We will discuss the GBMI verdict and the abolition of the NGRI plea later in this chapter.

There is still significant variation in the insanity tests in use today. Most states and the federal government follow some form of M'Naghten. But at least 11 states omit the first component of the test—whether the defendant "knew the nature and quality of the act." A substantial number of jurisdictions use some form of the American Law Institute (ALI) test, under which a defendant is excused from liability if "as a result of mental disease or defect he lack[ed] substantial capacity either to appreciate the criminality [wrongfulness] of his conduct or to conform his conduct to the requirements of law." A few states follow M'Naghten as supplemented by the irresistible impulse test or the second part of the ALI test. Georgia does not include the "nature and quality" language of M'Naghten. New Hampshire continues to use the "product" approach. And four states have abolished the insanity defense altogether and instead consider mental illness in assessing mens rea (*Clark v. Arizona*, Brief for the United States, 2006).

Effects of insanity defense reforms. In theory, altering the legal standard from the M'Naghten to the ALI standard should have resulted in more insanity pleas and more acquittals; changes from the ALI to the stricter IDRA standard, which is more like M'Naghten, should have decreased NGRI acquittals (Ogloff, 1991). Shifting the burden of persuasion to the defendant requiring that he or she introduce proof of insanity should have decreased acquittals, especially with a strict standard of proof (clear and convincing evidence versus a preponderance of the evidence).

It is difficult to assess the real-world impact of legal reforms on the rate of use of the insanity defense or on its rate of success. When politicians instituted insanity defense reforms, they responded to public opinion, not empirical data. Many states did not keep useful records regarding the frequency of insanity pleas or their outcome (Circincione and Jacobs, 1999). There was no good way of determining if public perceptions of overuse and abuse of the defense were correct, or if the reforms were successful. Empirical studies yielded equivocal results. After a change from M'Naghten to ALI standards, insanity acquittals increased in several states, but not in all (Keilitz, 1987; Ogloff, 1991; Sales and Hafemeister, 1984). The rate of use of the defense changed after both ALI and IDRA reforms, but changed in different ways in different states (Borum and Fulero, 1999; Steadman et al., 1982). Administrative and procedural changes in the handling of mentally ill defendants may also have affected how the system worked in different states.

⊠ How Jurors Think about Insanity Cases

Although they do not provide information about real-world effects, analog or simulation studies help us understand how changes in legal standards affect people's reasoning about insanity cases. In these studies, subjects playing jurors are given a written vignette describing evidence presented at a trial, or are shown a video of a simulated trial. Mock jurors in different conditions are given a different insanity standard. The mock jurors choose a verdict individually, or they deliberate until they agree on a verdict or a preset time is up. For the same case facts, mock juror verdicts are similar, no matter the insanity standards (Borum and Fulero, 1999; Ogloff, 1991). These results are not surprising because mock jurors do not understand instructions very well. Rates of accurate comprehension and recall of instructions range from 31 to 58 percent (Borum and Fulero, 1999).

If the legal standards do not influence mock juror verdicts, what does? While it is not clear whether the results of jury simulations generalize to real trials, these analog studies offer a good way to examine how ordinary people think about justice. Because most mock jurors agree on a verdict for any given case, they are not just flipping coins. The subjects seem to base their judgments on their own ideas about madness and responsibility rather than on specific legal instructions (Finkel, 1991). Pennington and Hastie (1986, 1990) applied the techniques of social cognitive psychology to study the jury process. Mock jurors seem to share culturally developed prototypical stories or schemata for different kinds of crimes and verdicts. When presented with a case, they organize the evidence into a story. To arrive at a verdict, they evaluate how well the trial story matches prototype stories for the crime. In an insanity case, mock jurors compare the elements of the crime story to prototypes which represent commonsense ideas about mental illness and criminal responsibility.

Factors Influencing Decisions by Mock Jurors

Do jurors who reach the same verdict reach it for the same reason? The question is important. When asked what influenced their decisions, mock jurors mention similar factors as affecting their decisions about mens rea and insanity, including understanding of right and wrong, capacity to make choices, intent, expert testimony, and past history of mental illness (Finkel, 1990; Ogloff, 1991). Mock jurors are more likely to find psychotic than nonpsychotic defendants NGRI (Finkel and Handel, 1988; Roberts, Golding, and Fincham, 1987). Schizophrenic defendants whose delusions were thematically linked to an unplanned crime were found insane more frequently than schizophrenics whose delusional systems were unrelated to the crime or whose crimes were planned (Roberts, Golding, and Fincham, 1987).

The mock jurors' constructs are similar to ones that legal thinkers consider important. However, the jurors' responses may have reflected the way the legal case was presented or the way they were questioned about their decision making.

⊠ The Insanity Defense in Practice

Social scientists have continued to track the uses and outcome of the insanity defense after the *Hinckley* reforms. Steadman and colleagues (1993) conducted a study of eight

Table 7.1

Some Facts about the Insanity Defense

- The public overestimates the frequency of the use of the insanity defense by a factor of 400; it is used in less than 2% of cases that go to trial[1]
- The public overestimates rate of success of the insanity defense—the defense succeeds rarely, in less than 10% of the cases in which it is raised[2]
- The rate of success of the insanity defense varies greatly from state to state, from almost zero in Minnesota (1 acquittal in three years) to 87% in Washington[3]
- The public underestimates the number of insanity acquitees who are sent to a mental hospital after trial; 84% are hospitalized after trial[4]
- The public underestimates the length of time insanity acquitees are hospitalized; in most studies insanity acquitees spend about the same time in confinement as do persons convicted of similar crimes[5]

[1]Pasewark and Seidenzahl (1979); Carter-Yamguichi (1998)

[2]Coleman (1999)

[3]Coleman, 1999; Carter-Yamauchi, 1998; Silver, Cirincione, & Steadman (1994)

[4]Silver, Cirincione, & Steadman, 1994

[5]Miller, Maier, Van Rybroek, & Weidemann, 1989

states where insanity reforms had been instituted. (See also McGinley and Pasewark, 1989; Cirincione and Jacobs, 1999.) The data collected by these researchers provide the best basis for measuring the accuracy of public perceptions of the insanity defense (see Table 7.1).

Misperceptions of the Insanity Defense

The vast majority of Americans believe the insanity defense is used far more often than it is, that it is successful more often than it is, and that NGRI acquitters are released sooner than they are (Borum and Fulero, 1999; Cirincione and Jacobs, 1999).

How often is the insanity defense invoked? Over 80 percent of the public overestimate the frequency of the insanity defense by 400 percent (see Table 7.1; Silver, Cirincione, and Steadman, 1994; Steadman and Morrissey, 1986). The actual ratio of NGRI pleas per 100 felony charges is less than 1 percent (Silver, Cirincione, and Steadman, 1994; Steadman et al., 1993).

For what crimes do defendants plead NGRI? Perhaps because bizarre murders involving mentally ill defendants receive a great deal of publicity, the public has a perception that NGRI pleas disproportionately involve murder. Attorneys also believe that the insanity defense is most frequently used for murder. In fact, murder accounts for one third or less of insanity defenses presented in felony cases (Borum and Fulero, 1999). In their study of data from eight states, Steadman and colleagues (1993) found that about 14 percent of NGRI felony pleas were for murder, 54 percent for other violent crimes, and 32 percent for nonviolent crimes. Insanity pleas for misdemeanors (minor crimes) are rare. In some jurisdictions police divert obviously ill people who have committed misdemeanors to the mental health system without charging them. When they are charged, defendants may be advised to plead guilty: they will probably spend less time in prison if found guilty for a misdemeanor offense than they would spend confined in a mental institution if they are found NGRI (Goldstein, 1967; Steadman et al., 1993; see case of Michael Jones, below).

How successful is the insanity plea? Among eight states, the percentage of NGRI pleas that resulted in acquittal ranged near zero percent to 87.4 percent averaging 26 percent (Borum and Fulero, 1999; Pasewark, 1986; Silver, Cirincione, and Steadman, 1994; Steadman et al., 1993). We don't have good data explaining the variability in success rates in the different states and countries.

Most NGRI cases are decided by a plea bargain or by a bench trial (trials by judges) rather than by juries. NGRI cases tried before a judge are more likely to be successful than those tried before juries (Steadman et al., 1993). In a majority of the successful cases, the prosecution agrees not to contest the NGRI verdict if the disposition of the case will ensure public safety (Rogers, Bloom, and Manson, 1984). The cases that go to juries are more likely to include those in which the prosecutor vigorously contests the insanity plea, perhaps because the claim is more doubtful.

Annual number of successful pleas. In 36 states, the mean number of insanity acquittees per state per year between 1970 and 1995 was 33.4; extrapolated to all 50 states, that would indicate about 1,670 NGRI acquittals per year (Cirincione and Jacobs, 1999). Those numbers are miniscule compared to the approximately 1 million people a year who are convicted of serious crimes (felonies) in state courts (Maguire and Pastore, 1999, Table 5.40).

The high rates of serious mental illness found among prison inmates are another indication that the insanity defense is not abused. About 16 percent of state prison inmates have stayed overnight in a prison mental hospital unit or treatment program (Bureau of Justice Statistics, 1999). Between 6 and 8 percent of prisoners have been found to be seriously mentally ill (Powell, Holt, and Fondacaro, 1997). In 1980 alone, 31,773 convicted offenders who were mentally ill were admitted to forensic mental health units for treatment when their mental state deteriorated in prison (Steadman et al., 1988). In that same year (1980), only 1,970 NGRI acquittees nationwide were admitted to mental hospitals. The annual number of sucessful NGRI pleas and the percentage of defendants who plead NGRI also varies from country to country. In Ireland, from 1850 to 1995, a period of almost 150 years, only 437 patients were admitted to a central mental hospital under guilty but insane criteria. There were many more serious crimes committed in Ireland by mentally ill people during that period (Gibbons, Mulryan, and O'Connor, 1997).

Malingering. One concern about the insanity defense is that defendants, especially those facing the death penalty, may try to *malinger,* or fake or exaggerate mental illness. Malingering of psychosis in a psychiatric population is a rare occurrence, although in the absence of a "gold standard" for detection, the best we can say is that mental health professionals suspect malingering in a low percent of the cases.

Malingering can be detected, even if imperfectly. In experimental tests, in which college student subjects are told to fake psychosis on tests, mental health workers using standardized instruments can identify fakers at above-chance levels. Some actual cases of malingering may be detected by using clinical signs (e.g., atypical content in reported hallucinations, conduct inconsistent with delusional thinking, presence of motivation to malinger, blatant contradiction between reported prior episodes and the person's psychiatric history, and sudden emergence of symptoms to explain antisocial behavior). It is not enough to fake psychotic symptoms in the evaluation interview. The *legal standard for the insanity defense* refers to mental defect or disorder at the time of the crime. However, there are enough instances of successful faking revealed later to support the assertion that mental health workers can mistake some feigned symptoms for signs of psychosis. It is not a very frequent problem, certainly, but it is a troublesome one when it occurs (Resnick, 1997). For a colorful example, see the case of Vincent "the Chin" Gigante, who sucessfuly escaped conviction for charges of murder and racketeering for many years by feigning mental illness and producing a series of mental health experts to testify on his behalf (Raab, 2005).

What Is the Outcome of a Successful NGRI Plea?

The question of what happens after a successful insanity plea is at the heart of the controversy about the defense. Many people mistakenly believe that violent NGRI acquittees are released immediately and go on to commit further crimes.

Legal context: Illness and dangerousness. An NGRI verdict rarely leads to the defendant's immediate release from custody. Since Hadfield's (1800) case, statutes have required that insanity acquittees be hospitalized immediately after the verdict, or be civilly committed to a mental hospital. They cannot be discharged from the hospital without judicial approval, and the prosecutor can object to discharge. M'Naghten evidently spent the rest of his life in a hospital. It does not appear as if John Hinckley, President Reagan's would-be assassin, will be released even after 25 years in a mental hospital.

A convicted criminal cannot be imprisoned longer than the maximum sentence for the crime he or she has committed. However, there is no legal limit on the length of time an NGRI acquittee can be hospitalized involuntarily. Theoretically, hospitalization is not punishment.

In 1983, Michael Jones challenged this practice of committing NGRI acquittees indefinitely. Jones had stolen a jacket from a department store, a misdemeanor that carried a sentence of one year or less. He successfully pleaded NGRI. He was committed to a mental hospital under a state statute that permitted indefinite commitment. After he had been held for more than a year, a longer time than he would have been confined if criminally convicted, Jones demanded his freedom.

The Supreme Court ruled against Jones. The majority said that the state did not have to prove by clear and convincing evidence (*Addington v. Texas,* 1979) that an NGRI acquittee like Jones was dangerous in order to keep him confined (*Jones v. United States,* 1983). By his NGRI plea, Jones had admitted to his insanity and his dangerousness. His plea was evidence that his commitment was appropriate. Because there is no correlation between the severity of the offense and length of time necessary for recovery, acquittees can be held indefinitely if they remain mentally ill. The length of the criminal sentence for the same offense was irrelevant. From the point of view of regaining his freedom, Jones would have been better served if he had pleaded guilty to the minor criminal offense.

In *Jones,* the U.S. Supreme Court said that a person found NGRI could be retained until he or she recovers from his or her illness regardless of the severity of the offense. The Court said mental illness was the key issue. In *Foucha v. Louisiana* (1992), the Court ruled that the state cannot continue to hospitalize an NGRI acquittee after he or she has recovered from his or her mental illness, even if he or she is still dangerous (see Box 7.3). Justice White wrote for the majority, "[T]he acquittee may be held as long as he is both mentally ill and dangerous but no longer." However, in *Kansas v. Hendricks*

(1997), the Supreme Court set a very low requirement for civilly committing a criminally convicted sex offender (not an NGRI) to a mental hospital after he finished his prison term. These rulings seem inconsistent in spirit; perhaps future cases will clarify the issues.

Doing time in mental hospitals. Theoretically, the law permits NGRI acquittees who are no longer mentally ill to return to the community sooner than defendants found guilty of the same crime, and, if they remain ill, to be held in a hospital longer than comparable convicts are held in prison. What happens in practice? (See Figure 7.3.)

Most studies have found that NGRI acquittees are confined for about as long as felons convicted of similar offenses (Steadman et al., 1993). However, research findings are not consistent; in some studies, NGRI acquittees spent less time in confinement than criminally convicted persons, and in other studies more. The differences may be due to differences in laws and procedures in the several states.

In light of Supreme Court rulings, the length of confinement of an NGRI acquittee should be related to treatment outcome, not the severity of the offense. There is no evidence that those who were found NGRI of murder had different or more difficult-to-treat mental disorders than those who were accused of other crimes. But Steadman and colleagues (1993) found that those accused of more serious crimes are confined longer. Borum and Fulero (1999) report that the average number of months insanity acquittees were confined in California and New York was 32.5 months. However, those acquitted of murder were confined an average of 76.4 months. It appears, then, that at least some insanity acquittees are not in the mental hospital just to be treated; they are there "doing time" (Miller et al., 1989). Clinical judgments about patient readiness for discharge may be affected not by the patient's present condition, but by concerns about public reaction to release (see *Hinckley* case, above).

BOX 7.3

A Legal Case in Point: *Foucha v. Louisiana* (1992)

Terry Foucha was acquitted of aggravated burglary and related charges by reason of insanity because he was suffering from a drug-induced psychosis at the time of the crime. He was committed to a mental hospital. After four years, he asked a court to be released because he was no longer suffering from his drug-induced psychosis or any other mental illness. He was not released. The trial court said he was still dangerous because he had been involved in fights in the hospital, and because psychiatrists had agreed that he had an "antisocial personality." The hospital psychiatrist refused to certify that Foucha was not dangerous. Foucha appealed because the mental illness for which he had been hospitalized (the drug-induced psychosis) had remitted. The case went to the U.S. Supreme Court.

The U.S. Supreme Court held that Foucha's continuing commitment violated due process. The majority ruled that "due process requires that the nature of commitment bear some reasonable relation to the purpose for which the individual was committed." Because Foucha was committed for evaluation and treatment of his mental illness, not punishment, the state had no basis for confining him when the illness had disappeared. Drug-induced psychosis, the illness on which Foucha based his insanity plea, is often a temporary condition, different from schizophrenia or other major mental illnesses that may persist even after treatment.

FIGURE 7.3

Lorena Bobbitt

Lorena Bobbitt cut off her husband's penis as he slept. She claimed she did it because he had raped her. The severed part of the penis was recovered and reattached. She successfully pleaded NGRI and was released after a brief time in a mental hospital. Was this a type of "jury nullification"?

One unintended consequence of indefinite commitments is that the mental hospital system over time may have a very high density of such individuals in the patient population. Missouri's standard for release of those who were hospitalized after a finding of NGRI is very rigorous. Over the previous ten years in Missouri, only nine NGRI patients were released unconditionally. As a result of deinsitutionalization policies for other patients, resulting in a reduced census, approximately 50 percent of Missouri's long-term beds in mental hospitals are now occupied by NGRI patients (Linhorst and Dirks-Linhorst, 1997).

Political considerations and the notoriety of the case may play a role in the decision to release an NGRI acquitee. John Hinckley, the man who attempted to assassinate President Reagan, was found NGRI in 1982 and has been confined in St. Elizabeth's Hospital in Washington, D.C., ever since. After a hearing before a federal judge in November 2004, Hinckley, now over 50 years old, was allowed six 32-hour unsupervised visits with his parents, just so long as they didn't go further than 50 miles from Washington, D.C. One of his parents must always be with him on the visits. Although mental health personnel treating Hinckley testified he was in remission from major depression and a narcissistic personality disorder, prosecutors argued he was still mentally ill. The federal judge ruled that Hinckley's request for much more free time away from the hospital was "too much, too soon, too fast" (Wagner, 2004). Members of the late President Reagan's family objected to his furloughs after they learned of the news (Davis, 2004).

Recidivism

The recidivism rate of NGRI acquitees and convicted felons is about the same (Borum and Fulero, 1999). Quinsey et al. (2005) reported that about 16 percent of females and about 29 percent of males were charged with another violent offense in an eight-year period subsequent to release from a mental hospital. Most of these patients (75 percent) were NGRI. The recidivism rates of released convicts with a history of mental illness and those without mental illness are quite similar. About 40 percent of each group commits a nonviolent felony after release. About 10 percent of each group commits a violent felony subsequent to release (Gagliardi et al., 2004). Even though NGRI acquitees' rates of recidivism and of subsequent violent crimes are little different from those of others convicted of crimes, the public appears especially concerned about recidivism by the violent mentally ill and particularly by those who have committed homicide. These cases alarm the public, lead to calls for tighter control of the mentally ill, and undermine support for community treatment generally (Wexler, 1985).

Borum and Fulero (1999) suggest that conditional release programs, which provide intensive monitoring of insanity acquittees, could enhance public safety without increasing commitment times. These programs, which are used in a few states, have as their aim increased surveillance aimed at earlier detection of those who need further treatment or rehospitalization. Preliminary research suggests that the programs can reduce rearrests of NGRI acquittees (Borum and Fulero, 1999). However, Patti Davis, the late President Reagan's daughter, noted that John Hinckley's supervised release program did nothing to relieve her feelings. More than twenty years after the assassination attempt, she wrote that Hinckley would never be out of her mind. She wondered how the Brady family, who had a member seriously wounded by one of Hinckley's shots; Jodie Foster, the actress who was the target of Hinckley's obsession; and Nancy Reagan, the late president's wife, would feel on learning that Hinckley might be seen on the streets of Washington, D.C. (Davis, 2004).

Expert Testimony

All the insanity standards assume that we can determine the defendant's mental state at the time of the crime. Courts have looked to psychiatrists and other experts to provide the necessary assessments. At least from the time of M'Naghten, expert testimony has been criticized as confusing and untrustworthy. For example, in 1873 the Board of Managers of a lunatic asylum, as psychiatric hospitals were called then, reported that

> this matter of the testimony of experts, especially in cases of alleged insanity, has gone to such an extravagance that it has really become of late years a profitable profession to be an expert witness, at the command of any party and ready for any party, for a sufficient and often exorbitant fee. . . . One expert, whether real or assumptive is set up against another. (Annual Report of the Board of Managers of the Utica, New York, State Lunatic Asylum, 1873, quoted in Levine, 1981, p. 111.)

Professionals in the field like to think that their understanding of mental illness has advanced at least a modicum in the last century. However, Robinson (1980) questions whether there is any more "expertise" about mental health. Even the strongest advocates of clinical science acknowledge that using expert testimony in insanity trials is problematic.

In the normal run of cases, collaboration between the courts and forensic clinicians is relatively smooth. When mentally ill people disturb the peace or break the law, more often than not, laypeople, including the offender's family and the police, mental health experts, and representatives of the legal system, will probably agree about the defendant's state of mind. Expertise is not necessary to see that an overtly severely disturbed person is unwell. When a clearly mentally ill offender is charged and pleads NGRI, the prosecutor very often accepts the plea. The most important factor in all NGRI adjudications is whether the prosecution's own pretrial forensic examiners found the defendant mentally ill and probably insane (Steadman and Braff, 1983). When an insanity case does go to trial, judges or jurors usually do not disagree with a court-appointed panel of experts who are unanimous in their opinions in insanity trials (Fukanaga et al., 1981). In all these instances, there is no **battle of the experts.** Unfortunately for the reputation of the insanity defense and the experts, the cases that receive the most publicity are those in which the crime is sensational, and there is no consensus about the accused's moral responsibility. Sometimes, people with antisocial personality disorder and perpetrators of bizarre sexual crimes plead NGRI for lack of any other plausible defense strategy.

What Counts as a Mental Disease for the NGRI Plea?

Mental illness is a socially constructed term; its meanings are quite elastic and tend to vary with context (Winick, 1995). Psychiatrists and psychologists use the term to refer to a broad range of behavioral, perceptual, cognitive, and affective problems that interfere with an individual's ability to perform important social roles or that cause the person distress. The law accepts that the professionals can (and, indeed, must) diagnose mental disorder or defect as part of the legal definition of insanity. However, what is most important for the law's purpose is whether the underlying disorder caused deficits in understanding or appreciation of wrongdoing sufficiently great to excuse the person from criminal punishment.

Which mental illnesses or dysfunctions are disorders likely to lead to the incapacity that defines insanity? The legal formulations deliberately leave the terms *mental diseases* and *mental disorder* undefined, giving professional mental health workers the greatest leeway in examining and in testifying. This leeway in insanity defense cases, and in other cases in which the defendant's state of mind is at issue, leaves room for justice to operate but also leads to some serious problems.

A large-scale study of psychological and psychiatric evaluations (over 200 evaluators and over 5,000 cases) for insanity found that about 12 percent of those referred for evaluation were found to be legally insane. Evaluators spent an average of 8.2 hours evaluating each case. There were no differences in rates of opinions of insanity between psychologists and psychiatrists, but less experienced practitioners tended to report more cases as insane. The most important correlate of the opinion that the defendant was insane was a diagnosis of psychosis. Although there were three possible reasons under Virginia law (where the study was done) for finding a person legally insane, most of the cases (91 percent) were said to have cognitive deficiencies (didn't understand nature or consequences of the act, or couldn't distinguish right from wrong). A relatively small percent were characterized as unable to resist an impulse. Overall, the study suggested considerable consistency in the criteria used over many years to render an opinion the defendant was insane, and thus not criminally responsible (Warren et al., 2004).

A person who was psychotic at the time a crime was committed would have a good case for an insanity defense. Most people recognize that the person is mentally ill when the person reports bizarre ideas or experiences, speaks incomprehensibly, and generally seems out of touch with reality. Unfortunately for diagnosticians and juries, not all mentally ill people, including the seriously ill, exhibit such dramatic symptoms. It is the relatively unusual case that obtains the publicity.

The *Diagnostic and Statistical Manual of Mental Disorders* (*DSM-IV*), the bible of mental health professions, divides disorders into two groups. One group (Axis I, the **clinical disorders**) includes all the disorders that are marked by psychotic symptoms and many others as well. These disorders are described, similarly to physical illnesses, as having an onset and a course of development over time.

Another group (Axis II) includes mental retardation and the "personality disorders." The **personality disorders** describe people who, rather than becoming ill and developing specific symptoms, appear to have had maladaptive personality traits and impaired interpersonal perceptions and relations since childhood. The pattern of maladaptive behavior is stable over time. Antisocial personality disorder, which is defined by rule-breaking behaviors in both childhood and adulthood, is a personality disorder.

By excluding those who commit repeated criminal acts, the ALI standard specifically excluded antisocial personality disorder as an underlying basis for the insanity defense. Similarly, in the *Foucha* decision, the Supreme Court seemed to suggest that antisocial personality disorder is not mental illness for purposes of the insanity defense (Winick, 1995; but see *Kansas v. Hendricks*, 1997).

What about the disorders on Axis I (the clinical disorders)? These include schizophrenia, which is defined by psychotic symptoms, and bipolar disorder, which frequently induces **psychosis**. Other Axis I disorders, for example depression or post-traumatic stress disorder, are sometimes associated with psychosis as well. Brakel and colleagues (Brakel, Parry, and Weiner, 1985) argue that a Vietnam vet who "reverted" to wartime behaviors under stress might qualify as legally insane. But many people who never have an overt psychotic episode suffer from Axis I disorders marked by impaired judgment and reasoning. At present, insanity or mens rea claims could be made on the basis of these symptoms. And, in jurisdictions where inability "to conform one's behaviors to the law" is a test for insanity, testimony about disorders of impulse control, such as intermittent explosive disorder, might well be admitted. Should professional mental health workers be permitted to provide testimony in a legal forum about any kind of mental or emotional problem?

"In states where evidence of mental retardation can be grounds for an NGRI plea, the judge or jury decides whether the mental handicap is severe enough to lead to incapacity to appreciate right and wrong in the particular case at hand" (see Anderson, 2004, for a discussion of a case brought under California law; see also discussion of mental retardation and the death penalty in the next chapter).

Part of the problem is that the diagnoses in the *DSM-IV* have expanded over the years. The inclusion of some of the additional disorders appears to be as much a political and economic decision as a scientific one. For example, some "disorders" may have been added, not because there is evidence that the problems or symptoms reflect a disease process, but because professionals must give patients an official diagnosis for treatment to be reimbursed by health insurance companies (Kutchins and Kirk, 1997). Moreover, even though the *DSM* system is widely accepted, in large part because of the claim that it would improve the reliability of diagnosis, that claim has not been verified by subsequent research. Critics have many questions about the use and development of the system (Spiegel, 2005).

Whatever the reasons for their inclusion, the appearance of new conditions in the *DSM-IV* has created opportunities to make novel insanity and mens rea claims. Sometimes novel claims discredit the defense in the public's eye (see Abplanalp, 1985; Morse, 1986, on premenstrual syndrome as a defense; and Cummien, 1985, on a case involving pathological gambling). These new conditions may present new legal problems within the insanity defense framework. For example, when Carl Lockhart was charged with sexual assault, battery, burglary, and assault, he wanted to claim he suffered from a dissociative identity disorder (multiple personality), but the trial court refused to admit the expert's testimony. The West Virginia appellate court agreed that evidence of such a diagnosis was relevant, but a diagnosis alone was not sufficient. The expert could not say how many or which of Lockhart's alter egos were or was active at the time of the offense, or how many of the alter egos were taking part in the commission of the crime. The expert was also unable to say whether the host personality as a unified person met standards of insanity and was unaware of the offense or unable to control the behavior. In other words, evidence of a dissociative personality disorder was insufficient in itself to meet standards of insanity. The court confirmed the criminal conviction (*State v. Lockhart*, 2000).

Filicide (killing one's own children). Two recent cases of filicide in which mothers killed one or more of their children illustrate problems with the insanity defense. Some of the defendants were found guilty of murder, and others were found NGRI. It is difficult to separate the factors that resulted in the verdicts in the several cases, but all of the actors are involved—defendants, defense attorneys, prosecutors, expert witnesses, family members, and judges—and their feelings may have played a role in the outcomes. The apparent inconsistencies raise questions about whether the success and failure of the insanity defense reflect real differences in defendant's culpability.

Andrea Yates had five children, ranging in age from 7 years to 6 months, all given biblical names in keeping with her religious beliefs. One morning, after her husband left for work, she drowned them one by one, even running after Noah, age 7, who had struggled free, to recapture him and hold his head under water in the filled bathtub. After drowning each one, she carefully laid four of the bodies on a bed face up, draped by a sheet, but left Noah in the bathtub where she had drowned him. She called the police and her husband telling them she had killed all the children. She said she thought she was a bad mother because the children were not developing correctly.

Although she seemed coherent on arrest, she seemed to deteriorate afterwards and was initially found incompetent to stand trial. A few months of treatment with medication restored her competence and she appeared normal at the trial. The state prosecutor decided to seek the death penalty. Psychiatric testimony was critical. Yates had been institutionalized several times, had been diagnosed as having major depression, had experienced psychotic hallucinations, made two unsuccessful suicide attempts, and had had several different antipsychotic and antidepression drugs prescribed. Three well-qualified defense psychiatrists, including Dr. Phillip Resnick, testified that on the day of the crime, she had a mental disease that prevented her from understanding what she did was wrong. She believed that killing her children was the right thing to do. One problem for the defense during trial was that medication had stablized her, and in court, she appeared normal.

Dr. Park Dietz, the prosecution's expert witness, agreed Yates was psychotic. She told him, that Satan was giving her directions on the day of the crime. By killing her children before they went astray morally, she was saving their souls and ensuring their entrance into heaven. However, she admitted to Dr. Dietz that she knew that what she had done was wrong. She had planned to kill the children for at least a month and she had waited until her husband had left home before she killed them. Dr. Dietz testified that although she was possibly schizophrenic, because the thoughts were attributed to Satan, she should have known that what she was doing was wrong. Dr. Dietz also testified that a *Law and Order* TV show presenting the case of a woman found NGRI for drowning her children was aired in the weeks before Yates drowned her children. That testimony was evidently incorrect. No such show aired (Ramsland, 2004).

Although the trial lasted three weeks, the death-qualified jury (i.e., a jury specially selected for a case in which the prosecution seeks the death penalty) deliberated less than three hours before they returned a guilty verdict. Some research shows that death-qualified juries tend to be particularly suspicious of the insanity defense (see Chapter 8). In the penalty phase, the same jury deliberated about 40 minutes before they returned a verdict recommending life imprisonment. Yates would be eligible for parole when she was 77 years old. She was incarcerated in a prison psychiatric unit. In January 2005, a Texas Court of Appeals overturned her conviction because Dr. Dietz's incorrect testimony about the *Law and Order* show could have affected the jury's views of whether her acts were premeditated (*Yates v. Texas*, 2005). The Texas high court confirmed the Appeals Court, and ordered a new trial. On retrial, she was found NGRI, and transferred from prison to a mental hospital. (See Ewing and McCann, 2006, ch. 19, for further discussion of this case.)

There was a different outcome in a very similar case, also tried under Texas law. Deanna Laney smashed the heads of her 6-year-old son Luke and her 8-year-old son Joshua with stones, killing them. She severely injured a third son, 14-month-old Aaron, who was left nearly blind. Smiling and wide-eyed shortly after the attacks, Laney told a psychiatrist, "I feel that I obeyed God and I believe there will be good out of this. . . . I feel like He will reveal His power and they will be raised up. They will become alive again. They will be healed completely. They will walk on the earth." Two of the key experts at the Yates trial also testified at Laney's trial. Defense psychiatrist Dr. Phillip Resnick, said Laney had psychotic delusions caused by a severe mental illness and didn't know right from wrong. In his opinion, she met Texas standards for insanity. Dr. Park Dietz, who testified for the prosecution, agreed Laney was mentally ill, but said she probably knew her act was illegal at the time. The jury deliberated six and a half hours before finding her not guilty by reason of insanity.

Do these two cases show the arbitrariness of the insanity defense? Andrea Yates said Satan was in her head. Deanna Lane said God told her to do it. Could that be the difference in the outcomes? The prosecutor in Laney's case did not request the death penalty, so the jury was not screened to be death-qualified. Could that discretionary choice make a difference? The same psychatrists agreed the two women had mental illnesses, but the diagnosis of mental illness was not the key issue. In addition to mental illness, the insanity defense in Texas requires proof of a cognitive defect related to the act, or an impulse that couldn't be controlled at the time the person committed the act. There was no hard data that could indisputably prove either point. The juries seem to make a moral judgment about whether the "crime" should be punished, or the person treated as ill.

How Is Mental Illness Diagnosed?

A diagnosis of mental illness, although not sufficient in and of itself to establish insanity, is a necessary prerequisite to raising the defense. How are diagnoses made? Psychologists use the term **reliability** to refer to the degree to which a measurement or classification produced by the same procedure is reproduced when it is used by different people or at different times. A diagnostic system or technique is reliable when two trained mental health workers given the same data about a patient agree on the diagnosis. Reliability depends on having clear criteria for the presence or absence of a disorder, and accurate and consistent tests for measuring the defining features.

Diagnosing mental illness is not as precise as diagnosing many physical illnesses. The *DSM* is continually being revised with the explicit goal of improving reliability by (1) establishing clearer behavioral criteria for disorders, and (2) empirically testing the reliability of the diagnoses. Progress, though real, is slow (see Kirk and Kutchins, 1992). Mental illness is simply not well understood, and disagreement or uncertainty among clinicians is common. The diagnosis of mental disorders depends on the observation of behaviors and symptoms whose meanings are often a matter of degree and context and may characterize more than one condition (Spiegel, 2005).

Levine (1985) summarized a number of studies that revealed moderate reliability for clinical diagnoses conducted for research purposes. When two mental health workers with similar training observed the same interview at the same time, interjudge reliability coefficients for ratings of specific characteristics averaged about .78 (where a reliability coefficient of 1.00 would indicate perfect agreement). When the sources of data were different or there was a time interval between the two interviews there was greater disagreement; the reliability coefficients dropped to an average value of about .45. Judgments of overall severity, which might be more important for some legal purposes, had somewhat higher overall average reliability coefficients, in the range of .6 to .7, but even correlations of that magnitude leave room for disagreement among clinicians.

Clinicians often base their opinions on clinical judgment rather than on empirically validated and commonly accepted assessment techniques like those used in research studies. The confidence with which they assert their opinions is not necessarily related to its accuracy or its clarity (see Box 7.4). Many clinicians acknowledge the limits of expertise and the difficulties of diagnosis. They regard diagnoses as tentative working hypotheses to be proved or disproved as they learn more about the patient. In a forensic context, however, clinicians as "experts" must quickly provide facts and conclusions, not hypotheses. Moreover, the forensic task is more difficult than the clinical task of undertaking assessment for treatment purposes. Forensic experts are asked to retroactively assess someone's mental functioning at the time of the crime. The standardized tests most highly recommended by a sample of diplomates in forensic psychology for mental state at the time of the *offense* evaluations (Lally, 2003) are tests which assess present, not past functioning. Experts may also be asked to give opinions about imprecisely defined issues like moral understanding, not a clinical concept. Because of their experience and training, expert testimony may be something more than mere speculation, but its reliability and validity are debatable.

Diagnostic Reliability and the Adversary Process

Responsible forensic examiners are not "hired guns." Most will not agree to deliver whatever assessment the side hiring them wishes. However, the adversarial system may compromise their objectivity in subtle ways. Zusman and Simon (1983) postulated a process

BOX 7.4

209

Expert
Testimony

Experts at the Hinckley Trial

John Hinckley had no history of psychiatric hospitalizations prior to his attempted assassination of President Ronald Reagan. He had been in psychotherapy because he wasn't working up to his potential or his parents' expectations. He functioned adequately as a student, traveled all over the country, and walked into a store to buy a weapon, all without arousing the slightest suspicion that he was mentally ill.

At Hinckley's trial, Dr. William T. Carpenter, a defense psychiatrist, testified that Hinckley fully or partially met the *DSM-III* (the then-current edition) diagnostic criteria for schizophrenia, for schiozotypal and schizoid personality disorders, and for major depressive disorder. He concluded that Hinckley suffered from "process schizophrenia." *Process schizophrenia* is not among the subtypes of schizophrenia listed in the *DSM*. Carpenter defined it as "an illness that usually begins during adolescence or early adulthood. It has usually a slow development so that the first years in the illness will be the illness manifestation, begin with fairly subtle disorders in social functioning and in personality functioning, and it progresses" (quoted in Reisner, 1985, p. 622).

Dr. Park Dietz, a prosecution psychiatrist, saw some of the symptoms Carpenter observed, but he disagreed with Dr. Carpenter's diagnosis. Dr. Dietz said that Hinckley fit three diagnostic categories, dysthymic disorder (Axis I), narcissistic personality disorder, and mixed personality disorder. He characterized these as falling on the "less serious side" of the range of disorders in the *DSM-III* (Reisner, 1985, p. 628). On cross-examination, Dr. Dietz refused to agree with the defense attorney's summary of the testimony of the several psychiatrists "that Mr. Hinckley on March 30, 1981 [the date of the assassination attempt] was suffering from a mental disease." Dr. Dietz agreed that mental disorders were included in the *DSM-III* as well as mental diseases, and that John Hinckley suffered from a mental disorder but not a mental disease (Reisner, 1985, 630). Was that sophistry in the use of language because of the legal standard, or did it refer to a real and valid distinction?

For an extended description of the case, see Ewing and McCann (2006), ch. 8, 91–101.

of "forensic identification" in which initially neutral experts become emotionally involved with the party that hired them because of frequent contacts with litigants and their attorneys. Without meaning to or even being aware of the process, they may develop a desire to support that side's case as much as possible. Levine (1985) showed that, over a series of cases, the adversarial contest undercut diagnostic reliability sharply.

Some critics of the present system have suggested that the court itself appoint experts to avoid the biasing effects of the adversarial process. But using only one set of experts would not ensure accuracy or objectivity. The judges who would appoint the experts have their biases and preferences, too. A judge may appoint an expert knowing that expert rarely finds any defendant is insane. The point of the adversarial system is to see that individual defendants get a vigorous defense and are protected from biases that work against them. The U.S. Supreme Court, in *Ake v. Oklahoma* (1985), held that a defendant was entitled to his or her own psychiatric witness if sanity is likely to be an issue at trial, or when the defendant's mental condition is relevant to sentencing in a capital punishment case. If the defendant is indigent, the state has to pay a reasonable fee for the defendant's psychiatric expert.

The Language Problem

Experts testifying under the stress of the courtroom may go into great detail about about irrelevant distinctions. Their testimony can be excessively theory ridden. Because of their culture and training, some clinicians are prone to use abstract terms that signify unconscious processes and structures (e.g., *poor boundaries, projected rage, chronicity,* and *regression*) that laypeople do not understand (Morse, 1982). Standard diagnostic terms like *formal thought disorder, pressure of speech,* and *hypervigilance* are jargon if they are not explained well. Experts may fail to provide what most judges and jurors need: their informed speculations about the nature and quality of the defendant's conscious thought processes, subjective experience, and observable behaviors and symptoms during the time the crime was committed. When jargon-laden expert testimony is long-winded and detailed, it can be boring as well as baffling, and, therefore, not very useful. Lawyers can avoid these problems by better organizing and preparing the testimony of their expert witnesses.

Mental Illness and Insanity: Ultimate Issues

The triers of fact (the judge or the jury) in an insanity trial must answer four questions:

1. Does or did the defendant have a mental disease or defect?
2. Was the defendant suffering from disabling symptoms of the disease at the time of the crime, and, if so, what were these symptoms?
3. Did the symptoms or deficits impair the defendant's ability to know or appreciate the wrongfulness of the act (and/or, in some jurisdictions, to conform the defendant's conduct to the requirements of law)?
4. Is the defendant legally insane (**ultimate issue**)?

Do triers of fact need the assistance of expert testimony to answer any of these questions? Morse (1978, 1982, 1985, 1986) contends that expert testimony will not improve jury decision making about any of these questions, all of which he sees as involving moral judgments about criminal culpability. Most legal and mental health professionals, however, believe that expert testimony may help juries address the first two questions. Many lawyers and experts agree that clinicians should not explicitly address questions (3) and (4), which are beyond professional competence (American Bar Association, 1983; American Psychiatric Association, 1983; Golding and Roesch, 1987; *Washington v. United States,* 1967). They argue that experts' opinions might unduly influence the jury. This is the reason why the Insanity Defense Reform Act (1984) prohibited experts from testifying directly on the "ultimate issue" of the defendant's insanity in federal courts. Several states have similar prohibitions.

The ban on offering certain opinions may not have had its intended effect. Rogers and Ewing (1989) argue that this reform is technical only; they believe that, when an "expert" offers a strong scientific opinion about the defendant's mental state, the jurors will know where the expert stands on the legal question of insanity. A mock juror study (Fulero and Finkel, 1991) confirms that view. Twenty-two percent to 69 percent of the subjects, depending on which experimental condition they were in, could not remember whether experts had offered an opinion about the ultimate issue of the defendant's insanity. Most of the subjects in the group for which the experts gave diagnostic testimony, but said nothing about insanity per se, misremembered the testimony as including a conclusion about the defendant's insanity.

The Guilty but Mentally Ill Verdict

In 1975, Michigan instituted a guilty but mentally ill verdict (GBMI) in response to public concern after two NGRI acquittees released by court order committed violent crimes (*People v. McQuillan*, 1974). To be found GBMI, a defendant must be found mentally ill, guilty, and not insane. By the early 1980s, 13 other states had instituted a GBMI verdict, generally in response to a well-publicized case where the perpetrator of a violent crime pleaded NGRI.

Legislatures intended the new verdict to reduce inappropriate NGRI acquittals and to ensure the detention and punishment of mentally ill criminals. GBMI is a guilty verdict, not a partial responsibility verdict. A defendant found GBMI is not charged with a lesser crime because of the illness. The court can impose the same sentence on a GBMI convict as on someone simply found guilty of the offense, including the death penalty. A conviction based on a plea of GBMI can count as a prior felony conviction (*United States v. Bankston*, 1997). In some states, provisions for probation or parole are stricter for GBMIs than for other convicts (McGraw, Farthing-Capowich, and Keilitz, 1985). Legal challenges to the GBMI laws in state and federal courts have been unsuccessful (McGraw, Farthing-Capowich, and Keilitz, 1985; *Neely v. Newton*, 1998, 1999).

Providing mental health treatment for mentally ill convicts was a secondary aim of the GBMI legislation. However, the GBMI laws do not contain provisions insuring that GBMI convicts will receive special mental health services and do not provide special funding for their treatment. In fact, GBMI convicts are not getting much special psychiatric treatment (Borum and Fulero, 1999; Keilitz, 1987; McGraw, Farthing-Capowich, and Keilitz, 1985; Steadman, 1985b; Coleman, 1999).

The American Bar Association, the American Psychiatric Association, the National Mental Health Association, and many legal scholars have objected to GBMI laws. They argue that the verdict gives juries an opportunity to take "the easy way out." They can compromise on the verdict and avoid confronting the issue of criminal responsibility. (See *Neely v. Newton*, 1998, for a legal response to criticisms of the GBMI verdict.) Jury simulation studies using college students as mock jurors suggest that this fear may be justified (Roberts and Golding, 1991; Roberts, Golding, and Fincham, 1987; Finkel, 1991; Finkel and Duff, 1989). When mock jurors are offered the GBMI option, it replaces both NGRI and guilty verdicts, even in cases in which NGRI or guilty verdicts traditionally would be appropriate. Roberts and associates (1987) concluded that, if the introduction of the new verdict leads to a reduction in the number of NGRI acquittals, the reduction "will be achieved not by eliminating inappropriate verdicts but rather by creating a new (and larger) class of inappropriate verdicts as a result of obfuscating the classic moral distinctions inherent in the insanity defense" (p. 223).

The effects of the introduction of the GBMI option on the outcome of real cases are not as clear. Both NGRI acquittals and GBMI convictions are relatively rare. In some GBMI verdict states, the rate of NGRI acquittals rose somewhat, while in other states the rate of NGRI acquittals decreased as intended (Slobogin, 1985; Coleman, 1999). The introduction of the GBMI verdict option in Georgia resulted in a small, perhaps temporary, increase in the number of defendants using insanity pleas. Three quarters of those who pled insanity bargained for a GBMI verdict (Steadman et al., 1993). In Michigan, 61 percent of the GBMI findings were obtained through plea bargains (McGraw, Farthing-Capowich, and Keilitz, 1985). In these states, then, the GBMI option appears to have added a new card to the plea-bargaining deck. Coleman (1999) cited a study claiming that the GBMI verdicts had all but eliminated the insanity verdict in Indiana. As a result, prisons in that state, and other states in which the use of the insanity defense is sharply reduced may be displacing mental hospitals as the institution in which the long-term mentally ill are held.

Mental health courts (MHC). The strict standards for NGRI pleas keep defendants out of mental hospitals. The policy inadvertently ensures that large numbers of mentally ill people enter the criminal justice system, often reoffending after release when they become ill again. One response has been the development of mental health courts (MHC). These are criminal courts which hear only cases where the defendant is mentally ill. The court diverts defendants from prison into mandatory community mental health treatment. It monitors the treatment and enforces sanctions for noncompliance (Redlich et al., 2005). These courts were instituted to ensure mentally ill defendants get care. They expanded as part of a trend towards problem-solving specialty courts that emphasis treatment and reintegration into the community.

There was one mental health court in 1997; today they number about 100 (GAINS Center, 2004). Where many of the original courts diverted mostly misdemeanor defendants out of the criminal justice system, later courts increasingly include felony cases. After adjudication, which requires a guilty plea for eligibility, the courts developed treatment plans and relied on probation officers to enforce compliance (Redlich et al., 2005; Steadman and Redlich, 2006). Steadman and Redlich (2006) found that, as with other jail diversion programs, older white women were disproportionately represented among cases accepted by the MHCs.

MHC supporters believe they are an effective and humane way to rehabilitate ill offenders. The MHCs have been criticized for being coercive, violative of due process, for not always ensuring adequate treatment is provided, and for potentially harming the people they are intended to rehabilitate by further stigmatizing and criminalizing illness. Methodological problems make it hard to gather good evaluation data (Stefan and Winick, 2005).

Abolishing the Insanity Defense

In 1979, Montana removed the insanity defense from its statute books. Idaho (1982) and Utah (1983) followed suit (Keilitz, 1987). The abolition survived constitutional challenges because there is no constitutional right to the defense (*Kansas v. Bethel*, 2003). Later, Nevada (1995) and Kansas (1996) abolished the insanity defense.

In all of these states, the traditional mens rea defense was left intact. A mens rea defense is concerned with the specific mental state that is an element of a crime. In contrast, the NGRI defense is concerned with the defendant's capacity to behave lawfully. Borum and Fulero (1999) give the hypothetical example of a schizophrenic who shoots a man he believes is going to kill him and take over the planet, not unlike the defendant in *Clark v. Arizona* (2006). If the defendant intended to kill the man, he had the requisite mens rea to be guilty of murder even if, because of his delusion, he did not know the act was wrong. In a real case, Michael Bethel shot and killed two women and his father. He claimed God told him to do it because one of the women and his father were responsible for his rough life. Bethel had a history of mental disorder. Under the revision of Kansas law, the psychiatric testimony that he was psychotic was not relevant because the defense had to show that the mental disease or defect was specifically related to the intention to perform the illegal act. The evidence was clear from Bethel's statements that he intended to kill his victims. That was sufficient to prove the mens rea element of the crime despite evidence of mental disorder (*Kansas v. Bethel,* 2003). A similar issue was addressed by the U.S. Supreme Court in *Clark v. Arizona* (2006). Arizona's statute barred evidence of mental disorder to show diminished capacity to undermine proof of mens rea or intent to kill. The Supreme Court held that Arizona's law was a constitutionally permissible variation of the insanity defense.

There are little data on the effects of the abolition. In Montana, the number of insanity acquittals dropped. However, the reduction may not have made much difference in the way mentally ill offenders were treated. Steadman et al. (1989) examined court records in seven Montana counties for three years before and three years after the NGRI verdict was abolished. While insanity acquittals markedly declined, dismissals based on competence to stand trial substantially increased. Those defendants whose cases were dismissed were then committed civilly. In Utah (Heinbecker, 1986), there were as many mens rea nonresponsibility acquittals in the two years after the abolition of the insanity defense as there had been NGRI acquittals in the nine years before. A prosecutor in Idaho, one of the states that abolished the insanity defense, said,

> It is probably incorrect to say that Idaho 'abolished' the insanity defense. The new tactic of defense attorneys in our jurisdiction is to challenge an individual's ability to aid his attorney in the preparation of his own defense. If successful in that endeavor, the defendant may never have to be tried under our statutory scheme. Thus our 'abolition' has shifted the emphasis from asserting the defense during the trial to pre-trial. Although the standards are different, it doesn't appear to be as difficult to have an individual certified to not be able to assist his attorney in preparation of his own defense as it would be to challenge the intent aspect of a particular crime. (Quoted in Geis and Meier, 1985)

It seems that, although the law changed, the belief of players in the justice system that mentally ill offenders should not be punished as other lawbreakers were did not change very much.

Summary

The definitions of most crimes include an explicit requirement of possessing a certain mental state (mens rea). The greater the degree of intentionality and malice, the more serious the crime and the greater the punishment. To prove that a person is guilty, the prosecution must prove every element of the crime charged (i.e., the act and the injury), including the mental state.

In our society and most others, those severely mentally ill at the time of the criminal act are presumed to have lacked the capacity for moral responsibility because of their disordered mental state. Legal formulations have varied from the 1723 "Wild Beast" standard, to the M'Naghten right or wrong test, to the **product test,** which required only that the defendant's behavior be "the product of a mental disease or defect." Today, most jurisdictions use a cognitive test for insanity: the defendant is insane if the person did not know what he or she was doing or did not know or appreciate that the act was wrong. Many jurisdictions also accept an additional volitional test: the defendant is insane if he or she can't conform his or her behavior to the requirements of law or is acting under an irresistible impulse.

When John Hinckley was found NGRI for his attempted assassination of President Reagan, there were calls to make it more difficult to plead insanity. The U.S. Congress and many states changed legal standards or procedural and commitment rules to reduce the rate of insanity defenses and to assure the public that they would be safe from mentally ill offenders. These changes may not have had the intended effects on the rate of insanity pleas or the outcome of insanity trials. Changes in legal standards do not significantly affect the verdicts of mock jurors, either.

Eighty percent of the public overestimates the frequency and success rate of insanity pleas and underestimates the amount of time NGRI acquittees are confined in mental institutions. Defendants plead NGRI more often in felony than misdemeanor cases, and they plead NGRI in less than 1 percent of felony cases. Most NGRI cases are decided by bench trials rather than by juries; NGRI cases tried before a judge are more likely to be successful, often because the prosecutor does not contest the plea. The success rate of NGRI pleas varies from state to state.

NGRI acquittees are rarely released immediately. After the trial, they are sent to hospitals for evaluation and are not released without judicial approval. An NGRI acquittee can legally be confined in a mental hospital longer than the prison term served by someone found guilty of the same offense. This may happen to NGRI acquittees of nonviolent offenses and violent offenses other than murder. Although in principle NGRI acquittees are confined for treatment, they may remain in hospitals longer than those who are convicted criminally for the same offenses remain in prison. The length of stay in confinement is correlated more closely with offense than with diagnosis.

The law assumes that expert testimony will help the judge or jury determine whether a defendant is suffering from a mental illness and how his or her understanding and behavior might have been affected by the illness at the time of the crime. In most cases in which a mentally ill person breaks the law, there is no "battle of the experts." However, there are enough trials in which mental health professionals offer contradictory or confusing testimony to raise doubts about their supposed expertise. The vagueness of the law, the relatively weak reliability of mental health diagnoses, the adversarial nature of a trial, and the need for the court to come to a definite decision may all tend to undermine a professional's objectivity and decrease agreement among clinicians participating in the adversary process.

To reduce inappropriate NGRI verdicts, while providing for the detention and treatment of mentally ill offenders, some states introduced a guilty but mentally ill (GBMI) verdict. This is a guilty verdict intended to ensure that violent mentally ill offenders will be incarcerated and punished. The verdict also acknowledges their illness and need for treatment. The GBMI verdict may confuse the issue of responsibility. It appears to promise treatment, but the promise has not been backed up with funds or facilities.

A few states have abolished the insanity defense altogether, retaining only the traditional mens rea defense. Even when abolished, there is resistance to finding the severely mentally ill guilty of crimes; as NGRI pleas decreased, the number of cases dismissed because the defendant lacked the competence to stand trial increased.

The legal system, the public, and clinicians have been struggling to develop a just insanity defense for two centuries. There is as yet no firm consensus about how the criminally insane should be treated, that is, how to balance our desire to help those who are helpless to control themselves, our belief that people are responsible for their actions, and our need for protection from irrational aggression. Intractable social problems are susceptible to better and worse solutions, but there may be no optimal solution (Sarason, 1978). Social science certainly cannot resolve philosophical questions of guilt and responsibility. Empirical knowledge can help us evaluate the realism of our fears and hopes, appreciate the nature and complexities of the dilemmas we face, and prepare for the consequences of the policy choices that we do make.

Discussion Questions

1. What justice principles are served by the insanity defense?
2. Polls indicate that people believe the insanity defense is used more often and is more often successful than it is. Why might this be?
3. How might you develop a measure assessing appreciation of right and wrong?
4. Do people understand and use the mens rea principle in everyday life? How could you find out whether parents use the principle in disciplining their children?

5. Can you devise a study to see if people's opinions about the insanity defense are influenced, as many believe, by fear of the mentally ill?

6. A mentally ill patient who attacked someone because voices told him the man was trying to poison the city's water supply is found NGRI. His delusions, paranoia, and auditory hallucinations are successfully treated with medication. He responds to psychotherapy aimed at helping him understand his illness and his need for medication, and at improving his ability to cope with stressful situations. He is released from the hospital, he stops taking the medication, the delusions and voices return, and he assaults somebody again. If you were a jury member, what information would make you more or less likely to find him NGRI?

Key Terms

affirmative defense
ALI standard
battle of the experts
clinical disorders
cognitive capacity
Durham rule
guilty but mentally
  ill (GBMI)
Hinckley trial
insanity

Insanity Defense Reform
  Act (IDRA)
intent
irresistible impulse
malice aforethought
manslaughter
mens rea
M'Naghten rule
murder
non compos mentis

not guilty by reason of
  insanity (NGRI)
personality disorders
product rule
product test
psychosis
reliability
ultimate issue
volitional capacity
wild beast standard

CHAPTER **8**

The Death Penalty

Capital punishment has been controversial for at least three centuries. Some people believe it is morally reprehensible, while others believe it is an essential element of criminal justice. Research cannot address the question of whether capital punishment is morally right or wrong. Social scientists have investigated whether or not decisions about capital punishment can be made fairly and whether the death penalty has a deterrent effect. This research provides another good example of the interplay between social science and the courts.

In this chapter, we will review

- the history of the death penalty in the United States, and the legal decisions ruling on its constitutional and fair use.
- research bearing on arguments for and against capital punishment, and research bearing on those arguments, in particular whether the death penalty deters capital crimes (crimes potentially punishable by execution) or crimes in general.
- research on the relationship between race and capital punishment, including social science data bearing on potential influences of cultural and institutional racism on the imposition of the death penalty.
- research investigating whether "death-qualified" juries, composed of jurors willing to impose the death penalty selected to serve in a capital case, are biased in favor of the prosecution.
- research on the penalty phase of capital cases, a second trial with the same jurors held after a person is convicted of a capital offense to decide whether or not execution is appropriate.
- controversy about the applicability of the death penalty to juveniles and to those with mental retardation.
- proposed reforms to make the death penalty fairer.

In the course of the chapter, we will highlight differences in the ways social scientists and judges think about data, about values, and about social problems. These differences have sometimes led judges to reject what social scientists believe are important implications of their research.

The History and Jurisprudence of Capital Punishment

Even though the Ten Commandments of the Old Testament include a prohibition on killing, that prohibition never included punishment for a crime or killing an enemy in warfare. Capital punishment was an accepted punishment for many crimes. Up through the eighteenth century in England, a great many crimes (e.g., animal poaching, pickpocketing, and practicing witchcraft) were punishable by death. Jurors often refused to convict rather than put to death a sympathetic defendant or one who had committed a relatively minor crime (see Green, 1985, for a history of the struggle between jurors who refused to convict in **capital cases,** cases in which the guilty could receive the death penalty, and judges who wanted the law to be standardized). Similarly, although the law on the books allowed execution for many crimes, the death penalty was seldom used in the North American colonies. Eventually, juror reluctance to convict led to a reduction in the number of capital offenses. But if people did not want the death penalty used frequently, they accepted it as a necessary part of the justice system.

In the early days of the Republic, most states in the United States did not make much use of the death penalty, either before or after they reduced the number of crimes that nominally could be punished by execution. However, there were important differences in the administration of the death penalty by race and by region. The occasional hangings that took place were public events held in broad daylight, before morbidly curious and sometimes festive crowds. A hanging was an occasion, a spectacle. People eagerly watched the trip to the gallows; and they listened closely to the condemned man, when, as sometimes happened, he made a last speech in the shadow of the gallows (Friedman, 1985, p. 283).

In the twentieth century, many people came to believe that the death penalty was immoral. After World War II, the penalty was abolished in what is now the European Union and by legislatures in some states in the United States. Subsequently, many states reinstated it. Although public support for capital punishment is generally quite strong, as a result of publicity about unfairness and error in death penalty sentences, support has fallen to 50 to 60 percent in various polls. Nearly half of respondents favored life without parole over the death penalty (Death Penalty Information Center, 2004). Death penalty proponents are now mounting a counteroffensive in support of the death penalty (Justice for All, 2004).

Based on the pattern of past rulings of the U.S. Supreme Court, it seems unlikely that the death penalty will be declared unconstitutional in and of itself any time in the immediate future. The justices have repeatedly held that it is constitutional. However, the Supreme Court, as well as federal courts and state courts have mandated an increasing number of exceptions and procedural requirements to ensure the fair application of the the death penalty. These may account for its decreasing imposition.

The Supreme Court has banned the death penalty for those who are mentally retarded and for those who committed their crimes before they were 18. Now there are questions about whether lethal injection is a permissible means of execution. The death penalty can be imposed only for certain types of murders specified in state legislation. It cannot be imposed for felony murder (where a death occurs during the commission of another felony) or for the rape of an adult woman. The death penalty cannot be a mandatory punishment for any crime. Each defendant's case has to be considered against specific state standards for a capital offense. Moreover, the jury is directed to take into account all mitigating circumstances. There is also a prohibition on executing those who are found incompetent to be executed. Because some exceptions (e.g., mental retardation or youth) are based upon psychological propositions, we will emphasize them in this chapter.

⊠ Challenges to the Death Penalty

In the 38 states with the death penalty, those sentenced to death routinely appeal. Challenges to the constitutionality of the death penalty have been made on two grounds. The first is that any execution violates the **Eighth Amendment**'s prohibition against "cruel and unusual punishment." This argument asks us to consider the purposes of punishment in criminal justice, and to consider what punishment fits what crime (**proportionality**). That argument has failed so far because the death penalty has a long history in the United States. However, we have eliminated torture and mutilation as punishments. Is it proper to consider "evolving standards of decency" when interpreting the constitution? If so, will execution be consonant with our values in the future?

Death row prisoners have also challenged the death penalty on the grounds that it is imposed arbitrarily or unfairly and, thus, violates the Constitution's Due Process and Equal Protection Clauses (both in the Fourteenth Amendment). This second argument has been more successful. A large number of death penalty convictions reviewed by appeals courts were judged by legal standards to have been wrongfully imposed (White, 1991). The American Bar Association (ABA) has recommended that the death penalty be suspended because it cannot be imposed fairly (Harris, 1997).

Furman v. Georgia

In *Furman v. Georgia* (1972), the U.S. Supreme Court reviewed three death penalty cases. A deeply divided Court found that, under then-existing state laws, the death penalty had been, as Justice Stewart put it in his opinion, "so wantonly and so freakishly

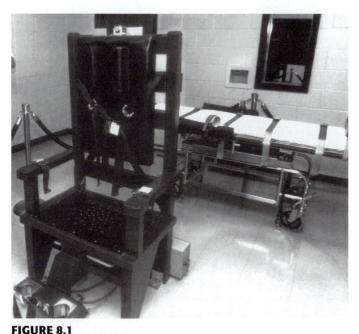

FIGURE 8.1

Electric Chair and the Lethal Injection Gurney: Two Common Methods for Execution

imposed" that capital punishment *as it was being administered in the states* constituted cruel and unusual punishment in violation of the Eighth and Fourteenth Amendments.

The *Furman* decision resulted in a national suspension of the death penalty. State legislatures rewrote their death penalty statutes to meet the Supreme Court's objections. The new legislation specified which crimes should be subject to the death penalty, and established guidelines for conditions that had to be met before imposing the death penalty. The guidelines were intended to ensure that like crimes would be punished equally.

Gregg v. Georgia

In *Gregg v. Georgia* (1976), the Supreme Court reviewed the death penalty statute that Georgia's legislature passed in response to *Furman*. The new law specified the offenses subject to the death penalty. It also provided for a split, or **bifurcated,** two-phase trial in capital cases. In one phase (the **guilt phase**), the jury determines guilt or innocence of the capital offense. If the jury finds the defendant guilty of a capital offense, in the second phase (the **penalty phase**) the jury determines whether to impose the death penalty on the defendant. The evidence is presented separately in each phase, but the same jurors may decide both phases of the case. In the penalty phase, the jury decides whether the evidence shows that one or more of ten **aggravating factors** (e.g., multiple murder, or wantonly brutal killing) specified in the legislation occurred during the crime. They also hear evidence presented by the defense (**mitigating factors**) making the crime seem less severe or more understandable, or the defendant more sympathetic. If the jury finds one or more aggravating factors to be present in the crime, and, in their judgment, these are not outweighed by the mitigating factors, jurors can impose the death penalty. Later challenges to the fairness of the death penalty centered on whether jurors who said they could not ever impose the death penalty could be excluded from the guilt-determining phase of the trial (see section on *Witherspoon* case), and on how mitigating factors were to be introduced and weighed.

Public Opinion and the Death Penalty

The Court upheld the constitutionality of the new Georgia statute. The majority opinion asserted that the death penalty was not in and of itself "cruel and unusual punishment" and did not violate U.S. standards of conscience. The representatives of the people in more than two-thirds of the state legislatures had enacted death penalty statutes. The Court concluded that the very willingness of jurors, who represent community sentiment in criminal trials, to impose the death penalty also showed that the death penalty was acceptable within modern society. On those grounds, the death penalty could not be said to violate American values or standards of conscience. The Court was following legal tradition in looking to such sources to gauge public opinion. Social scientists use scientific, public opinion sampling surveys to gauge attitudes toward the death penalty.

Capital Punishment Today

In the 1970s and 1980s, other states, including some that had abolished the death penalty in the past, adopted death penalty legislation similar to the Georgia law approved by the Supreme Court in *Gregg.* By 1998, 38 states and the federal government (for treason and a few other offenses) permitted capital punishment.

BOX 8.1

Professors and Students Exonerated Death Row Convicts

David Protess, a journalism professor at Northwestern University, assigns his investigative reporting classes to investigate death row cases. In 1999, the class found information exonerating Anthony Porter, who had spent 20 years on death row. Porter was cleared two days before his execution date. Other students helped clear four men in Illinois who had been convicted of a double murder (McCormack, 1999).

Law professors Barry Scheck and Peter Neufeld, formerly members of O. J. Simpson's "dream team," founded and directed the Innocence Project at the Benjamin Cardozo School of Law. They represent convicts on death row who have been wrongfully convicted. Experts in DNA evidence, they used it to demonstrate that a number of innocent people had been sent to death row. Their book, *Actual Innocence,* vividly describes their cases and the reasons for wrongful convictions (Scheck, Neufield, and Dwyer, 2000).

After an initial up-tick, the number of death sentences imposed by juries has declined since 1976, when the death penalty was reinstated (Liptak, 2004; Greenfield and Stephan, 1993). In 2004, 3,314 state and federal prisoners were held on death row. In 2004, 98.4 percent were men; only 1.6 percent (a total of 52) were women. Fifty-six percent were white, 42 percent were black, and about 2 percent were Native American or Asian American (Bonczar and Snell, 2005). Latinos (otherwise classified as black or white in this survey) constituted 13 percent of those under sentence of death. From 1930 to 2004, 4,803 people were executed in the United States. Since 1977, 66 percent of the executions have taken place in just five states: Texas (336), Virginia (94), Oklahoma (75), Missouri (61), and Florida (59). Because most death penalty cases are appealed several times in the state and federal court systems, only a few people are executed each year. In 2005, 60 people were executed. Among all prisoners under sentence of death, the median time in prison exceeds nine years (Bonczar and Snell, 2005).

Mounting evidence that innocent people may have been executed and that legal representation for defendants in capital cases is often poor has led many to reconsider its fairness and eroded popular support for the death penalty (see Box 8.1). Since 1976, 114 persons sent to death row were exonerated before they were executed, some by the use of DNA evidence (Scheck, Neufeld, and Dwyer, 2000; see also Chapter 6; see Figure 8.2). After eighteen people were found to be wrongfully convicted of capital charges in Illinois since 1977, then Illinois Governor George Ryan, suspended the death penalty in his state (Johnson, 2000; see Figure 8.3). The television evangelist Pat Robertson called for a moratorium on executions on the grounds that it was unfair to minorities and to poor people (Holmes, 2000). The Nebraska legislature placed a moratorium on executions.

Arguments for and against Capital Punishment

The Constitution does not prohibit or require capital punishment; states may and have abolished the death penalty. How should state legislatures decide whether to abolish or adopt capital punishment? One line of argument looks at the rationale for punishment in criminal justice. A second line of argument examines the morality of the death penalty (see Box 8.2).

A Divisive and Painful Issue

On April 19, 2000, Tennessee held its first execution in 40 years, killing a 44-year-old man convicted of raping and murdering an 8-year-old child. The mother of the victim said, "My child will finally rest in peace." A 16-year-old boy, arrested while participating in a demonstration protesting the execution, said, "I don't see the reason behind killing people who kill people to show that killing people is wrong."

From an account by Yellin (2000).

FIGURE 8.2

Darby Tillis
Darby Tillis was wrongfully convicted and spent nine years on death row for a murder he didn't commit.

Rehabilitation

One goal of punishment is to reform or rehabilitate the offender. The goal of **rehabilitation** reflects humanist arguments that human life always has value, or a religious belief that a guilty person should be allowed to repent and heal spiritually. Even a person sentenced to life without parole has an opportunity to develop a meaningful life within the prison walls. In the penalty phase, death penalty juries may be instructed to consider the likelihood that the convicted person could be rehabilitated in deciding whether to impose the death penalty.

FIGURE 8.3

Governor George Ryan
*Governor George Ryan of Illinois suspended the death penalty in his
state because so many wrongful convictions involving the death
penalty had come to light. New York, by order of its high court, and New
Jersey, by legislation, suspended the death penalty pending further study.*

Not everyone can be rehabilitated, but assuming we did not want to execute those
who had truly changed, how could we measure a change of heart or detect faked or
superficial changes? Moreover, for many death penalty advocates, rehabilitation is not
the most important purpose of punishment. Some who apparently reformed have still
been executed. For example, Carla Faye Tucker spent 14 years on death row while
appealing her death sentence for a brutal and sadistic double murder. She appeared to
undergo a deep religious conversion manifested in good deeds toward others. Prominent religious leaders pled that she not be executed. The courts and a state commission
refused to grant a stay of execution. Governor George W. Bush of Texas refused to grant
clemency. She was executed in 1998 (Figure 8.4).

Stanley "Tookie" Williams, a cofounder of the notorious Crips gang, was convicted in 1981 of killing four people. He subsequently wrote nine children's books
while on California's death row, warning of the dangers of gangs; he also created an
international Internet project for at-risk youth. He was nominated for a Nobel
Peace Prize by a member of the Swiss parliament (Sevcik, 2003; Harris, 2000). Despite
pleas from many, including Reverend Jessie Jackson and prominent Hollywood stars,
the governor of California, Arnold Schwarzenegger, refused to grant him clemency.
Williams died by lethal injection in December 2005 (Finz, Fimrite, and Fagan, 2005).

Retribution

Another purpose of punishment is **retribution,** or legal revenge. The idea of "just
deserts" and taking revenge is deeply rooted. Proponents of capital punishment argue
that the murderer's execution settles the score for victims' loved ones and helps bring

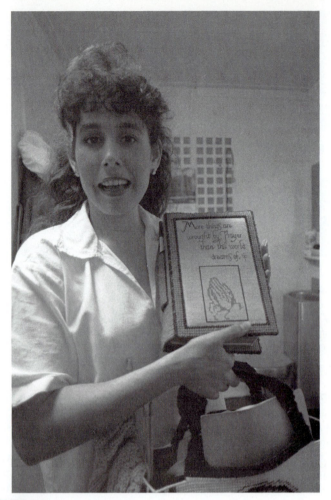

FIGURE 8.4

Carla Faye Tucker

Carla Faye Tucker was excuted in Texas despite appeals mounted on her behalf by many prominent people. Among her advocates were fundamentalist religious leaders who believed she had undergone a religious conversion and was reformed.

a painful episode to a just end. The principle of proportionality (the punishment should fit the crime) provides a basis for legal retribution. The pro–death penalty website, Justice for All (2004), underscores the point by presenting vivid and graphic depictions of the crimes those executed have committed. Without the death penalty, how can the system preserve proportionality of punishment when the crime is horrendous? Is life imprisonment without parole adequate punishment for a mass murderer or a serial killer or someone who kills a child? Does life imprisonment undervalue the magnitude of the crime and undervalue the victim's life?

Community Safety

A third purpose of punishment is to provide for community safety. Imprisoning a defendant who has committed numerous or particularly brutal crimes may not suffice to protect the community. Willie Bosket (see Chapter 9) was convicted as a juvenile of killing two people. He committed many more crimes after his release from a juvenile institution. He is now serving a life sentence as a persistent, dangerous felon. He is considered so hostile and dangerous that he has been in solitary confinement continuously. Corrections officers never approach him alone because of his tendency to attack them (Ewing, 1990a). He has attempted to kill a corrections officer. The prosecutor in the Jasper, Texas, trial of John King, a white supremacist convicted of dragging an African American man to death behind a pickup truck, argued to the jury that King should be executed to ensure public safety: "By giving Mr. King a life sentence, you're giving him at least forty years to catch a black guard, a black nurse, a black doctor, a Jewish guard, a Jewish nurse, a Jewish doctor, or anybody else. You're giving him a chance to catch anybody . . . who doesn't believe in his satanic, racist views" (Langford, 1999).

Deterrence

The fourth purpose of punishment is general **deterrence.** Proponents of capital punishment argue that the death penalty discourages people from committing violent crimes, especially if execution is swift and relatively certain. Deterrence advocates assume that criminals use the same mental calculus as noncriminals. If the thought process of criminals is different, the risks won't have the same deterrent effect (Zimring and Laurence, n.d.). If criminals do reason like anyone else, then in theory they will be deterred by potential consequences only if they rationally weigh the pros and cons of their actions. When a person kills someone else impulsively, while intoxicated, in a moment of strong passion, or while insane, he or she is not thinking rationally about possible consequences. But death penalty advocates argue that the threat of execution will, at the least, deter those criminals who plan to kill, or who might consider killing someone in the course of committing armed robbery or another planned crime.

Empirical studies of the deterrent effects of capital punishment have had conflicting results. In the past, most studies have found no deterrent effect (Forst, 1983). West (2002) studied the effect of a Louisiana statute that permitted the death penalty for convicted child rapists. Its primary effects were in increasing plea bargains, reduction in charges, and dismissals of cases. No deterrent effect was detected. In later studies, economists using mathematical models used in economics research examining large data bases claim to have found some deterrent effects of the death penalty on homicide rates, but not on other crimes (Liu, 2004; Mocan and Gittings, 2003). One study found deterrent effects were limited to the use of electrocution as the method of execution (Zimmerman, 2005). There are formidable difficulties in conducting definitive research that identifies and measures variables that may be related to the number of executions, with the availability of a death penalty, and with changes in the rate of serious crime generally. For example, in states with the death penalty, the rate of executions rises in gubernatorial election years (Lubik and Moran, 2003). The deterrent effects may show up in the econometric studies because of the use of powerful statistical and mathematical methods to find relationships that were not observed by less powerful methods.'

BOX 8.3

The Dollar Costs of the Death Penalty

The safeguards built into modern death penalty statutes make executions expensive to carry out. All death penalty cases become jury trials, and all involve the second, penalty phase trial if the defendant is found guilty. There are two to six times as many pretrial motions as in other cases. There are fees for investigators and often for mental health experts. Jury selection takes five times longer in capital cases. Trials last 3.5 times longer by an average of thirty days. Appeals may consume 800 to 1,000 attorney hours. In Los Angeles County, capital trials cost on average $1.9 million, in Texas $2.3 million, and in Florida, $3.2 million. The costs of the trial are so high that they exceed the costs of life imprisonment. It is cheaper in dollars for society to incarcerate for life than to conduct a death penalty trial (Death Penalty Focus of California, n.d.). These figures don't count the costs of incarceration in maximum security death row facilities for years awaiting the outcome of appeals (Garey, 1985). Though some of the costs may be offset by defendants who plea-bargain to avoid facing a capital charge, society pays a high dollar price for executions. Is the dollar cost a persuasive argument against the death penalty?

Proponents say that if the death penalty is just, any deterrent effect at all is a bonus:

If we execute murderers and there is in fact no deterrent effect, we have killed a bunch of murderers. If we fail to execute murderers, and doing so would in fact have deterred other murders, we have allowed the killing of a bunch of innocent victims. I would much rather risk the former. This, to me, is not a tough call. (J. McAdams, 1997, p. 9.)

(His "risk assessment" assumes that no innocent person is executed, or that the deterrent effect outweighs the "costs" of erroneous executions.)

Opponents of the death penalty are not persuaded. First, no research has convincingly shown that the existence of the death penalty has a general deterrent effect over and beyond the effect of a long prison term or a life sentence. In Canada, homicide rates actually *fell* after the abolition of the death penalty in 1976. Southern states with the greatest number of executions have the highest murder rates. In the United States, states without the death penalty, compared to adjacent states with the death penalty, have on average lower homicide rates (Death Penalty Information Center, 2004). Not all other things are equal in adjacent states, of course, so the comparison may be misleading (Justice for All, 2004). Nonetheless, the fact that the homicide rate is lower on average in states and countries without capital punishment than in those that have it demonstrates that the threat of execution is neither necessary nor sufficient to prevent crime. If some persons fear life imprisonment more than death, then the death penalty is less effective as a deterrent.

Second, punishment is an effective deterrent only if it is swift and certain. The risk of being executed for a killing is low. In 1996, there were 19,650 cases of murder or manslaughter nationwide (Ringel, 1997), but only 45 people were executed that year (Maguire and Pastore, 1998, Table 6.75). The median time between the commission of the crime and the date of execution is 16 years (see Justice for All, 2004), hardly "swift punishment."

How often is the death penalty sought in murder cases? Virginia is second only to Texas in the number of people it has executed since 1976. A state commission reviewing Virginia's system of capital punishment provided data on the flow of capital cases from 1995 to 1999 (Joint Legislative Audit and Review Commission, 2001). Of 970 arrests for murder, 215 (21.1 percent of the total) were eligible for capital punishment. One hundred and seventy (170) (17.5 percent) cases were indicted for capital murder. Of those indicted, 64 (6.6 percent) were prosecuted as death-eligible cases. Of those prosecuted, 46 (4.7 percent) were convicted of a capital murder offense; and of those, 24 (2.5 percent) were given a death sentence. It is of interest that 22 out of 46 of those convicted of a capital offense were not given a death sentence by the jury hearing the penalty phase of the trial. The death penalty is sought in only a small percent of murder cases and actually imposed on a still smaller number. The death penalty for the crime of murder is not only slow but also far from sure, raising further questions about its effectiveness as a deterrent.

Morality

For many opponents of the death penalty, deterrence is not the important issue. Some people oppose capital punishment on the grounds that it is morally wrong to risk executing an innocent person. Capital punishment leaves no room for error. Executed prisoners cannot appeal for a new trial.

Others argue against capital punishment on the moral ground that the state should not engage in killing even if the person has been convicted of a capital crime. They assert that the justice system should represent our highest values. These values include respect for human life and dignity and the rejection of violence. The great advocate Clarence Darrow expressed his opposition to the death penalty in these terms: "I would hate to live in a State that I didn't think was better than a murderer. . . . I am against it" (quoted in Katkin, 1982, pp. 241–42).

Justice Antonin Scalia (2002) believes the death penalty is not immoral. He has said that if it was immoral, as an individual, he could not participate in death penalty cases, and would have to resign from the Court. He argues that the morality appropriate for individuals (e.g., the Ten Commandments) is not appropriate for evaluating the actions of governments. Justice Scalia points out that historically, Christian teaching has not opposed the death penalty, and the death penalty was acceptable to those who wrote our Constitution. If capital punishment was acceptable then, it is acceptable today. His argument is with those who believe the Constitution is a "living document" subject to change from time to time. He does not believe the concept of "evolving standards of decency" is appropriate in death penalty jurisprudence.

Capital Punishment and Race

Historical Overview

African Americans constitute about 13 percent of the U.S. population, but they constitute 42 percent of those on death row. Of the 60 persons executed in 2005, 31.7 percent were African Americans (Bonczar and Snell, 2005). Due to a long history of racial discrimination, there is disagreement about whether or not any part of these figures are direct results of present-day discrimination, a long legacy of racial discrimination, or both.

After the Civil War, black codes designed to keep former slaves in a state of subjugation, and later Jim Crow laws guaranteed unequal justice (Woodward, 1966). The death penalty for rape was imposed almost exclusively when an African American man was convicted of raping a white woman. Despite constitutional guarantees ratified after the Civil War, African Americans were disenfranchised. With no vote they had little influence on the political system and, thus, on the police or the justice system. Until the 1960s civil rights laws, African Americans did not serve on juries in the South.

In 1964, Myrdal published a study on race and murder. He found that the majority of homicides by both whites and African Americans were within race. Black-on-black crimes were viewed as a less serious matter by (white) authorities. Crimes committed by blacks on whites were punished most severely, an unfair discrimination.

In *Furman* (1972), the U.S. Supreme Court ruled that the death penalty was unconstitutional if "wantonly," or arbitrarily, imposed. One factor the justices considered was racial discrimination in capital sentencing. Since *Furman*, political developments may have reduced racial bias in capital sentencing. Juries were integrated everywhere in the United States following federal civil rights legislation in the late 1960's and legal requirements that jury panels represent a cross-section of the community (e.g., *Duren v. Missouri,* 1979). These and other political developments were expected to reduce racial bias in capital sentencing. Prosecutors, responsive to a growing African American electorate, may have become more selective in seeking the death penalty.

Gross (1985) reviewed ten studies of race and capital cases conducted in different jurisdictions after Furman. Race of the criminal had little relationship to the imposition of the death penalty in these post-*Furman* cases, an encouraging finding. However, Gross did find evidence of continuing racial discrimination related to the race of the victim, not the race of the perpetrator. Those of either race who killed a white victim were more likely to receive the death penalty than those who killed an African American victim (Gross, 1985; White, 1991). This issue of discrimination in capital sentencing related to the victim of the crime reached the U.S. Supreme Court in 1987.

McCleskey v. Kemp

In 1978, Warren McCleskey, an African American, was convicted in Georgia of killing a white policeman during a robbery. On appeal of his death sentence, McCleskey argued that, had he killed a black victim, he would not have been given the death penalty. His claim that the sentence was influenced by racial factors was based on an elaborate statistical analysis of homicide convictions in Georgia between 1973 and 1979 (Baldus, Pulaski, and Woodworth, 1985). In 1987, McCleskey's appeal reached the U.S. Supreme Court (*McCleskey v. Kemp,* 1987).

Proportionality. In order to achieve equal protection (i.e., similar cases being treated similarly), state appeals courts review death penalty cases for proportionality. Rather than rely on appellate judges' subjective views, Baldus, Pulaski, and Woodworth (1983) used sophisticated statistical techniques to examine proportionality in Georgia over a six year period, during which McCleskey was sentenced. They wanted to use statistical regression to isolate the effects of the race of criminals and the race of victims from the effects of variables such as the characteristics of the crimes and the harm done to victims, which should properly influence sentencing.

The Baldus study. The **Baldus study** measured variables such as the certainty the defendant was a deliberate killer, the closeness of the relationship between the defendant and victim, and the viciousness of the killing. They combined these elements into

Table 8.1

229

Capital
Punishment
and Race

Death Sentence Rates by Race of Victim Taking into Account Culpability

		White Victim (Death Penalty/No. of Cases)		Black Victim (Death Penalty/No. of Cases)	
		Race			
Culpability					
Low	1	.02	5/207	.005	1/192
	2	.19	8/43	.05	1/22
	3	.44	15/34	.23	3/13
	4	.71	20/28	.40	2/5
	5	1.0	18/18	.56	5/9
High	6	1.0	31/31	1.0	4/4

This work, copyright 1985 by D. G. Baldus, G. Woodworth, and C. A. Pulaski, was originally published in 18 *U. C. Davis Law Review,* 1401 (1985), copyright 1985 by the Regents of the University of California. Reprinted with permission.

a "culpability" scale. Assigning a culpability rating to each homicide, they compared the frequency with which murderers with the same level of culpability were given a death sentence when the victim was white and when the victim was black. The results are summarized in Table 8.1.

The greatest disparity between death sentences for killing whites and death sentences for killing blacks occurred in the middle range of culpability, where judges and juries are most likely to exercise discretion. If we add together culpability levels 2 through 5, when the murder victim was white, the death penalty was imposed in 49.6 percent (61 out of 123) of the cases; when the murder victim was black, the death penalty was imposed in 22.4 percent (11 out of 49) of the cases. There was no discrimination by race of victim when the level of culpability was very low on this scale, nor when the crime was horrifying (very high score). Even with the effects of more than 200 other variables controlled statistically, race of the victim was one of the strongest independent predictors of whether a criminal received the death penalty.

Most homicides were not punished with the death penalty. Culpability scores aside, the death sentence rate for all homicides was about 9 percent when the victim was white and about 3 percent when the victim was black.

The majority opinion. By a five to four majority, the U.S. Supreme Court rejected McCleskey's appeal. Both the majority and the minority discussed the statistical data and their implications for the constitutionality of the death penalty, although the Court's understanding of the technical statistics is questionable (see Faigman, 2004, p. 258).

Justice Lewis Powell's majority opinion said that, to have his death sentence overturned, McCleskey had to show direct evidence that legislators, the prosecutors, or the jury acted with discriminatory intent. It is rare that one can obtain direct evidence of racial bias. The U.S. Supreme Court had accepted statistical proof as prima facie (initial) evidence of discrimination in cases challenging the racial or ethnic compositions of juries and in cases challenging employment discrimination. Here, the Court would not accept the correlation between race of victim and the imposition of the death penalty as evidence of racial discrimination. Some other variable could have accounted for the relationship.

There was no evidence in the record that McCleskey had been subject to overt discrimination in his trial and sentencing. McCleskey's case was not one to win sympathy. He had shot a policeman in the course of a planned robbery. In the Court's view, there was no direct evidence that McCleskey's death sentence resulted from racial discrimination. The general statistics said nothing about McCleskey's particular case.

Since 1985, studies in Indiana, Kentucky, Maryland, New Jersey, North Carolina, Texas, and Washington have confirmed that imposition of the death penalty is more likely if the victim is white than if the victim is black (Death Penalty Information Center, 2004). Not all studies confirm the victim effect (see Baime, 2001; see also Scheidegger, 2003, for a critique of the Maryland study).

Differences in Judicial and Social Science Reasoning

The Supreme Court and the social scientists reasoned differently. The social scientists took a **systems approach.** The death penalty was part of the larger criminal justice system that included police, prosecutors, defense attorneys, trial judges, jurors, and appellate judges. The opportunity for racial bias to influence the outcome arises at each point in the legal process where the actors exercise discretion. Just a little bit of relatively invisible bias at each point, for example in police discretion in the vigor of an investigation, in a prosecutor's discretion to select the charge on which to prosecute, or on a judge's decision on issues of procedure, can go a long way to produce a biased result. The statistical data supported an inference that when examined from a systems approach, discretionary decisions had subtly introduced an impermissible factor, race of the victim, into death penalty trials. The bias found by Baldus and his colleagues (1985) was visible statistically because they compared many cases using the same measuring instruments.

The Court's majority explicitly rejected the systems approach based on statistical data and the relevance of institutional racism. The history of racial discrimination had no bearing on whether there was discrimination in the application of the death penalty in the present case. The majority said courts should review decisions individually to determine if there is evidence of discrimination in the case.

To social scientists, the justices were missing the point: if each case is examined by itself, without reference to others, it will be impossible to detect patterns. The majority opinion seemed to deny that legal outcomes are affected by history and culture and are embedded in a social system. But the Court's majority noted that accepting the systems approach would mean that no death penalty scheme could yield "fair" results as long as society was imperfect. Justice Powell wrote, "McCleskey's claim, taken to its logical conclusion, throws into serious question the principles that underlie our entire criminal justice system." It was the states' right and responsibility, the majority affirmed, to determine appropriate punishments for crimes and to apply that punishment on an individual basis.

The Court decided that legal and policy considerations outweighed McCleskey's data. Though rejecting the empirical findings as irrelevant, reviewing them led the Court to clarify the values and reasoning underlying their support for the death penalty (Faigman, 2004).

Postscript. In a federal system of government, each state can adopt its own evidentiary standards. In 1998, Kentucky passed a Racial Justice Act providing for a pretrial hearing in death penalty cases. The Kentucky legislation explictly allowed the consideration of statistical evidence to determine racial discrimination against the defendant, or in relation to the race of the victim. If the judge found that the decision to seek the death penalty was racially biased, the case would still be prosecuted, but not as a capital offense (Kentucky Racial Justice Act, 1998). Although the social science evidence did not persuade the U.S. Supreme Court, advocacy based on the research caused the Kentucky legislature to respond (Coalition for Prisoners' Rights Newsletter, 1998). (Kentucky executed only two people since 1976; as of January 2006, 34 convicted persons were on Kentucky's death row.)

⊠ The Guilt Phase: Death Qualification

In a capital case, the jury is **death qualified.** Prosecutors of capital cases can challenge prospective jurors for cause during the voir dire if their opposition to the death penalty would prevent them from reviewing evidence impartially or from voting for the death penalty. A death-qualified jury is one selected after jurors unwilling to impose the death penalty have been eliminated. Social scientists hypothesized that jurors who accept the death penalty and jurors who oppose it may differ in other attitudes that could affect their decision making when determining guilt. Death-qualified juries might be more likely to convict. Jurors have been classified into five categories based on attitudes toward the death penalty (see Box 8.4). There is little controversy about excluding jurors in Category I because they would not follow the law, nor about including jurors in Category IV, because they would clearly follow the law. The fairness of excluding or including jurors in the remaining categories has been questioned.

Witherspoon v. Illinois

In the 1960s, William C. Witherspoon was convicted in Illinois of murdering a police officer, and was sentenced to death. He appealed on the grounds that the procedure for death-qualifying jurors in Illinois violated his rights under the Sixth and Fourteenth Amendments. At that time, Illinois law permitted the exclusion for cause from capital cases of prospective jurors in Category II and in Category III (see Box 8.4) as well as those who said they were so opposed to the death penalty that they would not vote guilty (Category I). The state used bifurcated trials in death penalty cases, with the same jury serving in the guilt-determining and the penalty phases.

BOX 8.4

Attitudes toward the Death Penalty and Death Qualification

Death penalty attitudes of prospective jurors can be classified in five categories:

  I. The prospective juror is so opposed to the death penalty that the juror would never vote guilty in order to avoid imposing the death penalty.

  II. The prospective juror could review the evidence impartially and vote guilty if the evidence warranted, but the juror would never vote for the death penalty.

  III. The prospective juror has some qualms about the death penalty, but could be fair and vote for the death penalty when it was appropriate.

  IV. The prospective juror has no qualms about the death penalty, could be fair during the guilt-determining phase, and could vote for the death penalty if the defendant was found guilty.

  V. The prospective juror favors the death penalty; if the defendant was found guilty, the juror would always vote for the death penalty.

BOX 8.5

A Legal Case in Point: *Witherspoon v. Illinois* (1968)

Illinois law provided that any prospective juror in a murder case could be challenged for cause if the juror "shall, on being examined, state that he has conscientious scruples against capital punishment or that he is opposed to the same." In 1960, when this law was in effect, William Witherspoon was tried for murder. The judge said early in the voir dire, "Let's get these conscientious objectors out of the way, without wasting any time on them." The prosecution then eliminated nearly half of the prospective jurors because they had expressed qualms about the capital punishment. Only 5 of the 47 jurors who were dismissed explicitly said that they would never vote to impose the death penalty.

Witherspoon was convicted and sentenced to death. He appealed, arguing that his due process rights had been violated because the selection procedure had led to a jury that was prosecution and execution prone (see text for discussion). The Supreme Court of the United States agreed that the selection procedure had resulted in a jury partial to execution. However, they said the social science data cited were "too tentative and fragmentary to establish that jurors not opposed to the death penalty tend to favor the prosecution in the determination of guilt." The majority opinion, written by Justice Potter Stewart, pointed out that ruling that the jury was prosecution prone would require "the reversal of every conviction returned by a jury selected as this one was." The court reversed the death penalty but affirmed his conviction. Witherspoon remained in prison. The cause resulted in a burgeoning of research on "death-qualified" juries.

Witherspoon argued that the Illinois death qualification procedure created, a biased jury. He claimed that a death-qualified jury would be biased toward finding a defendant guilty in the first phase of the trial and biased toward executing him or her in the second phase (see Box 8.5).

Justice Potter Stewart, writing for the majority, agreed that the Illinois procedure for death-qualifying jurors produced "a jury uncommonly willing to condemn a man to die . . . a hanging jury." The Court specifically objected to the exclusion of the Category III jurors, who had said they had some qualms but were willing to follow the law. The court held that "a sentence of death cannot be carried out if the jury that imposed or recommended it was chosen by excluding potential jurors for cause simply because they voiced general objections to the death penalty, or expressed conscientious or religious scruples against its infliction." Since *Witherspoon*, juror Categories I and II have been called *Witherspoon* **excludables** (may be excluded in capital cases). Categories III, IV, and V are *Witherspoon* **includables** (acceptable for jury duty in capital cases).

The Court did not accept Witherspoon's other claim that a death-qualified jury is "necessarily biased in favor of conviction." Witherspoon's brief referred to three psychological studies in support of the claim. The Court said the studies were "too tentative and fragmentary" to be persuasive. However, a footnote (n. 18) invited further research. If the research bore out the prosecution proneness of death-qualified juries, perhaps it would be fair to require a different jury for each phase of the death penalty trial. Jurors in Category II could sit on the guilt-determining phase, and another jury, not including jurors with those attitudes, could sit on the penalty phase.

The footnote stimulated psychological research on whether a juror's attitude toward the death penalty affected the juror's behavior in determining guilt or innocence. In the 12 years after *Witherspoon,* about two dozen studies tested the theory that death-qualified jurors were prosecution prone.

Hovey v. Superior Court

In *Hovey v. Superior Court* (1980), the California Supreme Court wrote a detailed review of the research on juror bias and death qualification. In California, the same jury heard both the guilt-determining and the penalty phases of the trial. Richard Adam Hovey argued for two juries during a 17-day hearing that produced 1,000 pages of exhibits and testimony from seven expert witnesses who reviewed some two dozen social science studies. Hovey lost the motion and subsequently was convicted of murder. His appeal eventually reached the California Supreme Court.

The California Supreme Court's opinion strongly resembled a review article in a social science journal. Thirty-five pages were devoted to a detailed description and methodological review of research in four categories: (1) juror behavior in voting, or conviction proneness; (2) attitudes correlated with attitude toward the death penalty; (3) demographic characteristics associated with attitude toward the death penalty; and (4) differences in the evaluation of evidence associated with differences in the attitude toward the death penalty.

Conviction proneness. The court opinion described studies by Hans Zeisel and Phoebe Ellsworth that showed a relationship between death penalty attitudes and **conviction proneness,** or the likelihood of voting guilty in an actual trial. Hans Zeisel surveyed jurors who had served on real criminal juries (not necessarily death penalty cases). After the trial, he asked each juror how he or she had voted on the first ballot. He also asked about their attitudes toward the death penalty. *Witherspoon* excludables (Categories I and II) voted more often to acquit than did death-qualified jurors. (Category I and II jurors could be jurors in non–capital offense criminal trials.) Ellsworth (1991) showed a sample of jury-eligible California adults a two-and-a-half-hour videotape of a simulated trial. Viewing the same trial, Category I and II jurors voted twice as often to acquit as did death-qualified jurors.

Pooling the results of 14 studies in a meta-analysis, Allen, Mabry, and McKelton (1998) found a small ($r = .17$), but statistically significant, correlation between death penalty attitudes and several measures of conviction proneness. They translated the correlation into an effect size. Of those who favored the death penalty, 59 percent voted for conviction in the simulations; of those opposed to the death penalty, 41 percent voted for conviction.

Results described in the next three sections are based on studies summarized in *Hovey.*

Attitudinal correlates. Compared to *Witherspoon* excludables, death-qualified prospective jurors were

- less inclined to accept the presumption of innocence;
- more inclined to believe that a defendant who did not testify at trial was concealing guilt;
- more inclined to believe the courts protected the guilty by legal technicalities;
- more distrustful of defense attorneys;

- less concerned about the danger of erroneous convictions; and
- more inclined to believe the insanity defense is a loophole that allows too many to go free.

These findings support the assertion that death-qualified jurors are more inclined to see defendants as guilty than are *Witherspoon*-excludable jurors.

Demographic correlates. Women are opposed to the death penalty more often than men, and African Americans are opposed to the death penalty more often than whites. Thus, selecting jurors with favorable attitudes toward the death penalty has the effect of disproportionately excluding women and African Americans from serving on capital offense juries.

Attitudes toward evidence. Death-qualified mock jurors were more likely to interpret "reasonable doubt" less stringently in a way favorable to the prosecution, to believe police witnesses more than defendants, and to believe prosecution witnesses more than defense witnesses.

Not "on point". The California Supreme Court agreed that the weight of social science evidence was persuasive. However, the court said that the research was not "on point" for California because the studies included Category V mock jurors who would always vote for the death penalty, a group excluded from capital juries under California law. Consequently, the court ruled that Hovey had not shown that the procedure actually used to select his jury was biased.

The voir dire and death qualification. Hovey raised a second issue of bias. During voir dire, prosecution and defense counsel questioned prospective jurors about their attitudes toward the death penalty in full hearing of the other prospective jurors. Moreover, the prospective jurors were told that, if the jury found the defendant guilty, they would go on to consider whether he should be executed. Hovey's lawyers argued that this voir dire procedure biased the jurors toward believing the defendant was guilty before the trial began. They introduced a study conducted by psychologist and lawyer Craig Haney to support their argument (see Box 8.6).

The California Supreme Court found Haney's research convincing. The court ordered that all death penalty voir dires in California should be conducted individually out of the hearing of other prospective jurors to prevent the introduction of biases. Here was a policy change in the California courts based on experimental evidence. Haney had provided "legislative facts," and the California high court responded by changing the state's voir dire rules.

Lockhart v. McCree

Ardia McCree was convicted of killing the proprietor of a store while robbing it, potentially a capital offense. He had been sentenced to life imprisonment without parole. McCree, like Hovey, objected to the trial judge's removal of prospective jurors who said they could not vote for the death penalty. McCree claimed that his right to have his guilt or innocence determined by an impartial jury, not a prosecution-prone jury, had been violated.

After *Hovey*, some defendants raised the issue of death qualified jurors in federal courts. The federal courts rejected the argument, as the California Supreme Court had. However the federal circuit court hearing McCree's appeal decided differently. After

BOX 8.6

235

The Guilt
Phase: Death
Qualification

The Power of Suggestion

Haney showed a two-hour videotape of a simulated voir dire to Californians qualified for jury duty. One group of randomly assigned subjects saw a videotape in which two prospective jurors indicated that they were opposed to the death penalty. In the video, they were challenged for cause. The subjects saw the two excused from service. A second group was randomly assigned to see the same video, but without the segment showing the two prospective jurors opposed to the death penalty being excluded.

Before they heard any evidence, the subjects were asked whether they thought the defendant referred to in the voir dire was guilty. Those who were exposed to the segment where jurors opposed to the death penalty were disqualified voted guilty more often than those who did not see the segment. The subjects exposed to the segment were more likely than those not exposed to say (1) that the prosecutor and defense attorney personally believed the defendant was guilty, and (2) that the judge believed the defendant was guilty. Fifty-five percent of those who saw the segment said they would impose the death penalty, compared to 22 percent of those not exposed to it.

Described in *Hovey v. Superior Court* (1980).

reviewing 15 studies, the court ruled that death qualification in a death penalty case produced juries more prone to convict than non-death-qualified juries. The U.S. Supreme Court agreed to resolve the conflicting death qualification decisions between circuit courts by reviewing the case, *Lockhart v. McCree* (1986). A conflict in rulings between circuits is a reason for the Supreme Court to agree to grant **certiorari** ("hear a case"). The American Psychological Association submitted an amicus brief for the U.S. Supreme Court case reviewing the psychological evidence that death-qualified juries were conviction prone (Bersoff and Ogden, 1987).

Chief Justice William Rehnquist, writing the majority opinion, systematically excluded the social science studies from consideration. While the circuit court had found "substantial evidentiary support" for McCree's claim, the Supreme Court majority found the evidence was seriously flawed. Chief Justice Rehnquist discounted 9 of the 15 studies as at best "marginally relevant" because they did not deal directly with guilt or innocence determinations. Eight of the studies dealt with attitudes toward the death penalty and other aspects of the criminal justice system rather than with verdicts. The ninth, Haney's study, dealt with the effects on jurors of voir dire questioning.

Chief Justice Rehnquist criticized the remaining six studies on methodological grounds. Three mock juror studies were rejected because they were not based on the responses of actual jurors acting under oath to apply the law in a specific case. Two of the three studies did not include deliberations, and none could detect the extent to which the presence of one or more of the excluded type of jurors would have changed the outcome. Finally, the chief justice faulted the six studies because they failed to identify and account for the subjects who were absolutely opposed to the death penalty and would never vote to convict in a capital trial (Category I jurors). They could properly be excluded from serving in capital cases. Because they were allowed in the simulations, the results did not generalize to the actual situation.

Having taken away with one hand, the chief justice then took away with the other. He said that, even if the studies were methodologically sound and showed that the process of death qualification did produce juries that were more conviction prone, it didn't matter.

> We will assume for purposes of this opinion that the studies are both methodologically valid and adequate to establish that "death qualification" in fact produces juries somewhat more "conviction-prone" than "nondeath qualified" juries. We hold nonetheless that the constitution does not prohibit the states from "death qualifying" juries in capital cases. (*Lockhart v. McCree*, 1986)

The principle that jurors should be selected from a representative cross-section of the population does not mean that each petit (trial) jury must be representative. Only the panels from which jurors are selected need represent a cross-section of the population, and these panels were representative, the chief justice said.

Challenges that systematically exclude people by race, ethnicity, or gender are unconstitutional. However, people who share psychological or social attitudes do not constitute a distinctive group whose interests should be legally recognized. "On a more practical level," Rehnquist wrote, "if it were true that the Constitution required a certain mix of individual viewpoints on the jury, then trial judges would be required to undertake the Sisyphean task of 'balancing' juries, making sure that each contains the proper number of Democrats and Republicans, young persons and old persons, white-collar executives and blue-collar laborers and so on."

In sum, the majority opinion said that *Witherspoon* excludables (Category II) could be excused from serving in the guilt determination phase of a capital case without violating the defendant's Sixth Amendment right to an impartial jury.

Epistemology and the Courts

The *Lockhart v. McCree* decision shows a difference in the **epistemological approach** (the philosophical study of what constitutes knowledge) of the APA psychologists and the Supreme Court justices. Chief Justice Rehnquist found the social science research unpersuasive because it didn't speak precisely to the legal point or because of methodological weaknesses. Social scientists acknowledge that all studies have flaws. But, in their view, research is persuasive when the results of many studies using different populations and methods converge on the same results. Most psychologists agreed that the research had produced valid, robust, and replicable knowledge that could be used for policy-making purposes (see Bersoff, 1987; Ellsworth, 1991). A few psychologists questioned whether the studies of death-qualified juries were strong enough to merit a policy recommendation. Even if the studies were valid, in the absence of a gold standard of truth, we don't know whether a decision made by a death-qualified jury is more or less valid than a decision made by a jury that included *Witherspoon* excludables (Elliott, 1991).

Chief Justice Rehnquist did not agree that consistent social science findings merited a judicial response affecting many future cases. In his view, practicality and legal precedents outweighed the possible value of changing through a judicial decision how juries were selected. Moreover, he wanted to reduce future challenges to jury selection procedures in capital cases by limiting what is legally cognizable discrimination. The majority ruling, so disappointing to psychologists, may simply have reflected the Court's policy decision at that time to get on with the death penalty, and to minimize legal roadblocks to carrying out executions.

Social scientists can take two useful, if somewhat humbling, lessons from *Lockhart v. McCree*. First, social science research designed to influence legal decision making should be ecologically valid and as much on point as possible. Second, when courts review social science testimony, they are as much concerned with its value relevance and its legal implications as they are with its scientific validity.

Postscript. Although the U.S. Supreme Court did not find legal significance in the evidence regarding the pro-prosecution bias of death qualification, the construct has entered popular culture. Even though courts have not been receptive, lawyers continue to challenge death qualification in one way or another. Prosecutors are sometimes accused of seeking the death penalty in order to obtain a prosecution-favorable death-qualifed jury, and then not pursuing the death penalty (Associated Press, 2003a). Even though the U.S. Supreme Court rejected the claim that death qualification biases a jury, some court or state legislature may recognize the claim in the future. Those interested in influencing the legal system through research should not look only at victories or defeats in court cases. Over the long run, the dissemination of the research-based construct may influence popular culture, thus having an effect.

The Penalty Phase: Mitigating and Aggravating Circumstances

In *Ring v. Arizona* (2002), the Supreme Court said it is the jury's responsibility (and not the trial judge's) under the Sixth Amendment to find aggravating and mitigating circumstances. Most states already followed the procedure required by the U.S. Supreme Court. However, the explicit statement in *Ring* emphasizes the role of the jury, the representative of the community, in deciding whether the crime warranted the death penalty. The jury makes that decision in the penalty phase of a capital trial.

Judicial instructions to jurors sitting on the penalty phase are supposed to reduce arbitrariness in the imposition of the death penalty. In the penalty phase, the jurors hear testimony about aggravating circumstances that warrant the imposition of the death penalty, and mitigating circumstances that would warrant life imprisonment. A penalty phase deliberation goes beyond establishing culpability. In the penalty phase, in theory, jurors who have found a defendant guilty of a capital murder should look beyond the conviction and the presence of "aggravating" factors. In theory, the defendant is to be treated as a unique individual. The jurors are asked to make a "reasoned moral response" in consideration of any mitigating circumstance that the death penalty is not morally appropriate in this case (Bentele and Bowers, 2002). The task is complex and vague. The jurors have no guidance but judicial instructions. The penalty phase has resulted in many court challenges (see Bonczar and Snell 2005). Here we examine the dynamics of death penalty deliberations and some evidence about whether jurors understand the instructions and the task.

The Defense's Task

The penalty phase poses problems for the defendant and defense counsel. The "death-qualified" jurors have already found the defendant guilty of a capital offense. One study showed that death-qualified jurors are less receptive to the influence of mitigating factors than are jurors with more concerns about the death penalty (Luginbuhl and Middendorf, 1988). Bentele and Bowers (2002) interviewed jurors who had imposed the death penalty. They found that jurors did not think much beyond the fact that they had unanimously found the defendant guilty of a capital offense. For many jurors, that settled the issue. Much of their deliberation consisted of reviewing the trial evidence and the aggravating circumstances. The jurors who voted for the death penalty spent much less time discussing mitigating factors; few had any clear idea of the moral dimensions of their task.

Lawyers' arguments at the penalty phase may be critical, but, having focused so much of their efforts on the guilt phase of the trial, they may be inadequately prepared to make the case for mitigation in the penalty phase (White, 1991). The defense has great leeway in introducing mitigating evidence in the penalty phase (*Lockett v. Ohio*, 1978). The jury may consider as mitigating factors the defendant's character, his or her record, or any trait or circumstance that might persuade them to spare the defendant's life. Psychologists, social workers, former teachers, friends, and relatives may testify (*Skipper v. South Carolina*, 1986).

The defense lawyer tries to put together a life story that will present the now convicted murderer as an individual human worthy of being spared. Lawyers are sometimes aided in this task by an "interpretive psychologist" who testifies at the penalty phase. The interpretive psychologist tries to develop themes that help account for why the defendant is different. For example, the psychologist might show that the defendant is a victim of child abuse or has had other terrible experiences (White, 1991). The goal of the testimony is to establish empathy, understanding, and compassion between the jury and the defendant. We know little about how jurors respond to psychological testimony. If the psychologist testifies that the defendant is mentally ill, mentally retarded, or had a dreadful childhood, will that lead jurors to feel sympathy, or concern that, if the person was ever released, he or she would kill again? To what extent does consideration of a defendant's disadvantaged background, rather than arouse sympathy, call forth negative reactions to the "abuse excuse"? Bentele and Bowers's (2002) jurors who voted for the death penalty said they were not very much influenced by expert testimony on the defendant's psychological background. Such jurors see responsibility for the death penalty as belonging to the guilty defendant who committed the crime.

The Prosecutor's Task

The prosecutor will counter the defense's efforts by emphasizing individual responsibility, the duty to provide justice for the victims, and the need to protect society from future crimes. He or she will stress that the defendant had choices, but made the wrong ones. He or she will give the jury information about the defendant's criminal history (if any). The jury may hear predictions about future dangerousness made by expert witnesses as required by some state statutes (*Barefoot v. Estelle*, 1983). The jury may also be told of the harm and pain the death caused to survivors (*Payne v. Tennessee*, 1991).

Are Judicial Instructions Understandable?

In the penalty phase, the jurors must find unanimously, beyond a reasonable doubt, that one or more of the aggravating circumstances defined in the statute was proven in the case (see *Ring v. Arizona*, 2002). Whichever procedures are followed in the state, the jury is instructed to "weigh" aggravating and mitigating circumstances in some manner to decide whether execution is justified. They are instructed that they can assign any moral or sympathetic value they wish to mitigating circumstances. After jurors hear evidence and argument in the penalty phase, the judge instructs the jurors on their task in deliberation. Do jurors understand the judge's instructions?

To complicate the matter, Bentele and Bowers (2002) identified three different types of penalty phase procedures. In states using so-called *threshold procedures*, "[J]uries are instructed that they may impose a death penalty once they find an aggravating factor and after they consider mitigating circumstances." In states using so-called *weighing statutes*, juries are told to decide whether aggravating circumstances outweigh mitigating circumstances. In states using so-called *directed statutes*, jurors told that they must focus on specific factors such as future dangerousness or the heinous nature of the crime, but they still must consider mitigating circumstances. Do jurors understand the judge's instructions? Do these different procedures have different implications for jury deliberation in the penalty phase? Simulations testing testing juror comprehension of different legal instructions would make an interesting experiment.

Because the jurors are given little specific guidance, it is important that they understand what they must do to achieve a just and moral decision. If they don't understand the instructions, the reason for having a penalty phase deliberation will not be satisfied. Unfortunately the instructions may be very difficult to follow. Diamond (1993) gives an example of a penalty phase instruction with four negatives: "If you do not unanimously find from your consideration of all the evidence that there are no mitigating factors sufficient to preclude imposition of a death sentence, then you should sign the verdict requiring the court to impose a sentence other than death." It is questionable whether jurors comprehend such language and understand their task.

Some psychologists have studied judicial instructions by creating reading comprehension tests. Mock jurors read the penalty phase judicial instructions and are asked questions about what they read. Other researchers have used survey methods. Respondents read vignettes giving the instructions and telling how a juror responded to a fact situation. They are asked whether the juror's response was in keeping with the instructions. The studies have uniformly shown that mock jurors have a low level of comprehension of the instructions (Diamond, 1993; Haney and Lynch, 1997; Luginbuhl, 1992; Wiener, Pritchard, and Weston, 1995). Subjects understand about half of what they have been told. Comprehension can be improved by simplifying the language.

Bentele and Bowers' (2002) posttrial interviews with actual jurors who had sentenced defendants to death showed that many of the jurors had misconceptions about what the law required. Under the law, to vote for the death penalty, jurors have to agree unanimously, beyond a reasonable doubt, on whether specific aggravating circumstances in the statute were proven by evidence. The individual juror has great power when a unanimous decision is required, if the jurors understand the penalty phase task and their role. The jurors don't have to agree on the mitigating factors. One juror can be swayed by one mitigating factor, and another by another. In arriving at a final verdict, each juror weighs aggravating and mitigating circumstances according to conscience. Yet, in one posttrial interview, 75 percent of jurors incorrectly believed that all jurors had to agree on a mitigating factor before it could be considered (see Diamond, 1993).

Although some lower courts have been convinced by research reports that jurors didn't understand the instructions (Diamond, 1993; Luginbuhl, 1992), this line of research may not go very far. In 1999, Justice Sandra Day O'Connor said in a speech that jurors are "finally to be read a virtually incomprehensible set of instructions and sent into the jury room to reach a verdict in a case they may not understand much better than they did before the trial began" (quoted in Berlow, 2002). Not long after making the speech, she signed on to an opinion that said it is a long-standing legal presumption that jurors understand and can follow a judge's instructions (*Weeks v. Angelone*, 2000). Justice O'Connor may have been convinced by the research that jurors don't understand judicial instructions, but that had no effect on her opinion in that case.

Judicial instructions are often at issue on appeal. It is a conceit of the law that it is the *wording* of the instructions that matters, and not whether jurors understand them. As a practical matter, appeals courts cannot engage in tests of juror comprehension of judicial instructions. Research won't be sufficient to overcome the very strong presumption that jurors do understand. Because of long-standing policy considerations, claims that jurors don't understand the instructions will not likely influence constitutional decisions regarding death penalty jurisprudence.

States are free to try to respond to the issue, however, and may alter instructions. For example, the California courts have had a commission of judges, lawyers and law professors revise all jury instructions under state law. They simplified jury instructions and tried to improve comprehension by using shorter sentences and more direct language and examples. The aim of the commission was to have instructions comprehensible to a person with a tenth-grade education. The California court administration strongly encouraged courts to use the new instructions by adopting them as the only "approved" instructions in the state in 2005 (i.e., these instructions are to be used unless a judge is convinced that there is a better instruction to use for a point of law applicable to a particular case). These new instructions have not yet been tested experimentally, but research opportunities exist.

The Death Penalty and Mental Retardation

In *Penry v. Lynaugh* (1989), the U.S. Supreme Court held the Constitution did not bar the execution of a mentally retarded individual. At the time, only two states explicitly barred the execution of those with mental retardation, not a sufficient number to indicate a consensus. The Court did say that mental retardation could be introduced as a mitigating factor for jurors to consider when deciding whether to impose the death penalty.

The Court reversed this ruling a few years later in *Atkins v. Virginia* (2002). Daryl Atkins was convicted of abduction, armed robbery, and capital murder. He robbed Eric Nesbitt of his cash, drove him to an ATM machine to withdraw additional cash, and then took him to an isolated spot, where he shot him eight times. Sentenced to death by a Virginia jury, Atkins' lawyers argued he shouldn't be executed because he was mentally retarded. In part, the argument hinged on whether people with mental retardation should be considered less "culpable": "there is abundant evidence that they [i.e., the mentally retarded] often act on impulse rather than pursuant to a premeditated plan, and that in group settings they are followers rather than leaders. Their deficiencies do not warrant an exemption from criminal sanctions, but they do diminish their personal culpability" (*Atkins v. Virginia*, 2002, p. 318). The Court noted (p. 321) that those with mental retardation are more susceptible to making false confessions, and are often poor witnesses when testifying on their own behalf in the penalty phase of a death penalty trial. The Court took changes in law in many states (19 and those states that have no death penelty) barring execution of the mentally retarded as powerful evidence that society now views mentally retarded offenders as categorically less culpable than the average criminal. The Court concluded that with changing societal attitudes it had become it "cruel and unusual punishment" in violation of the Eighth Amendment to execute a mentally retarded person. Justices Scalia, Rehnquist and Thomas dissented, arguing that only the severely and profoundly retarded were excused from guilt (the equivalent of not guilty by reason of insanity), not more mildly retarded persons.

Justice Scalia's dissenting opinion said that the fact that the U.S. Supreme Court had agreed to hear the case would bring forth many new appeals from death row inmates. Those with mental retardation may constitute as much as 10 percent of the death row population. Justice Scalia also objected because the symptoms of mental retardation may be feigned (*Atkins v. Virginia*, 2002, p. 353). The standards for diagnosing mental retardation put forth by both the American Psychiatric Association and the American Association of Mental Retardation are similar. They both require subaverage intellectual functioning (Atkins had an IQ of 59) and two or more limitations in social adaption or self-care. These deficiencies must have been manifested before age 18. The psychologist in the *Atkins* case, Dr. Evan Nelson, administered a Wechsler Adult Intelligence Scale (WAIS), reviewed school records, and interviewed members of Atkins's family and deputies at the jail, in addition to examining other records. Dr. Nelson testified that Atkins's deficiencies were lifelong, and that the obtained IQ of 59 was not an aberration.

After the Supreme Court's decision, Virginia held a new trial for the sole purpose of determining whether Atkins was retarded. The trial lasted seven days. Virginia law defines a mentally retarded offender as a person with an IQ below 70 who also has significant limitations in adaptive behavior observed before the offender was age 18. The jurors heard testimony from psychologists who examined his school and prison records, and heard from friends, family, and teachers about his everyday adaptive behavior. The psychologists testified that Atkins had IQ scores of 59, 64, 74, and 76 (Glod, 2005). We don't know whether these results are from the same test, nor do we know whether the psychologists took into account any practice effect that might have raised his scores. It would be ironic if the fact that he had improved on subsequent testing justified his death sentence. The jury decided that Atkins was not metally retarded. His attorneys argued to the Virginia Supreme Court that that conclusion was tainted by the fact that the new jurors were told that the previous jury had convicted him (Hardy, 2006). The Court agreed, criticized the phychologist's methods of examining Atkins, and ordered still another hearing on whether Atkins is mentally retarded (Atkins v. Commonwealth, 2006).

Several new research questions are posed by the case. Can mental retardation be feigned, as Justice Scalia contended? Can forensic psychologists reliably detect feigning? Will the requirement that the deficiencies be manifest before age 18 be a limiting factor that will minimize faking? What sort of records should a psychologist review to determine whether the condition was manifest before age 18? If IQs vary from time to time by as much as 10 or 15 points, or if different tests yield different results, which results should be used?

Death Penalty for Juveniles

Under the common law in England and in the United States, children over seven could be tried as criminals, and, on rare occasion, even executed. Between 1642 and 1983, 287 of the 14,029 people executed in the United States were under 18. As late as 1885, a ten year old was executed in Little Rock, Arkansas (Streib, 1988). In the late nineteenth century, our attitudes changed. We created the juvenile court as a civil, not a criminal, court to try to help youth who offended (see Chapter 9). But should we deal with diffeently with children and adolescents who commit especially horrible crimes? World opinion is clearly opposed to applying extreme penalties to young people (Streib, 1988). The United Nations Convention on the Rights of the Child (United Nations, 1990) bars capital punishment and life imprisonment without the possibility of release for offenses committed by persons under 18 (Article 37). The U.S. Senate did not ratify this UN convention and until recently youths were subject to execution in this country for crimes committed before they were age 18.

BOX 8.7

Public Opinion and the Execution of Younger Children

Crosby et al. (1995) conducted a vignette study by mailing a case description and questionnaire to a large sample of former jurors. One hundred and seventy-nine responded. The defendant in the hypothetical case had been found guilty of first-degree murder for the premeditated killing of a clerk during a robbery. The defendant's age was given as 10, 15, 16, or 19 years. Respondents were asked to read the vignette and then to vote for or against execution. The results were startling. Fully 60.5 percent of respondents voted to execute the 10 year old, 73.2 percent the 15 year old, 90 percent the 16 year old, and 97 percent the 19 year old defendant. The authors say, "In light of the societal perception that the rate of violent crime has risen in the United States, have our standards of decency evolved to establish a societal consensus that heinous murderers deserve the death penalty regardless of their age?" (257).

Since 1976, seven states have executed youths for crimes they committed when they were over 16 or under 18 (Rimmer and Bonner, 2000; see also Stephan and Brien, 1994).

In September 1993, then 17-year-old Christopher Simmons, along with a 15-year-old companion, entered Shirley Crook's home in the middle of the night. She awoke and recognized Simmons. He and his companion then dragged her out of her bed, abducted her from her home, and drove her to a railroad trestle over a river. They then hogtied her, and covered her head and face completely with duct tape. While she was still alive and conscious, they threw her off a bridge into a river, where she drowned. An autopsy showed that prior to death, she had sustained several fractured ribs and other bruises.

Simmons was tried and convicted of first-degree murder and sentenced to death. His first appeal to the Missouri Supreme Court failed. His death sentence was upheld. The Missouri Supreme Court found no merit in any of his many assertions of error in the trial (*Missouri v. Roper*, 1997). (Simmons had asserted that his lawyer was ineffective because of the way the lawyer had handled the penalty phase of the trial. We discuss that claim in Box 8.8 for what it reveals about trial tactics in penalty phase hearings.)

The Missouri Supreme Court heard Simmons's appeal for a second time (*State ex rel. Simmons v. Roper*, 2003) after the U.S. Supreme Court had decided *Atkins*. The opinion in *Atkins* said that the national consensus had changed, as shown by the trend in legislation in the states barring execution of the mentally retarded. Executing the mentally retarded was "cruel and unusual punishment" by contemporary standards. The Missouri Supreme Court now found that the national consensus had also changed as far as executing those under 18 at the time of the crime. They noted that 16 states, and the federal civilian and military courts, barred execution of those under 18 at the time of the commission of the crime. When added to the 12 states and the District of Columbia, which have no death penalty, 28 states bar execution of youth who committed their crimes when they were under 18. The Missouri Court believed the U.S. Supreme Court would find the execution of youth in violation of the Eighth Amendment. It set aside Simmons's death penalty and sentenced him instead to life imprisonment. Missouri authorities appealed the decision, and the U.S. Supreme Court accepted it for review in 2004.

BOX 8.8

243

Death Penalty
for Juveniles

Penalty Phase Trial Tactics

On appeal in *Missouri v. Simmons* (1997), Christopher Simmons claimed his trial attorney was ineffective because the attorney failed to present evidence of child abuse Simmons had suffered at the hands of his father, psychological abuse because his parents underwent a bitter divorce, and Simmons's abuse of alcohol and drugs. The trial attorney employed Dr. Daniel Cuneo to examine Simmons to determine the presence of mitigating factors, but did not call Dr. Cuneo as a witness in the penalty phase. At a hearing not in the presence of the jury to assess the effectiveness of counsel, Dr. Cuneo said, "My perceptions of Christopher at that time was he had borderline personality traits and . . . his accounting of the alleged offense or crime to me was extremely cold and that would not be in his best benefit. . . . It was their [attorneys'] decision at that point that there were some things that were bad that I could say. The bad that I could say would outweigh what I could say that could be helpful." Again, Dr. Cuneo was not called to testify in the penalty phase.

At the same hearing, Mr. Burton, his trial attorney, outlined his penalty phase strategy. He indicated that "he wanted to . . . appeal to the sympathies of the jury and ensure the jury knew Movant [Christopher] was only seventeen. He intended to present [Christopher] as one who was liked or loved by his brothers, his mother, his father and Christy Brooks [a friend]. He also sought the testimony of other friends, school teachers, or former employees but learned that none of them could offer any thing substantive. In fact, some appeared . . . unwilling to discuss anything positive about him. . . ." Another plan was to allow Christopher's family to demonstrate their sorrow in contemplating the possible recommendation of death. Mr. Burton believed that if the jury chose not to like Christopher, they may choose to like his family and spare Christopher's life for the family's benefit.

Dr. Robert Smith did some psychological tests and interviewed Simmons and persons familiar with him. He diagnosed Simmons as having "a borderline personalty disorder and a schizotypal personality disorder." His testimony was also not used at the penalty hearing. The Missouri Supreme Court commented, "Missouri juries have often rejected such testimony as the sort of compelling psychological mitigating evidence that warrants a life sentence. . . . Simmons' experienced trial counsel, no doubt aware of the likelihood of the success of the psychological evidence, chose a strategy they believed might give Simmons's (sic) better chance for a life sentence."

All facts in the box were in the report of the case *Missouri v. Simmons* (1997, 182–85).

From a legal perspective, Simmons's case was a good one to decide the issue of the constitutionality of executing a youth who was under 18 at the time of the commission of the crime. By its earlier decision, the Missouri Supreme Court had eliminated all his other challenges to his death sentence. The only remaining issue was Simmons's age at the time he committed the crime. In *Atkins*, the U.S. Supreme Court agreed that persons with mental retardation were less culpable because of their limitations. The American Bar Association (2004) submitted an amicus brief in Simmons's case. The brief argued, "Like the mentally retarded, juveniles have decreased abilities to regulate their actions, understand the correlation between their actions and the consequences of those actions, and to appreciate the impact of the resulting punishment for their actions. Moreover, recent scientific research supports the conclusion that the brains of juveniles are less developed than those of non-mentally retarded adults." The American Medical Association and eight other professional organizations, including the American Psychological Association, submitted a similar brief. A review of pertinent research is found in Beckman (2004). Beckman also cited other scientists who said that the data are insufficient and that too little data connect behavior to brain structure.

In *Roper v. Simmons* (2005), the Supreme Court issued its 5–4 opinion saying that executing a person who had committed a capital crime before the person was 18 was cruel and unusual punishment, in violation of the Eighth Amendment. The Court emphasized that the consensus had changed, with 30 states now prohibiting the execution of a juvenile. Even in states that had allowed the death penalty for juveniles, the death penalty was imposed infrequently. In an argument that created controversy, the Court noted that the United States was the only country in the world that still executed juveniles. Some dissenting justices objected to using foreign law to interpret the U.S. Constitution. The majority opinion also cited research showing that adolescents have not achieved mental and emotional maturity and have an underdeveloped sense of responsibility. The Court did not note studies of brain development but referred to research demonstrating that people in their late teens were vulnerable to peer pressure, and that their personalities and characters were less firmly formed. Because of these characteristics, juveniles were less culpable than the average criminal. The majority opinion held in light of all these factors evolving standards of decency dictated that execution of a juvenile violated the Eighth Amendment's prohibition against cruel and unusual punishment. States will no longer be allowed to execute those who committed capital crimes before their eighteenth birthday. In 2004, there were 63 on death row who had been under 18 at the time of their arrest (Bonczar and Snell, 2005). Their sentences were changed life in prison. By this decision, the category of persons who could be executed had been reduced.

Death Penalty Reforms

Perhaps because of their professional acquaintance with chance and human error, social scientists may be more open to question the justice, if not the morality, of capital punishment. Researchers and advocates have taken active roles in studying and publicizing the reasons for flawed convictions, and in suggesting reforms. For example, Scheck, Neufeld, and Dwyer (2000) review reasons for flawed convictions:

- Mistaken eyewitness testimony
- False confessions (see Chapter 6)
- The use of jailhouse snitches and informants
- Forensic fraud, "junk" science, and sloppy science
- Misconduct by prosecutors and police
- Bad defense lawyers (incompetent, poorly paid, and/or inexperienced with homicide or death penalty cases)

To ensure that innocent people are not executed, the authors recommend the following reforms:

- Implementation of National Institute of Justice recommendations to change police practices to safeguard against faulty identification
- Better use of DNA testing

- Victim services and compensation for the wrongfully convicted as well as for crime victims
- A moratorium on the death penalty
- Case review commissions to review wrongful convictions to determine the causes of such convictions with a view toward recommending remedies
- Projects in law schools and other schools to investigate and represent convicted persons where there is reason to believe justice miscarried

In light of the distressing number of falsely convicted death row inmates, more states appear open to considering such reforms. Jennifer Joyce, a prosecutor in Missouri, reopened a murder investigation after 25 years. Larry Griffin had been executed for the crime 10 years earlier, but many were convinced that the evidence against him was

FIGURE 8.5

Barry Scheck, Peter Neufield, and Jim Dwyer

Attorneys Barry Scheck (r) and Peter Neufield (c) are lawyers expert in DNA evidence. They were members of O. J. Simpson's "dream team" that successfully defended him in his criminal case by challenging the DNA evidence in that case. They founded and direct the Innocence Project at the Benjamin Cardozo Law School. The project represents wrongfully convicted persons when DNA evidence is a factor in the cases. Law students work with them. Dwyer (l) is a Pulitzer Prize–winning Journalist who coauthored the book Actual Innocence (2000) with the lawyers.

seriously flawed. If exonerated, this would be the first case of the execution of a demonstrably innocent person (Zernike, 2005). Governor Ryan of Illinois placed a moratorium on executions. No one has been executed in 7 of the 38 death penalty states since 1976 when this penalty was reinstated. Twenty-four states are considering changes in their death penalty laws (see Bonczar and Snell, 2005). Although some call for extending the death penalty to new crimes, most call for limiting the imposition of the penalty (e.g., in the cases of juveniles and the mentally retarded, and when there is evidence of racial bias), for investigating its fairness, or for establishing further safeguards such as using DNA testing. Many of the recommendations, which are more directed to legislators than the courts, would rely on psychologists and other social scientists to study the flaws in the justice system, and how they could be corrected. There is much work to be done.

Summary

Many people passionately oppose capital punishment as inconsistent with our national values, but, in surveys, a majority of U.S. citizens favor the death penalty. Historically, the trend in the United States had been to restrict the use of the death penalty to fewer types of cases. Nonetheless, whereas all the Western European nations have eliminated capital punishment, 38 states and the federal government permit it. Recent publicity about wrongful convictions in death penalty cases appears to have led some former proponents of capital punishment to reconsider their position.

The death penalty should be considered in light of the four goals of punishment: rehabilitation, retribution, deterrence, and community safety. One argument for capital punishment is that it will deter other crimes. Social scientists have not found consistent evidence supporting the hypothesis. In discussions of capital punishment, however, pragmatic considerations are secondary to moral concerns.

The Supreme Court refused to rule that execution is cruel and unusual punishment in violation of the Eighth Amendment. However, executions were briefly suspended in the United States in 1972 after the Supreme Court, in *Furman v. Georgia*, found that the death penalty procedures used by the states resulted in arbitrary and capricious decisions. Executions were resumed in 1976 after the Court approved new death penalty laws designed to overcome constitutional objections.

The death penalty continues to be challenged on grounds that it is not applied fairly. In two cases, *McCleskey v. Kemp* and *Lockhart v. McCree*, the U.S. Supreme Court rejected the relevance of what social scientists considered strong evidence of bias in capital sentencing. In *McCleskey*, the Court ruled that discrimination in imposition of the death penalty based on race of the victim arising from systemic bias was irrelevant. There was no violation of due process rights if there was no direct evidence of discrimination in the defendant's trial. In *Lockhart v. McCree*, the Court said a strong body of evidence indicating that death-qualified juries are conviction prone was unpersuasive because it was not directly on point. The Court added that, even if persuasive, the finding would not mean death qualification was unconstitutional. In those cases the Court based its determinations, not on data, but on other policy considerations.

Psychologists have also studied the comprehensibility of instructions explaining to jurors how they are to weigh aggravating and mitigating circumstances in the penalty phase of a capital trial. Jurors' comprehension of these instructions is poor. Judicial instructions do not seem to control arbitrariness in capital sentencing. Challenges based on incomprehensible instructions have not yet reached the U.S. Supreme Court. The belief that jurors understand and will follow instructions is so deeply embedded in legal tradition that courts might be unresponsive to such arguments. However, in the future, states may modify standard jury instructions to make them more comprehensible, as California has recently done.

The U.S. Supreme Court has ruled that the death penalty is constitutional as long as state legislators pass laws regulating its implementation that meet constitutional standards for fairness. However, the Court has said that "evolving standards of decency" control whether the death penalty is considered cruel and unusual pnishment. The Court has been slowly reducing the categories of capital crime and the categories of individuals who can be executed. Recent decisions barred execution of the mentally retarded and juveniles under 18 at the time of the crime. Social science research has had some influence on these decisions. It has been less influential in other types of cases, but has called attention to areas where capital trials are prone to bias and miscarriage of justice.

Discussion Questions

1. Why is it difficult to assess the deterrent effect of capital punishment?
2. What do you think of Justice Powell's comment that "McCleskey's claim, taken to its logical conclusion, throws into serious question the principles that underlie our entire criminal justice system"?
3. Can you think of some ways researchers could conduct new studies to address the Supreme Court's criticisms of the social science research presented in *Lockhart v. McCree?* Do you think research that was more "on point" would have greater impact in the courts?
4. How could one test whether using different juries in the first and second phases of a bifurcated trial would change the rate of capital sentences?
5. What is meant by the weighing of aggravating and mitigating circumstances? How could you get information about how real juries have interpreted this instruction?
6. What is the rationale for treating child criminals differently from adult criminals? Locate the experiment described in Box 8.7. Are there any aspects of the design that might explain the very high rates of respondents willing to execute defendants under 16?
7. How can juror comprehension of legal instructions be tested, especially now that states are revising their instructions?
8. Do you think the reforms suggested by Scheck, Neufeld, and Dwyer (2000), taken together, could ensure that the death penalty was administered fairly?
9. What do you think about the arguments that the mentally retarded and juveniles are less culpable because of their psychological characteristics?

Key Terms

aggravating evidence	Eighth Amendment	penalty phase
Baldus study	epistemological approach	proportionality
bifurcated trials	*Furman v. Georgia*	rehabilitation
capital cases	*Gregg v. Georgia*	retribution
conviction proneness	guilt phase	systems approach
death qualified	*McCleskey v. Kemp*	*Witherspoon* excludables
deterrence	mitigating evidence	*Witherspoon* includables

CHAPTER  9

Juvenile Court and the Legal Processing of Children and Adolescents

249

Juvenile Court
and the Legal
Processing of
Children and
Adolescents

The juvenile court is a U.S. invention, a product of the late nineteenth-century Progressive era reformers' faith in the possibility of solving social problems with institutional reforms. Before juvenile courts were created, children under 7 were exempted from criminal responsibility. Children 14 and over were held criminally responsible as if they were adults. Those between 7 and 14 could be held criminally responsible if they seemed mature. The juvenile court laws introduced the concept of delinquency, the idea that juveniles who break the law should not be treated as adult criminals, but placed in a special legal category. This was a legal and social innovation.

Juvenile courts were created by state legislatures when the political climate was favorable for reform. The court's purpose was to keep offending youth out of the criminal justice system while helping them grow into responsible adults. When the political climate changed, legislators changed the laws. Over time, we have come almost full circle; recently, states have amended their laws first to try and then to punish more young people in the adult criminal justice system. Each change brought its own psychological and social problems.

In this chapter, we will review legal and psychological issues in juvenile justice. We will look at

- the history, origins, and philosophy of the juvenile court.
- the creation of delinquency and the decriminalization of young offenders.
- the political fallout from rising rates of juvenile crime.
- status offenses.
- due process considerations in juvenile court.
- the recriminalization of young offenders.
- psychological assumptions underlying the policy of treating juveniles differently from adults.

250

CHAPTER 9
Juvenile Court
and the Legal
Processing of
Children and
Adolescents

- laws governing the transfer from juvenile to adult courts, and their consequences.
- the contribution of mental health professionals to the transfer decision.
- juvenile competence to waive rights and to stand trial as adults.
- new reforms, including teen courts and family group conferences.

Historical Context

By the middle of the nineteenth century, immigration, industrialization, and urbanization had increased the number and visibility of unsupervised children. Poor people, living in crowded, dirty, disease- and crime-ridden slums, couldn't always care for their families. Orphaned, neglected, and runaway children lived on the streets of all the major cities, begging, peddling, selling newspapers, or working at other odd jobs, and also stealing, selling themselves into prostitution, and drinking. In 1852, police in New York City estimated that the city's population of 500,000 included 10,000 homeless children. Charles Loring Brace, a minister in New York City who offered faith-based services to poor youth, estimated there were 30,000. They were classified as "street arabs" (bands of predatory children), "guttersnipes" (weaker children who survived by scavenging), and "waifs" (lost property no one claimed) (Levine and Levine, 1992). Eighty percent of the felony complaints were against minors (Clement, 1996). The public feared young criminals but nonetheless generally accepted the idea that children and adolescents who committed crimes should not be treated the same as adult criminals.

Before juvenile courts were established in 1899, children who committed crimes were punished through adult courts (Feld, 1999; Nurcombe and Partlett, 1994). The modern concept of childhood, the idea that children were not little adults, but had to be nurtured, educated, and socialized to prepare them to take on adult roles in society, only developed during the seventeenth century (Aries, 1962). By the nineteenth century, reformers were arguing that putting young people in adult jails was cruel and would promote their criminal tendencies. States and cities began devising ways to separate offending children from adults. Some cities (e.g., New York in 1825) established houses of refuge or reformatories to control and correct youthful offenders. Adolescents went through the adult court system, but were sent to the new juvenile institutions instead of to adult jails. Though their original purpose was rehabilitative, reform schools quickly acquired a reputation for harshness and authoritarianism.

The Origin and Philosophy of Juvenile Court

In 1899, Illinois passed legislation establishing a court to deal with the problems of youth. The idea for the court grew out of the late nineteenth-century settlement house and community improvement movements (Levine and Levine, 1992).

The first juvenile court was instituted in Chicago. Instead of adjudicating guilt or innocence and providing for punishment of crime, the juvenile court aimed to promote child welfare and to prevent future crimes by intervening early in the lives of "wayward" and "delinquent" youth (Levine and Levine, 1992). The court was to be a benevolent agent of rehabilitation (see Box 9.1).

The Chicago court came under criticism very early on (Ryerson, 1978). The first probation workers, volunteers, were replaced by civil service employees with limited powers of action. Their numbers were small, but probation caseloads were large. The workers could do little by way of rehabilitation or prevention. They were not very

BOX 9.1

251

Historical
Context

The Juvenile Court Judge as Social Therapist

Most juvenile courts, following the original Chicago court, adopted the pathology/deviancy theory of delinquency. The juvenile court established in Denver, Colorado, also in 1899, operated with a very different model. The Denver juvenile court judge, Ben Lindsey, was a unique, charismatic personality who made himself "the leader of every kid's gang in Denver." His court, deeply embedded in the community, took the lead in attempting to correct social conditions that affected youth and their families, assisting pregnant teenagers, helping youth with employment and recreation, and supervising mothers' pensions, a forerunner of welfare. Sadly, Lindsey's approach did not survive after he left the court (Levine and Levine, 1992).

Judge Ben Lindsey
Charismatic and controversial, Lindsey was one of the first juvenile court judges serving Denver, Colorado, from 1899 to 1927.

effective youth supervisors (Levine and Levine, 1992). The recidivism rate was high. Nonetheless, the juvenile court model appealed to people's sense that children could and should be "saved." Juvenile courts were soon established by other jurisdictions throughout the country, and in other countries as well.

252

CHAPTER 9
Juvenile Court
and the Legal
Processing of
Children and
Adolescents

Not criminal courts. The Chicago Juvenile Court and the juvenile courts subsequently established in other states were not criminal courts. They were established under the state's *parens patriae* (state as higher parent) powers to legislate in the interests of people's welfare. In theory, the state, through the juvenile court, seeks to protect and help the child offenders rather than prosecute them (see Weithorn, 2005). The court is to treat the child as a "wise parent treats a wayward child." For this reason, juvenile courts are civil, not criminal.

The language used by the juvenile courts emphasized that the proceedings are not criminal. A complaint against a juvenile brought to juvenile court is not called an *indictment* (a charge in a criminal offense), but a **petition on behalf of a child,** or some similar term reflecting benign and therapeutic intent. Cases are not titled *People v. Smith,* as they are in criminal court. Juvenile cases are often called *In re* J.R ("In the matter of J.R."). The youth is usually called a *respondent,* not a defendant. Proceedings are confidential and records sealed to protect young offenders from permanent stigma (Feld, 1999).

For a long time, legal procedures were informal to allow juvenile court judges acting as "wise parents" to develop individualized "treatment." It almost didn't matter if the youth had committed the offense. If the youth was in court, the youth needed help.

Due process rights. Early juvenile courts were run rather informally, with few procedural rules. Consistent with the belief that children are more vulnerable and less competent than adults, the young respondents weren't accorded the same **due process rights** as adults in criminal courts. In theory, because the juvenile court judge was supposed to be protecting the youth's interests, procedural protections were unnecessary. Moreover, youth do not have full adult civil rights and liberties in most contexts (*In re Gault,* 1967; *Schall v. Martin,* 1984).

The original juvenile court model withstood legal challenges for many years (Ryerson, 1978). Appellate courts ruled that the ameliorative purpose of juvenile court and the corollary need to keep the court flexible and responsive to each child's situation trumped due process concerns. Juvenile court was not a criminal court, so constitutional protections appropriate to criminal trials didn't apply. This legal view changed with *In re Gault* (1967; see next section).

Creating delinquency. The statutes that created the juvenile court changed the very way people thought about juvenile crimes (Levine and Levine, 1992). The laws created a new social category, *delinquency,* by lumping together different types of children.

From earliest colonial times, the government supported parents who needed help controlling "disobedient," "idle," or "congenitally stubborn" children. The principle that a parent can call on the community to deal with a drunken, disobedient, stubborn, and rebellious child is ancient (see Deuteronomy 21:18–21).

The practice of using the legal system to support parents was incorporated into laws defining delinquency (see Status Offenses, below). The early statutes gave jurisdiction to the juvenile court for a broad range of crimes and problematic youth behaviors. By putting them in one category, the law assumed that sullen, impulsive, difficult, mischievous, oppositional, and resentful children were on a path that ended with criminality, no less than those youth who actually committed crimes. The Progressive Era reformers believed that the juvenile court could best fulfill its purpose of helping children avoid criminal careers as adults by taking jurisdiction over them all.

Pathologizing bad behavior. The effect was to pathologize certain youthful behaviors (Kutchins and Kirk, 1997; see also Weithorn, 2005). When we **pathologize** a behavior, we focus attention on the individual deficits or character traits associated with the behavior. That focus obscures the social factors that may initiate and sustain the behavior.

By defining a class of deviant "delinquent" youth, the juvenile court statutes brought this class of young people to the attention of mental health professionals. William Healy, a pediatric neurologist and psychiatrist, established a clinic within the Chicago Juvenile Court about ten years after the court began its operations in 1899. One of the clinic's purposes was to study the *Individual Delinquent*—the title of a book by Healy (1915). The clinic was a forerunner of community child guidance clinics established in the 1920s (Levine and Levine, 1992). Because delinquency was defined as a product of individual pathology, it made sense to provide mental health services to young people. In some cities, mental health and social service agencies worked very closely with juvenile courts.

The Juvenile Court System Today

Today every state has a special court system to handle cases involving juveniles. The age at which young people are considered adults for purposes of criminal justice varies from state to state. In most states juvenile courts supervise young people until they are somewhere between 15 and 17 years of age. Many states extend juvenile court jurisdiction to allow continued supervision to age 20 or even 24 to fulfill a disposition order. For example, a youth may have been ordered to stop harassing a parent as a condition of release. That order may continue past the age of juvenile court jursdiction (OJJDP, 2003a).

Crimes committed by youth. Crime committed by youth is a major social problem. The percentage of violent crimes involving juveniles grew from about 10 percent of all crimes in the early 1980s to 14 percent in 1994 (U.S. Bureau of the Census, 1994). The rise was related to the crack epidemic and to the ready availability of guns (Feld, 1999; Zimring, 2005). Although the overall crime rate has declined some since 1994 (Snyder, 1998), the crime rate among people under 18 remains high. In 2002, juveniles under age 18 accounted for 21.1 percent of arrests for index crimes (serious crimes tracked nationally by the U.S. Department of Justice). Juveniles under age 17 constitute 23.2 percent of reported sexual assault offenders. A great many males entering the juvenile justice system have been charged with sexual offenses (Snyder, 2000). Given contemporary societal concerns about sex offenses, the juvenile courts are faced with new problems of how to deal with youthful sex offenders in a way that acknowledges societal concerns about safety and pays attention to the developmental state of youth.

Juvenile court remains our primary institution for dealing with young people who commit crimes. In 2000, juvenile courts processed 1.7 million cases (Sourcebook of Criminal Justice Statistics, 2002, Table 5.61). About 50 youth per 1,000 in the age range 10 to 17 are involved in juvenile courts. Male offenders (75.4 percent of offenders in juvenile court) far outnumber females (24.6 percent) (Sourcebook of Criminal Justice Statistics, 2002, Table 5.61), but females may be catching up (Hoyt and Scherer, 1998).

254

CHAPTER 9
Juvenile Court
and the Legal
Processing of
Children and
Adolescents

Females and delinquency. Arrests of females for juvenile delinquency have increased rapidly in recent years. In particular, the number of *violent* crimes charged to females went up; it is still quite low compared to the number charged to males. Eighty-seven females under 18 were charged with murder in the United States in 2002, compared to 724 underage males. In 2002, 2,308 females under 18 were charged with carrying or possessing a weapon, compared to 19,075 males. Formerly the almost exclusive domain of young males, more female juveniles are now arrested for robbery, assault, drug trafficking, and gang activity ("Female Offenders," n.d.). Serious crimes of violence constitute a small proportion of offenses committed by female juveniles. About half of assaults charged to girls involved a girl hitting her mother (Okamoto and Chesney-Lind, 2004). Some female offenses may occur when the youth is trying to survive on the street after having run away from home.

Because violent girls are becoming more prominent in the juvenile justice system, courts and treatment programs are beginning to assess their special needs. Efforts to develop more gender-appropriate treatment methods in juvenile facilities have had only modest success. Gender-specific programs emphasize victimization issues and promote self-awareness, prevention, and empowerment. The use of male staff is carefully limited and supervised. Some programs include training in assertiveness and conflict resolution to improve interpersonal and relationship skills (Okamoto and Chesney-Lind, 2004).

Political consequences of rising violent juvenile crime. In 1995, 53.5 percent of adjudicted delinquents were placed on probation (Maguire and Pastore, 1998, Table 536). In 1999, over 60 percent of those adjudicated delinquent were placed on probation (Juvenile Court Statistics, 2003). The juveniles who were sent to institutions for serious crimes were released after a relatively short confinement. These relatively mild dispositions seemed inadequate to many people, especially in view of the high rate of youth violence. Public awareness of the high crime rate among young people and publicity surrounding particularly shocking cases of youth violence led to pressures to reform the juvenile courts or "recriminalize" (Singer, 1996b). Politicians and members of the public charged that the juvenile justice system was encouraging crime by offering adolescent offenders immunity from serious punishment. Legislators increased the severity of penalties for juveniles to make the system "tougher." For example, in Georgia, when a youth convicted of rape and murder as a juvenile received a sentence of five to nine years, the victim's family was outraged, and successfully advocated for a change in the law (Brown, 2003) to increase sentences (Auer, 2003; Georgia Department of Corrections, 2004). Legislators also passed laws to allow juveniles to be prosecuted as adults in response to the argument "If they are old enough to do the crime, they are old enough to do the time" (Singer, 1996a; Feld, 1999). The problems are similar in the UK and in other European Union countries. Prime Minister Tony Blair of Great Britain has introduced legislation to get tough on so-called "yobs", youthful wrongdoers (Morris, 2006).

How successful are juvenile courts? There are reasonable grounds for questioning the efficacy of the juvenile court system. Juvenile courts have had only modest success in achieving their aim of rehabilitation. **Recidivism** rates (reappearances in court, or further offenses after assignment to a treatment program or to probation) ranged from 30 percent to 70 percent in different studies (Champion, 1998). The recidivism rates in newly developed programs range from 2 percent to 32.2 percent. However, these are model programs, and it seems unlikely that there will be sufficient training, support and funding to ensure they are adopted faithfully in the field. Most treatment programs do not have funds to conduct evaluation research (Roberts, 2004). The situation is similar in England and Wales where, "As a result of low political priority and a lack of resources, effective social programs to provide necessary support for young offenders are not being adequately developed" (Arthur, 2004, p. 323).

But if the results are unsatisfactory, it is debatable whether it is the concept of the juvenile court that is at fault. Defenders of the juvenile justice system are not ready to write off large numbers of teenagers as hopeless, hard-core criminals. They point out that many young people who become involved in crime mature into law-abiding citizens. Half of those who commit an initial delinquency don't repeat it, and of those who commit a second delinquency, 34 percent do not offend further (Feld, 1999). For these youth, the juvenile court is a workable answer. Supporters believe that with greater social support, more children could be effectively served through the courts.

Delinquency and Status Offenses

When juvenile courts were first created, they were given broad authority over troubled youth. In the 1960s, states drew legal distinctions between categories of juvenile offenders (see Singer, 1996b). Today, juvenile courts have jurisdiction over three legally distinct classes of young people: delinquents, status offenders, and abused and neglected children (Clement, 1996).

Status Offenses

Delinquency now refers to acts that are defined in the state's criminal code, and would be a crime if committed by an adult. **Status offenses** refer to acts that are offenses only because of the juvenile's age (status). These acts may be immoral or harmful, but they would not be crimes if done by an adult. Children who run away from home, drink or smoke, are truant from school, "keep bad company," are sexually active, are "beyond control of their parents," violate curfews, or are simply "incorrigible" are status offenders. Status offenders (often called **minors in need of supervision**) are brought to the attention of the court when someone (parent, guardian, school official, etc.) petitions the court to help them supervise the child. The proportion of female status offenders has always been higher than the proportion of female delinquents.

Despite apparent vagueness in the law, appeals courts upheld the states' efforts to reinforce parents in carrying out parental responsibilities and to support parents whose reasonable and lawful commands were being disobeyed by their children (see *In re Walker,* 1972; *District of Columbia v. B.J.R.,* 1975).

Deinstitutionalizing status offenders. In the past, juvenile courts handled delinquents and status offenders in much the same way. Both were frequently sent to detention centers for "rehabilitation." In the 1970s, half of all youth who juvenile courts ordered into out-of-home placements were status offenders, not delinquents (Handler and Zatz, 1982; Murray and Rubin, 1983).

As youth problems became more difficult, expensive out-of-home placements increased, and courts became overcrowded. Some observers questioned whether juvenile courts should have jurisdiction over status offenses at all, maintaining that these were family problems that should be handled by social agencies. Child advocates argued that putting status offenders in detention homes or in secure facilities with

256

CHAPTER 9
Juvenile Court
and the Legal
Processing of
Children and
Adolescents

delinquents was unfair and harmful. The U.S. Congress found that argument persuasive. Guidelines under the federal Juvenile Justice and Delinquency Prevention Act of 1974 required the states to **deinstitutionalize** status offenders—that is, to reduce the number incarcerated—and to keep status offenders out of secure detention or correctional facilities if the states were to receive federal funds (Murray and Rubin, 1983).

After the 1974 Act, states made important changes. First, juvenile courts sharply reduced the use of detention in local closed facilities. Most status offenders now remain at home pending their final hearing. Youth who run away may be detained more often than other categories of youth in order to ensure an appearance in court.

Second, after adjudication, the placement of status offenders in secure public facilities, including state schools for delinquents (reform schools, industrial schools), has just about been eliminated. Status offenders who go to court are still at risk of being placed away from their families in group homes or in foster care under the aegis of social services (Handler and Zatz, 1982), but not in state reform or industrial schools. As time went on, the effectiveness of the law in keeping status offenders out of institutions decreased. The number of youth in public facilities declined, but the number held in private facilities increased (McNeese and Jackson, 2004). The decrease in the number of status offenders held in public institutions was offset by an increase in residential treatment programs, private psychiatric hospitals, and private "correctional" facilities. There were about 12,000 girls in private residences in 1995, mostly because of status offenses (Chesney-Lind, 1999).

Sometimes, a change in law that solves one problem creates other problems. Some parents felt they needed the authority of the court to control their adolescent children, especially their daughters. When the law no longer allowed young people to be confined for status offenses, parents and others looked for new ways to get children perceived as out of control and in danger into custody. There have been reports of police advising parents to block the door when their daughters try to leave and, when the girls push past, to charge them with assault. Judges are inclined to "bootstrap" to protect females. A juvenile court judge may find a youth guilty of contempt when the youth, brought in for a status offense not subject to confinement, violates some court order, including curfew violations or running away from a therapeutic placement out of the home. The youth can then be confined because contempt is a crime (Chesney-Lind, 1999).

Parents have also sought state help controlling teenagers too old to fall under status offense jurisdiction. In response, some states (e.g., New York and Georgia) extended the age. In Georgia, a parent was criminally charged with unlawfully restraining her 17-year-old daughter when she tried to stop her from leaving the house. The case was described to the Georgia Legislature, which then extended the age of jurisdiction for status offenses to 18 (Gianni, 2003). This may be another good example of problem creation through problem solution. Even though more youth with differing service needs will come into the court, no new funds are typically attached to the legislation. The change was made in response to political pressure from parents (Leiter, 2001; Bruck, 2003).

The changes in law that resulted in the deinstitutionalization of status offenders were also directed toward keeping juveniles out of adult jails. Despite the law, on any given day, perhaps as many as 2,000 youth are held in adult lockups (McNeese and Jackson, 2004).

A third change which followed the 1974 Juvenile Justice and Delinquency Prevention Act was the increased use of **diversion** programs. **Diversion** programs divert young people who have committed minor offenses away from the courts and steer them toward social service agencies. The programs are intended to protect adolescents who are not dangerous from the negative consequences of involvement with the juvenile justice system. Diversion programs have sharply reduced the proportion of status offenders who enter the juvenile justice system. It is ironic that we now divert youth from an institution that itself was created to divert youth from the criminal justice system.

Diversion programs. Diversion programs make sense in principle. Status offenders have not necessarily taken the first step toward delinquency. Only a minority of status offenders ever make a subsequent appearance in juvenile court on a felony charge (Murray and Rubin, 1983). Their rate of reappearance in court for any offense may be lower than the reappearance rate of delinquents (Butts, 1996). Status offenders as a group may also be more psychologically disturbed than delinquents (Lopez-Williams et al., under review). If they are less dangerous than delinquents, and have greater mental health needs, diversion is a sensible policy.

While it makes sense to distinguish between status offenders and delinquents, diverting status offenders to social agencies may not do them any good. Some youth, who in the past would have been let off with a warning from the police or dismissed by the court, or whose case would have been resolved by negotiation at the intake level to the court, may now be referred to service agencies or other alternative programs. The result is **net widening,** the involvement and "enmeshment" of more young people, including many whose problems are transient, in the social service system. Research is needed to see if some or all of these status offenders would have been better off with no or minimal interventions. Critics question whether there are sufficient services, sufficiently diverse services, and sufficiently appropriate services to actually help the youths who are diverted (Murray and Rubin, 1983; see Box 9.2).

BOX 9.2

Diversion or Radical Nonintervention?

In 1989, New York State changed its law to limit access of status offenders to juvenile court, and to divert people applying for status offense petitions in juvenile court to service agencies. The petitioners were mostly parents who wanted the court to help them control their children. The petitioners wanted to have the child declared a person in need of supervision (PINS). The new law allowed an intake officer to delay processing a PINS petition for 90 days while the worker attempted to "adjust" the problem or refer the family to an appropriate social agency.

Under the new law, PINS cases were successfully diverted. The number of status offense cases that reached juvenile court declined. The rate of out-of-home placement also declined because there was less risk of out-of-home placement when a case didn't get into court (Patchel, 1996).

The law might have saved the taxpayer money in court time and in out-of-home placement, but we don't know the cost to the family in time and trouble. There was no systematic follow-up to see if those diverted from court to social services actually received any services. Erie County, which processed 1,200 status offense cases annually, had reserved only nine spots in social agencies for status offenders diverted at intake. The law as implemented was an inadvertent experiment in "radical nonintervention." Few received any services.

258

CHAPTER 9
Juvenile Court
and the Legal
Processing of
Children and
Adolescents

Diversion for status offenders was a legal reform that addressed the problem created by existing legal structures: the problem of hurting rather than helping status offenders by grouping them with delinquents, institutionalizing them unnecessarily, or punishing them harshly. However, the reform failed to address the underlying social problem. Some parents have difficulty raising and controlling their children, and some young people have difficulty learning necessary social behaviors. Without any real change in access to help for families, and in the effectiveness of the help, any legal change may, in the end, prove merely cosmetic.

Delinquency and Due Process

When juvenile courts were first established, judges had considerable discretion to develop individualized dispositions and nearly unrestrained power to incarcerate the youth. The young respondents did not have the due process rights of adults in criminal court. Critics questioned whether the tradeoff of procedural rights for good intentions was worth it, especially because good intentions were not fulfilled. The U.S. Supreme Court noted, "There may be grounds for concern that the child receives the worst of both worlds: that he gets neither the protection accorded to adults nor the solicitous care and regeneration treatment postulated for children" (*Kent v. United States,* 1966, p. 556).

In *In re Gault* (1967), the Supreme Court decided that due process rights were not for adults only (see Box 9.3). The majority opinion said that more stringent due process

---

BOX 9.3

A Legal Case in Point: Due Process Rights for Juveniles

Gerald Gault, a 14 year old with a history of minor delinquent behavior, was taken into custody by Arizona police after a neighbor complained that someone had made a lewd or indecent telephone call to her. The police filed a petition saying merely that the youth was under 18 and was in need of the court's protection. The petition didn't allege any offense. Gerald was placed in a juvenile detention center. His parents were not notified. When Gerald's family succeeded in locating him, they were told a hearing was scheduled for the next day. Gerald's mother was present, but he had no attorney. No record was kept of the hearing. Gerald remained in detention for three more days, and then another hearing was held. Gerald still had no counsel. The woman who received the call allegedly made by Gerald did not appear. At the conclusion of the hearing, the judge sent 14 year old Gerald to the State Industrial School "for the period of his minority" (i.e., until he was 21). Had Gerald been an adult convicted under Arizona criminal law of making an obscene phone call, his maximum punishment would have been a fine of no more than $50 or imprisonment for not more than two months.

Gault's appeal reached the U.S. Supreme Court. The Court ruled that a young person appearing in juvenile court was entitled to many of the same due process protections as adults. These rights included (1) timely written notice of charges "setting forth the alleged misconduct with particularity," (2) the right to counsel, (3) the Fifth Amendment privilege against self-incrimination (testifying against oneself), (4) notification of the right to counsel and to silence when first taken into custody and when interviewed (a juvenile "Miranda" warning), and (5) the right to confront and cross-examine sworn witnesses.

From *In re Gault* (1967).

protections would reduce the number of cases in which a young person lost his or her liberty because of an erroneous or arbitrary determination. The Court was less indignant about the failure of the system to provide appropriate treatment.

Changes after *Gault.* As a result of *In re Gault* juvenile court proceedings throughout the country became more like criminal trials. Subsequent cases further strengthened procedural rights for juveniles. In *In re Winship* (1970), the U.S. Supreme Court established that an **adjudication** (a trial or hearing to determine whether the youth committed the offense) of delinquency, like adjudication of guilt in criminal court, required the high standard of proof beyond a reasonable doubt. On the other hand, courts continued to recognize a special paternalistic role for juvenile court, as when the Supreme Court specifically declined to grant juveniles the right to a public jury trial (*McKeiver v. Pennsylvania*, 1971). Some of the advantages of informal process and some special protections for young offenders were continued. For example, appellate courts upheld the practice of sealing juvenile court findings so that a young person would not be stigmatized by a criminal record as a result of a delinquency adjudication (Feld, 1999).

Providing formal due process protections for youth may in some instances undermine what the juvenile court was intended to accomplish, that is, a disposition that would help the youth. Youth are now represented in juvenile court appearances mostly by attorneys who are public defenders. A significant number of youth (in one study, about 16 percent) waive their right to an attorney. There may be some wisdom in their decision to do so. An examination of the dispositions showed that youth *not* represented by an attorney were most likely to have their charges dismissed and less likely to receive secure confinement. Guevara, Spohn, and Herz (2004) suggest that without an attorney, juvenile court judges may feel more inclined to act as a wise parent toward a wayward child, while with an attorney representing the youth, legal formalities take precedence and the judge may feel less sympathetic toward the youth.

Recriminalizing Delinquency

By the 1960s, many citizens believed, rightly or wrongly, that juvenile courts were ineffective. As rates of juvenile crime went up in the 1980s, criticisms increased. Politicians and members of the public complained that the system was encouraging crime by offering adolescent offenders immunity from serious punishment. They believed young criminals knew they would not be punished harshly and were thumbing their noses at the justice system. There is some basis for this charge. In the late 1980s and 1990s, gangs and crack cocaine dealers in large cities deliberately employed people under age 16 to commit felonies. The youth knew they would not receive severe punishment (Kotlowitz, 1999).

In response to public concern about juvenile crime, legislatures throughout the country moved away from rehabilitation toward greater personal accountability and greater concern for public safety. In New York, the legislature set a minimum period of confinement in a secure institution and terms up to five years for specified offenses by juveniles. Other states followed suit, making juvenile court dispositions harsher (Feld, 1999). Legislatures also changed the jurisdiction of juvenile courts by providing for the direct prosecution of adolescents in adult criminal court for some crimes (Feld, 1999). To use Singer's (1996b) apt phrase, they "recriminalized" delinquency (see Box 9.4). By 1996, all 50 states and the District of Columbia had authorized longer periods of confinement for those adjudicated as juveniles and established procedures for transferring

260

CHAPTER 9
Juvenile Court
and the Legal
Processing of
Children and
Adolescents

BOX 9.4

A Legal Case in Point: A Violent Offender Triggers Legal Change

The impetus for recriminalization often is public indignation when a particularly violent young offender or a delinquent who received lenient treatment in juvenile court commits further offenses. Willie Bosket is a case in point. When he was 15 years old, Bosket murdered two passengers on a New York subway. Under the laws of the time, he could only be charged as a delinquent, and could be detained for no more than five years. Members of the public were indignant that a double murderer received such a short sentence. In response, the state legislature amended the law in 1978 to allow for the transfer of juveniles who committed certain serious offenses to adult court. The transferred youth would be tried as adults and face the same penalties that adults faced for comparable offenses. Bosket committed other felonies shortly after he was released, as the public feared. He is now serving a life term in a maximum security penitentiary.

juveniles to adult criminal courts or for initiating prosecutions there (Heilbrun et al., 1997; Weissman, 1999).

The original juvenile court laws were based on assumptions that adolescents are less responsible for their actions than adults and more responsive to rehabilitation (Weithorn, 2005). The **transfer laws** (sometimes called *waivers*) recriminalizing juvenile offenses, in contrast, assume that youth understand the nature of the offenses and the consequences of their actions in the same way as adults. Moreover, laws linking transfers to specific offenses imply that certain crimes are by their nature "adult." In theory, adolescents capable of appreciating the wrongful nature of these crimes deserve the same punishment as adults. The laws also assumed that more drastic consequences would have a deterrent effect. Symbolically, the laws were intended to show that the legislature has greater concern for the victim than for the perpetrator of a crime.

Adolescent Immaturity

We treat offending youth differently than adult criminals on the assumption that they are more immature, have less appreciation of the nature of their offenses, and will, for the most part, eventually mature into good citizens. Many youth do things they would not do later in life. So many boys and, increasingly, girls, engage in delinquencies that it is almost normative for teens (Reppucci, 1999). About two-thirds of those who commit delinquent acts stop after their first or second offense (Feld, 1999). There is a correlation between age and crime rates, with rates peaking in the mid- to late teens, and then dropping off by age 25. Youth grow up (see Box 9.5).

The juvenile court system represents social recognition of the usefulness of providing what Erik Erikson (1968) called a "psychosocial moratorium." It would not serve us as a society to allow criminal convictions to reduce the opportunities available to a great many young people who are likely to grow up to be good citizens. We hope that, while we wait for troubled youth to grow up, they won't do anything that would irretrievably ruin their lives or the lives of others. Unfortunately, sometimes young people do destroy or seriously harm the lives of others. Society demands protection and justice. When we ask for different treatment for juveniles than for adults, we are

BOX 9.5

261

Recriminalizing
Delinquency

A Legal Case in Point: A Youthful Offender Is Rehabilitated

When she was 14, Gina Grant killed her mother. Her mother was probably an alcoholic and abusive. Gina served a year in a correctional facility and then was on probation until she reached 18. While on probation, she did very well. The record of her past was supposedly sealed. Gina was admitted to Harvard, among other first-rate schools. But the information about her crime "leaked." Harvard denied her admission ostensibly because she failed to reveal her record on her application. Gina was admitted to Tufts where she was greeted with some student protest, but with strong support from the administration and other students (Kraus, 1995).

Gina is an example of a juvenile offender who was successfully rehabilitated. It seems doubtful she would have done as well if she had gone to prison for several years. The laws protecting juvenile records were intended to ensure that someone like Gina could go on to have a maximally productive life, although they failed to do so in her case (Reppucci, 1999).

asking: How accountable for their actions are juveniles? Do the psychological characteristics of youth make them less "culpable?" If so, what are those characteristics?

Adolescent thinking, attitudes and decisional competence. Adolescents' cognitive capacities need to be evaluated independently in each legal area where their rights and responsibilities are in question. Competence to make medical decisions (see Grisso, 1981; see Chapter 14), competence to engage in sexual activities (see Chapter 4), and criminal responsibility may involve different abilities. Scott, Reppucci, and Woolard (1995) and Reppucci (1999) point out several ways in which adolescents differ from adults that are pertinent to judging their culpability relative to adults (see also Steinberg and Cauffman, 1996). Some of these developmental factors may be related to brain maturation (Reppucci, 1999). (See also Chapter 8 on the death penalty.)

Because of their shorter time perspective, adolescents may be less likely than adults to think about possible long-term consequences of their actions for themselves or others. For example, a young person may not fully appreciate that an action in the present can affect his or her occupational or educational opportunities ten years hence. Similarly, many adolescents have a sense of invulnerability ("I can smoke because I won't get sick") that makes them more likely to take risks, or to be less aware of risks (Reppucci, 1999). Whereas an adult would worry, an adolescent may feel excited when riding in a car with a drunk driver who is speeding or weaving in and out of traffic recklessly. Adolescent risk-taking attitudes are associated with self-reported delinquency, and self-reported alcohol and drug use (Levine and Singer, 1988).

Adolescents are more oriented toward peers and more socially conforming to peer groups than adults. They are more likely to commit crimes in groups than they are to commit them alone (Zimring, 2005). Their judgment may be impaired because of a desire to be accepted by the group or not to appear "chicken" in front of friends.

Adolescents may be responsible for their actions, but still be less fully culpable than adults. Feld (1999) suggests that adolescents should be treated as adults for the sake of establishing criminal responsibility, but, because of their psychological characteristics, they should receive discounted sentences.

262

CHAPTER 9
Juvenile Court
and the Legal
Processing of
Children and
Adolescents

Adolescence is not an excuse. Opponents of the view that adolescents should not get special treatment argue that adolescents know right from wrong, have foresight (hence, capacity for criminal intent), and have the capacity for self-control; many adult suspects are no wiser. Transfer to adult criminal court reflects the concept that youth should be held fully accountable for their acts.

There is also a new emphasis on accountability within the juvenile court system itself among those who believe that juveniles should not be punished as harshly as adults. For example, some jurisdictions are experimenting with expanded community service and reparation/restitution programs (McNeese and Jackson, 2004; and see Restorative Justice, below). The juvenile not only is placed on probation, but also experiences some consequence. Congress has provided grants to encourage states to develop accountability-based sanctions for juveniles (Griffin, 1999).

The Transfer Laws

All states have laws that exclude some juveniles from prosecution in juvenile court for some serious offenses, permit juvenile court judges to transfer youth to criminal court from juvenile court, or give the prosecutor discretion to try a youth in either juvenile or criminal court. In recent years over 200,000 youth below age 18 were subject to criminal prosecution as a result of transfer laws whereby juveniles may be sent directly to adult court for some crimes, or as a result of changes in the age of juvenile court jurisdiction.

Types of transfers. Most people under 18 who are tried in adult court are there because the state legislatures simply lowered the age of juvenile jurisdiction, thus making more youth eligible for prosecution and for punishment as adults. By setting an age of 16, 14, or even less as the juvenile "cutoff," the legislatures were saying that youth above that age don't deserve any special consideration or leniency because of psychological immaturity.

Most states also established **legislative offense exclusions,** whereby anyone charged with certain specified offenses may be tried as an adult, even those young enough to be considered juveniles otherwise. The first hearing in these cases may be in juvenile court, but the juvenile court judge can transfer the case to adult court after the hearing. In some states the reverse is also true: the case may begin in adult court; but the judge can transfer the case to juvenile court. In about a dozen states, the prosecutor can choose whether to prosecute initially in adult criminal court or in juvenile court. Judges in states with prosecutorial discretion still have the power to transfer in either direction after a hearing (Feld, 1999).

Age of eligibility for transfer. The transfer laws are aimed at the more violent young offenders; eligibility for transfer is related to the offense. Murder is treated as a special case in many states. In most states, juveniles become eligible for transfer to criminal court for specifically designated serious offenses at age 14. Nine states do not have a minimum age, and three additional states don't specify any age. For example, in Pennsylvania, which has no minimum age for a charge of murder, a 7-year-old boy was charged with arson and second degree murder (Associated Press, 2004a). In North Carolina, 11-year-old twins were charged with killing their father and wounding their mother and sister. Eleven states require adult trials for defendants 13 or older accused of murder, the most serious offense. Seventeen states have no minimum age or have a minimum age under 13 for transferring a murder suspect to adult court

(Firestone, 1999). In Michigan, Nathaniel Abraham was tried as an adult when he was 13, and was found guilty of a murder he committed when he was 11 (See Figure 9.1). Arkansas, the scene of a well-publicized school shooting where the youthful perpetrators were 13 and 11, had no provision for trying the youths as adults. They could only be tried and punished as juveniles. Arkansas since changed its law to permit juveniles to be charged as adults for murder and other serious crimes (Brummer, 2002).

Even some prosecutors have qualms about the prosecution of a very young person as an adult for murder. Marc Shiner successfully prosecuted Nathan Brazill, who at age 14 shot and killed a teacher in school in Florida. Shiner felt he did his duty when he prosecuted the boy and won a 28-year sentence, but privately he struggled with his role. He didn't feel quite right about prosecuting such a young person. After 12 years as a prosecutor, Shiner went into private practice and zealously defended a 16-year-old girl accused of murdering her baby (Canedy, 2002).

Due process and judicial transfers. In *Kent v. United States* (1966), the Supreme Court ruled that a case could not be transferred (waived) from juvenile to adult court without a hearing. In an appendix to the *Kent* opinion, the Supreme Court instructed juvenile court judges making a transfer decision to consider eight specific factors, many of them psychological in nature (Box 9.6).

FIGURE 9.1

Nathaniel Abraham

Nathaniel Abraham, then age 11, shot and killed Ronnie Greene Jr., an 18-year-old stranger. When he was 13, he was tried as an adult and convicted by a jury of second-degree murder. The judge exercised discretion and sentenced Nathaniel as a juvenile. He will serve seven years in a maximum security juvenile detention facility. Judge Eugene Arthur Moore believed the laws trying youth as adults were too harsh and did not sufficiently emphasize rehabilitation. Nathaniel has had hearings requesting early release. Michigan judges declined to release him until he reaches age 21 in January 2007.

264

CHAPTER 9
Juvenile Court
and the Legal
Processing of
Children and
Adolescents

BOX 9.6

Factors to Be Considered in a Decision about Transfer to Adult Court

1. The seriousness of the alleged offense
2. Whether the protection of the community required the transfer
3. Whether the alleged offense was committed in an aggressive, violent, premeditated, or willful manner
4. The prosecutorial merit of the complaint (likelihood of an indictment by a grand jury)
5. The desirability of trial in one court when the juvenile's associates in the alleged offense are adults
6. The maturity of the juvenile as determined by home life, environmental situation, emotional attitude, and pattern of living
7. The record of past contacts with the criminal justice and juvenile justice systems
8. The likelihood of protection of the public and of reasonable rehabilitation of the juvenile if the case is handled by juvenile court

From *Kent v. United States* (1966).

State transfer laws specify similar criteria. Consistent with *Kent*, judges are expected to look at the issues of individual dangerousness, maturity, responsibility, and potential for being rehabilitated. The judges may look to mental health professionals for assistance in making their determinations, which have important consequences for a youth's life. Young people tried as adults can potentially be sentenced to life in prison. The death penalty for juveniles has been declared unconstitutional (*Roper v. Simmons*, 2005; Weissman, 1999).

Is the Transfer System Fair and Effective?

The transfer laws have three main purposes: (1) to do justice by ensuring that young people mature enough to be responsible for their crimes receive punishment more proportional to their crimes; (2) to protect the public by incapacitating violent young offenders; and (3) to deter crime by other young people.

To function as intended, the juvenile justice system is dependent on the wise exercise of discretion by various actors: the police who apprehend the youth and decide whether to warn and release, or to detain; the prosecutors who decide which charges will be prosecuted, and defense lawyers who plea-bargain; the probation workers who make reports about the youth; and the judges who make the transfer decision. Singer (1996b) describes the juvenile justice system as a **loosely coupled system,** meaning that different actors have different roles, tasks, and goals, and pursue their role-related interests with only loose integration.

While some objective factors affect transfer (e.g., defendant's age and the type of offense) and may reduce discretion, other criteria, such as dangerousness or amenability to treatment, are poorly defined and difficult to measure. This vagueness gives judges and others much room for discretion. Whenever legal actors have discretion, we can ask how it is exercised. Three questions can help us evaluate the real-world functioning of the transfer laws. First, are the transfer laws being applied fairly and equitably—are similarly situated youth treated the same way? Second, do young people indeed receive more severe sentences when waived to adult court? Third, do transfer provisions with potentially severe penalties actually deter crime by young people as intended?

Are the transfer laws applied equitably? In most states, juvenile defendants first appear in juvenile court and the judge decides whether to transfer the case to adult court. In 1999, about 1.1 percent of those *charged* with crimes against persons were transferred from juvenile to criminal court, compared to 0.8 percent of those charged with property crimes. However, of those *transferred* to adult criminal court from juvenile court, 33 percent were for offenses against persons (e.g., assault) and 40 percent for property offenses (auto theft, burglary, etc.). Only a small proportion of those transferred to criminal court were charged with a violent crime (homicide, rape, robbery, and aggravated assault). Thus the transfer laws are applied to about as many youth who committed property offenses as they are to those who have committed crimes against persons. In theory, youth should be transferred for the most serious crimes, but apparently they are transferred for less serious crimes as well.

Offender age was a predictor of transfer; the younger the offender, the less likely he or she would be tried in criminal court (Howell, 1996; Singer, 1996b). In 1999, 0.3 percent of youth under 15 were transferred, compared to 1.5 percent of youth 16 and older (Juvenile Court Statistics, 2003). A history of previous offenses also predicted the transfer decision (Singer, 1996b). Two factors, the youth's "dangerousness" and resistance or amenability to "rehabilitation," might be reflected in a history of previous offenses. These factors closely follow some of the criteria the U.S. Supreme Court said should be followed in **judicial transfer** decisions (*Kent v. United States,* 1966).

The criteria of offense severity and offender history were not applied consistently by the courts (Howell, 1996). Researchers examining different jurisdictions in the same state, or different judges in the same jurisdiction, found wide variation in the proportion of juveniles who were transferred to adult criminal court. Howell cites one national study showing that the percentage of juveniles transferred to adult court ranged from 1 percent in Newark, New Jersey, to 44 percent in Miami, Florida. Singer (1996b) found that the percentage of youth who were removed to juvenile court from adult court (reverse transfer) varied widely (2 percent to 42 percent) in different counties within New York State.

Salekin et al. (2002) reported an elaborate study of the constructs judges use when transferring juveniles to adult court. The researchers examined the judges' evaluations of youth transferred to adult court: transferred youth received high scores on dangerousness, low scores on amenability to treatment, and low scores on sophistication and maturity. Clinicians' thinking for the most part fit nicely with judges' thinking with the exception of the sophistication and maturity factors. The researchers believe the results should help to make the criteria for transfer clearer. If judges give greater recognition to developmental considerations, the already low rate of transfer may be reduced still further.

There also may be inconsistencies between decisions made by different judges because of decisions made by other players in the system who interact with the judges. In one jurisdiction, over 90 percent of the transfers were decided without a full adversary hearing. The legal actors (prosecutor, defense attorney, and probation officer)

266

CHAPTER 9
Juvenile Court
and the Legal
Processing of
Children and
Adolescents

apparently agreed about what the outcome of these cases should be, and the judges accepted their unanimous recommendations (Howell, 1996). This suggests that repeat players in the system come to mutual accommodations. Whether these serve or sometimes override the interests of individual defendants is an empirical question, although it is difficult to investigate.

Howell (1996) found that minority youth were more likely to be transferred to adult court than majority youth. In 1999, there was also a small racial disparity in transfer decisions. About 0.7 percent of white and 1.6 percent of African American youth who appeared in juvenile court were transferred to criminal court (Juvenile Court Statistics, 2003).

The availability of appropriate treatment resources (see Weithorn, 2005) may also play a role in the decisions. A judge may be less willing to transfer a youth to criminal court if the judge has confidence there is an appropriate treatment program in the community. A decision with very serious consequences for a youth may be made on the basis of the resources the community has available, not on the basis of individual culpability (Kruh and Brodsky, 1997). These factors lead us to question how well and how fairly the transfer system is meeting its objectives.

How often are juveniles convicted in adult court? Many states have changed their laws to require that juveniles be sent directly to criminal court to be charged there. Most juveniles tried in criminal court were charged there in the first place as required by statute, not transferred from juvenile court. Juveniles have to be convicted before they can be punished. Young people tried in adult court have greater due process rights than those tried in juvenile court, including the right to a jury trial. Greater procedural protections can make conviction more difficult, but still, in 1998, 66 percent of juvenile *felony* defendants in criminal court were convicted. Not all were sent to prison (Strom, Smith, and Snyder, 1998; Howell, 1996; Singer, 1996a).

Are young people punished more severely in adult than in juvenile court? Howell's (1996) review showed that serious and violent young offenders do receive longer sentences when convicted in criminal rather than juvenile court, an indication that the transfer policy has succeeded in "getting tough" with young offenders who are convicted (Grisso, 1996; Bureau of Justice Statistics, 2003). About 40 percent of all the juveniles tried in adult criminal court were *convicted and sent to prison.* Of juveniles tried as delinquents in family court, 55 percent were adjudicated delinquent, and of those adjudicated delinquent, 40 percent received a residential placement. Thus, all other things being equal, the odds of being incarcerated were somewhat greater if a juvenile was tried in an adult criminal court (40 percent) compared to a family court (40 percent x 55 percent = 22 percent).

Serving the sentence. In most states, juveniles are not immediately incarcerated with adults when convicted of adult crimes. They begin their sentences in high security juvenile facilities. Upon reaching their majority, they are transferred to adult prisons. In states that now require long mandatory sentences after adjudication of serious crimes in juvenile court, the same procedure is followed. The convicted youth begins serving the sentence in juvenile facilities and "graduates" to adult prison (Grisso, 1996). Some states are experimenting with *blended sentences.* Juveniles are held in juvenile facilities until they reach their majority. If they are deemed rehabilitated, they may be released. If not, they will go on to serve the remainder of the sentence in an adult prison.

Trials in juvenile court where a blended sentence is possible present some unique due process issues. The trial has to blend components of juvenile process with those of adult process. If an adult penalty is possible, what due process protections should be used in juvenile court to avoid erroneous conviction (Brummer, 2002)? Certainly adjudicative competence and fitness to stand trial must be determined early in the process, especially for very young children who have committed serious offenses.

The Contribution of Mental Health Professionals to Transfer Decisions

The procedures governing transfers continue to recognize the rehabilitative ideal of juvenile justice (Heilbrun et al., 1997). Before making a transfer decision, judges in either juvenile or criminal court may order a forensic mental health professional to evaluate a juvenile suspect and make recommendations to the court. In many jurisdictions, mental health examinations are required by law before a transfer hearing. However, the statutes rarely provide clinicians or courts with clear guidelines for the evaluations. The clinician is asked to provide information relevant to the transfer decision. The clinician evaluates the young person's mental health status, his or her "treatability" (rehabilitation potential), maturity (related to criminal responsibility), dangerousness (related to the issue of public safety), and competence to stand trial. A young person considered treatable and not dangerous is less likely to be transferred to adult court.

Mental health professionals have given little attention to the juvenile justice issues, and to legally as opposed to psychiatrically defined problems. Evans and colleagues (2005) note that a comprehensive volume on treatment of disorders of adolescence ignores or barely mentions the juvenile justice system, delinquency, or status offenses and does not discuss the use of standardized diagnostic methods with this population (Evans et al., 2005).

The clinical knowledge base is not strong enough to support confident assessments. It is difficult to evaluate juvenile candidates for transfer. "Treatability" is an example. It is difficult to identify who needs what kind of treatment, if any at all. We don't know how to match individuals with treatment programs. Some treatment programs for some delinquent young people are effective (see Bartollas and Miller, 1998; Tate, Reppucci, and Mulvey, 1995). It is difficult to say whether a particular individual will be "treatable" and therefore should remain in family court. And suppose we know that a young offender could benefit from a certain kind of treatment, but it is not available. As a practical matter, the individual is not treatable. Should the clinician estimate the likelihood of the young offender benefiting from an ideal rehabilitation program or from the services that are actually available in the district (Kruh and Brodsky, 1997)?

Forensic examiners also find it difficult to respond to a court's request for advice when dangerousness is one of the standards for the decision. Predictions of dangerousness of individual adults are flawed (see Chapter 3). Research and evaluation strategies are improving for the assessment of adults, but it may not be valid to apply the new instruments and techniques to the evaluation of juveniles. Some studies show that psychometric measures of psychopathy have statistically significant predictive value for dangerousness, but the predictors still make both false positive and false negative errors. We don't have good data for adolescents (O'Neill, Lidz, and Heilbrun, 2003; Corrado et al., 2004; Spain et al., 2004). Measures of psychopathy may not have the same predictive value for females (Nicholls and Petrila, 2005). How much error can we tolerate in a prediction that will determine whether a person is treated as a youth or as an adult? We need research with adolescent populations to establish the validity and

268

CHAPTER 9
Juvenile Court
and the Legal
Processing of
Children and
Adolescents

usefulness of different assessment tools and methods. Forensic examiners are often asked to ascertain a young person's cognitive and social maturity. We have instruments for assessing children and adolescents' reasoning and general cognitive ability. Maturity, however, is ill defined. Is the law referring to the same thing as reasoning ability? Even if it is, reasoning ability is probably domain specific: someone can be smart about cars, and stupid about people. Suppose a 14-year-old computer whiz develops a virus that disrupts local businesses and then says she didn't realize how many people she was hurting. As a computer whiz, she would probably have scored well on tests of abstract reasoning ability, but, if she was truly unable to foresee the social and financial consequences of her prank, was she cognitively mature? Social and emotional maturity are even harder to measure (see Salekin et al., 2002). In the absence of psychometric instruments, clinicians must rely on social histories to determine social maturity. Interpreting these without age-based norms for emotional and social skills is a difficult task.

The adequacy of forensic examinations of juveniles raises important ethical and methodological questions, especially because examinations by psychologists and psychiatrists are given great weight in many courts. However, even though the research base may be less full than desirable, it makes sense for judges making decisions as important as a transfer to adult court to make use of whatever expertise is available to them.

Does Recriminalization Reduce Juvenile Crime?

One purpose of the transfer laws is to prevent juvenile crime. The threat of harsher penalties should make juveniles less likely to commit serious crimes. The available research does not tell us whether the new laws deterred crime.

Youth who have been punished more harshly don't necessarily improve as a result of the experience. Researchers have found that adolescents tried as adults were rearrested at a greater rate than youth processed through the juvenile court system (Fagan, 1996; Howell, 1996; Weissman, 1999). The originators of the juvenile justice system may have been correct when they said that serving time in an adult prison would simply harden the juvenile's identification with the criminal role. However, we can't do a controlled experiment. Even if we use statistical controls, we may not be able to measure the most pertinent characteristics. Youth who are tried as adults are more likely to be dangerous and less likely to respond to rehabilitation in the first place than those whose cases are handled in juvenile court. One would expect them to have a higher recidivism rate.

We can assess deterrent effects of harsher penalties better by comparing overall juvenile arrest or conviction rates before and after the implementation of the laws. Singer (1996b) reported that in New York, recriminalizing delinquency had no effect in deterring crime among juveniles as measured by the juvenile arrest rate. Juvenile arrest rates in New York City and in the rest of the state were about the same before and after **recriminalization.** There was no evidence that youthful offenders in New York were deterred by the knowledge that they could be treated as adults and subject to longer sentences in secure facilities. However, Weissman (1999) cites research suggesting that, in some jurisdictions, the availability of transfer may have had a deterrent effect. Economic theorists hypothesize that the rate of crime is a function of the probability of being caught and the costs of being caught and punished. Some economists, testing this theory, have shown that the larger the number of youth incarcerated, the lower the violent crime rate. However, these analyses don't distinguish between a deterrent effect and an incapacitation effect (the more incarcerated, the fewer available to commit crimes) (Rashid, 2004). It is not clear that longer sentences have a greater deterrent effect than shorter sentences (Lippke, 2002). Given that it is difficult to prove deterrent effects, those who assert that harsher penalties will deter other youths from committing crimes have at best a weak database to support that proposition.

Psychological and Developmental Issues in Juvenile Competence

Since *Gault* (1967), respondents in juvenile court receive many of the same due process protections accorded adults in the criminal justice system. But questions about the competence of juveniles to exercise—or waive (voluntarily give up)—due process rights remain.

Competence to Waive Due Process Rights

In *Gault* (1967), the U.S. Supreme Court in effect said that youth were entitled to *Miranda*-style warnings (***Miranda v. Arizona,*** 1966). Juveniles taken into custody, like adults, must be informed of their rights before they are interrogated. Specifically, suspects must be told that they have a right to remain silent, that any statements they make can be used as evidence against them, that they have the right to have an attorney present, and that the court will appoint an attorney for them if they can't afford one. A suspect, adult or juvenile, can waive these rights, but must do so "voluntarily, knowingly and intelligently." The Supreme Court in *Gault* and other courts (e.g., *People v. Lara,* 1967) assume that young people, like adults, do have the **competence to waive** their procedural rights. This assumption is open to question.

Juvenile interrogation. Juveniles taken into custody and interrogated arguably face a more complex situation, psychologically and even legally, than adults. Usually, juveniles who are arrested appear in juvenile court or are brought to a designated court officer first. The parents are supposed to be notified when their children are taken into custody. Parents are not always present at the interrogations. Sometimes a court representative (e.g., an intake probation officer) or someone appointed by the court to represent the child's interest as a legal guardian may be present. About two-thirds of juveniles are subject to some interrogation shortly after being taken into custody (Grisso, 1981).

In contrast to adults, juveniles may be subject to questioning by the police, by social workers, by probation workers, by psychologists or psychiatrists, and later by court guardians, by defense attorneys if they ask for them, and, eventually, by the juvenile court judge. Many of the rules for confidentiality, except for the attorney-client relationship, do not apply. What a young person says to the various adults who question him or her may affect his or her adjudication in juvenile court and may have other serious legal consequences as well. The case may be transferred to criminal court. And if the case is transferred to criminal court, a confession made in juvenile court may be admissible in the criminal trial (*State v. Benoit,* 1985).

The *Miranda* warning is supposed to be given to a juvenile taken into custody by every adult who interviews the youth. But is it given in such a way that its significance

270

CHAPTER 9
Juvenile Court
and the Legal
Processing of
Children and
Adolescents

is clear? Does the young person understand why he or she might want to remain silent? Does he or she understand that it is all right to remain silent, even if talking to an adult authority, or a "helper" like a social worker? Parents are supposed to be notified of children's rights, but what if the parent says, "Just tell them the truth," or the youth assumes this is what the parents want? Does the youth realize he or she can change his or her mind, stop talking, and ask for a lawyer at any time? That the state will get one and the youth doesn't have to worry if parents don't want to or can't pay for the lawyer? Does the youth really understand what a lawyer is supposed to do? What a "right" is? That a right is unconditional and that one can't be punished for asserting it?

Waiver of rights. Grisso (1981) reviewed juvenile court records after the *Gault* decision. He found that youth either had orally waived rights or had signed a waiver of rights in 60 percent of the cases. Almost no adolescent under age 15 exercised the right to remain silent. Attorneys were almost never present at early interrogations of juveniles. Were these waivers voluntary, knowing, and intelligent? A confession will not be admitted into evidence if the waivers don't meet legal standards. When should we accept a waiver of rights by a juvenile?

Grisso (1981) addressed this question systematically, applying psychometrics to develop a measure of legal and psychological ability to waive or to exercise due process rights. The work is a model for good law/psychology research. Grisso reviewed the legal standard of "knowing, intelligent, and voluntary" and developed tests to measure these issues as they had been defined in court decisions. He then developed a measure to test comprehension of the *Miranda* rights and of how rights played out in a legal context. He gave the tests to 359 recently arrested juveniles, a group for whom the issues were salient. He assessed their comprehension of the provisions of the *Miranda* warning in three ways: (1) he asked them to paraphrase the elements of the warning; (2) he tested their understanding of the vocabulary used in the warnings; and (3) he asked them which of several alternative wordings was most similar in meaning to the wording in the *Miranda* warning. The several types of indicators had been mentioned in court cases.

To measure the subjects' understanding of "legal rights in context," Grisso used hypothetical vignettes and drawings. Subjects were asked questions about each scene shown in a drawing and about what they thought would be the consequences of decisions made in the hypothetical stories. Grisso developed scoring standards for the more open-ended questions and asked experienced attorneys and psychologists to review them. Interrater reliability (consistency) was adequate.

Grisso examined the relationship between test scores and various respondent characteristics that courts said should be taken into account when considering the validity of a waiver of rights (e.g., age and intelligence). He found that age and IQ made independent contributions to predicting competence scores. Race, gender, socioeconomic status, number of prior felonies, number of prior referrals to juvenile court for any reason, and number of prior detentions made very little difference.

Only a very small percent of Grisso's youngest subjects obtained perfect scores on the measures. Many understood some but not all of the warnings and words, or correctly interpreted some but not all of the vignettes. Grisso concluded that children under 12 had a poorer understanding of the issues involved in waiving *Miranda* rights than older children. About half of juveniles over age 13, and most of those who were older but who had low intelligence, appeared deficient in their understanding of *Miranda* warnings.

Because adults are presumed to have the capacity to waive their rights, Grisso used adult understanding as the benchmark to judge how well juveniles understood their

rights. He administered the same tests to a large number of adults who had been convicted as offenders in the past.

Comparing the scores of adult and juvenile subjects, Grisso found that 16 year
olds showed about the same level of comprehension on his various measures as those
17 to 22. Those below age 15 obtained significantly lower scores than those who
were 17 or older. Grisso concluded that those under 15 on average lacked the competence to waive rights. Youths below age 16, compared to adult offenders, also showed
poorer understanding of the lawyer's role and the significance of the right to remain
silent. The differences were more likely to occur with juveniles whose IQ scores fell
below 90.

Grisso recommended that waivers by youth under 14 should not be accepted without substantial inquiry. Similarly, juveniles under 16 with IQs below 80 probably lack
competence to waive their rights. His research may have had some influence on
defense attorneys and, perhaps, on courts by alerting judges to critical problems in protecting juveniles' rights.

271

Psychological
and
Developmental
Issues in
Juvenile
Competence

Juvenile Competence to Stand Trial as Adults

The question of competence to stand trial in juvenile court, as opposed to in criminal
court, did not receive early consideration because juvenile court hearings were supposed to be helpful and not punitive. Since the *Gault* decision introduced due process
into the juvenile court, however, about one-third of the states have explicitly recognized
the necessity for juveniles to be competent to stand trial in juvenile court. In juvenile
courts, as in adult courts, incompetence has been interpreted to involve deficits in
understanding of one's legal situation secondary to mental illness or mental defect;
incompetence does not refer to deficits related to an immature developmental stage
(Grisso, 1997; see Chapter 4).

A juvenile defendant tried as an adult is treated the same way as an adult. Transfer laws presume that juveniles whose cases are transferred to criminal court have the
capacity for criminal intent. At present, most states also presume that juveniles tried as
adults are competent to stand trial (Chapter 4). If there is evidence that the juvenile
being tried as an adult has a mental illness or mental defect, his or her lawyer can
request a competency evaluation. However, there is usually no provision in state laws
for raising questions about a transferred juvenile's competence to stand trial simply on
the grounds that he or she is immature. Arkansas is an exception. There, if questions
are raised about an older juvenile's fitness to proceed in adult criminal court, the
juvenile must be examined by a psychiatrist or a clinical psychologist. But if the
juvenile is under age 13, he or she is automatically presumed unfit to proceed. Then,
the state must have a psychiatrist or a clinical psychologist evaluate the youth's competence to stand trial. The Arkansas statute does not seem to require a finding of mental illness or defect. The factors to be evaluated by the mental health professional
apparently focus on the youth's developmental level.

Under Arkansas law, the written report of the examination must include statements
about:

> (a) ability to understand and appreciate the charges and their seriousness; (b) ability to
> understand and realistically appraise the likely outcomes; (c) reliable episodic memory
> so that he can accurately and reliably relate a sequence of events; (d) ability to extend
> thinking into the future; (e) ability to consider the impact of his actions on others;
> (f) verbal articulation abilities or the ability to express himself in a reasonable and
> coherent manner; and (g) logical decision-making abilities, particularly multi-factored

272

CHAPTER 9
Juvenile Court
and the Legal
Processing of
Children and
Adolescents

problem solving or the ability to take several factors into consideration in making a decision. (Brummer, 2002, p. 813)

Should it be possible to request a competency evaluation of a juvenile simply on the basis that the defendant is too mentally immature to participate in his or her own defense? The reasons for not trying a mentally incompetent defendant should apply equally to a defendant whose understanding of his or her situation is limited because of immaturity. If a youthful defendant does not understand the trial process or is not **competent to assist counsel** fully in his or her defense, the trial will be unfair. Based on his literature review, Grisso (1997) concluded that the competence of younger juveniles should not be presumed. He recommends a competency evaluation whenever

> (a) the juvenile is less than fourteen years old; (b) the past history of the youth or observation of persons working with the youth (e.g., counsel) indicate the possibility of emotional disturbance, mental illness or mental retardation; (c) records indicate the possibility of below average intellectual functioning or a learning disability; or (d) the possibility of deficits in memory, attention, or other cognitive functions has been identified by counsel, court personnel or others who have had contact with the youth. (Grisso, 1997, p. 23)

If we are to evaluate youth, special instruments might be needed. Emotional as well as cognitive components of judgment should probably be assessed. Youthful defendants may be influenced in their decision making by their propensity for immediate gratification as against contemplating the future, or to please friends rather than to see and act on their own best interests. Some research suggests that measures of adjudicative competence and measures of competence to waive *Miranda* rights correlate strongly. The correlations support the view that competence is a general construct, but there are still some differences that make generalization difficult (Redlich, Silverman, and Steiner, 2003).

Using the same research methods developed to evaluate juvenile competence to waive *Miranda* rights, Grisso et al. (2003) created two new instruments, the MacArthur Competence Assessment Tool—Criminal Adjudication (MacCAT-CA) and the MacArthur Judgment Evaluation (MacJEN), to assess psychosocial influences on making legal decisions. The research team obtained samples of males and females, ages 11 through 24, who were detained or who were living in the community and had never been charged with an offense. About 30 percent of those 11–13, 19 percent of those 14 or 15, and 12 percent of those over age 16 were considered sufficiently impaired on the tests to raise questions about their competence to stand trial in an adult court.

The research team concluded that "juveniles aged 15 and younger are significantly more likely than older adolescents and young adults to be impaired in ways that compromise their ability to serve as competent defendants in a criminal proceeding" (Grisso et al., 2003, p. 356). Further, "[a]pproximately one third of 11- to 13-year olds and approximately one fifth of 14- to 15-year olds are as impaired in capacities relevant to adjudicative competence as seriously mentally ill adults who would likely to be considered incompetent to stand trial by clinicians" (p. 356). The competence of 16- and 17-year olds was comparable to that of young adults (p. 356).

This research did not deal explicitly with the relationship between juveniles and their lawyers. Some have theorized that adolescent struggles with identity and independence create suspicion of adults. Youth may not be as cooperative with their lawyers as is desirable. They may withold information or be unwilling to reveal information to lawyers they do not trust. Youth may also lack in appreciation of the role of attorneys and their ethical rules, and many lawyers may be unskilled in communicating

273

Psychological
and
Developmental
Issues in
Juvenile
Competence

with youth. Pierce and Brodsky (2002) studied 163 males between the ages of 12 and 20 who were in correctional institutions or in facilities for delinquent youth. Each participant had been represented by a defense attorney. Pierce and Brodsky developed a Trust in My Lawyer scale including items such as "I could be honest with my lawyer," "My lawyer was too busy to see me," and "My lawyer was good at doing his/her job" (2002, p. 94). They also created a second scale, Understanding about Lawyers. This scale was designed to assess understanding about the role of the defense counsel. Those with a poorer understanding of legal matters and less understanding of the role of defense attorneys were less trusting in their lawyers. Legal understanding did improve with age and with higher levels of IQ. These relationships suggest that younger defendants with lower IQs may have great difficulty in assisting their attorneys. The ability to assist an attorney is an important aspect of adjudicative competence.

Schmidt, Reppucci, and Woolard (2003) examined responses to two MacCAT (see above) items assessing juvenile's beliefs about their lawyer's effectiveness and the likelihood that they would disclose fully to their lawyer. The measures were administered to 101 younger juveniles (12–15), 102 older adolescents (16 and 17), and 110 adults (19–35). All were males and were incarcerated at the time of the study.

The majority of participants (77 percent) recommended that the character in the vignette admit the offense to his lawyer. More juveniles (about 28 percent) than adults (17 percent) selected refusal to talk as an option. More juveniles (23 percent) than adults (11 percent) recommended that the character deny involvement in the offense. About a quarter of all participants felt negatively about the attorney's effectiveness. Age-related differences in willingness to talk to an attorney suggest that courts with jurisdiction over adolescents and particularly younger adolecents need to exercise caution to insure that youth can cooperate with an attorney, one of the key aspects of adjudictive competence. The results of studies of adolescent relationships with attorneys suggest that attorneys representing youth in adult criminal court should be alert to the problems of working with youth. Perhaps they should have training in understanding psychological development.

Treating Incompetence to Stand Trial

Psychiatric treatment, combined with teaching about the legal system, can help adults found incompetent become competent to stand trial. But can someone be helped to competence if the problem is immaturity? The question is related to an important theoretical question: are adolescents simply young adults with deficits in knowledge and experience that can be rectified, or are there qualitative differences in the ways adults and adolescents think and make judgments that will change only with time, experience, and brain maturation?

Cooper (1997) tested whether an intervention that provided information about the juvenile justice system would enable juveniles to achieve a reasonable level of competence. She used a version of the Georgia Court Competency Test (GCCT) developed for juveniles. The test is written at a fourth-grade reading level. Experts agreed that a number of items were critical for the adolescent to answer correctly if we were to say a youth met legal standards of competence.

Cooper's subjects were 112 delinquents ranging in age from 13 to 16, in their first residential placement. The subjects were given the juvenile version of the GCCT in small groups, and then shown a 50-minute videotape providing information about juvenile court personnel and proceedings. One day later, the subjects were given the GCCT again.

274

CHAPTER 9
Juvenile Court
and the Legal
Processing of
Children and
Adolescents

The first time they took the test, only 2 of the 112 delinquents scored above the competency level set by the forensic experts. Test scores improved at the posttest, especially for 13 year olds. However, even at posttest, only 12 youths obtained scores above the cutoff of correct answers on the critical items. Cooper (1997) concluded that "children are functioning differently from adults within the court system, and do not have an understanding of legal process necessary for competence to stand trial. . . . Competence to stand trial cannot be presumed for juveniles, as it is for adults" (p. 178).

Cooper's study suggests that a simple intervention to provide information may "cure" incompetence for a few youth who do not understand how the legal system works. However the simple intervention would not affect cognitive skills or attitudes based on psychosocial maturity. Even more extended interventions may be ineffective with youth with mental retardation (Mumley, Tillbrook, and Grisso, 2003).

What should be done? Assuming brief interventions would not compensate for developmental limitations in many cases, should incompetent juveniles be held without a trial until they have matured? Would a youth living in an institution be exposed to conditions that promote "maturing"? One suggestion following from the research is that the minimum age for adult criminal adjudication should be set at age 14 to minimize the risk that juveniles incompetent because of immaturity would be tried in adult court. Assuming brief interventions would not compensate for developmental limitations in many cases, should incompetent juveniles be held without a trial until they have matured? Grisso et al. (2003) believe that the vast majority of juveniles would be found competent for juvenile court proceedings because the standards are not as stringent as for criminal court. Youth found incompetent for trial in an adult criminal court because of immaturity would not be held indefinitely. They would be tried in juvenile court, and if found guilty would be punished according to the prevailing penalties for juveniles. This would have the effect of reducing the number of youth transferred or tried in adult criminal court. Here, as in many areas of law, practical policy considerations and psychological insight leave us with very difficult questions and few answers.

New Reforms

Critics are justified in complaining that the overloaded juvenile courts have not been holding many of the juveniles who appear before them accountable for wrongs they have done. Well over half of those adjudicated delinquent are put on probation or receive an **adjournment in contemplation of dismissal** (charges dismissed if the youth doesn't get into further trouble within some specified period of time; Maguire and Pastore, 1998; OJJDP, 2003b). Often, probation is not very rigorous because probation workers have high caseloads. The youth receive little in the way of punishment for socially undesirable behaviors and little support in adopting prosocial behaviors (see Weithorn, 2005).

At the same time that legislatures have adopted "get-tough" policies for youth who commit serious crimes, some communities have been experimenting with innovative ways to hold status offenders and minor delinquents more accountable for their actions (Singer, 1996a). Some communities use restorative justice methods with some who have committed more serious offenses as well. These programs are an extension of Victim–Offender Mediation programs, in which victims confront offenders in the presence of a mediatior and attempt to work out some form of restitution or reparation. The goal of the new experiments is to increase accountability while also fostering social integration by moving the justice system back to the community.

Restorative justice theory contrasts with the theory of retributive justice. Retributive justice emphasizes punishment for an offense against the state. The criminal act is interpreted as creating an "imbalance" in the social order that will be redressed by punishing the offender. The victim has little role, except as a complaining witness. The prosecutor represents the community. Restorative justice emphasizes that wrongdoing has created a wound in the victim and in the social order. Restorative justice approaches give greater prominence to the victim, emphasize healing the breach, and involve offender and community in the process (OJJDP, 1996). Nuzum (n.d.) identified legislation in 29 states addressing restorative justice issues either directly or indirectly. Evaluation of restorative justice programs has lagged although some promising results are reported (Umbreit, Coates, and Vos, 2002). Implementation problems, including gaining acceptance from juvenile court judges, remain to be worked out (Bazemore, 1998).

Juvenile Justice and Moral Development

Moral development is a process of internalizing community values. Internalization replaces the external controls imposed by authority figures with internal self-control and self-regulation. It takes place in part through experiences that lead an offender to feel shame or guilt. In theory, this developmental approach can be applied to juvenile justice. Braithwaite and Mugford (1994) argue that the rehabilitative goals of juvenile justice can be served by legal rituals involving shaming followed by reintegration in the social group. Seen from this perspective, a juvenile justice disposition is most likely to be rehabilitative if it: (1) creates the conditions for shame by calling the offender to account before valued others, (2) imposes a penalty tailored to the specific offense, and (3) uses the offenders' participation in the accountability process to confirm membership in the community. These principles are consistent with definitions of restorative justice.

Some new juvenile justice programs are building on these concepts. The programs enlist peers, family members, and, sometimes, victims to design sentences to penalize young offenders and to help the youth to feel they are part of a community. In theory, the process should encourage youth to internalize community values. Two innovations incorporating these ideas have generated growing interest: teen courts, and an alternate form of conflict resolution developed in New Zealand called Family Group Conferencing (FGC). Both are good examples of **therapeutic jurisprudence,** a legal process designed to achieve a therapeutic end.

Teen Courts

The first **teen court** was organized by juvenile authorities in Odessa, Texas, in 1983 in response to the perception that the overburdened juvenile court was ineffective. The Odessa court invited juveniles to help administer and contribute to juvenile justice. The idea was to give young people what adults have: a jury of their peers. The concept captured public attention. Teen courts have subsequently been introduced in numerous jurisdictions throughout the country. They have grown from about 50 programs in 1991 to over 1,050 programs in 2005 (National Youth Court Center, 2005). Most teen courts

276

CHAPTER 9
Juvenile Court
and the Legal
Processing of
Children and
Adolescents

handle between 50 and 100 cases a year. In some states, the teen courts are established by law and have statutory authority. In most, they are set up under the state's diversion statute.

Jurisdiction. In most jurisdictions, the teen court only takes cases involving minor infractions or misdemeanors: truancy, vandalism, shoplifting, assault, disorderly conduct, defacing property with graffiti, and possessing alcohol (Butts, Hoffman, and Buck, 1999). A few may accept cases involving theft or burglary (Shiff and Wexler, 1996). The vast majority (87 percent) of teen courts accept only first offenders, not those with prior arrest records, especially for felonies (Butts, Hoffman, and Buck, 1999).

Different court models. Teen courts are more for disposition than adjudication. Most do not determine guilt or innocence (Butts, Hoffman, and Buck, 1999). The youth must admit to the charges or the case is processed through normal legal channels. There are different teen court models. In all of them, young volunteers participate in a court that hears cases involving their peers. They receive training in aspects of law from volunteer community lawyers. In some programs the cases are presented to a panel of three youth "judges," and in others the case is presented to a peer jury who can ask questions (Butts, Hoffman, and Buck, 1999). The defendant's peers sometimes serve as lawyers, bailiffs, and clerks, and manage the programs. In most programs, an adult judge rules on procedure and clarifies legal issues.

Procedure. Youth are referred to the teen court following agreements with police, with probation, with other social agencies, and with the local juvenile court. Only those who are young enough to be covered by status offense or delinquency statutes are eligible. The youth must admit to the charges or the case is processed through normal legal channels. Admitting to charges publicly may be a first step in the restorative justice process. After doing so, the youth is given a choice between having the offense adjudicated in juvenile court or in teen court. The possibility of appearing in juvenile court, with potentially harsher punishment and greater stigma, probably adds incentive for the teen to agree to have the case disposed of in teen court.

Teen courts differ in procedural complexity and formality. The teen jurors or the panel hear testimony about the offense, the circumstances of the offense, and any mitigating factors. Panel members or the jury can ask questions of the defendant. In many of the courts, teenage defense lawyers represent defendants and teenage prosecutors sum up the case for the jury. After the case is presented, the jury or panel retires to deliberate to decide on a "sentence."

Teen court sentences are intended to educate and reform. The sentences often involve a process of restoring the offender to the community, and may serve to provide some reparation for the victim if appropriate. Typical sentences include

- a term of community service, used in 99 percent of the programs;
- jury duty on teen court, used in 75 percent of programs;
- written apologies to the victim, used in 86 percent of programs;
- essays on the harmful effects of the offense or apology essays, used in 79 percent of programs; and
- assignment to **peer mediation** (use of peers trained in mediation techniques to mediate a dispute between youths). (See Butts, Hoffman, and Buck, 1999.)

The teen court and therapeutic jurisprudence. Teen court, in keeping with the tenets of therapeutic jurisprudence, is intended in and of itself to have a therapeutic effect on participants (Shiff and Wexler, 1996; Singer, 1997). Ideally, both the trial process itself and the implementation of the sentence should lead all concerned to accountability, to a better understanding of the mechanics of the legal process, and also to a deeper understanding of the law. In theory, peer disapproval and the shame it produces will prevent recidivism more effectively than the disapproval of adult authority figures. At the same time, the process integrates the offending teen into the community of peers. Although defendants in teen court may be shamed and sentenced by their peers, they are not rejected by them.

In contrast to the "exclusionary" thrust of punishment in the criminal justice system, the teen court is "inclusionary." Teens are included in the legal process itself. Offenders are eligible or even required to serve as jurors on the court. Requiring teenager offenders to serve on the teen court is an application of Reissman's helper therapy principle. In the process of taking the role of giving help, one develops a deeper understanding of the problems and of receiving help (Reissman, 1965). Helping and working with others may change young offenders' attitudes about their offenses and about the legitimacy of social institutions. It may also help them develop new social and communication skills, and may enhance their capacity to empathize with victims (Shiff and Wexler, 1996). Moreover, giving the young offenders an active role in the community empowers them. Some teens who stay with youth courts say that they learn a great deal, feel part of a group, learn to be appropriately assertive in their court roles, learn to prepare cases, learn public speaking skills, and gain a credential for college applications (National Youth Court Center, 2005).

Program evaluation. But does all this really happen? Does teen court work well in practice? On the basis of observation, and a review of some literature, Shiff and Wexler (1996) concluded that teen courts "lighten the juvenile justice system's load, provide community service volunteers, process cases more quickly and cheaply, result in very low rates of recidivism, discourage juvenile delinquency, reduce street crime, and educate teens about the legal system" (Shiff and Wexler, 1996, p. 346). Weisz, Lott, and Thai (2002) found that juveniles and their parents exposed to a teen court program expressed a high degree of satisfaction with the experience.

However, Shiff and Wexler's (1996) assertion of low recidivism and reduced street crime requires better documentation. We have just a few highly limited studies evaluating teen courts. The results are inconsistent (Godwin, Steinhart, and Fulton, n.d.). Weisz, Lott, and Thai (2002) found a relatively low rate of recidivism among teens sentenced in teen court for shoplifting (13 percent) compared to teenage shoplifters sent to other diversion programs. However, they could not control for bias stemming from the referral process. Youth were not randomly assigned to the new teen court or to juvenile court. The only offense studied was shoplifting, and the results might not generalize to other offenses. Youth, for some of whom shoplifting is almost normative, may not believe that prosecuting the offense is reasonable. Weisz, Lott, and Thai (2002) did not find any attitude change consistent with the theory underlying the teen court.

The teen court experiment provides an excellent opportunity for social scientists to cooperate with the juvenile justice system to evaluate program effectiveness, test theories of juvenile justice, and improve the system itself. The teen court may also be a means of rejuvenating the juvenile court by freeing it to concentrate on harder cases in which it may be more important to make full use of the coercive power of the court.

277

New Reforms

278

CHAPTER 9
Juvenile Court
and the Legal
Processing of
Children and
Adolescents

The New Zealand Family Group Conference Model[1]

In 1989, the New Zealand Parliament passed a law establishing the **Family Group Conference (FGC)** as an alternative to court hearings in both the juvenile justice and the child protection systems. The model includes all the features of a restorative justice intervention—confrontation between victim and offender, a prominent role for the victim, participation of the community, and a restorative, healing orientation. It is also a good example of therapeutic jusiprudence because the legislation was written with a therapeutic purpose in mind. The FGC process has a number of potentially therapeutic effects, some similar to those involved in the teen court. The innovation has attracted substantial attention in the United States and in many other countries, although it is difficult to say in how many countries or communities in the United States the procedure or something like it is in routine use.

The FGC is an adaptation of methods of dispute resolution used by the Maoris, the indigenous people of New Zealand. In traditional Maori culture, it is less important to ascertain guilt and to exact punishment than to resolve a conflict in a way that satisfies the community. The priority is to avoid feuds and rifts within the relatively small tribal groups. When someone has a grievance, a meeting is held before the whole community. All who wish to participate can do so, and the community arrives at a suitable disposition by consensus. The FGC follows this model. The option of using this alternative method of resolving juvenile cases is available to all New Zealanders, whether or not they are of Maori ancestry.

The FGC, like the teen court, does not decide questions of guilt or innocence. An admission to the offense is a precondition of the conference. Its basic purpose is to hold the offending youth accountable. Whatever else is accomplished, some penalty is imposed as a consequence of the conference.

Jurisdiction and referral. When a person under age 17 commits an offense in New Zealand, the police can respond informally by cautioning the young person, speaking to the family, or sending a letter to the family. If the police feel that informal methods of resolution are inappropriate, they can refer the case for an FGC or bring it to the youth court (New Zealand terminology). If the juvenile pleads not guilty, a hearing must be held in the youth court. If he or she admits the offense, the judge may decide to order an FGC. All but the most severe offenses may be referred for an FGC.

Procedure. An FGC is convened and facilitated by a youth justice coordinator. The juvenile, the juvenile's lawyer, members of the nuclear family, a police representative, a social worker, the victim, and a victim support person participate. Members of the youth's extended family, members of the subtribe, tribal representatives, ministers, school officials, or counselors may also be invited. The youth policeman tends to support the victim in the FGC.

The youth justice coordinator opens the conference, outlining the rules and procedures. The coordinator explains that communication in the FGC is privileged. **Privileged** means that new information obtained in the conference cannot be used in court against the youth. Next, the youth police representative reads the charge and asks the youth to admit to it. If the youth admits to the charge, the process continues. The

---

[1]The material in this section is drawn largely from M. Levine (2000) and references contained in that article.

victim may confront the offender and tell the FGC how he or she was harmed by the offender's actions.

The youth and the other participants, including the victim, offer their views of what should be done. Then the youth and the extended family meet alone. They develop a plan that includes a penalty and a rehabilitation program. The proposal is discussed with the other participants. If the plan achieves a consensus, it becomes the official disposition or sentence and is written down. Copies are distributed to participants and to relevant agencies. The youth justice coordinator may put a follow-up plan into place to monitor implementation. If the FGC doesn't arrive at a resolution satisfactory to the police, the social workers, the victim, or family members, the case may be returned to the youth court for disposition, or another FGC may be convened.

Therapeutic jurisprudence implications. The legislation establishing the FGC is an example of applied therapeutic jurisprudence, of a law enacted with the explicit goal of healing and empowering the people affected by it (see Wexler, 1995). The FGC empowers the victim by creating a structure for the victim to confront the offending youth and to have a say in the disposition. The system is intended to elicit shame, to help youth internalize social values and social control. The young offender who might feel disdain and disconnection from the authority figures in juvenile court may feel ashamed when his or her offenses are revealed in detail to people he or she loves and respects. The processes of face-to-face social control are invoked.

By asking the family to come up with a plan, the law puts the family in a cooperative rather than an adversarial relationship with the juvenile justice system and with social service and mental health professionals. The law empowers the family and community, and even the offending youth, by providing a way for them to take an active role in solving a community problem. Empowerment was an explicit legislative goal of the new program.

Program evaluation. Although there is widespread interest in the FGC model, there is little systematic research testing its underlying propositions or its effectiveness. The limited formal research in New Zealand has revealed both advantages and limitations.

Youth accountability. Juveniles who go to FGCs are held more accountable for their offenses than juveniles whose cases are heard in the youth court by a judge. The latter usually receive probation only, while most offenders who go to an FGC at least apologize to the victim. A high percentage are assigned community service or even required to make monetary repayments to the victims. Observers believe that most elements of the FGC plan seem to be followed. However, no one really sees to it that the plan is followed. There is no automatic action if the disposition plan is not followed.

Satisfaction. Family members and community participants, including police and social workers, express a great deal of satisfaction as a result of their participation.

The young offenders are not as satisfied with the FGC as their families. However, satisfied or not, they do participate actively in the conferences. In the formal youth court, the young offenders hardly participate at all. Observers of the youth court say that, typically, youth are asked only a few questions that they answer with few words. Most of the time, the young people just stand there while the judge lectures them. If it is important for youth to participate in matters affecting their lives, the FGC is an advance over youth court.

280

CHAPTER 9
Juvenile Court
and the Legal
Processing of
Children and
Adolescents

Victim satisfaction. Some victims say they were emotionally moved by the confrontation with the offender, understood the offender better, and felt reconciled. However, many victims are disappointed in the FGC program. They complained that their voices were not sufficiently heard, that the offender's punishment was insufficient, and that they did not receive sufficient restitution for financial losses. The victims probably would not have fared any better had their cases gone to youth court, where offenders are typically placed on probation. To increase victim satisfaction and empowerment, the FGC law was amended to allow the victim to bring a support person to the conference. Others have also reported generally favorable, but mixed, results from the viewpoint of crime victims in family group conferencing (Umbreit, 2000).

Reduction in out-of-home placements. The adoption of the FGC program has resulted in a sharp decrease in out-of-home placements in New Zealand. Cases of youth who formerly would have been sentenced to residential care are now settled more informally, sometimes by family members taking responsibility for the youth's supervision. The FGC has increased family involvement in discipline and rehabilitation of troubled and troubling young people. In theory, more community agencies are also involved in rehabilitation of youth offenders, but some complain that the state has not created sufficient and appropriate community services to fully support the community program.

Recidivism. About 48 percent of youth who participate in an FGC reoffend within six months of the conference. It is difficult to say if this rate of recidivism is higher or lower than the recidivism rate for comparable cases heard in the formal youth court. There have been no controlled studies investigating the question. Simply comparing recidivism rates before and after the new law went into effect isn't enough. Many other changes occurred at the time the FGC was introduced. Moreover, the 1989 law created more options for diversion. As a result, cases involving milder offenses, which were handled in youth court before 1989, are now siphoned off, and the pool from which the police choose FGC candidates contains a higher proportion of difficult cases.

New Zealand authorities evaluating the FGC have weighed measures of community participation and satisfaction as heavily as behavioral outcome measures. They believe the rate of recidivism is at least no worse since FGC was introduced, and they are satisfied that the new system has brought other benefits that make it worth retaining. The FGC has succeeded in increasing satisfaction of participants with the juvenile justice system. If that means that people feel less alienated from the justice system, then the FGC is contributing to social cohesiveness, no small matter in these days of divisiveness and separation.

Summary

In our society, children's behavior is supposed to be controlled by their parents and their schools. Courts have been willing since colonial times to step in and help when parents and schools cannot control unruly or aggressive children. Until the beginning of the twentieth century, teenagers and even younger children were tried in adult criminal courts under adult rules.

Social and economic changes in the nineteenth century increased the number of troubled and troubling youth. Reformers believed that "incorrigible" children and children who performed criminal acts could grow up to be productive citizens if they received help. Illinois established the first juvenile court in Chicago in 1899 to provide that help. Similar courts were soon established all over the country. The juvenile court laws created the idea of "delinquency" as a problem to be treated rather than punished.

Almost from the beginning, juvenile courts were criticized for ineffectiveness and arbitrariness. In the 1960s, the U.S. Supreme Court noted that youth got the worst of both worlds, receiving neither due process nor adequate help. The Court's decision in *Gault* granted youth due process rights, making delinquency hearings more like criminal trials. Subsequently, states introduced reforms to ensure that status offenders, unruly juveniles who had not engaged in any acts prohibited by the adult criminal code, were treated differently from delinquents.

In the second half of the twentieth century, the rising rate and violence of juvenile crime led to increased criticism of the effectiveness of the juvenile justice system. Although the rate of juvenile crime peaked in the mid-1990s, public concern continues. To "get tougher" on juvenile crime, state legislatures have "recriminalized" delinquency, authorizing the transfer of juveniles charged with murder or other felonies to adult criminal court where they can be tried and punished as if they were adults. The transfer laws created new questions about the competence of youth to waive their basic rights and to stand trial. Psychological research suggests that young minors may well be incompetent in these areas for developmental reasons. However, acknowledging the implications of the research would create new problems for the system.

At the same time that they have been increasing penalties for juveniles who have committed serious felonies, states have been experimenting with more effective ways to handle minor offenses and to promote community involvement with juvenile justice to increase its effectiveness. New methods of handling these cases include the teen court and the family group conference.

Juvenile justice policies and procedures make explicit or implicit assumptions about how children and adolescents differ from adults and when they should be considered criminally responsible. The questions of when young people are competent to make decisions or engage in activities on their own and when they need guardianship permeate all areas of juvenile law and are based on beliefs about children's judgment. These beliefs are not necessarily highly consistent in different areas of law, but people hold their views about personal responsibility very strongly. These strongly held attitudes may not be changed by new research-based psychological knowledge.

Discussion Questions

1. Do you agree with the philosophy behind juvenile court? Whether you agree or not, how could its implementation be improved?
2. Do you think having a juvenile declared a minor in need of supervision is a good way to help parents who are having trouble controlling their children? Can you think of any alternatives?
3. Do you think capacity for criminal responsibility is related to seriousness of the crime? What are the arguments for and against the proposition that a 14-year-old who commits murder is more likely to have an adult capacity for criminal responsibility than a 14-year-old who shoplifts?
4. A judge has to decide whether to transfer the case of a 14-year-old alleged to have killed someone to adult court. The judge asks a psychologist to evaluate the youth and submit the report. What information could the psychologist provide that would be helpful to the judge? What problems would the psychologist face in deciding how to do the evaluation?
5. Can you think of any changes that could be made to help arrested juveniles understand their rights better? How could you test your proposed reforms to see if they worked?
6. How could the efficacy of teen courts be studied? What specific elements of the teen court programs do you think are likely to be most important, and how could you test your hypothesis?
7. Could the New Zealand Family Group Conference model be established in the United States? Would it work better in small towns than in big cities?

282

CHAPTER 9
Juvenile Court
and the Legal
Processing of
Children and
Adolescents

Key Terms

adjudication

adjournment in contempla-
  tion of dismissal

competence to assist
  counsel

competence to waive

decisional competence

deinstitutionalize

delinquency

diversion

due process rights

family group conference

In re

In re Gault

judicial transfer

Kent v. United States

legislative offense exclusion

legislative transfer

loosely coupled system

minor in need of
  supervision

Miranda rights

net widening

pathologize

peer mediation

petition on behalf of a child

privilege against
  self-incrimination

privileged

recidivism

recriminalization

restorative justice

status offenses

teen courts

therapeutic jurisprudence

transfer laws

CHAPTER **10**

Protecting Children: Child Protection Proceedings

The Child Protection System
>Historical Background
>>Early efforts • Societies for the prevention of cruelty to children
>>• Rediscovery of child abuse • Mandatory reporting laws • The police and
>>child abuse • Increase in number of reports • Foster care • Family preser-
>>vation • Indian Child Welfare Act (ICWA)
>Child Protection Today
>>Child abuse and criminal prosecution • Typical child protection statutes
>>and procedures • Hotline • Sources of reports • Types of reports
>>• Investigation • Substantiated reports • Hearing and disposition • Court
>>Appointed Special Advocates (CASA) • Research on CASA programs • Ter-
>>mination of parental rights (TPR) • Infant safe haven laws
>The Child Protection Services (CPS) Worker
>>Life-and-death decisions • Risk assessment • Testifying in court
>>• Criticisms of CPS workers
>Mandated Reporting, Role Conflict, and Professional Practice
>>Underreporting • Corporal punishment • Sexual abuse • Neglect
>>• Emotional abuse • Psychotherapy and mandated reporting • Therapists'
>>fear of negative consequences
Children's Rights, Parents' Rights
>Procedural Differences in Civil and Criminal Court
>Issues of Proof in Family Court
>>Children's testimony • Empirical basis for professional validation testimony
>Disposition
>>Mandated psychotherapy
>Termination of Parental Rights
>>Due diligence • Mental illness and mental retardation • Parents in prison
>The Adoption and Safe Families Act of 1997

284

CHAPTER 10
Protecting
Children: Child
Protection
Proceedings

Summary
Discussion Questions
Key Terms

Our survival as a society and a culture depends on our ability to socialize children to take their place in the social world. The family, the child, and society as represented by the state all have important interests in this process of human socialization. We would like to believe that these interests are compatible. In practice, they sometimes conflict (Goldstein et al., 1996).

When a family member allegedly mistreats a child, the situation is complex legally and psychologically. Parents have a constitutionally protected right to bring up their children as they choose. A state can intervene in family life only if the family is accorded due process of law. All states have laws defining a parent's minimum responsibilities toward his or her children and authorizing intervention if the parent fails to meet these obligations. Each state has an agency to implement the laws.

Child protection laws can profitably be considered within the framework of therapeutic jurisprudence (Wexler and Winick, 1996a). The laws have the clear therapeutic purpose of protecting children from harm, helping families, and preventing long-range negative consequences of child maltreatment. Children with histories of abuse or neglect are at risk of poor performance in school, diminished attachment, low self-esteem, physical aggression, delinquency, crime, sexual problems, and alcohol and drug abuse; the victims too often grow up to abuse their children (English, 1998; Kaufman and Zigler, 1989; National Research Council, 1993; Widom, 1992).

The child protection system affects the lives of millions of children and families. The investigations are costly for the public, painful for the families, and not always beneficial for the children. Clearly, child protection has helped a great many children, but many observers believe it is foundering badly (U.S. Advisory Board on Child Abuse and Neglect, 1993; Wexler, 1990).

In this chapter, we will describe the child protection system and discuss some of the legal and psychological issues that arise as states try to balance the protection of children and family autonomy. Topics covered will include

- the history of the child protection system and its rediscovery in the 1960s.
- problems created by the new laws: family preservation policy and children in foster care.
- the child protection system today.
- the child protection worker's job and risk assessment.
- mandated reporting in principle and in practice.
- psychotherapy and mandated reporting.
- prosecution of child maltreatment in criminal and in civil court.
- problems of proof in child maltreatment.
- dispositions after adjudication.
- termination of parental rights.
- the Adoption and Safe Families Act of 1997.

Historical Background

Under English common law, the king, as ***parens patriae*** ("parent of the state"), had the power to act as guardian to incompetent citizens, including orphaned children. When the Crown exercised its prerogative of guardianship, it was usually over infant heirs to powerful estates. Families were responsible for caring for their own young, sick, or disabled. Without family, orphaned children and adults unable to care for themselves were at the mercy of private or religious charity, such as it was. Within the family, parents could raise and discipline their children pretty much as they wished. Until the modern era, the power of parents over children was almost absolute.

Early efforts. The Elizabethan Poor Laws of 1601 in England established local, public responsibility for those unable to care for themselves. Colonists coming to America brought English customs and laws with them. Local government was responsible for the care of abandoned or orphan children. Colonial American communities also imposed some limited duties on parents to educate and maintain their children, but virtually no restriction on the discipline they could administer. Until well into the nineteenth century, states and local communities extended their protection only to destitute, abandoned, vagrant, or wayward children who were placed in institutions. As the cities grew, statutes were passed authorizing local government to intervene in cases of parental cruelty, gross neglect that seriously endangered a child's health or morals, or serious neglect of the parents' minimal duties to educate the child. The laws were not enforced very much (Folks, 1902; Myers, 2004).

In the mid- and late nineteenth century, urbanization, immigration, and rising urban poverty led to an increase in child neglect and abuse as well as juvenile crime. Large numbers of homeless children lived on the streets of the big cities. Charles Loring Brace (1880) estimated that there were 30,000 homeless children and youth in New York City alone when the city's population was perhaps 500,000. Brace, a minister, pioneered in developing faith-based community services for homeless and abandoned children. Overwhelmed by the number of children and the severity of the conditions of their lives, he questioned the value of institutional care. His primary method was to put abandoned children on "orphan trains" and ship them west to be adopted by farm families who valued them for their labor. From 1854 to 1929, Brace's and other agencies sent 100,000 children, many not technically orphans in the sense of having no living parent, to the West. Some of the children were adopted by the families with whom they were placed. Adoption law was much more informal in those days. Although a seemingly harsh intervention, follow-up research showed that many placements were quite successful (Myers, 2004). Brace's solution did not cover children still in their own homes who were poorly treated by their caretakers.

Societies for the prevention of cruelty to children. In 1874, Etta Wheeler, a mission worker, learned that an orphan child named Mary Ellen was being badly abused by her caretaker Mrs. Connolly. Because there were no child protective services, Mrs. Wheeler went to the Society for the Prevention of Cruelty to Animals (SPCA). SPCA officials obtained a special warrant from a court to remove Mary Ellen from the home. Mrs. Connolly was prosecuted for assault; Mary Ellen testified against her (Figure 10.1). The caretaker was convicted and sentenced to prison (Myers, 2004). Mary Ellen was

286

CHAPTER 10
Protecting
Children: Child
Protection
Proceedings

FIGURE 10.1

Mary Ellen

Mary Ellen was an abused child in nineteenth-century New York City. A court issued a special warrant to the Society for the Prevention of Cruelty to Animals to remove her from her foster home. At that time, there were no agencies for children empowered to intervene in their homes for the children's safety.

eventually placed with Etta Wheeler's family. When Mary Ellen grew up, she married, had two children, and lived to a ripe old age (Lazoritz, 1990; Stevens and Eide, 1990).

The publicity from Mary Ellen's case led to the formation of the **New York Society for the Prevention of Cruelty to Children (NYSPCC)** in 1875. Existing charitable agencies could aid abandoned or destitute children, but they had no legal authority to intervene with children in their own homes. The NYSPCC, a private agency with a state charter and public funding, was given legislative authority to seek out abused or neglected children and take them into custody. They were also authorized to initiate criminal prosecutions against those who abused or neglected children (Myers, 2004). That was the beginning of child protective services in the United States.

The New York law establishing the NYSPCC was novel in asserting the superiority of the child's claim to protection over the parent's right to raise the child as the parent saw fit. By 1910, almost every state had passed a similar law (McCrea, 1910), but many agencies had very limited resources and didn't cover all parts of the state (Myers, 2004). The courts routinely denied challenges to the authority of the state to intervene in intact families (U.S. Bureau of Education, 1880; Mason, 1972).

The SPCC's agents, who saw themselves more as police officers than social workers (Myers, 2004), were soon charged with excesses of their own. Critics claimed the agents exercised power arbitrarily against the children of the poor. The NYSPCC removed children from their homes, placed them in institutions, and was reluctant to return them even when the situation at home changed (*Matter of Knowack*, 1899). Many poor families referred to the societies as the "Cruelty" (Folks, 1902; Gordon, 1988). Nonetheless, the NYSPCC worked to obtain state legislation to regulate child care facilities, to stop some of the worst exploitation of children, and to prosecute parents who refused to obtain necessary medical care for their children (Myers, 2004).

Rediscovery of child abuse. The Social Security Act of 1935 made public welfare departments responsible for child protection. However, child abuse was not high on the public agenda. The problem was rediscovered in the 1960s when President Lyndon Johnson's War on Poverty brought renewed attention to poor people. The federal Children's Bureau took note of an increase of reports of physical abuse of children. The increase reflected advances in radiology that enabled physicians to detect healed fractures due to physical abuse. Child abuse was more prevalent than anyone had thought.

Kempe and associates (1962) investigated the problem by surveying hospital officials and district attorneys' offices. These officials responded to the survey by reporting they saw many cases of children with severe, nonaccidental, physical injuries. Many had brain damage; some child deaths were attributed to abuse. Kempe's group identified **battered child syndrome,** which was characterized by signs of multiple injuries inflicted at different times. Battered child syndrome was quickly accepted, and the concept received a great deal of publicity. Feldman (1997), for one, believes that repetitive injuries occur less frequently today than they did some years ago.

Mandatory reporting laws. Because of patients' rights to confidentiality, and because they had difficulty believing that parents would deliberately harm their children, physicians were reluctant to report possible child maltreatment. To overcome physician reluctance, child advocates proposed that physicians be mandated to report suspected cases of child abuse to a child protection hotline. By the early 1970s, every state had adopted a reporting law, an unusually brief period of time for the wide diffusion of a legislative innovation (Nelson, 1984).

The federal Child Abuse Prevention and Treatment Act of 1974 and later amendments (see National Adoption Information Clearinghouse [NAIC], 2003, for a list of these amendments and their provisions) encouraged states to further develop reporting laws and hotlines. The reports were made to state agencies responsible for child protection.

This system continues today. We will refer to these agencies generically as **Child Protection Services (CPS).** The laws extended the list of mandated reporters, professionals required by law to report suspected child maltreatment, to include almost everyone who worked with children. (The list of mandated reporters varies from state to state.) Suspected problems that could be reported included neglect and sexual,

288

CHAPTER 10
Protecting
Children: Child
Protection
Proceedings

emotional and physical abuse. The CPS worker has had two objectives from the beginning: to protect children, but also to help the families.

The police and child abuse. Police officers are mandated by state law to report suspected child abuse. They may be called to the scene when children are apparently abandoned, or when there is domestic violence in the home. Child protection workers may request that a police officer accompany them when responding to a child abuse call in a potentially dangerous neighborhood. Because there may be criminal charges involved in a child abuse case, some have suggested that the police have primary responsibility for investigating child maltreatment cases. Some police departments (e.g., Austin, Texas, and San Diego, California) have created child abuse or domestic violence units which incorporate the department's child abuse investigation responsibilities. In an experiment conducted in four counties in Florida, a child protection investigator employed by the county, together with a deputy sheriff, prepared the initial assessment of a reported case of abuse. They could refer the case to the Department of Children and Families for follow-up for social services, or to the police for further criminal investigation. An evaluation study showed there was no increase in emergency placements or in placement in foster care (Gelles, Kinnevy, and Burton, 2002).

Efforts at joint teams working together have not always been as sucessful as in the Florida experiment. Simply putting people together in "joined-up" activities doesn't mean that active cooperation will automatically follow. In England, which does not have mandated reporting, many communities have police-based child protection teams. These came under review after the well-publicized murder of an eight-year-old child, Victoria Climbie, by her caretakers. Her case had been known to police and social service authorities before the murder. At least in this case, the special police-based units did not prevent the child's death (Barrett and William, 2004). Garrett (2004) reported a study in three locations in England of "police/social work relationships" in police child protection units. He reported tensions in the relationship with social workers, with police perceiving themselves to be the "lead agency." He found a blurring of the social work role in the joint units. Freeman (2003) discussed similar organizational issues that emerged in the U.S. in efforts to "privatize" child protection services in private sector agencies that were not originally specialists in child maltreatment. An understanding of the process of change and of organizational dynamics is necessary to make such an experiment work.

Increase in number of reports. There were 669,000 reports nationally in 1976 of child abuse and neglect, including sex abuse, and 2.9 million in 2003, involving 5.29 million children. In 2003, cases involving over 906,000 children were **substantiated** (or **founded**): on investigation, there was sufficient evidence of maltreatment to support a determination for the record. Substantiated cases of child sex abuse increased rapidly from the mid-1970s to the early 1990s. In the mid-1990s both reports of suspected and of substantiated sexual abuse declined and now seem to have levelled off (Jones and Finkelhor, 2001; Finkelhor, 2004). The data sources reveal a smaller decline in reports of neglect and physical abuse as well.

We can't fully explain the decline in reported and substantiated child sexual abuse. There may be a real decline in the incidence of sexual abuse as a result of publicity and law enforcement. However, policy and standards for reporting may also have changed in response to what some perceived as an overemphasis in child protection on sexual abuse (Jones and Finkelhor, 2001). Terminology and procedures are so variable from state to state and from year to year that precise comparisons are difficult (Peddle and Wang, 2001).

Foster care. The increasing number of substantiated cases throughout the 1970s quickly overwhelmed the system. Child protection agencies had few community-based resources for family treatment. However, the federal government reimbursed states for **foster care** placement. Partly as a result, as the number of substantiated child abuse reports grew, the number of children in foster care also grew. Other problems in addition to maltreatment led to foster care placement. About 20 percent of children in foster care were placed there because their parents were abusing substances, were ill, or were in prison (Craig and Herbert, 1997). Originally, foster care was meant to be a temporary expedient to care for children when a parent was ill. It was not meant to be a semipermanent disposition for large numbers of children who entered the system because of a variety of social problems.

In 2003, 523,000 children were in foster care. Of these, about 46 percent were white, 38 percent African American, and the remainder Latino or members of other ethnic groups. Children stayed in foster care a median of 33 months. About a quarter were in foster care with relatives. More children entered the system each year (about 300,000) than left it (about 278,000). About 15,000 "age out" of the system each year, because they are no longer eligible for foster care. Half who had "aged out" had not completed high school. After leaving the system, thirty-eight percent were without employment for a year or more. After leaving the system, 60 percent of the young women had a child out of wedlock. Many former foster care children become homeless young adults (National Clearinghouse on Child Abuse and Neglect Information 2005).

When a child is taken into foster care, the court awards custody to the department of social services which finds and supervises the foster parents. Each child who is in care must have a case plan including a treatment goal. Reunification with parents is the goal in about 44 percent of the cases. Adoption is also a frequent goal for foster children. The treatment plans are reviewable by a court when custody is given to the department of social services. About 70,000 children a year are eligible for adoption because parental rights have been terminated in a court action. In 2003, about 49,000 children were adopted from foster care placements (Administration for Children and Families, 2004).

With more children entering every year than leave through reunification or adoption, the foster care system in most states is under stress. Some of these often troubled children are again abused or neglected in foster care, or the foster parents find they cannot handle them or get fed up dealing with false accusations of abuse (see National Foster Parent Association website to learn more about needs of foster parents). To ensure children will be well cared for, foster parents are licensed and many states require training. However, these measures are not always adequate. Children may be moved from placement to placement because of further abuse, because the foster parents lose their license, or because they do not wish to continue to foster the child. Children's sense of immediate safety and ability to develop attachments is undermined when they switch from home to home. High levels of turnover among social service staff in this stressful field make continuity and good case management more difficult. For example, foster parents in Connecticut keep licenses for 2.7 years on average (Biklen, 1999). This short tenure means that the state must continue to recruit foster parents. Where the need for foster parents outstrips the supply, standards for accepting people as foster parents (e.g., family stability and criminal history) may go down. Young children may be placed inappropriately in group homes or institutions for want of an alternative.

Because most of the children entered foster care as a result of abuse, neglect, or other difficult circumstances in the home, they have many needs for services while in care and after they leave. Their families also have needs for services to prepare for the return to the home. The prevalence rate of psychiatric disorder is probably over 20 percent in

290

CHAPTER 10
Protecting
Children: Child
Protection
Proceedings

children in foster care. Because the service system is complex (e.g., one private agency supervises foster care, another agency provides mental health services, and a third agency provides medical care), many receive inadequate services or struggle with the bureaucratic complexity. The U.S. Surgeon General issued a report in 2001 detailing the inadequacies of services for children, emphasizing that children involved with the welfare, juvenile justice, and mental health systems are the most poorly served (Levine, Perkins, and Perkins, 2005).

Family preservation. To stem the growth of foster care, the federal government passed the Adoption Assistance and Child Welfare Act (1980). The 1980 law was aimed toward keeping children in their homes, and toward returning children home as soon as it was feasible. This act required states to make reasonable efforts to prevent placement, and to make reasonable efforts to return children to their families when placed out of the home. This was called the **family preservation policy.** Before children could be placed out of the home, a judge had to be satisfied that CPS had made efforts to keep the family together. When children were placed in foster care cases had to be reviewed annually at hearings now called Child and Family Services Reviews to show that CPS was making efforts to reunite the children with their families (Horn, 2004).

The 1980 law temporarily reduced the number of children in foster care, but within a few years, in part because of the absence of funds for community services, the foster care population grew. The family preservation policy was attacked because of well-publicized cases of children who were injured or killed after they were kept with an abusing family or returned to an abusing parent. Although these cases are tragic, our ability to predict such cases accurately is very poor, because the base rate of abuse related deaths and injuries is very low. That hasn't prevented critics from accusing CPS workers of incompetence or lack of caring.

To try to correct the problems, Congress passed the Adoption and Safe Families Act of 1997 (see below). The law specified seven service standards that all state welfare authorities must meet. These include reducing the incidence of abuse and neglect, reducing the time children spend in foster care, reducing the number of changes of homes (to promote permanency and stability), and providing permanency plans (e.g., adoption) for children in the state's custody. However, the law on the books may not be yielding the therapeutic consequences its designers hoped. No state met all of the standards, and the states were required to submit program improvement plans. States that do not eventually meet the standards may be subject to loss of federal child welfare funds (Horn, 2004). One aim of the law is to enhance the adoption of children in foster care. While there has been some improvement in the number of adoptions in many states, there are not enough people willing to adopt children from foster care, especially older children (PR Newswire, 2004a).

Indian Child Welfare Act (ICWA). In the last decades of the twentieth century, a large number of Native American children were placed in foster care with non-Indian families as a result of child protection laws and many Indian children were adopted by non-Indian families. Tribal spokesmen and activists claimed that child welfare authorities simply did not recognize traditional Indian child-rearing practices when they removed children from their parents. In Native American culture, children are often cared for by the tribe and live with different family members over time. These children are not abandoned or homeless. The critics contended that if an Indian child did have to be removed, the child should be fostered by an Indian family because placement with non-Indians would alienate the child from his or her culture. In response to these criticisms, Congress passed the **Indian Child Welfare Act (ICWA)** (Jones, 2000). The law intends that Native American culture be respected and taken into consideration when decisions are made about the out-of-home placement of children.

The law requires that placement cases involving Indian children be heard in tribal courts if possible, and permits a child's tribe to be involved in state court proceedings. It requires testimony from witnesses who are familiar with Indian culture before a child can be removed from his or her home. If a child is removed, either for foster care or for adoption, the law requires that Indian children be placed with extended family members, other tribal members, or other Indian families (Pine Tree Legal Assistance, 2002).

It is not clear how well the act is accomplishing its purposes. Indian children, who constitute 0.9 percent of the child population, make up 3.1 percent of the population in various forms of substitute care. Twenty to 30 percent of Indian children are still being placed out of their tribal and family environments. Surprisingly, tribal Indian Child Welfare programs, which receive federal subsidies for supervising foster care placements, may be responsible for a large number of out-of-home placements. These agencies do not receive payments if children are adopted, but they do receive funds when children are in foster care. But cultural prejudice about Indians may also play a part in placing children with non-Indian families. Some wish to amend the legislation to make it easier for non-Indians to adopt Indian children without tribal consent (Special Report, n.d.). Once again, the law on the books is not the same as the law in action. Legislation passed with good intentions may be undermined by organizational, social, and economic forces that are not taken into account in the words of the law.

Child Protection Today

The state can intervene in family life to protect children through either the criminal or the civil law system. In this section of the chapter, after briefly looking at criminal prosecutions, we will emphasize the civil child protection system.

Child abuse and criminal prosecution. The purpose of a criminal proceeding is to establish guilt and to punish the offender. A family member can be prosecuted criminally for murdering or assaulting a child, for homicide resulting from excessive punishment or from neglect (e.g., a young child left alone dies in a fire), for incest, and for endangering the welfare of a child. About 5 percent of all child maltreatment reports handled by child protection agencies are referred for possible criminal prosecution (Besharov, 1988). The criminal defendant accused of harming a child is entitled to full due process protections, and is presumed innocent until proven guilty beyond a reasonable doubt.

All criminal prosecutors prosecute child abuse cases (DeFrances, 2002), but not many cases reach the prosecutors from CPS. For example, in Utah, fewer than half of the cases investigated by CPS are substantiated. Many of the cases referred for criminal prosecution are for child sexual abuse. In this Utah sample, only 20 of the substantiated cases were referred for criminal prosecution. Although 17 of 20 pleaded guilty, only 5 went to prison. Other substantiated cases involved juveniles who were referred to juvenile court and processed as juveniles (Tauteoli, Oldroyd, and Lewis, 1992).

Children are protected if an imprisoned offender has no further access to a child. However, criminal prosecution may compound psychological and social problems when the perpetrator is the child's parent or another family member. A convicted offender may receive a prison term, but the child victim or the family receives no help as a direct result of a criminal prosecution. Because the child often loves the abusing

292

CHAPTER 10
Protecting
Children: Child
Protection
Proceedings

person, the child may feel guilty or abandoned when the offender is imprisoned. The family may lose a breadwinner. The other parent, having failed to protect the child, may be considered neglectful, and the child may be placed in foster care.

When maltreatment occurs within the family, the state most often intervenes through its child protection system rather than the criminal justice system. The aim of the child protection system is to protect children, but also to help the family care for its children better. (The courts that have jurisdiction over offenses against children have different names in different states [Edwards, 1987]. We will follow New York practice, and use the name **family court**.) When child protection cases do go to family court, the hearing is a civil, not a criminal, proceeding. Nationally, about 15 percent of substantiated child maltreatment reports go to a hearing in family court (Besharov, 1988). The rest are officially recorded, but parents and the CPS worker agree on a treatment plan without going to court.

Typical child protection statutes and procedures. All states have similar laws and procedures because all states receive reimbursement from the federal government for child protection services. The laws establish a public CPS with authority (jurisdiction) to investigate cases in which a child was harmed by someone in or close to the family and to provide services for child victims and their families. If the offender is not a family member, CPS has no jurisdiction; the case is referred for criminal prosecution.

In recent years, in response to criticism of public agencies, some states have experimented with "privatizing" child protective services. Many of the initial experiments were unsuccessful because of the private agency's lack of experience with the problems. Problems similar to those experienced by the public agencies emerged. Based on a review of a number of experiments over several years, Freeman (2003) commented that "turning over responsibilities to private agencies with the hope that they would be able to do the job better, without providing any more funding or training . . . would be a fool's errand at best" (p. 452).

Hotline. CPS receives reports on a central hotline. Persons who work with children are mandated by law to call the hotline when they suspect that a child they see in a professional context is being maltreated. Hotline telephone numbers are often listed in the front of the telephone book with other emergency numbers (Figure 10.2). Ordinary citizens may report, but in most states citizens are not obligated to report. The hotline screens reports and forwards to a local CPS agency for investigation those that seem to make out a prima facie (on its face) case of abuse. Nationally, in 2005, there were 2.6 million referrals forwarded to local CPS agencies. About two thirds were accepted for further investigation (Administration for Children and Families, 2006).

Sources of reports. A little more than half of reports come from professionals and mandated reporters. The remainder of the reports come from parents, relatives, friends, or neighbors, or are anonymous (Administration for Children and Families 2006).

Types of reports. The hotline staff transmits reports to a local CPS, which investigates each report promptly, usually within 24 hours. The CPS worker will talk with the person who made the report and interview the parents and child. The CPS worker is authorized to see the child at home or at school with or without parental permission, and can call on police support if necessary.

Most reports (about 60 percent) are for neglect. Examples of neglect include leaving a child alone; failing to provide food, clothing, medical care, or shelter for

infoline 1-800-203-1234 or 860-355-0023

Note: Some telephone numbers may be toll calls, please refer to the local calling area map(s) beginning on page 2.

Abuse
Child Abuse Care-Line
1-800-842-2288
Commission on Child Care,
Rights & Abuse 748-4542
Domestic Violence Service
(Women's Center) 731-5206
Nursing Home Ombudsman
596-4473
Protective Services for Elderly
596-4242
Susan B Anthony Project
860-482-7133 or 860-672-3291

Alcohol/Drug Abuse
Al-Anon/Alateen 743-8967
Alcoholics Anonymous
860-354-0843
APT Foundation 426-3344
CT Valley Hospital Addiction
Services 868-344-2420
Danbury Hospital 797-7905
Danbury Treatment Center
731-0730
MCCA 792-4515
Narcotics Anonymous
1-800-627-3543

Children/Youth
Child Care Connections 740-2445
Child Care INFOLINE
1-800-505-1000
Child Support Line: CT Dept of
Social Services
1-800-228-KIDS
CT Adoption Exchange
1-800-842-6347
CT Department of Children &
Families 1-800-842-2288
National Runaway Switchboard
1-800-621-4000
New Milford Teen Center
860-355-0087
New Milford Youth Agency
860-354-0047

Civil Rights
Commission on the Status
of Women 860-566-5702
CT Human Rights & Opportunities
Commissions 579-6246

Community Action
Committee of Danbury
744-4700

Consumer Services
Better Business Bureau
1-800-955-5100
CT Dept of Consumer Protection
1-800-842-2649

CT Dept of Public Utility Control
1-800-382-4586
Consumer Credit Counseling
798-9504
Consumer Product Safety
Commission 1-800-638-2772

Counseling
See Yellow Pages or
Call INFOLINE 860-355-0023

Disabilities
Birth to Three INFOLINE
1-800-505-7000
Brain Injury Association of CT
1-800-278-8242
Bureau of Rehabilitation Services
797-4174
Converse Communications, see
Disabilities page 20.
CT Board of Education & Services
for the Blind 1-800-842-4510
CT Commission on the Deaf &
Hearing Impaired
(Voice/TDD/TT) 860-566-7414
CT Office of Protection &
Advocacy for Persons with
Disabilities 1-800-842-7303
DATAHR Rehabilitation Institute
775-4700
Easter Seal Society 860-226-9438
WECAHR 792-3540

Disaster Services
American Red Cross
860-354-3415

Elderly Services
See the
Senior Citizens pages 22-23.

Energy Assistance
Community Action Committee
of Danbury 748-5422

Environment
CT Dept of Environmental
Protection 860-424-3000
Oil & Toxic Chemical Spills
1-800-424-8802
(Voice/TDD/TT)

Food
Elderly Hot Lunch Programs/
Meals-On-Wheels 748-2148
Food Stamps 1-800-842-1508
Food Pantries, Call INFOLINE
860-355-0023

Health Information
AIDS Counseling & Testing
796-1613

AIDS Project, Northwestern, CT
1-800-381-AIDS
Alzheimer's Association
1-800-356-5502
American Diabetes Association
1-800-842-6323
American Heart Association
1-800-242-2666
American Lung Association
1-800-992-2263
CT Cancer Information Service
1-800-4-CANCER
Juvenile Diabetes Foundation
860-561-1153
Also see "Health Agencies"
section in the Yellow Pages

Legal Services
CT Women's Education And Legal
Fund (CWEALF) 860-524-0601
Lawyer Referral Services
860-525-6052
Legal Services (low income)
1-800-453-3320

Medicare
Claim Info (Part B)
1-800-982-6819
CONNMAP (Assignment)
1-800-443-9946

Mental Health
CT Council on Compulsive
Gambling 1-800-346-6238
CT Valley Hospital 860-344-2666
Mental Health Association of CT
1-800-842-1501
Psychiatric Emergency Services/
Crisis Intervention Center
797-7899
Call INFOLINE 860-355-0023
or 1-800-203-1234

Poison Control
Danbury Hospital 797-7300
Poison Control Center (24 hrs)
1-800-343-2722

Social Security
In Connecticut 860-489-1633 or
1-800-772-1213

Suicide Prevention
Psychiatric Emergency Services/
Crisis Intervention Center
797-7899
Call INFOLINE 860-355-0023

**Support/Self-Help
Groups**
Call INFOLINE 860-355-0023
or 1-800-203-1234

Gambler's Anonymous
777-5585

Transportation
METROPOOL Ridesharing
1-800-346-3743

**Unemployment
Benefits**
CT Labor Department
797-4150

**Veterans
Administration**
US Dept of Veterans' Affairs
1-800-827-1000
Veteran's Advisory Center
797-4620

Victims
Commission on Victims'
Services
1-800-822-8428
Sexual Assault Crisis Service
(Women's Center)
731-5204
Susan B Anthony Project
860-482-7133
or 860-672-3291

Volunteers
Literacy Volunteers
1-800-345-READ
RSVP 792-8200
Voluntary Bureau of Greater
Danbury 797-1154

Voter Registration
State of CT Secretary of
State 1-800-540-3764

Welfare
CT Dept of Social Services
797-4034
For local assistance,
see Blue Pages

infoline
24 Hours
Every Day

*Don't Know
Where to
Turn?*

*Need Help
With Health
& Social
Services?*

- **Information**
- **Referrals**
- **Help**
- **Crisis
  Intervention**
- **For All Human
  Services Needs**
- **En Espanol**
- **Voice/TDD/TT**

There is no charge for
INFOLINE help and all
calls are confidential.

INFOLINE is a service
of your UNITED WAY
and the STATE OF
CONNECTICUT.

Call INFOLINE for infor-
mation on other available
services which are not listed
above. For questions about
telephone service, please
call your local SNET
service representative.

FIGURE 10.2

The Hotline

A page similar to this is found in almost all telephone directories. The page has hotline numbers for a variety of services, including a hotline for the public to report suspected child abuse.

294

CHAPTER 10
Protecting
Children: Child
Protection
Proceedings

children; or leaving a child in a filthy or dangerous environment. The statutes provide that **excessive corporal punishment** is abuse, but *excessive* isn't defined. About 19 percent of substantiated reports involve physical abuse. Fortunately, a smaller number allege serious physical injury (e.g., cigarette burns, scalding, and broken bones) to children. About 7 percent involve emotional abuse. About 10 percent of substantiated reports are of sexual abuse (Administration on Children, Youth and Families, 2005).

Investigation. The investigating CPS worker, who (as discussed above) usually visits the home within 24 hours of receiving the report, must assess the immediate risk of injury to the child if left at home. The CPS worker has authority to take a child into protective custody in an emergency. As a matter of **due process** of law, the CPS worker's actions have to be reviewed by a judge soon after the emergency removal. If it is not an emergency, but the worker feels the child is at serious risk of harm at home, the CPS worker must seek a court order to remove the child. About 20 percent of substantiated cases are placed in out-of-home care (Administration on Children and Families, 2006). If a child is removed from the home, parents must receive notice, and they can challenge the CPS worker's action in a hearing in front of a judge. The due process requirement of court orders is an important protection for parents, who may fear losing their children the minute they see a CPS worker at their door.

After the initial visit, the CPS worker continues to investigate. The system is "front-loaded" for investigation, not treatment, although many families encountered during the initial investigation period are in need of services (Levine et al., 1996; U.S. Advisory Board on Child Abuse and Neglect, 1993). The worker must complete the investigation within a specified period of time (e.g., 60 days). The worker decides whether abuse is "**founded**," "**indicated**," or "**unfounded**," typically with only a little oversight from a supervisor. A case is classified as *unfounded* or *not substantiated* when there is no credible evidence for CPS to assert that maltreatment, as defined by statute, occurred. Some states use the term *indicated* for cases where insufficient proof of maltreatment is present, but where the worker suspects maltreatment has occurred. The founded or substantiated rate varies state by state (U.S. Department of Health and Human Services, 2003). Reports coming from professionals are substantiated at a higher rate than reports coming from other sources. Overall, about two out of three referrals from the hotline to child protection agencies are unsubstantiated after investigation (Administration on Children and Families, 2006). If a case is unfounded, the report may be kept confidential for a period defined by statute and available only to CPS workers. It may later be expunged.

Substantiated reports. A case is founded or substantiated if there is some credible evidence to substantiate a charge of maltreatment. Some credible evidence is a very weak **standard of proof.** It is not comparable to a finding of criminal guilt. The law casts a wide net under the assumption that the investigation will be benign and the intervention beneficial. If this assumption is true, the large number of false positives won't matter because the family will be helped.

The CPS worker's judgment that a case is substantiated has consequences for the parent. In addition to state intervention in his or her family life, the subject of a substantiated report may be barred from working with children or from adopting a child (see *Valmont v. Bane*, 1994). The parent has a right to appeal the worker's decision through an administrative proceeding and in the courts after having exhausted administrative remedies.

If the case is substantiated, the CPS worker will offer the parent a treatment program. Substantiation may be a risk factor for subsequent maltreatment, especially for neglect, and such cases may warrant closer monitoring (U.S. Department of Health and Human Services, 2003). Almost 60 percent of substantiated cases receive some type of service. The CPS worker can't order the parent to participate in treatment, only a court can. However, the CPS worker will notify the parent that the case can be brought to court if the parent doesn't cooperate with the CPS worker. If the parent does not cooperate with the treatment plan, the CPS worker may petition the family court for a hearing. At the hearing, CPS has to prove that maltreatment occurred. CPS, through its attorney, will ask the court to mandate treatment. As stated above, about 20 percent of substantiated cases result in foster care placement; this usually occurs after a hearing in court. A few parents may relinquish custody voluntarily to obtain services for a child. The number of out-of-home placements is about 6.6 percent of investigated cases.

Hearing and disposition. There is no jury trial in civil child protection cases. CPS's petition alleging abuse or neglect is heard in an adversary hearing before a judge. The purpose of the hearing is to adjudicate whether the parent has abused or neglected the child. CPS has to prove the accusation by a **preponderance of the evidence,** a somewhat higher standard than *some credible evidence.* The parent, the child, and CPS have legal representation. Witnesses, including experts, may testify. The parent, through an attorney, is entitled to cross-examine witnesses and to call witnesses. In most states, a parent's therapist or a physician may be required to testify even if the testimony would be privileged in other legal contexts. (**Privileged** means that the disclosure by the professional of communications received in confidence cannot be compelled in a legal forum. Privileges are granted by statute and may be limited by statute as well.) In contrast to a criminal trial, the judge can use the parent's refusal to testify as evidence of maltreatment.

After a finding of neglect or abuse, the judge will then preside over a disposition hearing to determine a treatment plan. The treatment plan may include substance abuse counseling, parent training classes, day care for the child, or participation in Parents Anonymous, a self-help group. The plan may include removing the child from the parent and giving temporary custody to the local department of social services (DSS), who will arrange foster care. The parent may be found in contempt of court and given a jail sentence if the parent does not follow through on a treatment plan. That occurs rarely. If the child is removed from the home, CPS works out a "contract" that the parent must fulfill before the child is returned home. If the child is placed out of the home, DSS also has to engage in **permanency planning** to develop a plan for the child's eventual return home or placement elsewhere.

Court Appointed Special Advocates (CASA). Since 1976, federal statutes (Child Abuse and Prevention Act, 1976; 1996 reauthorization) required that children in neglect and abuse proceedings have a court-appointed *guardian ad litem* (a person appointed to represent the child's interests for that case only). In 1977, to reduce the costs associated with using attorneys, one court began appointing citizen volunteers as guardians ad litem. By 2004, with federal support, 70,000 volunteers were representing over 280,000 children a year. The National CASA Association oversees a network for the volunteer programs. It provides grants to local groups to enhance and promote services.

Most of the CASA volunteers are white women. About 8 percent of volunteers are African Americans. About 48 percent of the children served are white, 31 percent African American, and the rest of other ethnic and racial backgrounds. They receive some

296

CHAPTER 10
Protecting
Children: Child
Protection
Proceedings

training in law and in the service system, among other matters. The CASAs are usually assigned to one case at a time, and agree to follow the case as long as the child is involved with the courts and the child welfare system. They serve about 3.2 hours per month for the duration of the case (an average of 17 months). CASAs may conduct an investigation, interview the child or children, make home visits, and interview key people including professionals, parents, neighbors, and foster parents. They make court appearances and offer recommendations to judges. CASAs may work cooperatively with the child's court-appointed attorney, serving as the official guardian ad litem. CASAs sometimes monitor court orders for compliance in specific cases. The volunteer may inform the court of failures to provide necessary services or noncompliance with other court orders.

Research on CASA programs. Studies of cases with a CASA compared to those without a CASA or with an attorney as a guardian ad litem show few differences in outcomes for children (Litzelfelner, 2000; Caliber et al., 2004). However, the children in the three groups may not be comparable. The children assigned CASAs were at greater risk or had more difficult histories than children without such representation. Children with CASA representatives were far more likely to be placed out of the home than comparison children, and if the child stayed in the welfare system, the child was more likely to be referred for adoption (Litzelfelner, 2000; Caliber et al., 2004). Judges accept most CASA volunteer recommendations. Children with CASAs received more services, and had fewer court continuances (going back to court because the issue wasn't resolved fully at the hearing), than children without CASA representation. The CASA children did at least as well in terms of obtaining services as those served by a court-appointed attorney. CASA volunteers usually have only one case at a time, while poorly compensated court-appointed attorneys may be too busy to give full attention to their cases. The CASA volunteer seems to be a cost-effective way of ensuring that a child's interests are brought to the attention of the court. There are apparently no studies about using random assignment of CASA volunteers to cases to assess outcomes of cases, or about the effects of serving as a CASA volunteer on the volunteer.

Termination of parental rights (TPR). As long as the parents comply with the treatment plan and remain actively involved with the child, they retain their parental rights, even if they do not succeed fully in meeting the conditions necessary to resume custody. DSS may petition for termination of parental rights if there appears to be little possibility that treatment will make the parent fit to care for the child within a reasonable period of time.

States are under federal pressure to reduce the number of children on the foster care rolls by increasing adoptions. The **termination of parental rights (TPR)** hearing is the vital first step in freeing a child for adoption. If the parents do not cooperate with a treatment plan, or if it appears unlikely they will be fit to resume custody, the local DSS may petition the court to declare the child **permanently neglected.** The parent, the child, and DSS all have legal representation at the hearing, and testimony, including expert testimony, is received. If the court makes this declaration, parental rights may be terminated, and the child released for adoption. After termination, the parent no longer has any rights to the child. Legally, it is as if the parent never existed. The decision to permanently end the legal relationship between a parent and child is very serious and can be emotionally trying. A *preponderance of the evidence* is sufficient to justify a finding of abuse, but the standard of proof in a hearing to terminate parental rights is **clear and convincing evidence** (*Santosky v. Kramer*, 1982), a more rigorous standard of proof but not as rigorous as *beyond a reasonable doubt*. Termination is not a rare event. Milwaukee, Wisconsin, with a population of about 600,000, processed 857 termination of parental rights cases in 2003. New York State disposed of 11,637 TPR cases in 2002, or about 224 cases per week, most of these in New York City.

To terminate parental rights, the state must demonstrate that the parent is **unfit.** The decision is easy if the parent abandons the child and has no contact over a prolonged period of time. Severe or chronic abuse and neglect, long-term mental illness or mental deficiency, long-term alcohol- or drug-related incapacity, conviction of a parent for a crime of violence against a family member or a child, or conviction of a felony carrying a long sentence are grounds for termination. Under the Adoption and Safe Families Act (1997), as mentioned earlier in this chapter, DSS may petition for termination of parental rights if a child has been in foster care for 15 of the preceding 22 months. Professionals necessarily participate in termination hearings when the reason for alleging parental unfitness is mental retardation or mental illness. However the research base for evaluating parenting skills and making predictions of future parenting conduct is not strong (Azar and Benjet, 1994; American Psychological Association—Committee on Professional Practice and Standards, 1999).

Infant safe haven laws. To prevent the death of unwanted babies who are left in trash cans and dumpsters, 43 states have passed **Baby Moses laws** to allow a parent to surrender a newborn, unwanted baby to a safe haven (e.g., hospital, police station, or church). The parent is guaranteed anonymity and, if not immunity from prosecution, then an affirmative defense against prosecution for abandonment, neglect, or child endangerment. Custody of the child will be given to the state's DSS, and its CPS which can petition for termination of parental rights so the infant may be adopted.

In the past, in Europe, many convents had what were called *tours*. These were infant baskets on a turntable set in the convent's wall. The person leaving the child would ring a bell and turn the turntable, placing the infant inside the walls and bringing an empty basket outside the wall ready to receive the next infant (Levine and Levine, 1992). In some places, foundling homes always had a basket in their entrance way to receive an abandoned infant (Meyers, 2004).

We do not know how many infants are abandoned each year. In recent years, mothers left as many as 31,000 infants in hospitals after they gave birth. In 1999, Texas reported 800 abandoned infants; 50 were placed in trash dumpsters (Bolling, 2003). We know very little about the mothers who abandon these newborns, their motivations, or the success of the new laws in preventing fatalities to the abandoned infants.

The Child Protection Services (CPS) Worker

CPS workers have important, difficult, and sometimes dangerous jobs. They usually have bachelor degrees, but not necessarily in psychology, social work, or related fields. They receive limited in-service training and supervision. Child protection investigators nationally average 75.8 new cases a year. Their new caseload ranges from 36 to 162 cases in different states. They are also carrying old cases that are still open (Administration for Children, Youth and Families, 2002). The CPS worker must enter many different homes, some where people are violent or are abusing alcohol or drugs, in all kinds of neighborhoods, day or night. They are rarely welcome, and sometimes greeted with open hostility. Physical attacks on CPS workers and threats of physical assault are rare, but they do occur. For example, in 2006, a caseworker in Texas was murdered, and

298

CHAPTER 10
Protecting
Children: Child
Protection
Proceedings

in another episode, a woman fired a shotgun at two caseworkers who had come to her home (AP, 2006).

Life-and-death decisions. An investigating CPS worker must decide whether to remove a child from the home at once, or whether it is safe to leave a child in the home while the investigation continues. This can be a life-and-death decision, often made with little information. The CPS workers must use their considerable power judiciously while managing their own emotions of anger, fear, and empathy. Workers want to be helpful, but must be prepared to break up a family if need be (Richards, 1992).

Workers may at times be faced with removing a newborn infant from its mother's arms if the infant tests positive for drugs. Fourteen states define prenatal drug use as child abuse, although often there has to be other evidence that the mother is unable to care for the infant (Alan Guttmacher Institute, 2004). California does not define prenatal drug abuse as child abuse. We were told by a California CPS worker that if authorities removed every newborn who tested positive for marijuana, especially in the San Francisco area, the system would be overwhelmed.

If a CPS agency has had contact with a child or a family, and the child was subsequently injured or killed, the CPS agency is often subject to strong adverse publicity. The agency and the worker may be liable for monetary damages in a civil suit, although the legal rules are complex. Sometimes, CPS workers may be scapegoated for failures of the system and subject to criminal prosecution, at times to deflect criticism from higher officials (*Barber v. State,* 1992). There are also many vocal critics of the system who claim that CPS workers use their authority in capricious ways. These criticisms and legal threats add to the background of stress on the job.

Risk assessment. CPS workers live with the knowledge that they will make mistakes and that some mistakes may be grievous. There is no foolproof way to assess risk (see Chapter 3). There are some standardized risk-assessment procedures consisting of interview guides and scales that focus on variables that differentiate abusing from nonabusing families. Risk-assessment scales include factors such as age of child (younger are more at risk), caregiver's history of abuse or neglect as a child, physical hazards in the home, support for the caretaker, and so on. Risk-assessment scales produce quantitative scores used to predict later repeated reports of maltreatment. The instruments may help workers make systematic risk assessments rather than rely on personal judgment, and may aid in treatment planning.

One study attempted to predict child abuse using expectant mothers as the sample (Weberling et al., 2003). Although statistically significant increments in accuracy of prediction of subsequent abuse were found using risk-assessment instruments, all of the instruments produced fairly high rates of false positives (i.e., they predicted future abuse, but no abuse occurred). It would be quite expensive to intervene in all cases predicted to be at risk. The use of risk assessment scales might make workers more efficient by concentrating effort on high-risk cases, risking that the rate of false negatives (i.e., the scales predict no abuse, but abuse occurs) will be low, and that false negative cases will not become a cause for public criticism of child protective services. The development and validation of better risk-assessment instruments are important and difficult areas of research (Doueck, Bronson, and Levine, 1992; Gambrill and Shlonsky, 2000).

Testifying in court. As part of their job, CPS workers testify in family court hearings. The workers are subject to cross-examination by the parent's attorney and by the court-appointed attorney or law guardian representing the child's interests. Occasionally, the workers may be scolded by judges for inadequate preparation, or because of bureaucratic delays in obtaining recommended services. Many are anxious about going to court, but others become quite expert in the courtroom.

Criticisms of CPS workers. Wexler (1990) is very critical of the child protection system. He believes that workers investigating a hotline call begin with a presumption that the child has been maltreated. He cites cases in which workers interviewed parents aggressively, and physically inspected and even strip-searched children to look for signs of physical abuse.

Levine et al. (1996) examined a random sample of 300 cases processed by the CPS in Erie County (Buffalo), New York. The allegation that CPS workers rush to judgment was not supported. About 70 percent of all investigated cases were not substantiated. Most of these cases had only one visit. About half of substantiated cases (15 percent) were closed without further action because the family was already under care, the family had moved away, or other such reasons. The remaining half (15 percent) were kept open for services. Sex abuse cases were processed no differently than other cases. They were substantiated at a somewhat lower rate than other types of maltreatment. Cases involving African American families were processed no differently than cases involving white families (Levine et al., 1996). Mandated reporters responding to an anonymous survey about their experiences with CPS workers said that most cases were handled in a professional manner (Compaan, Doueck, and Levine, 1997). These findings suggest that the excesses complained of by Wexler (1990) are likely to be the exception rather than the rule. On occasion, some workers may not track their cases adequately, or even fail to make the visits they claimed they made. The system undoubtedly needs review.

CPS workers often carry very large caseloads. They must complete voluminous paper work. The work environment is too often not supportive. Changes in legislation and other policies occur with some frequency and affect the worker's job. There are limited opportunities for promotion. Promotion may require the worker to take on management responsibilities and give up direct service. Public criticism of the system may result in poor morale. Media coverage of a child's death is sensationalized and often blames the worker. Workers are not always treated with respect by judges and lawyers. Workers are also concerned about personal safety (AP, 2006) and sometimes are subject to civil litigation (Child Welfare League, 2002). This difficult, demanding, and stressful job is not highly paid, Understandably, in many agencies there is a high worker turnover (Fryer et al., 1988).

Mandated Reporting, Role Conflict, and Professional Practice

Every state has a reporting statute (Kalichman, 1999). The statute requires reports to a hotline whenever the mandated reporter has a reasonable suspicion (the terminology differs slightly in different states) that the child the professional is seeing has been maltreated. A professional may also be obligated to report suspicions of abuse based on what is learned from a parent even if the professional never saw the child. The reporting statutes include civil and criminal penalties such as imprisonment for failure to report, and they provide **immunity from suit** for reporting in good faith (Small, 1992).

Advocates agreed that a reporting law was necessary; young victims could not seek the help of the law themselves. However, the reporting statutes created a problem because the laws authorized a breach of the confidential relationship between a professional and a client. The laws created a conflict between their helping and their policing or social control roles.

300

CHAPTER 10
Protecting
Children: Child
Protection
Proceedings

Underreporting. Mandated reporting laws resulted in more reports, more investigations, and more discovery of abuse. However, not all professionals comply with the law. Some exercise professional discretion about reporting, even though the law has no provision for discretion. Kalichman (1999) reviewed the results of reporting studies using different methods (e.g., surveys, or responses to hypothetical vignettes in an experimental design manipulating conditions). The results were quite consistent across different studies: about 30 percent of practitioners at some time elected not to report child maltreatment that they probably should have reported. About a third of schoolteachers also failed to report when they probably should have reported (Anderson, 1996). Physicians, who are more likely to have physical evidence as a basis for suspicions, do not always report when they should (Morris, Johnson, and Clasen, 1985).

What accounts for the unwillingness of professionals to comply strictly with the law? Among the reasons cited for sometimes failing to report are the vagueness of statutory standards, a fear of losing patients or losing the therapeutic alliance, and concerns that reporting may do more harm than good (Kalichman, 1999). Some professionals fear that, if they make a report, the parent may pressure the child to recant the allegation. Some are concerned that the inadequate foster care system may expose the child to more risk than remaining at home with support. A few may want to avoid becoming involved in time-consuming investigations or trials. Based on vignette studies, psychologists are more likely to say they will make a report when the alleged victim is younger and when the evidence is clear (Kalichman and Craig, 1999).

Corporal punishment. Many parents believe in the efficacy of corporal punishment. In contrast, some experts favor banning corporal punishment as inevitably harmful and believe it should be treated as a criminal assault (Straus, 1994). In deference to the normative acceptance of minor corporal punishment (such as spanking), CPS can intervene only when corporal punishment is "excessive" (see Nelson, 1984). But when is corporal punishment excessive? Morris and associates (1985) listed 23 methods of disciplining children ranging from taking away privileges to hitting a child with a belt; tying the child up as a form of physical restraint; striking the child with a fist, leaving marks; and knocking the child unconscious. They asked a sample of physicians to say whether the method of discipline was inappropriate, and whether it should be reported as abuse. Many physicians said most of the methods were inappropriate punishments. However, not all who said it was inappropriate also said they would report the case. If there was a visible mark such as redness, a bruise, or a more serious injury, more of the physicians said they would report. They were not unanimous until the descriptions included burn marks, evidence of fractured ribs, or indications of a blow to the head leaving the child unconscious.

Child-rearing methods and beliefs about corporal punishment vary with ethnicity and social class (Box 10.1). African Americans view reporting of mild or moderate corporal punishment as more unfair than do whites (Chavez, 1999). However, if professionals adapt the definition of abuse to the client's norms, they are not protecting all children equally.

Sexual abuse. Sexual abuse is defined in child protective statutes similarly to sexual offenses in the criminal code. However, what constitutes reportable sexual abuse is not that clear. Atteberry-Bennett and Reppucci (cited in Haugaard and Reppucci, 1988) asked legal professionals, child protective workers, probation and parole workers, mental health professionals, and parents not in those professions to rate descriptions of activities with a possible sexual component. These ranged from hugging to kissing a

BOX 10.1

301

The Child
Protection
System

Cultural Differences

Elian Gonzalez *was* a six-year-old Cuban child who was at the center of a political and legal controversy. His mother lost her life trying to flee Cuba with him in a small boat. Elian survived and landed in the United States. His Cuban American relatives wanted Elian to stay in the United States. Because of the political controversy, his Cuban grandmothers were permitted to visit him in the United States. On her return to Cuba, his paternal grandmother described on a Cuban television interview her efforts to warm him up when he seemed shy. She said she teased him by biting his tongue and by unzipping his pants to "see if it's grown." It is a custom among Cuban mothers and grandmothers to tease young sons and grandsons affectionately in this way, and no one in Cuba thinks it is wrong. However, a spokeswoman for a group strongly opposed to the boy's return to Cuba said, "I cannot understand that kind of behavior from a grandmother with a 6-year-old child, and in this country that's understood as child molesting" (Kerry, 2000).

child on the lips, sleeping in the same bed with the child, entering the bathroom while the child is bathing, nudity in front of the child, photographing the child in the nude, touching the child's genitals, and having sexual intercourse with the child.

All agreed that touching the child's genitals in an erotic way and having intercourse with a child constituted sexual abuse. However, mental health professionals and legal professionals differed in whether they considered other acts sexually abusive (Haugaard and Reppucci, 1988).

About 40 percent of all sexual abuse reports to CPS came from social agencies (Levine et al., 1996). Only 9 percent came from schools, and about 11 percent from medical professionals. Steinberg (1994) found that fully 40 percent of reports made to CPS by psychologists involved suspicions of sexual abuse. Mental health professionals sometimes infer sexual abuse from psychological symptoms, and not just when the victim makes a disclosure (Levine et al., 1996). As noted before, reports of suspected child sexual abuse and substantiated cases have both declined from their peak in the early 1990s (Jones and Finkelhor, 2001), suggesting mandated reporters may have become more cautious about what they report.

Neglect. About 60 percent of substantiated cases in 2004 involved neglect (Administration for Children, Youth and Families, 2006). **Neglect** is reported far more than other forms of maltreatment, but is substantiated at a lower rate than other types of maltreatment. It is difficult to define neglect. Under the law, children are entitled to a minimum level of care, but not the best level of care. The reporters believed they had observed neglect. However, after investigation by CPS, a high percentage of the reports were not founded.

People may have different standards for neglect because of differences in lifestyles, in personal or cultural standards, and limitations related to poverty. Poor housekeeping may create the appearance of neglect to someone with a high standard of cleanliness, but that is usually not enough to warrant state intervention. Is it neglect if a child is dressed in ragged, dirty clothes and torn sneakers? Neglect is most often associated with poverty, and poor families are most often investigated for neglect (Drake and Zuravin, 1998). How do we distinguish between financial inability to provide for a child

302

CHAPTER 10
Protecting
Children: Child
Protection
Proceedings

appropriately and neglect? It is easy to justify intervening when several small children are left alone in filthy and dangerous conditions while a parent is out socializing. It is a more difficult decision when a younger child is left in the care of a nine-year-old because the mother has no other babysitter when she needs to work.

Emotional abuse. Emotional abuse is difficult to define and prove. Garbarino, Guttman, and Seeley (1988) make a persuasive case for the harmfulness of rejecting, openly castigating, scaring, or ignoring and isolating a child. However, mandated reporters claim that the CPS hotline often rejects emotional abuse and emotional neglect reports. CPS investigators respond that they are bound by the law in the complaints they investigate (Levine et al., 1996). The legal system, with its requirement of proof, may be in conflict with professional understanding of what is harmful for children's psychological development.

Psychotherapy and mandated reporting. Therapists are ethically and legally required to obtain informed consent from clients before beginning therapy. They should warn clients at the beginning of treatment of their obligation to report suspicions of child maltreatment. Often they give a warning in written consent forms. The form may meet the legal requirement for informed consent, but do clients truly understand what they are agreeing to? Some therapists explain their legal duty to make the report in an initial session with the client. Others, working with high-risk populations or working with children or adolescents, emphasize confidentiality, mentioning the limits to confidentiality only in passing. A substantial number don't tell the clients of their status as mandated reporters until after some incident has arisen that would trigger a report (Levine et al., 1995; Steinberg, 1994; Weinstein, 1996).

Therapists who avoid calling clients' attention to **mandatory reporting** may be concerned about scaring clients off or inhibiting disclosure (Berlin, Malin, and Dean, 1991). Does client knowledge that a therapist is a mandated reporter inhibit disclosure or willingness to seek therapy? Wallach (1993) tested different informed consent statements with women who were at risk for having child maltreatment calls made because they were in drug treatment programs. A detailed statement of the limits of confidentiality did not seem to deter women from being open in a simulated psychotherapy test (see also Steinberg, 1994; Weinstein, 1996).

Therapists' fear of negative consequences. Therapists are aware that reports have consequences for the child and the family. Levine and associates (1996) interviewed 30 psychotherapists who had made a mandated report of suspected child maltreatment on clients they had in treatment (see also Steinberg, 1994). Many said that making a mandated report on a client in treatment was stressful for them personally. They were distressed because of the uncertain consequences for the child and family. Some feared that more harm than good would result. Some lacked faith in the child protection system altogether; they believed that placing a child in a less than adequate foster care system made the child a double victim. Some believed that parents pressured or punished children to recant after CPS began an investigation. Therapists had mixed experiences with reporting. Some CPS workers consulted with therapists and handled investigations with sensitivity, tact, and a concern for future therapeutic efforts; according to the therapists, other CPS workers did not handle the investigation well.

Therapists fear that a client will drop out of treatment after a report is made. The legal reporting requirement impinges directly on the therapist's ethical duty to preserve confidentiality. Even if a client has given informed consent, therapists fear that report-

BOX 10.2

303

Children's
Rights, Parents'
Rights

What Happens in Therapy after a Mandated Report?

Watson and Levine (1989) looked at outpatient case records in 65 cases for which a report had been made. Patients dropped out of therapy in only 24 percent of the cases. In about 20 percent, the report had a positive effect: patient self-disclosure increased, and cooperation with therapy improved. The remaining cases showed no change. (See also Steinberg, 1994; Steinberg, Levine, and Doueck, 1998; Weinstein, 1996.)

There was a higher percentage of positive outcomes and a lower percentage of negative outcomes in cases in which the alleged abuser was a third party (i.e., mother's boyfriend) not in treatment than in cases in which the alleged abuser was in treatment, or the whole family was in treatment (Steinberg, 1994; Weinstein, 1996). On balance, therapists characterized the duty to make a mandated report as a "necessary evil" (Levine et al., 1995).

ing will destroy the client's trust and with it the therapeutic relationship, one predicated on trust and the expectation of confidentiality (see Box 10.2).

Harper and Irvin (1985) examined 107 cases in which a report of medical neglect was made about child patients in a pediatric hospital. Contrary to expectations, very few of the parents fled or removed their children from treatment. Watson and Levine (1989) found the rate of dropping out of treatment after a report was made was about one in four (see also Steinberg, 1994).

✉ Children's Rights, Parents' Rights

The complex problems of protecting children by state intervention into family life are enmeshed in fundamental conflicts of values and priorities. We want to be fair to parents and to avoid erroneous adjudication of fault or unnecessary intrusion into private matters. The law uses different procedures to ensure fairness in different situations.

Procedural Differences in Civil and Criminal Court

Family court uses civil procedure rules. For example, the standard of proof for an adjudication of child maltreatment is the lenient one of *preponderance of the evidence*. In criminal court, it is the more stringent *beyond a reasonable doubt*. In a criminal trial, the defendant has a Fifth Amendment right to remain silent, and no inference may be drawn from the defendant's exercise of that right. A parent's refusal to testify in family court is accepted as evidence against the parent.

The process described in Box 10.3 is very different from a criminal proceeding in which the burden of proof falls solely on the prosecution. In a criminal trial, the prosecution must present positive evidence that a crime (nonaccidental injury) occurred, and that the defendant was responsible. The defendant would not have to prove anything, offer any alternative explanation for the injury, or even testify.

In family court, it does not matter which parent in the household actually inflicted the injury. The law holds both parents liable for the child's safekeeping. If the child is not kept from harm, the law allows the judge to infer parental responsibility and

304

CHAPTER 10
Protecting
Children: Child
Protection
Proceedings

BOX 10.3

Parent Must Explain in Family Court

When a child is injured physically, a physician may testify that the injury was nonaccidental. If so, the parent then has to explain the injury. The court weighs the parent's explanation against the physician's and other testimony. For example, an infant may have a severe head and neck injury. The expert states that an injury of that kind could only have come from the parent shaking the child violently (shaken baby syndrome). The expert disputes the parent's explanation that the injury resulted when the infant fell from the parent's lap when he fell asleep on a couch while feeding the infant. According to the parent's explanation, the fall was only a foot or two, and onto a soft carpet. The expert states that such an injury could not have resulted from that kind of fall. The parent may have an expert who will support the parent's explanation. The parent has to provide an adequate explanation. If the parent refuses to testify in a family court, in contrast to a criminal court, the parent's failure to testify may be used by the judge as evidence in arriving at an adjudication.

intervene even in the absence of proof of which parent inflicted the harm. Under criminal law, a person can almost never be found responsible for a crime committed by another. Absence of proof of which parent inflicted the harm would very much limit a criminal prosecution for assault on a child or for homicide if the child died.

In short, the standards for evidence in family court and for proof make it easier to find that a parent has abused a child than it would be to prove the same charge in criminal court. In the criminal context, we often say it is better to let many guilty persons escape justice than to convict one innocent person. But legislators have weighed the importance of protecting children as greater than the importance of unjustly finding against an innocent parent. A "false positive" in family court is seen as less serious than in criminal court. Although the parent may lose custody of a child, the parent is not subject to criminal penalties such as imprisonment in a family court proceeding. It is assumed that intervention in a family by court order will be helpful to the child and to other family members.

Issues of Proof in Family Court

The petition to family court specifies the maltreatment allegations. If the case goes to trial in family court, even with less stringent procedural burdens, the allegations have to be proven. The parent is entitled to an attorney. The proof of the allegations is sometimes difficult, and often involves professional mental health workers and experts.

Children's testimony. Sex abuse allegations arouse great emotion. In the past, many people, including professionals, simply did not want to believe that parents would sexually abuse their own children. Summit (1988) believed that popular and professional resistance was so strong that he termed the resistance a "negative hallucination."

It is particularly difficult to prove that a child has been sexually abused. The problems of proof in sexual abuse cases may be more difficult than in physical abuse. Without penetration, there are few or no physical signs of sexual activity. The abuse may have consisted of fondling or of oral sex. Even physical signs may be equivocal (Nohejl, 1992).

BOX 10.4

305

Children's
Rights, Parents'
Rights

The Importance of a Child's Disclosure

A child's disclosure can be important even when there is physical evidence. An eight-year-old girl was brought to an emergency room with vaginal bleeding. The physician who made the initial report to CPS observed a gash in her vaginal wall. The mother said that the injury had occurred when the child fell on a folding chair, and that it was reopened by bumps on a hay wagon ride. The doctor did not accept this explanation; he believed that the injury could only have been made by something about the size of an erect penis penetrating the girl. The child denied that the mother's boyfriend had ever done anything to her. The mother produced witnesses who testified they had seen the child fall on the chair and testified that the boyfriend was never alone with the girl. The family court judge found insufficient evidence to support an adjudication of abuse and dismissed the petition.

In most cases of sexual abuse, the child victim may be the only witness. A great deal depends on the child's account (see Box 10.4). If the physical evidence is equivocal, a child's denial of abuse can be an important factor in the judge's decision to dismiss the case.

In some jurisdictions, young children are not required to testify in family court cases involving sexual abuse because of concerns that the experience will be upsetting (see Chapter 11). Others can testify as to what the child allegedly revealed. The allegation of abuse may be introduced through the testimony of someone to whom the child disclosed the sexual abuse. The person could be a parent, a teacher, the CPS worker, a police officer, a neighbor, or even another child. The disclosure might have been made long after the abuse allegedly occurred. The witness can testify even though the person did not see the abuse, and does not know whether the acts described actually happened. The witness can testify about what the child said. Such hearsay (an out-of-court statement introduced as proof of the matter asserted, e.g., "He told me he was sexually abused, therefore he was sexually abused") while admissible in this context, is legally insufficient to support an adjudication of abuse. The hearsay usually has to be corroborated by other evidence. (For hearsay in the criminal context, see *Crawford v. Washington,* 2004.)

Empirical basis for professional validation testimony. The **corroborative evidence** in a sexual abuse proceeding in family court can be any evidence, physical or testimonial, that tends to establish the offense, and that the accused committed the act (Levine and Battistoni, 1991). Testimony by an expert witness, based on a psychological examination or interview, that a child was sexually abused is called validation testimony. Such testimony may be legally sufficient corroboration (*Matter of Nicole V.,* 1987).

On what basis could an expert testify with professional certainty that the child was sexually abused? One court (*Matter of Nicole V.,* 1987) cited Sgroi, Porter, and Blick (1982) approvingly, but didn't really examine the underlying science. Sgroi and colleagues listed 20 behaviors found in child victims of sexual abuse. Of course, not all sexually abused children show all 20 symptoms. Symptoms exhibited by sexually abused children vary with sex and age. Of the list of 20 behaviors, 17 are general

306

CHAPTER 10
Protecting
Children: Child
Protection
Proceedings

BOX 10.5

The Child Discloses

The divorced father of a six-year-old son had a very middle-class background. The mother, who had custody, came from a lower-class background. She also had a history of drug use, and was allegedly promiscuous. The child disclosed something to his father's present girlfriend suggesting the boy had engaged in some kind of sexual activity at his mother's home. The girlfriend, who lived with the father, questioned the child for several hours before deciding to file a report with the hotline. The CPS worker testified that he interviewed the child for two hours using anatomically detailed dolls. The child revealed knowledge of sexual activity in his play.

A mental health professional, who had seen the child for treatment several times following the disclosure, also testified. Further disclosure came after several interviews. The child, she said, spontaneously drew a picture of two people in bed, one on top of the other, and identified himself as the one on the bottom. There was no videotape of the interview to know exactly how the mental health professional had elicited either the disclosure or the drawing. (See Box 11.2 for a discussion of interviewing techniques that might lead to false statements by the child.) The mental health professional was impressed that the child knew words like *pussy*, and said that a "pussy" was wet and smelled. The professional wasn't aware of cultural differences in children's knowledge of sexual terms (see Childers, 1936). The mental health professional also testified that several of the factors identified by Sgroi, Porter, and Blick (1982) as indicative of sexual abuse were present. Most of those symptoms, however, also characterize troubled, nonabused children. These include acting out aggressive behavior, poor peer relationships or inability to make friends, running away from home, sleep disturbances, regressive behavior, wthdrawal, clinical depression, and suicidal feelings (Sgroi, Porter, and Blick, 1982, 40–41). The mother's attorney did not cross-examine vigorously or even knowledgeably. No one discussed alternative hypotheses. The symptoms might have been related to instability in the child's relationship with his mother or with his father, or instability regarding the father's pending remarriage. The child did not testify. The judge found the mother had sexually abused her son. He then gave custody to the father and sharply limited the mother's visitation rights.

indicators of distress. The symptoms include sleep and eating disturbances, regression in toilet habits, fears and phobias, depression, shame, guilt, anger, school problems, and running away. These symptoms may be exhibited by emotionally disturbed children who have not been sexually abused, and by normal children under stress (Browne and Finkelhor, 1986). Some sexually abused children show no signs of emotional disturbance. Some children who were not abused may exhibit symptoms because they were distressed by the investigation.

Sgroi, Porter, and Blick, (1982) also found that a sexually abused child may show inappropriate sexual behavior. Three of the 20 symptoms are directly related to sexual activity: hints about sexual activity; persistent and inappropriate sex play with peers, toys, or themselves; and sexually aggressive or seductive behavior toward men. Friederich (1988) studied differences between sexually abused children, children seen clinically for other reasons, and normal children. Although both of the first two groups of children differed from normal children on many measures of emotional disturbance, the sexually abused children differed from the nonabused clinical group only on the frequency of the sex behaviors. However, sexually inappropriate behavior is not a reliable marker of sexual abuse either. As few as a quarter of sexually abused children may show the behavior (Browne and Finkelhor, 1986). Moreover, some children who were not abused may hint about sexual activity or engage in sexual play. They may have witnessed sexual activities or been exposed to adult movies. There may be class and cultural differences in sexual knowledge and behaviors among children (Childers, 1936).

There is little research to enable an expert to base an opinion that a child who did not disclose was sexually abused. Even if a child discloses something, we have few substantiated methods for determining true from false allegations, and experts can disagree sharply (Corwin et al., 1987).

Disposition

Following an adjudication of child maltreatment, the judge holds a disposition hearing. We will focus here on dispositions of mandated therapy, and the termination of parental rights.

After hearing testimony and reviewing the record, the judge issues a treatment order. The judge may order the parent into psychotherapy or counseling, an alcohol treatment program, or parent training, or may set other conditions the parent must meet. A parent who abused a child may be ordered to live outside the home. A noncustodial parent may have visitation rights curtailed, or may be permitted to visit only under supervision. The judge may give custody of the child to DSS for placement in a foster home. Parents in family court may eventually be faced with the possibility of losing parental rights.

Mandated psychotherapy. Family court judges frequently order parents into treatment or counseling. Those who work with sexually abusing families and offenders believe compulsion is essential to engage the abuser in treatment. Compulsion, however, may interfere with the development of a therapeutic alliance. Some therapists complained that courts ordered parents into therapy with the unrealistic expectation that therapy could "fix" complex and multidimensional problems (Levine et al., 1996). How effective is treatment when it is involuntary? What effects does compulsion have on the process of treatment itself?

If the judge finds that the parent abused the child, the judge can order the parent to enter psychotherapy even if the parent continues to claim innocence. If ordered into treatment, confidentiality is limited. Psychotherapists who work with abusive parents believe that progress in treatment requires the person to admit to the offense, if not apologize to the child. Many psychotherapists do not consider treatment a success unless the client admits the abuse. But what if the person is innocent? On occasion, mandated therapy can raise Fifth Amendment problems of self-incrimination (see Levine and Doherty, 1991).

We don't know much about the success of different rehabilitation programs. Sometimes, a child who is restored to a parent after the parent completed treatment is injured again or even killed. These notorious cases raise questions about our ability to make good predictions about child safety (see Box 10.6).

Risk-management strategies, such as long-term, frequent supervision of potentially dangerous situations, and more supportive services may be better than prediction. Agencies already use this approach for some high-risk families to prevent out-of-home placement (Waldfogel, 1998). All solutions to this problem are costly in different ways. The expense forces reconsideration of the balance between the desire to preserve the autonomy and privacy of the family, and the right of the child to be protected from harm.

308

CHAPTER 10
Protecting
Children: Child
Protection
Proceedings

BOX 10.6

A Legal Case in Point Unsuccessful Treatment

A Florida man was found guilty of the murder of his two-year-old stepson, who had been returned to the family by DSS. The child had been in foster care as an infant because the parents had neglected him. The mother and stepfather were ordered into a treatment program, including parenting classes. The child was returned to the mother and stepfather when DSS believed the program had been successfully completed, and a judge acquiesced. The child died after the stepfather, who had been trying to toilet train the two year old, took him out in the yard to hose him down after an accident. Then, in order to teach him not to have an accident again, the stepfather, despite having successfully completed parenting classes, held the child's head in the toilet bowl while he flushed it. The child died of a brain hemorrhage (*Barber v. State*, 1992).

Termination of Parental Rights

Child protective statutes recognized "the superiority of the moral over the legal qualification of the home in securing the child's welfare" (Kelley, 1882, p. 96). However, biological parents have certain rights as parents. These rights cannot be terminated without proving parental unfitness with clear and convincing evidence (*Santosky v. Kramer*, 1982). Unwed biological fathers who have acknowledged and cared for a child have parental rights that cannot be terminated without good cause (*Stanley v. Illinois*, 1972; *Lehr v. Robertson*, 1983).

Due diligence. Even if a child is removed from a home, parents have a constitutional right to the companionship of their children. The state cannot terminate parental rights unless it tries with **due diligence** (see Box 10.7) to reunite the family. Judges are under a legal mandate to oversee the child's return to the natural family. Social services must provide a treatment program (e.g., help locate a safe place to live and teach parenting skills) for a parent to remedy adverse conditions. The parent has an obligation to maintain contact and to plan realistically for the child's future. If the parent neither abandons the child nor succeeds in establishing a safe and stable home, the child is in limbo in long-term foster care. The child has no permanent home, but cannot be adopted until parental rights are terminated. If the parent successfully completes the treatment program, the court may approve the child's return to parental custody.

Some parents show little interest in the child, or do not follow through on the treatment program. The parent may not visit the child for long periods, even though able to do so. The parent may not attend required parenting classes, or an alcohol rehabilitation program. Sometimes the parent may attend sporadically, and not benefit. After a time, the agency can petition to have the court declare the child permanently neglected. That means parental rights can be terminated and the child freed for adoption. Older children are less attractive to adoptive parents, however. In 2003, of the 542,000 children in foster care, 115,000 were potential adoptees. Of this number, in 67,000 cases parental rights had already been terminated, but only 49,000 were actually adopted (AFCARS, 2003).

Star, the little girl described in Box 10.7, remained in foster care with no real parent, adopted or biological, for her developmentally crucial first five years. Under the 1997

BOX 10.7

309

Children's
Rights, Parents'
Rights

A Legal Case in Point: Parental Rights Terminated

Star Leslie W. was a few weeks old when she was voluntarily placed in foster care by her 20-year-old unwed mother. In the next five years, Star resided with her natural mother once for one week and once for about a month. When Star was five, family court responded to DSS's petition and terminated her mother's parental rights. The mother, who did not want to lose Star altogether, appealed. Eventually the case reached New York's highest court, the Court of Appeals.

The Court of Appeals found that the agency did exercise due diligence. The state offered counseling. Workers arranged for the mother to visit the child. They offered an educational and vocational program. They kept the mother informed of Star's development. She saw the child only a few times each year. She changed her residence frequently and did not keep DSS informed of her whereabouts. She made no plans for obtaining suitable housing, and failed to follow through on referrals from the DSS housing office. DSS helped her obtain public assistance, find day care, and return to school, and they then restored Star to her. Within a month, the mother returned Star to the foster home.

There was nothing in the record to suggest that the parent would change. The state offered expert witness testimony based on psychiatric examination and psychological tests that the respondent suffered from a chronic mental illness, and was of borderline intelligence. The court concluded that the parent had failed to meet her responsibilities and upheld the termination of parental rights. The child was released for adoption (*Matter of Star Leslie W.*, 1984). Under today's law, DSS might have moved to terminate parental rights sooner because Star was in foster care for 15 of 22 months.

Adoption and Safe Families Act, parental rights could be terminated much sooner; she would have been eligible for adoption much sooner.

Mental illness and mental retardation. Parents with mental retardation and chronic, difficult-to-treat major mental illness present special issues. Mental retardation in and of itself is not a sufficient reason to terminate parental rights. It must be demonstrated that mental retardation affects the parent's fitness or the child's well-being. How much mental retardation puts the child at a sufficiently high risk that parental rights should be terminated? The problem arises at the margin, not when the parent with mental retardation is severely limited. Psychologists and psychiatrists are called to testify about the extent of the parent's disability. Can a parent with mental retardation care for a child with some help and supervision? If so, how much effort and money is the state obligated to spend to protect the parent's constitutional right to privacy and autonomy in bringing up a child (Pollack, 2002)?

A similar problem arises when the state seeks to terminate the parental rights of a person with severe and persistent mental illness. The law requires testimony from a psychiatrist, and sometimes other mental health professionals, that the individual will never recover to the point of being able to care for the child or children. Many mentally ill people can care for their children. Most parents who have abused or neglected their children are not mentally ill. What kind of mental illness, and what validated

310

CHAPTER 10
Protecting
Children: Child
Protection
Proceedings

prognostic indicators, justify the termination of parental rights so that a child may be eligible for adoption?

Parents in prison. It is difficult when a parent is serving a long prison sentence and can't cooperate with a treatment plan. In order to fulfill its responsibilities, the state must make diligent efforts to strengthen the parental relationship. Does this mean the child should be brought to the prison to visit the parent? What effect does that have on a child's psychological development? Should a long prison sentence be grounds for terminating parental rights when the child is in foster care and the parent won't voluntarily agree to release the child for adoption? Some state laws do make a long-term prison sentence for some crimes grounds for terminating parental rights.

The Adoption and Safe Families Act of 1997

The federal Adoption and Safe Families Act of 1997 made important changes in family preservation policy. Under previous law, CPS workers and family court judges were required to make "reasonable efforts" to help maintain a child in the home before removing the child (**family preservation**), and were to restore the child to the family as soon as feasible (**family reunification**). Under the new law, CPS is not required to make reasonable efforts to preserve or reunify the family if the parent has subjected the child to "aggravated circumstances" (e.g., abandonment, torture, chronic abuse, and sexual abuse). The provision also applies if the parent has killed or seriously injured a child, or if parental rights to another sibling were terminated. A permanency planning hearing is held soon after the determination to place the child out of the home. At the hearing, where parents are represented, the judge approves a permanency plan and chooses among possible goals: the child should return home, a termination of parental rights petition should be filed, the child should be referred for adoption, or the child should be referred for legal guardianship or another permanent placement. Social services then must follow that plan. If the goal is reunification, but progress is not made and the child is in foster care for 15 of the previous 22 months, under the Adoption and Safe Families Act (1997) the state can seek to terminate parental rights. Once parental rights have been terminated, the state must expedite adoptions.

The 1997 law has had varying success in accomplishing its aims. More youth in care now have permanancy plans reviewed by courts. Foster care rates decreased in some states, but increased in others. The length of stay in foster care increased in a number of states even as the number of termination of parental rights procedures increased in many states (White, 2003). The length of time until reunification of children in foster care with their own families may have increased since the act was passed (Wulczyn and Hislop, 2002). The new law (as amended in 2001 and 2003) also has the aim of increasing adoptions by providing performance-based incentives to states to increase the number of adoptions from foster care. This act has had some success in increasing adoptions from foster care from 31,000 in 1997 to 51,000 in 2002. There may be a limit because of the difficulties in finding adoptive homes for older children.

Summary

The child protection system does not have the visibility that criminal courts have because much of what goes on is kept confidential. Yet the lives of millions of children and parents are affected by that system each year.

Historically, the state provided some aid for orphaned and abandoned children but did not intervene within the family. The idea that children had some rights to protection from maltreatment by parents developed gradually during the nineteenth century. The first child protection organizations were the Societies for the Prevention of Cruelty to Children, private organizations authorized by the state to "rescue" children. The SPCCs were distrusted by poor people, who saw them as arbitrarily breaking up families.

Children are removed from the home in a minority of cases. In most cases, when a report is substantiated, CPS offers a voluntary treatment plan to the parents. If the parents do not comply, CPS can petition a court to mandate treatment.

When a child has been removed by court order, the court develops a plan designed to make the home safe and reunite the family. The plans often require parents to enter counseling, drug or alcohol treatment, or parent education programs. When the parents meet the requirements set by the court, their children will be returned. Abuse sometimes recurs. If parents do not make efforts to fulfill conditions set by a court, or seem unable to do so, parental rights may be terminated. A new Federal law makes it easier to terminate parental rights than was true in the past.

Despite failure of professionals to strictly follow the law and report every suspicion, the number of mandated reports has increased steadily, straining the child protection system. Child protection is stressful for almost all the professional participants. CPS workers must carry out a dangerous, emotionally demanding job, often with insufficient training and support. Mental health and other professionals must violate client confidentiality to make mandated reports. Many do not always report when they should because of concerns about the effects of reporting and uncertainty about the meaning of neglect and abuse. Some clinicians also feel uncomfortable with being assigned the task of "fixing" parents and making the home safe through a simple treatment program. The effectiveness of treatment programs generally, and the practical and ethical problems of mandating treatment, have not been well evaluated.

Mental health professionals also participate in the system by evaluating alleged child victims of sex abuse and by evaluating the parenting capacities of mentally retarded and mentally ill parents. The empirical foundation for evaluations of this kind is not strong.

CPS was established to help children and strengthen the family. It does not always succeed. The laws must steer between the sometimes conflicting rights of parents and children and must do so within a diverse and culturally complex society. We need to approach the complex problem of protecting children with wisdom based on facts. Research might help us improve our child protection systems, but information alone won't resolve all the issues. In the end, we may be able to evaluate what we do in this area only by examining the degree to which we can feel we are acting compassionately and in keeping with our highest values.

Discussion Questions

1. What are the pros and cons of policies emphasizing family preservation? Of policies encouraging child safety and permanency planning?

2. Assume there is a hearing in family court to determine whether or not a two-year-old child has been sexually abused by her father during visitation. There is no physical evidence of abuse. A psychologist presents **validation testimony,** based on interviews with the child and observations of the child's doll play. If you were assisting the father's lawyer, what questions would you want the lawyer to ask the psychologist during the cross-examination? If you were consulting with the CPS lawyer, what questions would you want the lawyer to ask the psychologist?

3. How would you define *physical abuse?* Is there any empirical research that would help judges trying to define when physical discipline becomes abusive?

312

CHAPTER 10
Protecting
Children: Child
Protection
Proceedings

4. How would you develop a measure for evaluating the parenting skills of mild to moderately retarded parents? Can you think of a way to evaluate parenting skills without using paper-and-pencil tests?

5. When people are ordered to go into therapy, do you think the therapy is likely to be more or less effective than when they decide to enter therapy voluntarily? Why? How could you test your hypothesis?

6. Do you think the child protection system should recognize cultural differences in child-rearing practices and family culture? In what ways? Can you design an experiment to assess cultural differences in the concept of *neglect*?

Key Terms

Adoption and Safe Families
  Act
Baby Moses laws
battered child syndrome
Court Appointed Special
  Advocates (CASA)
Child Protective
  Services (CPS)
clear and convincing
  evidence
corroborative evidence
due diligence
due process
excessive corporal
  punishment
family court

family preservation
family preservation policy
family reunification
foster care
founded/substantiated
hearsay
immunity from suit
Indian Child Welfare
  Act (ICWA)
indicated
mandatory reporting
neglect
New York Society for the
  Prevention of Cruelty to
  Children (NYSPCC)
parens patriae

permanency planning
permanently neglected
preponderance of evidence
privileged
some credible evidence
standard of proof
termination of parental
  rights
unfit
unfounded
validation testimony

CHAPTER **11**

Children and the Criminal Process

With the sharp rise in sex abuse charges, and more aggressive prosecution of various forms of family violence, children are being called on to testify in criminal trials with increasing frequency. A child may testify most often as a victim of a crime, or less often as a witness to a crime committed against another.

Concerns about children's capabilities to observe, to interpret, to retain and recall experiences, to communicate their memories (think of the limited language ability of a three-year-old), and to be influenced by others arise at every point in the long process leading to trial. Those issues have stimulated a large body of research that has reached the courts through expert testimony and in amicus briefs.

Much of the research has focused on the central issue of children's capabilities as witnesses. The defendant in a criminal trial is entitled to all of the due process protections designed to prevent the conviction of an innocent person. Due process protections for the defendant include the rules of evidence, which are intended to keep from the jury unreliable testimony or testimony that might induce prejudice against the defendant without adding to the proof of the issues in the trial. One class of evidence that might be considered more prejudicial than probative is children's testimony. If children are poorer witnesses than adults, or if their memories or statements are more easily manipulated, allowing children to testify might lead to unfair convictions.

Notable instances of false testimony by some children in the past increased the legal community's suspicion of child witnesses. The fantastic accusations made by adolescent girls in colonial times against so many members of their community in the Salem, Massachusetts, witch trials is a case in point (Richardson, 1983; Ceci and Friedman, 2000).

To help the legal system understand the strengths and weaknesses of children's testimony, researchers have investigated the accuracy of children's memories, their understanding of truthfulness in a legal context, their **suggestibility,** and whether false memories can be induced. Research workers have looked at ways the investigative and the trial processes can be conducted to elicit the most accurate testimony.

Psychologists have also been concerned with the effects on children of being subjected to repeated interviews during the investigation before trial. Because of the stress, some argue that the criminal justice system revictimizes the child who comes forward as a witness. With the exception of establishing the competence of a young child to testify, courtroom procedure made little distinction between adult and child witnesses. In *Maryland v. Craig* (1990), a case we will discuss below, the U.S. Supreme Court authorized some adaptations for child witnesses, and acknowledged psychological research on the child as a witness in formulating its opinion.

In this chapter, we will look at some representative research on various aspects of children's capacities as witnesses, at efforts to protect child witnesses, at jurors' reactions to children as witnesses, and at expert witness testimony in this area. Topics covered will include

- the history of the study of the child as a witness.
- legal tests of a child's competence to testify in court.
- research on children's memory and cognitive competence as they relate to testifying.
- studies with enhanced ecological validity.
- research on whether children fabricate stories of abuse.
- psychological impact of the trial process on children.
- closed-circuit video testimony: its constitutionality, advantages, and disadvantages.

- preparing children to testify.
- the credibility of child witnesses to jurors.
- child witness research, expert witnesses, and the *Daubert* decision.

315

History of the
Study of the
Child as
a Witness

History of the Study of the Child as a Witness

The scientific study of the capabilities of children as witnesses began in the early 1900s when psychology was still a new science. Most psychologists of that time did not believe children were credible or reliable witnesses. Not long before, however, the general view was different. For example, no question of competence or suggestiblity arose in 1874 when nine-year-old Mary Ellen, whose case precipitated the child protection movement, testified in a criminal assault charge against Mrs. Connolly, the woman who was caring for her (see Figure 10.1). In addition to her verbal testimony, Mary Ellen bore scars and bruises from beatings. Mrs. Connolly was convicted (Myers, 2004).

Alfred Binet, the originator of the intelligence test, studied the suggestibility of children from age 7 to 14 in the late nineteenth century (see Figure 11.1). He showed children pictures and objects, then asked them increasingly suggestive questions about what they had seen. Children accepted the misleading suggestions more frequently than adults (Goodman, 1984; Ceci and Friedman, 2000). Binet also noted individual differences in responsiveness to **leading questions.** Leading questions are questions that suggest an answer that might be false, for example, "He had a green hat on, didn't he?"

FIGURE 11.1

Alfred Binet (1859–1911)
Alfred Binet, the French psychologist who devised the first intelligence test in the early 1900s, experimented with children's suggestibility and memory. These experiments were forerunners of today's research on children.

Around the turn of the twentieth century, psychologists in Germany, where experimental psychology began, were called as expert witnesses in trials in which children testified, including cases involving allegations of sexual abuse. Some psychologists used tests similar to the ones Binet employed to demonstrate that children were unreliable witnesses.

Members of the legal community objected to the picture tests. They said that the children's memory of pictures was not an adequate measure of performance in the type of situation that would be the subject of testimony. In contemporary terms, the legal community was challenging the ecological validity, or the "fit," of the research methods to legal cases. How applicable, they asked, were the findings of a laboratory experiment to a situation with very different characteristics? This problem of ecological validity continues to be raised whenever courts consider the applicability of laboratory research to the real world (see discussion of *Daubert* case in Chapter 2).

In response to the criticisms, research workers studied the reliability and vulnerability to suggestion of children's memories of staged live events. Goodman (1984) (Figure 11.2) provided a translation of an early series of studies of this kind by a psychologist named Varendock. Varendock's method of exposing children to live situations and studying how their reports could be influenced or manipulated remains an important approach to research today.

The early research workers touched on many problems that continue to be of interest (see summary of the early research in Ceci and Friedman, 2000). Psychologists have gone on to study other issues, including balancing defendant's rights with protecting children from unnecessary emotional distress, determining the best and least traumatic methods of eliciting accurate testimony from children, assessing the degree to which children's memory and testimony may be influenced, and understanding how jurors respond to child witnesses. Over time, research workers have tried to improve the ecological validity of the experimental procedures. Research workers hope this growing body of knowledge about child witnesses will help guide policies affecting children in the legal system (Goodman, 1984).

⬚ The Child in Court: Competence

Concerns about children's **competence to testify,** their credibility, and the effects of testifying on the children themselves can arise in all kinds of cases. Most controversy, and a good deal of the research, however, have focused on cases of alleged sexual abuse (Faigman et al., 2005). In a national survey, prosecutors said that by far the most common cases in which children testified involved child sexual assault or incest (Goodman et al., 1999). Episodes of sexual abuse generally occur in private, so there may be no other witness than the child–victim. Sometimes there is no physical corroborative evidence, or there is evidence that does not lend itself to clear inferences about what happened. Under these circumstances, the child–victim's testimony is critical for a criminal prosecution. A recent example is the accusation of child molestation brought against singing star Michael Jackson; the district attorney's case, which did not persuade the jury, hinged on the credibility of the main child witness. But the very fact that the child's testimony can be the main basis for conviction, combined with the intense emotions aroused by the alleged crime, heightens concerns about the child's reliability as a witness and about the stresses of testifying on the child.

In fact, most children who are victims of abuse are not exposed to the courtroom as witnesses. The majority of cases are plea-bargained and do not go to trial. The threat of the child's testimony is enough to persuade many defendants to plead guilty to a lesser

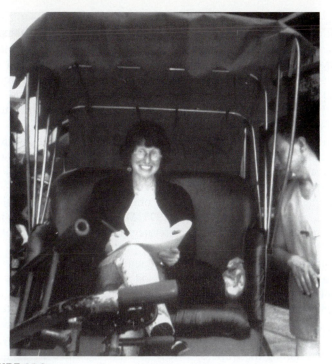

FIGURE 11.2

Gail Goodman

Professor Gail Goodman is a leading research worker on children's testimony. Her work is significant in the development of the modern field of research on children's memory and suggestibility, as these factors affect testimony. Her studies of children's testimonial abilities have been cited in two U.S. Supreme Court decisions. She received two major awards from the American Psychological Association for her research on children and the legal system.

charge or penalty, and the child does not have to testify in court. In other cases, parents choose not to proceed because of concerns about the emotional impact on the child of participating in a long pretrial process and later in a trial. In still other cases, there is no corroborative evidence and the prosecutor, exercising prosecutorial discretion, decides that the witness is not sufficiently strong or credible to warrant going ahead. In one sample of 316 sexual offense cases involving a child witness, only 16.8 percent were disposed of by trial (Lipovsky et al., 1992). The low rate of trials is similar to the low rate of trials in criminal cases generally. On the other hand, a minority of cases do go to trial, and when they do, children may have to testify. Much research has been concerned with the child as a witness in a criminal trial, even though criminal trials with children are relatively infrequent.

Competence to Testify: Legal Standards

Under common law rules, very young children could be excluded from testifying (McGough, 1994; Myers, 1987). However, the rule was far from absolute, and children of any age were allowed to testify if the presiding judge found them to be sufficiently capable. In the past, the judge might have probed to determine if the child understood the oath. The oath was considered critical in placing moral pressure on a witness to tell the truth. If a child was too young to understand that not telling the truth under oath put his or her soul in peril of eternal damnation, the child was considered incompetent to testify. Goodman (1984) quotes a colloquy from a 1684 case in which a child of 13 was permitted to testify after he acknowledged that he would go to hellfire if he told a lie after swearing to God to tell the truth.

Today, laws in many states set an age at which competence to testify is presumed. A child above the established age, usually 10 or 12 but sometimes 14, is presumed competent to testify and is allowed to testify in the same way as an adult. Children under the statutory age will be allowed to testify if the judge, after questioning the child or listening to an examination conducted by the attorney offering the witness, is satisfied that the child has the capacity to testify (McGough, 1994; Myers, 1987). (Note that there is no requirement of competence for a child to be interviewed in an investigation of suspected crimes.)

A witness is considered competent to testify if the witness can observe the events about which he or she is to testify, has a sufficiently good memory to recall events, and can express him- or herself reasonably intelligently and coherently. The witness must also know the difference between truth and lies, understand the importance of telling the truth, and understand that he or she may be punished by the court for not telling the truth (Myers, 1987). To determine underage children's competence to testify, the judge, or the attorney presenting the witness, usually asks the child to state his or her name, age, and address, and perhaps asks the child to answer some questions about his or her schooling. The judge may ask the child questions to see if the child knows the difference between a lie and the truth. In order to tell whether a young child knows the difference between a truth and a lie, the judge may show the child a green book, call it a red book, and ask if that is the truth or a lie. The tests are not very rigorous. The U.S. Supreme Court permitted a five year old to testify in a murder case provided the judge, on examination, found that the child possessed the relevant abilities (Myers, 1987).

Goodman, Aman, and Hirschman (1987) showed that the ability of a child to respond to the type of inquiry used to assess child witness competence has little or no correlation with performance on tests of memory of stressful events that a child experienced. Talwar et al. (2002, 2004) found that many 3- to 7-year-old children could reasonably define a lie. Between 57 and 76 percent of 3 year olds, and well over 80 percent of older children (4–7), could correctly identify a lie in an experimental procedure. They were asked to say whether given the information in a story, the child character in the story had told a lie (Talwar et al., 2002; see also Haugaard et al., 1991; Strichartz and Burton, 1990). However, the children's knowledge of what was a lie did not relate very well to whether the children actually told a lie about a transgression in an experimental procedure. Asking children to promise to tell the truth helped in promoting truth telling, but in the experiments, a majority of children who could say what a lie was still told a lie under the conditions of the experiment. Knowledge of what a lie was did not in and of itself foster truth telling in the experimental situation. The findings of these studies support those who say it is preferable to do away with the competency examination, and to allow the child to testify. It is then the responsibility of the fact-finder (jury, or judge in a bench trial) to decide how much weight to give to the child's testimony. Modern law has been moving in this direction.

Children's Memory and Cognitive Competence

The question of the accuracy of children's understanding, memory, and reporting of events is central to evaluating their competence to be witnesses and how a jury might weight their testimony. It is not very meaningful to discuss children's memory and cognitive competence in general and in isolation from context. Think about a story told by a three year old, a nine year old, or an adolescent. Their storytelling will reflect their ages and also, in different ways, the situation and the social context. Telling a story about a crime depends on memory, but as soon as we introduce other actors who interact with the child—a parent, a judge, a jury, a police investigator, or a prosecutor—the story is potentially subject to social influence.

Memory and errors of memory. Witnesses testify about what they remember of events they have seen or participated in at some time in the past. Memory, however, is a complex phenomenon. The laboratory study of memory has strongly influenced research in the psycho-legal context.

Memories may change "spontaneously," depending on whether the experience is retained with clear detail, or whether just the gist of the experiences is retained in a "fuzzy trace" (Brainerd, Reyna, and Poole, 2000). Memories can vary from a "true" record of the event that is available in an experiment. Memories may also change as a result of social influence. The memory as conveyed later may be false because it has been subtly influenced by intervening events, or because the person remembering has a conscious or unconscious reason to falsify it. The memory that is ultimately given as testimony may have been affected by cognitive and social factors at each stage, beginning with the preliminary investigation. The memory may be wholly true, partially true, partially false, or wholly false. One psycho-legal problem is to develop principles to help determine when a memory conveyed as testimony is likely to be accurate and when it might be faulty.

Typical experimental paradigms. In a typical study of children's memory, children are asked to read a passage, or to view a film or a slide show telling a story. In other studies, they may watch a staged event, or play games with a confederate. The games may involve the confederate touching the child, photographing the child, or putting stickers on various body parts. Shortly afterwards, the children are asked questions about what they saw, experienced, or read. Sometimes they are just asked to describe the events in their own words. Afterward, they may be asked specific questions about the events.

In many research designs, the experimenter is interested in seeing what might affect memory. Leading questions that suggest answers may be compared with non-leading questions to see if the manner of questioning affects the accuracy of the report. Preschool children especially may be influenced by leading questions (e.g., Krackow and Lynn, 2003). In some designs, the experimenter is interested in whether the answers suggested within the leading questions will be incorporated into the child's memory. Later (a week, a month, or sometimes longer), the subjects are asked to remember the "stimulus" (the original story or the events) again. The researcher checks to see whether the initial questioning resulted in systematic memory distortion, that is, if the suggestive questions changed the subject's memories.

In other research designs, children are repeatedly questioned about an episode they witnessed to see if such questioning changes their stories. In some studies, the children are given suggestions or false information in the repetitions (Leichtman and Ceci, 1995)

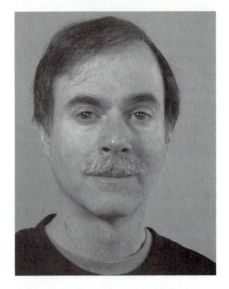

FIGURE 11.3

Stephen Ceci
*Professor Stephen Ceci, a leading researcher on children's testimony,
challenges the position that children don't lie about sexual abuse. His
experiments and demonstrations have raised our skepticism about the
reliability of children's testimony. He and psychologist Maggie Bruck
organized a committee of concerned scientists to submit an amicus
brief on behalf of Kelly Michaels, (see Box 2.3) who had been
convicted on the basis of flawed children's testimony.*

(Figure 11.3). Some researchers have given children suggestions about experiences they
were told they had. They then again subjected the children to repeated questioning over
subsequent weeks to see if the children came to say they saw or remembered things
that didn't actually happen to them.

Leichtman and Ceci (1995) undertook one of the few studies to examine children's
memories over a period of more than a few weeks. The stimulus event was a very short
visit to the children's classroom from a man called Sam Stone. After the visit had taken
place, the children were given suggestions over a period of ten weeks about what had
happened during the visit. In that study, 74 percent of preschoolers, 47 percent of 6 to
8 year olds, but only 7 percent of the 9 to 14 year olds agreed with a false description
of the visit. When asked to confirm that the false event really happened, 13 percent of
all the children said, "Yes," and another 28 percent said they just didn't know. In other
words, many of the children reported something they knew wasn't or might not be true,
but knew they were doing it. A small number of the children were apparently convinced of the truth of their "memories" of events that did not occur. In Leichtman and
Ceci's studies, a significant proportion of younger children, and some older children,
could be influenced to describe with confidence events that never happened, but were
only suggested.

Researchers have also examined children's ability to differentiate something
they imagined from something that actually happened. **Source monitoring** (Where did

I hear that, did I make it up, or did I just dream it?) can be a problem for adults as well as children. The problem is especially important because children may report fantastic events as true, as some have in well-publicized day care cases (see Ceci and Bruck, 1995). In a typical study, children of different ages will be asked to perform an action, watch someone else perform an action, or think about an action, and then asked to say whether they did the action, watched the action, or thought about the action (Johnson and Foley, 1984).

The studies demonstrating suggestibility and the induction of false memories have been influential, even though the studies have some design problems that limit their interpretation. The type of memories induced in an experiment may have little legal relevance because of ethical limitations on study designs. The dissemination of the results of research demonstrating how memory may be influenced may be affecting how jurors respond to child witnesses. Jurors may be more inclined to disbelieve child witnesses because of the dissemination of information about false memories (Schaaf et al., 2002). However, in one study of actual trials in which children testified, 92 percent of the defendants were convicted. Of course, these were cases that prosecutors selected to prosecute, and there was other evidence in the trials as well as the child witness' testimony (Myers et al., 1999).

Ecological validity. If research is to inform the legal system about children as witnesses, under the *Daubert* standards for the admission of expert testimony the research should have **ecological validity**. A *Daubert* inquiry asks whether there is a scientific base, appropriate to the issue in the case, for admitting expert testimony. The ecological validity of laboratory-based studies, the generalization of the results to the real situation about which children will testify, is open to question (Goodman, Aman, and Hirschman, 1987). Goodman et al. (1990) point out that the personal significance of experimental stimulus events and real-life abuse will differ in the degree to which revealing the memories may be embarrassing, thus affecting the ecological validity of the experiment. An episode of sexual abuse may involve nudity and genital contact, matters that are embarrassing to relate; sometimes a child's personal safety may be threatened, stimulating strong feelings of fear and anxiety. In contrast, the laboratory studies involve relatively brief interactions with the experimenters. The time periods between exposure to the experimental stimulus and recall are generally short, especially compared to the months or years between the time a crime occurs and until a child testifies at trial. Research workers are constrained by ethical considerations in the degree of stress that can be employed in an experiment, or the kinds of stimulus materials they can use. It would be questionable ethically and legally to expose a young child to sexually explicit stimulus materials for the sake of conducting an experiment.

Children's memory of medical procedures. To investigate children's memory under more ecologically relevant conditions, researchers have studied children after they have been exposed to naturally occurring stressful or embarrassing situations. Goodman, Aman, and Hirschman (1987) assessed children's memories of what occurred when they went to a clinic to be inoculated. Children are often frightened of procedures that involve being touched and held by strangers. Saywitz et al. (1989) did a similar study with five and seven year old children who had a physical that involved a genital and anal examination, or a physical in which they were examined for evidence of scoliosis (curvature of the spine).

The three- to six-year-old children in Goodman and associates' study (Goodman, Aman, and Hirschman, 1987) came from low socioeconomic status families. Their parents accompanied them into a clinic examining room. The children then received one and sometimes two shots, and often a dose of an oral polio vaccine. The entire episode took three to four minutes. Researchers interviewed some of the children about their visit three or four days later, and others seven to nine days later. The children were questioned using a combination of free recall, suggestive or leading questions, and nonsuggestive questions about what they remembered about the inoculation visit.

The children were asked four questions of relevance in an investigation of child abuse: (1) "Did the person kiss you?" (2) "Did the person hit you?" (3) "Did the person put anything in your mouth?" and (4) "Did the person touch you anywhere other than your arm/thigh?" Goodman and associates report that the children were quite accurate in response to these questions. Ninety-six percent of the children answered the first question correctly, all of the children answered the second question correctly, 81 percent answered the third correctly, and 50 percent answered the fourth question correctly. When they made errors, children were more likely to say, "No," to a question about something that did happen (error of omission) than to say, "Yes," to a question about something that didn't happen (error of commission). No child made a false report of abuse, even when asked questions that might elicit such reports. Five- and six year olds answered more questions correctly than three and four year olds; the longer period of delay affected the younger children's accuracy more than the older children's (see also Saywitz et al., 1989).

Goodman and her colleagues concluded that children were far more likely to fail to disclose touching than they were to state falsely that they had been touched. The use of anatomically detailed dolls did not influence children to disclose falsely. The research workers properly noted that the rigors of a police investigation were not in effect, and that the children in the study had no motivation to lie.

Another investigation of children's memory of medical procedures found that children make false identifications, just as adults do, and under similar conditions of viewing suspects. Peters (1987) examined the ability of young children ages three to eight who went to a dentist's office for checkups or for a cleaning to identify the dentist and the dental hygienist 24 to 48 hours after the visit, and after three to four weeks. In a suspect-absent lineup (see Chapter 6), as many as 65 percent of the children made a false identification.

The applicability of these resourceful experiments to the actual conditions under which children's memory is tested in real-life legally oriented situations is still problematic. Goodman's research has often been used to support the proposition that children do not lie when reporting child sexual abuse, and that they are relatively immune to suggestion about key events in which they have participated. Goodman does not make that claim. Goodman and colleagues studied younger children who were not under any great pressure to respond to the interrogator. Ceci and Friedman (2000) reviewed other studies, which showed a much higher rate of influence than Goodman and her colleagues reported. Nonetheless, they agree that there is a greater likelihood that a child's assertion that he or she has been sexually abused is correct than it is false. The problem is the degree to which any particular child has been subject to influence that might affect the child's testimony. Even if we agree that some children can be induced, albeit with difficulty, to make false assertions, that understanding doesn't help us in the specific case. Was the child accurate in the case at hand? An innocent defendant might be falsely convicted by statements made by a child that were induced, or a guilty person might be let free because of juror unwillingness to credit a child's statements.

BOX 11.1

323

The Child in
Court:
Competence

False Allegations in Schools

It is rare, but not unheard of, for a group of adolescents, or even preadolescents, to get together and accuse an unpopular teacher of molesting them (Poole and Lamb, 1998). A well-publicized case came up in a Germantown, Maryland, middle school. Six girls and one boy, who were 11 and 12 years old, accused Ronald Heller, a physical education instructor, of having gone into the girls' locker room. They said he hugged one girl in her bra and panties, slapped another on her behind, and called another "hot sexy momma." The girls were annoyed because he had disciplined two of their friends two days before they made the accusation. Mr. Heller was immediately suspended, while police investigated. The girls conspired with each other so that their stories would be consistent. The police became suspicious, and eventually the girls admitted they had made everything up. After one month, Mr. Heller returned to school. The girls were arrested on charges of making false statements to the police (Schulte, 2000).

Do Children Fabricate Stories?

A number of highly publicized cases involving false or highly improbable accusations of sexual abuse by children has led to a "backlash" against the proposition that children don't lie about matters such as sexual abuse (see Doris, 1991). The fact that children understand the difference between truth and falsehood doesn't mean that they never lie. No one doubts that children, like adults, sometimes deliberately lie (see Talwar et al., 2002), or that older children and adolescents can lie quite convincingly. Deliberately false allegations are infrequent, but they do occur, as Box 11.1 shows. Occasionally, adolescents with a grievance against a teacher may deliberately make a false allegation (Anderson and Levine, 1999).

Deliberate self-serving lies of children and adolescents are not, however, the main concern of those who question the reliability of children's accounts of sexual abuse. The critical problem is whether children can be induced by pressure from others to make up events that didn't happen.

In the 1980s, sexual abuse charges were brought against day care workers on the basis of testimony by children as young as three and four. The day care cases came up when initial allegations of abuse reached a number of parents. A preschooler may have made statements to a parent that suggested the children may have been abused by their teachers. The very young children were questioned repeatedly by many people, including therapists. In some cases, the children made fantastic accusations: charges of satanic ritual abuse, of videotaped sodomy (but no videotapes were ever found), of mutilations of animals or people, or of riding on sharks (Ceci and Bruck, 1995). In some cases, interviewing practices and the conditions under which the children finally made statements were so questionable that charges were dropped and juries failed to convict. In other cases, however, children's testimony resulted in criminal convictions despite the fantastic quality of their accounts, (Rosenthal, 1995). Kelly Michaels's conviction in the Wee Care case, is an example (see Box 2.3). Michaels's conviction was eventually overturned on appeal. An amicus brief prepared by a committee of concerned scientists was instrumental in bringing research to the appellate court's attention. When they voted to convict Michaels, the jurors seemed to discount the fantastic

BOX 11.2

A Legal Case in Point: The Fells Acres Day School Case

In 1987, Cheryl Amirault LeFave was convicted in a jury trial of four counts of indecent assault and battery on a child under 14, and three counts of rape of a child under 16. Nine children testified against her. Children who had been repeatedly interviewed by therapists and, before that, by parents and law enforcement officials gave the main testimony against her. Two children spoke of a robot that would hurt them if they failed to cooperate with the investigation. Another said he was tied naked to a tree in full view of classmates and teachers. There was no corroboration. A girl said she was penetrated with a 12-inch knife. She never exhibited any signs of injury. Prosecutors claimed that the operators of the day care center were producing child pornography, but no photographs or videos were found.

In 1998, after having served ten years in prison, a Massachusetts judge overturned LeFave's conviction. The judge heard testimony by psychologist Maggie Bruck and psychiatrist Diane Schetky, who testified that research published since Amirault LeFave's conviction cast doubt on the veracity of children's testimony obtained under the conditions described in the trial.

In his opinion, Judge Borenstein said that prosecutors argued that children never lied or made up stories about sexual acts, and wouldn't talk about these unless they had experienced them. These are common beliefs shared by many professionals, but they are inconsistent with subsequent research. At the original trial, prosecution expert witnesses also testified that it was a pattern for children to deny abuse, then disclose, recant, and disclose again (child abuse accommodation syndrome). This pattern, they said, made it necessary for interviewers to use suggestive techniques. However, in briefs and at the appellate hearing, experts testified that suggestive techniques could lead children to make inaccurate reports.

Judge Borenstein concluded that the prosecutor's attitudes and practices enhanced the "risk of convicting innocent people for acts that probably did not occur." The judge described the suspect techniques:

1. Interviews with high-status adults such as police: children defer to these adults, and the relationship increases their vulnerability to suggestion.

2. Stereotype induction: the interviewer repeats characterizations of the alleged perpetrator until the child comes to believe the characterizations.

3. Use of leading questions rather than open-ended questions: the child is likely to answer even if he or she does not know or doesn't have an answer.

4. Pretending, speculation, and fantasy: the interviewer asks the child to pretend or to imagine, encouraging the child to stretch the bounds of reality or to believe that the interviewer is not interested in the truth.

5. Repetitive questioning: interviewers refuse to take "no" for an answer and imply by repeated questioning that the child's answer was "wrong."

6. Repeated interviews: inaccurate reports emerge after repeated interviews because the interviewer may plant suggestions that can emerge later as the child's memory of an event.

7. Source monitoring problems: when young children are asked to pretend about an event, they may have difficulty later distinguishing the pretended event from a "real" memory.

8. Use of anatomically detailed dolls and drawings: the research, the judge said, showed that their use fosters inaccurate reports. A single exposure may result in an increased interest in sexual play and in a discussion of sexual themes.

9. Emotional tone of the interview: interviewers may create an atmosphere of fear by telling the child, "You're scared," or by leveling accusations.

10. Use of rewards: interviewers may reward children when the children produce stories that are consistent with the interviewer's expectation.

11. Peer pressure: interviewers may tell children that others have already told in an attempt to elicit disclosures from them.

Judge Borenstein said that these techniques reflected "interviewer bias," "were suggestive and dangerous to the truth-finding process," and could result in false narratives that cannot be distinguished from true narratives. Children may come to believe what they say, making it more compelling for jurors to believe them. Based on his review, he said Cheryl Amirault LeFave had been convicted on unreliable evidence and ordered a new trial.

The state appealed Judge Borenstein's decision and won (*Commonwealth v. Cheryl Amirauit LeFave*, 1999). The appeals court said that the issues had been covered in the trial, and the new research was not really "new evidence" as it is defined in the law. A policy issue was behind this ruling: "to hold otherwise would provide convicted defendants with a new trial whenever they could find a credible expert with new research results supporting claims that the defendant made or could have made at trial" (p. 181). However, Cheryl LeFave was released from prison when the prosecutor agreed with a motion she filed to reduce her sentence.

elements of the children's testimony or to believe that these elements must have been stimulated by real experiences. Some clinicians would agree that real experiences can be altered by children into seemingly tall tales. Everson (1997) argues that bizarre, improbable, and fantastic elements in children's stories may be understood as systematic transformations of experiences interacting with the abusive event. He concluded that children's stories of abuse should not be dismissed simply because they contained improbable or fantastic events.

In actual cases of alleged abuse, however, children are not simply transforming stories on their own. They may be subjected to a great deal of pressure and influence. Cole and Loftus (1987) describe a three year old who allegedly was sexually abused. The child was interviewed by parents, police, social workers, prosecutors, attorneys, and physicians more than 30 times, and, in addition, had been in psychotherapy. The child's story developed in the course of the interviews, but details of the story could not be confirmed. The judge in that case disallowed the child's testimony. In a case in Jordan, Minnesota, children were separated from their parents during interrogation, and told that they wouldn't be able to go home unless they revealed information about abuse. They were interrogated as many as 50 times, over weeks and months. Answers were suggested to the children by telling them what others had said. Under those conditions, the initial allegations of sexual abuse turned into stories of mutilation and murder that could not be confirmed. Zealous child protection workers, police, and prosecutors have also been implicated in cases in which allegations of abuse were compounded by allegations of satanic practices, none of which could be corroborated by independent evidence (Van De Kamp, 1986). Ceci and Friedman (2000) argue that repeated interviews with strong suggestions and pressure on the child to reveal abuse occur much more frequently than we would like to think.

A similar problem of influence may arise when children first disclose to parents. In general, parents are reasonably good reporters of what their children have told them (Schaaf et al., 2002), but in some studies, they are not (see Ceci and Friedman, 2000, for a review of this area of research). We have very little good information on how parents or others who may be the initial recipients of disclosures handle the disclosure.

One response to the problem of repeated interviewing of children has been the development of the Child Advocacy Center. In communities that have such centers, police, prosecutors, child protection workers, physicians, and mental health workers cooperate to minimize the number of interviews and the intrusion and pressure on the child. There is now a National Children's Advocacy Center to help people in local communities develop such centers. In theory, interviewers are trained to avoid suggestive interviewing techniques, and many interviews are videotaped. Another solution, prompted by the Kelly Michaels case, has been the use of pretrial "taint hearings" that focus on interviewing practices. A judge may exclude the child's testimony if the child had been exposed to overly suggestive questioning.

The taint hearing is controversial. Children may come to agree with false statements as a result of repeated or leading questions, but the hearing may protect a defendant at the cost of losing valuable evidence. However, children produce more accurate information when responding to direct as opposed to open-ended questions. Moreover, the statements they make under repeated questioning may, in some instances, still be true even if elicited by questionable interviewing practices (Schaaf et al., 2002; Ceci and Friedman, 2000). If the testimony is excluded because of taint, then an offender may go free. Ceci and Friedman suggest that the child who has been exposed to questionable interviewing practices should be permitted to testify, but so should an expert on child suggestibility to provide a context for understanding the child's testimony.

In the majority of cases, however, when children do reveal abuse, it is highly likely that their reports are accurate, and they have not been subject to undue pressure from overzealous child protection workers. For example, 70 percent of suspected child maltreatment reports, including reports of sexual abuse, are dismissed as unfounded after a single interview by child protection workers, and very few cases are referred for criminal prosecution (Levine et al., 1998). These data suggest that children are not routinely subject to undue pressure from overzealous child protection workers. Nonetheless, many interviews in cases that do go forward show evidence of questionable practices.

Ceci and Friedman (2000) note,

> Thus at one extreme we can have more confidence in a child's spontaneous statements made prior to any attempt by an adult to elicit what they suspect may be the truth. At the other extreme, we are more likely to be concerned when a child has made a statement after prolonged, repeated, suggestive interviews. Unfortunately, most cases lie between these extremes and require a case-by-case analysis (p. 59).

We can agree that it may be possible to induce false memories. We can also agree that professionals cannot reliably distinguish between induced false memories and real memories in any individual case. Because the legal system operates on a case-by-case basis, we try to bring to bear the best information we can. The best information is population based; it doesn't answer questions about the individuals before the court. Perhaps this is one reason prosecutors do not rely on expert witness testimony routinely in sex abuse cases (Goodman et al., 1999).

327

Protecting
Children
Against the
Stress of
Testifying

The problem of balancing children's needs to be heard and helped with defendants' rights to due process of law is fraught with difficulty. We wish to make it easy for children to report their concerns and to obtain protection against those who would exploit them by using positions of trust or authority, but the goal is hard to achieve. In the sex abuse cases involving Catholic priests, the children were reluctant to come forward while they were being abused, and some didn't reveal the abuse until several years later when they were adults. Had they revealed the abuse at the time and been believed, they and other children would have been protected. On the other hand, even a low rate of false allegations can have serious consequences over a population of accused persons. Any allegation that becomes public and leads to prosecution will profoundly affect the alleged abuser's reputation, may cost thousands of dollars in legal fees to defend, and in some instances may result in very expensive damage suits against employing institutions (Dokecki, 2004). It is difficult to strike the right balance between encouraging children to reveal abuse and protecting defendants' rights.

Research showing the dangers of some approaches to interviewing, accompanied by training materials and interview protocols, may help professionals working with children to avoid the worst excesses (Poole and Lamb, 1998). New research is also increasing our understanding of the personal and situational determinants of the accuracy of children's response to questioning about their memory for events, and how these are affected by individual differences (Quas, 2005).

Better-trained child protection workers, specialized law enforcement personnel, and prosecutors better attuned to the hazards of overly zealous interviewing and more knowledgeable about the characteristics of children might reduce the use of egregiously inappropriate investigation techniques. Video recording interviews may also be helpful. Interviewers, knowing their work can be reviewed, may be more careful. However, the existence of the video record may open the child's testimony to more question because it is difficult for any interviewer to avoid some practices that could be criticized.

Protecting Children Against the Stress of Testifying

The atmosphere of a courtroom is designed to symbolize the authority, the dignity, and the solemnity of the proceedings. The courtroom itself, often impressively decorated in wood and marble, and often of imposing size, expresses the formality of the occasion. The judge sits high up on a bench and wears a black robe. A U.S. flag and a state flag will be prominently placed. Except for spectators permitted in the public courtrooms, none of the adults—attorneys, clerks, court stenographer—will be dressed informally. One or more bailiffs will be in police uniform. The setting can be awesome if not intimidating for adults, and much more so for children. In criminal trials and related pretrial hearings, the child witness, most often as a victim, is subject to direct examination by the prosecuting attorney, and to whatever amount of cross-examination the defense attorney wishes to conduct. The accused will be sitting nearby, readily visible from the witness stand. Children, no less than adults, may be anxious about participating in a criminal prosecution, and testifying in court in front of strangers.

If participating in prosecutions harms some children emotionally, then the state has some responsibility to protect them. Moreover, children who are anxious and upset may not be able to participate fully and adequately in prosecutions, so a guilty party may go free. States have been experimenting with law reforms to find ways for prosecutions to go forward without subjecting children to harmful or debilitating stress. Many jurisdictions are developing Child Advocacy Centers; the centers try to coordinate child protection and law enforcement investigations to reduce the number of times children are exposed to questioning. Some state laws permit a child witness to have a supportive person present during testimony (Whitcomb, Shapiro, and Stellwagen, 1985), a reform consistent with research that shows that in general, young children report on their experiences more accurately and resist misleading questions better when interviewed by a supportive person (Carter, Bottoms, and Levine, 1996; Quas et al., 2005). Prosecutors say they often encourage the presence of a support person in the courtroom (Goodman et al., 1999). However, new research by Quas and her associates suggests there may be important individual differences in children's response to support that may have a basis in autonomic nervous sytem responses to stimulation. In the next section, we will review several other techniques used to help make child witnesses feel more comfortable. Courts are faced with the problem of deciding when procedures intended to protect the child witness may impinge on a defendant's rights.

Closing the Courtroom

Some states have experimented with laws that exclude spectators from trials in which the testimony may be particularly difficult or embarrassing for the witness. For example, suppose a 13 year old allegedly raped by her father has to testify. In addition to the difficulty of testifying about sexual activity with her father, should she have to tell her story in a courtroom full of strangers? (The question has also been raised with regard to adult victims of sex crimes.)

State laws allowing the public to be excluded from trials have encountered constitutional challenges because the Sixth Amendment to the Constitution guarantees "the right to a speedy and public trial." A public trial is a safeguard against arbitrary government actions. However, spectators are not permitted in grand jury proceedings, and the judges may at their discretion require a **closed courtroom** during pretrial motions. The U.S. Supreme Court prohibited states from establishing blanket rules excluding the press and the general public from all criminal trials involving victims of sex offenses who were under age 18. The courtroom could be closed, but only after an individual determination that the child witness in the particular case will suffer injury over and above that involved in simply testifying (*Globe Newspaper Co. v. Superior Court*, 1982).

In actuality, prosecutors rarely request that spectators be excluded (Goodman et al., 1999). The problem is more one of protecting children from exposure in the media, and that requires self-restraint on the part of the press. Moreover, many observers do not believe that the audience is a major source of anxiety for children who testify (Whitcomb, Shapiro, and Stellwagen, 1985).

Avoiding face-to-face confrontation

Confrontation with the defendant can cause great distress to many children and youth who are called to testify. Because of the distress, a number of states have tried to limit direct confrontation with the defendant. These efforts have encountered constitutional obstacles. The Sixth Amendment to the Constitution gives all criminal defendants the right "to be confronted with the witnesses against him."

Hearsay evidence. One way to protect a child witness from face-to-face contact with the defendant is to allow the child witness's statements made to others (e.g., doctor, teacher, and friend) to be introduced into court in testimony made by the person who heard the statement, without the child testifying. That kind of testimony is technically

329

Protecting
Children
Against the
Stress of
Testifying

BOX 11.3

When Is Hearsay Allowed?

In *Idaho v. Wright* (1990), the U.S. Supreme Court disallowed a statement given by a two-and-a-half-year-old child to an examining pediatrician. The pediatrician testified that the child told him that her daddy touched her with his "pee pee" and said, "Daddy does this with me, but he does it a lot more with my sister than with me." The Court found that in this case, the statements and the conditions under which they were reported did not have sufficient "indicia of reliability" to be admitted. However, the Court said that stringent safeguards to ensure reliability of hearsay (videotaped examinations, no leading questions, and conduct of the interview "blind," without knowledge of what allegedly had happened) were not necessarily required for hearsay testimony to be admitted. (See McAuliff and Kovera, 2002, and Lyon, 2002, for discussions of hearsay evidence and child witnesses.)

hearsay (statements made out of court, not under oath, and not subject to cross-examination, introduced as proof of the proposition in the statement). The use of hearsay may deny the defendant the Sixth Amendment right to confront witnesses. Under the rules of evidence, hearsay is generally not admissible at trial, unless one of the few recognized exceptions for hearsay testimony applies. The hearsay testimony may be admitted, but only if the evidence has sufficient indicia of reliability (see Box 11.3). Myers et al. (1999) interviewed actual jurors about their response to hearsay testimony about child sexual abuse. The results were complex. If anything, hearsay testimony by a confident adult witness about what the child said was rated as credible as direct testimony by a child. If legally admissible, hearsay can protect the child, and can be used with little damage to the case against the defendant, but whether such testimony would prevail in the absence of testimony by a child is an open question.

Closed-circuit video testimony. Another strategy for protecting child witnesses is to find a way for them to testify without having to look at, and be looked at by, the alleged abuser. A simple screen in the courtroom between a child witness and a defendant was ruled an unconstitutional infringement on a defendant's right under the **confrontation clause** of the Sixth Amendment (*Coy v. Iowa*, 1988). Another method used by states to protect child witnesses is to allow the child to testify by means of **closed-circuit video testimony.** In that procedure, the child, the prosecutor, and the defense counsel go into a nearby room. The judge, jury, and defendant remain in the courtroom. The child witness is questioned by the prosecutor and cross-examined by the defense attorney, who can communicate with the defendant by a telephone. The child's testimony is relayed to the courtroom by closed circuit, where the judge, jury, and defendant view it on television screens. The approved procedures may vary in detail in the 37 states that permit some form of videotaped testimony (McAuliff and Kovera, 2002).

Maryland law permitted such a procedure if the trial judge first determined that the child testifying would suffer such emotional distress when confronting the defendant that the child could not "reasonably communicate." Sandra Craig, owner of a private kindergarten and prekindergarten center, challenged the law. She was indicted for having sexually abused a six year old who had attended her center. The prosecutor asked the judge to allow child witnesses to testify by means of closed-circuit video.

BOX 11.4

A Legal Case in Point: How Will a Child Respond in Court?

David Gottwald III, age ten, was attacked by his mother with a pickax. She killed his two half sisters in the same attack. David suffered nightmares about the attack. The prosecution wished to have him found vulnerable so he could testify by closed-circuit video. The defense wanted David to testify face-to-face with his mother in open court because she was planning an insanity defense. The defense thought the mother's insanity defense might be helped by the boy's appearance in court. The trial judge refused to declare David a vulnerable child and would not permit him to testify against his mother by closed-circuit video. The judge said New York law only authorized closed-circuit video testimony in cases of child sexual abuse.

David Gottwald testified in open court. He described how his mother attempted to kill him by hitting him with a pickax and cutting his throat. He testified to seeing the dead bodies of his younger sisters on a bed. His mother had killed them a little while earlier. According to a newspaper report, he testified clearly. At least on the surface, he did not appear to be overly stressed by the ordeal of testifying. We have no information about the emotional after-effects on David, positive or negative, of reliving the events while testifying against his mother.

No one examined David Gottwald beforehand to determine how he would respond while testifying. However, a prediction of how well he could testify, based simply on the horror of the situation, would have been wrong. Montoya (1995) claims that mental health professionals are biased toward seeing children as vulnerable in order to try to protect the children. They may "overpredict" vulnerability.

The judge heard testimony from expert witnesses who said that the children would suffer emotional distress and would be unable to communicate in the defendant's presence. The children testified using closed-circuit video, and Craig was convicted.

The case reached the U.S. Supreme Court. At this point, the American Psychological Association (APA) decided that psychology as a science and a profession had sufficient interest in the case that it was willing to file an amicus curiae (friend of the court) brief. The brief summarized its view of psychological and other social science research that had some bearing on the legal issues in the case (see Chapter 2 for more on amicus briefs).

APA's brief (Goodman et al., 1991) argued that protecting potentially vulnerable child witnesses is an important state interest. The brief reviewed data showing that a significant number of child victims of sexual abuse exhibit symptoms of distress. Testifying in court seemed to maintain some children's symptoms and impeded their recovery (Goodman et al., 1992). Goodman and her associates used standard behavior checklists (Child Behavior Check List, or CBCL) filled out by the child and the parent to measure the children's degree of emotional disturbance initially and seven months later, on follow-up. Goodman and her colleagues were careful to point out that not all children suffered, and, in fact, some showed decided improvement as a result of testifying.

Research cited in the APA brief showed that children mention confrontation with the defendant as the most difficult part of testifying. This point was important for the legal case because it pinned the children's distress to the confrontation itself. The brief also cited laboratory research showing that, when children testified under conditions of heightened emotional arousal, their testimony was likely to be less accurate and less

331

Protecting
Children
Against the
Stress of
Testifying

FIGURE 11.4

Justice Sandra Day O'Connor
U.S. Supreme Court Justice Sandra Day O'Connor wrote the majority opinion in Maryland v. Craig *that permitted child sexual abuse victims to testify before closed-circuit TV under some conditions. Her opinion cited research conducted by psychologist Gail Goodman and the amicus brief submitted by the American Psychological Association. Justice O' Connor retired from the Court in 2006.*

complete. If children's testimony when faced with the defendant was less accurate and less complete, the APA brief argued, the child's confrontation with a defendant might in some cases "actually disserve the truth seeking rationale that underlies the Confrontation Clause" (Ogden, 1990, p. 4).

APA brief cited in majority opinion. The Court ruled that the closed circuit video procedure could not be used automatically, only when there was indication that it was necessary to protect the child, and to ensure that the child would give his or her best testimony (*Maryland v. Craig*, 1990). Justice Sandra Day O'Connor (Figure 11.4), who wrote the majority opinion, noted that it was an important state interest to protect the physical and psychological well-being of child abuse victims. Her opinion included citations to the APA brief and to Goodman's research in support of the proposition that testifying in court may be psychologically traumatic for some children. Her opinion cited APA's brief when she acknowledged that a confrontation that causes significant emotional distress to a child would "disserve the Confrontation clause's truth seeking goal." Justice O'Connor also upheld the use of expert witnesses to advise the court about the potential trauma to the child and about the potentially adverse effects on the child's testimony.

In this case, an interpretation of a constitutionally based right, the Sixth Amendment right to confrontation, was influenced, at least in part, by a summary of psychological data. The APA's arguments were important enough in shaping the rationale of the case to warrant citations in the body of the Supreme Court decision. The Court doesn't always use psychological data provided to it or use the data correctly (Faigman, 2004). However, the attention given to psychological research in judicial opinions shows that psychological research can have very important and far-reaching effects in the legal system.

Criticism of the APA amicus brief. Underwager and Wakefield (1992) were sharply critical of the APA's amicus brief in *Maryland v. Craig.* They argued that the APA's brief took a stronger advocacy position than the underlying research warranted. They said the research was not sufficiently developed to warrant an authoritative recommendation to the Court that a constitutional right should be curtailed. They argued that using video because of a child's fear of testifying face-to-face with the defendant assumed the defendant's guilt. In addition, they were highly critical of the proposition that children's behavior on the witness stand could be predicted with any degree of accuracy (see Box 11.4). (For a response to these criticisms, see Goodman, Levine, and Melton, 1992.)

Is video testimony unfair to the defendant? Justice Scalia, who wrote in dissent in *Maryland v. Craig,* also asserted that it was unfair to defendants to have the children testify by closed-circuit video because jurors could infer that the children were afraid of the defendant, and that the defendant was therefore guilty. If true, it is an important criticism of the ruling.

The hypothesis that having children testify by video would lead jurors to infer guilt was put to the test by Goodman and a group of her doctoral students in a huge simulated jury trial project. The experiment involved 186 children and 1,201 mock jurors selected from the community (Goodman et al., 1998). Five- and six-year-old (mean age six years, one month), and eight- and nine-year-old (mean age eight years, four months) children participated in a play session with a confederate who was called a "babysitter." In a second session, the "babysitter" made a movie of the child putting a costume on over the child's clothing. In one condition, the children also placed stickers on their bare arms, toes, and bellybutton ("guilty" condition). In a second condition, the "babysitter" videotaped the children, but the children didn't expose any body parts ("not guilty" condition). The "crime" was videotaping children's exposed body parts.

Two weeks later, the children came to an actual city courtroom, where they were told that the babysitter was "perhaps not supposed to make the movie and might be in a little trouble because of it." They were then asked if they would be willing to be witnesses in a trial to find out what happened when the child was with the babysitter. Half the children testified in open court, and half testified using closed-circuit video.

This was an extraordinarily elaborate study. It was held in an actual courtroom. Jury-eligible citizens from the community were invited to participate as mock jurors. Experienced lawyers acting as prosecutors and defense attorneys questioned and cross-examined the children. A judge gave the mock jurors standard instructions and defined the crime as photographing exposed body parts. Attorneys made closing statements, and 12-person juries deliberated. (The IRB approved study was so expensive and so elaborate that it is unlikely ever to be replicated, although in principle it could be.)

The jurors more often found the defendant guilty when the defendant was "guilty," and not guilty when the defendant was "not guilty." The evidence was the most important factor in predicting verdicts. The use of closed-circuit video did not affect this relationship or undermine the presumption of innocence. Moreover, juror ratings of the fairness of the regular procedures and of the closed-circuit video procedures did not differ.

Another perspective. Montoya (1995) disputes the fairness of one way closed-circuit video to the defendant. She described a criminal case in which the children's **demeanor** when testifying in open court strongly influenced the jury's decision making. The defendant, Akiki, was accused of kidnapping and sexually abusing children he watched in a church nursery school. The prosecution wanted to use closed-circuit video, and mental health experts testified that the children would not be able to testify accurately in front of the defendant. Based on a hearing and personal interviews with the children, the judge did not allow the use of closed-circuit video, despite the expert testimony. Ten child witnesses took the witness stand in the courtroom with the defendant present. Each child testified for between an hour and a half to a little over three hours, including direct and cross-examination. None of the children appeared overly distressed by giving testimony, nor did they appear to be afraid of the defendant. Their behavior on the witness stand was in sharp contrast to the predictions made by the experts.

After a seven-month trial, the jury deliberated less than seven hours to return a "not guilty" verdict on 35 counts of child abuse and kidnapping. Interviewed afterward, jurors said they were impressed with the children's lack of fear of the defendant, and the defendant's calm behavior during the children's testimony.

Inferences from witness demeanor. If asked, many people would probably say (incorrectly) that they can always tell when someone is lying because they watch the person's body language. The belief that direct observation of witness and defendants will help jurors arrive at the truth is part of our legal culture. One argument against the use of closed-circuit video is that jurors would not have the same opportunity to observe witness demeanor that they have when a witness testifies in front of them. According to Montoya (1995), the jurors in the *Akiki* case were much impressed by the defendant's and the children's demeanor in court.

Jurors certainly pay attention to witness demeanor in arriving at judgments about guilt or innocence (Myers et al., 1999; Aubrey, 1989), but the interpretations of demeanor can cut both ways (Aubrey, 1989). We have very little evidence that jurors can detect truthful from untruthful or inaccurate from accurate testimony on the basis of a witness's demeanor. One reviewer of the social science evidence concluded that observing witness demeanor did not help jurors detect either lying or inaccurate testimony (Wellborn, 1991). (See also Goodman et al., 1989; Wells, Turtle, and Luus, 1989.) In Leichtman and Ceci's work (1995), 119 experts failed to distinguish videos of children who had made up stories after having been influenced by repeated questions from those who hadn't. Jurors in the Goodman and associates (1998) study were unable to detect which children had been told to lie (one of the conditions in this very elaborate study) and which were told to tell the truth, whether or not closed-circuit video was used.

Will video testimony be more complete? The APA brief was explicit in noting the lack of evidence as to whether anxious children's testimony would be improved by the use of closed-circuit television. The Goodman and associates (1998) simulated trial included a test of the effects of closed-circuit video on children's testimony. In this study, there were no significant differences in accuracy of free recall in the video condition or in the regular trial condition. Complex interactions of witness age, condition of the trial, and type of questions asked precluded any simple answer to the question of whether closed-circuit video improved children's testimony. However, because of ethical considerations, children who were so anxious they were unwilling to testify (47 of the 186 called) were not urged to try. They were excluded from the research. Therefore, the very children that *Maryland v. Craig* said should be the beneficiaries of closed-circuit video could not be included in the study. We don't know whether they would have benefited. The question of whether closed-circuit video testimony would help the most anxious children to testify more completely is far from settled.

Limits on use of closed-circuit video. The question whether the use of closed circuit video testimony would help anxious children testify may be of little practical importance because prosecutors infrequently use video. For one, some state constitutions are explicit in requiring a face-to-face confrontation (Grearson, 2004). Closed-circuit video testimony would be barred in those states. (States cannot diminish rights protected by the federal Constitution, but they can give their citizens rights beyond those the Constitution protects.) Even in states where it is allowed, video is little used. Although prosecutors accept that closed-circuit video may reduce trauma for some children, they do not believe that closed-circuit video is very helpful in producing guilty verdicts. Closed-circuit video procedures are expensive and intrusive.

Prosecutors are more willing to use other techniques to help children deal with the stresses of a trial: victim advocates, preparation of the child to testify by familiarizing the child with the actual courtroom, having a support person for the child in the courtroom, and using age-appropriate language in questioning children. Children might be taught to say, "I don't understand," when faced with confusing questions. None of these approaches impinge on defendants' confrontation rights. There is some evidence that these procedures reduce children's stress while testifying and enhance communication (Goodman et al., 1999; McAuliff and Kovera, 2002).

Preparing Children to Testify

Some clinics and some prosecutors' offices employ child advocates who help prepare children to testify. The advocate will develop a relationship with the child, and spend time explaining the nature of a courtroom and the role of the judge, the attorneys, the bailiffs, the court stenographer, and the defendant. The advocate will try to answer the child's questions, and, in some programs, allow a child to play with dolls and a toy courtroom. The advocate will also take the child to visit the courtroom before the child is scheduled to testify so that the child will be familiar with it. The advocate provides support for the child and the family, but will not talk to the child about what he or she might be asked in order to avoid a charge that the testimony was coached. Prosecutors rate these procedures favorably and say they use them frequently (Goodman et al., 1999). This type of preparation, which may be characterized as teaching coping skills for a specific stressful situation, may help overcome the child's discomfort in testifying (Sas, 1991; McAuliff and Kovera, 2002). Defense attorneys typically do not have the opportunity to build rapport with child witnesses before a trial, even though it might be helpful to their cases if they could (Montoya, 1995).

Lawyer's language. Lawyers may also benefit from preparation when they will be working with children. Two studies (Carter, Bottoms, and Levine, 1996; Perry et al., 1995) examined the effect on children's testimony of *lawyerese*, complex questions with many parts and with extraneous language ("You don't know if any of your brothers or sisters or if I was your brother—well any of your brothers or sisters didn't really tell what happened, didn't quite tell the truth once, you don't know of any of that happening in your family?" Quoted in Perry et al., 1995, p. 610). In both the Carter et al. and the Perry et al. studies, all children, but younger children especially, were much more accurate in responding and were misled less often by leading questions when the questions were simple. The children had more difficulty responding to questions when they included multiple clauses, negatives, double negatives, and difficult vocabulary.

Making children confused may have an effect on how jurors evaluate their testimony. Mock jurors give higher accuracy estimates to child witnesses who appeared more confident regardless of the child's age (Nigro et al., 1987). Child witness demeanor, certainty, and consistency in testifying are correlates of a child witness' believability to real jurors (Myers et al., 1999). Some lawyers, zealously defending their clients, may adopt complex language as a tactic to elicit hesitant reactions that can undercut children's credibility as witnesses to jurors. When this happens, we must raise questions about the degree to which moral considerations, as opposed to narrow legal-ethical considerations, should permit questioning tactics that will not clarify but only confuse. However, many lawyers may use inappropriate language simply because they lack understanding of how children perceive and think and of what is developmentally appropriate.

How Credible Are Child Witnesses to Jurors?

A child's credibility to an adult is important at many points before a case ever gets to trial. A potential child abuse case often begins when a child discloses what appears to be abuse to a teacher, a parent, or a neighbor who may or may not believe the child. If the case goes forward, the child will be interviewed by one or more police officers and, perhaps, a child protection worker and a mental health professional. Each of these will, in turn, speak to a prosecuting attorney, who will also interview the child. The prosecutor must decide whether or not to prosecute. The prosecutor's perception of the child's potential effectiveness as a witness may well affect that decision.

Once the case goes to trial, the jurors must evaluate the child's testimony and weigh that testimony in arriving at a decision. The problem of how a child witness is perceived by jurors has been studied by a variety of research methods. In some experimental studies, the child witness is cast in the role, in simulations or in vignettes, of a bystander witness, but not an active participant in the events. In other studies, the child witness testifies in the role of a victim (complaining witness). The issues that may be important to jurors when the child is testifying as a bystander and as a victim may be quite different. In mock jury studies, younger children as bystander witnesses tend to be less believable to mock jurors than older children or adults (Goodman et al., 1989; Ross et al., 1990). In practice, prosecutors say that children are rarely used as witnesses in other than sexual assault or incest cases where the child is a victim (Goodman et al., 1999).

Child as Complaining Witness (Victim)

Goodman and colleagues (1989) studied the perceived credibility of victims in a sexual assault case using a one-page written scenario in which the alleged perpetrator was a 28-year-old schoolteacher, and the victim was characterized as either 6 years old, 14 years old, or 22 years old. In this study, the mock jurors were more likely to say the defendant was guilty when younger victim–witnesses testified.

In another study (Duggan et al., 1989), mock jurors selected from the community watched videotaped simulated trials of the sexual abuse of a child. In the videos, the complaining child witness was 5 years old, 9 years old, or 13 years old. When individual juror votes were analyzed by the age of the complaining victim–witness, the 13-year-old complaining witness drew fewer guilty votes than either the 9 year old, who was most effective, or the 5 year old. In this study, the 13-year-old victim was the least credible both in eliciting guilty votes and in the mock jurors' ratings of witness credibility.

The mock jurors tended to attribute more responsibility to the 13 year old than to the younger witnesses for what had happened. Content analysis of transcripts of videos of the deliberation sessions showed that mock jurors discussed sexual fantasies and sexual interests that the 13 year old might have had, even though consent is not a relevant legal issue in a child sex abuse case. The 5 year old was viewed as cognitively less competent than the older children, and more subject to influence by a parent or by attorneys, but the jurors thought the 5 year old too unsophisticated to make up a story of sexual abuse. The 9 year old was cognitively more competent than the 5 year old, but not seen as having sexual interests (Aubrey, 1989). Several other studies using different methods supported these findings (Isquith, Levine, and Scheiner, 1993).

The tendency to attribute responsibility to the adult victim of a rape is well-known. However, these results and those obtained by Goodman and colleagues (1989), by Nightingale (1993), and by Gabora, Spanos, and Joab (1993) suggest that mock jurors may attribute responsibility for a sexual act to victims as young as 13 years old (but see Crowley, O'Callaghan, and Ball, 1994). In actual cases, based on court records, the rate of conviction is higher when a rape or sexual abuse victim is under 12 or over 40 (Williams, 1981). The results of the simulations parallel the outcomes of real cases in suggesting that, in rape or sexual abuse cases, the victim's sexuality may become an issue for jurors, even when it is not considered pertinent by the law.

Gender Differences among Jurors

There are important differences between male and female jurors in how they view sex crimes against children (e.g., Bottoms and Goodman, 1989; Goodman et al., 1998; Isquith, 1990). Females are more likely to believe the alleged victims than men, more likely to see the crime as serious, more likely to believe the victim suffered, and less likely to attribute responsibility to the child victim. Gabora and associates (1993), Crowley and associates (1994), and Goodman and associates (1998) reported gender differences in guilty votes and in ratings of the credibility of child witnesses and defendants. Are the results of studies strong enough to warrant advising defense attorneys to use peremptory challenges to female jurors in these cases? Probably not. Evidence is still critical in judgments of guilt.

⊠ Expert Witnesses, Child Witness Research, and the *Daubert* Decision

The *Daubert* and subsequent decisions (see Chapter 2) enhanced the trial judge's role as gatekeeper for the admission of expert testimony. The judge is to look to the scientific soundness of the research underlying the testimony the expert may give, and decide whether the science is a "fit" to the facts of the case on hand (Lyon, 2002). Because rules in state and federal courts differ, and because different states have differing evidentiary codes and case law, generalizations about what courts will and will not permit experts to testify about are somewhat limited (Lyon, 2002).

Expert testimony in child abuse cases is used for several purposes (Berliner, 1998). First, courts have generally admitted social framework testimony relating general information about child abuse and child sexual abuse, about how victims might react (e.g., delayed disclosure), and about children's susceptibility to factors that influence their memory (Lyon, 2002). Such testimony is accepted on the grounds that it helps the fact-finder (judge or jury) to understand testimony in the case. Judges look to cross-examination and presentation of opposing witnesses to show up any underlying weaknesses in testimony. The *Daubert* decision, making the judges gatekeepers, may limit the admission of some expert testimony, although the trend seems to be to admit it in child sex abuse cases (Lyon, 2002). Ceci and Friedman (2000) suggest courts should admit an expert to testify about the potential significance of circumstances surrounding a child's disclosure of sex abuse if that evidence is introduced.

Second, experts may be asked to give testimony presenting evidence that a child is exhibiting clinical symptoms which child victims of abuse often exhibit. This testimony has been admitted, but sometimes without careful scrutiny of the underlying scientific base. There is too little reliable evidence to permit a conclusion about whether a child was abused based on the presence of clinical symptoms (Berliner, 1998). When evidence of this kind was scrutinized by the Louisiana Supreme Court (*State of Louisiana v. Hypolite Foret,* 1993), the appellate court said that expert testimony based on the **child abuse accommodation syndrome** (in which children who have been abused deny abuse, then disclose, recant, and disclose again) should not have been admitted at trial.

Weighing the testimony by the *Daubert* factors, the Louisiana Court found the testimony inadmissible: (1) it was not generally accepted in the scientific community, and controversy existed about its use and validity; (2) based as it was on clinical and psychodynamic formulations, the concepts were "irrefutable" and could not be tested for accuracy; and (3) the clinical picture was prevalent in 68 percent of cases, and the 32 percent margin of error was too great to permit testimony about the syndrome to influence a criminal trial (error rate factor in *Daubert*). The Louisiana Supreme Court found the expert testimony prejudicial, reversed the conviction, and ordered a retrial.

McGough (1998) and Lyon (2002) discussed the effect that *Daubert* and related cases might have on the admission of expert testimony in child abuse trials in the future. Challenges to expert testimony, whether offered by the prosecution or the defense, may become more pointed. Experts, many of whom are clinical social workers with minimal scientific training, will have to be more cognizant of the scientific base for their testimony, and they can expect vigorous cross-examination. A deep appreciation of the research base will become increasingly important for experts, judges, and lawyers.

Expert's style. The issues go beyond whether or not the expert testimony will be admitted. The expert's style of testifying is also important (Kovera et al., 1997). In a trial in England (*Lillie and Reed v. Newcastle City Council et al.,* 2002) two nursery school teachers sued for libel because of a report the Council published accusing them of sexually abusing six children in their care. With his decision, the judge included an extensive statement (paras. 382–472) reviewing his reactions to two well-known, highly qualified American experts who testified about evidence related to the "disclosures by the children, and the potential significance of child behaviours as possible indicators of sexual abuse."

The judge responded positively to one of the experts' testimony:

> She was a careful and moderate witness. She was always ready to acknowledge the limitations of her experience or skill and to recognise that some of her opinions might have to be revised in the light of later knowledge or second thoughts. She was not in the least dogmatic. She seemed to me to be objective and measured in her assessments.

She did not claim to have all the answers, and she emphasized the limited value of some of the literature. In particular, she stressed more than once that there is often difficulty, when assessing data, in determining how certain one can be that any particular child or class of children has been abused. . . . I found her approach illuminating and in no way undermined in cross-examination. In particular, I did not find her prone to overstatement or exaggeration. Quite the opposite. She seemed especially keen to be as accurate as she possibly could while recognising the limitations of scientific studies into very young children. It is true that she had an informal, almost casual style. She tended to smile and laugh a good deal—certainly more than the average expert witness. But I did not construe this as in any way undermining the rigour of her analysis or the seriousness with which she approached her task. (paras. 418, 421)

The judge was less favorably impressed with the expert witness on the opposing side, a very well-qualified and well-recognized clinical researcher. The judge remarked, "I am wary of an expert who is prepared to clutch at straws . . . on the basis of incomplete information" (para. 430). He described his observations of the expert:

Professor F. seemed objective but so cautious as to be non-commital—making such observations as that it was a very complex case and that he was glad he did not have to decide the facts. When pressed in cross-examination, as to his methodology, he spoke very slowly and cautiously, his answers being circumlocutory and difficult to follow. For the most part, they seemed to amount to little more than saying that one had to gather as much information as possible before attempting to make a judgment. He seemed to experience particular difficulty when asked to explain with what degee of probability he was advancing his conclusions of sexual abuse; whether it was uniform in respect of all of the children or varied from child to child, and the extent to which his conclusions were based on individual cases or global impression. It was all a bit vague (para. 435).

The judge described a number of other parts of the testimony in which Professor F. seemed to be shifting the grounds for his statements. "At this stage, I could hardly keep up wth Professor F.'s footwork. At all events, I realised finally that I could place no reliance on him at all. It was a complete waste of time and money" (para. 450).

The plaintiffs in the case were each awarded $170,400 pounds ($310,000 U.S. dollars) (the maximum legal award) in their libel suit (FMS Foundation, 2002).

Summary

Historically, children below a certain age were considered incompetent to testify in court because of beliefs that their memories were less accurate and reliable than adult memories, and that they were more suggestible. Exceptions have always been made in individual cases, however. Today, the trend is to evaluate children's competence to testify on a case-by-case basis. The issue of their competence is especially important when the child is allegedly a victim of sexual abuse. In these cases, the child's report is often the only direct evidence of the crime. If the child's testimony is excluded, the case cannot go forward. But, if the testimony is included and the child's account is inaccurate, an innocent person may be convicted on the basis of flawed evidence.

Since the late nineteenth century, psychologists have conducted research to help judges and juries make decisions about the credibility of children's testimony. This field of study, still rapidly developing today, shows the potential of research to influence legal policy. It also shows how questions that arise in the legal arena set an agenda for psychological research. When early experiments involving tests of children's memories of objects or pictures were criticized for being irrelevant to memories of real events, psychologists were diligent and ingenious in working out sound research designs with improved ecological validity. Research groups have developed careful and elaborate studies of children's memory using staged events and unpleasant medical procedures.

By about the age of four years, most children understand the difference between truth and lies, but this doesn't mean they always tell the truth. The results of studies of accuracy and suggestibility are inconsistent and harder to interpret. Most studies have found that the accounts of children below age five are less reliable and accurate than those of older children, and younger children are more susceptible to influence. The variety of methods, and the variety of study conditions, make interpretation of conflicting results difficult. We are not warranted in concluding that children never lie, or that they always lie, or that they are or are never susceptible to influence. Unfortunately, we also can't conclude that professionals or laypeople can discriminate between inaccurate and accurate witnesses, those whose statements may have been influenced by suggestive procedures from those whose statements have not been influenced, or those who may be lying from those telling the truth. Studies suggest that jurors consider a witness's age when evaluating his or her testimony. Jurors and mock jurors give accounts of younger child bystanders less weight than accounts by older witnesses. However, when the child is the alleged victim of sexual abuse, younger child victim witnesses are more likely to be believed than adolescent victims.

Psychologists have also investigated the question of whether testifying will have harmful psychological effects on child victims or will upset them in ways that will make their testimony less credible. In one study, testifying did inhibit recovery from symptoms of distress among some, but not all, children. States have been experimenting with a number of procedures intended to protect children from the rigors of the courtroom or to make them better witnesses. These procedures include closing the courtroom, using closed-circuit video testimony, and preparing the child to testify. The APA brief was cited in the U.S. Supreme Court decision that permitted closed-circuit video in some cases. These approaches to protecting children are not used very often in the courtroom.

This is an active and changing field of research. The research has not yielded any simple answers but has helped to analyze the issues. The courts have been open to expert testimony, but given *Daubert,* we may well see more challenges to experts, which means that judges, lawyers, and experts will have to know a great deal more about the science underlying their testimony than before.

Discussion Questions

1. Why is the testimony of children, especially the testimony of alleged victims of sexual abuse, so controversial?
2. Research suggests that preschool children (ages two to four) report less full memories than older children, are more suggestible, and are less clear about the difference between truth and lies, memory, and imagination. Given these findings, can you think of any ways prosecutors could successfully make a case against an alleged abuser of a small child?
3. One of the assumptions underlying the Sixth Amendment right to confront witnesses is that it will be harder for someone to lie when the person they are accusing falsely is looking them in the eye. Can you design an experiment to test the validity of that assumption for adults? For children?
4. Do you think that children are more likely to be influenced by their parents' beliefs about an event than by other people's? How could you test that proposition?
5. What ethical constraints make it difficult to study child eyewitnesses?
6. Suppose that a physically mature-looking 13 year old is going to testify that she has been sexually abused. Can you think of anything the prosecuting lawyer could do to counter the tendency of jurors to find older child victims of sexual abuse less credible than younger victims? How could you test the effectiveness of this tactic?

Key Terms

child abuse accommodation
   syndrome
closed-circuit video
   testimony
closed courtroom

competence to testify
confrontation clause
demeanor
ecological validity
hearsay

leading questions
source monitoring
suggestibility

CHAPTER **12**

Intimate Partner Violence

In this chapter, we will discuss **intimate partner violence (IPV),** which is violence directed toward a spouse, partner, or former partner. Men as well as women, and homosexuals as well as heterosexuals, can be victims of IPV. IPV affects all members of the household, is frequently associated with child abuse, and has far-reaching social and medical costs. Parties to violent partnerships may become involved with the criminal or family courts; with the child protection system, if children appear abused or neglected; and with the civil law system, if divorce and custody issues arise. States have been experimenting, with mixed success, with legal and social policies intended to reduce the problem of IPV.

IPV is a subject about which people feel strongly. Strong feelings are often associated with strong opinions and a preference for seemingly simple solutions. In this chapter, we will emphasize some of the complexities of the problem and the limits of solutions. We will see how legal processes can shape behaviors even in the private zone of personal relationships and also see the limits of legal interventions as a means of controlling or preventing IPV. We will look at

- the nature and extent of IPV.
- different ways of thinking about IPV.
- victim and abuser characteristics, and the dynamics of abusive relationships.
- the effects of IPV on children.
- the effectiveness of various social service and legal policies in stopping and deterring violence, including mandatory arrest, orders of protection, "no-drop" prosecutions, diversion-to-treatment programs, and child protective services interventions.
- IPV and custody and visitation disputes.
- partner murder and the battered woman defense.

The Discovery of Intimate Partner Violence (IPV)

Wives had few rights of any kind in the United States before the second half of the nineteenth century. A single woman lost the right to enter into contracts, to sue, to be sued, and to manage and control her own property when she married. A wife could not work outside the home without her husband's permission, and her wages belonged to him (Small and Tetreault, 1990).

Though home was the woman's sphere, it was the man's "castle" where he could rule with little fear of state intervention. Acts that would be treated as criminal **assaults** if the victim were a stranger or even a lover were not crimes if they involved husband and wife. Until the late nineteenth century, U.S. courts followed the **rule of thumb** promulgated in England in the seventeenth century by Lord Matthew Hale. To protect women, Hale ruled that a man was permitted to beat his wife so long as he didn't use a switch bigger around than his thumb. Hale also declared that marital rape was impossible because, with the marriage contract, a wife "hath given herself in this kind unto her husband, which she cannot retract" (Small and Tetreault, 1990).

Attitudes changed. After the Civil War, states enacted legislation giving married women basic economic rights. By the end of the nineteenth century, wife-beating was criminalized, but was rarely subject to prosecution. Well into the twentieth century, police and courts continued to view many intimate partner assaults as cases of natural passions getting a little out of control rather than as ordinary criminal behavior. (Figure 12.1)

In the 1970s, the women's movement challenged traditional notions of gender and family. Women's **advocates** reframed IPV as a public issue as well as a private problem. Women's groups organized **shelters** for battered women and developed grassroots support and advocacy programs. Scholars and clinicians undertook the first research investigating domestic violence as a crime and a social problem, not just a symptom of disturbed family relations.

In the 1980s, the states introduced legal and administrative reforms to enable prosecutors to use the criminal justice system more aggressively to curtail domestic violence. But changes in the laws were not implemented consistently, nor did they always have their intended effects (Bell, 1990; New York State Bar Association, 1988; U.S. Commission on Civil Rights, 1978). Further reforms followed. The federal government provided financial support to state programs, which instituted specified reforms and

FIGURE 12.1

Jane Addams and Ellen Starr

In the earliest years of Hull House, established in 1889, Jane Addams and her companion Ellen Starr took in a 15-year-old bride who was desperate to escape the nightly beatings administered by her husband.

funded new research initiatives (e.g., the Violence Against Women Act, reauthorized in 2005). The incidence of domestic assaults has gone down in recent years (Rennison, 2003). However, because the rate of all kinds of assaults has also gone down during this period, and because of other social changes, it is difficult to know how much of the drop is attributable to the policy of criminalizing IPV. Evaluations of specific police, prosecution, and court innovations have yielded mixed and confusing results (Buzawa and Buzawa, 2003).

States and localities are still considering whether and how to make the justice system more responsive to the needs of victims, and whether they may have relied too much on the criminal justice system to "fix" a multidimensional problem. They are looking to the social and clinical sciences for help. Meanwhile, social scientists have moved beyond their initial focus on abused wives and cohabiting partners, to look at abuse among dating couples, including adolescents; abuse among homosexual and lesbian couples; and abuse of men by women. They are also looking more critically at the feminist model of IPV and are considering other models that illuminate different aspects of this complex and persistent problem.

Domestic violence is a legal term, defined differently in different jurisdictions. We follow recent researchers in using the more comprehensive terms *intimate partner violence* (IPV) and *partner abuse* when discussing the problem. When speaking of government initiatives that use the term *domestic violence,* we will use that term also.

Models of IPV

Four models of IPV have dominated our thinking: feminist, psychotherapeutic, systemic or family and criminal justice. These theoretical models have implications for remediation and have shaped research agendas (Healey and Smith, 1998).

Feminist models. Proponents of feminist models believe IPV arises in the context of patriarchal society. Individual abusers use violence and the threat of violence to affirm their gender status by controlling their partners. They believe that abused women are not helpless victims, but are "survivors" coping and seeking help in whatever ways are available to them.

Psychotherapeutic models. Proponents of psychotherapeutic models see IPV as a symptom of underlying interpersonal problems or psychopathology. Interventions in this model focus on individual behavior and personality, emphasizing that IPV is not the social norm. In this theory, the combination of high emotion, dependency, and low external restraints characteristic of intimate relationships increases the likelihood of violent and domineering behaviors.

Systems and family-interaction models. Proponents of systems models apply the biological concept of a system to social units, including the family. A *system* is a unit maintained by the interactions of its components (Weihe, 1998). According to systems theory, behavior of each individual or each subunit within a social system is influenced by and in some way influences the behavior of the other components in the system.

Family interaction models conceptualize violence as a product of a dysfunctional system of conflict resolution to which the behaviors of both partners contribute. Thus, the family system as a whole is the object of study and intervention.

Criminal justice models. Much of the money assigned to IPV interventions and research has been channeled through agencies allied with the justice system. As a result, criminal justice concepts and approaches have influenced how we think about IPV. The mission of police and prosecutors is to protect society as a whole. In the criminal justice model, IPV is a crime against the state. Legislatures define crimes as distinct acts with a clear dichotomy between victim and perpetrator (Buzawa and Buzawa, 2003). Most states have defined IPV as physical assault or threat of physical harm. Victims have little control over the outcome of events in the criminal justice system.

These different models are complementary, rather than conflicting. However, each model leads researchers to ask different questions, and to develop and evaluate different types of interventions including legal interventions.

Defining and Measuring IPV

Prevalence is a term used in public health to refer to the percentage of the population who ever had a disorder or problem. **Incidence** refers to the number of new cases of a disorder or problem coming into the population in a period of time (e.g., in one year). Measures of the incidence and prevalence of a problem help policy makers decide how important it is, what resources should be allotted to it, and how much progress is being made in addressing it.

Because of differences in how IPV is defined and measured, studies of IPV yield different results. Advocates may choose to emphasize figures showing a higher prevalence, while the budget-minded or ideological critics of feminist models of IPV may emphasize lower estimates.

To measure IPV, researchers have to define it. Some researchers connected with the criminal justice system are interested in measuring acts that match statutory definitions of crimes. Their definitions involve intentional acts causing injury, or intimidation by threats of inflicting injury, with clear-cut victims and perpetrators. Social science researchers may want to study the continuum of violence, including relatively minor aggressive behaviors like shouting and throwing things. With narrower definitions, the prevalence rate is lower. With broader definitions, the rate is higher.

How social scientists define the problem of IPV is also influenced by their theoretical orientation and, if they are also activists, by their social and political agenda. In addition to acts that are defined as crimes, some researchers use the term *abuse* to include any verbal, physical, or sexual actions or threats by one partner used to psychologically *control* the other. Psychological abuse would include domineering behaviors like placing restrictions on a partner's access to money or social support, limiting their freedom to come and go freely, driving recklessly to scare someone, monitoring and questioning them about their movements, criticizing everything they do, hurting their pets, engaging in public humiliation and verbal belittling, and initiating legal harassment after a relationship has ended (e.g., bringing lawsuits, or making repeated anonymous calls to child protection, the fire department, and other agencies leading to investigations).

Definitions of *intimate or domestic partner* also vary among jurisdictions and among researchers (Fray-Witzer, 1999). The different definitions in these laws may affect the collection of statistics. State domestic violence laws generally cover unmarried couples living together as well as spouses, and former partners. Same-sex partners, those in dating relationships, including long term partners who do not cohabit and engaged couples, and rejected suitors may or may not be included. Violence in those relationships can still be prosecuted as crimes. Special provisions of law addressing domestic violence may not apply to same-sex couples in those states that have passed state constitutional amendments to define marriage as between a man and a woman.

Violence against minors is measured in some surveys and not others. For example, the National Crime Survey (NCS) includes violence against all women 12 and older, while the National Violence Against Women Survey (NVAWS) includes violence committed against women 16 and older. The National Family Violence Survey (NFVS), published by the U.S. Justice Department's Bureau of Justice Statistics, examines violence against people 18 and older. Violence between teenage boyfriends and girlfriends is thought to be quite high (Buzawa and Buzawa, 2003). When younger women or girls are included, child abuse by parents or assaults by brothers, dates or strangers may be counted as IPV along with abuse by partners, depending on how the questions are worded.

Research methods also affect findings. Some researchers base estimates on police, social agency, hospital emergency room, doctor, or hot line records. An example is the Uniform Crime Report compiled by the FBI using police department statistics. These approaches are limited by selection bias: they count only those victims who use public resources. Researchers estimate that at least half of the incidents of reportable IPV do not come to the attention of public agencies (Abate, 1997; Healey and Smith, 1998; Rennison, 2003). Record-keeping practices may be different even in similar agencies.

To overcome the selection and recording biases in official records, some research workers use sampling survey methods. They conduct telephone or face-to-face interviews or mail questionnaires to individuals randomly selected or to representative households. Household surveys always report much higher prevalence and incidence of IPV than counts from agencies or police. Surveys also present methodological problems. The findings will reflect what questions are asked and how they are worded (e.g., "Have you ever been 'assaulted'?" versus "ever been 'hit'?") Willingness to participate, willingness to disclose and the respondent's understanding of questions may differ among subgroups and subcultures.

How Common Is IPV?

The two most important governmental surveys are the NCVS and the NVAWS. Both include measures of physical and sexual assaults by intimates, family members, and nonfamily members, but their methods differ in some important details. A consumer of research has to pay careful attention to a study's methods. The NCVS, repeated yearly, asks a sample of men and women representative of the population as a whole whether they have been the victim of various crimes, including IPV, during the last year (incidence). The NVAWS, a state-of-the-art, random digit–dialing telephone survey, was conducted just once between November 1995 and May 1996 by the National Institute of Justice and Centers for Disease Control and Prevention. The respondents, 8,000 women and 8,005 men, were randomly selected within each U.S. Census region of the 50 states and the District of Columbia. It asked questions about rape, assault, and stalking by intimates and nonintimates in two time frames: over the person's life (prevalence), and during the last year (incidence).

The NVAW survey counted only people 18 and older in the IPV statistics. The NCVS included victimizations of people 12 and older. The NVAW survey used five questions to screen respondents for rape victimizations, and the NCVS only two. NVAW queried about a range of possible threatening and assaultive acts using the modified Conflict Tactics Scale (CTS; Straus, Gelles, and Steinmetz, 1980; see next section). The NCVS asked fewer questions about more serious incidents. If a respondent was assaulted or raped several times, the NVAW survey counted each attack as a separate incident. The NCVS counted reports of six or more crimes within a six-month period for which the respondent cannot recall details (e.g., "I can't remember when he beat me up; it was after some argument") as a single victimization.

Because of these and other differences, the NVAW survey (Tjaden and Thoennes, 1998) reported higher incidence and prevalence of violence against women than the NCVS of that year (Tjaden and Thoennes, 1998; Buzawa and Buzawa, 2003).

The most important nongovernmental surveys of IPV are the National Family Violence Surveys (NFVS) conducted by Straus and Gelles in 1976 (personal interviews with 2,153 respondents), 1985 (telephone interviews with 6,002 respondents), and in 1992 (telephone interviews with 1,970 respondents). Straus distinguishes the NFVS, a family conflict study, from crime studies. The NFVS and most other studies conducted by conflict researchers use the CTS (Straus, Gelles, and Steinmetz, 1980). Many of the items on the CTS are not crimes. The CTS asks questions about how people behave when they are settling arguments. It asks about reasoning, negotiating, and verbal aggression. The original version does not include questions about sexual humiliation, violence or rape. Straus (2000) reported that in 1992, the rate of minor violence was about 91 per 1,000

Table 12.1

Percentage of Persons Physically Assaulted by an Intimate Partner in Lifetime and by Type of Assault and Sex of Victim

Type of Assault	Women (n = 8,000)	Men (n = 8,000)
Total physical assault by intimate partner	22.1	7.4
Threw something	8.1	4.4
Pushed, grabbed, shoved	18.1	5.4
Pulled hair	9.1	2.3
Slapped, hit	16.0	5.5
Kicked, bit	5.5	2.6
Choked, tried to drown	6.1	0.5
Hit with object	5.0	3.2
Beat up	8.5	0.6
Threatened with gun	3.5	0.4
Threatened with knife	2.8	1.6
Used gun	0.7	0.1
Used knife	0.9	0.8

From Tjaden and Thoennes (1998).

(9.1 percent), and the rate of serious violence 19 per 1,000 (1.9 percent). This was considerably higher than the 1.3 percent of women and 0.9 percent of men who reported being physically assaulted in any way by an intimate partner in the prior year in the NVAW survey; it was also higher than the incidence reported by the NCVS respondents.

In deciding whether the "true" estimate of violence is closer to one percent or 11 percent, it is vital to pay close attention to the methods employed in the studies. Whatever the data source, IPV is a common crime. According to the relatively conservative NCVS figures for 2001 (Bureau of Justice Statistics, 2003), IPV made up 20 percent of all nonfatal violent crimes experienced by women in that year, and 33 percent of female murders. IPV also constituted 3 percent of nonfatal crime experienced by men, and 4 percent of male murders. The incidence of IPV declined from 1993–2001, as did other types of family violence and violent crime generally (Bureau of Justice Statistics, 2003; Bureau of Justice Statistics, 2005). In 2002, the number of women who reported in the NCVS being victimized by an intimate was down to about half a million. Men were the victims of about 73,000 assaults by partners (Bureau of Justice Statistics, 2005). The NCVS may undercount because it measures relatively serious acts only, and does not necessarily count repeat episodes separately.

About a quarter of the women in the NVAW survey said they were assaulted (22 percent) or raped (8 percent) by an intimate at some time in their lifetime (prevalence), compared with 8 percent of the men who said they were assaulted (Tjaden and Thoennes, 1998). Milder forms of assault were more common than serious ones.

A Chronic Problem

IPV is often chronic, affecting victims and their family for years. Between 20 and 65 percent of perpetrators arrested by the police will assault the same victim again within 6 to 12 months (Buzawa and Buzawa, 2003; U.S. Bureau of Justice Statistics, 1988; U.S. House of Representatives, 1990). The abused partner is at the same or greater risk after separation than before (Geffner and Pagelow, 1990). Between 1993 and 1998, the incidence of IPV was 30 per 1000 divorced or separated women, compared to about 2 per 1000 married women, and about 11 per 1000 never married women (Rennison and Welchans, 2000). Stalking, by definition repetitive, is often perpetrated by a former partner or date. Eight percent of the women and 2 percent of the men in the NVAW survey said they were stalked at some time in their lives (Tjaden and Thoennes, 1998). Stalking is now a criminal offense in many states.

A high percentage of the most violent batterers have high rates of mental health problems, alcohol and drug abuse problems, and histories of violence against strangers and acquaintances, as well as partner assaults (Buzawa and Buzawa, 2003; Kropp and Hart, 2000).

IPV does not necessarily continue or escalate over time. It is predominantly a problem of younger people. Women aged 16–24 are more likely to be severely victimized than any other group. The rate of intimate partner assaults declines with age and was down to about 10 percent for both men and women by age 40 (Healey and Smith, 1998; Straus et al., 1996). The rate of intimate partner murder, however, does not go down with age (U.S. Department of Justice, 2005).

Gender, Violence, and Abuse

The feminist model of IPV construes women as victim-survivors of male violence and intimidation. Women are unquestionably more likely to be seriously physically injured and to be terrorized by their partners than men (Straus, Gelles, and Steinmetz, 1980; Tjaden and Thoennes, 1998). Women account for between 65 percent and 95 percent of those seeking medical help for injuries resulting from partner violence (Stark, 1990; Zuger, 1998). Women are far more likely than men to be victims of sexual violence by intimate partners than men (NVAW survey; Tjaden and Thoennes, 1998).

While it is clear women suffer greater injury from intimate partners than men, findings about the relative rates of all aggressive acts by male and female partners are inconsistent. The NCVS and the NVAW survey both found that male perpetrators hugely out number female perpetrators. Women were the victims of 84% of spouse abuse and 86 percent of boyfriend or girlfriend abuse reported by justice system agencies and in crime surveys (U.S Department of Justice, 2005). However, men do report being attacked. The NCVS found that 15 percent of the victims of IPV and about one third of IPV murder victims were men (Rennison, 2003; Bureau of Justice Statistics, 2004; Straus, 2000).

In contrast with the two big government surveys, the National Family Violence Survey and 100 others studies using the Conflict Tactics Scale (CTS) have found rates of violence by women against men to be as high as rates of violence by men against women (Buzawa and Buzawa, 2003; Felson, 2002; Straus, 2000, 1999; Archer, 2000). In many households, both partners are violent. When a woman assaults a man who has previously not assaulted her, the chances that he will assault her in the future goes up. Severity of abuse and the recidivism rate among male abusers is also higher when the women engage in violence (Buzawa and Buzawa 2003; NIJ, 2004).

High rates of violence and abuse by women of men do not accord with the feminist patriarchal model unless the violence is defensive. Some activists fear that reports of female violence will create a blame-the-victim mentality and reduce support for terrorized women (McHugh, 1993). They noted limitations of the CTS which might explain the findings of high rates of female violence. Straus and colleagues (Straus et al., 1996) revised the CTS scale in 1996 to address some of these criticisms. Studies using the new scale continued to find high rates of abuse by women against men, and lower levels of serious injuries caused by women. There are however, cases of battered men. Four different studies have found that women hit first as often as men (Straus, 2000).

IPV Among Minorities

Methodological problems make it difficult to generalize research on IPV to minority groups. Members of some minority groups are more likely to have been left out of surveys altogether because they had no phones, they were more likely to refuse to be interviewed, or interpreters were not available. Sometimes researchers pool data from different minorities. For example, Mexicans, Puerto Ricans, Colombians, and Cubans may all be pooled as *Hispanic* or *Latin;* Chinese, Koreans, and Indians may be pooled as *Asians.* Immigrants from these very different countries may have different attitudes and experiences regarding IPV. An ethnic category may include first-generation immigrants and native-born Americans, and combine immigrants of very different class and education levels. Means for these groups may not give much useful information. Members of some minority group members may be prone to different self-reporting biases than other groups.

Measures have not been validated for different minority groups. For example, one study found no differences in severity and frequency of abuse between Latina and Anglo-American women. However, Latina women were less likely than Anglo women to label behavior as abusive unless it occurred frequently (Swan, 2000). Some minority women accept a gendered division of authority and power, as do some religious groups. Researchers need to distinguish the concepts of authority intrinsic to tradition or religiously-based patriarchy from concepts of coercion, aggression, and mistreatment. The belief that there is honor or spiritual merit in fulfilling assigned social obligations may also influence some minority women's responses to questions on surveys.

Intimate Partner Murder. IPV sometimes ends in death. Between 1976 and 2002, about 11 percent of all murder victims were killed by a current or former spouse or boyfriend or girlfriend (U.S. Department of Justice, 2005). This type of murder accounted for about one-third of murders of women of all races and about 3–4 percent of murders of men (U.S. Department of Justice, 2005). Murder by an intimate is the leading cause of death for African American women aged 15 to 45, and the leading cause of premature death for U.S. women overall (Chang et al., 2005). Pregnancy, delivery of a baby or the victim's decision to terminate the relationship may be triggers for partner homicide (Campbell et al., 2003). For example, an analysis of 57 spouse murders in New York State between 1990 and 1997 found that 75 percent of the victims had ended or indicated they wished to end the relationship at the time of the murder (Commission on Domestic Violence Fatalities, 1997). Girlfriends of all races are more likely to be murdered by partners than any other group of intimates (U.S. Department of Justice, 2005).

In recent years, the number of intimate homicides has been going down. Rates of murders of men by women have gone down much faster than the murder rates of women by male intimates. Thus, in 1976 women were the victims in 54 percent (1,600) of intimate murders and the perpetrators in 46 percent (1,357). In 2002, females were the victims in 76 percent (1,202) of intimate murders, and perpetrators in 24 percent (388).

Many women who killed their partners were, or claimed that they were, abused themselves. The declining rate of male intimate murders indirectly supports the hypothesis that many women who killed their male partners did so to escape an abusive relationship. The decline is associated with the availability to women of other resources for avoiding or escaping abuse, including legal advocacy programs, shelters, and hotlines (Browne, 1990; Zuger, 1998; Dugan, Nagin, and Rosenfeld, 2003). Women's economic status also improved in the period in which partner murders by women declined; economically independent women are more likely to leave abusive relationships, and less likely to feel that murder is the only way out. An extensive Chicago study found that compared to other abused women, abused women who killed their partners had experienced more severe and increasing violence, had fewer resources such as employment or education, and were more likely to be married with children or in a long-term relationship (Block, 2003).

Deaths might be prevented if lethality could be predicted accurately. Risk factors for lethality when there is prior physical abuse include a past history of violence, threatening behavior, excessive jealousy, stalking, and controlling daily activities. The use of drugs, especially "uppers," and gun ownership are additional risk factors. Some relationship factors also increase risk: the woman recently leaving or trying to leave, or a woman having had a child by another man. Researchers have been developing risk assessment instruments based on such predictive factors (Kropp et al., 2000; Campbell et al., 2003; Murphy et al., 2003).

These measures have promising psychometric properties. But because the proportion of violent relationships that end with one of the partners being killed is relatively small (i.e., a low base rate), any prediction measure and interventions based on it are likely to have a large number of false positives. For example, a recent study of one instrument found that 83% of women who were killed had scored above 4, but 40 percent of the abused women in the study who were not killed also scored 4 or above. (Campbell et al., 2003; see McClosky and Grigsby, 2005, for a good discussion of assessment and risk planning). Another problem is that few victims or perpetrators present for assessment prior to the murder. In 30 of the 57 homicides analyzed by the New York State Commission on Domestic Violence Fatalities (1997), there was no known physically violent behavior prior to the homicide.

IPV and Children

IPV is a problem for children as well as adults. In this section, we will describe relationships between IPV and child welfare. These data support the efforts to define witnessing abuse as a form of child maltreatment. In later sections, we will discuss social and legal reforms intended to coordinate child protection and battered women services.

Co-occurrence of partner abuse, child abuse, and neglect. Many homes in which IPV occurs include children (Rennison and Welchans, 2000). Between 30 percent and 60 percent of the children living in homes where there is violence between partners are abused (Browne, 1990; Edelson, 1997, 1999b, 2001; New York State Bar Association, 1988; Stark, 1990; Wohl and Kaufman, 1985). In 30 percent to 60 percent of the families where children are victims of physical abuse, mothers are also abused (Edelson, 2001; Fields, 1986). Usually it is the man who abuses the children; but abused women also abuse their children (Edelson, 1997, Ross, 1996). Women who are beaten are twice as likely to abuse their children as other women (Edelson, 2001).

Very small children may suffer directly from effects of violence against their mothers. Pregnant victims are four times more likely to deliver low-birth-weight babies than other women (Epstein, 1999). Women who are frightened, depressed, isolated, or in physical pain because of IPV have more difficulty providing emotional nurturing for their children.

IPV is also associated with homelessness in children; of female-headed homeless families, 43 percent listed physical abuse as one reason they were homeless. Workers at shelters for the homeless have identified IPV as a significant factor in homelessness (Kelly-Dreiss, 1990). The majority of the residents of shelters for women fleeing domestic violence are children (Edelson, 2001).

Children who witness violence are at risk of getting hit accidentally or if they try to intervene. About 62 percent of sons over age 15 living in families where there was IPV were injured while trying to protect their mothers (Epstein, 1999). A New York State study of 57 partner homicides (Commission on Domestic Violence Fatalities, 1997) found that in 24 of 36 cases, at least one child was present at the homicide.

Witnessing violence between parents. If partner abuse is chronic, children will probably know about it. Even if they do not see the abuse, it is likely they will hear the sounds of fighting, see their mother's injuries the following day, and make the connection. About 10 percent of the domestic violence 911 calls are made by children (Weithorn, 2001).

Children who have witnessed their mothers being assaulted, especially boys, show an elevated rate of emotional, developmental, and behavioral problems (Dutton, 1988; Fantuzzo and Mohr, 1999; Fields, 1986; Keenan, 1985; Rosenberg, 1987a, 1987b; Wohl and Kaufman, 1985). Exposure to both domestic violence and to violence in the community during childhood predicts poorer future adjustment (Edelson, 2001).

Some children develop "externalizing" symptoms such as aggressive behavior, defiance, and delinquency, while others show a high rate of "internalizing" symptoms like depression, anxiety, and withdrawal. Despite methodological problems (see Edelson, 1997, 1999a, 2001, for a good discussion of methodological issues), the consistency and strength of the findings (Fantuzzo and Mohr, 1999) strongly support the theory that witnessing violence between parents is associated with a higher incidence of behavioral problems. When appropriate comparison groups are used, the rates of severe psychiatric and behavioral difficulties exhibited by children living in violent homes exceed those exhibited by the children of unhappy but nonviolent marriages (Rosenberg, 1987b). However, only about 30 percent of children who witness parental violence exhibit problem behaviors (Lewis, Mallouh, and Webb, 1989). Most children in the studies coped with a very difficult situation.

One can hypothesize that witnessing their mothers abuse their fathers or other partners (Archer, 2000) or witnessing mutual couple violence puts children at some risk of distress and adjustment problems. However, research has generally looked at children of abused women who, as we have seen, are most often the victims of the most serious violence.

Is violence transmitted across generations? Children not only suffer from living in violent homes; there is also distressing evidence that children from violent homes are more likely than others to live in violent households as adults. Studies of the family of origin of male abusers consistently find that they were more likely than other men to have witnessed violence between their parents (Dutton, 1988; Edelson, Eisikovits, and Guttman, 1985; Geffner and Rosenbaum, 1990; Rosenbaum and O'Leary, 1981; Straus,

Gelles, and Steinmetz, 1980; Wohl and Kaufman, 1985; Buzawa and Buzawa, 2003; Ehrensaft et al., 2003). We don't know if women who abuse men witnessed parental violence as children. Abused women frequently have histories of having experienced abuse as children (Gelles, 1977; Rosenbaum and O'Leary, 1981).

We should be thinking preventively, but if we tried to intervene preventively we would encounter the same problems in prediction discussed in earlier chapters. Although a disproportionate number of spouse abusers grew up in violent homes, it does not follow that most boys who grow up in violent homes become abusive men. Nor are most abusers from violent homes: 85 percent of child and partner abusers did not witness violence between parents when they were children (Stark, 1990). Moreover, proposals for involuntary preventive interventions to protect health raise civil liberties issues (*Jacobson v. Massachusetts*, 1905).

Victims, Abusers, and the Dynamics of Abusive Relationships

Information about the characteristics of victims, abusers, and their interactions is helpful in developing appropriate legal interventions in IPV and related child custody and protection cases.

Social Factors Relating to IPV

IPV is higher in urban areas characterized by high rates of social problems and high unemployment (Healey and Smith, 1998). Conversely, an individual's likelihood of being victimized or victimizing a partner is related to what researchers sometimes call **stake in society variables.** The risk of IPV is reduced, but not absent, in more stable households characterized by marriage (as opposed to divorce or separation), home ownership, less frequent moving, and income that is adequate and stable. Factors that increase the risk of IPV include living in a disadvantaged neighborhood, having a partner who had two or more periods of unemployment, being young, divorced, separated, black, or living in rental housing (Rennison and Welchans, 2000; Buzawa and Buzawa, 2003). So-called *stake in society variables* also predict who will respond favorably to criminal justice and psychosocial interventions.

Typologies of Abuse

Better understanding of different patterns of violence and better ways of assessing the characteristics of individual abusers can help in assessments of dangerousness and in determining which men are likely to be responsive to treatment, court orders, or legal sanctions.

Studies using criminal justice sources have found that perpetrators of IPV are likely to have histories of mental illness, substance abuse, juvenile delinquency, and adult criminal arrests (Buzawa and Buzawa, 2003; Keilitz, Hannaford, and Efkeman, 1998; Klein, 1998; Simon, 1995). For example, a study of 663 restraining orders issued against alleged abusers in Massachusetts found that the men subject to the orders had an average of 13 previous arrests. More than half had been convicted of drunk driving or alcohol- or drug-related crimes at least once. Most of the men who had histories of violence had been violent with men as well as women (Klein, 1998). These were men who did not seem to respect the law, or to be restrained by contacts with it. However, family conflict studies made it clear that milder aggressive acts between arguing couples were far more common than the severe incidents reported to the police, and might differ from reported incidents in quality as well as severity.

Holtzworth-Munroe and Stuart (1994) and colleagues (Holtzworth-Munroe et al., 2000) have built on these findings to develop a typology of male perpetrators. They proposed four subtypes, which they elaborated using intrapersonal models of aggression:

1. Family-only batterers: least severe violence, little psychopathology
2. Borderline-dysphoric batterers: moderate to severe abuse, psychologically distressed, may engage in violence outside the family
3. Low-level antisocial batterers: moderate to severe abuse, mild-moderate extrafamilial aggression and criminal behavior
4. Generally violent antisocial batterers: moderate to severe abuse, highest levels of extrafamilial aggression and criminal behavior, likely to have antisocial personality disorder traits, substance misuse problems, impulsivity

This typology has held up well in validation studies using male subjects (Holtsworth-Munroe et al., 2000).

Johnson (1995, 2000) developed classifications based on an interactionist approach, looking at behaviors of both partners. He identified four groups based on a study with low-income African American and Latino women in Chicago (see also Cook, 2000; Swan, 2000a, 2000b):

1. Intimate terrorism (formerly "patriarchal terrorism"): one partner, usually the male, is violent and controlling. Responsible for most of the injuries reported.
2. Mutual violent control: both partners are violent and controlling.
3. Common couple violence: either partner is violent, or both are violent, but neither is generally controlling. Injury rates the same as in nonviolent relationships.
4. Violent resistance: one partner is violent and generally controlling, and the other is violent in response.

The "intimate terrorists" constituted 11 percent of the sample. Eighty percent were male.

From these studies of types of abusers, it seems clear that 10–20 percent of men who assault their partners are responsible for most incidents of severe violence (Buzawa and Buzawa, 2003). They are likely to have significant psychopathology, often have substance abuse problems, are violent with more than one partner and with people outside the family, and are often excessively controlling (Buzawa and Buzawa, 2003). Arguably, these men constitute the more serious threat to their partners, to public safety and are less likely to respond to rehabilitation than other perpetrators of IPV. Thus, one important policy question is whether the justice system should develop legal interventions targeted to this subgroup of repeat severe offenders.

Victims

Social and demographic factors put some women at greater risk of being hurt by partners. Poor women, African American women, American Indian women, women who live in urban areas, and women whose relationships are ending or have recently ended are most likely to be victimized (Healey and Smith, 1998). Women aged 16 to 24 are more likely than other women to be severely victimized, while women between the ages of 35 and 50 are at the greatest risk of being murdered by their partner (Rennison and Welchans, 2000; U.S. Department of Justice, Bureau of Justice Statistics, 2005).

Chronically abused women exhibit psychological symptoms of distress at higher rates than nonabused women (Stark, 1990). When an abused woman is a mother, symptoms of depression, anxiety, and substance abuse (as well as physical injuries) may interfere with her ability to care for her children. The questions of whether her psychological problems predated the abuse, and whether these problems will continue after the abuse ends, can become important for legal and social service decisions about the welfare of the children (see Yoshihama, Hammock, and Horrocks, 2006).

Information about the personal traits or behaviors of abused women before they were abused is rarely available. However, studies indicate that when women get out of the abusive situation, their psychological symptoms tend to abate or remit (Stark, 1990).

Abused women are not a homogeneous group. The majority do not appear to have preexisting psychological problems or personal characteristics that make them predisposed to enter and reenter abusive relationships. Only 13 percent of women interviewed in a hospital emergency room had been physically abused in a previous relationship (Dutton, 1988; Stark, 1990). A subset of women does repeatedly enter abusive relationships, and exhibits persistent psychological and interpersonal problems. Many of this group had been physically or sexually victimized by family members (National Institute of Justice, 2004).

Although abused women do not share common personality traits or family backgrounds, they may develop similar responses within the abusive relationship. Walker (1984) postulated that chronically abusive relationships are characterized by a repetitive three-stage cycle of interactions: (1) tension building and placation, (2) "contrition" after beatings, and (3) escalating violence. Walker believes that women caught in this cycle develop a cluster of distorted cognitions and symptoms she calls the "battered woman syndrome." Walker claims that women suffering from this syndrome feel depressed, helpless, ashamed, chronically afraid, and come to believe there is no escape. The symptoms are made worse by the abuser's attempts to isolate the woman socially. Other social and economic factors (e.g., not having savings or an income, poor employability, poor English, and immigrant status) may contribute to her feeling of being trapped and helpless.

Critics point out that there is little evidence to support the hypothesis of a distinct clustering of symptoms among battered women, or the assertion that IPV induces symptoms associated with learned helplessness in the victims (Faigman and Wright, 1997; Gordon, 1998; Schuller and Vidmar, 1992). Faigman and Wright (1997) argued that Walker's interview procedure was highly suggestive, and even in Walker's original data, no more than 58 percent of the women showed the three-stage cycle (see also Faigman et al., 2005).

Many women do suffer severe stress-related symptoms as a result of the abusive relationship. These sometimes, but not always, fit the criteria of posttraumatic stress disorder. However, there doesn't seem to be any one pattern of symptoms or syndrome that is typically experienced by abused women. We will discuss these issues below in light of psychologically based legal defenses put forward by abused women who assault or kill their partners and in relation to custody awards.

Ending Abuse: Why Don't Victims Leave?

All IPV does not necessarily continue or escalate over time. Sometimes IPV is a one-time event; the victim leaves after the first episode, or the abuser is never violent again. More often, aggressive acts are repeated in an ongoing relationship; the level of violence may remain the same, escalate, or dissipate (Block and Skogan, 2002). Only 25 to 30 percent of abused women leave the relationship after the first incident of violence (Stark, 1990). When a woman remains in a violent relationship, the general public and prosecutors, judges, and police may find her behavior puzzling. They sometimes assume that the abuse must not be serious.

Most victims eventually do succeed in changing the relationship or escaping it (NIJ Gender Workshop, Johnson, 2000). Leaving the relationship and legal termination of the marriage are the most common means of stopping the violence (Geffner and Pagelow, 1990). However, many abused women leave and return to their partners several times before separating permanently (Stark, 1990). The pattern of leaving and returning is frustrating and confusing for courts and service agencies trying to protect women and children.

Many women remain in or return to abusive relationships because they believe that ending the relationship will make them even less safe. This fear is reasonable. Many serious spouse-on-spouse assaults and most murders take place after divorce or separation, or when a woman tries to leave the relationship (U.S. Bureau of Justice Statistics, 1988; Block, 2003a, 2003b). Another reason is a fear their partner will kill himself. In one large study of women obtaining protective orders, 45.5 percent of the male partners had threatened suicide in the past; 13 percent had histories of attempted suicide (Conner, Cerulli, and Caine, 2002). Women's motives for staying with or returning to their partners include: love and affection, a sense of honor or religious duty, regard for children who love their fathers, and fear of family or community disapproval. Women fear the effects of divorce on their children, or, if their husband threatens a custody battle, they fear losing their children (Orloff, 1990; Stark, 1990). Efforts to reconcile are not unreasonable: beatings are rarely a daily event, many abusers express remorse after a violent incident, and some abusers may indeed be good husbands in other respects. Violence in many relationships, especially milder "common couple violence," declines over time. In short, many victims want to end the violence but not the relationship (Buzawa and Buzawa, 2003; Coker, 2001).

Women, especially when they have children, may stay with abusive men or return after leaving because they don't have the financial and other resources to start a new life. Employed women and those of higher socioeconomic status are likely to leave an abuser sooner and are less likely to return than housewives and women of lower economic status (Saunders, 1994; Stark, 1990; Saunders, 1988).

Responding to IPV: The Systems Network

An effective response to both IPV and child abuse requires extensive collaboration among the police, family and criminal courts, child protection services, battered women's shelters, corrections, medical and mental health services, welfare and social services, and housing agencies (Campbell, 1998). Unfortunately, cooperation among agencies, although easy to recommend, is hard to implement. If we adopt a systems orientation, we can appreciate that, even when they share a commitment to reduce IPV, actors in different systems have different tasks and different cultures, complicating their relationships.

Despite the problems, officials in different localities have been developing multisystem networks to help abused women and children. Here, we will look briefly at how legislative or administrative reforms of the medical and welfare systems may affect services to abused women. Reforms of the justice system and of child protective procedures intended to improve services to abused women and their children will be discussed in separate sections.

The Medical System

Physicians are among the first outside the family to recognize the most severe incidents of spousal abuse. The American Medical Association and the Centers for Disease Control recommend routine screening of female patients for abuse (American Medical Association, 2001; National Center on Women and Family Law, 1990). A physician's recognition of the problem may be the first step to obtaining help. Dentists, too, are

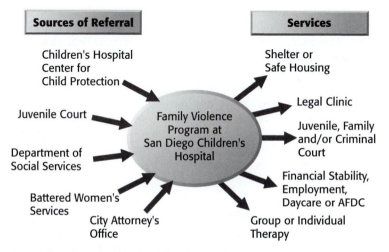

Battered mothers receive the following services:

INTENSIVE ADVOCACY
This includes accompaniment to all court hearings (criminal, juvenile, and family); assistance with obtaining legal services, emergency shelter, and long-term housing; help achieving financial stability through employment, child support, and welfare; and facilitation of access to child-care and medical services.

LEGAL CONSULTATION
This may consist of a one-time consultation with an attorney at the project, or referral to Volunteer Lawyers for *pro bono* representation.

FIGURE 12.2

The Family Violence Program (FVP) at San Diego's Children's Hospital

FVP provides services to mothers and their children who have experienced spousal abuse and child abuse. Women who are court-ordered and those without children are not accepted. Referrals for voluntary services come from the courts, law enforcement, Child Protective Services, schools, hospitals, shelters, and self-referrals.

From National Council of Juvenile and Family Court Judges, (2005).

being trained to recognize signs of abuse because the majority of the victims suffer face and head injuries (Little, 2004).

Some have proposed that medical personnel be required legally to report suspected IPV cases even if the woman denies abuse. However, advocates fear that abused women will not seek treatment if they know their cases will be reported to the police (Abbate, 1997).

Welfare and Social Services

The problem of IPV is embedded in other social problems (Lewin, 2001). Poverty increases the risk of IPV. About 20 percent of welfare recipients reported being physically abused by partners in the previous year (Pears, 2003). Many abusive men discourage their partners from working. If physical and mental health are affected by chronic abuse, then the ability to maintain employment is also adversely affected (Yoshihama, Hammock, and Horrocks, 2006). To leave the violent relationship and survive, women who don't work must rely on public welfare and on shelters (Albanesius, 2004; Dao, 2004; Yoshihama, Hammock, and Horrocks, 2006). Advocates fear that new eligibility and workfare requirements for welfare may make it more difficult for abused women to leave.

Partner abuse is widespread among some immigrant groups and presents special problems. Many immigrant women fear that if they leave their partner, they will lose custody of their children and may not be eligible for welfare services. Their position is even more complicated if they are not legal immigrants themselves, but, as often happens, are brought over by a husband who has established residency or obtained citizenship for himself (Abbate, 1997; Thompson, 1999).

◻ The Justice System's Response

As the public came to view IPV as a crime rather than a private problem, a consensus grew that new laws reforming the justice system were needed. Unfortunately, changes in the laws on the books didn't always lead to intended changes in the law in action. New laws were unevenly implemented, and where they were implemented, the effects were sometimes unintended and undesirable.

Police Response

Victims, witnesses, or neighbors often call the police to stop an incident of IPV. Police are frequently injured intervening in these emotionally intense conflicts. Historically, police officers were reluctant to make arrests when IPV involved less serious injuries. Instead, they acted as mediators or sent the abuser away to cool off. Some of the victims may have been encouraged by police not to bring charges or by prosecutors to drop less serious charges (Buel, 1990).

Advocates argued that perpetrators should always be arrested to make it clear that partner assault is a criminal offense. They believe that many abused women did not request arrest because they were fearful of retaliation (American Bar Association, 1995; New York State Bar Association, 1988). Mandating arrest takes the onus off the victim. Consequently, many jurisdictions adopted policies to limit police discretion, and to encourage or mandate arrests on the spot in IPV cases. In 1994, Congress provided funds to encourage local police departments to adopt **pro-arrest policies**, or **mandatory arrest policies**.

Deterrent effects of arrest policies. In 1981–1982, the first study testing the effectiveness of mandated arrest for misdemeanor IPV on increasing victim safety was conducted in Minneapolis (National Institute of Justice, 1999). Arrest seemed to have an effect: 24 percent of those sent away from the scene of spouse abuse for eight hours, 19 percent of the subjects given some form of advice, but only 10 percent of the subjects arrested were involved in another violent incident in the next six months. These initial results suggested that mandatory arrest reduced repeated incidents, at least in the short term.

Results of later studies were not so clear. In the 1990s, the Spouse Assault Replication Program (SARP) collected data from five jurisdictions around the country to assess the deterrent effects of mandatory arrest and several other alternative dispositions. Schmidt and Sherman (1996; see also National Institute of Justice, 1999) found that, *regardless of the police intervention,* about 60 percent of the suspects *did not reoffend* in the follow-up period (between six months to three years in different studies). Arrest appeared to reduce the repeated incidence of violence by 30 percent according to victim reports, less according to official records. Although arrests were associated with reduced repeat incidents if the abuser was employed and was older, arrests *increased* the frequency of repeated violence if the abuser was unemployed or if the victim was African American (Schmidt and Sherman, 1996). Some data suggested that arrest might actually increase the incidence of violence in the long term. Almost all the SARP studies had design limitations, including nonrandom assignment of cases to alternative treatments (Zorza, 1998).

Problems with mandated arrests. What appears to be a good idea from the perspective of one actor in a system may not be a good idea when perceived by another actor with a different perspective. Mandated arrest policies cannot be assessed without understanding how people actually live, how the system functions, and without looking at unintended effects.

Although victims of IPV want the police to come when called, unlike victims of stranger assaults, most do not want the perpetrator arrested (Buzawa and Buzawa, 2003). A mandatory arrest policy may reduce the number of new incidents *reported* to the police, not the number of actual incidents. A victim whose partner was arrested previously might decide not to call the police again, or not to disclose information about a later attack if she felt the initial arrest led to undesirable outcomes (Birnbaum, 1989; Dugan, 2002).

The Wisconsin Mandatory Arrest Monitoring Project (Birnbaum, 1989) found that the arrest program was not popular with those it was meant to help. Sixty-eight percent of the women who had police contact said they would not call the police again. The women said the police failed to respond, or responded inappropriately. Some women reported financial problems because of the arrest of the abuser, whose income their families needed. Arrests of both partners occurred when police saw each partner physically attacking the other (Birnbaum, 1989). When both parents were arrested the child was placed in the temporary custody of child welfare authorities. In other words, many of the intended beneficiaries of the new mandatory arrest policy said it had done them and their children more harm than good.

Rates of arrest of both partners in recent years varied from 5.5 to 33 percent of all IPV arrests (Buzawa and Buzawa, 2003). Some jurisdictions have tried to prevent dual arrests by specifying that when both parties are injured, only the "primary" assailant will be arrested. However, it is not easy to determine the primary assailant, and sometimes it is or appears to be the woman. An unintended consequence of mandated arrest policies is that more women (usually the primary caretaker of the children) have been arrested either solely or in dual arrests. In some jurisdictions, more than a quarter of all arrests of domestic violence suspects are of women (Buzawa and Buzawa, 2003; Goldberg, 1999). The rise in arrests of women has raised new questions about mandatory arrests and about rates of IPV assault by women.

Mandated arrest may pose special problems for African Americans. African American women who live in urban areas are more likely to be severely victimized by partners than other women. They call the police more often (Rennison and Welchans, 2000). While arrest deters violence among the employed, it leads to *more* incidents of violence among unemployed men who live in socially disorganized neighborhoods (Coker, 2001). When convicted, African Americans and Latinos are more likely to be imprisoned for a misdemeanor IPV offense, in part because they are more likely to have prior arrests, which reduce eligibility for **diversion** or probation. Many African American women don't want more men from their community imprisoned (Coker, 2001; Epstein, 1999). African American women are also more likely to have their children taken away because of IPV (Buzawa and Buzawa, 2003).

Prosecution

Local prosecutors (district attorneys, or DAs) have considerable impact on how laws and policies are translated into action. They decide which cases to prosecute and what charges to bring. In the past, prosecutors did not vigorously pursue IPV cases involving lesser criminal charges (misdemeanors). Arguments between intimate partners, even violent ones, were regarded as private affairs.

Abused women do not often petition the DAs to bring criminal charges against those who assault them (Rebovich, 1996). Police can ask the prosecutors to charge a person they have arrested, but even after aggressive arrest policies were implemented, perpetrators were rarely charged. When charges were brought, women frequently asked the prosecutor to drop the charges (Hotaling and Buzawa, 2001).

Women may drop charges for fear of retaliation. They may also drop charges because of hope for reconciliation, cultural and religious misgivings, financial concerns, and the belief that prosecution will not help their children. If the partner was employed, prosecution and conviction may affect his future job opportunities and the family's financial status. Prosecution in itself is stressful. The victim may be required to repeat painful or humiliating stories over and over. Prosecution may take her away from her job and cost her money in transportation and child care.

Until quite recently, most prosecutors automatically dropped charges at the victim's request, especially in misdemeanor cases. IPV assaults are often classified as misdemeanors, even when there was a history of prior attacks (Buzawa and Buzawa, 2003). Recently, in response to legislative mandates, jurisdictions have been trying to increase prosecution of all IPV offenses and make the system more "victim friendly." One important reform instituted in some jurisdictions is vertical prosecution (Abbate, 1997), where a single prosecuting attorney is assigned for all stages of the case instead of dividing up responsibilities. This spares the victim the task of repeating her story and facilitates safety planning. Prosecutors' offices are also experimenting with specialized IPV programs where the victim is offered court preparation and education, social services, counseling, safety planning, and in some places an advocate to help her through the system (Rebovich, 1996; Buzawa and Buzawa, 2003).

"No-drop" policies. Another approach is to limit freedom of prosecutors and victims to drop cases. Prosecutors may proceed without victim cooperation and can subpoena victim testimony. The **"no-drop" policy** has two aims: to establish that the state considers IPV a serious crime against the public order, and to protect victims through incarceration of the offender.

Rebovich (1996) conducted a mail survey of 200 local DAs offices, of which 68 percent responded. All the prosecutors pursued some cases without victim cooperation. Prosecuting cases without a cooperative victim is difficult (Davis, Smith, and Nickles, 1998). Prosecutors can subpoena a reluctant victim to testify and bring punitive charges if she does not respond, but this is problematic. In *Crawford v. Washington,* (2004), the U.S. Supreme Court made prosecution of IPV cases with reluctant victims even more difficult. The Court prohibited introduction into a criminal trial of "testimonial" statements, such as a statement made by a potential witness in a police interrogation, unless the defendant had the chance to confront and cross-examine the person who made the statement.

Prosecutors have tried other methods for gathering evidence to help them make a case without the victim's help. One is to submit photographs of a victim's injuries as evidence. So far, use of these photos even without victim testimony has withstood legal challenges (Kershaw, 2002).

A few weeks after *Crawford v. Washington,* a judge ruled (*People v. Moscat,* 2004) that the prosecutor in a domestic violence case could use 911 recordings of the woman's call for help as evidence without her testimony. The 911 call was not "testimonial" in the judge's opinion. (Tavernise, 2004). In *Washington v. Davis* (2006), the U.S. Supreme Court agreed that calls to 911 are not "testimonial" and may be introduced into evidence even if the victim does not otherwise testify.

Prosecution and victim safety. Aggressive prosecution has symbolic value, but are the victims safer? The main outcome measure in most studies is reported incidents of reabuse; rates of unreported incidents or nonviolent harassment are not assessed. Even without considering unreported cases, if the outcome sought is victim safety, empirical support for prosecution without victim cooperation is weak; in some circumstances increased prosecution rates are associated with increased IPV (Epstein, 1999; Dugan et al., 2001; Ford and Regoli, 1998; Davis, Smith, and Nickles, 1998; Davis, Smith, and Taylor, 2003). Aggressive prosecution, like mandatory arrest, is not popular with victims who may want to use the justice system to safeguard themselves and their interests rather than feel they are being used by it to promote policy ends.

The Courts

The judicial system is a complex of courts with different jurisdictions, powers, and limitations. IPV cases can enter the system in several ways and end up in different places. In New York State, a person who has been threatened or assaulted by a spouse or a partner with whom she has a child can seek relief by initiating a family offense case in the civil family court. Family offenses include child abuse, harassment, menacing behavior, and assault involving family members. The victim can also ask the prosecutor to pursue a family offense in criminal court. If divorce, custody, or visitation is at issue as well as IPV, the case may also go to a civil divorce court or to the family court.

The same family can be involved with more than one court, sometimes without the judge's awareness, especially if computerized records of all the cases pending are not available to each judge.

In family court, a victim can receive an order of protection from the judge requiring the alleged abuser to stay away from the person claiming victimization whether or not an arrest has been made. A temporary order of protection can be issued **ex parte** (on behalf of one party only, without the other person appearing). A full hearing with both parties appearing is held later. Family courts, in theory, are better able than criminal courts to handle children's problems. Family courts may have links with social service agencies; family court judges can order treatment for batterers. However, family court judges cannot impose fines or jail terms except when an order of protection has been violated.

If a victim of partner violence is not married to her alleged abuser or doesn't have a child with him, in most states, the family court does not have jurisdiction (e.g., Criminal Procedure Law, 530.11). The victim must go to criminal court. Some serious violent crimes (e.g., assault in the first degree, use of a deadly weapon or instrument, intent or actions to disfigure someone, and murder and attempted murder) also must be prosecuted in criminal court.

To initiate a criminal prosecution, the victim brings a complaint to the prosecutor. The criminal court judge can't issue a protective order until an arrest is made. The prosecutor can decide whether to prosecute at all, what charge to bring, and whether to plea-bargain. The prosecutor can also request a high bail to try to keep the defendant in jail. If the defendant violates an order of protection, the criminal court judge can impose a prison sentence.

In New York, the victim may pursue prosecution of family offenses simultaneously in criminal and in family court. This complexity can be confusing to the victim, who is under stress and not easily able to evaluate which course of action is best. Courts may sometimes issue inconsistent rulings. For example, one court may order a man not to go to his former partner's house, while another may order the woman to allow the man to come to the house to pick up the children for reasonable visitation (Epstein, 1999).

Specialized IPV courts. States have been experimenting with integrated **intimate partner violence courts** (commonly called *domestic violence courts*) in which all aspects of a case—criminal issues, custody disputes, orders of protection, family law matters, child protection issues—are assigned to a single specially trained judge. Delays may be reduced, and judges can monitor compliance with orders and coordinate with community agencies. Some advocates (Mazur and Aldrich, 2002) are concerned that "domestic violence courts," like other "problem-solving courts" (e.g., drug courts or mental illness courts), will focus on rehabilitating the offender rather than on the safety of the victim.

Orders of Protection

Almost all states have legislation establishing relatively simple procedures for abused women to obtain an order of protection (restraining order) against an alleged abuser from a judge (U.S. Senate, 1990). **Orders of protection** can direct the alleged abuser to stop abusive conduct, to leave or stay away from the family home, or to have no contact with the victim. Judges can customize the orders specifying what the alleged offender must do (e.g., pay the rent) or refrain from doing (e.g., stop following the victim around). The order may give custody of the children to the victim, or may restrict visitation. Sometimes abusers are ordered to give up their firearms (Dugan, 2002). An order of protection is functionally like an arrest warrant. For example, if the order requires an alleged abuser to stay away from the block where the woman lives, and she sees him there, she can call the police. In theory, police are to come immediately and arrest him.

It is far easier for a victim to obtain an order of protection in a family court than to wait for a criminal arrest and court appearance. *Easy* is a relative term, however. Obtaining a temporary order of protection requires knowledge, initiative, and getting to court safely. The process can be time-consuming and stressful. The most severely abused woman may have the most difficulty using the system. Women who are economically dependent on their abusers may be reluctant to seek a restraining order because support provisions may not be included. The victim must return to court for another hearing a few weeks or months after receiving the temporary order to request a permanent order.

About 20 percent of the women who experience IPV obtain protective orders (Holt et al., 2002). In Erie County, New York, a jurisdiction with just under 1,000,000 in population, containing urban (City of Buffalo), suburban, and rural areas, 6,153 orders of protection were active each day (Warner, 2000). Many victims who obtain temporary orders of protection do not return to court to obtain permanent orders.

BOX 12.1

Some Legal Cases in Point: When Orders of Protection Fail

Three Erie County, New York, cases illustrate the limited power of orders of protection, even those backed by cooperative authorities, to protect women from very violent men.

Norma Roman obtained an order of protection against her husband. The city police and the county sheriff's department were aware of the order and were willing to support her. She moved into a new home and fitted it with a burglar alarm. Her husband, who was a sheriff's deputy, chased her into an elementary school building and shot her to death in the school.

Margaret Valdez obtained an order of protection against her former boyfriend. When her boyfriend was given the order, he crumpled it up in the courtroom and stuffed it into his pocket, indicating his attitude toward the court's authority. The judge warned him strongly that he would get a year in jail if he violated the - order. About two weeks later, he stabbed Margaret 29 times during an argument, killing her.

Jetaun Devers refused to prosecute her husband. The prosecution proceeded nonetheless. Devers bailed her husband out of jail, and continued to live with him while he awaited trial. He was convicted of having assaulted her. The judge issued an order of protection, put him on probation for three years, and ordered him into a batterer intervention program. He didn't show up for a date in intimate partner violence court. The judge issued a warrant for his arrest, but, before he was found, he stabbed his wife to death in their home in front of their six-year-old son.

Despite these failures, Erie County's efforts to deal more effectively with IPV may be showing some results. The number of IPV deaths in this county dropped from 14 in 1995 to 7 in 1999 (Warner, 2000).

Systems and enforcement problems. Women who have been threatened and stalked but not physically injured may have trouble obtaining orders. Some judges may require physical evidence of abuse—bruises, lacerations, or black eyes before granting them. The alleged abuser has to be found and then formally served with the order by a process server before it becomes effective. Sometimes judges issue **mutual orders of protection** (i.e., restraining both parties). When the court has issued a mutual order of protection, the victim may be reluctant to call the police if she is threatened. Officers must arrest both parties, and take children to social services. Abused women sometimes agree to the violation of the order meant to protect them by letting their former partner into the home to see the children, to deliver money for child support, or to pick up his things, or because they may want to reconcile. Judges have ruled that a victim who agreed to contact with the subject of a protection order waived the order by her action (National Center on Women and Family Law, 1990; Liptak, 2003).

Protective orders have not been consistently enforced in many jurisdictions (Finn and Colson, 1998; National Institute of Justice, 1999). States have been changing their laws to try to ease these problems, but it is unclear how effective the legislation has been (National Institute of Justice, 1999). For example, some states have passed laws mandating police to enforce orders of protection or to make an arrest if there is probable cause to believe an order has been violated. In *Gonzales v. Town of Castle Rock* (2005), the U.S. Supreme Court considered whether a person who is injured in such a

---

BOX 12.2

A Case in Point: Betty Lucas

Joseph Lucas was convicted on a domestic violence charge after he assaulted his wife, Betty. The court issued a permanent protective order for Betty Lucas. The order prohibited Mr. Lucas from having any contact with her. The couple subsequently divorced.

A year later, Betty Lucas invited Joseph to a birthday party for one of their children. They started drinking and then fighting at the party. The police were called.

Joseph was charged with violating the protective order. He pleaded no contest and was fined $100. Betty, whose case was heard by a different judge, was charged with domestic violence. She pleaded guilty. "It was very much of a mutual combat situation," her lawyer, Andrew T. Sanderson, said. "It resulted in Ms. Lucas kicking his butt." She was sentenced to 90 days, the sentence was suspended.

Betty was, charged with aiding in the violation of the protective order. She pleaded no contest and was sentenced to another 90 days in jail, also suspended, and to two years' probation.

The County Municipal Court ruled that Betty had violated the protective order. An appeals court confirmed the decision, holding that Ms. Lucas had "recklessly exposed herself to the offender from whom she sought protection." The Ohio Supreme Court reversed, holding that Betty was immune from prosecution for complicity in Joseph's violation of the order because she was the protected person (*Ohio v. Lucas*, 2003).

What are arguments in favor of or opposed to charging her with aiding in the violation of the order?

From Adam Liptak, "Ohio Case Considers whether Abuse Victim Can Violate Own Protective Order," *New York Times*, May 30, 2003.
www.nytimes.com/2003/05/30/national/30ABUS.html.

state can sue the city for money damages when police fail to enforce an order. The case originated in Colorado, where a statute directed police to arrest a violator of a valid court order. Jessica Gonzales had a valid order limiting her husband's contact with their three children. Her husband kidnapped the girls one afternoon while they were out, violating the order. At about 5:30 P.M., Ms. Gonzales made the first of several calls and visits to the police station complaining and asking to have her husband arrested. The police repeatedly advised her to wait to see if the girls were brought home.

At 3:20 A.M., her husband went to the town police station and opened fire with a semiautomatic handgun. The police killed him. The police found the dead bodies of the three girls in the back of his truck. He had murdered them earlier that evening.

The U.S. Supreme Court ruled that the order of protection did not entitle Ms. Gonzales to seek money damages from the town for the failure of the police to enforce the order and for the death of her children. How can orders of protection be enforced if the police are lax in pursuing enforcement and the victim has no recourse against the police or the city?

Evaluating the effectiveness of orders of protection. Studies in this area face the same methodological problems as other policy evaluations. Three large-scale studies used court records and telephone interviews to evaluate the effectiveness of orders of protection (Harrell and Smith, 1998; Keilitz, Hannaford, and Efkeman, 1997; Klein, 1998; National Institute of Justice, 1998; Holt et al., 2002; Buzawa and Buzawa, 2003). Dugan and colleagues studied correlations between changes in order of protection procedures and policies and rates of IPV and intimate partner murder in different states (Dugan, 2002; Dugan, Nagin, and Rosenfeld, 2003). Once again, the results were complex. Orders of protection made some women safer, but under some conditions obtaining an order aggravated violence (Buzawa and Buzawa, 2003).

One indicator of the limitations of orders of protection is the number of partner murders that take place when an order is in force. There was a current order in force in 21 of a sample of 57 intimate partner murders in New York State (Commission on Domestic Fatalities, 1997). Some jurisdictions are experimenting with space-age monitoring of protective orders using devices that automatically signal both abuser and victim if the abuser gets too near the victim. These provide a record of violations for further legal action.

A restraining order does not confer 24-hour police protection. Orders of protection do provide victims with a means of seeking immediate relief; deter some abusers and potential abusers, especially in the short term, and, if enforced vigorously, can be a valuable tool in safety planning (Dugan, Nagin, and Rosenfeld, 2003).

Diversion and Treatment

Because IPV is so prevalent and tends to recur, many advocates believe violence against women can only be reduced if abusers can be rehabilitated. Since the 1970s, women's organizations and clinicians have been developing **"batterer" intervention programs (BIPs)** to be used by courts. The programs are designed to (1) ensure victims' safety by monitoring abusers, (2) hold abuser's accountable for their behavior and attitudes, and (3) do so without incarceration. The criminal justice system is referring more and more defendants to BIPs (Healey and Smith, 1998; Rebovich, 1996; Healey, Smith, and O'Sullivan, 1998). By agreeing to attend the BIP, the defendant avoids criminal prosecutions or prison; participation is not entirely voluntary (Simon, 1995).

In the majority of IPV incidents when victims call the police, the victims say they would prefer mandated counseling and reconciliation to arrest and conviction

(Buzawa and Buzawa, 2003). A perpetrator's attendance at a batterer's program is a strong predictor that his partner will remain with him (Gondolf, 1988). For this reason, good decision making about who can safely be diverted to a BIP is vital if victims are to be kept safe. Researchers are developing empirically based classifications of the defendants with different levels of risk of dropping out of treatment and of reoffending (Healey and Smith, 1998; Williams and Houghton, 2004). However, like all assessment and prediction instruments, these will not eliminate false negative and false positives.

Different intervention models. Most intervention programs are based on one of three theoretical models of IPV described earlier. The earliest BIPs were based on feminist models of IPV. These programs try to change participants through feminist education. They use a group format and incorporate personal examples from abused women into the curriculum. The most widely recognized feminist program is the Domestic Abuse Intervention Project, also known as the Duluth model.

Family systems models try to equip both partners with communication and conflict resolution skills. The usual mode of family interventions for other problems is joint couple or family counseling. Couples counseling has been rejected by victim advocates because it blurs accountability, implies that the victim shares responsibility for the violence, and might increase the risk of further psychological and physical abuse. Couples counseling is actually prohibited in 80 percent of the states (Healey and Smith, 1998; Association of the Bar of the City of New York, 2003). However, family systems models need not involve couples counseling (Laing, 2001; Almeida and Durkin, 1999; Stuart, 2005).

Psychotherapeutic models include cognitive-behavioral (CBT) and psychodynamic psychotherapy. Proponents of these models argue that since most men are not violent towards their partners, patriarchal attitudes alone cannot account for the behavior; personality issues must also be addressed. Cognitive behavioral therapy programs use a group educational format. They focus on teaching participants new ways of relating, communicating and resolving conflicts with partners. Many teach anger management. They have been criticized for implying that the perpetrators lost control when angry and are therefore not fully responsible. They have also been criticized by feminists for teaching abusers new techniques of manipulation and control, which are not subject to legal sanctions. Psychodynamic programs theorize that violent behaviors stem from childhood problems that can be addressed through individual therapy or counseling. Victims' advocates criticize this approach for focusing on the ways in which the abuser has been victimized in the past rather than on his present victimization of others.

The most popular psychotherapeutically oriented programs combine psychoeducational, cognitive behavioral, individual, and sometimes victim and community elements. Perhaps the best known is the Denver Program AMEND (Abusive Men Exploring New Directions) (Stuart, 2005).

Effectiveness of intervention programs. Everyone would like BIPs to be effective, but there is little evidence that they are. One-quarter to one-half of the men who enter BIPs do not complete the programs (Schechter and Edelson, 1994). Examining results based upon completers only introduces biases (Feder and Forde, 2000). Dropouts are more likely than completers to have complicating problems such as substance abuse, mental disorders, personality disorders, and unemployment (Bennett and Williams, 2001). Single-group studies without controls that examine reabuse by completers only are studying the people least likely to reoffend anyway; since there is no comparison group, good results can't be attributed to BIP attendance. Large scale studies, some employing random assignment to treatment and control conditions, have not found any evidence that BIPs were useful (Palmer, Brown, and Barerra, 1992; Dunford, 2000; Feder and Forde, 2000; Taylor, Davis, and Maxwell, 2001; Jackson et al., 2003). Babcock, et al. (2004) conducted a meta-analysis of the findings of 22 studies of BIPs. There was a minimal impact on recidivism, compared to just arresting the defendant. Research on which elements of what programs work for which abusers would be useful (Babcock, Green, and Robie, 2004).

If diversion programs are as effective as jail time for misdemeanor offenses, they have some advantages over jail: they are cheaper (the offender pays), may be preferred by victims who are interested in possible reconciliation, and may prevent batterers from losing their jobs. Diversion programs are not appropriate for very violent men or men with long criminal histories (Goldkamp et al., 1998).

The system's response and immigrant groups. IPV in immigrant groups presents special problems for research and for practice (Garcia, Hurwitz, and Kraus, 2005). The system is especially difficult for many members of immigrant groups to negotiate. Immigrant women may fear deportation or loss of custody of their American born children if they contact the police. There are tangled interrelationships between immigrant status and social services that can complicate women's lives and compromise their willingness to seek protection (Epstein, 1999; Coker, 2001). In addition, immigrant communities are often close-knit. Taking an action that brings the state into the community seems to show the community in a bad light. Immigrants often maintain ties to extended family in foreign home communities. These ties can be affected if a woman's prosecution of her husband causes trouble for family members at "home." Separated or divorced women have low social status in some groups.

Many members of immigrant groups are not comfortable going to shelters, especially if they don't speak the language. Members of ethnic groups may participate in spiritual traditions not readily accommodated in shelters. Observant Muslim, Jewish, and Hindu women may be unable to eat in shelters without violating dietary rules. Courts in urban areas are becoming increasingly sensitive to the diversity of family forms and cultures (Bograd, 1999).

Child Protection and IPV: System Responses

Protecting children is another goal of an aggressive justice system response to IPV. With knowledge of the high rates of co-occurrence of partner and child abuse, police called in on IPV cases have been trained in some jurisdictions to consider risk to children. Child protection workers investigating reports of possible child maltreatment are increasingly likely to look also for IPV.

Is Witnessing IPV Reportable Child Abuse?

Because children who witness IPV often suffer from psychological problems, some advocates have argued that IPV occurring in front of a child should be considered child abuse even if the child is not hurt (Weithorn, 2001). Assaulting one's partner in the presence of children may qualify for prosecution for the crime of endangering the welfare of a child (*People v. Johnson*, 2000), but not lesser expressions of anger (*People v. Ventura*, 2005). Georgia and Utah have statutes that make assault and battery of a partner in the presence of a child a form of criminal child abuse (Weithorn, 2001).

In many states, allowing a child to witness partner abuse can be reported as suspected maltreatment (Weithorn, 2001). A few states have amended reporting laws so that professionals are *required* to report suspicions that a child has been exposed to domestic violence. These laws proved unworkable. Resources were not allocated to investigate every incident of IPV, many of which did not pose serious threats to children's welfare (Weithorn, 2001). Many advocates for women and children oppose a legal requirement to report IPV witnessed by children to child protection authorities because it highlights the role of the victim parent. Authorities may bring charges against the mother for neglecting the child by (allowing him or her to witness IPV) or remove the children. In New York City, child protection authorities had often removed a child from the home, charging neglect because the mother had not prevented the child from witnessing IPV. When the practice was challenged in a lawsuit, the high court in New York said that a child's exposure to domestic violence is not sufficient in and of itself to constitute neglect warranting removal of the child (*Nicholson v. Scoppetta*, 2004).

Changing Approaches

Two important policy documents published at the turn of the twenty-first century, *Effective Intervention in Domestic Violence and Child Maltreatment Cases: Guidelines for Policy and Practice* (National Council of Juvenile and Family Court Judges, 1999) and *Safe from the Start: Taking Action on Children Exposed to Domestic Violence* (also known as "The Green Book"; U.S. Department of Justice, 2000), recommend that children should remain in the custody of a non-offending parent whenever possible. If anyone is to be removed from the home, it should be the offending party. Child protective services should be mandated to protect the victim parent as well as the child.

Child Protection and Battered Women's Services

Child protection services in many states have been working to develop programs consonant with newer principles of protecting victims and children, and prosecuting abusers. Domestic violence and child protection workers are trying hard to coordinate their services, a task which has sometimes proved problematic.

Historical Background

Laws and service programs protecting the vulnerable are devised piecemeal as problems reached the public agenda, and as political decision makers choose to act. A person's problems are interrelated. The patchwork nature of the service system is an obstacle to effective interventions. The uneasy interactions between child protection and battered women's services serve as an example. Child abuse and partner violence are handled by separate agencies. The agencies have different missions, operate within different legal constraints, and have developed different cultures.

Differences Between IPV Workers and CPS Workers

Grassroots women's advocates first set up IPV programs and opened battered women's shelters in the 1970s. From the beginning their purpose was to protect and empower women victims; until recently, they considered the needs of the women's children only secondarily. CPS, in contrast, is a hundred year old governmental quasi-policing agency whose mission is to protect children from abuse or neglect by family members (see

Chapter 10; Weithorn, 2001). For a long time, there was little communication and some distrust between these two very different agencies. This lack of understanding reduced the ability of either to deal effectively with families in which both women and children were abused, and made it difficult to implement changes to coordinate services.

CPS workers distrust women's advocacy groups and shelters because the IPV staff has sometimes tended to deny or minimize abuse and neglect perpetrated by abused mothers. Sometimes they refuse to cooperate with investigations. Many shelters frustrate CPS by refusing to accept referrals of women with substance misuse problems or troubled older children, groups the shelters feel ill equipped to help. On the other hand, many IPV workers believed that CPS workers are insensitive to abused women's situations.

Many abused women, especially poor women, fear being charged with neglect by CPS, and fear that CPS might remove their child. If an abused woman escapes to a shelter, planning to pick up her children later, she may be charged with abandoning the children. Prosecutors in some jurisdictions used the threat of a felony charge of child endangerment to "encourage" women to cooperate with the prosecution of the abuser (Whitcomb, 2002, in Buzawa and Buzawa, 2003).

Hopefully, with the greater implementation of the "Green Book" approach, prosecutions of women are occurring less often (Epstein, 1999). However, the "policing" character of CPS conflicts with the empowering culture of IPV agencies. Domestic violence programs and shelters were organized to serve women who voluntarily seek help (Aron and Olsen, 1997). The programs may not wish to accept a woman who is coerced or pressured by CPS into going to a shelter. Mandated treatment and monitoring are not consistent with their empowerment ideology or with their security and safety rules. The preservation of security and safety is important for victim's advocates. CPS has a legal mission to preserve families and protect children (Schechter and Edelson, 1994). Consequently, CPS workers may insist that a woman cooperate with visitation, mediation, and any other court-ordered actions to restore the family. Most IPV organizations encourage women to separate from abusers, and they support women who hide themselves or their children from a former partner.

Shelter workers also fear that CPS involvement may compromise the safety of all the women at the shelter. Shelter locations are kept secret to prevent batterers from finding the women. Shelter workers fear that a woman who comes to the shelter because of CPS pressure, but not because she wants to leave the batterer, may give out the address (Aron and Olsen, 1997).

Service coordination. Despite many problems, both women and children's advocates are very aware of the high co-occurrence of child and partner abuse, and of the need to address both problems. Child Protective Services and IPV programs are experimenting with service coordination (Davidson, 1995). CPS workers are increasingly being trained to develop safety plans for victimized parents, and IPV workers are increasingly willing to recognize that some abused women may be poor parents.

IPV, Divorce, Custody, and Visitation

IPV complicates the difficult problems of custody and visitation. The most dangerous period for a woman is around the time of divorce or separation. During this time, victims have to interact with their former partner around custody and visitation issues, and often experience ongoing intimidation and abuse during these encounters. As a result of advocacy and research, legislation and court decisions now recognize the relevance of spouse abuse to custody and visitation orders. However, developing effective policies and shifting institutional cultures are slow processes.

Custody and Orders of Protection

Many states have statutes that require judges to award immediate custody of children to the victim after a protective order is issued. However, Dugan (2002) and colleagues (Dugan et al., 2003) found that the odds of a household being victimized by a spouse or an ex-spouse are higher in states which grant custody to the victim when an order of protection is issued. It is unclear why risk increases after a custody order.

Custody and Divorce

The dynamics of violent relationships carry over into custody and visitation negotiations that are part of a divorce or separation. The victimized spouse may be in a weakened legal position in a custody dispute because of how he or she copes with the violence (Gordon, 1990; Keenan, 1985). Some states have "friendly parent" provisions that instruct the judge to consider the likelihood that a parent will facilitate the child's contacts with the other parent when awarding custody. In these states, a woman who refuses to cooperate with a visitation order or who takes the children away runs the risk of appearing an unfriendly parent and losing custody. She may even be charged with contempt of court (see the Morgan-Foretich case in Figure 13.2).

Victims may be anxious and depressed secondary to the violence. They may have a substance abuse problem. They may appear psychologically less fit for parenting than their partners (Geffner and Pagelow, 1990). Some victims may be at an economic disadvantage in a custody dispute because their partner has discouraged them from working or the violence has affected their work (Orloff, 1990).

Today, courts are instructed by legislation or appellate precedents to consider any history of violence between the parents as a factor when awarding custody or making visitation orders (ABA, 1995; Orloff, 1990; Weithorn, 2001). Some states have a **rebuttable presumption** (a legal rule whose effect can be overcome by evidence) against giving custody, including joint custody, to a parent who had abused his or her spouse or partner. However the laws tend to be vague and leave much to judicial discretion.

Fathers' rights advocates are concerned that a legal rule favoring an abused spouse will lead to false allegations of spouse abuse as a ploy to obtain custody or restrict visitation (McNeely and Robinson-Simpson, 1987, 1988; Tobesman, 1990; Turner, 1990; Weithorn, 2001). Women's advocates are concerned that victims' complaints are being dismissed as unimportant because the couple has separated or complaints are wrongly treated as a ploy. Judges have to order temporary custody and visitation arrangements. Absent strong evidence, some judges may hesitate to prejudge a case where IPV is alleged. Integrated domestic violence courts may help judges handle some of these problems better by providing them with more background information.

Mediation

Many jurisdictions offer, encourage, or even require parents who are disputing custody to try to settle the dispute through mediation before they can proceed to litigation. The policy is based on the belief that mediation is less likely than litigation to aggravate conflict between parents, and that it spares the family and the system the emotional, temporal, and financial costs of a court case (see Chapter 13 on child custody). Victims' advocates have long argued that mediation is not appropriate where there has been domestic violence. They believe that because of the power differential between victim and abusers, voluntary agreement is impossible and mediation may even become a forum for further psychological abuse. Proponents of mediation acknowledge these concerns. Most mediation programs have procedures to screen for domestic violence and enhance mediation safety (Pearson, 1997).

However, these precautions may not be having the intended effects. Mediation is mandated in California. Saccuzzo, Johnson, and Koen (2003) conducted a content analysis on a sample of 200 mediations in San Diego where there was a past record of domestic violence, and 200 cases where there were no indicators of violence in the mediator's case file. The researchers found that the court screening form often failed to detect violence or abuse. When violence was noted, it was often not addressed. Mediators recommended primary physical custody for the perpetrator father as often in cases where there had been domestic violence as in other cases. Mediators define success by finding an acceptable resolution to a problem. They appeared reluctant to recommend anything other than joint *legal* custody, where both parties "win," except in cases of very extreme problems (e.g., drug abuse plus extensive psychiatric history and suicide attempts).

Supervised Visitation

Divorced parents' relationships continue after a custody decision because the noncustodial parent is legally entitled to visit his or her children. The parents encounter each other when the custodial parent gives over the child to the noncustodial parent, or when the noncustodial parent returns the child after a visit. When a relationship has been violent, these transitions can be an occasion for further partner abuse, often in front of the child. Judges can deny visitation altogether to parents who pose a serious risk of violence. However, they are loath to cut off a parent's contact with a child altogether. In most cases, children benefit from contact with both parents and the parent has a right to the companionship of their children. And, in fact, many people who abuse their partners do not abuse their children. The children may value their relationship with both parents.

Courts can order supervised visitation when there has been IPV. **Supervised visitation** means the parent is not permitted to see the child alone; a person or agency appointed by the court must be there with him. Visitation is provided at day care centers, or other community centers or even at some domestic violence courts. The custodial parent drops off the child before the other parent arrives, and picks up the child after the other parent has left. The visitation situation is structured to limit face-to-face contact between actively hostile parties (Edelson, 1998b).

There are now 350 supervised visitation programs in 15 states. The centers are largely staffed by trained volunteers or counseling interns. However, there are not nearly enough programs to meet the need. In addition, because of security issues charity and child-advocate-run facilities may not accept cases where violence is a serious concern.

It is unclear how seriously courts make systematic attempts to ascertain degrees of risk. A study conducted in New York City and a nearby suburban county found that family offense petitions and protection orders had little impact on courts' decisions regarding visitation and custody. Courts granted visitation in most cases where there was an allegation or evidence of ongoing violence or threats. Fathers were somewhat more likely to be granted visitation when they were the subject of a protection order than when no family offense petition was filed. Lawyers said they were rarely able to persuade the court to suspend visitation or order supervised visitation (O'Sullivan, 2002).

⊠ Partner Murder

In the past, in the United States, men who killed their partners or wives were sometimes let off leniently. Today, women who kill their partners are more likely to get lenient treatment. Women's advocates challenged the legal rules of self-defense when women were tried for killing an alleged abuser. Clinical research on abused women and the battered woman defense entered the courtroom through expert testimony. Courts and juries have not always been receptive to the defense arguments, but the arguments may change the terms of the debate.

The Battered Woman Defense

Fifty to 85 percent of the women charged with killing their husbands or partners claim the **battered woman defense:** they say that they were acting to defend themselves from abuse (Kasian et al., 1993). Ewing (1987, 1990) collected data on allegedly battered women who killed their partners and were charged with criminal homicide. In one-third of 87 cases, the killing took place during a violent attack by the partner, the classic self-defense scenario. The other killings occurred while the partner was asleep or otherwise preoccupied. These circumstances created an almost insurmountable obstacle to the women's legal claims of self-defense.

A defendant claiming self-defense has to prove that she had a reasonable apprehension of imminent death or grievous harm at the time of the killing, and that the force she used was reasonable and necessary to protect against serious injury or death. Courts have traditionally used the "reasonable man" standard in defining "reasonable and necessary." Is that standard reasonable when the conflict is between a man and a woman? Women's advocates argue that a woman who faces a much stronger partner intent on hurting her can't just punch back. They argue that she must use a weapon to compensate for her lesser strength, or strike when the man cannot strike back. The delay presents the legal problem. If she strikes when the man is sleeping or not paying attention, why couldn't she just leave instead? Why didn't she leave earlier?

Leonore Walker (1979, 1984) developed the **battered woman syndrome** to explain why the woman didn't leave (see section on "Victims" at the beginning of the chapter). Defense lawyers seized on it. They called on experts (see Chapter 2) to testify about the syndrome to the jury. (For the first use of the defense, see *Ibn-Tamas v. United States*, 1979.) In an amicus curiae brief submitted in *State v. Kelly* (1984), the American Psychological Association argued that there was a sound basis for a diagnosis of battered woman syndrome.

The trend over the 1980s was to admit expert witness testimony on the battered woman syndrome (Parish, 1998). Some courts allowed the expert to provide "social framework" testimony to help the jury put the case in context (Schuller and Vidmar, 1992). The expert testimony was used to support the defendant's claim that given her terrifying experiences with the batterer, she was acting reasonably in self-defense. In other cases, the syndrome was introduced as part of an insanity defense, or to show "diminished capacity" to form the intent to kill, and thus to qualify for a reduced charge. The battered woman syndrome has also been used in defense of women who were partners in crime with their abuser. The women claimed they participated in the crime under "duress" (Faigman and Wright, 1997; *People v. White*, 2004; *Dixon v. United States*, 2006).

Is the Syndrome Valid?

It is highly questionable whether the evidence supporting the existence of a battered woman syndrome or a pattern of learned helplessness among abused women can meet *Daubert* standards of falsifiability and reliability (Faigman et al., 2005; Faigman and Wright, 1997; Gordon, 1998; Schuller and Vidmar, 1992). Moreover, the act of killing is inconsistent with "learned helplessness." However, even though there may be no "syndrome," expert testimony about abuse and its effects can assist a jury in putting an abused woman's actions in context (Schuller and Hastings, 1996; Gordon, 1998). Dutton (1998) recommends replacing references to *"battered woman syndrome"* with *"battering and its effects."*

Dahir et al. (2005) found that most state trial judges had had at least some experience with battered woman syndrome testimony. Most said admissibility was an issue, but they often admitted the testimony. In some states, courts have excluded testimony on the syndrome on the grounds that it adds little to jurors' ability to evaluate the circumstances of the crime.

How Effective Is the Defense?

The short answer is "Not very effective." Although it worked in a quarter to a third of the cases, most of the time expert testimony on the battered woman syndrome was not sufficient to overcome standard judicial instructions on self-defense (Dutton, 1998; Ewing, 1987). Mock jurors don't seem to accept the defense either. Simulation studies where college student subjects were asked to make judgments based on written trial scenarios showed that expert testimony about the battered woman syndrome had, at best, weak effects on mock juror votes (Ewing, 1990; Schuller and Hastings, 1996; Schuller and Vidmar, 1992).

Battered Women May Be Sentenced Less Harshly

While it doesn't increase acquittals in mock trials, expert testimony about battered women leads mock jurors to more lenient verdicts (e.g., manslaughter rather than murder; Schuller, 1992; Schuller and Hastings, 1996; Schuller and Rzepa, 2002). Judges and juries, though not often swayed to acquit on self-defense grounds, seem to treat women who kill their partners far more leniently than men. Men convicted of intimate partner homicide are sent to prison more often and receive longer sentences than women (U.S. Bureau of Justice Statistics, 1995; Beaulie and Messner, 1999; Curry, Lee, and Rodriguez, 2004). Some state governors have also given clemency to abused women who had been convicted of murdering their spouses.

⊠ Excluded Victims

Male Victims of IPV

Some victims of domestic violence have been effectively excluded from services offering support or protection. They receive less attention in research as well.

Men assaulted by women. Male victims of IPV are almost invisible. The general cultural view of women as victims and men as aggressors makes it difficult to see men as victims. Abused men may be hesitant to call the police or to request orders of protection because of shame. In our culture, the woman-dominated man is seen as amusing at best, and weak and contemptible at worst. If they do call the police, they are less likely to get protection than a woman. Research workers reviewing domestic violence cases in one large county found that when the victim was male, the female perpetrator was five times less likely to be arrested than a male perpetrator of violence against a female partner (Buzawa and Buzawa, 2003; Buzawa and Hotaling, 2000).

Men and Women Assaulted by Same-Sex Partners

Men are also victimized by male intimate partners, and women by women. Victims of gay and lesbian IPV are only now becoming visible. In the National Violence against Women Survey (NVAWS), 11 percent of women in same-sex relationships reported IPV, compared to 30 percent of women in heterosexual relationships. About 15 percent of the men in relationships with men reported being attacked or stalked, compared to 8 percent in heterosexual relationships. (See also Weihe, 1998; Renzetti, 1993; Greenwood et al., 2002.)

Several states have eliminated provisions excluding same-sex couples from statutes defining family offenses (Fray-Witzer, 2000). But even where they can seek police protection, abused lesbian and gay people may hesitate to do so. Homosexuals suspect that police and courts would not take their claims seriously. BPI programs designed for heterosexual men may not be appropriate or comfortable for gay men and lesbians.

IPV among same-sex couples is just beginning to receive more attention from researchers. IPV among gay men and lesbians appears to involve similar dynamics as among heterosexuals; control is a key motive, providing a challenge to feminist theories of patriarchy (Weihe, 1998).

Teenagers

IPV is a serious problem among teenagers. In one large scale survey, 20 percent of girls age 14 to 18 reported that they had been hit, slapped, shoved, or forced into sexual activity by either a boyfriend or a date (Silverman et al., 2001). Seeking protection and justice through police or juvenile courts may bring the young woman's activities to parental attention. Counseling and support services may not be available or be seen as friendly. Teenagers often fall in a service gap because neither child- nor adult-oriented services fully address their problems (Silverman et al., 2001). Clearly, if shifting social attitudes toward IPV is a goal, we should somehow address violence among teenage dating partners.

Socially Excluded Groups

Other victims of IPV who have remained in the shadows might loosely be described as *stigmatized:* prostitutes, drug addicts and alcoholics, incarcerated criminals and partners of criminals, people with mental illness or mental retardation, homeless people, and illegal immigrants. There is little information about the rate of IPV in these stigmatized groups. One suspects that because of their low social status, they are especially vulnerable to abuse with little recourse to police or courts. They risk getting themselves in further trouble if they seek help. Their marginality makes it hard to research their problems and hard to reach them with services or to protect them through the police or the courts.

Summary

IPV was recognized as a significant social problem only in the last quarter of the twentieth century as ideas about family and women's social position changed. The new attitudes led to new research and to systematic studies that influenced public policy. Depending on the definition of violence and method of study, as many as a quarter of women have been assaulted by a partner at some point in their lives. Perhaps 20 to 35 percent of the women treated in emergency rooms were injured by intimate partners. Men are also victimized by intimate partner violence in significant numbers, but are less likely to be seriously hurt or killed. In many families, both partners sometimes behave violently during conflicts.

In 75 percent of partner murders, the victim is the woman. Twenty years ago, as many husbands were murdered by wives as wives by husbands. Perhaps due to better resources to aid women, and women's greater economic independence, they can leave abusive relationships more easily today. The rate of husband murders has gone down about 30 percent.

Women's advocates used the hypothesized "battered woman syndrome" to bolster the self-defense claims of the women who killed abusive husbands. However, most abused women do not develop any clear-cut "syndrome" or grouping of symptoms. Many battered women do not exhibit mental health problems. The majority of the men who are the most violent towards their partners have prior criminal histories or substance abuse problems. In response to women's advocates, the justice system has reversed its historical stance toward minimizing IPV. Orders of protection have been developed as a vehicle for protecting victims, with mixed success. Victims do not always cooperate with justice system policies intended to help them. Police, prosecutors, and courts, frustrated by frequent refusals of victims to cooperate with prosecution, have adopted policies like "no-drop" prosecution and mandated arrests. When the policies are examined in the context of the victims' real lives, however, their lack of cooperation does not appear misguided or unreasonable.

Children of families in which there is IPV are also victimized. Some believe that witnessing IPV should be reportable as child abuse. Women's and children's advocates have been struggling to find ways to integrate women's IPV services and CPS with different histories, values and legal authorization in order to serve the many families who need both.

Many localities are experimenting with multisystem networks that bring welfare, health, mental health, housing, immigration, education, and law agencies together to address the problem of IPV. They have also been experimenting with specialized courts.

Discussion Questions

1. How would you define *intimate partner violence?* Why is it difficult to agree on a definition?
2. What are the pros and cons of requiring professionals to call the child protection hotline if they learn that a child's parents have a violent relationship? Could you design a program to investigate the outcomes of a reporting policy?
3. How might the new workfare laws limiting time on welfare affect abused women? How could you monitor the effects of the laws to see if your predictions are correct?
4. Why do you think women are at the same or greater risk of being hurt or killed after they leave an abusive husband as before? How might knowledge of that risk affect women's decision making? What are the implications for the justice system and social service IPV programs?

5. Why have child protection and battered women's services had initial difficulties coordinating services? How do you think the system responds to families in which spouse abuse and child abuse co-occur?

6. Suppose a woman shoots her husband while he is sleeping. Do you believe that a history of abuse should be the basis for a legitimate self-defense plea? That it could be grounds for a diminished capacity defense? Why?

Key Terms

advocates

assault

battered woman defense

battered woman syndrome

batterer intervention
   programs (BIPs)

child witnesses

diversion

ex parte

incidence

intimate partner
   violence (IPV)

intimate partner
   violence courts

mandatory arrest policies

mutual orders of protection

"no-drop" policies

orders of protection

prevalence

pro-arrest policies

rebuttable presumption

rule of thumb

safety planning

shelters

stake in society variables

supervised visitation

CHAPTER **13**

Child Custody

Custody is a legal term. It refers to guarding, controlling, and maintaining a person or an object. Whoever has custody of a child has the right to make all decisions about the child, including his or her education, health care, religious practices and other affiliations.

Children are normally in the custody of their biological parents. Courts become involved in determining custody of a child only when it is in dispute. In Chapter 10, we discussed cases in which the state wishes to take custody of a child away from a parent temporarily or permanently because it believes the child is in danger. Here, we will deal with disputes arising when the child's divorcing parents both want custody.

Custody disputes between divorcing parents are adversarial proceedings. Divorce cases are heard initially in a state court where, until recently, custody issues were settled along with issues of property and support issues. Subsequent legal actions (e.g., requests for change in visitation or support) may be heard in a state court or in a family court. Custody and support issues involving unmarried parents are also heard in courts. Whatever the forum, the hearings are regulated by divorce and custody laws (e.g., the Uniform Marriage and Divorce Act). The laws have some consistency across jurisdictions, but they differ in detail from state to state. Many states have attempted to separate custody from other issues arising at the time of divorce. As of 1992, most states have either voluntary or mandated mediation to resolve custody disputes prior to going to court, unless there is a history of spousal or child abuse (Krauss and Sales, 2000; ALI 2000, Sec. 2.07). Social change has added greatly to the complexity of custody disputes. More mothers, even of very young children, work. Our ideas about gender roles are changing. Our attitudes toward extramarital sexual relationships and homosexual relationships are also changing. Remarriages and cohabitation of unmarried couples complicate custody decisions. Foster parents who wish to adopt and grandparents in divorced families who wish to maintain relationships with grandchildren are asking courts to reconsider the rules for awarding custody and visitation.

In this chapter, we will look at the problem of deciding who will have custody of children after parents separate. We will discuss

- the historical context of custody disputes.
- research on children's adjustment to divorce.
- standards and decision rules applied by courts to decide custody cases, including presumptions favoring primary caretakers, joint custody, and biological parents.
- research about different custody arrangements.
- specific custody issues, including accusations of sexual abuse, parental alienation syndrome, relocation, dilemma created by new reproductive technologies, and the question of how to determine and weigh the child's preferences.
- custody evaluations: practical, ethical, and scientific issues.
- mediation and other alternative approaches to settling custody disputes.

The presentation here owes much to the discussion of the issues in Mnookin and Weisberg's (2005) and Ellman et al. (2004).

Historical Background: Paternal and Maternal Preferences

Broken and reconstituted families were probably as common in the past as they are today, but for different reasons (O'Neill, 1967). In the past, families were broken much more frequently than today by parental death from disease and industrial accidents, and by desertion. Many women died in childbirth well into the nineteenth century. Both single-father and single-mother homes were common. Extended families helped care for their own, and widowers frequently remarried.

Divorce, however, was uncommon until the last half of the twentieth century (O'Neill, 1967). Traditionally, states granted a divorce only if one party to a marriage could prove that the other was guilty of a gross violation of the marriage contract or of highly reprehensible behavior—adultery, physical or mental cruelty, desertion, habitual drunkenness, or criminality. Divorce was time-consuming, expensive, and socially shameful.

Paternal Preference

When a marriage dissolved, the common law contained a presumption that the father should have custody of the children. The **paternal preference** followed from the common law and Roman law principle that all marital property, including children, reverted to the father or his family if a marriage was broken. Children belonged to the father because the father bore the responsibility for their support. The mother might be given custody if she could show that the father was not a fit or appropriate custodian (Nurcombe and Partlett, 1994). When a divorce was granted based on serious fault, courts sometimes awarded custody to the innocent party.

Tender Years Doctrine

In the nineteenth century, paternal preference began to give way to a concern with the child's best interests. In *Helms v. Franciscus* (2 Bland. Ch. 544, Md. 1830, quoted in Nurcome and Partlett, 1994, p. 91), the court wrote, "While the father is the rightful and legal guardian of his minor children, it would violate the laws of nature to snatch an infant from an affectionate mother and place it in the coarse hands of the father." The belief that the mother was the natural custodian of small children, called the **tender years doctrine,** became the basis of **maternal preference.** By the end of the nineteenth century, the tender years doctrine was the rule. A child's tender years could end anywhere between 5 and 13, depending on the state (Nurcombe and Partlett, 1994).

The tender years doctrine separated the issues of financial support and custody. The doctrine implied that a child's needs are best served by giving custody to the parent who is the best nurturer rather than to the parent with the most money, who could still supply financial support. Courts today continue to treat financial responsibility and child care responsibilities as separate issues. The separation is not always easy to preserve in practice. Disputes involving support payments, property, and the distribution of tax benefits can become entangled with custody issues, complicating negotiations and increasing resentments.

Increase in Divorce and Separation

As people lived longer, disease and death failed to intervene in a timely fashion to dissolve unhappy unions. To many, it made no sense to force unhappy people to live together indefinitely. Over time, our culture became more tolerant of divorce (O'Neill,

---

BOX 13.1

Divorce and Custody: Some Statistics

There are now about 1,000,000 divorces a year in the U.S. involving about 900,000 children. The divorcing parents usually try to minimize the hurt to their children. In 80 to 90 percent of the cases, the parents and their lawyers work out a custody arrangement on their own that the court makes official. The remaining couples contest custody issues in court. That means that about 100,000 children each year are involved in disputes about who will care for them and where they will live.

About 31 percent of children whose parents are married are expected to be involved in parental divorce (Braver, Ellman, and Fabricius, 2003). A large number of children whose parents were not married may also be involved in custody disputes. Children who are the subject of custody agreements are young. Over half the children who experience divorce are under 6, and most of these are under 3. (Pruett, Insabella, and Gustafson, 2005)

1967). When a couple agreed to divorce, custom dictated that the husband protect the wife's more vulnerable reputation. She was allowed to charge him with adultery or other misbehavior, and received custody of the children and alimony (support payments) (Mnookin and Weisberg, 2005). Gradually, the laws changed to make it easier to obtain a divorce. During the 1970s, most states began permitting **no-fault divorces** as well as "fault" divorces. Couples could divorce, after a cooling-off period, simply on the grounds of "irreconcilable differences" or because the marriage was "irretrievably broken."

With the legal changes and greater social acceptance of divorce, the number of divorces doubled. Between 1950 and 1960, there were about 10 divorces per 1,000 married women. Since 1975, there have been about 21 divorces per 1,000 married women every year, with a peak of 23 per 1,000 in 1980 (U.S. Bureau of the Census, 1998a, Table 156). The divorce rate seems to have leveled out since then.

"Best Interests" Standard

Maternal preference remained the rule until the 1970s. First feminist writers and later fathers' rights groups questioned assumptions about gender. They maintained that fathers also bond with their children and do a good job of nurturing. By the 1990s, most states adopted a straightforward **best interests of the child** standard (Box 13.2 lists factors to be considered in determining "best interest"). These standards often include a determination of which parent had primary daily caretaking responsibilities independently of gender (**primary caretaker**). The abolition of maternal preference led to an overall increase in custody litigation (Nurcombe and Partlett, 1994). The changes in divorce law resulted in sharp curtailments of alimony for divorced women, an unintended consequence of the 1970s political thrust toward gender equality under the law.

Custody is not a unitary concept: different aspects of child care and child companionship can be divided up in different ways (see Box 13.3). Courts continue to award joint **legal custody** (shared decision making) with **physical custody** to the mother or **sole custody** to mothers most of the time (Santilli and Roberts, 1990). However, in recent years, many more fathers have taken on more child care responsibilities. In the event of a divorce, these fathers are more likely than fathers in the past to seek ongoing involvement in their children's daily lives whether or not they want the child to reside primarily with them (Pruett and Pruett, 1998).

The increase in divorce combined with the somewhat vague and gender-free "best interests of the child" custody standard has opened up a large market for the services of mental health professionals. Courts often refer the divorcing parties to mental health professionals for custody evaluations. A mental health professional evaluation is often seen as an alternative to mediation. However, the role of mental health professionals in custody determinations has been sharply criticized.

BOX 13.2

Gender-Free Best Interest Standard

The New York State Domestic Relations Law contains a typical custody standard: "In all cases there shall be no prima facie right to the custody of the child in either parent, but the court shall determine solely what is for the best interest of the child and will best promote its welfare and happiness and make award accordingly" (Article 5, Section 70, paragraph [a]).

BOX 13.3

Custody Arrangements

Several different custody arrangements are recognized.

- *Legal custody* is the authority to make decisions about the child's welfare and upbringing.
- *Physical custody* refers to the right to reside with the child and to have the authority to make decisions about the child's day-to-day care and instruction.
- In *sole custody,* one parent is given legal and physical custody of the child; the other parent is granted rights to visit the child and to have other contacts, and the child may reside with the noncustodial parent for summer vacations or holidays.
- The court can also grant *joint custody.* In one arrangement, sometimes called *joint custody with primary placement with one parent,* the court gives one parent physical custody of the child but divides legal custody between both parents. The court order requires the two parents to consult with one another about major child-rearing decisions. If parents can agree to cooperate, joint custody solves the problem of the noncustodial parent feeling left out; however, if the parents cannot cooperate, joint custody may sustain and feed conflict. In a relatively infrequent variant of joint custody, sometimes called *joint custody with shared placement,* or split or divided custody, the child resides with both parents, alternating between their homes. Sometimes, the children live in the parental home, and the two parents alternate in residing there.
- *Divided custody,* sometimes used to refer to arrangements in which the same child lives with each parent at different times, is also used to refer to arrangements in which custody of siblings is assigned differently. In a divided custody arrangement, the father might be given sole custody of one or more children and the mother sole custody of the other(s). Typically, the father is given custody of the older children or boys and the mother custody of the younger children or girls.

Unless their relationship with the child is legally terminated, parents are obliged to support their children whether or not they have custody. Child support payments are a frequent source of conflict in divorced families and in custody disputes.

Custody Disputes, Social Values, and Social Science

Social scientists play a significant role in shaping custody policy as well as decisions in individual cases. Because of the frequency of divorce and the problems that emerge, legislatures revise divorce and custody laws from time to time. Legislators are in need of useful information about these topics. Social scientists and developmental psychologists who study children and families in the midst of conflict and transition may provide an important component of that information. Courts deciding individual cases struggle to balance questions of fairness, parental rights, and workability of a plan when determining the best interests of the child. Family court judges, probably more than judges in other areas, use a therapeutic jurisprudence approach, seeking to come to decisions or settlements that will serve the well-being of all the participants. They routinely turn to clinicians to help them in this task.

Legal View of "Best Interests"

The key legal concept of "best interests" shapes the evaluations that mental health professionals do when they participate in custody evaluations. The **Uniform Marriage and Divorce Act** (Section 402) instructs courts to consider the following factors when determining the best interests of the child:

1. The wishes of the child's parent or parents as to his or her custody
2. The wishes of the child as to his or her custodian
3. The interaction and interrelationship of the child with his or her parent, his or her siblings, and any other person who may significantly affect the child's best interests
4. The child's adjustment to his or her home, school, and community
5. The mental and physical health of all the individuals involved (see also Chapter 2; ALI, 2000)

Three of the five factors—the child's adjustment, the mental health of the individuals, and the quality of the child's relationships—refer to psychological concepts. Judges do not routinely receive training in evaluating individuals along these dimensions. They frequently call on the expertise of mental health professionals. The participation of a mental health professional was noted in 38 percent of published decisions on issues in divorce and custody (ALI, 2000). The demand for clinical expertise also stimulates research to provide an empirical basis for the expert's testimony (see *Daubert* and *Kumho Tire Co.* decisions in Chapter 2).

Effects of Divorce on Children's Psychological Well-Being

Judges, lawyers, and professionals who undertake custody evaluations may use what they have learned from research about the adjustment of children after divorce.

Issues in research. Developmental research in divorce poses special research problems. It is difficult to separate psychological problems preexisting the divorce from the effects of divorce and of normal adjustment and development. Random assignment is not possible; in its absence, it is difficult to determine the factors influencing outcomes. Moreover, immediate or short-term psychological effects may not predict long-term psychological and behavioral problems.

Researchers have used various methods including surveys, intensive interviews, and psychological testing to compare the **adjustment** of children from broken and intact families. Sometimes researchers conduct more extensive **longitudinal studies**. Longitudinal studies are useful because they provide information about children's adjustment over time in the postdivorce period. Sampling selection biases may limit the generalizability of the information, however. The people who participate and remain in longitudinal studies over many years may not be representative of all divorced families. Study participants may be recruited exclusively from people seeking help after a divorce. They may be different than people who don't seek help. For example, when Luepnitz (1979) interviewed children from divorced families who had not sought psychological help, many reported that the divorce brought relief from conflict and emotional turmoil.

Researchers must also define and assess adjustment. They may measure happiness, school achievement, peer relations, self-image, family conflict, physical health, or rates of various problems (e.g., aggression and depression). Studies have measured maladjustment more often than health. The assumption that if a factor is associated with maladjustment, its opposite will be associated with better health is not warranted, however (Krauss and Sales, 2000).

Differences in results between studies may reflect the use of different measures or different samples. Despite these problems, enough studies have been conducted using enough different designs and measures to confidently draw some conclusions. The important work of Wallerstein and Kelly (1980) and the work of the researchers who followed them are summarized and discussed in Hetherington, Bridges, and Insabella's (1998) review of the literature on children's adjustment after divorce. We rely heavily on that review here.

Negative effects of divorce. The assumption that divorce is bad for many children is supported by the evidence. Divorce is a proxy for a large number of physical, social, economic, and emotional changes that inevitably accompany it and challenge adaptation. Divorce is weighted heavily on stressful life-event scales (e.g., Bloom, Asher, and White, 1978; Holmes and Rahe, 1967).

Children in divorced and remarried families have more emotional, interpersonal, and behavioral problems than children from intact families. Twenty to 25 percent of children whose parents have divorced exhibit ongoing psychological problems compared to about 10 percent of children from intact families.

The problems vary with the child's age and gender, and may continue or change throughout the life span. Children of divorce, whatever their age at the time of the divorce, have more problems *on the average* than people from intact families when they reach adolescence and in young adulthood. They are more likely to divorce themselves, and are less satisfied with their lives. However, the *majority* of children of divorce weather the transition, adapt to divorce (and to any remarriage), and go on to be well-functioning adults (Hetherington, Bridges, and Insabella, 1998).

Problems before divorce. Many children and parents of divorcing families had problems before the divorce. Children in families that later break up have more psychological, social, and behavioral problems than children in comparable nondivorcing families. The children's problems may be related to family conflicts in the predivorce period and to parental problems. Parents who later divorce are more likely to have emotional, psychological, economic, and substance abuse problems, and poorer interpersonal and parenting skills, than parents who stay together. When the adjustment of the children before the divorce is controlled, the negative effects of divorce on children shrink considerably. What we see after divorce may be related to what happened before the divorce as much as to what happened after the divorce (Heatherington, Bridges, and Insabella, 1998).

Postdivorce changes. Divorce and remarriage affect children by changing the roles, relationships, and interactions of family members. Two parents support each other in many ways. A couple can provide more varied role models and more resources of many kinds for their children than a single parent.

One theory attributes the poor adjustment of some children of divorce to the personal and economic stresses divorce places on the parents and the family. The income of custodial mothers drops 25 percent to 50 percent after divorce; the drop for custodial fathers averages about 10 percent. The loss of income doesn't account for children's postdivorce problems; children in divorced families have higher rates of adjustment problems even when income is statistically controlled. However, child and parent behavior, changes in family structure, socioeconomic decline, and parents'stress may all contribute to the disruption of family processes, which, in turn, affects children's adaptation. Financial, legal, social, and emotional problems may interact and may be exacerbated when the noncustodial spouse fails to keep up with child support payments, or later refuses to contribute to the cost of a child's college education because the child is no longer a minor.

High-conflict families. Most parents work out a custody arrangement on their own or with lawyers, which is simply ratified by the court. Only 6 to 20 percent of custody cases are actually decided in the courtroom (Krauss and Sales, 2000). Nine to 15 percent of all divorcing families, and 25 to 40 percent of those obtaining court-imposed decisions, engage in extreme conflict (Pruett and Hoganbruen, 1998; Johnston, 1994). Procedures and policies, especially in family court, are intended to promote stability and resolve conflict, but the court can become another battleground for warring couples. These include couples who refuse to settle and who relitigate again and again, taking up an inordinate amount of court time and creating costs and emotional distress for themselves, their children and everyone else involved.

Research and theory with divorcing couples and children suggest policies that might mitigate negative effects of divorce. For example, some jurisdictions have experimented with mandated counseling or parent training to try to reduce maladaptive changes in family processes at the time of divorce. Efforts to enforce child support orders may help alleviate the custodial family's financial distress. The noncustodial spouse may be required in the divorce agreement to contribute to the costs of the children's college education. While mental health professionals' (MHPs) role as evaluators has come under considerable fire, they are being welcomed as collaborators in experiments in court-based therapeutic interventions.

Custody Standards

The best interests of the child standard provides the basic framework for custody decisions and for custody evaluations. Within this framework, judges may choose between a variety of custody arrangements (see Box 13.3).

Vague Standards

The vagueness of the best interest standard creates several problems. Without clearer legislative guidance, judgments about what constitutes the child's "best interests" tend to be based on the judge's values (see *Painter v. Bannister*, 1966, discussed in Box 13.4). The judge must also decide whether to consider the child's needs at the time of the custody dispute only, or to weigh considerations about the child's future needs.

When the law is clear, the outcome of cases is more predictable. When the law is clear, people tend to avoid the time and distress of litigation. (They think, why bother to litigate if the outcome is fairly certain?) On the other hand, because the "best interests" standard is vague, is applied with reference to the child's individual circumstances, and with a high degree of judicial discretion, the outcome of custody cases is difficult to predict: similar custody cases can be decided very differently. In consequence, more people may choose to litigate, prolonging the conflict and leaving children unsettled longer.

Vague standards also limit the potential validity of psychological evaluations. It is easy to agree when one parent has severe problems: a parent who abuses the child, an alcoholic parent, or a parent with a history of frequent hospitalizations for mental illness should probably not receive custody. But in most cases, judges must choose

BOX 13.4

A Legal Case in Point: Who Is the Better Parent for a Child?

In *Painter v. Bannister* (1966), grandparents were granted custody of a child over the claims of a natural father. The case illustrates the fallibility of expert predictions. It also illustrates how courts may weigh conventional values strongly in arriving at a decision. After his wife died, Mr. Painter asked the Bannisters, his wife's parents, to care for their five-year-old grandson, Mark, until he could find satisfactory child care. When he remarried a year and a half later and asked for Mark to be returned, the Bannisters refused. They filed for custody in their state court. A psychologist, Dr. Glenn Hawks, testified that Mark "had already made an adjustment and sees the Bannisters as his parental figures in his psychological makeup . . . ." Dr. Hawks concluded that a change in custody would be detrimental: "The chances are very high [Mark] will go wrong if he is returned to his father." The judge, giving great weight to the psychologist's testimony, awarded custody to the Bannisters. The judge never characterized the father as unable to care for the child. He was open about his preference for the grandparents' more conventional lifestyle. After Mark visited his father a few time he expressed a desire to stay with him. His grandparents did not oppose the change in custody. Two years after the hearing, Mark went to live with his father, with no apparent ill effects.

between (and the consulting psychologist must evaluate) two reasonably fit parents; both have strengths and weaknesses as parents and as people. Here, psychological evaluation can offer only limited help. For example, there is no empirical basis for choosing between a warm, stimulating, but somewhat anxious and moody parent and a cool, unexpressive, but stable and reliable parent. Psychology cannot say which of these parents has more or less of a quality called "mental health," nor what the relationship of such characteristics is to good parenting skills. There is no algorithm to predict how a child will do in one of two "good enough" but imperfect homes, no matter how much information is available.

Legislation has provided some guidance for judges. The Uniform Marriage and Divorce Act lists factors to consider, but does not tell judges how to weigh them. Sometimes legislators provide more guidance. Laws may structure the decision process by enumerating more specific factors to consider or procedures to follow (e.g., weigh preferences of children over 14 heavily) in coming to a decision. They may establish default decision rules or "presumptions" favoring certain arrangements. A preferred arrangement is to be presumed best for the child absent evidence that it would not be best in the case at hand. Courts have also promulgated guidelines intended to reduce arbitrariness in decision making while retaining flexibility. In the following section, we will discuss the most widely used preferences or presumptions.

Primary Caretakers and Stability

Primary caretaker doctrine. In 1981, a West Virginia appeals court discarded the tender years doctrine on the grounds that it violated equal protection to make the sex of the parent a basis for awarding custody (*Garska v. McCoy*, 1981). Instead, the court said that, other things being equal, the interests of young children are best served by awarding custody to the parent who has been their primary caretaker ("in most cases in West Virginia still the mother"). The opinion defined the primary caretaker as the person with responsibility for care of the child, including providing meals, grooming, arranging for social interaction after school, and educating. The primary caretaker doctrine was readily adopted by other states, often incorporated in a best interests standard. Some legislatures and courts established a rebuttable presumption that children of divorcing parents would do best if custody remained with the parent who spent the most time caring for them, typically the mother.

The doctrine was appealing. It acknowledged the importance of the mother's traditional role, but at the same time it gave those men who had been deeply involved in the day-to-day care of their children grounds for requesting custody. It acknowledged the importance of psychological bonding. Under the principle, men can claim primary caretaker status if, for example, the mother has a demanding job requiring long hours or frequent travel.

Continuity, attachment, and psychological parents. The primary caretaker preference was consistent with a preference for a custody arrangement that maximized continuity or stability (or minimized disruption) in the child's life. Fathers' advocates, however, challenge restrictions on visitation or shared physical custody based on this preference. They question the belief that disruption caused by frequent visitation and overnights is harmful for children (Pruett, Ebling, and Insabella, 2004).

Change accompanied by loss is harmful to children. Such changes include divorce, parental death, prolonged hospitalizations of a parent, frequent moves in and out of or between foster homes, and separations from parents in wartime. Change doesn't necessarily interfere with long-term development. Sometimes change can have positive effects as children learn to cope. Overcoming problems can contribute to personal growth by enhancing openness, resilience, and future adaptability. Change can be accompanied by gain as well as loss. Children can benefit from the dissolution of a violent marriage, or from moving to a safer neighborhood or a better school. Development is itself a change process.

No body of psychological work allows anyone to say precisely when and how much stability and continuity should be figured into the best interests of the child. There is no clear empirical answer to the question of whether maintaining stability in the child's life should be weighed more than the value of spending time with both parents. However, the beliefs that a child has one primary caretaker and that a strong stable relationship between young children and their primary caretaker is essential to normal development are strong tenets of psychoanalytically based developmental theories (Goldstein, Freud, and Solnit, 1973; Goldstein et al., 1996).

In their book *Beyond the Best Interests of the Child* (1973), Joseph Goldstein (a law professor), Anna Freud (the daughter of Sigmund Freud and herself a noted child analyst), and Albert Solnit (a professor of child psychiatry) maintained that in deciding custody disputes, courts should choose "the least detrimental available alternative" for the children. This alternative would maximize the child's opportunity for maintaining a relationship with the principal "psychological parent," the person who provided daily attention to the child's needs for physical care, nourishment, comfort and intellectual stimulation. More controversially, they agued that the child's relationship with the psychological parent should not be disrupted, even for the sake of maintaining or developing other relationships. Therefore, they contended that the rights of the noncustodial parent had to be minimized in order to avoid damaging the all-important primary relationship with the psychological parent.

Beyond the Best Interests of the Child received a mixed reception. Many psychologists were skeptical of psychoanalytic theories of child development because these theories had a weak empirical base (see Katkin, Bullington, and Levine, 1974). Moreover, there is evidence that children form multiple **attachment**s to fathers, siblings, grandparents, other relatives, and other adults. These contribute to their emotional growth.

Goldstein, Freud, and Solnit's recommendation to sharply restrict the rights of the noncustodial parent was not adopted by the courts as a new legal standard. Nonetheless, the book had considerable influence on the way judges thought about individual cases in the 1970s and 1980s. Their ideas have entered into current debates about how the courts should respond when a custodial parent wishes to relocate (see relocation discussion, below) or when stepparents (including gay stepparents) request custody in a divorce.

Primary Caretakers, Male and Female: Empirical Findings

As a practical matter, sole or physical custody is rarely given to a "nonprimary" parent when the other parent is a fit primary caretaker. The mother as the primary caretaker becomes the parent with whom the child principally resides in 84 percent of divorces (Hetherington, Bridges, and Insabella, 1998).

Fathers with custody. Most fathers do not ask for sole or primary physical custody. But father-headed single-parent families are the fastest-growing type of family in the United States. Some researchers have compared outcomes for children when fathers have custody and when mothers have custody (Hetherington, Bridges, and Insabella, 1998). Even when income (higher for custodial fathers than mothers) is statistically controlled, custodial fathers report less child-rearing stress than custodial mothers after an initial adjustment period. Single fathers may be less stressed than mothers with sole custody because the men are more likely to receive support from other family members (e.g., their mothers) (Luepnitz, 1982). The children of fathers with sole custody have fewer problems than children raised by single mothers (Hetherington, Bridges, and Insabella, 1998).

Children may do better on average with custodial fathers because these fathers are "self-selected." They care about the parental role and feel competent in it. Most custodial mothers do well for their children, but they are not self-selected caregivers; maternal custody is still the socially expected "default" arrangement in the United States.

Same-sex parent. A strong relationship with the same-sex parent is important for the adjustment of adolescents of both sexes, but the same-sex parent need not be the primary caretaker or custodial parent. A policy of granting custody to the same-sex parent may mean dividing male and female siblings, which courts are reluctant to do. Sociologists Powell and Downey (1997) found no evidence in a large-scale national survey that living with a same-sex parent was better for the child. There is also evidence that positive relationships with fathers (opposite-sex parent) are associated with academic achievement and good interpersonal relations among adolescent girls and young women.

Joint Custody

Both parents and children do better when the parents develop a cooperative, mutually supportive coparenting relationship after divorce. Children of cooperative parents adapt better to their parents' remarriages as well as to the divorce (Hetherington, Bridges, and Insabella, 1998). Some children's advocates urged a preference for **joint custody** arrangements in the belief that joint custody would keep both parents involved with the child and contribute to postdivorce cooperation between them. Moreover, with both parents working in many families, and some men more involved in parenting, the concept of the primary caretaker has become less compelling.

Advocates of joint custody rejected Goldstein, Freud, and Solnit's (1973) recommendation that the role of the noncustodial parent be limited. Advocates reasoned that joint custody (see Box 13.3) would help families avoid the problems associated with fatherless households (Pearson and Thoeness, 1990). They believed that joint custody would encourage children's continuing relationship with both parents, increasing social support. The coparenting relationship would have positive effects on parents as well as children because it would keep both parents involved in the child's care, providing the parents with gratification and support. Many parents who were unhappy with one another as partners could still cooperate as parents, which in turn would lead to diminished hostility over time. Joint custody has the added advantage of appearing fair because it allows both parents to have a meaningful place in the child's life.

Although there was little solid research on the actual outcome of different custody arrangements, many legislatures and courts found the arguments in favor of joint custody persuasive. By 1990, 34 states had enacted statutes that favored joint custody rather than sole custody (Mnookin and Weisberg, 2005; Pearson and Thoeness, 1990). However, judges, following legislative directive or legal precedent, consider the ability of parents to cooperate, communicate, and make decisions before awarding joint custody (see *Matter of Reed v. Reed*, 1997; *Taylor v. Taylor*, 1986). Adopting a therapeutic jurisprudence approach, family court professionals use the term *parenting plan* rather than *joint custody award*. The new term signals that the custody arrangement is an agreement between parents about how to work together rather than a property settlement.

Psychologists also appear partial to joint custody. Bow and Quinnell (2001) conducted a nationwide survey of 198 psychologists who frequently do custody evaluations. On average, the respondents recommended joint legal custody in 73 percent of their cases; in effect, it was the default recommendation. They recommended joint physical as well as legal custody about a third of the time. However, the frequency of the joint custody recommendations might have reflected legal requirements to favor this arrangement barring counterindications. The three primary reasons the psychologists gave for recommending sole custody were lack of cooperation or inability to coparent, severe mental illness of one parent, and abuse or neglect.

Problems with joint custody. Although a popular solution to the problem of maintaining a child's relationship with both parents, not everyone sees joint custody as an ideal or even a feasible arrangement, at least not for all families. Many lawyers and clinicians do not think it is reasonable to expect hostile parents who couldn't get along before divorce to engage in ongoing shared decision making afterward. Joint custody, they say, will exacerbate parental conflict, continue the unhealthy emotional relationship between former partners, and make it difficult for them to move on. It may also expose children to more occasions of parental conflict, making it more likely that children will become pawns in arguments between their parents (Pearson and Thoeness, 1990). Inability to coparent was a major reason why psychologists in the Bow and Quinnell (2001) study recommended sole legal custody.

Some women's advocates believe policies favoring joint custody are harmful to women, usually the primary caretaker and primary residential parent. When custody, support payments, and property division are all in dispute, a parent, usually a father, who doesn't really want custody may seek joint physical custody as a bargaining ploy, knowing that the court is likely to award it. That parent might then agree to give up custody in return for lowered child support payments or a larger share of marital property. Women's advocates have expressed similar concerns about "friendly parent" policies (physical custody to the parent most likely to support visiting with the other parent). The parent, usually the mother, who wants sole custody may agree to joint custody rather than risk losing physical custody altogether by seeming "unfriendly" (Mnookin and Weisberg, 2005). Advocates for abused women strongly oppose joint custody on the ground that it provides violent men with a way of continuing to control and threaten their ex-wives.

Joint Custody: Empirical Findings

Much of the research on joint custody has focused on the workability of the arrangement and on parents' satisfaction with it rather than on the outcome for children (McKinnon and Wallerstein, 1986; Pearson and Thoennes, 1990; Pruett and Hoganbruen, 1998). Researchers do not always make it clear whether they are referring to joint legal or joint physical custody (Kraus and Sales, 2000). Moreover, since joint physical custody need not involve an even 50-50 division of the child's time, it may not in practice differ from joint legal custody with generous visitation arrangements.

Children do best when they have good relationships with both parents and the parents are cooperative. Amato and Gilbreth's (1999) meta-analysis of studies of nonresident father involvement found that authoritative involved parenting by the father was correlated with better child adjustment. Joint custody arrangements may be linked to greater closeness with the father and more contact with the father. Children may have less of a sense of loss and may maintain contact with both parents better when custody is shared. But it can't be assumed that awarding joint custody is always the best way to achieve good relationships, or that children in joint custody arrangements necessarily do better than children in sole custody arrangements.

Bauserman (2002) did a meta-analysis of 33 studies that compared joint physical or joint legal custody with sole custody. On average, children in joint physical or legal custody were better adjusted than children in sole custody, and were just as well adjusted as children in intact families. However, the differences in adaptation between children in joint and sole custody arrangements were small, and the results may reflect biases in the selection of samples; custody arrangements are not made randomly. There may be gender differences in children's adaptation to different custody arrangements as well (Luepnitz, 1982; Pruett and Hoganbruen, 1998).

Pruett and Santangelo (1999) undertook an extensive review of the empirical literature on joint custody. They concluded that

- parents who choose joint custody voluntarily tend to be older, wealthier, and better educated than sole custody parents;
- joint legal custody and joint physical custody fathers feel more satisfied after divorce, and that has a positive effect on their involvement with their children over time;
- joint physical custody provides benefits in satisfaction and adjustment among educated child-centered families that are most likely to choose it;
- custody arrangement does not affect parental cooperation or conflict;
- when families are in high conflict, joint custody of any sort does not heal the relationship, and when parents cannot contain their conflict within the marital

dyad, it can be destructive for children; school-age children may be the most vulnerable; and

- based on the widely used Child Behavior Check List, custody arrangements made no difference on scales measuring children's depression, aggression, delinquency, social withdrawal, and somatic complaints (pp. 398, 415–416; see also Pearson and Thoennes, 1990).

Joint custody and parental conflict. The research does not support a presumption that joint custody is the best arrangement for the child in all cases (Felner and Terre, 1987; Pruett and Santangelo, 1999). Most participants in studies of joint custody were parents who voluntarily chose the arrangement. They were more likely than other divorced couples to have had a good parenting relationship at the time of separation. Children in families with cooperative divorced parents tend to do well regardless of the custody arrangement.

When mandated to accept joint custody, parents in conflict continue the conflict post divorce. They report negative experiences with joint custody (Pruett and Santangelo, 1999). These parents continue their conflicts in single custody arrangements as well. Joint custody does not make the conflict worse, but some children may be more likely to experience divided loyalties. Joint custody may make violence worse and is counterindicated in violent families (see Chapter 12). The evidence is strong that involvement in hostile conflicts between parents is harmful to children no matter what custody arrangement is made (Kraus and Sales, 2000).

About 50 percent of divorced parents have neither highly cooperative nor highly conflicted relationships (Hetherington et al., 1998). Many disengage. They don't interact much, and consequently do not have conflicts. The pattern is similar for families with joint custody or sole custody (Pruett and Santangelo, 1999). The fidelity to the original parenting plan fades as the parents enter into new relationships, remarry, or develop a lifestyle that accommodates to their circumstances. The initial custody arrangement may serve as a bridge to a new life during a transition period.

Natural and Psychological Parents

In most custody disputes, the child has been living with both parents and has some attachment to both. But sometimes a nonparent custodian and a natural parent both claim custody. The presumption that custody should go to the natural parent is strong but can be overcome. "A parent has a prima facie right to custody of his child. . . . Only where the best interest of the child would be served will this right be forfeited and custody awarded to a non-parent third party. Therefore, the burden of proof is on the third party to show the best interest of the child would be served by her receiving custody" (*Ellerbe v. Hooks*, 1980).

Nonparents seek custody. Third parties have most often petitioned for custody when they have been the child's caretaker because a parent and child were separated. They argue that the child is doing well with them, that they have bonded, that they love the child, that the child regards them as a parent, and that it would hurt the child to take the child away. These can be dramatic and heartbreaking situations.

The law long recognized de facto parent–child relationships (*de facto* refers to an actual state of affairs accepted for practical purposes and is the opposite of *de jure*, "by act of law"; see *Guardianship of Shannon*, 1933). Goldstein, Freud, and Solnit's (1973)

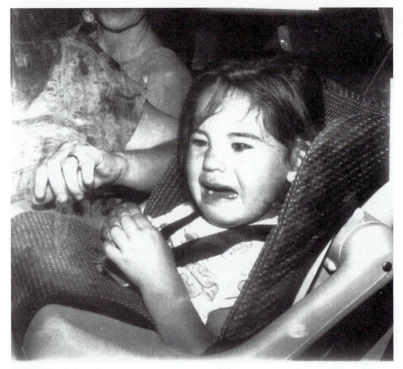

FIGURE 13.1

Baby Jessica DeBoer

Baby Jessica DeBoer was placed in custody with adoptive parents by her natural mother. Her natural father had never given permission for her to be adopted. Months later, the father petitioned to have the child restored to his custody. Had the child bonded to her adoptive parents, and would her adjustment be harmed if the relationship was severed? There was a very public and emotional fight. The infant was eventually restored to her birth parents. Ironically, the couple divorced a few years later. Baby Jessica changed her name and went to live with her father after the divorce.

concept of the "psychological parent" contributed to the judicial recognition of de facto parent–child relationships. The emphasis on children's developmental needs may have paved the way for cases like *Bennett v. Jeffreys* (1976), in which the court spoke matter-of-factly of the "rights" of a child. When she was 15, Ms. Bennett had a baby girl named Gina out of wedlock. She gave the child to Mrs. Jeffreys to raise. When she was 23, Ms. Bennett asked Mrs. Jeffreys for the child. Mrs. Jeffreys refused to give her back. Ms. Bennett was not unfit to be a parent. Nonetheless, the New York Court of Appeals ruled that where there was a prolonged separation between mother and child, the best interests standard should be applied. "A parent's right to rear its child is not absolute. Extraordinary situations may require a different result. The rights of the child must be considered." Mrs. Jeffreys received custody of the child.

Stepparents are the most common "psychological parents." At least one court has awarded custody of a child to a stepparent rather than a parent (*Stanley D. v. Deborah D.*, 1983). Grandparents who have been raising children have sometimes sought custody, especially if the parent was neglectful. Grandparents, concerned because divorce may separate them from grandchildren, have also sought enforceable visitation rights. They argue that they have a psychological and a familial relationship with the child and it is in the child's interests that this relationship be maintained. Some states have recognized grandparents' standing to seek visitation. However, the U.S. Supreme Court affirmed a State of Washington Supreme Court ruling limiting grandparents' rights. The Washington high court overturned a lower court decision requiring a mother who already allowed some grandparent visitation to allow more visitation than the mother wished to grant. The court ruled that the requirement violated the mother's due process right to make decisions concerning the care, custody, and control of her daughter (*Troxel v. Granville,* 2000).

Is it time for a less ambitious standard? There is a long tradition of family privacy and protection from state interference in child rearing. Protecting children from neglect or abuse has been established as a compelling reason to limit parental rights. In the case of custody disputes, the parents are themselves turning to the state for help in resolving a conflict, and the state chooses the principles on which the resolution is based. The states have placed children's interests rather than the parents' rights at the center of the law.

Some advocates for both fathers and mothers have argued that fit parents' interest in and right to companionship of their children should figure more in custody decisions. They question whether there is any basis for judges to decide or for mental health professionals to advise them how to choose between fit parents.

Father's advocates would like an end to what they see as a system biased toward women: they would like courts to recognize parental rights and to see that fathers have access to their children even if this is inconvenient or disruptive for the child and mother. Some women's advocates would prefer a return to a primary caretaker standard. They argue that most of the time, it is the mother who has the greater emotional predivorce investment in the child. Consequently, the mother will inevitably make greater concessions to retain custody (Krauss and Sales, 2000). In their view, a presumption awarding custody to a primary caretaker would overcome the weakness in the mother's bargaining position.

Krauss and Sales (2000) recommend replacing *best interests of the child* with "least detrimental alternative" (originally coined by Goldstein, Freud, and Solnit, 1973). They argue that the least detrimental alternative is what in reality all judges can look for and mental health professionals can honestly claim to evaluate.

Controversial Factors in Custody Decisions

Social and cultural changes have affected custody decisions and created controversy. Underlying many of the specific controversies is the question of the extent to which custody awards should be influenced by social norms. Courts recognize that custody cannot be decided solely "on the premise that the child's best interest would be served by assimilation into the dominant culture" (*Johnson v. Johnson,* 1978), but they will consider evidence that a child can be harmed in concrete ways if in the custody of a parent with unusual beliefs or practices. Controversy regarding suitability to adopt orphaned or foster children has often highlighted issues that are later reargued in the context of a custody dispute in a divorce.

In the past, judges agreed that sexual activity outside of marriage was immoral, and they would not give custody to a parent who had extramarital sexual relationships. Today, courts regard sexual activity outside of marriage, substance abuse, or other "immoral" behaviors as relevant to custody determinations only if they are witnessed by the child or disrupt child care (Nurcombe and Partlett, 1994).

Gay Parents

Many men and women who consider themselves homosexual have had heterosexual relationships at some time in their lives; some become parents. In the past, a homosexual parent had little chance of obtaining custody. Homosexuality was regarded as either moral unfitness or mental illness. Today, homosexuality per se, without evidence of conflict or anxiety about one's sexual identity, has been removed from the *DSM-IV* (American Psychiatric Association, 1994) and is no longer characterized as a psychiatric disorder. The rise of the gay rights movement and greater openness about homosexual behavior and relationships led homosexuals to challenge rulings that denied them custody or visitation because of their sexual orientation.

Some courts continue to view homosexuality in and of itself as evidence of parental unfitness. The majority of courts have held that a parent's homosexuality is relevant to a custody determination, but that adverse impact on the child must be shown (see *D.H. v. J.H.,* 1981). Courts differ about whether homosexual parents should be required to keep their sexual orientation secret, and whether restrictions should be placed on visitation with homosexual parents. The ALI statement (2000) recommending future legislation would prohibit courts from considering the sexual orientation of a parent in reviewing a parenting plan.

Research on gay parents. Some psychologists undertook research to see if children raised by homosexual parents exhibited more adjustment problems than other children. The APA and allied professional organizations summarized this research in an amicus curiae brief submitted to the Supreme Court of Virginia on behalf of Sharon Bottoms (*Bottoms v. Bottoms,* 1994). Sharon's mother, had filed for custody of Sharon's two-year-old son, her grandson, on the grounds that Sharon's lesbian relationship with her partner rendered her an unfit parent. The brief summarized research indicating that there are no significant differences between children raised by homosexual parents and those raised by heterosexual parents. The overall psychological health of the children in these two groups is the same. Moreover, children raised by homosexuals are not more likely than other children to become homosexual themselves. The children show no differences from other children in their social relationships. The evidence on these points was very consistent, especially for lesbian mothers. (The relatively small number of studies of children raised by gay fathers made the conclusions about these children's well-being more tentative.) The limited research suggested that social harassment and social stigma, a concern of some judges, were not severe. Friends of gay parents were rarely accused of molesting children, and gay families were confident that their children were not at elevated risk. However, the Virginia Supreme Court (1995) gave custody to the grandmother finding the mother an unfit custodian for behaviors other than her lesbian relationship.

Courts have not always found the research persuasive, however. As is often the case when the APA files a brief, some psychologists felt that the current knowledge was insufficient to justify a policy recommendation (Cameron and Cameron, 1997). They noted a number of weaknesses in the research into homosexual parenting. The studies used small samples, and many lacked appropriate comparison groups. The research suffers from selection bias: most of the subjects were middle-class, formerly married lesbians. The results might not generalize to gay men. The subjects volunteered; parents whose children were doing poorly may have been less likely to volunteer to participate than parents whose children were doing well. Moreover, gay parents might have been reluctant to cooperate with researchers they felt were unfriendly or skeptical about their parenting abilities. Stacey and Biblarz (2001) reviewed 21 studies. They noted that while there were some differences between children raised in heteroseuxal and gay families, the research indeed showed that childrens' adjustment, development, and well-being—the important custody considerations—were unrelated to parental sexual orientation.

New technologies have made it possible for homosexual men and women to arrange to become biological parents without engaging in heterosexual intercourse. Homosexual women can have their eggs fertilized in vitro by an anonymous donor and implanted in their own womb. Homosexual men can arrange for a friend or surrogate to carry a donor egg fertilized by their sperm in vitro to term. Alternate reproductive technologies, and the problem of deciding who are parents with standing when disputes arise about children born through their use, are discussed in the section below.

Gay psychological parents. Gay men and women who are biological parents retain some rights as parents even in jurisdictions that are less tolerant of their sexual preferences. In some states, gays may also seek to become parents by adoption. Some gay couples become foster parents and seek to adopt hard-to-place children. Gay partners of biological parents, usually female partners of lesbian mothers, may also seek to adopt their companion's child or, in the event of separation or the partner's death, seek custody of or visitation rights with the children they helped raise. The American Academy of Pediatrics and the Child Welfare League of America support the right of gay people to adopt their partner's children, arguing that this will insure that the child has access to health insurance benefits and social security benefits as well as a continuing legal relationship with both (biological and psychological) parents in the event of separation (Goode, 2002; see also the American Academy of Pediatrics website, www.aap.org).

Most states leave it to the courts to decide second-parent adoption petitions, and to agencies or courts to evaluate petitions to adopt orphaned children. Vermont, Connecticut, and California have passed laws allowing gay people to adopt their partner's children. Appellate courts in Illinois, New York, New Jersey, Massachusetts, and Washington, D.C., have sanctioned the right of gay partners to adopt. Mississippi, Florida, and Utah effectively ban these adoptions.

Florida evaluates adoption applications from people with a history of drug abuse or domestic violence on a case-by-case basis. Its adoption laws no longer contain a preference for married couples. But the state absolutely and categorically prohibits adoptions by gay people (Goode, 2002). In a case, which illustrates how ideology may trump other considerations, a gay couple in Florida attempted to adopt a child they had raised from infancy. The child was the eldest of three HIV positive children they were fostering. When the boy was ten, his mother died. The gay couple's petition to adopt him was rejected. The Supreme Court refused to hear an appeal. (*Lofton v. Secretary of the Florida Department of Children and Families,* 2005.)

Alternative Reproductive Technologies (ART)

There are many ways to make a baby nowadays. To name some: in vitro fertilization of a woman's own eggs by her male partner's sperm, with subsequent implantation of the eggs in the mother's womb (used when women have blocked fallopian tubes); artificial insemination by the male partner or, if his sperm is defective or infertile, by a donor; surrogacy, which may involve a surrogate carrying her own egg fertilized by the male partner's sperm, a surrogate carrying her own egg fertilized by a sperm donor through birth, transfer of the surrogate's ova (fertilized by the husband's sperm or a donor) to the wife's womb for gestation, transfer of the wife's egg fertilized by the husband's sperm to a surrogate's womb, or the use of donated egg and sperm carred to gestation by a surrogate.

These new reproductive technologies are beginning to raise new legal issues and new psychological questions. The United Kingdom, Australia, Canada, Denmark, the Netherlands, and some other European countries have passed legislation specifying the rights and responsibilies of the parties involved in surrogacy and ART. In the United States, the states and often individual state courts are addressing these questions and coming up with inconsistent answers. Here are some examples of legal dilemmas introducted by ART.

Suppose one partner is infertile and a donor is used in his or her place. Does the genetic parent have greater claim to custody? In a New York case, a woman had a baby from a female donor's eggs fertilized by her own husband's sperm. The husband later sued for divorce and demanded custody as the only natural parent. He lost (*McDonald v. McDonald,* 1994).

Some lesbian couples now have the egg from one partner fertilized with donor sperm and then carried to birth by the other partner. Does the child have two legal mothers? Whose name goes on the birth certificate? Whose name goes on the birth certificate as the father and mother? Does it matter what the child has been or will be told (Schwartz, 2003)? What are parental rights if the couple separates and a custody dispute ensues? What psychological issues enter in such a dispute?

A child cannot be regarded as a market commodity about whom contracts can be made, but courts have treated surrogacy as a contractual relationship. Three tests have been used to determine which parents will receive legal recognition in a dispute between a surrogate and a parent for custody of the child: preconception intent to raise the child, the child's best interests, and genetic relationship to the child (Schwartz, 2003). Should carrying the child be included in the list since, arguably, this process creates a biochemically based bond?

ART suggests new areas for psycholegal research as well. We will restrict our comments here to a few problems relevant to custody disputes. Does it matter what children born of ART are told about their origins? Golombok et al. (2002) followed a group of children conceived by artificial insemination up to age 12 and found no evidence that secrecy negatively affected family relationships. How will the children be affected if court cases, custody or visitation disputes, or public records list different parents from the ones they recognize? If the carrier or donor is a relative, does the contributing family member feel or want a special relationship with the child? How do extended families feel about children conceived with gametes donated by strangers, and will these issues affect the disposition in a custody dispute?

Mental illness in itself does not make a parent unfit, and courts have not presumed that custody should go to the nondisabled parent. Courts look at whether the parent's illness affects his or her parenting ability or relationship with a child. The other parent's ability to parent and involvement with the child may be a factor in the decision (*Moye v. Moye,* 1981).

Mental health professionals evaluating parents in a custody dispute try to assess how a parent's mental health status and personality might affect child rearing. It is a complex problem. Clinicians have concepts, tests, and interview techniques to assess psychopathology, but diagnosis doesn't predict parenting. A parent may have problems in one realm of life, but may be highly competent in another role. A person who might have disastrous relationships with adults may relate very well with children. Moreover, some children prove resilient. They can adapt to parental limitations. With adequate support, they may grow into healthy adults who have learned to cope successfully with stresses.

Should parents' therapists be allowed to testify? Separation and divorce are highly stressful life events (Bloom, Asher, and White, 1978). Many people, including those with no prior history of mental health problems, seek help at that time.

A parent's mental health is considered relevant to a custody determination. If one parent is in therapy and the other alleges that the parent in therapy has psychological problems that affect the child, the psychotherapist may be subpoenaed to testify. This situation poses ethical and practical problems. Is one parent gaining an advantage simply from not being in therapy, even though he or she may have as many or more problems than the former spouse? Is the breach of confidence and confidentiality required for the therapist to testify justifiable? The subsequent course of treatment may be affected if the therapist testifies frankly about the client's strengths and weaknesses. However, a parent's therapist may not really know much about what kind of parent the client is. Shuman et al. (1998) argue that, because of the many potential problems, therapists should be excluded from testifying about their patients in custody disputes.

Race and Ethnicity

With the elimination of legal barriers to racial intermarriage, and diminished cultural barriers to interracial relationships, courts are sometimes faced with deciding custody involving an interracial couple. In *Palmore v. Sidoti* (1984), the U.S. Supreme Court ruled that, as a matter of public policy, custody decisions cannot turn on racial considerations. The case was brought by a white father who sued for custody of his daughter after her mother married an African American man. He claimed that the girl would suffer social pressures and stigma because of the mixed marriage. Chief Justice Burger said, "A natural mother cannot be divested of the custody of her child merely because of her remarriage to a person of a different race. . . . Racial discrimination is wholly contrary to public policy and custody decisions cannot turn on racial considerations."

Race can nonetheless become an issue in custody disputes between partners of different races and with regard to transracial adoption. Some African American social workers and children's advocates have argued that black children need to be raised by or have frequent contacts with black parents to help them develop a positive understanding of their racial identity and cultural heritage and to learn how to cope with prejudice (Fenster, 2004). Evidence on this point is not well established.

Religion

The First Amendment prohibits courts from weighing the relative merits of different religions or basing a custody decision on the parents' religious beliefs alone (*Prince v. Massachusetts,* 1944). Similarly, lack of professed religious belief is not in and of itself a barrier to custody (*Gould v. Gould,* 1984). Evidence of a person's religious beliefs or practices is relevant and admissible in a custody proceeding if it is shown that such beliefs or practices are reasonably likely to cause present or future harm to the physical or mental development of the child. The ALI (2000) recommends that religious practices of a parent or child should be considered in parenting plans only to protect the child from "severe and almost certain harm" (Sec. 2.12(1)(c)).

When physical health of a child is at issue, courts have changed custody or conditioned it on some modification of the custodial parent's religious practices. For example, a Christian Science mother was granted custody provided she allowed her child to receive medical examinations and care (Nurcombe and Partlett, 1994). Developmental psychologists have paid scant attention to religion in child rearing. In the absence of a research base, psychologists involved in custody cases in which religion is at issue risk passing on personal preferences and prejudices as scientifically based judgments.

Relocation

Americans, including separated parents, move frequently. A 2000 U.S. Census Bureau study found that 43 million Americans relocated in a 12-month period (Eaton, 2004). People are more likely to move after divorce or a separation. About 17 percent of custodial parents moved away within a year, and about a fourth within 4 years of divorce (cited in Kelly and Lamb, 2003; Braver, Ellman, and Fabricius, 2003). Fathers move at similar rates to mothers.

Parental moves, especially those that involve long distances, may interfere with joint **custody** (both parents can make decisions about the child) and visitation arrangements. The courts can consider such a relocation a change in circumstances and a basis for modifying the parenting plan (ALI, 2000, Sec. 2.17). When the noncustodial parent moves the change does not become a legal issue. The parent has voluntarily altered the circumstances affecting his or her contact with the child; the former partner is unlikely to go to court and demand that the parent who has moved visit the child as before. However, when the custodial parent wishes to relocate, the noncustodial parent may go to court and request that if the other parent moves, the custody arrangement be changed. When the custodial parent has good reason (e.g., to take a better job, to be closer to extended family, or to pursue another relationship) to move to a distant location where it will be very difficult for the noncustodial parent to visit or to exercise joint custodial responsiblities, the courts must choose between one parent's right to change and to improve his or her circumstances and the other parent's right to have a relationship with the child. Both factors are thought to be related to the child's adjustment and welfare.

Psychological arguments have figured strongly in relocation cases, but the arguments are hypotheses based on indirect evidence or theory (e.g., the joint custody literature). Braver, Ellman, and Fabricius (2003) conducted one of the few studies to examine the issue directly. The researchers gave a number of self-report measures to college students in introductory psychology classes whose parents had divorced. Students from families in which no parent moved away reported fewer personal problems and better family relationships, though the magnitude of the difference was not great. The students who had experienced a move by a parent rated the distant parent less favorably as a source of emotional support and received less financial help for college from their fathers. The findings might have reflected preexisting differences in the parents who relocated and those who did not; when fathers were emotionally and financially involved with the children in the first place, both parents might have been less likely to relocate.

As yet, no consistent and coherent legal approach to the problem of relocation has emerged. During the 1980s and early 1990s, case law made it difficult for parents with primary custody to move even for a good job or a new marriage. In 1996, a trend to permit relocation began with a California case, *In re Marriage of Burgess* (1996). The court in *Burgess* relied heavily on an amicus brief filed by Judith Wallerstein, who is known for her studies of the long-term sequelae of divorce. Wallerstein argued that the child's best interests depended on maintaining the stability and continuity of the unit composed of the custodial parent and child and on the primary caretaker's psychological well-being. She contended that what was good for the parent with physical custody was good for the child. The court, influenced by her argument, reversed California's former standard and held that the parent with primary custody has a presumptive right to relocate.

Other researchers strongly criticized the court's reasoning in *Burgess*. They challenged Wallerstein's contention that involvement of nonresidential parents was unimportant for children's adjustment compared to the well-being of the custodial parent. They noted that the majority of studies strongly indicates that children actively involved with both parents do better on measures of adjustment and achievement (Kelly and Lamb, 2003; Kirkland, 2003).

A few years after *Burgess,* the trend toward permitting custodial parents to relocate began to reverse. Wallerstein submitted a brief in another California case, *In re Marriage of Navarro v. LaMusga* (2004), repeating her argument about custodial stability. For this case, Richard Warshak, another respected researcher with an interest in the role of divorced fathers, submitted an opposing brief. The California Supreme Court ruled that the parent with physical custody has a right to choose the child's residence unless the other parent could show detriment to the child. They held that the father did so in the case by demonstrating that the move would alienate the boys from him. Legislatures and courts in other jurisdictions also became less tolerant of relocation. For example, in 2001, the Colorado legislature abolished a legal presumption that the custodial parents have the right to move. The Colorado Court of Appeals placed the burden on the custodial parent of showing the move would directly benefit the child, a very difficult standard to meet (Eaton, 2004).

At present, the law and the conditions permitting a move as a basis for modification of a custody order vary from state to state. The disposition may depend on whether the custody order is for joint custody, shared physical custody, or visitation only. In the absence of clear and consistent criteria, parents fear that the outcome of their case will depend not on law but on the values of the judge to whom they happen to be assigned.

Kirkland (2003) believes that parents will move no matter what the legal standard may be. Mental health professionals should turn their attention to developing ways to maintain parent–child relationships across distances. Kelly and Lamb (2003) argue that moves in the first three years of life, when children are forming attachments, are not generally in the young child's best interests. If the custodial family does relocate, they suggest using videos, faxes, photos, and phone calls and rethinking visitation schedules to maintain contact after moves.

Relocation highlights another limitation of using the legal system to address social problems. When courts hear a request to modify a parenting plan due to relocation, they do not usually consider the interests of other children who are not involved in the custody dispute (e.g., children of moving parent's future spouse), but may be affected by its outcome. When a custodial mother makes a decision to move, she may be considering the interests of all the members of a new **blended family,** which might include a second husband, a child they have had together, and his children from an earlier marriage who rely on his financial support. A decision for or against relocation will impact on all these family members and possibly new step- or half-siblings on the father's side as well. Because of social changes in family structure and formation, courts are being presented with highly complex issues, whose outcomes are very difficult to predict.

Paying Attention to a Child's Wishes

The Uniform Marriage and Divorce Act (UMDA) directs judges to consider the child's wishes. In most states, custody statutes list children's preference as a factor, but it is not determinative. Many judges involve children in custody cases, but that involvement differs across jurisdictions and cases. The wishes of older children (those aged 12, 13, 14, or older) are given more weight than those of younger children. Some judges try to assess the child's maturity and decisional competence (Crosby-Currie, 1996; Nurcomb and Partlett, 1994). Sometimes, a child's change of preference for parental custody is sufficient to trigger a modification of the original custody decree.

Role of the guardian ad litem. In disputed custody cases, courts may appoint a **guardian ad litem** ("guardian for this litigation") to represent a child's interests. When the child is a baby, the guardian ad litem obviously thinks for the child. When the child is older, the guardian ad litem must decide what role to play. Should the guardian ascertain the child's wishes and represent them to the court, as the guardian would with an adult client, or should the guardian represent the disposition the guardian thinks would be best for the child, even if the child disagrees? The mental health professional preparing a report must also decide how much consideration to give to the child's opinions.

Weighing the child's preferences. Judges, professionals, and guardians ad litem alike have to assess and weigh the wisdom of a child's preferences. Most children are under six at the time of divorce, and many are under three. We know little about how children of different ages make choices about custody, or how to assess a child's maturity or competence to select the parent who will be best for his or her development. For example, suppose one child wants to live with the parent who makes firmer rules and limits, another child prefers a parent who gives the children greater freedom, and a third with the parent the child believes needs them most; there is no obvious way to determine which choice will be better. Small children are less able than adults to anticipate the future. However, even small children know as well as anyone what is emotionally important to them at any moment. Some child advocates believe that the court should be most concerned with the child's present needs, and that the views and desires of young children should be heard as well as those of teenagers.

Problems with asking the child's opinion. It is a problem to ask a child to express a preference between parents. As a young friend once said with eloquently bad grammar, "The one thing children of divorced parents don't want the most is to have to

BOX 13.5

401

Controversial
Factors in
Custody
Decisions

Asking Children's Wishes

Crosby-Currie (1996) surveyed about 400 family law attorneys and mental health professionals in several states to learn more about the actual involvement of children of different ages in the resolution of disputes about their custody.

Judges said that they were more likely to ascertain the wishes of children of all ages through interviews than through the use of mental health professionals or law guardian reports. Michigan judges asked children about their wishes in 69.9 percent of the cases; Virginia judges asked children about their wishes in 33.4 percent of the cases.

Almost ninety-six percent (95.5 percent) of the mental health professionals and 89 percent of the judges indicated that whether or not they asked a child specifically about his or her wishes was dependent on the child's age. Michigan judges said they were likely to ask children about their wishes starting at age eight to nine while Virginia judges were not likely to begin asking children directly about their wishes until the children were 12 or 13. Both judges (99 percent) and mental health professionals (91.9 percent) stated that the weight they gave a child's wishes depended on the child's maturity. Forty-three percent of the judges said they would give the wishes of 16- to 17-year-olds controlling weight although the laws of their states did not require it. Bow and Quinnell (2001) asked a nationwide sample of psychologists who do frequent custody evaluations at what age they would give serious consideration to a child's preference. The average response was 11.6 years with 12 as the most frequent age given.

choose." Most judges and clinicians believe that asking a child to choose will affect them adversely. One tactic is to avoid asking children the "ultimate" question and instead to ask them indirect questions (e.g., "Which parent do you like to put you to bed?" and "Which parent helps you with your homework?"). To limit stress, judges in some states can interview a child privately in chambers rather than have the child testify in open court in front of the parents (Crosby-Currie, 1996; see Box 13.5). Some states require that a record be kept of the interview or that the parents' attorneys be present. These procedures are intended to protect the parents' right to hear and respond to all the testimony on which the decision will be based. But using them means that the parents may learn what the child said, something the child may not want. An alternative is to leave the interviewing of children to a mental health professional or a law guardian who presents a report to the court. The presenter can be cross-examined. However, this deprives the child of the opportunity to present his or her views to the judge unedited and the parents of the opportunity to respond to those views. The dilemmas are clear, but the solutions are far less obvious.

Parental alienation syndrome. What if the child doesn't wish any contact at all with one of his parents? In 1985, Richard Gardner, controversial psychiatrist, coined the term **parental alienation syndrome (PAS)** to describe a pattern of child behavior he and other clinicians had observed developing during hostile, high-conflict divorces (Warshak, 2001). In PAS cases, the child persistently, vehemently, and unambivalently rejects and denigrates one parent, usually the noncustodial father; the rejection is not a reasonable response to the rejected parent's behavior; and the child's behavior is assumed to be strongly influenced by the mother, who persuades the child to ally with her, "programming" or "brainwashing" the child to share his or her hostility or para-noia about the other parent. Interest in PAS should be understood in the context of the problem of PAS, as described by its proponents, can vary in severity. In extreme cases, children may make or support false accusations of sexual abuse, physical abuse, neglect, or abuse of the custodial parent. Other researchers have described similar phe-nomena (e.g., the "Divorce related malicious mother syndrome"; Sexual allegations in divorce: the SAID syndrome"; and the "Medea syndrome"). If a court accepts that the child is suffering from PAS, the PAS literature recommends that children be forced to visit the rejected parent or, in extreme cases, that custody be given to the rejected par-ent and contact with the alienating parent cease.

Not surprisingly, PAS receives a lot of coverage in the fathers' rights literature. PAS may be considered a variant of the problem of interfering with a custody provision under a parenting plan (see ALI, 2000, Sec. 2.19). The most controversial problem concerns children who resist visitation. During custody hearings, parents are required to adhere to a temporary visitation schedule pending agreement on a permanent arrangement. Sometimes children say they do not want visitation with the noncustodial parent, usu-ally the father. However, children sometimes change their feelings about visitation as they get older. Fathers' advocates argue that they have a right to see the child, and can-not build a better relationship with the child if this right is taken away. They claim the refusal of the child to visit often reflects the child's desire to please the custodial parent. A custodial mother may make the counterclaim that the father is insisting on a particu-lar pattern of visitation to control her, not to see the child who really doesn't want to see the father. Allegations of PAS, allegations of domestic abuse or harassment, and allega-tions of child abuse or neglect may be raised.

Though few doubt that children can be caught up in parental hostility at the time of divorce, PAS testimony has been criticized by mental health professionals, children's advocates and lawyers, as lacking in scientific validity and reliability (Warshak, 2001; Emery, 2003; Kelly and Johnston, 2001; Rand, Rand, and Kopeski, 2005; See also http://www.leadershipcouncil.org/). Many but not all courts have rejected testimony on PAS. The National Council of Juvenile and Family Court Judges, condemned PAS as "discredited" in its publication "Navigating Custody and Visitation Evaluations in Cases with Domestic Violence: a Judge's Guide." Jennifer Hoult (2006), argues that there is no empirical data supporting the existence of PAS and that testimony about it ought therefore to be inadmissible. She traces PAS origins in Gardner's theory of human sex-uality which views adult-child sexual contact as natural.

While PAS is increasingly viewed as "junk" science, the observation that children become caught up in hostile triangle continues to add to the difficulty courts face eval-uating the child's wishes. These cases are even more troubling when the court is pre-sented with allegations of child sexual abuse, child physical abuse, and partner abuse made in the context of custody and visitation disputes. (For discussion of custody and intimate partner violence, see Chapter 12 on the latter.)

Allegations of Sexual Abuse in Divorce Cases

At the initial custody hearing, one parent sometimes alleges that the other sexually abused their child. The allegation may come later; a parent refuses to cooperate with visitation or custody orders because she or he suspects the other of sexually abusing the child. An allegation of sexual abuse is powerful. It makes the nasty business of custody disputes nastier. When comedian Woody Allen was accused by actress Mia Farrow of abusing their daughter, the personalities of both celebrities were savaged by

FIGURE 13.2

Dr. Elizabeth Morgan

Drs. Elizabeth Morgan and Eric Foretich engaged in a bitter custody battle over their daughter, Hilary. Dr. Morgan accused her former husband of sexually abusing Hilary. Experts disagreed as to whether the child was abused. Dr. Morgan was adamant in refusing to follow court orders: she would not let Dr. Foretich visit Hilary, and eventually secreted the girl away to New Zealand. Morgan was held in contempt of court and spent 25 months in jail. In 1989, she was released as a result of an act of Congress.

lawyers in a well-publicized trial. Another famous case, in which Dr. Elizabeth Morgan alleged that her husband, Dr. Eric Foretich, had sexually abused their daughter, went on in public view for years (Farber, 1990).

The children in both the Allen–Farrow and the Morgan–Foretich cases were examined by outstanding experts on both sides. The experts in neither case could agree on whether the children had been sexually abused; this sort of disagreement is not an unusual result when there is no physical evidence of abuse. Absent a clear finding of abuse, courts are reluctant to deprive a parent of custody or of constitutionally protected visitation rights. The need for proof can be painful for a parent who believes that the child has been maltreated. Dr. Morgan was convinced she needed to protect her child; she spent two years in jail for contempt of court because she refused to honor her husband's court-ordered rights to visitation (Farber, 1990).

False accusations in custody disputes. Allegations of sexual abuse in the course of a custody or visitation dispute, true or false, are comparatively rare. When an accusation of sexual abuse is made, there are four possibilities:

1. Abuse occurred, and there is adequate evidence.
2. Abuse occurred, but there is no adequate evidence and the charge is dropped.

FIGURE 13.3

Woody Allen and Mia Farrow

Woody Allen and Mia Farrow were contestants in a bitter custody dispute involving charges of sexual abuse and sharply conflicting testimony by expert witnesses.

See Ewing and McCann (2006, ch. 13, 153–64) for further details about this case.

3. Abuse did not occur, but the spouse making the accusation genuinely believes it occurred and therefore is worried about the child.

4. Abuse did not occur; the spouse makes a false accusation deliberately.

Many lay people and judges (Thoennes and Tjaden, 1990) believe that false accusations are made frequently and knowingly for strategic reasons. Some clinicians believe that disturbed parents also make sincere but deluded accusations fueled by hostlity and paranoia.

Thoennes and Tjaden's research (1990) suggests that most allegations are made in good faith and may be true, or at least are based on reasonable suspicions. Although some allegations may be made strategically, deliberate false allegations of sexual abuse during custody and visitation disputes are relatively infrequent. They undertook a two-year study on the incidence, characteristics, and validity of sexual abuse allegations in custody and visitation disputes. They collected detailed data over six months at eight courts in different states about all cases involving allegations of abuse. During this time, the courts heard 9,000 custody–visitation disputes. Overall, less than 2 percent of the contested cases (a range of less than 1 percent to 8 percent in different jurisdictions) involved an allegation of sexual abuse. Court personnel believed that sexual abuse allegations had increased but linked this to the general increase in reports of suspected sexual abuse made by public and professionals. However, even 2 percent is higher than the rate of sex abuse allegations in the general population (Thoennes and Tjaden, 1990).

Thoennes and Tjaden (1990) collected detailed information from court counselors and from family court and CPS agency files on 169 custody cases in which sexual abuse was alleged. Forty-five percent involved initial divorce agreements; in the remaining cases, the couple had divorced and one parent was trying to change the original custody or visitation order. Sixty-seven percent of the allegations were brought by mothers, and 28 percent by fathers. Fathers were accused in 51 percent of the cases, but mothers, mothers' new partners, and extended family members were also accused. Sixty-two percent of the children were age six or under.

There is no "gold standard" for determining what really happened in a case of alleged abuse. Because they had no way to verify or disprove the allegations, Thoennes and Tjaden used professional beliefs as their standard. In 129 cases, the CPS worker or a court clinic evaluator were asked to say if they thought it was "likely that abuse occurred," that it was "unlikely that abuse occurred," or that they "could not determine whether abuse occurred." Overall, 50 percent of the cases were rated as likely to involve abuse, 33 percent were found unlikely to involve abuse, and 17 percent were indeterminate. In half the cases in which abuse was judged likely, there had been prior reports of abuse; prior reports appeared in only 5 percent of the cases where it was judged unlikely that abuse occurred (Shepard, 1998; Thoennes and Tjaden, 1990).

Thoennes and Tjaden's (1990) detailed investigation suggests that deliberately false accusations of abuse probably occur infrequently (see also Shepard, 1998). However, they do occur. Sincere allegations that might be true but are difficult to substantiate occur more often; they present dilemmas for courts and evaluators.

⊠ Custody Evaluations: Problems and Ethics

Where there is no clear legal rule, judges have a lot of discretion in ordering a custody arrangement in the "best interests" of the child. Many judges, understanding "best interests" to be largely a matter of psychological health, consider reports of mental health professionals to be of critical value. The professional examiner, a psychologist, social worker, or psychiatrist, may be an employee of a forensic or social services unit affiliated with the court, a private practitioner hired by the court, or hired by the parties at the request of the court. The judge specifies the scope of the investigation (e.g., to evaluate a parent with a history of mental illness or to do a complete forensic assessment of the family and its members). The judge may order the parties to the dispute to cooperate. Parties can refuse to cooperate with an evaluation if it is not court ordered, but they run the risk of appearing uncooperative to the court.

Ethical and Procedural Guidelines

Custody evaluations are challenging. The disputes can be highly emotional for everyone: parent, child, evaluator, and sometimes the attorneys. When there are accusations of child sexual abuse, neglect, or family violence, the emotional stress is even greater (APA, 1994). Evaluators have to keep powerful feelings of empathy or anger toward parents from undermining their fairness and their good judgment. The parents may feel angry at being ordered to undergo an intrusive evaluation involving disclosure of very personal and sensitive information about their history and current family relations. Courts have ruled that when parents dispute custody, they put their fitness as parents at issue, waiving the right to keep mental health information confidential. The parents may have to sign releases permitting the evaluator to interview or obtain records from schools, doctors, therapists, employers, family, and other people who might be able to provide useful information (Glassman, 1998).

To protect families and to help professionals avoid ethical complaints, the American Psychological Association (APA, 1994) and the Association of Family and Conciliation Courts (AFCC, n.d.) have issued standards or guidelines for custody evaluations. They call for the evaluator to remain objective, neutral, and honest, and to strive to demonstrate respect for the parents or guardians.

Neutrality and the best interests of the child. No matter who hires the evaluator, the evaluator's paramount concern should be the child's best interests. Evaluators should generally steer clear of relationships that might compromise objectivity (APA, 1994; AFCC, n.d.). To minimize adversarial conflicts, many established private practitioners will not undertake a custody evaluation unless both parties agree and unless the court appoints the professional as the sole evaluator (Glassman, 1998). The evaluators should avoid doing a custody evaluation if they have had a previous professional relationship with any member of the family, nor should they accept any member of the family as a client after the evaluation is complete. They should also avoid **ex parte** communications (communicating with only one side) during the assessment (e.g., copies of any letters should be sent to both parents). Evaluators should assess both parents and should use similar assessment techniques with both (Glassman, 1998).

Informed consent. The evaluator should obtain written informed consent from everyone involved beforehand (APA, 1994; AFCC, n.d.). The purpose of the evaluation, the procedures, the evaluator's credentials, the costs and who will pay, and the possible uses of the information should be discussed. All parties, including children, should understand that what they say may be disclosed to the court and to the other parties and their lawyers now and in the future.

Thorough evaluation. Both the APA and the AFCC guidelines recommend that the custody evaluator assess three different factors:

1. The psychological and developmental needs of the child, including assessment of the child's wishes (the AFCC guidelines proscribe asking children to choose between their parents and recommend obtaining information "through techniques which will not be harmful and guilt inducing");
2. The parents or guardians' strengths and weaknesses as parents; and
3. The interactions and relationships between all the family members (see Jameson, Ehrenberg, and Hunter, 1997, for a family systems assessment model).

The APA and the AFCC recommend that the evaluator use several methods of obtaining data. Evaluations should include interviews with each of the parents; interviews with each child alone, using age-appropriate methods (e.g., play and drawings with younger children); and joint interviews with and observations of one-on-one interactions between each parent and each child. The interactions should be both structured and unstructured. The parent and child may be asked to play a game or plan a trip in order to see how the parent and child communicate and whether they enjoy a shared activity. A structured task also allows the evaluator to compare the interaction styles of the two parents. The evaluator may ask the parent of a very young child to leave the room briefly to observe if the child can tolerate a separation (attachment style). The evaluator has to decide whether what he or she observes is typical or reflects the parent's or the child's attempt to cope with the evaluation.

Reports and testimony. The AFCC guidelines recommend reviewing all the findings and conclusions directly with both parents and children before submitting the report. When completed, the evaluator's report is given to the court. The evaluator may be called as a witness, can be cross-examined, and may be asked to submit raw data or records of interviews for review.

Ultimate Issues. Sometimes the process of assessment itself leads the parties to resolve the dispute (Lee, Beauregard, and Hunsley, 1998; Nurcombe and Partlett, 1994). When the dispute continues, it is the judge, not the mental health professional, who ultimately makes the custody determination. However, courts often order evaluators to make a specific recommendation about custody arrangements. Some psychologists believe that it is inappropriate for psychologists to make custody recommendations. Clinicians may be able to identify a parent who is unfit, but, in the majority of cases in which both parents are fit, there is no scientific basis for choosing between them. Evaluators say that when a judge asks them to offer an opinion, each evaluator should instead explain only what the data suggest about the advantages and disadvantages for the child of different possible awards (Nurcombe and Partlett, 1994). However, some judges may be impatient with the evaluator's ethical niceties and insist on a recommendation. Whatever the reason, it appears psychologists do address the ultimate question. Bow and Quinnel (2001) surveyed 198 psychologists from 38 states who frequently undertook custody evaluations. Ninety-four percent said they made explicit custody recommendations, a higher percentage than in a similar 1997 survey (Ackerman and Ackerman, 1997).

Legal and Ethical Problems

Bow and Quinnell (2001) found that the practice of their national sample of psychologists on the whole conformed with the APA Guidelines (APA, 1994). Eighty-four percent of the evaluations undertaken by respondents were court ordered. The respondents had been trained to work with both adults and children and had specific training in custody evaluation. They conducted thorough investigations using diverse assessment methods (see Box 13.6). The average number of hours for a case involving one child was 24.5 hours, and for two children it was 28.5. The respondents placed a high weight on domestic violence and on child abuse and neglect as important considerations in making recommendations.

Conforming with the guidelines did not protect these psychologists from suits or ethical complaints. Ten percent of the respondents reported that they had been the subject of malpractice suits, and 3 percent had been sued two or more times; 35 percent reported at least one complaint filed against them. Seven to 10 percent of the ethics complaints made to the APA involve custody evaluations.

Given the important issues involved, it is not surprising that the evaluative process has been criticized from inside the professions and from outside for being biased, subjective, or otherwise unprofessional. Most states have not established standards regarding qualifications of evaluators or content of assessments. (California is an exception; Eaton, 2004.) Forensic assessment is in effect unregulated in many jurisdictions (Eaton, 2004).

Because the evaluator is supposed to be a neutral expert, the parents in most jurisdictions can't request a different or additional evaluator. Even if a parent believes that the evaluator chosen has a history of biased recommendations or is not disinterested, he or she can only complain after the fact. Furthermore, it is not clear what "neutral" means in this context. Neither the APA or AFCC guidelines nor the law specify what the child's best interest is in a measurable way (e.g., school performance, happiness, stability of family, or emotional adjustment), nor what is meant by a good parenting or a good fit between child's need and parent's ability. Because custody standards are vague and the research findings complex, the evaluators' values and beliefs, like those of judges, can make a difference in the outcome of a case. There are other fairness and due process issues. When the evaluator is not a court employee, in most jurisdictions the parents have to pay for the court-ordered evaluation. Bow and Quinnell's (2001) national sample charged an average of $3,335 for their assessment and report, a serious sum of money for struggling parents. Many aggrieved parents cannot afford the expense of yet another professional fee, on top of the costs of a lawyer and a trial (see section on pro se representation below).

Some parents may never see the report they paid for. The judge and, if the parents are represented, their attorneys will be given copies of the evaluation. Parents are not generally given copies; though the evaluator is supposed to give them verbal feedback and their lawyers also will summarize the contents. Ninety-five percent of the respondents in Bow and Quinnell's (2001) study distributed the report to attorneys, and 83 percent to judges, but only 17 percent gave a copy to parents. It is likely attorneys shared reports with parents.

If parents want to challenge a report, they can only do so by having a full trial and having their lawyer cross-examine the evaluator. They may be put to the expense of hiring their own expert for the trial. The attorneys may ask to see therapists' notes, transcripts, test scores, statements of third-party interviews, or any other data on which the report was based. Many psychologists for ethical reasons (see APA Code of Ethics, 2002) will only give the data to another licensed psychologist for review.

But perhaps the central issue is whether there is a real scientific basis for custody evaluations: are they a valid way to predict which of several possible arrangements is most likely to be best for a child?

Custody Evaluations: Validity

What procedures do custody evaluators use, and how valid are they? Over 90 percent of the respondents in Bow and Quinnell's survey (2001) took histories and conducted clinical interviews with both parents and children, observed parent–child interactions, and conducted psychological testing of the parents. Sixty-one percent also tested children. They used both structured and unstructured questions and tasks. However, absent definitions that can be operationalized, different psychological evaluators, like different judges, may look at different factors and weigh them differently. There have been, to our knowledge, no studies of interrater consistency (whether different psychologists assess the same dimensions of behavior) and interrater reliability (whether they make the same judgements given the same asessment information) in custody evaluations. Interrater reliability in clinical fields is generally not impressive.

In addition to interviews and observations, psychologists routinely use standardized tests and measures. Psychologists presumably use tests and rating scales to increase the objectivity and accuracy of the evaluation and to have rational grounds on which to base an inherently difficult recommendation. Predictions based on objective measures are usually more accurate than those based on clinical judgment alone. But is what the tests measure relevant to custody decisions, and do they measure it well?

General Tests

A survey of 201 psychologists in 39 states experienced with custody evaluations found that the most frequently used tests were general assessment instruments developed to screen for psychopathology, assess personality, and assess cognitive functioning in clinical contexts (Ackerman and Ackerman, 1997). Tests specifically designed to assess behavior and attitudes relevant to custody issues were not used as often as the general measures. The custody instruments most often given to children were the **Bricklin Perceptual Scale** and the **Bricklin Perception of Relation Test** (Bricklin, 1984) administered to children in about 26% of the evaluations (Ackerman and Ackerman, 1997; Hagen and Castagna, 2001). The Bricklin scales were used to assess children's perceptions of their parents as caregivers. The **Ackerman-Schoendorf Scales for Parent Evaluation of Custody (ASPECT)** was the most frequently used instrument intended specifically to assess parenting skills and parent–child relationships (Ackerman and Ackerman, 1997; Hagen and Castagna, 2001).

Tests are interpreted by comparing the test taker's response with the average responses of a normative sample (a sample representative of the group to which the individual being tested belongs). The validity of the interpretation depends in part on the appropriateness of the norms. One set of tests used in about 25 percent of evaluations, the Millon Clinical Multiaxial Inventory (MCMI II and III), was designed for use with clinical populations (subjects being treated for mental disorders). Their use in custody evaluations of parents who are not being treated for psychological problems is questionable. Moreover, the score on the Millon test may not correlate with any measure of good parenting. The norms used to score the MMPI, the test most commonly used by custody evaluators in the Ackermans' (1997) study, was also developed for clinical use, but the norms are representative of the population as a whole. However, people's feelings, responses, and behaviors are affected by the situation they are in. Comparing the responses of parents in a custody dispute with average scores of a "normal" population not in the midst of an emotionally charged, highly consequential adversarial process may not be sound. Most importantly, a measure of psychopathology may have little validity for predicting parenting skills or other relationship issues.

Bathurst, Gottfried, and Gottfried (1997) used the MMPI profiles of 508 parents involved in custody disputes to develop norms for interpreting the test in this population. In the adversarial legal environment, people taking the test were more prone to deny negative aspects of their personalities than the "normal" population and endorsed more indicators of hostility, suspiciousness, and mistrust. These context-specific norms will help evaluators to interpret the MMPI for custody evaluations. But the profiles still need to be validated against measures of parenting skills or other measures of children's and parents' adaptation to and coping with divorce.

Custody-Specific Measures

Heinze and Grisso (1996) did a thorough review of the instruments developed specifically for use in custody evaluations, and concluded that the measures were not adequately supported by validation studies. We will restrict our discussion here to summarizing their conclusions about the ASPECT and the Bricklin scales, the two most widely used instruments.

The ASPECT is a procedure for quantifying and weighing information about parents and parent–child interactions that appears to be related to parenting effectiveness. The clinician collects data from tests, interviews, and observations of parent–child interactions. On the basis of these data, the clinician answers 56 forced-choice (i.e., yes or no) questions for each parent. The 56 items yield scores on three subscales: an Observational Scale, a summary of the clinician's impressions of the subject's effectiveness as a parent; a Social Scale, which measures the parent's interactions with the child, with the other parent, and with the community; and a Cognitive–Emotional Scale, which measures parental ego strength, adjustment, social judgment, and intellectual competence. These summary scores are weighted and summed to provide an overall Parental Custody Index. The index can be interpreted in light of cutoff scores and "critical items."

The summary score has adequate internal reliability. Ackerman and Schoendorf, the creators of the system (cited in Heinze and Grisso, 1996), reported that two raters who independently reviewed the same notes and test results achieved a very high degree of interrater agreement. The degree of agreement between two evaluators who assess the same parents by each obtaining the data anew has not been tested. Nor are there data on how reliable the scores on the instruments are over time (test–retest reliability). This is important because the ASPECT is used to predict behavior in the future. Using it for that purpose assumes that the level of a trait it measures today will be the same in the future.

A prediction can be made reliably, and the prediction can be wrong (invalid). To assess the correctness of the prediction, we need a criterion measure and a validity study. The only validation reported in the Heinze and Grisso (1996) review shows that predictions based on the ASPECT agreed with the judge's orders a very high percentage of the time. We don't know whether the judge's orders were made independently of knowledge of the evaluator's recommendations. Assuming that they are independent, it still does not follow that either the judge or the test is correctly predicting the child's future adaptation in the home: both the judge and the test could be wrong. There is also a base rate problem. If judges award sole custody or physical custody to mothers 84 percent of the time, and the ASPECT is biased toward favoring women over men, then, by predicting the woman will get custody, the evaluator will be right most of the time—not because of the ASPECT, but because of the high base rate of custody awards to women. This is a variant of the base rate problem discussed in Chapter 3.

Similar issues arise with the Bricklin Perceptual Scale (BPS) and Perceptions of Relationships Test (PORT), which measure the child's perception of his or her parents. A measure of a child's preferences, considered with other measures, might contribute to good decision making, and is one of the factors judges consider in making custody determinations.

The BPS purportedly measures the child's assessment of each of his or her parent's "warmth, competency and empathy, consistency and admirable character traits" (p. 298). The child indicates how well each of 64 descriptors describes each parent by punching a hole along an eight-inch line with one end marked *not so well* and the other *very well*. Bricklin makes an untested assumption that this nonverbal form of responding is superior to a verbal response in revealing a child's "real" feelings. Each parent's score is the total of the number of items on which that parent "won." That parent becomes the "parent of choice," and the difference can be stated quantitatively. Although this test is in wide use, there are very little psychometric data supporting it (Heinze and Grisso, 1996). The seven-day test–retest reliability is only modest. When the scores are close, the parent of choice may well change over two administrations of the test even from day to day.

The PORT is a projective test that attempts to measure the psychological closeness each child feels toward each parent. The child is asked to draw pictures of himself, his family and family members, and other families and homes. The test is scored by measuring the physical distance on the page between the child's drawing of self and each of the parents or parent figures. Heinze and Grisso (1996) question the validity of using the distance between drawings as a measure of emotional closeness. Although the procedure is in general use, according to Heinze and Grisso, there are little basic psychometric data available to aid in interpreting scores.

In short, the tests used in custody evaluations have not been well validated for that purpose. Professionals are making predictions about a child's adaptation with one or the other parent on the basis of clinical judgment with little statistical evidence or substantial research to back up their decisions.

Coin Flipping versus Evaluation

Because the best interest standard is vague, and there are no validated empirical bases for decision making, judges are awarding custody on the basis of unspoken values and unproved intuitions. Even if there were an adequate body of research, the best predictors based on it might account for perhaps 50 percent of the variance, leaving much room for mistaken predictions (Kraus and Sales, 2000).

Kraus and Sales (2000) suggest switching to a "least detrimental" standard. They argue that such a standard would be more realistic, better represents the expertise of mental health professionals doing custody evaluations, and is more related to existing research that has focused primarily on factors associated with maladjustment and pathology. Robert Mnookin (1975) suggested, rhetorically, that we decide custody by a state-administered coin flip. Flipping a coin has advantages. A coin toss would be at least as fair as present procedures. Mnookin argues it would be quicker and cheaper, spare the parents from a painful process of evaluation and litigation, and, perhaps, spur them to settle privately.

The proposal is rational given the psychometrics of prediction. However, a coin toss would change one outcome. With a coin flip, men would receive custody 50 percent of the time, which would be a huge change from the status quo. Although Mnookin made his proposal just to highlight the difficulties of our present system, his point is well taken: custody evaluations by mental health professionals in the context of adjudication may be simply an elaborate ritual.

Rituals may be valuable, however. Thorough evaluations contribute to the appearance that courts are being careful and fair in making custody awards. Maintaining that appearance may be more socially useful than acknowledging that the decision is based on methods of dubious validity. Mnookin (1975) rejected his own coin flip solution for that reason. "While forceful arguments can be made in favor of the abandonment of adjudication and the adoption of an openly random process," he wrote, "the repulsion many would probably feel towards this suggestion may reflect an intuitive appreciation of the importance of the educational, participatory, and symbolic values of adjudication as a mode of dispute settlement" (pp. 290–291).

The Changing Legal Landscape

Pro Se Representation

The 1990s saw the acceleration of a nationwide movement for people to represent themselves (pro se representation) in family disputes (Wilgoren, 2002), motivated primarily by a desire to avoid large legal fees. Litigants in matrimonial actions do not have a constitutional right to counsel paid for by public funds. On the other hand, the right to represent oneself is well established (e.g., *Faretta v. California,* 1975).

A 1992 study of courts in 16 different parts of the U.S. found that one or both parties were representing themselves in between 53 and 88 percent of cases; both parties had a lawyer in only 28 percent of the cases (Goerdt, 1992, in Beck and Sales, 2000).

Unfortunately, the courts are not easy for untrained people to negotiate. Judges report that pro se litigants make a lot of mistakes. They may not understand civil procedure; they often do not know what motions and other papers to file, use the wrong forms, complete them incorrectly, or file them late. They may also make substantive mistakes, for example, miscalculating child support payments. Some judges are concerned that the high level of emotion elicited by divorce cases makes it difficult for parties to represent their interests clearly and objectively. Lawyers are concerned that that pro se parents may not fully understand the issues (Beck and Sales, 2000; Wilogren, 2002).

Courts are experimenting with policies to manage pro se litigants. In the early 1990s, Maricopa County, (Phoenix) Arizona, opened a self-service center and a 24-hour hotline for individuals wishing to represent themselves. Other jurisdictions have begun setting up clinics or providing other forms of support for people going to court without lawyers. Websites, books, and public and private "divorce kits" have proliferated. However, significant problems remain. Not least is the potential problem of unfairness where one party is represented by a lawyer and the other, probably less effectively, represents him- or herself.

Mediation

Litigation takes time. (Remember the safest prediction about the legal system is that there will be delay!) The family's living arrangements are uncertain until the case is settled. The delay can be especially difficult for children, whose time sense is different from adults. The delays that accompany litigation can also make the process appear less fair. The party with temporary custody benefits because courts are reluctant to change children's living arrangements and disrupt their lives without good reason. On the other hand, when there is a disparity of income or when conflict is high, the party with more money or power may be tempted to drag the litigation process out to pressure the former spouse. Litigation is expensive. Finally, litigation is not on its face the most sensible way to resolve a dispute between two parents about custody of their child.

Ordinary civil litigation resolves conflict between parties who, as a general rule, will no longer deal with one another once the dispute is resolved. But the parties to a custody dispute will continue to have a common interest in the child's health, welfare and education for a lifetime. They may meet at the child's school or at important milestones such as confirmation, graduation, and wedding, and at the birth of their common grandchildren. The adversarial process, by encouraging each side to portray the other in worst light, is not the high road to future cooperation. Sometimes parties begin a divorce intending to cooperate, but end up angry and fighting. And acrimony and conflict between parents are associated with poorer adjustment in children—hardly in anyone's best interest. When one or both parties to a divorce refuse to settle, litigation can become a way to maintain a conflictual relationship instead of dissolve it. Even low-conflict parties who work out settlements on their own often find the rules and constraints of the system expensive and time-consuming. In the 1980s, jurisdictions began experimenting with mediation as an alternative to adversarial litigation.

Mediation is a way of resolving disputes without resort to litigation. Mediation is also an alternative to custody assessments by mental health professionals (Lee, Beauregard, and Hunsley, 1998). In mediation, a neutral third party works with two contending parties to help them negotiate a settlement. The mediators are specially trained, and can have backgrounds in many different fields. Most family law mediators come from law, sociology, and the helping professions. The mediation process is private: no records are kept in most states, and mediatiors are generally not allowed to testify or submit recommendations to courts related to the content of mediation (Beck and Sales, 2000; see ALI, 2000, Sec. 2.07).

By the mid-1990s, most states had mandated mediation or encouraged voluntary mediation in child custody disputes. If divorcing couples can't agree to a solution in mediation, they are still able to go to court. In most states, but not all, the mediation concerns custody and visitation only; the idea is to discourage couples from using these issues as chips in financial bargaining. The development of custody mediation programs is part of a more general movement that looks for alternative, nonadversarial ways of resolving disputes to reduce costs and encourage outcomes likely to contribute to social reconciliation and individual health.

Theory of mediation. In litigation, the custody decision is imposed on warring parties by a judge, or negotiated under threat of a court-imposed settlement. In mediation, no solution is imposed. The mediator serves as a facilitator. The goal is for the parents to agree on a parenting plan, often including nonjudicial means for resolving subsequent disputes. Mediation theory assumes that, because the agreement is voluntary, parents will feel they "own" it and will adhere to it better. (In the 1980s, the noncompliance rate with court-imposed orders of support and custody was greater than 40 percent.) In theory, mediation should bring faster settlements, reduce time in court, reduce costs, reduce stress on all the parties, empower parties by allowing them to air all their grievances and be heard, focus parties on the needs of their children, and, by teaching dispute resolution skills, reduce conflict in future contacts.

Mediators vary in style and philosophy (Mnookin and Weisberg, 2005). Some are very nondirective, emphasizing the importance of the parents coming to a decision autonomously. Others are more directive; they will intervene to try to strengthen the position of the weaker party or to veto an agreement they consider unfair or not in the child's interests. They emphasize sucessful problem solving over neutrality. A few programs are experimenting with therapeutic models of mediation, which allow a greater number of sessions and focus on changes in the quality of the parental relationships (Beck and Sales, 2000).

Research on custody mediation. Mediation is difficult to evaluate. The programs vary considerably from jurisdiction to jurisdiction with regard to the rules and procedures, including the qualifications of the mediator, rules about who will be excluded from mediation, the number of sessions, the absence or presence of lawyers, and who bears the cost. Most mediation clients are required to attend court-sponsored mediation. Divorcing couples who voluntarily attend and pay for private mediation are wealthier and, on average, better educated than mandated couples. Because of these and other differences in different programs, it is unclear how much the results of research conducted in one locality will generalize to another. In jurisdictions where mediation is mandated, group comparisons are difficult: all those who go to court will have failed to reach a mediated settlement or will have been assessed as inappropriate for mediation. In these jurisdictions, the mediation group presumably had fewer conflicts or better communication to begin with than the group who went to court.

These methodological problems make it difficult to draw firm conclusions. Nonetheless, research suggests that mediation programs achieve some of their goals. Most parents reach an agreement in mediation. This reduces the number of cases going to court and allows settlements to be reached in about half the time (Emery, Matthews, and Wyer, 1991).

BOX 13.6

Gender and Mediation

Emery and colleagues undertook a series of studies in which parents were randomly assigned to negotiate settlements in mediation or to the adversarial system (Emery, Matthews, and Wyer, 1991; Kitzmann and Emery, 1993). The majority of couples assigned to mediation were able to work out an agreement. Fathers reported more satisfaction with mediation than litigation. They felt the process was fairer. They felt they had more control over the final decision even though physical custody to the mother with visitation by the father was the outcome in most cases in both the mediation and the adversarial groups. Fathers also reported more positive effects on themselves and on their relationship with their ex-spouse. Mothers were equally satisfied with litigation and mediation. The women in the mediation group felt the outcome for them would have been better in litigation but believed that the mediation process was better for the children.

Mediation leads to more joint custody awards (Kitzmann and Emery, 1993; Pearson and Thoennes, 1990; Emery et al., 2001). The most common mediated custody arrangement is joint legal custody, with physical custody going to the mother (see Box 13.6). Joint custody is generally more satisfying to the noncustodial parent, usually the father, than is sole custody with visitation (Pearson and Thoennes, 1990). However, physical custody to the mother with joint legal custody is becoming more common generally. Noncustodial fathers are more likely to see their children regularly, more likely to be involved with decisions about them, and more likely to make regular support payments when mediation is used (Hetherington, Bridges, and Insabella, 1998; Emery et al., 2001). Mediation results in higher compliance with provisions of the agreements over the short term (Lee, Beauregard, and Hunsley, 1998). Studies of long-term results are conflicting. Some researchers find that fathers in mediated cases remained more involved with their children than fathers in families who went to court, but others report that mediated child custody agreements tend to break down at a higher rate than other custody agreements (Emery et al., 2001; Pruett and Santangelo, 1999).

A survey by Lee, Beauregard, and Hunsley (1998) of 161 Canadian family lawyers found that the lawyers saw mediation as a good way to develop viable parenting plans, and strongly agreed that mediation was preferable to going to court. They also rated mediation as a better alternative than assessment. They believed mediation, but not assessment, enhanced relationships between parents, increased parental compliance, and increased the emphasis on shared parenting. (Not surprisingly, they thought parents in mediation should have lawyers.) Child adjustment has not been used as a direct outcome measure of mediated parenting agreements.

Problems with mediation. Since much mediation is mandated, it is not fully voluntary. This can be distressing for a parent who does not feel comfortable negotiating with their former spouse. ALI (2000) recommends that courts should not compel any service requiring a face-to-face meeting with the other parent (Sec 2.07(3)). Speeding up divorce and saving money were among the express goals of mediation. The number of sessions of mediation is limited in some jurisdictions, and the mediator's job is to facilitate settlement. It is not surprising that some clients report feeling pressured to reach an agreement or felt the mediator was dictating the terms (Pearson and Thoennes, 1989). Mediators also differ individually in how they see their roles. Mediators may press parties to achieve an agreement in order to count the mediation as successful. Many lawyers, mental health professionals, and mediators agree that, in some cases, mediation should be terminated after it has begun or shouldn't be undertaken at all (see ALI, 2000, Sec. 2.07(2)).

Whatever the circumstances, if the parties are not negotiating in good faith, the case should go to court. Mediation generally does not work for very high-conflict families, who are likely to go on to engage in lengthy ligtigation anyway (Benjamin, Andrew, and Gollan, 2003). It may be unrealistic to expect the most troubled couples to resolve disputes in a few mediation sessions.

The theory of mediation assumes that the parties have relatively equal bargaining power. When one parent has considerably less economic power than the other, has less education, speaks English less well, has less skill in negotiating, is less assertive, or is less willing to take risks, the imbalance may preclude fair negotiations. The stronger party may subtly bully the weaker, or the weaker may feel obliged to comply even when the other party is not acting in good faith.

There may also be differences in access to counsel. The professional and ethical standards issued by various organizations to guide mediation generally assume that the parties are receiving legal advice and are fully informed, and that there has been full disclosure. Beck and Sales (2000) argue that these assumptions are not warranted. Pro se representation in divorce proceedings is increasingly common. If one party has a lawyer providing advice about issues and the other does not, an obvious power imbalance has been created. There is little research on how the absence of legal advice affects the process; effectiveness studies do not compare spouses in mediation with and without lawyers. Most mental health professionals believe that mediation is strongly counterindicated when there has been violence between parties or by one party toward children. They fear that the aggressor will use the mediation sessions as a forum to continue to threaten and control the other, and that negotiated compromises may put the victim at risk of further violence or harassment (Fischer, Vidmar, and Ellis, 1993).

While in many jurisdictions mediation is not used where there is a history of violence, child abuse and intimate partner violence are often not discovered by the courts or mediators. If violence or threats of violence do not begin until the time of separation, there is no history to be discovered (Beck and Sales, 2000; see also Chapter 12 on intimate partner violence). Some mediators are attempting to develop mediation strategies and procedures that can safely be used in cases of IPV (Lee, Beauregard, and Hunsley, 1998). Others are attempting to develop procedures to screen out inappropriate cases (see Fuhr, 1988; and Tan, 1991).

If, for whatever reason, one or both of the parties to a mediated agreement feel the mediator was incompetent or unfair, or that they were pressured into compliance or ill informed, they have little recourse. Mediation needs to be private and informal so clients can resolve difficult emotional issues without fear that disclosures will later be used in a court (see ALI, 2000, Sec. 2.07(4),(5)). A negative consequence of the protection of confidentiality is that there is virtually no oversight, and no way the mediation process can be reviewed. Despite all the problems, most legal and mental health professionals agree that mediation still has advantages over the uncertainty, emotional trauma and expense of litigation for many couples.

Alternative Dispute Methods: New Roles for Clinicians and Researchers

Both individuals and courts have been experimenting with new approaches to resolving custody and visitation issues. The goal of these approaches is to move beyond settling disputes to develop procedures that actively help parents make the transition to a new relationship.

Collaborative family law. Collaborative family law is another alternative to adversarial litigation. The movement, which began in the early 1990s, is a process of lawyer-assisted negotiated resolution of family and marital issues outside the court system (Tesler, 1999). Each of the parties and their specially trained attorneys formally agree not to litigate and bind themselves to prearranged ground rules. The attorneys represent their clients, but share a commitment to keeping the process honest and respectful. Other professionals, such as financial planners or mental health professionals, may be jointly engaged by the couple to help them work out a satisfactory agreement. If negotiations fail, the attorneys initially hired to negotiate will no longer represent the parties. Unlike mediation, the parties in a collaborative law negotiation will each have an advisor and an advocate. They can be confident they fully understand the agreement and know the qualifications of the person they have hired to represent them. They do not have to bargain face-to-face with a former spouse if this is difficult for them. There is no pressure to reach a settlement quickly.

Collaboratative law would probably not work with high-conflict couples. It is intended for people who are committed to amicable settlement. The parties also have to be relatively well off. In most jurisdictions, mediators, though not lawyers, are paid by the court, but the divorcing couple pays the collobrative family lawyers and any other professionals (e.g., financial planners or mental health professionals) they agree to use. However, it is probably less costly for wealthy couples than litigation. To our knowledge, there are as yet no studies of the effectiveness of collaborative law settlements.

Procedural reforms. Some family courts are experimenting with procedural reforms and new programs to manage high-conflict couples. Collaborative law principles, initially developed as an alternative model to the court system, are being applied experimentally by courts to resolve the custody disputes of more and more troubled families. The Collaborative Divorce Project (CDP) in Connecticut, a court based research and development program, is a good example (Pruett, Insabella, and Gustafason, 2005). The project compared parents of children six years or younger in a research-based intervention designed to help them develop and implement a custody plan with a control group of families who completed the usual court procedures. The intervention combined psycho-education parenting classes, clinical intervention, mediation, and case management by a coparenting counselor available to help the family with parenting decisions. The intervention was found to be helpful for European American but not minority parents. The European American parents reported less distress and conflict, increased parental cooperation, and more noncustodial parent involvement. The researchers, collaborating courts, and mental health professionals believe the pilot experience supports collaborative divorce.

Various jurisdictions have experimented with other therapeutic dispute resolution processes involving some combination of parental education, therapy or counseling, and active assistance in developing and implementing a coparenting plan (Johnston, 1994; Lebow, 2003). In families where there is very high conflict, where there has been partner or child abuse, or there are mental health problems, courts and social services may be involved with the family on an ongoing basis, establishing and monitoring a parenting and safety plan (Johnston, 1994). These plans can include visitation enforcement, supervised visitation, or visitation conditional on compliance with mental health or substance abuse treatment.

Summary

The divorce rate doubled in the last quarter of the twentieth century. Custody is disputed in 10 to 20 percent of the divorces involving children and in many other cases where the parents never married. The courts, having discarded the early preference for paternal custody and later the tender years doctrine that favored maternal custody, have looked to the social and clinical sciences for help in determining where the best interests of children might lie.

Social science has yielded no easy or simple answers. There is strong, rather unsurprising, evidence that children will do well when they have contact with both parents; when both parents are warm, authoritative, and involved; and when the custodial and noncustodial parents are friendly and cooperate in child care decisions. But children do well in these circumstances regardless of the custody arrangement. When parenting is poor, when there is continued conflict between the parents, and when any of the parties have interpersonal problems, the children are vulnerable whatever the custody arrangement. The research investigating and comparing different custody arrangements offers no clear evidence for the utility of any particular rules or arrangements. Joint custody does not appear to decrease or increase levels of cooperation and conflict, and does not affect child adjustment per se. However, joint custody arrangements appear to have some advantages for couples who are cooperative in the first place.

Professional mental health workers participate in custody evaluations. It is a difficult and complex task made more difficult by the lack of clearly valid instruments for making predictions about adaptation in the future in different custody arrangements, or indeed without clear understanding of what good adaptation would be. It is especially difficult when the dispute is between two otherwise fit parents. There may be no one "correct" custody award. Children with normal resiliency may be able to adapt successfully in many different types of reasonably healthy family arrangements.

Many jurisdictions have been experimenting with mediation to find ways of resolving custody disputes that will be less expensive and will increase parent cooperation, or at least avoid the risk of exacerbating conflicts through adversarial litigation. These approaches are promising.

Clinical, developmental, and social psychologists studying divorce and its consequences have been examining development in the context of adaptation and coping in changing circumstances. Work on this applied problem has the potential to expand theories of healthy development.

Discussion Questions

1. Why is it important to have a legal standard that provides guidelines for courts making custody decisions? Do you think cases would be decided differently if judges were just told to decide what they think is best?

2. How much do you think a child's preferences should be counted in deciding custody arrangements? If you were a judge, how would you go about finding out what the child wished? Can you think of a study that would allow you to determine whether or not following a child's preference did or did not contribute to postdivorce adjustment?

3. Do you agree with Shuman et al. (1998) that a parent's therapist should not be required to testify in a custody case, or do you believe that the therapist should testify if the parent's

mental health is at issue? Suppose you wanted to find out whether therapists are able to accurately assess parent–child relationships or parenting skills on the basis of knowledge gained from seeing a parent in individual therapy. How would you go about it?

4. As we have seen, 80–90 percent of divorcing parents work out custody issues between themselves, perhaps with the help of lawyers. That means that many of the studies of custody decisions focus on a minority of families. Would more information about the arrangements of parents who didn't contest custody be helpful to judges? To mental health professionals?

5. Joint custody arrangements are now sometimes referred to as *parenting plans* to stress the active and ongoing nature of the parent–child relationships. Do you think the change in language is meaningful? What could courts do to make the process of resolving custody issues more therapeutic?

6. What are the pros and cons of using mediation instead of litigation to resolve custody issues?

7. Suppose you wanted to find out how many parents are still following their initial custody agreement five years later. How would you go about it? Would that kind of information be useful to judges? To mental health professionals?

Key Terms

Ackerman-Schoendorf Scales
for Parent Evaluation of
Custody (ASPECT)
adjustment
attachment
best interests of the child
blended families
Bricklin Perceptual Scale
custody
exparte

guardian ad litem
joint custody
legal custody
longitudinal studies
maternal preference
mediation
Minnesota Multiphasic
Personality Inventory
(MMPI) I or II
no fault divorce

parental alienation
syndrome (PAS)
paternal preference
physical custody
psychological parent
shared custody
sole custody
tender years doctrine
Uniform Marriage and
Divorce Act

CHAPTER **14**

Abortion

The abortion controversy is among the most intense in contemporary life. On one end of the debate are those who believe that human life begins at the moment of conception. They say that a fetus of any gestational age is entitled to the same legal protections as a newborn child. To them, abortion is murder, for some, even if the procedure is done to save the mother's life. On the other end are those who believe that life begins at birth, and that women should have the option of aborting a fetus as a matter of their autonomy. There are many views in between these poles, as well.

Social science cannot provide a factual basis for settling disputes about irreconcilable values and beliefs, though social science methods can be used to study correlates of these opposed beliefs (Luker, 1984; Tribe, 1990). However, both proponents and opponents of abortion sometimes make claims with empirical referents to support their positions. These can be assessed.

In this chapter, we will review research on social and psychological issues related to abortion. Much of this research was conducted within a framework established by *Roe v. Wade* (1973) and subsequent laws regulating abortion. Our focus will be adolescent pregnancy. Adolescent pregnancy is a serious social problem. Many states have promulgated laws affecting adolescents, and courts have allowed greater limitations to be placed on adolescent than on adult rights to privacy and choice. Adolescent pregnancy touches on critically important and emotion-laden topics—adolescent sexuality, the meaning of motherhood to a woman's life, and the authority of families to make decisions for their children. We will discuss

- the historical background of the abortion controversy.
- the constitutional background of the right to privacy that underlies the right to an abortion.
- the *Roe v. Wade* decision.
- laws and decisions limiting privacy rights established in *Roe v. Wade*.
- the problem of teenage pregnancy and abortion.
- adolescent abortion rights and parental consent.
- the effect of parental notification and consent statutes.
- the judicial bypass, and adaptations to notification and consent statutes.
- personal consequences for adolescents of having an abortion or having a child.
- the Welfare Reform Act of 1996.
- research on teenage competence to give informed consent in health matters.
- controversy about using the research base to attempt to affect legal decisions.

⊠ Historical Context

The rights to have an abortion and to contraceptive information and devices are linked. Since antiquity, men and women have sought to limit family size by a number of methods, including abortion and contraception, and also neonaticide, infanticide, child abandonment, selling infants, and giving infants up for adoption (Petchesky, 1984). Under common law (the law as interpreted by English and later U.S. judges), abortion before quickening (when the mother could feel the fetus moving, generally in the second trimester) was not a crime.

Until **Roe v. Wade** (1973), the states could regulate or not regulate abortion as they chose. Most did not regulate the procedure until the nineteenth century. In the nineteenth century, physicians pressed for legislation regulating abortion. Often, they tied the need for licensing physicians with governing and controlling abortions performed by unqualified people. Some physicians were also becoming uneasy about abortions because advances in biological knowledge showed that quickening had no special significance in fetal development. Another factor may have been the declining fertility of white U.S.-born women. Some physicians of the nineteenth century wanted these women to have more babies so that the "native stock" would not be overwhelmed by "inferior" immigrants (Mohr, 1978).

The early antiabortion laws were directed against quacks and apothecaries offering medications to induce abortion. The mostly young and unmarried women who sought abortions were not subject to criminal penalties. In the last quarter of the nineteenth century, activists concerned with public morals pressed for laws criminalizing the provision of contraceptive and abortion services and information to anyone. One leader was Anthony Comstock, a salesman living in New York City after his service in the Union Army during the Civil War. He was shocked by the open advertisement of birth control devices, which he concluded promoted evils including lust, lewdness and prostitution. Comstock was responsible for an 1873 federal law that prohibited the dissemination of information about the "obscene" matters of contraception and abortion through the U.S. mails. Many states passed their own restrictive laws in this period (Garrow, 1994).

For much of the nineteenth century, it was difficult to prosecute doctors or other abortionists functioning at the borders of legality because it was difficult to develop proof that the woman was pregnant or to determine how long she was pregnant at the time of the abortion. After 1880, statutory changes in evidentiary standards and burdens of proof made it easier to undertake criminal prosecution of abortionists. The laws succeeded in driving abortion and contraception underground, though not so far under that the upper middle class couldn't find what they needed (Olasky, 1992). By the 1880s, middle- and upper-class women were using increasingly effective contraception, including the rubber condom. When contraception failed, they had access to abortions through discreet private physicians. Poor women sought assistance where they could. Women who could not find an accommodating physician were at the mercy of anyone willing to terminate the pregnancy (see Mohr, 1978; Reed, 1978; Tribe, 1990).

The nineteenth-century laws prohibiting abortion continued on the books in most states until the 1960s, when 17 states, beginning with Colorado and California, reformed their abortion laws (Tribe, 1990). Several factors contributed to abortion law reform in the 1960s. The sexual revolution, especially the introduction of the birth control pill, opened many formerly taboo subjects to public discussion, and made more people open to the use of medical technology to control reproduction. Growing knowledge and concern about birth defects led to greater recognition of abortion as an option for women and couples who knew they were at risk of having a deformed child. After an epidemic of rubella, or German measles, a disease that can cause fetal deformity in infected pregnant women, some physicians urged reform of abortion laws (Geis, 1972).

Discussion of whether parents should be allowed to abort an abnormal fetus received further attention when Sherry Finkbine, the star of the children's TV program *Romper Room,* unknowingly used Thalidomide, a powerful teratogenic agent (inducer of birth defects). When she realized what had happened, Finkbine tried unsuccessfully to obtain an abortion in the United States. She went to Sweden to have the pregnancy terminated there. Because she was a celebrity, the press covered her case extensively (Geis, 1972).

The women's movement took up the abortion issue (Jaffe, Lindheim, and Lee, 1981; McKnight, 1992). Pregnancy counseling services created by local women's groups in the 1960s referred women to adoption agencies or to safe sources for abortion, often in foreign countries where abortions were legal (Faux, 1988; Tribe, 1990). Then, in 1973, *Roe v. Wade* changed the rules, preventing states from prohibiting abortion.

The Constitutional Context

In *Roe v. Wade* (1973), the U.S. Supreme Court limited the traditional authority of states to pass laws governing abortion. The Court said that a woman's constitutional right to privacy included the right to have an abortion. States cannot deny citizens the exercise of a constitutional right without a compelling reason.

A Constitutional Right to Privacy. The right to privacy is at the heart of the abortion controversy. This right is not expressly stated in the Constitution. The justices of the Supreme Court "found" privacy to be a fundamental right by interpreting the Fourteenth Amendment and other amendments to the Constitution in cases they heard on appeal from lower courts (see Box 14.1). The Court had earlier established a right to privacy in some matters involving the family (see Box 14.2).

Once a right like "privacy" is articulated, legislation can be challenged for allegedly limiting the right unnecessarily. The U.S. Supreme Court develops the contours of the right as it decides subsequent cases. Several years before *Roe v. Wade,* the Supreme Court extended the boundary of the right to privacy to include reproductive matters through its rulings on the constitutionality of the laws restricting access to contraception.

Privacy and Contraception: *Griswold v. Connecticut* (1965). Estelle Griswold, executive director of a newly opened Planned Parenthood clinic in New Haven, Connecticut, and Dr. C. L. Buxton, a professor of gynecology and obstetrics at Yale

---

BOX 14.1

Fourteenth Amendment

The Fourteenth Amendment was passed in 1868 to protect the rights of the newly freed slaves, but it was written in broad language to support ideals of liberty. The amendment states, in part,

1. . . . No State shall make or enforce any law which shall abridge the privileges or immunities of citizens of the United States; nor shall any State deprive any person of life, liberty or property, without due process of law; nor deny any person within its jurisdiction the equal protection of the laws.

The Fourteenth Amendment's Due Process and Equal Protection Clauses has provided legal grounds for legislation and for litigation to protect the rights of African Americans and other ethnic minorities, women, illegitimate children, aliens, and, within limits, stigmatized groups such as prisoners, persons with mental illness, and persons with retardation.

BOX 14.2

Abortion: Some Legal Cases in Point—Right to Privacy in Family Matters

The following three landmark cases contributed to the establishment and articulation of a constitutionally protected right to privacy in family matters:

- *Meyer v. Nebraska* (1923): The U.S. Supreme Court overturned the conviction of a parochial school teacher under a World War I law that barred the teaching of the German language in schools. The Court used the case to enunciate a broad definition of liberty including "the right of the individual . . . to marry, establish a home and bring up children" among other freedoms.

- *Pierce v. Society of Sisters* (1925): The Supreme Court overturned a state law requiring parents to send their children to public schools, reaffirming the right of parents to direct their children's education.

- *Skinner v. Oklahoma* (1942): The Supreme Court struck down a state law requiring sterilization after a third criminal conviction as arbitrary. The majority opinion, defined marriage and procreation as fundamental to liberty.

University, deliberately challenged a Connecticut statute making it a crime to assist someone in the use of contraceptives. They appealed their convictions, and the case reached the U.S. Supreme Court.

A majority of the Court agreed to strike down the law, which one justice characterized as "uncommonly silly." In his majority opinion, Justice William O. Douglas "found" a right of privacy in the "penumbras, formed from emanations" of the First Amendment right of association, the Third Amendment right to be protected against forced quartering of soldiers, and the Fourth Amendment right to be secure in one's own home and to be protected against unreasonable searches and seizures, as well as in the sanctity traditionally accorded the marital bedroom.

The right to privacy in intimate relationships was affirmed by the Court in a second case involving access to contraception, *Eisenstadt v. Baird* (1972). In the majority opinion, Justice William Brennan wrote,

> If the right to privacy means anything it is the right of the individual, married or single, to be free from unwarranted governmental intrusion into matters so fundamentally affecting a person as the decision whether to bear or beget a child.

Privacy and Abortion: *Roe v. Wade* (1973). Justice Brennan's ruling encouraged abortion activists to challenge other laws on right to privacy grounds. Two young lawyers, Sara Weddington and Linda Coffee, wanted to challenge a Texas statute prohibiting abortion except to save the mother's life. In Norma McCorvey, allegedly pregnant as a result of rape, they found the ideal person to make such a challenge. Norma McCorvey was "Jane Roe." She could not obtain an abortion in Texas.

Building on previous privacy decisions, the U.S. Supreme Court struck down the Texas law. Justice Harry Blackmun wrote the 7–2 majority opinion for the Court. He said, "This right of privacy . . . is broad enough to encompass a woman's decision whether or not to terminate her pregnancy." The opinion addressed several controversial issues: is a fetus a "person" under the Fourteenth Amendment? Justice Blackmun wrote that, in the Constitution, the term *person* had a postnatal referent, and did not apply to a fetus. (In contrast, the Supreme Court has found corporations to be "persons" entitled to protection under the amendment.) Moreover, under common law, fetuses had very few, if any, protections of the kind accorded to infants who were born alive. Justice Blackmun reviewed arguments that life begins at birth, not at conception, and eventually settled on a compromise: the fetus could be protected at the point when it was viable outside of the mother's womb.

The State's Interests. Justice Blackmun agreed that the state had a **compelling interest** (a purpose for legislation that could be considered highly important) in protecting the health of the pregnant woman. Because the risk to the mother's health of carrying a child to term was greater than the risk of a first-trimester abortion, he said the state had no legitimate interest in regulating first-trimester abortions. The state could regulate second-trimester abortions, but only to preserve and protect maternal health. After the point of viability, the state's interest in protecting potential life grew; states could regulate or even proscribe third-trimester abortions, provided that abortions were permitted to save the mother's life or preserve her health. (Because 90 percent or more of abortions are performed in the first trimester, legal regulation later in pregnancy has only a small effect on the choice to have an abortion.) These limits on how the state could regulate abortion were later modified to some extent in *Planned Parenthood of Pennsylvania v. Casey* (1992).

Norma McCorvey ("Roe") later become a pro-life activist and tried to persuade the U.S. Supreme Court to overrule its *Roe v. Wade* decision (Burchfiel, 2005). The Supreme Court declined to hear her petition.

FIGURE 14.1

U.S. Supreme Court Justice Harry S. Blackmun (1908–1999)
U.S. Supreme Court Justice Harry S. Blackmun wrote the 7–2 Roe v. Wade *decision for the U.S. Supreme Court in 1973. The decision was and is controversial. Justice Blackmun served on the court from 1970 to 1994.*

Roe v. Wade stimulated the growth of a large, highly active pro-life political movement (Luker, 1984) that continues its efforts today. States quickly passed laws restricting abortion to test the limits of the individual right to reproductive choice. The Supreme Court overturned many of the most restrictive provisions. However, it upheld the right of any state to elect not to fund abortions under Medicaid, the federally funded health benefits program for indigent persons, even though the same state elected to fund the costs of bearing a child (*Harris v. McCrae,* 1980; *Maher v. Roe,* 1977).

Appointments by Presidents George H. W. Bush and Ronald Reagan tilted the Court toward greater tolerance for state laws restricting abortion. In **Webster v. Reproductive Health Services** (1989), the Court upheld a Missouri statute requiring expensive testing to determine if a fetus was viable, and prohibiting abortions in publicly funded facilities. The *Webster* decision galvanized the pro-choice forces, and made the abortion issue a matter of concern for everyone running for state and local offices. In 1992, the U.S. Supreme Court decided **Planned Parenthood of Southeastern Pennsylvania v. Casey.** (Pennsylvania had passed a law with a number of restrictions and conditions before a woman could obtain an abortion, and Robert Casey was governor of Pennsylvania at the time of the litigation.) Abortion opponents were hoping the more conservative U.S. Supreme Court would overturn *Roe v. Wade.* Pro-choice proponents feared that if the Court in *Casey* overruled *Roe* and eroded the right to privacy, states might be free to restrict the use of contraception, as well as abortion, as they did earlier. Many people were surprised when three justices nominated by Republican presidents, Sandra Day O'Connor, Anthony Kennedy, and David Souter, refused to overturn *Roe v. Wade* on the basis of *stare decisis* (see Chapter 1). Their joint opinion helped reaffirm the basic concept of privacy in reproductive matters.

The Court's opinion in *Casey* opened the door to some restrictions on abortion rights, however. Where the *Roe* opinion held that states could only restrict abortion for a compelling reason, the *Casey* decision now permitted restrictions that did not place a **substantial obstacle** or **undue burden** on women seeking an abortion. In the Court's view, the following provisions of the Pennsylvania statute did not create substantial obstacles to seeking an abortion:

- A 24-hour waiting period.
- Informed consent procedures that must include provision of information about the nature of the procedure, the health risks of childbirth and abortion, and the "probable gestational age" of the unborn child; about medical assistance benefits for childbirth, child support, and adoption agencies and services; and about the availability of materials published by the state describing fetal development.
- Information must be given by a physician.
- A woman must sign a statement affirming that she knew of the availability of the materials.
- In addition to signing an informed consent form themselves, minors under 18 seeking an abortion must have a parent or guardian sign the informed consent form as well, or use a judicial bypass.

In permitting these restrictions on abortion, the Supreme Court gave the green light for other state legislatures to impose the same ones in their own statutes.

FIGURE 14.2

Pro-Choice Escorts and Pro-Life Protesters
*Pro-choice escorts taking a woman through pro-life protesters into an abortion clinic.
Scenes such as this took place in many cities throughout the United States in the 1970s
and 1980s. To this very day, one can still see a few protesters with signs outside
women's services clinics on days the clinics are performing abortions.*

The Court ruled that a provision of the Pennsylvania law requiring a woman to
notify her spouse prior to having an abortion did create a substantial obstacle and
was struck down. The Court cited literature on domestic violence in support of its
decision.

⊠ Psychological Propositions and Concepts of Liberty and Privacy

A key psychological proposition is central to the *Casey* Court's analysis of a woman's
interest in terminating her pregnancy:

> At the heart of liberty is the right to define one's own concept of existence, of mean-
> ing, of the universe, and of the mystery of human life. Beliefs about these matters
> could not define the attributes of personhood were they formed under the compulsion
> of the State. (p. 10)

The Court also recognized that "[t]he ability of a woman to participate equally in
the economic and social life of the Nation has been facilitated by their ability to control their reproductive lives" (p. 14). (See later in this chapter on consequences for adolescents of choosing to bear a child or to have an abortion.)

The pro-life movement opened a new front when it got legislation passed banning
what it labeled "partial birth abortions." However, while third trimester abortions

⊠ Adolescent Pregnancy and Abortion

Adolescent Pregnancy

Teenage pregnancy is an important problem in the United States. The rates of pregnancies for teenagers vary greatly from state to state and by race and ethnicity. In 2002, nationwide, about 685,000 females under 19 became pregnant. Most pregnancies for those under 19 are unintended (82 percent—Finer and Henshaw, 2006) and undesired. For those under 15, there were 7,315 births and 5,442 abortions. For those between 15 and 19, there were 425,491 births and 153,778 abortions (National Center for Health Statistics, 2004). The remainder, about 15 percent of all the pregnancies, ended in spontaneous miscarriages. About 40 percent of unintended pregnancies experienced by teenagers terminated in an abortion (Finer and Henshaw, 2006).

The Abortion Rights of Minors

The U.S. Supreme Court has always been ambivalent about granting full constitutional rights to minors, who are not considered competent to make their own decisions in many areas (see Chapter 4). In a series of rulings between 1976 and 1990, the Court affirmed that minors do have a right to privacy in reproductive matters, but said their right is more limited than that of adults.

Parental consent. In *Planned Parenthood of Missouri v. Danforth* (1976), the Court struck down a provision in Missouri law requiring that all unmarried women under 18 obtain **parental consent** for an abortion. The Court said that the provision gave too much power to a third party (the parent) to veto the adolescent's privacy right to decide on an abortion. However, in his opinion, Justice Blackmun (the author of *Roe*) acknowledged that the state might have a different interest in regulating the right of an immature minor than in regulating the right of an adult woman. The comment invited states to pass laws restricting the rights of minors. In subsequent cases, the Supreme Court modified its original position, ruling that states could require parental consent, provided the minor could obtain permission for the procedure from a state court judge (a **judicial by-pass**) without first going to her parents (*Belloti v. Baird,* 1979).

Parental notification. For a while, the Court distinguished between parental consent and **parental notification** statutes. Distinguishing between notification and consent implies that teens are essentially independent of their parent's influence when it comes to making a decision. Yet, can an adolescent act independently when her parents are aware of the decision she wants to make?

In *H.L. v. Matheson* (1981), Chief Justice Warren Burger wrote the opinion upholding a statute requiring a physician to notify "if possible" the parents of girls under 15, living at home, and not emancipated. He reasoned that the state had a compelling interest in protecting immature and dependent minors and in preserving family integrity. Chief Justice Burger wrote that parental notification protected the child because the parents could supply medical information and history to the physician that the minor did not know. It didn't matter if notice to the parent led to pressure on the girl to forgo the abortion because the state could elect policies to support childbirth rather than abortions, and notification was not the same as the veto involved in a statute requiring consent.

The chief justice saw no contradiction in the fact that, under most state laws, a pregnant minor can consent to medical procedures related to carrying a pregnancy and to childbirth. Citing some literature, he said abortion was different because

> If the pregnant girl elects to carry her child to term, the medical decisions to be made entail few—perhaps none—of the potentially grave emotional and psychological consequences of the decision to abort. (pp. 412–413)

Melton and Pliner (1986) disputed whether the literature in fact supported that contention.

The *H.L. v. Matheson* (1981) opinion discussed the immature minor. How is maturity to be determined? The courts and legislatures accept simple chronological age as an adequate basis for determining competence to drive, to purchase alcohol, and to consent to sexual relations. In the abortion area, however, the Supreme Court refused to set a bright line of age, calling for a case-by-case determination of maturity (*Akron v. Akron Center for Reproductive Rights,* 1983). The Court again addressed the issue of determining maturity to obtain an abortion in *Planned Parenthood v. Ashcroft* (1983). In his opinion, Justice Lewis Powell listed the requirements for a valid parental notification or consent statute including the availability of a judicial bypass procedure:

- To protect her privacy right, the minor who doesn't wish to obtain parental consent or doesn't want her parents to know must be allowed to go to court directly.
- Once in court, the minor must demonstrate to the judge that she is sufficiently mature to make the decision.
- If the minor demonstrates maturity, the judge will waive the provisions for parental notification or consent.
- Even if the judge finds the minor too immature to make the decision, the judge may authorize an abortion without parental notification or consent on the basis that this would be in the child's best interests.

Justice Powell set out some factors for the court hearing the minor's petition to consider: her emotional development, her maturity, her intellect and understanding, her understanding of the consequences of an abortion and of alternatives, and anything else the judge found pertinent to consider. These were vague, but they offered at least some minimum guidelines to judges and researchers.

Two-parent versus one-parent notification. In *Hodgson v. Minnesota* (1990), the U.S. Supreme Court reviewed a Minnesota law requiring that a minor notify both parents of her intent to have an abortion. The statute is another example of a state law designed to test the limits of restrictions on abortions. The legislature passed two versions of the bill, one version without a judicial bypass provision and another version with one.

The American Psychological Association submitted an amicus curiae brief to the Supreme Court arguing that the two-parent notification statute had harmful effects on minors. The brief reviewed research showing that the two-parent notice requirement did not reestablish relationships with an estranged parent, and could result in threats to renew custody disputes. It could provoke violence or harassment in dysfunctional or abusive families. Some adolescents who might have notified one parent went to court only to avoid notifying the other one. The evidence at the trial opposing the implementation of the law supported the conclusion that the statute did not enhance communication with parents, and might well have impeded that goal. In addition, Minnesota state court judges who administered the law testified that they saw no good in it. The judges and other professionals who worked with adolescents told the initial trial court that the procedure was nerve-wracking for youth, and stimulated feelings of anger, shame, guilt, and embarrassment.

The Supreme Court was deeply divided. Justice John Paul Stevens wrote for a five-justice majority finding the two-parent notice without judicial bypass unconstitutional. A different five-person majority agreed that the statute including a judicial bypass provision was constitutional.

Justice Anthony Kennedy wrote the five-justice majority opinion upholding the two-parent notification and 48-hour delay provisions with judicial bypass. Justice Kennedy was unimpressed with the empirical evidence. In his view, the values embodied in the statute were more important than assessing empirically whether the statute was achieving its goal. He saw the Minnesota law as a permissible, reasoned attempt to further the state's legitimate interest in protecting minors and protecting the parental role without placing an absolute obstacle to abortion in an adolescent's way. Imperfections in the application of statutes are inevitable, he said. The Court should defer to the state legislature's wisdom in supporting a "tradition of a parental role in the care and upbringing of children that is as old as civilization itself" (pp. 141–142). Justice Kennedy reflected the opinion of a strong majority of Americans who, in public opinion polls, support laws requiring teenagers to obtain parental consent or notification before obtaining an abortion (Carlson, 1990).

Justice Thurgood Marshall, who was in the first five-justice majority, entered a vigorous dissent to any two-parent notification provision, with or without bypass. In support of his position, Justice Marshall cited research findings extensively, including the APA brief and articles by Gary Melton (1987b) and by Catherine Lewis (1987) published in the *American Psychologist*.

Research Issues Raised by the Decisions

For many people, including many of the Supreme Court justices who decided *Hodgson*, legislatively selected social values should be the primary determinants of adolescent abortion policy. But, for many others, the underlying factual basis for laws and facts about the real-life consequences of laws should shape policy making. These approaches may be summed up as a matter of beliefs versus facts when selecting policies. The legal cases and the controversy they generated stimulated research into several questions:

- Are adolescent minors competent to make a decision about terminating a pregnancy?
- How often did pregnant adolescents communicate with their parents about abortion prior to mandatory notification laws?
- What are the consequences for minors and their families of laws that require parental notification or consent, or a court order for an abortion?
- What are the short- and long-term educational, occupational, economic, social, and psychological consequences for an adolescent of having an abortion or of having an out-of-wedlock baby?

- Do minors have the emotional and cognitive maturity to make competent decisions about whether or not to have an abortion?

Laws regulating adolescent access to abortion have sometimes played out in unexpected ways. How adolescents make decisions; how family members, judges, and lawyers who may represent adolescents in hearings respond; and the availability of abortion services determine what the laws mean in action.

Minors' Competence to Make a Decision about Abortion

The question of whether teenagers should be considered competent under the law to decide whether to have an abortion is a special case of the general problem of the competence of minors to consent to health care (see Chapter 4). Consent to health care must be informed; that is, the patient must have "received adequate information about the risks associated with the particular treatment and the alternatives that might be selected in place of it" (Wadlington, 1983, p. 64). The patient receiving the information must be able to use it intelligently, to understand the information, and to draw inferences about the probable implications of any proposed treatment for his or her future.

The law presumes that adults are competent to make decisions about medical care, but that minors are not. In theory, giving the parent the authority to consent for the minor helps make up for what the minor lacks in experience, emotional maturity, or the ability to make a complex judgment. The states recognize that many older minors do have the competence to give consent to treatment in some areas. Many states also recognize that minors may not seek treatment or may delay treatment for conditions that, if known to the parents, might result in family conflict. Depending on state law, minors under age 18 may seek treatment without parental consent for substance abuse or addiction, family planning, pregnancy care, venereal disease, and, sometimes, psychotherapy or counseling.

Research on adolescent decision making. Research suggests that young people 15 and older are fairly competent cognitively to make general health care decisions. They respond to questions about health care dilemmas and use information in a manner not too different from adults (Lewis, 1981; Weithorn and Campbell, 1982). However, the young people who participated in the studies were not actually faced with a health decision. Many health decisions, including how to respond to an unwanted pregnancy, are made in a highly charged emotional context. Emotion may affect people's ability to bring reason to bear on a decision and may affect people of different ages differently. Decisions regarding abortion can involve the clarification of values and religious beliefs as well. Lewis (1980) was one of the few researchers who interviewed both adolescent and adult women who had come to a clinic for a pregnancy test. About 20 percent of both groups planned to have the baby. The younger and older women had about the same knowledge of the laws governing abortion. But the two groups differed in some ways. Minors were less likely to think of consulting a professional for assistance, less likely to consider their own parenting abilities when deciding what to do, and more likely to feel that a decision was being forced on them by others.

Ambuel and Rappaport (1992) studied adolescents who came to a woman's medical clinic for a pregnancy test. They found that minors under 15, compared to older minors, were on average less able to answer questions about the advantages and disadvantages of an abortion or of parenthood, and about how a pregnancy or abortion might affect others in their lives. Minors over 15 had about the same knowledge and information as those over 18. Ehrlich (2003) studied adolescents who had sought judicial bypasses. She reported that adolescents as young as 14 had fairly well thought through reasons for their choice and that most could state several cogent reasons for seeking an abortion.

Controversy about the use of research. Some psychologists (e.g., Melton, 1983, 1984; Melton and Russo, 1987) argue that, based on intellectual competence alone as demonstrated in developmental studies, there is little basis for limiting the right of older adolescents to participate in medical decisions. They maintain that the research, though imperfect, is well enough developed to provide useful information to judges who need to make immediate decisions in the cases before them. The APA agrees with this position. The organization summarized research on adolescent competence as part of amicus curiae briefs presented to the Supreme Court in *Hartigan v. Zbaraz and Charles* (1987), *Thornburgh v. American College of Obstetricians and Gynecologists* (1986), and *Hodgson v. Minnesota* (1990).

Gardner, Scherer, and Tester (1989) believe that the APA's use of the studies on adolescent competence in a legal forum was inappropriate. They argued that the research was too sparse, the methods oversimplified, and the conclusions not well enough accepted in the scientific community to warrant confident assertions in a brief to the U.S. Supreme Court. The debate continues about when the database is sufficient to warrant an amicus brief and when it is sufficient to support a policy preference.

Effects of Parental Notification and Consent Statutes

Parental notification or consent statutes are intended to protect the minor from unwise decisions, and to promote the integrity of the family and the authority of the parent. No law prohibits adolescents from informing their parents. The laws permit adolescents to avoid notifying parents if the adolescent so chooses by going to court. The statutes present an important opportunity to see how a law shapes human behavior, and how people adapt to a law when vital interests are at stake.

Did adolescents notify parents before they had to? Clary (1982) studied 141 adolescents who had requested abortion services at a clinic in the Minneapolis–St. Paul area in 1979, before Minnesota implemented its law requiring parental notification (see *H.L. v. Matheson*, 1981). Seventy-six percent of the sample was either 16 or 17. The rest were younger. Two-thirds came from intact families.

Thirty-seven percent of Clary's interviewees had informed their mothers of their pregnancy and intent to obtain an abortion, and 25 percent had informed their fathers. Younger minors, perhaps because of greater financial and emotional dependence, were more likely to inform their parents than older minors. Other studies reported that a little over half of adolescents involved one or both of their parents, even if the hospital or abortion clinic had no policy requiring parental consent or notification (Cartoof and Klerman, 1986; Lewis, 1987). On the other hand, Monsour and Stewart (1973) found that only 15 percent of college women who had abortions and were not underage informed their parents. Thus, it appears that dependent minors are more likely than older adolescents to seek parental help even without a legal requirement to do so.

Smith (1973) found that most adolescents who confided in their parents felt the experience increased communication and brought them closer together. However, those who expected their parents would have a negative reaction were less likely to inform them of the pregnancy in the first place. About a third of those who did not tell their parents believed that, if they had, their parents would have punished them or prevented them from having the abortion (see Box 14.3). Some young women said they feared upsetting their parents or making them feel bad. One of Monsour and Stewart's interviewees explained her reluctance to tell her parents: "my mother would never stop crying about how she had failed, what her friends would think, how mad my dad would be if he found out, how I had been irresponsible and ruined my life and on and on" (Monsour and Stewart, 1973, p. 811). Ehrlich (2003) found that adolescents under 18 who sought judicial waivers under the law in Massachusetts expressed many of the same reasons for not notifying their parents. In addition to concerns about physical abuse, many feared their parents would lose respect for them or lose trust. Many who sought the waivers said that they had had little communication with their parents about sex and that communication now would be very difficult.

Advise, consent, or coerce. Adolescents who want an abortion and fear their parents will oppose their wishes can try to obtain the abortion by getting court permission or by seeking the abortion in another state without parental notification or consent laws. Eighteen states have consent statutes, while 14 states have notification statutes. In 9 states, the parental involvement law was not enforced because the law was challenged in court (Alan Guttmacher Institute, 2004). Adolescents must have the option of seeking a court waiver without notifying their parents if the state's consent or notification law is to be upheld as constitutional. Adolescents who want to have the baby don't need their parents' permission under the law. But in real life, adolescents who do notify their parents may be pressured by their parents into either having or not having the baby against their will.

Whom do adolescents consult? Adolescents are more likely to share problems with friends than with parents or professionals. Seventy-one percent of adolescents seeking an abortion in Cartoof and Klerman's (1986) sample told their best friend, and about

---

BOX 14.3

Becky Bell: A Victim of Parental Consent Laws?

When Becky Bell was 17, she became pregnant. She lived in Indiana, where the law requires a minor to obtain parental consent before having an abortion. Becky didn't want her parents to know. According to the Bells, Indiana judges had reputations for refusing petitions of minors claiming to be mature enough to make an abortion decision independently. Becky investigated making an appointment at an abortion clinic in Kentucky, a state with no parental notification law, but didn't follow through. Instead, she apparently attempted to abort the child herself. She died from a uterine infection. Had there been no parental notification or consent law in Indiana, Becky could have obtained a safe, legal abortion. A pro-life spokesperson said that, if Becky had obeyed the law, she would not have died. Becky Bell might have misjudged her parents' reaction to her plight. Had she consulted them, they might have been helpful and supportive. Her parents have since become active in opposing parental notification and consent laws (Carlson, 1990; Tribe, 1990).

90 percent told their boyfriends, though only about half told a parent. Ehrlich (2003) reported similar findings based on a large sample of adolescents who sought a judicial bypass waiver in Massachusetts.

We do not know what teenage friends have to offer by way of sage counsel or practical advice to a pregnant adolescent (Lewis, 1987). In 1995, 14 percent of sexually experienced adolescent males were involved in a pregnancy, but we have very little information about the male adolescent response to knowledge they had fathered a child (Siecus Report, 2002). A majority of the 15- to 19-year-old males in a national survey, the vast majority of whom had not fathered a child, were not sympathetic to abortions and said abortion was not acceptable if the woman wanted one, but the man did not (Marsiglio and Shehan, 1993). Adolescent male attitudes toward abortion in general have become increasingly negative (Bogess and Bradner, 2000). We don't know how the partner's attitude influences the decision to abort and how it might affect the adolescent's postabortion emotional state.

How Adolescents Adapt to the Law

Researchers have investigated the effects of parental notification laws in Massachusetts and Minnesota, and there are some data from other states as well.

The judicial bypass option. Before parental notification or consent laws took effect, 33 to 50 percent of minors seeking an abortion informed their parents. Mnookin (1985) estimated that, after Massachusetts instituted a parental consent requirement with judicial bypass in 1981, about 75 percent of minors seeking abortions in the state obtained parental consent, and about 25 percent sought judicial bypass. However, a significant number of young women got abortions in neighboring states without those restrictions to avoid both the consent provision and a court hearing (Cartoof and Klerman, 1986). If we take into account adolescents who went out of state, after the law went into effect, only about 42 percent of Massachusetts minors getting abortions were notifying their parents.

Blum, Resnick, and Stark (1990) studied the impact of the Minnesota law that required minors to notify both parents or seek a judicial bypass. They concluded that the law probably resulted in more adolescents telling their parents about their pregnancy. However, about 43 percent of minors seeking abortions used the court bypass. About a quarter of these had notified one parent, but didn't want to notify the other. Most of the group that went to court was over 16 (85 percent), and the majority came from economically better-off families.

The judicial waiver provisions of state laws on parental notification or consent, a constitutional requirement, provide good examples of the difference between the law on the books and the law in action (Ehrlich, 2003). In Massachusetts, the judicial waiver worked reasonably smoothly, although the adolescents who went through the procedure found it stressful and embarrassing. Other states also have such laws, but the mechanics were such that there were obstacles to using the court, especially if the judge reviewing the petition personally opposed abortion.

Silverstein et al. (2005) studied how well the Tennessee parental consent law operated. In theory, the law had several provisions that should make it easier for adolescents to access the judicial bypass option (e.g., a state-supported advocate, court-appointed counsel to assist the adolescent, and courts with jurisdiction conveniently located in each county). The research team called each county's court, saying, "I am calling to find out how a girl who is not eighteen who wants an abortion can get a judge's permission to avoid telling her parents."

If the respondent in the court referred the caller to someone else, the research team pursued that call to see where it led. The research team measured "preparedness" by noting whether or not the court personnel acknowledged their obligation to conduct waiver hearings and mentioned the availability of legal counsel or an advocate. Based on the telephone inquiry, they classified 45 of Tennessee's 95 county courts (47 percent) as being unprepared to handle inquiries. Many of the courts simply recommended contacting an attorney, a social service agency, or an abortion clinic. Eight informants in the 45 unprepared courts expressed doubts that a judge could waive parental consent, although state law explicitly gives judges that authority.

Most of the court advocates designated by the Department of Social Services to work with minors on the petitions were prepared to do so. However, it took repeated telephone calls to contact many of the advocates. Adolescents would not or could not leave home numbers to receive callbacks from advocates. They feared their parents would learn what they wanted to do. For many adolescents, these administrative flaws made the waiver procedure accessible only with difficulty. Similar problems were reported in Alabama and Pennsylvania (Silverstein et al., 2005).

What happens when adolescents go to court? In those states for which we have data, judges almost never reject the petitions of minors seeking abortions. From 1981 to 1983, about 1,300 Massachusetts minors sought judicial authorization for an abortion. The hearings were short. The judges found the minor was "mature" in about 90 percent of the cases. When the minor was not mature, the judge was required to consider her "best interests." The Massachusetts judges found that an abortion was in the minor's best interests in all but five cases. All five managed to obtain abortions, one by going to another judge, three through an appeal, and one by going out of state (Mnookin, 1985). Ehrlich (2003), working with Massachusetts adolescents in subsequent years, reported similar rates of judges allowing minors to obtained abortions. Though judges in Massachusetts almost always granted the petition, the young women who went to court experienced it as aversive and punitive. Many were embarrassed and angered by the experience. Going to court in and of itself invaded adolescent privacy (Melton, 1987; Ehrlich, 2003). Judges asked the young women intimate questions about their sex lives, their menstrual cycles (to determine how advanced the pregnancy was), about abortions, about how they made their decision, and sometimes about their relationship with their parents. Young petitioners were also afraid they might see someone they knew in the courthouse building.

In Minnesota, petitions were usually granted after a hearing lasting an average of 15 minutes (see Justice Marshall's dissent in *Hodgson v. Minnesota*, pp. 14–17). However, the judicial bypass procedure was burdensome. In addition to delays arising from court schedules, judges who had conscientious objections to abortion refused to hear the petitions. Minors sometimes had to travel as much as 500 miles to get a hearing. Undertaking a journey of that distance in itself sometimes compromised a teenager's privacy (Donovan, 1983). None of the groups involved in judicial bypass thought the procedure was satisfactory. The young women who went to court were angry and resentful at having to report intimate details of their lives to strangers, and many reported feeling anxious and guilty in court as well. Judges didn't see the point of the proceeding; if the young woman was mature, she could have an abortion as she wished. If they found that she was not mature enough to make her own decision, how could they decide she was mature enough to bear a child? Lawyers assigned to aid the petitioning minors also disliked the task. They received no fee or were paid low fees by the state and not very promptly (Donovan, 1983; Mnookin, 1985).

While judges in Massachusetts, Minnesota, and Michigan tend to rubber-stamp petitions by minors, this may not be the case in other states. There are very little systematic data for other states. When judicial approval of petitions is more difficult to obtain, one can hypothesize that more pregnant minors will inform their parents or go out of the state if they can to avoid the requirement (see Box 14.3). Virginia's bypass statute gives the judge discretion to inform the adolescent's parent or parents. There are no data on the effect of this Virginia law. The District of Columbia, which borders Virginia, has no parental consent or notification law. However, the District of Columbia has the highest number of teenage abortions in the country. Some of the adolescents who had abortions in the District of Columbia came from neighboring Virginia. In Texas, adolescents advised by lawyers or counselors may go "judge shopping." For example, two counties with judges with antiabortion reputations had 19 and 13 cases respectively. Two adjacent counties handled 191 and 110 cases respectively ("Planned Parenthood," 2002). Federal legislation is pending to make it a crime for any one to assist an adolescent to cross a state line in order to evade parental consent or notification provisions in their home state's law.

Delay in seeking abortion. Abortions are riskier and more costly as a pregnancy progresses. A first-trimester abortion costs between $350 and $500, while second-trimester abortions can cost $1,000 or more. Because the period between the first suspicions that they are pregnant and the decision about what to do is the most stressful for women, delay also increases stress and anxiety. Most abortions (87 percent) take place within the first 12 weeks of gestation. However, adolescents, especially younger ones, more than older women, delay seeking an abortion. For adolescents under age 15, 74.7 percent obtain abortions within 12 weeks; for those ages 15–19, 82.9 percent obtain abortions within 12 weeks; while for those ages 20–24, 87.5 percent have their abortions within the first 12 weeks. Although the numbers are small, a higher percent of adolescents compared to older women obtain abortions in the period 16–20 weeks after gestation (Elam-Evans et al., 2002). Concern about their parents' reactions and reluctance to go to court may be among the reasons adolescents delay seeking an abortion, to their detriment. In Texas, following a parental notification law, fewer minors became pregnant, but minors who were pregnant and were within six months of reaching their eighteenth birthday showed an increased likelihood of obtaining a delayed, second trimester abortion (Joyce, Kaestner, and Colman, 2006).

There seems to be a general trend to delay seeking an abortion among women in those states with laws that require a waiting period or a return for a second consultation, as approved in *Casey*. In Mississippi, the proportion of second-trimester abortions increased from 7.5 percent of abortions to 11.5 percent among women who relied on providers within the state. The rate increased somewhat less among those able to seek abortions in nearby states that did not have a law requiring delay (Joyce and Kaestner, 2000).

Does parental notification reduce the number of abortions? Pro-life advocates hoped that parental notification and consent statutes would reduce the number of abortions (Mnookin, 1985), but the law did not appear to have that effect in Massachusetts. Cartoof and Klerman (1986) used the Massachusetts Department of Health database to examine changes month by month in the number of adolescents who obtained abortions within the state, and also obtained data on the number of minors who obtained abortions in five neighboring states that at that time did not have parental consent or notification requirements. The number of women under 17 having abortions in Massachusetts

Table 14.1

Effects of Parental Notification and Consent Laws on Adolescent Abortions, Births, and Pregnancy Rates in Massachusetts

Abortions in Massachusetts:	
The year before the law went into effect	4,560
The year after the law went into effect	3,940
Out-of-state abortions:	
The year before the law went into effect	29 per month
The year after the law went into effect	95 per month
Number of births to adolescents in Massachusetts:	
The year before the law went into effect	2,712
The year after the law went into effect	2,481

Adapted from V. G. Cartoof and L. V. Klerman (1986). Parental consent for abortion: Impact of the Massachusetts law. American Journal of Public Health, 76, 397–400. Material adapted from Table 1, p. 378; Table 2, p. 399; Table 3, p. 399. Used with the permission of the authors and the American Public Health Association.

went down about 43 percent the year the notification requirement was implemented. However, the number of Massachusetts minors seeking abortions in neighboring states went from an average of 29 a month to an average of 95 a month. The researchers concluded that the law had done very little, if anything, to reduce the number of abortions among Massachusetts adolescents. In Texas, the number of abortions obtained by teenagers did decline following passage of a parental notification law (Joyce, Kaestner, and Colman, 2006), but it is difficult to attribute the decline to the operation of the law alone. The number of abortions has been declining nationally for several years now.

Do notification laws affect sexual behavior? The pregnancy rate is equal to the birthrate plus the legal and illegal abortion rate, plus spontaneous miscarriages. In the years from 1991 to 1994, right after the Supreme Court affirmed the constitutionality of parental notification with bypass laws, there was a small nationwide annual decline in both the birthrate and the abortion rate among minors (Centers for Disease Control, 1997a, 1997b). The decline has continued and has been somewhat greater among females under 17 than among those 18 or 19. The decline means that minors had changed their sexual behavior: either more young people were postponing intercourse, sexually active young people were having intercourse less often, or they were using contraception more effectively.

The new notification laws may have contributed to the change in sexual behavior. However, many factors other than notification or consent laws could be responsible for the changed behavior. During the same period in which state laws changed, adolescents were hearing more about the dangers of AIDS. The pregnancy rate became lower as the rate of AIDS went up (Altman-Palm and Tremblay, 1998). Teens were exposed to more information about contraception, including oral contraception, and more recently information about emergency contraception. Although there is some variation among white, African American, and Latino teens, contraceptive use at last intercourse among sexually active high school students ranged from 78 to 91 percent. The risk of pregnancy in the sexually active group declined by 21 percent between 1991 and 2003 (Santelli et al., 2006).

Table 14.2

Effects of Parental Notification and Consent Laws on Adolescent Abortions, Births, and Pregnancy Rates in Minnesota

Age	Prenotification and Consent Law (1978–1980)	Postnotification and Consent Law (1982–1985)
Abortion Rate per Thousand Females		
15–17	19.0	13.6
18–19	38.2	34.6
20–44	13.3	13.9
Birth Rate per Thousand Females		
15–17	17.7	15.5
18–19	57.3	50.2
20–44	78.0	76.2
Total Pregnancies (abortions + births, not counting miscarriages)		
15–17	36.7	29.1
18–19	95.5	84.8
20–44	91.3	90.1

Adapted from J. L. Rogers, R. F. Boruch, G. B. Stoms, and D. DeMoya. (1991). Impact of the Minnesota parental notification law on abortion and birth. American Journal of Public Health, 81, 294–298. Material adapted from Table 2, p. 297 and Table 3, p. 297. Used with the permission of the authors and the American Public Health Association.

In more recent years, teens have been exposed to abstinence education as well. Since 1993, over 2.5 million adolescents have taken "virginity pledges" to abstain from sexual relations until marriage. These pledges may have a short-term effect of delaying the initiation into sexual behavior for those who took the pledges (Bearman and Bruckner, 2000).

Personal Consequences of an Abortion

Teen expectations. Teens have unrealistic expectations about how their lives would be affected by carrying a child to term. Ninety-four percent believe they could stay in school if they became pregnant, but only 70 percent of pregnant teens actually do stay. Fifty-one percent believe they would marry the father of the child, but 81 percent of teen mothers are unmarried (Siecus, 2002).

Options. A pregnant adolescent has three options. She may have the baby and keep it, have it and give it up for adoption, or have an abortion. To make a wise choice, an adolescent must consider her values, including her religious and moral beliefs, and the possible medical, psychological, and practical consequences of each alternative course of action. Research provides some information about the consequences of the alternatives.

Health risks of abortion and childbirth. One consideration for the adolescent considering abortion is her health risk. The question of comparative health risks is surrounded by political controversy (see Family Planning Perspectives, 1989, 21, pp. 31–32). However, the best available studies indicate that the risk of death from a first-trimester abortion is less than 1 in 100,000 procedures. Childbirth is seven times more likely to cause death to the mother (see *Roe v. Wade*, 1973).

Pro-life supporters point out that comparing the risks of death from abortion and pregnancy implicitly weighs the rights of the mother over the rights of the fetus. They claim that the health risks of abortion are underestimated and that women are not fully informed of those risks (e.g., Johnson, 2003); however they have not provided scientifically derived risk estimates themselves.

Emotional and psychological consequences of abortion and childbirth. Another concern pregnant adolescents may factor into their decision is their emotional reaction following an abortion. The evaluation of psychological consequences of abortion and pregnancy is also enmeshed in political controversy (see Family Planning Perspectives, 1990, 22, pp. 36–39; U.S. House of Representatives, 1989). Many investigations of the question have methodological weaknesses. However, several lines of research converge to yield a fairly consistent picture (Adler et al., 1990).

Most studies of women's reactions to abortion did not examine adolescents separately, or factor age into the findings (Adler and Dolcini, 1986; Melton and Pliner, 1986). We will review the general research first, and later, the smaller group of studies focused on adolescents.

After abortion became legal, it was possible to study women who came to counseling centers for difficult pregnancies, to abortion clinics, or to hospital-based ob-gyn units. In a typical study, the women were given a questionnaire while in the waiting room before the abortion and then were asked to repeat the questionnaire after the abortion. The questionnaire might be repeated again when the women returned a few weeks later for a follow-up examination. Those who gave consent might be sent mail questionnaires at a future date, or be interviewed in person or by telephone.

One methodological problem is that the researchers usually had no good way of determining the woman's psychological status before she became pregnant. The woman's level of well-being before the pregnancy may be a factor in her postabortion level of well-being (Russo and Dabul, 1997). Another problem is that some women who participated in the first assessment didn't respond to follow-up requests. It is difficult to determine the effects of the **attrition,** or reduction in the number of participants. Attrition will result in a **selection bias** (unrepresentative sample) affecting the final conclusions if drop outs differ in important ways from completers. On the other hand, follow-up rates in some studies have been good enough so that there would have to be a very high concentration of strong reactions among the nonresponders for the results to be affected significantly.

Research indicates that most women seeking abortions experience the most stress after the discovery of the pregnancy and before the decision to terminate (Adler et al., 1990). The predominant emotion immediately following an abortion was relief. A small but not an insignificant number of women, perhaps 15 percent, also suffered some negative emotions such as guilt, remorse, or depression in the short run (Adler et al., 1990; APA, 2005). Factors associated with postabortion distress in adult women included a negative reaction from their partner, disapproval from people they turned to for advice, and low confidence in their own coping skills (Cozzarelli, Sumer, and Major, 1998; Major et al., 1998).

In general, emotional distress after abortion was relatively mild, short-lived, and self-limiting in the sense that the women themselves came to terms with the abortion (Major, Mueller, and Hildebrandt, 1985; Mueller and Major, 1989). Psychiatrists surveyed by David (1972) agreed that adverse psychological reactions attributable to abortions were infrequent and not severe. In fact, 75 percent of the sample of psychiatrists had never seen any psychological symptoms they could attribute to an abortion. There is no category of mental disturbance thought to be precipitated by abortion.

By contrast, in a minority of women, giving birth can precipitate an episode of **affective disorder,** a category of serious mental illness that includes depression or mania. Childbirth can also precipitate a brief psychotic episode without the presence of clear-cut symptoms of mood disturbance (according to the *DSM-IV;* American Psychiatric Association, 1994). One in 500 to 1 in 1,000 women experience mood episodes with psychotic features within four weeks of birth.

Even if there are few short-term adverse emotional reactions to abortion, some women may suffer from delayed or long-term emotional consequences. However, few women reported any change in work or school status attributable to the abortion one to two years later. Only 6 percent of women in follow-up studies reported seeking professional help after an abortion, often for problems related to their partners' or their family's responses to the unwanted pregnancy (Adler et al., 1990). We do not have evidence of the effects of abortion over more than two years.

Planned Parenthood (2001) reviewed the literature on emotional effects of induced abortion. They concluded most women adjust well following an abortion, and that while severe emotional reactions to abortion may occur, they are not frequent. Contrary to the claims of pro-life advocates, there is no known epidemic of women seeking psychological treatment postabortion either in the short term or in the long term. Keep in mind that approximately 1,000,000 women a year have had abortions. If there was an epidemic of emotional disorders following abortions, it should have been noted in the public health literature.

Pro-life groups believe that questionnaires typically used in the studies are insensitive to the emotional nuances that emerge when women discuss their experiences with sympathetic listeners (Robinson, 2004). They claim that women who have abortions may suffer posttraumatic stress disorders and "anniversary reactions" on the date of the abortion or on the date that might have been the baby's birthday. These reactions might well occur among some women. However, pro-life groups have not produced much systematic research to document claims that these adverse reactions occur frequently or are emotionally disabling.

Emotional responses in adolescents. The long-term response of those who have an abortion as young adolescents may be different from the long-term responses of those who have an abortion as young or middle-aged women. Zabin, Hirsch, and Emerson (1989; see Box 14.4) followed a large group of African American women under age 17 who thought they might be pregnant. Over a two- to three-year period, emotional distress, measured by standard scales, among the young women who chose to have an abortion at age 17 or younger was comparable to the rate for older women and no different from the rate among same-age controls who learned they were not pregnant or who carried a child to term.

Pope, Adler, and Tschann (2001) studied 96 females between the ages of 14 and 21 who sought counseling for an unwanted pregnancy. Four weeks post abortion, those under 18 were somewhat more uncomfortable with their decisions than older females, but there were no other differences on a variety of psychological measures. Members of both age groups improved on a number of psychological measures over the four-week follow-up period.

BOX 14.4

Follow-Up Study of Adolescents

Zabin, Hirsch, and Emerson (1989) studied 360 African American women under 17 who came to a university-based or a Planned Parenthood center in Maryland for pregnancy tests in 1985 and 1986. The research team identified three groups: (1) those who were not pregnant, (2) those who were pregnant and chose an abortion, and (3) those who were pregnant and chose to have the baby. The research team obtained baseline data before the women knew the results of their pregnancy tests. They were able to follow 334 of the 360 original participants: 141 who had abortions, 93 who had babies, and 100 who were not pregnant. All the participants were assessed by telephone every six months for two years and by extensive personal interviewing and testing one year after the initial assessment and again at the end of the two-year follow-up period.

Initially, the groups were comparable on many but not all demographic variables. The group electing the abortion had mothers who were better educated, came from somewhat better-off families, were less likely to have repeated a grade of school, and were more likely to have plans to go to college than those who elected to continue the pregnancy.

Most of the young women who chose to have an abortion, like the women in other studies, reported that once the abortion was over, they felt relieved. Two or three years after the initial assessment, subjects in all three groups showed a decline in measured anxiety, a small increase in self-esteem, and an increase in internal locus of control. Only 4 percent of the abortion group showed a negative change in emotional well-being at one year, and 4.5 percent at two years. The other two groups that had not had abortions had comparable, but slightly higher, rates of negative change in emotional well-being. The research designs generally preclude strong conclusions. There are important initial differences in social background and in attitudes between those who chose childbirth and those who chose abortions. These initial differences, rather than abortion or motherhood, may account for differences in the women's lives at follow-up.

Personal Consequences of Having and Keeping a Child as an Adolescent

Keeping a child. Almost all (97 percent) adolescents who give birth keep the babies (Bachrach, Stolley, and London, 1992). Perhaps for this reason, the emotional and social consequences of giving a child up for adoption, as opposed to keeping the child, have received little study. The social and personal correlates of early motherhood are considerable, and, in theory, these should be considered by adolescents making an abortion decision.

Educational and occupational attainment. Teenagers who have out-of-wedlock babies are much less likely to complete high school than those who elect an abortion or who don't get pregnant during their high school years (Ahn, 1994; Bachrach, Stolley, and London, 1992; Maracek, 1986; Upchurch and McCarthy, 1989; Zabin et al., 1989).

Teenagers who return to school after having a baby face a number of barriers, including difficulty in finding child care and, often, disapproval, hostility, or ridicule by school personnel or other students (Maracek, 1986). However, the greater educational success of those who had abortions cannot be attributed only to their decision to terminate the pregnancy. The teenagers who chose abortion appear more motivated to succeed in school to begin with (Olson, 1980). Women who give birth as teenagers are less likely to enter the labor force, more likely to be dependent on welfare, and more likely to be homeless than other women (Duncan and Hoffman, 1990; Maracek, 1986; Weitzman, 1989).

Furstenberg, Levine, and Brooks-Gunn (1990) followed a group of 404 pregnant inner-city teenagers. They succeeded in maintaining contact with about two-thirds of the women for 20 years. Because of their low socioeconomic status, these women were at higher than average risk of developing social and personal problems to begin with.

The women who became mothers in their teens "generally suffered considerable short-term handicaps as a result of an early first birth, including low levels of education and employment" (Furstenberg, Levine, and Brooks-Gunn, 1990, p. 55). Twenty years later, those who became mothers when they were very young remained less well adapted than comparable women who didn't have their first children until their twenties. However, over 20 years, the gap narrowed. Many who became young mothers eventually returned to school or found stable employment. Furstenberg, Brooks-Gunn, and Morgan (1987) concluded, "Many teenage mothers manage to break out of the seemingly inevitable cycle of poverty, but the majority did not make out as well as they probably would have had they been able to postpone parenthood" (p. 47).

Children of teenage mothers. Another consideration for teens deciding whether to have an abortion or to have and keep a baby is whether they can raise a happy and healthy child. Infants born to out-of-wedlock teenage mothers are more likely to be premature and have low birth weight than infants born to older mothers. Premature birth and low birth weight are, in turn, associated with higher rates of infant neurological impairment and consequent school and behavioral problems for those who survive to school age (Maracek, 1986; Maynard, 1996). Younger mothers are not at higher risk of neglecting or abusing young children than older mothers when other socioeconomic factors are taken into account (Gelles, 1986).

Furstenberg, Levine, and Brooks-Gunn's (1990) follow-up of inner-city teenage mothers included assessments of their children. The children of the teen mothers showed a higher frequency of school failure, delinquency, emotional problems, and teenage pregnancy than children born to older mothers from the same neighborhood.

Changes in welfare law. The availability of financial support through welfare may be a factor in the young mother's adaptation. The Welfare Reform Act of 1996 contained funds for state programs to reduce out-of-wedlock births without increasing abortions. The welfare law awarded an "illegitimacy bonus" to states that showed the greatest statewide drop in out-of-wedlock births without an increase in abortions. The statute provided a large sum for "abstinence-only" sex education programs. States were allowed to impose a "family cap." The law permitted states to deny welfare benefits for additional children born or conceived while their mothers were on welfare. The law requires teen mothers under 18 to remain in school and to live with their parents. Minors could be denied welfare benefits, but few states did so. The law had additional provisions for enforcement of paternal responsibilities, and to encourage states to enforce statutory rape laws. State welfare departments have used the new laws, but have been emphasizing the work-related provisions more than the pregnancy prevention provisions.

It is difficult to assess whether the new welfare law has contributed to slow decline in teen pregnancy rates over the last 15 years. There may be a general change in sexual norms among teens that obscures the effects of any single program (Sawhill, 2000; National Campaign to Prevent Teen Pregnancy, 2004).

Summary

For most of our nation's history, abortion was the province of state governments. In the twentieth century, the Supreme Court developed a constitutional right to privacy that it extended first to the use of contraception and then, in *Roe v. Wade,* to abortion. By making the right to get an abortion part of a constitutionally protected right to privacy in reproductive matters, the decision limited the power of the states to prohibit abortion. After *Roe v. Wade,* a growing right-to-life movement worked toward the passage of state laws regulating abortion in ways that would be likely to discourage women from terminating their pregnancies. Some of the restrictions survived challenges brought to the Supreme Court, but the Court refused to overturn the basic ruling that abortion could not be banned. The Supreme Court did allow states to limit adolescent rights to privacy and to obtain an abortion (*Hodgson v. Minnesota,* 1990). States can now require adolescents to notify parents or to obtain parental consent in order to obtain an abortion, providing the adolescent can bypass the requirement by first going to a court. The restrictions on adolescent rights raised many research issues about the effects of the notification and consent laws. Researchers found that, prior to the new laws, 33 to 50 percent of adolescents chose to tell their parents about a pregnancy, and that younger teenagers were more likely than older teenagers to do so. The new laws may have increased the number of adolescents who notified their parents. However, many chose the judicial bypass option, or traveled to nearby states that have no restrictive laws regarding an abortion. Contrary to the concerns of some, the birthrate among adolescents did not rise with parental consent and notification laws. Since 1990, the pregnancy rate among teenagers (live births + abortions + miscarriages) has declined. The change in pregnancy rate must reflect some change in adolescent sexual behavior; young people either are engaging in intercourse later or less often or are using contraception more effectively. The change cannot be linked directly to changes in abortion policy as too many other factors have also been at play.

Early abortions are associated with fewer health risks than pregnancy. Abortion does not seem to be associated with long-term emotional problems. Short-term emotional distress secondary to abortion occurs relatively infrequently and is usually resolved reasonably quickly. In contrast, childbirth may precipitate an episode of severe mental illness in a very small percentage of women. Adolescents age 15 or older seem to be as cognitively competent to make the decision to have an abortion as adult women.

Women who become mothers as teenagers have lower educational and occupational attainment than teenagers who choose abortion and those who have children later in life, and their children have higher rates of health and social problems. However, the adolescents who choose abortion are different in a number of characteristics from those who elect to give birth (e.g., parental background and ambitions to complete schooling). These differences may account, in part, for the differences in outcomes.

The abortion story is far from over, and social science and psychological studies will continue to play a part in the debate. The social science community will be divided about when the research base is sufficiently strong to be a basis for policy recommendations. Nevertheless, activists of all persuasions will use social science and psychological studies to try to persuade the public to support their causes. Research may well have both direct and indirect effects on legislative debates and judicial decision making.

Discussion Questions

1. In the *Casey* opinion, the Supreme Court linked the right to control one's reproductive life through contraception and abortion to equal opportunity for women in the nation's economic and social life generally. Do you agree that these rights are linked? Why?
2. Suppose you wanted to find out whether, on average, parents notified that their 15-year-old daughter had requested an abortion are more likely to agree with their daughter's decision or more likely urge her to give birth. How could you go about studying this question?
3. Why do you think so few pregnant teenagers decide to have the baby and give it up for adoption? How could you investigate this question?
4. Imagine you are a judge asked to hear a petition from a minor requesting an abortion without seeking parental consent. What would you do to determine if she were a "mature" minor? If you decided she was immature and confused, what would you do?
5. Suppose you wanted to find a way to study the reasoning processes that lead adolescent women to decide to have an abortion or decide to have a baby. How might you go about it?

Key Terms

affective disorder
attrition
compelling state interest
Fourteenth Amendment
judicial bypass
parental consent

parental notification
*Planned Parenthood of
Southeastern
Pennsylvania v. Casey*
privacy
Roe v. Wade

substantial obstacle/undue
burden
selection bias
*Webster v. Reproductive
Health Services*

CHAPTER **15**

Sexual Harassment

In the last half of the twentieth century, record numbers of women began working outside the home. Between 1960 and 1997, the number of men in the labor force went up from 46.4 to 73.3 million, an increase of 58 percent. In the same period, the number of women in the labor force went from 23.3 to 63 million, an increase of 172 percent (U.S. Bureau of the Census, 1998). Supported by a women's movement demanding equal opportunities, some women entered blue-collar, managerial, and professional occupations in which workers had been mostly or exclusively male in the past. The newcomers had few female colleagues, and were not necessarily welcomed by their male peers. In almost all fields, women were almost always supervised by senior men. Women identified the problem of sexual harassment and sought protection and relief in the context of this changing working world.

The legal term **harassment** refers to repeated use of words, gestures, and actions to intentionally annoy, alarm, threaten, or verbally abuse another person. **Sexual harassment** refers to behaviors intended to manipulate or upset a person because of his or her sex. In the 1980s, civil rights legislation banning discrimination in employment on the basis of sex, race, national origin, or religion was interpreted to include a right to be free of harassment. This meant that a person who is subjected to annoying or upsetting behaviors because of gender can now seek legal redress when the effect of the behaviors is to deny equal opportunity at work or in school.

In keeping with the tenets of therapeutic jurisprudence, we can say that the law and policies prohibiting sexual harassment have a "therapeutic" purpose. They were designed to alter a systemic power imbalance between men and women in the workplace by giving the socially and occupationally less powerful victim of harassment a compensatory legal resource. Because a company can be held financially liable for the harassing behaviors of its employees, especially its supervisors, the company has an incentive to adopt effective policies to control sexual harassment. But the law in action is not necessarily the same as the law on the books. One problem is whether real people in real settings can use the remedies the law provides. Another problem is that sexual harassment is difficult to define.

Harassment is an intrinsically psychological offense: the goal of the harasser is to create a negative mental state in another person, to make the target of the behavior upset, angry, humiliated, or frightened. But perceptions and interpretations of gender- and sex-related interpersonal behaviors vary in complex ways. Behavior that is experienced as serious sexual harassment by one woman may not bother another woman much and may not look harassing at all to a man. There are no clear standards for making judgments: the norms for social relations in the workplace are still being worked out. The law is providing a tool for defining and changing norms.

In this chapter, we will summarize how law and social science have interacted in developing the doctrine of sexual harassment. We will look at

- the prevalence of sexual harassment.
- the development of the concept of sexual harassment as a form of gender-based discrimination.
- the Supreme Court's recognition of two types of harassment, quid pro quo and hostile environment.
- the influence of gender stereotypes in the workplace.
- the question of whether a victim of harassment must establish that she or he has been psychologically harmed to claim relief.
- gender differences in perceptions of potentially harassing behaviors, and the problem of establishing objective standards for harassment.
- the relationship between sexual desire and sexual harassment.
- liability issues involving hostile environment harassment.
- harassment of men, and same-sex harassment.
- harassment in the schools, including harassment of gay students.

▧ Prevalence and Costs of Sexual Harassment

Surveys of government, university, and private sector employees indicate that about half of working women have been subjected to some form of harassment at some time in their working lives (APA, 1993; Fitzgerald, 1993). The definitions of harassment used by the researchers conducting these studies are often quite broad. The surveys query subjects about a range of experiences, including some that are distressing, annoying, or upsetting, but that would not be **legally actionable** ("of a nature or severity to provide grounds for a lawsuit"). Nonetheless, the surveys clearly indicate that unwanted sexual attentions or hostile behaviors related to gender or gender role make the workplace more stressful for many people.

During 2004, 13,136 sexual harassment claims were filed with the federal **Equal Employment Opportunity Commission (EEOC)** and the state and local fair employment agencies. This probably represents only a small proportion of legally actionable episodes of harassment, since not everyone who has grounds for legal action in any area chooses to make a claim (see Figure 15.1).

Women in Male Environments

Sexual harassment can occur in any workplace. However, women who are a small minority in traditionally male blue-collar work settings (such as construction and machine operation) are more likely to be harassed (APA, 1993). Women on these jobs complain of being taunted, jeered, threatened with physical harm, given defective equipment, or denied important information (Fitzgerald, 1993; Goodman-Delahunty, 1998). The popular book *Class Action* (Bingham and Gansler, 2002) and the film

FIGURE 15.1

U.S. Supreme Court Justice Clarence Thomas and Professor Anita Hill

Law professor Anita Hill had been an aide to Justice Thomas when he was head of the Equal Employment Opportunity Commission. She testified during Thomas's Senate confirmation hearing that he had made sexually offensive remarks to her while she was his employee. Although she did not accuse him of discriminating against her, her testimony almost caused Thomas's nomination to the U.S. Supreme Court to fail. The sensational case raised the nation's consciousness about sexual harassment.

based on it show these problems in iron mining. The branches of the armed forces are traditionally male preserves. A 1995 survey distributed to 90,000 active duty men and women found that, overall, 55 percent of the women reported some kind of harassment. Nearly one in ten women in the Army or Marine Corps said they had been sexually assaulted within the past year (a crime as well as an actionable civil offense), and nearly two in ten reported that they were the targets of sexual coercion (Compart, 1996).

Consequences of Harassment

Sexual harassment in the workplace can cause serious consequences for victims, for the organizations for which they work, and for society at large. These include absenteeism, dropping out of work or school, changing jobs or programs, low morale, and lowered productivity because of poor interpersonal relationships at work. Harassment may trigger depression, anxiety, somatic symptoms, and sleep disorders in some victims (Fitzgerald, 1993; Fitzgerald et al., 1999). The costs can be measured in dollars. A 1988 U.S. Merit Systems Board study estimated that the cost to the government of sexual harassment of government employees over a two-year period came to about $267 million in lost productivity, investigative and legal costs, and damage awards (APA, 1993). A 1991 study found little change (U.S. Merit Systems Protection Board, 1995).

⊠ Historical and Legal Context

Civil Rights Legislation: Title VII

The legislation that became the basis for sexual harassment suits was passed by Congress almost by accident. In 1964, a coalition composed of members of the Lyndon Johnson administration and liberal members of Congress proposed a Civil Rights Act intended to combat racial discrimination and segregation. **Title VII** of the proposed law banned discrimination in employment on the basis of race (see Chapter 16).

To kill a bill, opponents sometimes add an amendment to make the bill unacceptable to its supporters. Howard W. Smith, a Republican congressman from Virginia and an opponent of Title VII, proposed an amendment to ban discrimination on the basis of sex as well as race. He believed the idea was so ridiculous that, if the amendment were attached, even the bill's proponents would reject it. To Smith's surprise, the few women in Congress and some male colleagues took the idea of equal rights for women seriously and helped Smith and his conservative allies pass the amendment. The Civil Rights Act became law in 1964, with provisions such as **Title VII** excluding discrimination in employment and education based on sex as well as race.

Sexual Harassment: An Extension of Employment Discrimination

The members of Congress who passed Title VII and later **Title IX** of the Civil Rights Act (the latter focused on educational institutions) wanted to ensure racial and gender equality in hiring, firing, pay, promotion, and educational opportunities. They were not thinking of sexual harassment as a form of sex discrimination. The concept did not as yet exist (Goodman-Delahunty, 1998). The vulnerability of working women to sexual abuse, solicitation, and seduction was common knowledge (e.g., Theodore Dreiser's *American Tragedy*). But sexual exploitation of employees was treated as a problem of individual immorality, not a problem of discrimination involving organizations or institutions. A victim could make a criminal complaint of sexual assault, battery, rape, or criminal harassment, or could sue for compensation for injuries or other harms in civil court—if she thought she could make a case and find another job.

The idea that exploitative or harassing behaviors in the workplace should be considered a form of employment discrimination did not develop until the 1970s (Duncan and Hively, 1998). As the number of women in the workforce increased rapidly and the women's movement gained momentum, working women began talking and writing, privately and in the media, about workplace discrimination, including sexual pressures, sexual bullying, and sexual hostility (Toobin, 1998). The term *sexual harassment* was introduced by feminists at Cornell University in 1975 at a meeting held in support of Carmita Wood, a 44-year-old university employee who quit her job because of unrelenting sexual pressure (Toobin, 1998; Weiss, 1998). In 1976, *Redbook* magazine surveyed its readers; 90 percent of the 9,000 women who responded said they had been subjected to some kind of unwanted sexual pressure or insult at work (Safran, 1976). The respondents were not a random sample, but the results were nonetheless startling.

Early suits. In the 1970s, women began suing under Title VII, seeking relief from discriminatory practices in hiring, firing, promotion, and pay. A few women tried to sue under the same law for relief from sexual harassment. These early cases were dismissed on the traditional grounds that the unwanted sexual advances were "personal" problems, not a form of discrimination (MacKinnon, 1979). Then Paulette

Barnes, a clerical worker, sued her employer, the Environmental Protection Agency, in federal district court under Title VII, alleging that her supervisor had retaliated against her when she refused to sleep with him (*Barnes v. Costle,* 1977). When the trial court dismissed the case because she had not stated a legally recognized claim for relief, Barnes appealed. In 1977, the appeals court reversed the trial court, ruling that the use of work-related threats or promises by a supervisor to demand sexual favors could and should be considered sex-based discrimination in employment.

Redefining sexual harassment. The appeals court might have been influenced by a paper written by then law student Catherine MacKinnon, arguing that the law should recognize sexual harassment as a basis for a sex discrimination claim. MacKinnon subsequently published the argument in her book *Sexual Harassment of Working Women* (1979). She reasoned that women are sexually harassed because they are women, that is, on the basis of their sex, meaning gender; therefore, sexual harassment is a form of sex discrimination.

The idea was influential and raised consciousness about the nature of the problem. One result was the EEOC's guidelines against sexual harassment in 1980. Another was

---

BOX 15.1

Examples of Sexual Harassment Cases

Sexual harassment is a problem that has affected women in both public and private sectors, at all levels of income and in all types of employment. Here are some examples of some of the more dramatic cases over the last few years.

- In 2001, the United States sued the Giuliani administration in New York City for failing to respond to complaints of sexual and racial harassment by four women in workfare jobs. Complaints included being repeatedly groped by a supervisor who went on to tell coworkers the victim was a lesbian because she wouldn't sleep with him (Greenhouse, 2001).

- In 2003, two senior bankers with J. P. Morgan Chase were fired for making inappropriate and unwanted advances to a more junior manager in a bar, enforcing a zero harassment tolerance policy (McGeehan, 2003).

- In another 2003 case, three Mexican immigrant sisters alleged that supervisors at City Solutions, a bakery owned by Lufthansa, demanded sex from them under threat of being fired (Greenhouse, 2003).

- In 2004, Morgan Stanley paid $54 million to settle a sex discrimination case out of court that was rumored to include allegations of sexual harassment as well as denial of equal pay and promotions. The settlement could cover 340 professional women (McGeehan, 2004).

- In 2004, a U.S. Air Force report acknowledged that over the prior ten years, sexual assaults against women at the Air Force Academy were reported 150 times, but little action was taken before the accusations were made public (Shanker, 2004). In 2005, the Pentagon acknowledged that sexual assault complaints were not followed up and victims were not supported in any of the armed services, and it announced plans to set up a new complaints system. David S. Chu, undersecretary for personnel and readiness, said that most victims and offenders did not seem to understand that assault was a crime, and not merely sexual harassment (Stout, 2005).

a lawsuit at Yale University which forced the university to establish a procedure for sexual harassment complaints. Congress held hearings on sexual harassment in the federal government and the military, and commissioned the U.S. Merit Systems Protection Board to conduct a survey of the federal civilian workforce to assess the **prevalence** of sexual harassment. The board's findings, published in 1981, showed that, in a two-year period, 12,000 female federal workers were victims of rape or attempted rape by supervisors (Fitzgerald, 1993); rape is, of course, a felony, not merely a violation of civil antidiscrimination laws. The board also found that 42 percent of the women and 15 percent of the men reported some kind of incident in the previous 24 months that could be considered harassing (Goodman-Delahunty, 1998).

Types of Discriminatory Harassment

In 1980, the EEOC issued guidelines characterizing sexual harassment in the workplace as a form of employment discrimination. *Harassment* was defined as unwelcome sexual advances, requests for sexual favors, and other unwelcome verbal or physical conduct of a sexual nature. The guidelines distinguished two kinds of actionable sexual harassment: quid pro quo harassment and hostile environment harassment (Fitzgerald, 1993; MacKinnon, 1979; Toobin, 1998). The meaning of these terms was later refined through court cases.

Quid pro quo. **Quid pro quo sexual harassment** refers to attempts to buy or extort sexual compliance by implicit or direct threats or promises of job-related consequences (e.g., sleep with me and I can make things easy for you). A single threat or promise is sufficient to constitute actionable quid pro quo sexual harassment.

It is the *company* that hires, demotes, promotes, fires, and grants raises and transfers its employees. A supervisor is acting as an agent of the company when he or she uses his or her power to make employment decisions to solicit sexual compliance. "A tangible employment decision requires an official act of the enterprise, a company act," Supreme Court Justice Antonin Scalia explained (*Burlington Industries v. Ellerth*, 1998). For this reason, courts have held that a company is liable whenever a supervisor demands sex from an employee on a quid pro quo basis (Greenhouse, 1998a, 1998d). It doesn't matter if the supervisor was violating a company policy; it doesn't matter if his or her superiors didn't know about the harassment. The company can still be liable.

Hostile environment. **Hostile environment sexual harassment** refers to ongoing sex-related verbal or physical conduct that is unwelcome or offensive (Fitzgerald, 1993). Examples of behaviors that could make the environment hostile include ongoing demeaning jokes, threatening behaviors, use of derogatory epithets or names, or prominently displayed written or visual materials of a threatening or insulting nature.

The concept of "hostile environment" is complex and not very precise. Employers complained that the EEOC guidelines did not make clear what they and their employees had to do or not do to steer clear of potential suits. The vagueness left many questions for the courts. For example, when was a company responsible for a hostile environment created by the plaintiff's coworkers? Did sex-related behavior mean behavior triggered by the victim's gender, or behavior motivated by sexual desire or either? What was an employee who was the target of the behavior expected to do to communicate that the behavior was "unwelcome"? Did a person bringing a complaint under Title VII have to prove psychological or other harm?

Meritor, discriminatory behavior, and liability. The U.S. Supreme Court addressed some of these questions in *Meritor Savings Bank v. Vinson* (1986). The Court affirmed that (non–quid pro quo) behavior creating a hostile work environment could be considered harassment and was actionable under Title VII. The opinion said that Title VII was intended to protect people not just from economic discrimination (such as lower pay and fewer promotions) but also from "discriminatory intimidation, ridicule, and insult" that are "sufficiently severe or pervasive to alter the conditions of employment and create an abusive working environment."

The Court also ruled, however, that a company's liability for a hostile workplace environment was not as absolute as it was for quid pro quo harassment. The trial courts should consider what a plaintiff had communicated to her employer about the undesirable behaviors and what she reasonably expected the employer to do in response to the problem. The decision presaged a later requirement that companies have policies spelling out sexual harassment, and procedures for receiving and investigating complaints.

In the *Meritor* (1986) opinion, the Supreme Court also said that women who gave in to pressures to comply with sexual requests could still sue under Title VII. The Court answered the argument that, because the woman went along, the advances couldn't have been unwelcome: "The gravamen of any sexual harassment claim is that the alleged sexual advances were 'unwelcome.' . . . The correct inquiry is whether (the victim) by her conduct indicated that the alleged sexual advances were unwelcome, not whether her actual participation in sexual intercourse was voluntary." This was acknowledgment of MacKinnon's argument that, when the parties have unequal power, "consenting" to sex under pressure or threats is not truly voluntary.

Gender Stereotypes and Discrimination

Sexual harassment is one form of employment discrimination based on gender. Title VII also protects women and minorities from direct employment discrimination, that is, discrimination in hiring, firing, promotion, and transfer; indeed, this was the law's initial purpose. The two forms of discrimination are related, and both may be mediated by the same biases.

Research on gender- and sex-related biases accelerated with the increased entry of women into the labor market (and into the social sciences) and with the development of social cognition research. *Social cognition* refers to how people think about other people, social activities, and the social environment. Social scientists have been studying how role expectations, role divisions, **stereotypes,** and situational and other factors interact to influence how women and men perceive each other. The Supreme Court recognized this research in an important case, *Price Waterhouse v. Hopkins* (1989). The case concerned discriminatory denial of a promotion. We review it here because the research on stereotyping cited by the plaintiff is relevant to sexual harassment cases. (For a description of stereotyping, see Box 15.2.)

Price Waterhouse v. Hopkins

Ann Hopkins was a senior manager at the worldwide accounting firm of Price Waterhouse. In 1982, she was the one woman among 88 employees proposed for partnership. At that time, only 7 of the 662 partners were women. When her candidacy was rejected,

BOX 15.2

Stereotyping

Stereotypes refer to a set of characteristics ascribed to a group and then attributed to all the individual members of the group. Stereotypes develop from a normal process of developing mental representations (schemata) to generalize information about people through categorization. The process is an efficient and necessary way to organize and simplify a complex social world. However, stereotypes may lead to overgeneralization. People tend to think that members of groups other than their own are more similar than they really are. They also tend to think more positively of members of their own group and to treat them preferentially (APA, 1988; for a good introduction to the idea of social schemata, see Fiske and Taylor, 1984).

There is no single, simple, female stereotype: rather, there are multiple stereotypes, negative and positive and mixed, encapsulating ideas about different "types" of women. A man's perceptions of a woman's individual behavior, his general beliefs about the work setting and about gender roles, and his own needs and concerns may combine to trigger sterotypes in his mind. The stereotype may then become a distorting lens through which the woman's behavior is perceived (Burgess and Borgida, 1997; Goodman-Delahunty, 1998). Similar cognitive processes might affect perceptions, judgments, and awards in sexual harassment suits (Goodman-Delahunty, 1998).

Psychologists often distinguish between descriptive and prescriptive stereotypes. *Descriptive gender stereotypes* are beliefs about differences in the attributes, roles, and behaviors of men and women. These are probably unavoidable and not necessarily harmful if people notice and accept when individuals don't fit the stereotypes. For example, many people believe that women are more emotionally expressive than men, and men more assertive than women, but they recognize many exceptions to this formula.

Prescriptive stereotypes are beliefs about attitudes, roles, and behaviors to which men and women *should* conform. A person holding prescriptive stereotypes would disapprove of emotionally expressive men and assertive women. Burgess and Borgida (1999) suggest that descriptive stereotypes result in often unintended discrimination and policies that have a disparate impact on men and women. For example, someone who thinks of men as leaders may not think of women candidates for managerial posts. Prescriptive stereotypes are associated with harassment. This kind of harassment is often aimed at women in traditionally male environments or roles, or at men who behave in ways that are not considered manly. These forms of harassment may be motivated by hostility against individuals who violate the gender prescriptions and by a desire to exclude them from the workplace society (Stockdale, Visio, and Batra, 1999).

she sued under Title VII, charging that, by not making her a partner, the firm had discriminated against her because of her sex. Hopkins claimed that she was denied the promotion because of behaviors that clashed with her employers' views of how women should comport themselves, and asserted that the same behaviors might have been viewed more positively in a man.

Although successful in business relationships, Hopkins had been counseled about abrasive relations with staff and colleagues. Both her supporters and opponents described her as sometimes overly aggressive, harsh, and impatient. Some of the comments suggested that her supervisor's evaluations were influenced by her gender. She was described as "macho" and as "overcompensating for being a woman." She was told not to use profanity "because it's a lady using foul language." She was advised to go to "charm school," and to "walk more femininely, talk more femininely, dress more femininely, wear make-up, have her hair styled and wear jewelry". Dr. Susan Fiske, a social psychologist, testified at the trial that the partnership selection process was probably influenced by sex stereotyping.

When Ms. Hopkins won at the trial and appellate levels, Price Waterhouse appealed to the Supreme Court. The APA submitted an amicus curiae brief pointing out that Dr. Fiske's testimony was supported by over 50 years of research on social stereotypes using a diversity of methodologies (field experiments, laboratory experiments, and surveys) in a variety of settings, including the workplace.

Cutting through the Double Bind

The majority opinion, written by Justice William Brennan, recognized the validity of sexual stereotyping as a potentially discriminating factor:

> As for the relevance of sex stereotyping, we are beyond the day when an employer could evaluate employees by assuming or insisting that they matched the stereotype associated with their group. . . . An employer who objects to aggressiveness in women but whose positions require this trait places women in an intolerable and impermissible catch 22: out of a job if they behave aggressively and out of a job if they do not. Title VII lifts women out of this bind.

The case was sent back to the lower courts for reconsideration on technical legal grounds. Ms. Hopkins ultimately received hundreds of thousands of dollars in back pay and her attorney's fees. She also won reinstatement to her partnership at the firm, where she worked until retirement in 2002 (Hopkins, 2005).

Psychological Injury

When Ann Hopkins charged Price Waterhouse with discrimination (*Price Waterhouse v. Hopkins*, 1989), the harm she alleged was clear-cut: she was refused a partnership. But the line from the alleged harassing behavior to tangible harm is not always so straight. Courts have had to distinguish between a hostile work environment that is discriminatory and one that is merely unpleasant. Some courts said that **psychological injury** was a good way to separate workplace behaviors that affected equal employment opportunity from those that did not. This raised the question of whether psychological harm was a necessary element of a claim of hostile environment harassment. The Supreme Court in *Meritor Savings Bank v. Vinson* (1986) ruled that, for behavior to alter the conditions of employment and create an abusive working environment, it must be more than merely offensive, but need not cause a tangible psychological injury. However, the opinion did not offer clear guidance. Federal appeals courts had issued inconsistent rulings about whether a victim of harassing behaviors had grounds for a suit if the behaviors did not seriously affect the victim's psychological well-being. The U.S. Supreme Court addressed the issue in *Harris v. Forklift Systems* (1993; see Box 15.3).

BOX 15.3

A Legal Case in Point: *Harris v. Forklift Systems* (1993)

Teresa Harris worked as a manager at an equipment rental company, Forklift Systems. After working at Forklift for about a year and a half, Harris quit. She then sued the company under Title VII. She claimed that the company president, Charles Hardy, had created an abusive working environment. He made remarks denigrating her abilities on the job ("You're a woman, what do you know?") and humiliated her by suggesting in front of others that they go to a motel to negotiate. Sometimes he asked Harris and other women employees to get coins from his front pants pocket, or he threw objects on the ground and asked the women to pick them up. He made sexual remarks about their clothes. In August 1987, Harris complained to Hardy. He said he was surprised she was offended, apologized, and promised to stop. But, in early September, after Harris completed a business deal, he said in front other employees, "What did you do, promise the guy . . . some [sex] Saturday night?" Harris then quit and sued under Title VII. Ms. Harris claimed that she had been economically harmed by discriminatory behavior, but she did not claim that her treatment at Forklift caused serious psychological harm or psychological problems interfering with her work performance. The U.S. Supreme Court held that as long as the environment was "hostile and abusive," Title VII was violated and a suit could be pursued without the plaintiff having to allege psychological injury.

The APA Amicus Brief

The APA submitted an amicus curiae brief informing the *Harris* Court of several lines of research on harassing behavior (APA, 1993). The brief discussed the impact of harassing behaviors on their targets and on the workplace, workplace conditions increasing the likelihood of harassment, and differences in men's and women's perceptions of workplace interactions. On the basis of relevant research, the APA argued that psychological injury should not be considered a necessary element of a hostile environment claim because psychological injury is a poor measure of the severity or persistence of harassment (see Box 15.4 for a summary of the arguments). The brief also addressed the question of whether the standard for determining if an environment is objectively hostile should be the judgment of a "reasonable person" or "a reasonable victim," an issue we will consider below.

In *Harris,* the Court reaffirmed the *Meritor* standard: "Title VII comes into play before the harassing conduct leads to a nervous break-down," Justice Sandra Day O'Connor wrote for the Court majority (p. 3). The opinion listed two requirements for harassing behaviors to meet the "hostile environment" standard: (1) the environment must be such that "a reasonable person" would find it hostile or abusive (the objective standard), and (2) there must be some evidence (this need not be psychological injury) that the victim must have subjectively perceived the environment as abusive (the subjective standard).

The *Harris* rulings eliminated any requirement that the plaintiff prove psychological injury to prove that a working environment was hostile. The plaintiff's mental health has nonetheless remained an issue in Title VII suits.

In harassment cases, the plaintiff has the burden of proving that advances were unwelcome or that hostile behavior was perceived as altering the conditions of employ-

BOX 15.4

455

Psychological
Injury

Insult and Psychological Injury

In a brief submitted to the U.S. Supreme Court hearing *Harris v. Forklift Systems* (1993), the American Psychological Association argued that psychological injury is not a good way to distinguish inconsequential and discriminatory harassment. The brief said,

1. Sexual harassment causes considerable nonpsychological injuries that seriously affect equal employment opportunities. The effects include changing jobs or transferring within companies, and abandoning efforts to obtain new positions or jobs. These changes, in turn, lead to losses of established work reputations, seniority, references, working alliances, and income. Victims may be excluded from informal associations with coworkers needed to gain information and support. The isolation may negatively affect their work performance, and the victims may suffer from loss of motivation, distraction, loss of confidence, or lowered self-esteem, and they may receive unfair negative evaluations. A psychological injury requirement would require women to continue to endure all these problems until they suffered serious psychological or mental health problems. Only then could they take legal action to protect themselves.

2. A psychological injury requirement would have the effect of penalizing victims who are hardy. While harassment reduces the psychological well-being of most victims, the presence and severity of psychological injury may be more related to the victim's characteristics than to the severity of harassment. Victims with good coping skills and strong social support can often handle harassment without developing severe symptoms of psychological distress. Women with low self-esteem are likely to experience harassment as more traumatic. Prior victimization also substantially increases the chances that a victim of harassment will be injured psychologically. Thus, using a psychological injury requirement would shift a court's focus from the harasser's behavior to the victim's resilience or vulnerability.

3. A psychological injury requirement would deter reporting and discourage use of Title VII rights. Women with low self-esteem are more likely to experience psychological problems in response to harassment but less likely to report the harassment to someone in authority. A psychological injury requirement, by preventing higher functioning women from pursuing remedies under Title VII, would mean that fewer cases of harassment would be exposed. Requiring victims to prove psychological injury in itself is likely to deter injured victims from reporting harassment because they may wish to avoid revealing their inability to handle the experience. Moreover, the process of having to prove psychological injury could itself exacerbate the injury for some victims.

4. By rendering legal recovery less likely and less predictable, a psychological injury requirement reduces the motivation of employers to establish and enforce policies against harassment. Because men who harass women are more likely to do so in settings where the behavior is accepted, the requirement would reduce the effectiveness of Title VII In ending discrimination.

There were a large number of amicus briefs in this case, but the Court's opinion mentioned none of them directly. The opinion was consistent with the position adopted in the APA brief.

ment (the subjective side of harassment). The *Meritor* majority opinion (1986, p. 69) said that the complainant's behavior, including her speech and dress, was relevant to whether she found advances welcome. Defense lawyers have consequently argued that a plaintiff's sexual history or psychopathology led her to invite advances or misinterpret office behaviors, or that the history undermines her credibility. Defense lawyers have also argued that the plaintiff overreacted even to admitted harassment because of psychological problems. This argument is not relevant legally; to meet the harassment standard, the acts must be ones that a reasonable person in the plaintiff's circumstances would perceive as harassing. Nonetheless, in some cases, arguments that the plaintiff was oversensitive have been admitted in determinations of whether harassment took place (Fitzgerald, 2003; Stockdale et al., 2002; Fitzgerald et al., 1999).

Although a plaintiff is not required to prove psychological damage to establish a hostile environment, she herself may choose to do so to strengthen her case, to counter defense claims, or to recover the cost of mental health treatment or other compensation. Psychologists may also be asked to give social framework testimony explaining, for example, why many victims of harassment delay reporting (Duncan and Hively, 1998).

The original Title VII contained no provision for plaintiffs to recover damages. Victims were eligible only for "equitable relief," such as awards of back pay and reinstatement. In 1991, Congress amended Title VII of the Civil Rights Act to allow alleged victims to sue in federal courts for both compensatory and punitive damages. It was thought the promise of higher personal reward and greater social impact would increase the willingness of victims to avail themselves of the law. This in turn would further the social goal of creating a fairer workplace.

Although harassment has negative psychological, health-related, and work-related consequences for victims as a group, the law does not presume that everyone who suffers discrimination is injured by it. To qualify for compensatory damages for harms (e.g., costs of psychotherapy), the victim must prove that she was harmed as well as harassed. When any plaintiff claims damages for emotional or mental suffering, courts may rule that she is putting her mental health at issue. In such cases, the court can order the plaintiff to submit to a psychological examination, even if she doesn't want one (Federal Rules of Civil Procedure, Rule 35; Kovera and Cass, 2002).

Child sexual abuse, borderline personality disorder, and revictimization. Defendants in harassment cases commonly allege that the plaintiff has a borderline personality disorder or has other psychological problems as a result of childhood sexual abuse. Fitzgerald (1999) calls this "the argument that a victim cannot be a victim because she already was a victim."

Defense lawyers sometimes maintain that victims of childhood abuse or people who have borderline personality disorders provoke revictimization by seductive behavior; in other words, they engineer their own harassment (Feldman-Schorrig, 1995; Solotoff, 1998).

What is the scientific basis for these arguments? There is great variability in people's resilience to stressors and adverse experiences. The APA brief in *Harris* acknowledged that all people will not be equally distressed by the same unpleasant experiences (Fitzgerald, 2003; Stockdale et al., 2002). There is evidence that prior exposure to trauma can intensify people's reaction to new trauma. Childhood abuse of any kind increases a person's risk of developing psychological problems. Women who have been sexually abused within the family in preadolescence are more likely than other women to be sexually or physically victimized by intimate partners or dates as adults (Neumann et al., 1996). This is not the same as saying that all women who experienced childhood sexual abuse will be victimized by intimate partners as adults or that child-hood experiences of abuse *causes* adult problems.

There is little empirical investigation of whether history of abuse increases the risk of victimization in the workplace or outside the workplace in intimate relationships generally (Stockdale et al., 2002). Some clinicians hypothesize that it might on the basis of psychodynamic theory (Feldman-Schorrig, 1995). Referring to this clinical literature, defense lawyers have argued that plaintiffs who have been victimized in the past are likely to invite sexual harassment, and at the same time are more sensitive to behaviors that might be regarded as harassment. They suggest that these plaintiffs experience excessive emotional distress as a result of trivial and minor teasing or flirtation and are likely to complain that these acts are harassing (Feldman-Schorrig, 1995).

Expert testimony supporting such speculations about plaintiff behavior and personality may fall well short of *Daubert* standards for admissibility. Even if there is some statistical association between background factors and susceptibility to sexual advances, the error rate in relying on a low correlation is necessarily so high that a judge may be reluctant to admit such testimony.

Sexual harassment and prior experiences of abuse. There is little empirical research investigating the relationship of prior sexual abuse or prior sexual harassment on perceptions of sexual harassment in the workplace. Fitzgerald and colleagues (1999) tested the proposition that women who had experienced sexual abuse in the past would be more sensitive to harassment and more likely to complain about it. They asked 307 college women to view a series of training videos showing potentially harassing situations. Thirty-five percent of the college women had experienced unwanted sexual touching by someone at least five years old before age 18. The women rated their emotional response, and how they thought they would deal with the aversive events had they been the woman in the videos. The abused and nonabused women did not differ in their emotional or projected behavioral responses. About the same percentage of women in both groups said they would complain.

In a second study, the researchers investigated the question of whether harassment plaintiffs who are abuse survivors report more distress than plaintiffs who are not. Fifty-six women involved in sexual harassment litigation were assessed using structured diagnostic interviews and standardized psychological inventories. They were also assessed for prior child sexual abuse, sexual victimization, or no victimization, and for trauma versus no trauma. The abused and nonabused groups were not distinguishable on the basis of psychological characteristics or diagnostic profile. The researchers concluded that symptoms exhibited by litigants with histories of abuse were more likely related to present harassment than to their past abuse.

Stockdale et al. (2002) investigated whether prior experiences of sexual harassment affected women's perceptions and judgments of new incidents that might be seen as harassing. They conducted five studies that presented written, video, or pictorial scenarios presenting the fact pattern of an actual case to undergraduate students and adults waiting to serve jury duty in the community. Each of the studies included a variety of experimental manipulations varying facts of the case, the legal standards, and characteristics of plaintiff, defendant, or workplace. Prior sexual harassment was unrelated to current sexual harassment perceptions.

"Shielding" plaintiffs from personal attacks. In 1994 (Fitzgerald, 2003), Congress extended the "rape shield law," Federal Rule of Evidence 412, to civil proceedings. Under this rule, information about a plaintiff's sexual behavior is only admitted if any prejudicial effect is outweighed by its value in proving the facts of the case. The purpose of the rule was to encourage complainants to come forward by sparing them an aggressive investigation of their private histories. The change in the law does not appear to have the intended effect in harassment cases.

Rule 412 is a statement about what information can be admitted as evidence in a trial. However, defendants are allowed to investigate the plaintiffs' lives and sexual behavior extensively through discovery before trial. For pre-trial purposes in any civil law suit, the legal standard for relevance is that the information sought is reasonably calculated to lead to the discovery of admissible evidence (Federal Rule of Civil Procedure 26). As part of this pretrial discovery process, the plaintiff may be interviewed for many hours by male defense lawyers who may be allowed to query her regarding therapy experience and gynecological records. Even if none of the information discovered is used as evidence at trial, the discovery process itself may put off many would-be complainants. The effect is probably to undermine one goal of Title VII, to encourage individuals harmed by discrimination to come forward and seek redress.

Compensation. One incentive for victims to come forward is compensation. Federal damage awards were capped at $300,000, a relatively low amount. Perhaps as a result, many more sexual harassment suits are brought in state courts under state law than in federal courts. A Supreme Court case increased the amount of compensation that could be awarded in federal courts to one kind of plaintiff. Sharon Pollard claimed that she had been fired by DuPont because she refused to return to a hostile work environment she had complained about. The trial court awarded her back pay and the full $300,000 in compensatory damages. The court wanted to give her compensation for lost future earnings ("front pay"), but stated that this would violate the award cap. On appeal, the Supreme Court reviewed the 1991 statute and held that courts could award "front pay" beyond the $300,000 limit in cases where the employee could no longer be reinstated to her job (*Pollard v. DuPont*, 2001; *Pollard v. DuPont*, 2005).

☒ Objective Standards: A Reasonable Woman, Person, or Victim?

To evaluate the social meaning of a behavior or event, the legal system uses the perspective of a **reasonable person standard.** In legal terminology, the objective view of a situation is the way that this hypothetical reasonable (normal, rational) adult would see it. This **objective standard** can be used alone or with a subjective standard. The **subjective standard** is how the particular person actually in the situation at issue viewed it. A claim of harassment must meet both an objective and a subjective standard.

Early research on perceptions of harassment suggested that an "objective" standard might be elusive. Studies consistently found gender differences in perceptions of potentially harassing behaviors (Blumenthal, 1998; Wiener et al., 2004). Women's advocates subsequently proposed that the "objective" measure of harassment should be the perceptions of a "reasonable woman," rather than a reasonable person or man. Some jurisdictions were persuaded by the argument and adopted the "reasonable woman" or "reasonable victim" standard to determine if an environment was "objectively" hostile. The Ninth Circuit Court of Appeals adopted the **reasonable woman standard** in its *Ellison v. Brady* opinion (1991): "in evaluating the severity and pervasiveness of sexual harassment, we should focus on the perspective of the victim. . . . A complete under-standing of the victim's views requires . . . analysis of the different perspectives of men and women" (quoted in Blumenthal, 1998, p. 35).

Gender Differences in Perceptions of Harassment

In its amicus brief to the *Harris* (1993) Court, the APA pointed out that, in hearing a hostile work environment claim, the Court might be fashioning an objective test for determining whether a work environment was actionable. To help the Court in this task, the brief summarized the findings on gender differences in perceptions of sexual harassment.

When asked how they felt or would feel about various harassing behaviors directed at them, men reported being less disturbed than women. The difference was most pro-nounced with regard to gender-based insults and less explicit sexual overtures. Though there was no research on the question, the brief suggested possible explanations of the differences. Because of well-founded fears of sexual assault, women may perceive harassing behaviors as potentially physically threatening where men do not. Women may be more likely to see sexual overtures as threatening their position at work, and may accurately perceive that sexual liaisons with coworkers will lower their status in the organization while such liaisons might raise a man's status. The brief also noted that men and women attribute different causes to harassing behaviors. Men are more likely to think the behavior is caused by characteristics of the victim (e.g., "She's seduc-tive"), women by characteristics of the perpetrators (e.g., "He's an animal"). Men are also more likely to attribute harassment complaints to an external factor or an ulterior motive ("She's trying to get even for rejection"). The APA recommended that the Court adopt a **reasonable victim standard,** an ungendered standard that recognized the rela-tionship between social position and social perceptions.

In the *Harris* opinion (1993), the Supreme Court maintained "reasonable person" as the "objective" standard but also encouraged trial courts to recognize the victim's circumstances in making their determination. In 1993, the EEOC defined a *harassing experience* as one "a reasonable person in the same or similar circumstances" would find "intimidating, hostile or abusive." They added the explicit instruction that the per-son's gender should be considered part of the circumstances (in Waldo, Berdahl, and Fitzgerald, 1998). In 1998, in a case involving male–male harassment (*Oncale v. Sun-downer Offshore Services,* 1998, discussed later in this chapter), the Supreme Court con-firmed the standard for hostile environment established in *Harris:* "the perspective of a reasonable person in the plaintiff's position, considering 'all the circumstances.'" However, other courts have used a reasonable woman or reasonable victim standard.

Magnitude of Gender Differences

Research on gender differences in perceptions of potentially harassing behaviors con-tinued (see issue no. 51 of the *Journal of Social Issues,* 1995). Gutek and O'Connor (1995) reviewed the literature. Most of the studies had used brief vignettes of workplace interactions. Subjects were asked to rate whether they thought various behaviors in the vignette should be characterized as sexual harassment. Subjects might also be asked to assign a degree of responsibility to each actor, or to assess the acceptability of the behav-iors. Another approach was to give subjects a list of behaviors and ask them to indicate which ones were harassing. In still other studies, subjects were given a description of a legal case and asked to rate the behavior at issue along legally relevant dimensions (e.g., is the behavior intimidating, hostile, or based on the target person's gender?). Most, but not all, of the researchers used student subjects. While some researchers found no significant differences in the perceptions of men and women, and some found large differences, most found small differences, all in the same direction: women were more likely to consider a given behavior harassing than men (Gutek and O'Connor, 1995).

To address the question of gender differences in perception more precisely, Blumenthal (1998) performed a meta-analysis of studies of perceptions of harassment published or completed between 1982 and 1996. (**Meta-analysis** refers to statistical techniques for pooling data from different studies by converting the results into standard deviation units that can then be combined for analysis across all the studies.) He did two analyses, one of studies of the effects of gender on perceptions of harassment, and one of studies of the effects of a power or **status** differential between the initiator of the behavior and the object of the behavior.

Blumenthal confirmed that the divergence between the sexes was not wide, and that the small differences were stable across age of subjects, suggesting that the use of undergraduate as subjects was not a factor in the outcome. Blumenthal found that status differences between the actor and victim had a larger effect than gender on ratings of what constituted harassing behavior. Higher status actors (e.g., supervisors) were more likely to be perceived as harassers than lower status actors (e.g., coworkers). Student participants were more influenced by harasser status than were workers in nonacademic settings (Blumenthal, 1998). A later meta-analysis (Rotundo, Nguyen, and Acakett, 2001) had similar findings.

The Effect of a "Reasonable Woman" Standard

Blumenthal's (1998) meta-analysis suggests that there is only weak empirical evidence in support of a reasonable woman standard. Not only were gender differences in perceptions of harassment small, but they were also smallest when researchers used legal scenarios. If not an artifact of method, this finding suggests that changing the standards may not make a difference in a legal context. Even if there were large differences in men's and women's general perceptions of potentially harassing acts, changing the standard from a reasonable person to a reasonable woman might not affect jurors' decisions about a given set of facts. Researchers interested in the question have generally focused on hostile environment cases, which are more controversial than quid pro quo cases since they require making a judgment about the character of the environment.

Wiener and his colleagues (Wiener et al., 1995, 1997) investigated whether using a reasonable person or a reasonable woman standard in a legal scenario of a hostile environment case actually influenced how mock jurors made legally relevant judgments about the case. Neither study used a simulated trial; in both, student subjects were given case summaries, a definition of legal standards, and rating scales to record their judgments (e.g., rate the extent to which the behavior was unwelcome, its severity, its pervasiveness, the likelihood of negative work effects, the likelihood of negative effects on well-being, and the likelihood the plaintiff was subject to a hostile work environment). Using different objective standards (reasonable person versus reasonable woman) did not affect decision making in either study. In a second study, Wiener and associates (1997) found that males noticed the reasonable woman standard less often than females. However, neither men nor women rated the likelihood that there had been sexual harassment higher under the reasonable woman standard than they did under the reasonable person standard. In short, both studies suggest that a change to a reasonable woman standard would be unlikely to affect case outcomes.

461

Objective
Standards:
A Reasonable
Woman,
Person, or
Victim?

In a third study, Wiener and colleagues used a videotape stimulus that included a detailed explanation of the legal standard (Wiener and Hurt, 2000, cited in Perry, Kulik, and Bourhis, 2004). Gutek and colleagues (Gutek et al., 1999) undertook a series of five studies using a hostile environment scenario presented in different formats to a range of participants. In the Wiener and Hurt studies (1999, 2000) and in two of the Gutek studies, the legal standard had an effect, but not a large one. In actual cases in federal courts, researchers found that there was higher probability (50 percent) of a favorable verdict for the plaintiff in courts using the reasonable woman standard, especially if it was previously established in a circuit court, than in courts where the reasonable woman standard was not used (probability of a favorable verdict 24 percent) (Perry, Kulik, and Bourhis, 2004).

Researchers have begun looking at other variables that might explain the weak but persistent gender effects (Wiener et al., 2004; O'Connor et al., 2004; Huntley and Constanzo, 2003). No single explanation has yet emerged.

Policy Considerations

An appreciation of how men and women perceive some events differently may be very useful for in-service training to sensitize managers and coworkers about sexual harassment as part of a company's actions to eliminate workplace sexual harassment (Parker, 1999). However, empirical grounds for changing to a reasonable woman standard of a hostile environment are not strong. On the other hand, there are strong policy arguments against using a reasonable woman standard. First, such a standard enshrines gender as a useful basis for judging behavior. This would seem to run counter to the spirit of civil rights legislation intended as a corrective for stereotyping in the workplace and elsewhere. A reasonable woman standard might actually perpetuate negative stereotypes of women as sensitive, delicate, and in need of protection; this stereotype could hurt them in the marketplace (Goodman-Delahunty, 1998). It implies all women perceive interpersonal workplace behaviors in the same way, which is not the case. It also obscures the fact that qualities of different women may lead them to be treated differentially by those men who have a tendency to harass (Hoffman, 2004; Gutek et al., 1999).

Second, one goal of Title VII is to establish standards so that both male and female employers and employees will know what behaviors are prohibited. Men cannot be expected to avoid behaviors that are harassing to women if their gender severely limits their appreciation of what women find harassing. Third, in the future, psychological differences between men and women may become smaller as their lives become more similar (Goodman-Delahunty, 1998) and as they are subjected to company policies and training in sexual harassment avoidance (Pickerill, Jackson, and Newman, 2006). This may already be happening. Widespread training seems to have been effective in narrowing the gap between men and women's views of what constitutes sexually harassing behaviors (Pickerill, Jackson, and Newman, 2006; Wiener and Hurt, 1999; Perry, Kulik, and Bourhis, 2004). Fourth, a reasonable woman standard gives courts little guidance as to what standard should be used when men are harassed by women or by other men because of their gender.

Blumenthal (1998), Hoffman (2004), and Goodman-Delahunty (1998) suggest that, if the reasonable person standard is changed, it should be changed to "reasonable victim," as the APA recommended in its *Harris* amicus brief. The reasonable victim standard places the emphasis on exploitation rather than on gender per se, which is the law's intent. That standard allows for cases of male victimization. It encourages the decision maker to put him or herself imaginatively in the victim's place and to try to see things through the victim's eyes. The reasonable victim standard, more easily than the reasonable woman standard, invites the study of other variables that may influence judge and juror perceptions of harassment such as attitudes to women and to homosexuals, sex-role stereotyping, and personal experiences of harassment.

Real-Life Fact-Finders

Most of the studies have investigated how potential coworkers or jurors assess sexual harassment. This approach reflects the researchers' interest in understanding social cognition and social change as well as legal decision making. If workplaces become fairer, it will be because of changes in the way ordinary people think about each other. But decisions about actual harassment claims are usually made by managers, by human resource workers, and by arbitrators. Title VII, as amended in 1991, also allowed for the use of mediation and arbitration to resolve discrimination claims, and some companies have put in place mandatory arbitration policies, depriving complainants of their chance to appear before a jury (Wiener and Gutek, 1999).

When complaints are pursued through the federal legal system, they are usually resolved by federal district judges (Kulik, Perry, and Pepper, 2003). Kulik, Perry, and Pepper (2003) looked at the effects of judge's gender, race, age, and political affiliation on outcomes of 143 hostile environment cases heard between 1981 and 1996 in federal courts. The plaintiffs won in only 35 percent of the cases. One hundred and twenty-eight of the judges in the sample were male, and 124 white. Neither judge's gender nor ethnicity was related to the decision in the case, but the small numbers of female and minority judges made this difficult to assess. The judges' mean age was 60.6 years. The probability of finding for the plaintiff was 16 percent among judges over 71 years of age and 45 percent for judges below 50. Sixty-one of the judges in the sample were appointed by Democratic presidents, and 87 were appointed by a Republican president. The probability of a decision for the plaintiff was 18 percent if the case was heard by a judge appointed by a Republican president and 46 percent when appointed by a Democratic president. The battles in the U.S. Senate over appointments of judges to the federal courts reflect concerns about the judge's predispositions, although the concerns may be expressed as issues of "judicial philosophy."

⊠ When Is Sexual Behavior Discriminatory?

A sex scandal involving former President Bill Clinton stimulated discussion among women's advocates and the general public about the proper focus of the sexual harassment law.

Discrimination or Merely Offensive Behavior?

Some women's advocates believe that sexual abuse and exploitation, that is, quid pro quo harassment, is the central gender-related problem of working women. Others express concern that a tendency to refer to all attempted womanizing, lechery, or vulgarity as "harassment" undermines the purpose of Title VII: They note that politicians and journalists sometimes referred to President Clinton's sexual relationship with former White House intern Monica Lewinsky as "sexual harassment." But Ms. Lewinsky never complained about the sexual encounters and, by her own account, had initiated them. (Consensual sex between an employee and a supervisor can be considered sexual harassment, but the employee must complain; Ms. Lewinsky never filed or expressed a complaint.) In an op-ed piece in the *New York Times*, Anita Hill, who during Supreme Court Justice Clarence Thomas's confirmation hearing had accused him of making inappropriate sexual comments to her, wrote, "We are in danger of forgetting that laws forbidding sexual harassment in the workplace are not about sex. They are about employment discrimination" (Hill, 1998).

Some critics noted that in discussions of sexual harassment, women were being portrayed as victims unable to cope with an unwanted come-on, easily offended by vulgar language, and without sex drives or romantic interest of their own, a paternalistic stereotype that might actually contribute to workplace discrimination. They also feared the emphasis on sex in the workplace had led the courts to neglect "hostile environment" harassment aimed at keeping women out of traditionally "masculine" jobs and positions of power. Schulz (1998), for example, argued that, by focusing on unwanted advances, the courts were misusing the sexual harassment laws "to protect women's virtue and sensibilities" rather than to promote "their equality as workers."

At the same time, members of the public increasingly expressed discomfort with policies developed by businesses to protect themselves against harassment suits, policies making it difficult for coworkers or even employees of the same company to have dates. The policies sometimes extended into company rules about jokes and language as well. In 1997, a Miller Brewing Company executive named Jerold Mackenzie was dismissed on the basis of harassment after telling a female coworker a racy joke from a sitcom. Mackenzie sued the company for wrongfully firing him. He won a $26.6 million damage award from a jury that included women (Lewin, 1998). The jury, in finding for Mackenzie, may have been expressing public sentiment that efforts to stop sexual harassment had gone too far. Stories like Mackenzie's, especially combined with corporate use of electronic surveillance of employees (Rosen, 1999), contribute to the feeling of many that a valuable zone of workplace informality, spontaneity, and privacy has been eroded.

Discrimination or Ordinary Socializing?

The Supreme Court, in a ruling on a same-sex harassment case, may have brought some reassurance to those concerned that the phrase *sexual harassment,* if not the law, was being used for inappropriate policing (*Oncale v. Sundowner Offshore Services,* 1998). The *Oncale* decision emphasized that Title VII was about discrimination, not sex. Justice Scalia, delivering the opinion of the Court, made it clear that sexual harassment need not refer to sexual behavior but must refer to harassing behavior engaged in because of the victim's sex. Justice Scalia wrote, "But harassing conduct need not be motivated by sexual desire to support an inference of discrimination on the basis of sex." The behavior, whether or not sexually tinged, must be discriminatory: "Whatever evidentiary route the plaintiff chooses to follow, he or she must always prove that the conduct at issue was not merely tinged with offensive sexual connotations, but actually constituted 'discrimination . . . because of . . . sex.'"

Justice Scalia made a point of describing some behaviors that do not constitute harassment: "The prohibition of harassment on the basis of sex requires neither asexuality nor androgyny in the workplace; it forbids only behavior so objectively offensive as to alter the 'conditions' of the victim's employment. . . . We have always regarded that requirement as crucial, and as sufficient to ensure that courts and juries do not mistake ordinary socializing in the workplace—such as male-on-male horseplay or intersexual flirtation—for discriminatory conditions of employment." These distinctions are apparently clear to Justice Scalia, but the line may be less distinct for employers and employees and for judges and juries. To be on the safe side, it is likely that all concerned will continue to be cautious as norms are worked out, a process that will necessarily take place through social change outside of the legal system.

Limiting Company Liability: Developing a Complaint Process

In two 1998 cases, the Supreme Court clarified the extent of company liability for harassing behaviors and, by implication, what kind of behaviors employers had to try to control to protect companies from suits. The Court reaffirmed that corporations (*Burlington Industries v. Ellerth*, 1998) and municipal employers (*Faragher v. City of Boca Raton*, 1999) are absolutely liable when any kind of harassment involves a tangible job action (hiring, firing, promotion, demotion, transfer, and so on) whether or not high-level personnel knew about the harassment.

In other circumstances, the company could defend itself against a harassment suit by proving (1) that the company had taken **reasonable care** to prevent and correct harassing behavior, for example, by developing an effective complaint and follow-up procedure; and (2) that the complaining employee "unreasonably" failed to take advantage of the procedures.

In other words, employers could protect themselves against suits by putting into place adequate written policies condemning sexual harassment, and complaint procedures so that employees who were sexually harassed by supervisors or by other employees knew what to do to bring a complaint or to seek relief. The decisions encouraged larger companies and schools to establish units or departments to deal with questions of sexual harassment (Parker, 1999). Corporate spokesmen said they felt the decisions gave them the guidelines they needed to protect themselves from liability (Greenhouse, 1998c). (See Box 15.5 for summaries of types of harassment and conditions of employer liability.)

Will the Complaint Process Be Used?

Once again, the law on the books may be different from the law in action. The decisions presume that effective education, complaint, and follow-up procedures can be designed and implemented to reduce discrimination and protect companies from liability. Is this presumption warranted?

Though there is some research on why victims do not always report or report promptly (Duncan and Hively, 1998), there is little research on the potential impact on victims of requiring that they complain, on the effectiveness of complaint procedures, and on whether employees will actually avail themselves of this kind of remedy. We do not know what factors make a process "user friendly," what kind of procedures will protect employees who report harassment from direct retaliation (see *Burlington Northern v. White*, 2006), what can be done to assuage victim fears that reporting will alienate other supervisors or coworkers, and how employees can be protected against a malicious or a misguided complaint. There is a need for general and applied research in all these areas. The goal should be to develop procedures that enhance feelings of safety in those they are meant to protect while preserving or promoting comfortable interpersonal interactions. (See Parker, 1999, for a description of how a large corporation implemented compliance and training procedures.)

BOX 15.5

465

Harassment of
Men and
Same-Sex
Harassment

Sexual Harassment: Definitions and Conditions of Liability Behavior

Quid Pro Quo Discriminatory Harassment

1. Demand by a supervisor for sexual favors in return for job benefits constitutes harassment.
2. Demand can be implicit or explicit but the job benefits must be tangible: e.g., retention, promotion, good assignments, desirable transfer, or leave.
3. One instance is enough to constitute actionable harassment.
4. Employers are liable whether or not they know about the harassment because a supervisor offering job benefits is acting as the employer's agent.

Hostile Environment Harassment

1. Discriminatory intimidation, ridicule, and insult sufficiently severe or pervasive to alter the conditions of employment and create an abusive working environment must be present.
2. Harasser(s) can be supervisors, coworkers, or nonemployees. Key issues include the following:

   - Frequency
   - Severity
   - Persistence
   - Negative effects on work

3. The behaviors must have been perceived by the plaintiff as harassment.
4. A reasonable person in the plaintiff's position, considering all the circumstances, would perceive the behaviors as harassment.
5. The plaintiff need not have suffered psychological damage or injury because of the harassment.
6. The harassment need not tangibly affect the plaintiff's job.
7. When the harassment affects a tangible aspect of the plaintiff's job (e.g., promotion, retention, firing, or transfer) the employer is liable whether or not it knew of the harassment.
8. When the harassment does not tangibly affect the plaintiff's job,

   - the employer is liable if it does not have procedures to prevent and correct the behaviors or if it responds to the victim's complaints with indifference.
   - the employer is not liable if it has reasonable procedures to prevent and correct harassment and if the victim "unreasonably" failed to take advantage of the procedures. (See *Pennsylania State Police v. Suders,* 2004).

⊠ Harassment of Men and Same-Sex Harassment

What Makes a Man Feel Harassed?

Sexual harassment is often thought to be primarily a woman's problem, but men also can be victims. About 9.9 percent of the harassment claims filed with the EEOC and the state and local Fair Employment Practice Agencies (FEPAs) in 1994 were filed by males (see www.eeoc.gov/stats). By 2004, the percentage had gone up to 15.1. Complaints do not reflect the extent of a problem. Presumably there are at least as many male as female harassment victims who do not take legal action.

Researchers have attempted to assess the prevalence of sexual harassment of men using the same scales developed to assess women's experiences (Fitzgerald and Shullman, 1985; Stockdale, Visio, and Batra, 1999). However, these instruments may not be valid measures of harassment of men (Waldo, Berdahl, and Fitzgerald, 1998). First, similar behaviors may have different meanings for men and women. Men are less likely than women to perceive the behaviors included in the scales as harassing, and find them less distressing. For example, a man may be flattered by a woman flirting with him, while a woman may find a man's flirting offensive (Wiener et al., 1995). These differences in attitudes and feelings might reflect differences in socialization. Also, there may be less of a power or status differential between men and their female harassers, making some behaviors less threatening.

Second, there may be behaviors that men experience as offensive or upsetting that are not measured by scales developed to assess women's experiences (Waldo et al., 1998). For example, men have reported feeling harassed by behavior that enforced traditional male gender roles. Such behavior includes ridiculing men for being "unmanly" or pressuring them to engage in "masculine" behavior (Waldo et al., 1998). Perhaps the major problem with women-oriented instruments is that they assume an opposite sex harasser (usually the case when the victim is female). In surveys of harassing experiences, men reported being most bothered by harassment by other men (Waldo et al., 1998; Stockdale, Visio, and Batra, 1999; Abelson, 2001).

Waldo and colleagues (1998) conducted a survey of 378 men who worked for a large public utility company, 209 male faculty and staff at a large midwestern university, and 420 men who worked in a food-processing plant. The survey contained items to assess the frequency and type of potentially harassing behaviors the men experienced. The survey instrument was the Sexual Harassment of Men (SHOM) scale, developed by revising woman-oriented Sexual Experience Questionnaire items and adding items related to pressure to be a traditional male.

Very few of the men reported experiences of sexual coercion. They reported being subjected to negative remarks about men and unwanted sexual attention more often from women than from men. They found behaviors related to the enforcement of heterosexual male gender roles (e.g., urging someone to be a "man") more disturbing than lewd comments, negative remarks about men (e.g., "men are stupid"), sexual coercion, and unwanted sexual attention. Most of the men rated most of the behaviors listed in the scale as only "slightly upsetting." The researchers concluded that the behaviors measured by the SHOM may not be experienced as harassment by men and may not be associated with negative emotional consequences.

Hostile Environment Harassment, "Masculine" Behavior, and Homosexuality

In most cases when men claim they are being harassed, the harasser is another man (Stockdale, Visio, and Batra, 1999; Abelson, 2001). Women are also bringing cases claiming harassment by women, but these are rare. Male–male complaints of quid pro quo harassment usually involve homoerotic demands. Hostile environment cases have also been brought by men, homosexual or heterosexual, who were harassed by other men for being "effeminate" or because of their sexual preferences. These victims were often men working in traditionally male or male-dominated fields who did not fit in with prevailing "macho" norms, and who became the object of male-on-male hazing, teasing, and sometimes vicious horseplay.

Prior to 1996, about 10 percent of the private sector sexual harassment claims filed with the EEOC were filed by male victims. The applicability of Title VII was not questioned when the alleged harasser was a woman, but was questioned when the alleged harasser was another man. Between 1994 and 1996, over 40 courts ruled on whether same-sex harassment claims could be brought under Title VII (Goodman-Delahunty, 1998). Courts generally found in favor of plaintiffs who were pressured or coerced by a homosexual supervisor to give or receive sexual attentions. These cases were considered actionable under Title VII because they involved a misuse of organizational power for sexual favors (quid quo pro; Waldo, Berdahl, and Fitzgerald, 1998). However, because the Civil Rights Act does not list homosexuals among the protected groups, many courts ruled that Title VII did not prohibit hostile environment discrimination (threatening, humiliating, and taunting behaviors) by heterosexual men toward homosexuals or toward heterosexual men who did not conform to gender expectations (Goodman-Delahunty, 1998).

In *Oncale v. Sundowner Offshore Services* (1998), the U.S. Supreme Court unanimously ruled that the issue in Title VII actions is the harassing behavior, not the sex or sexual orientation of the alleged victim. Oncale worked with an all-male oil rigger crew on an oil platform in the sea. He brought suit in federal court against three other crew members and two supervisors, alleging that these men singled him out for crude sex play, unwanted touching, and threats of rape. The trial court ruled that Oncale, a male, had no cause of action under Title VII for harassment by male coworkers. The federal appeals court affirmed, but the U.S. Supreme Court reversed. The Supreme Court ruled that nothing in the law barred a claim of discrimination because the defendant and the plaintiff were of the same sex. The harassing conduct need not be motivated by sexual desire to support an inference of hostile environment discrimination in the workplace on the basis of sex.

Objectivity: A Matter of Context

The Court in the *Oncale* opinion confirmed that the standard for harassment required the fact-finder to consider that the same acts may have different meanings to different people and in different situations. Thus, the decision recognized that context and gender differences may affect the perceptions and responses of both men and women. Without using the terms, the Court adopted a social psychological or cultural anthropological approach to *objectivity:*

> The objective severity of harassment should be judged from the perspective of a reasonable person in the plaintiff's position, considering 'all the circumstances'. In same-sex (as in all) harassment cases, that inquiry requires careful consideration of the social context in which particular behavior occurs and is experienced by its target. A professional football player's working environment is not severely or pervasively abusive, for example, if the coach smacks him on the buttocks as he heads onto the field, even if the same behavior would reasonably be experienced as abusive by the coach's secretary (male or female) back at the office. The real social impact of workplace harassment behavior often depends on a constellation of surrounding circumstances, expectations, and relationships which are not fully captured by a simple recitation of the words used or the physical acts performed.

Whether judges will find reasonably consistent ways of deciding when horse play, haz-ing, locker room–style teasing, and bullying are sufficiently offensive, humiliating, or scary to constitute discrimination remains to be seen.

Harassment in the Schools

In 1972, Congress extended the Civil Rights Act, adding Title IX to prohibit discrimina-tion on the basis of race and sex in schools and universities that receive federal funds. Although the initial focus of the legislators was on race, one important effect of the new statute was the expansion and promotion of athletic programs for female students. Later, the concept of sexual harassment, developed in employment cases, was applied to harassment in schools. In 1997, the U.S. Department of Education, which adminis-ters Title IX, issued guidelines for the application of the law to sexual harassment in educational settings.

Pupil Age and the Harassment Laws

The considerations governing findings of harassment in the workplace developed through administrative and case law translate relatively easily to college and university settings. However, the problems and issues faced by elementary and secondary schools are somewhat different, morally and practically. Fear of lawsuits or loss of federal funds certainly influences school policy and practice. But schools presumably do not imple-ment sexual harassment policies merely out of fear (Short, 2006). The job of schools is to educate and socialize students. During the school day, schools are acting in the place of parents. Education includes teaching about good citizenship, equal opportunity for all, and acceptable and unacceptable behaviors. It is not only legitimate for a school to criticize and correct personal and interpersonal behaviors in a child or youth, it is also part of their job of socializing youth. Employers do not have a similar responsibility to socialize adult employees.

On the other hand, defining appropriate and inappropriate behavior in educational settings presents special problems. It may be difficult for teachers of young children with retardation or with a disability to avoid touching their students altogether. Affec-tion between teachers and older students is an element of mentoring, though the close-ness of the mentoring relationship may now be limited by fears of charges of sexual abuse or sexual harassment (see Anderson and Levine, 1999). Children also normally touch each other in play and tease each other in a way adults do not.

The Supreme Court's rulings in two cases involving school harassment cases helped clarify the extent and limits of a school's liability in these areas.

Harassment by Teachers

In 1998, the Supreme Court heard a case that involved a teacher having sex with a stu-dent. This situation is equivalent to quid pro quo sexual harassment by an employment supervisor (Greenhouse, 1998c, 1999). A 15-year-old, whose teacher initiated an affair with her, sued the school district after a police officer caught the two and arrested the teacher (*Gebser v. Lago Independent School District,* 1998). The teacher's acts were obviously immoral, unethical for an educator, and criminal because the student was below the legal age of consent. The question taken to the federal courts was whether, under Title IX, the school district was financially liable for the actions of its employee.

In the past, the Supreme Court ruled that an employer is always liable for a supervisor's actions when a quid pro quo complaint is upheld. But the Court did not hold that schools were automatically liable when teachers used the power of their position to sexually exploit a student. The Court ruled that schools do not have to pay damages for sexual harassment of a student by a teacher unless school officials knew about the behavior and responded with deliberate indifference. In holding that schools had to have learned of the harassment to be liable for it, the Court evidently did not weigh the pragmatic argument that teachers who sexually exploit children may make them fearful of complaining. We have little information about how complaints against teachers surface, and what might be the personal and organizational constraints facing students who seek relief in schools through a complaint.

Harassment by Peers

The second case concerned a school's liability for protecting students from harassment by other students. This kind of harassment can create the equivalent of a hostile environment, adversely affecting the victim's ability to learn, rather than to earn. It is a far more common problem than teacher–student seduction. Most people need only consult their own memories of school to know that children can be very cruel. Recent lawsuits included a big-bosomed girl who was followed throughout the school halls day after day by boys mooing at her, an eighth-grade girl who was groped on the school bus repeatedly by a boy, and a seventh-grade girl made the subject of a rumor campaign involving sex acts performed with hot dogs (Gorney, 1999).

Stories of vicious teasing are usually contrasted with the "going too far" story of the six-year-old boy in North Carolina who was suspended from school in 1996 because he kissed a classmate on the cheek. But the North Carolina incident appears the exception and not the rule; common sense prevailed, and the school's decision was reversed (Gorney, 1999). Yet the question remains: where does "kids being kids" who need to work things out among themselves end and school responsibility to intervene begin?

In *Davis v. Monroe County Board of Education* (1999), a 5 to 4 majority of the U.S. Supreme Court affirmed the liability of a school district for failing to protect a student from severe and ongoing harassment. The suit was filed by the mother of a fifth-grade girl who was harassed by a classmate who sat next to her. For months, the boy taunted her and repeatedly put his hands on her breasts and pubic area. The girl's mother complained repeatedly to the school, to no avail. The girl repeatedly asked to have her seat changed, with no response. Her grades dropped, and she wrote a suicide note. Later, the boy was convicted of sexual battery against the girl in juvenile court.

Harassment in the Schools

The Court's ruling confirmed that a school district's liability attached only if school officials knew of the harassing behavior and, acting with **deliberate indifference,** did not take steps to stop it. Justice O'Connor, who wrote the majority opinion, stressed that "damages are not available for simple acts of teasing and name-calling among school children" but for behavior "so severe, pervasive and objectively offensive that it denies its victims the equal access to education." Most school districts had already voluntarily implemented sexual harassment policies before the decision (Short, 2006), but the decision undoubtedly made such policies more salient for schools (Greenhouse, 1999).

The requirement that the school know about the behaviors creating a hostile environment for learning is troubling because it is unclear what this means in everyday practice. How is the school to know? Is the school liable for harassing behaviors observed by a school employee who then tells the appropriate supervisor? Is it liable only when the parents complain to the school? When the child or adolescent complains to the appropriate authority? Who is the appropriate authority? Empirical information about how often children and adolescents perceive themselves as harassed and how they respond would be useful here. Do children and adolescents always tell their parents when they are being teased, especially about something sexual? When do children want teachers or parents to protect them? Will they be better off or worse off within their peer culture with parental or teacher protection?

Bullying is a common and sometimes severe problem, especially in schools, but it is not always a civil rights problem. *Oncale* was actionable as sexual harassment because it included an attack on the plaintiff's masculinity. The child plaintiff in *Davis* was subjected to behavior later deemed sexual battery. Ordinary bullying without a distinct sexual (or racial) component would probably not be actionable under the Civil Rights Act.

The dilemmas faced by children who are subject to pervasive hostile harassment by their peers may be resolved only by efforts to change the norms of conduct among youth. Sexual harassment appears consistent with teenage norms for behavior, at least in some schools. For example, the New Jersey "jocks" who sexually assaulted a retarded 17 year old (discussed in Chapter 4) routinely harassed female students in their high school, as if it was their privilege (Lefkowitz, 1997). Perhaps schools should be teaching girls to cope with unwanted advances, and boys to be more civil.

Gay and Lesbian Youth

Antiharassment policies may be especially difficult to implement when harassing behaviors are directed at gay youth. Openly gay youths are probably at greater risk than heterosexual youths of being called demeaning names, subjected to verbal attacks, and physically assaulted in school corridors or stairwells. Others struggling with their sexual orientations may reasonably fear they will receive the same treatment. The negative consequences of a hostile environment may also be greater for homosexual adolescents and teenagers than for other adolescents. Garofalo et al. (1999) reviewed self-report data on sexual orientation and suicide attempts among 4,167 ninth- to twelfth-grade Massachusetts students who responded to a Youth Risk Behavior Survey. The 3.8 percent of the students who identified themselves as homosexual, lesbian, bisexual, or confused about sexual orientation were 3.4 times more likely than heterosexual youth to report a suicide attempt within the previous year (Garofalo et al., 1999; see also Harbeck, 1997).

If teasing and harassing behaviors are contributing or precipitating factors in suicidal attempts among gay youth or increase the likelihood that they will engage in high-risk behaviors like drug and alcohol use, then the harassment is contributing to a serious health problem in addition to interfering with education. Moreover, because homophobic attitudes are common, gay young people may be especially reluctant to complain. They may fear that adult reactions will be unsympathetic or colored by prejudices. For example, a young gay man in Wisconsin brought suit against his school for failing to prevent vicious teasing even when informed about it. The school administrators allegedly told the boy's parents that this is to be "expected" when a student is openly homosexual (Gorney, 1999). Jamie Nabozny brought suit against the school district and won a substantial award for damages (*Nabozny v. Podlesny*, 1996).

The Supreme Court's *Oncale* decision, holding that same-sex harassment qualifies as actionable sexual harassment, may provide a legal basis for gay youth to bring suits against schools. But this is another area where more data would be useful. In the Wisconsin case, the school was aware of the harassment because Jamie Nabozny told his parents, who complained. How many young men who realize they are homosexual would be willing to inform their parents of their sexual orientation? Would they complain without family backup to a possibly unsympathetic school administration? As minors, could they complain without their parents being notified? Even if they believed the school administration would be helpful, would fear of hurting or angering their parents deter them from complaining? Gay youths may have good reasons to feel anxious about revealing their sexual orientation to their families: about 26 percent of gay and lesbian youth have faced homelessness as a consequence of doing so (Harbeck, 1997).

Educational efforts in schools to increase tolerance of gay youth might help reduce harassment. The National Association of School Psychologists (2004) issued a position paper encouraging school-based programs to educate students, teachers, and staff about the problem and to provide counseling and advocacy for sexual minority youth within public schools. However, conservative or fundamentalist religious groups who view homosexuality as sinful may object to such programs. As long as hostility toward homosexuality remains widespread in the larger society, eliminating hostile environment harassment of homosexuals in the schools will be difficult.

Summary

Women working outside the home or venturing into historically male institutions have probably always been subject to unwanted sexual attentions and various forms of threat and insults. In the past, these behaviors were seen as simply rudeness and immorality. They can also be understood as mechanisms for enforcing traditional gender roles and protecting the norm of male ownership of the workplace.

In the 1970s, women began entering and reentering the labor market in unprecedented numbers, and a new women's movement challenged traditional gender roles. By the 1990s, working outside the home had become a norm for women. These late-twentieth-century working women saw sexual demands and sexually based abuse not as mere bad behavior, but as a serious barrier to their full participation in the economy and in the education system—in short, as a form of discrimination. Through case and administrative law, the 1964 Civil Rights Act and the Education Acts banning discrimination on the basis of sex as well as race, national origin, and religion became the basis for claims of discriminatory harassment. The EEOC and the courts defined two types of discriminatory harassment: quid pro quo harassment and hostile environment harassment.

Work by psychologists and other social scientists has contributed to the ongoing development of the concept of discriminatory sexual harassment. In keeping with a position adopted by the APA in an amicus brief, the *Harris* Court held that a person alleging harassment need not prove psychological injury. The brief's summary of work on gender and situational differences in perceptions of harassment, on stereotypical thinking, and on situational and personal factors that tend to trigger biases may also have influenced judicial decision making. The courts have adopted standards of harassment that take situational factors, personal characteristics, and cultural context into account in evaluating the meaning of potentially harassing behaviors, including the harassment of men by other men.

As a policy matter, the right to seek relief and redress for harassment was instituted to rectify a power imbalance in the workplace between men and women by giving the weaker victimized individual a way to fight back. The threat of lawsuits encouraged employers to take steps to prevent harassment. The law has succeeded in this regard. Fear of litigation has motivated many companies to establish programs educating employees about harassment and informing victims about complaint procedures. Schools have also established education and complaint procedures to avoid lawsuits. But it is not clear whether these procedures will be used and whether they will reduce the incidence of harassment. The problem of developing effective complaint and relief procedures for homosexual youths harassed by schoolmates may be especially acute.

The sexual integration of the workplace constitutes a radical change in U.S. society. The problem of sexual harassment is part of the culture's struggle to accommodate this change. The law has provided some initial basis for confronting the problem and has stimulated action to control it, but the eventual solution may well require a change in social norms. Social science research can potentially contribute to our understanding of how norms can be changed. Research into the relationship between social norms, situational factors, personal factors, and cognitive biases has already helped by providing men and women with a language through which to discuss these issues.

Discussion Questions

1. What are the arguments for treating sexual harassment as a civil rights issue?
2. Police Detective X has an excellent record of solving cases and collecting evidence that holds up in court. However, X is aggressive and brusque, uses foul language, and is intolerant of even small mistakes in support staff. Think of two experiments that would allow you to investigate if (a) people's emotional responses to this description differ depending on X's gender, (b) people would make different hiring or promotion decisions about X depending on their gender, and (c) the type of job (police detective or school principal) affects the relationship between the personal characteristics described above, the person's gender, and the likelihood that others would hire or promote him or her.
3. Which "objective" standard do you think fact-finders should refer to in deciding whether a behavior was sexually harassing: the viewpoint of a reasonable person, a reasonable man or woman, or a reasonable victim? Can you think of an experiment that would help you to evaluate which standard the average citizen would find most fair, and whether men or women prefer a different standard?
4. What do you think schools can and should do to protect students from sexual harassment? Where would you draw the line between "boys being boys" or "children being children" and harassing behavior that the victimized child shouldn't be expected to deal with on his or her own? Is there any developmental research that would help you with this task?
5. What characteristics would define a "successful" complaint procedure? Suppose you wanted to conduct a study to evaluate a complaint procedure? What would you do? How would you define and measure good and bad outcomes?
6. Are there any positive functions served by sexual stereotyping?

Key Terms

deliberate indifference
Equal Employment Opportunity Commission (EEOC)
harassment
hostile environment sexual harassment
legally actionable
meta-analysis

objective standard
prevalence
psychological injury
quid pro quo sexual harassment
reasonable care
reasonable person standard
reasonable victim standard

reasonable woman standard
sexual harassment
status
stereotypes
subjective standard
Title VII
Title IX

CHAPTER **16**

Psychological Tests and Discrimination in Education and Employment

474

CHAPTER 16
Psychological
Tests and
Discrimination
in Education
and
Employment

Psychological tests are among the proudest accomplishments of psychological science. They have a highly developed conceptual and mathematical basis and have useful real-world value. However, their practical application has produced controversy. Testing has been viewed variously as a vehicle for, or as an obstacle to, achieving a fairer and better society.

In the United States, psychological tests have been an important tool for allocating educational and occupational opportunities and resources among individuals and institutions since the turn of the last century. Their use favors some groups more than others. The findings from psychological tests influence our beliefs about the nature of class, ethnic, racial, and gender differences (Haney, 1981). Because of its social impact, testing became an object of litigation. Challenges to tests brought on political and ideological grounds are also challenges to the value-free stance of science. The challenges question the role of testing in rationalizing inequality in society. The challenges have taken place in the context of efforts to overcome racial discrimination and its legacies by engaging in affirmative action.

In this chapter, we will look at how social and political agendas have been pursued through the use of tests and through legal challenges to the use of tests. We will discuss briefly

- the history of tests of intelligence.
- achievement and tests used for employment selection.
- the legal attack on intelligence tests.
- tests used for college admission and affirmative action.
- gender differences in tests used for National Merit Scholarships.
- achievement and minimum competence tests, and high school graduation.
- legal attacks on tests used in the employment context as discrimination.
- possible adverse effects of affirmative action on minorities.

History of Psychological Testing

The psychological test is one answer to Immanuel Kant, who in 1786 claimed that psychology could never be a science because mathematics is inapplicable to its phenomena (Levine, 1976). Within 60 years of Kant's assertion, Ernst Weber and Gustav Fechner in Germany had developed methods for measuring units of mind (sensory perceptions) and relating them mathematically to physical units such as weight, brightness of light, and distance (Boring, 1957).

In the mid-nineteenth century, Sir Francis Galton set out to measure individual differences on "mental tests" of sensory and perceptual functions. Galton took psychological measurement out of the realm of abstract science and into the world of politics and policy. Influenced by his cousin Charles Darwin's ideas about evolution, Galton believed that many mental characteristics were inherited; measurements of human capacities could ultimately be used to improve the human race through selective breeding (Boring, 1957; Peterson, 1926). Galton developed the methods of statistical correlation that remain central to test construction and evaluation today.

Intelligence Tests

Alfred Binet and Théophile Simon (1905, 1948) developed tests of higher functions rather than the sensory processes measured by Galton or, later, by Cattell (1890). Initially, they wanted to develop a measure that would predict success in school. In 1882, France passed a compulsory school attendance law. It soon became apparent that some children were not able to keep up with the government-mandated curriculum. In 1904, the French government commissioned Binet and Simon to devise methods for identifying children who could be better taught in special classes or special schools.

Binet had shown that performance on tests of judgment and reasoning, using tasks similar to those of everyday life, varied systematically with age. They developed a complex test composed of subtests that they combined into an overall score. Binet and Simon collected data to **norm** the test (to find average scores and standard deviations) for children of different ages. They validated the test by seeing how well it correlated with student performance in school. Binet and Simon did not study the predictive validity of tests for performance calling for intelligence in other than school contexts.

Binet and Simon developed their test initially to help define the lower, pathological end of the intellectual scale so that "slow" children could be diverted to special classes, and to measure progress in special education facilities (Binet and Simon, 1905, 1948). Although they started out to measure school-related abilities, they soon claimed they were measuring general intelligence. Test scores not only identified the deficient but also predicted school performance of children who were not deficient. Not surprisingly, poorer children—who on average did less well in school compared to children from better-off families—also had lower scores on the intelligence test.

The Binet and Simon test met a need. Psychologists and educators elsewhere in the world quickly took them up, modified them, and developed similar tests to use in their own cultural contexts. The American version of the IQ (intelligence quotient, measuring mental age divided by chronological age) test, the Stanford Binet, was standardized by Lewis Terman (Terman, 1916). It was validated by showing that groups assumed to be less intelligent—lower social class children, juvenile delinquents, and children rated as problem students by teachers—had lower scores. Teachers' judgments were used as criteria even though one of the arguments for the test was that it would have greater validity than teacher's judgments. Since all subsequent intelligence tests were validated against a Binet-type test, the influence of a school context on the measurement of intelligence persists to this very day. In this way, "general intelligence" has come to mean in effect the ability to do well in an academic setting. Wealthier children continue to do better both on intelligence tests and in school than children from poorer homes. Some argue that IQ is also a strong predictor of general adaptation to work and to life in the community (Rushton and Jensen, 2005).

476

CHAPTER 16
Psychological
Tests and
Discrimination
in Education
and
Employment

BOX 16.1

Testing in the Military

By January 31, 1919, 1.73 million servicemen had been tested. Some were recommended for discharge because of mental inferiority as shown by very low test scores. Others were assigned to labor battalions because of low intelligence test scores. Still others were selected for military training schools or colleges or technical schools because of high scores. Some minority recruits benefited from tests. "In numerous cases, where requisitions called for the transfer to another camp of Negro recruits capable of becoming noncommissioned officers or of filling other positions of social responsibility, personnel officers made their selection solely on the basis of psychological rating" (Yerkes, 1921, 536). His statement reflects the argument that tests can be used to select people for jobs on merit alone, even though that ideal was contradicted by rigid racial segregation in the armed forces at that time.

Use of Intelligence Tests for Vocational Selection

Terman (1916) suggested that intelligence tests could be used for vocational selection. The U.S. armed forces took up the idea during World War I (Yerkes, 1921). A group of psychologists assisted the armed forces in developing a testing program. The tests were administered in large groups to measure recruits' intelligence. The military services then assigned recruits to different jobs or training on the basis of their scores (see Box 16.1). No attempt was made to assess job-specific skills. The psychologists in the armed forces conducted only minimal validity studies.

After World War I, industries worldwide took hold of the idea that tests of general intelligence could improve personnel selection (Viteles, 1932). Industrial-organizational psychologists showed that people in different civilian occupations showed differences in average scores on the Army intelligence tests. They also reported correlations between intelligence test scores and various criteria of occupational success or adjustment, though the correlations were not strong (Viteles, 1932). Morris Viteles, an early industrial-organizational psychologist and a psychology faculty member at the University of Pennsylvania, wrote, "Although there is growing agreement on the limited influence of general intelligence test score [*sic*] in determining the success of groups in specific jobs, there is still a tendency to attach considerable importance to *minimum intelligence level* as a significant factor, although little has been done to establish valid minimum intelligence levels for individual jobs" (Viteles, 1932, p. 126).

Intelligence Tests and Social Power

The social Darwinist notions that mental traits are heritable (i.e., can be inherited) and that social power reflects the "survival of the fittest" continue to pervade thinking about psychological tests (Rushton and Jensen, 2005). Calling the tests *measures of intelligence* provided a subtle justification for the existing social hierarchy. Psychologists working in the military in World War I found correlations between intelligence test scores and social class, ethnicity, and race. When publicized, those findings provided a scientific-appearing basis for making invidious comparisons among ethnic and racial groups (Crafts et al., 1938, Ch. 15; Kamin, 1974). In the 1920s, the results were used to argue for restrictive immigration legislation. Intelligence tests also provided a rationale for institutionalizing and sterilizing the "mentally defective" to protect society (Sarason and Doris, 1969). At the same time, proponents argued that tests leveled the playing field. Their use led to the award of "merit-based" opportunities for talented individuals from poorer homes. The arguments continue today, but in more sophisticated form (see Rushton and Jensen, 2005).

Achievement Tests

Intelligence tests purport to measure general cognitive skills that might be applied to different tasks. Achievement tests purport to measure the extent to which test takers have mastered specific bodies of knowledge or skills. They were developed to assess the degree to which children learned the content of what they were taught in school curricula. Achievement tests differ from teacher-made classroom tests because items on the test are selected mathematically; the tests are standardized and normed. Finding a way to measure that intangible thing called *educational progress* helped psychologists demonstrate that psychology was a quantified science. Educators who adopted tests could claim a scientific basis for their practices. Proponents of achievement tests argued that testing would make educational decisions, such as promoting children from grade to grade or evaluating how well schools were educating children, more objective. The tests were widely used for these purposes early in the twentieth century, when schools became the focus of political conflicts between Progressive reformers and local party bosses whose political base was often the immigrants in their districts (Levine, 1976; Ravich, 1974).

Tests are put to similar uses today. President George W. Bush pressed for the No Child Left Behind Act, which emphasizes annual testing in all grades, as the centerpiece of his educational program. Schools, responding to federal guidelines, are required to adopt testing as a means not only to evaluate schools but also to determine funding (No Child Left Behind Act, 2001).

The provision of the act requiring publication of test results by specific schools generated great controversy. Under the new law, the schools must publish test scores for African Americans, Latinos, immigrants, low-income students, and students with disabilities separately. In theory, the detailed publication of test results enhances accountability. However, the published results affect not only teachers but also parents, government officials, and public school officials. Real estate values may change as parents judge the desirability of residential areas by test scores in the school district.

The charter school movement advocates a "free market" solution to troubled schools by breaking the public school monopoly and creating choices for parents of all income levels. Privately established charter schools, freed from the bureaucratic control of the school district, in theory, have greater opportunity for educational innovation. The No Child Left Behind Act included support for this highly touted reform. Charter schools are also required by the act to test students and publish the results. In one review, students in charter schools were doing worse on academic achievement tests by about half a year[1] than comparable public school students. The charter school

---

[1] Achievement test results are reported in terms of years and months of educational attainment represented by the score on the test. Test results are actually based on the number of correct responses. Two months of educational progress may mean nothing more than that the student on average had one more right answer on the test. The significance of one more right answer is unclear. See Levine (1976) for a discussion of this issue.

478

CHAPTER 16
Psychological
Tests and
Discrimination
in Education
and
Employment

reform, based in part on political ideology, continues to be evaluated by standardized test scores (Winslow, 2004). Test scores thus enter into political discussion at every level from national politics to local school boards.

The Legal Attack on Tests

Psychologists found that intelligence test scores correlated with indications of racial and ethnic identity and with measures of social class. Because of the racial disparity in mean test scores, any cutoff score used for selection purposes disqualified a higher percentage of African Americans and members of some other minorities than of whites and many Asian Americans. Consequently, the tests had **disparate impact:** they made opportunities or resources more available to one group than another. If the scores have no (or limited) predictive validity, the use of tests denied opportunities to some individuals who would do well in classes or on the job if given the chance. The use of tests for selection purposes was challenged in the 1960s when the civil rights movement, backed in part by civil rights legislation, used the courts to challenge unfair practices and to bring about social change.

There are literally thousands of personality and psychopathology tests and attitude scales that are used in employment selection. The use of these instruments for employment selection presents analogous issues to disparate impact. Some of these tests ask deeply personal questions about sexual orientation, social or political views, or religious beliefs. They present issues of invasion of privacy. Tests of psychopathology used in an employment context may violate the Americans with Disabilities Act, especially if used for screening prior to offers of employment (Menjoge, 2003; Camara and Merenda, 2000). However, these tests have not been subject to much legal challenge. We will not discuss them in this chapter, focusing instead on tests of intelligence and achievement that have been subject to extensive litigation.

The meaning of some of the terms important to these cases is reviewed in Box 16.2.

Testing in Education Settings

Tracking in Schools

In 1954, the U.S. Supreme Court ruled that segregated schools were unconstitutional (*Brown v. Board of Education of Topeka,* 1954). Integrating the schools proved to be a slow process (*Brown v. Board of Education of Topeka,* 1955; *Keyes v. Denver School District No. 1,* 1973; see Levine, Perkins, and Perkins, 2005). Some school districts deliberately adopted tracking based on intelligence tests to maintain segregated classrooms. Because their average test scores were lower, African American students were disproportionately placed in the lower tracks and in special education classes. The practice of using test scores to maintain segregated tracks was challenged in court (*Hobson v. Hansen,* 1967). The judge in the case accepted the argument that tests were culturally and racially biased, and restricted their use.

The *Hobson v. Hansen* (1967) decision led to other challenges to the use of intelligence or ability tests for special class placement and for tracking. Spanish-speaking plaintiffs who were disadvantaged by tests administered in English successfully brought similar suits (Bersoff, 1980). These cases helped shape later challenges to the use of tests for employment selection.

BOX 16.2

479

Testing in
Education
Settings

Test Validity

Many of the legal challenges to psychological tests put test validity at issue. Following are some definitions that will be helpful in understanding the arguments:

Validity: A test is **valid** if it reliably measures what it is supposed to be measuring.

Construct validity refers to evidence that the test measures the "construct," or the psychological characteristic it purports to measure. Construct validity is established by showing that a test correlates with other measures that purport to measure theoretically related characteristics, and that it predicts real-world performance related to the characteristic it measures.

Content and face validity refer to whether the items on the test are a representative sample of the domain of abilities the test purports to measure. They also mean that the test items on their face look relevant to the characteristics the test is meant to measure (e.g., a secretarial test includes samples of skills such as mastery of word processing).

Predictive validity is assessed by seeing if subjects' scores on the test predict how they perform after a time interval on one or more independent measures (criteria) of the characteristic being assessed.

Criterion validity: since the criterion is used to validate the test, the criterion itself must be accepted as a good measure of the characteristic being assessed.

Differential validity: this is a technical term for measures to ascertain whether a test is **biased.** A test has differential validity for two groups if the **validity coefficients,** the correlation of test scores with criterion scores, are different for the two groups. For example, a test may not predict college GPA for girls, but it might for boys.

Disparate Impact: If the use of a test adversely affects opportunities for one group more than another, it has disparate impact. It has an **adverse impact** on members of the group that performs less well. A test need not have differential validity to have disparate impact.

Fairness: This is neither a legal nor a technical psychological term, but it is an important concept in discussions of uses and misuses of testing. Tests are said to be unfair for use if members of some cultures are more familiar with the items than members of others. When a test score predicts performance on a future criterion measure of all groups equally well, the test shows **prediction fairness.** However, even if tests are not biased, they are **unfair** if they have disparate impact and are not valid for the purpose for which they are being used (e.g., a test score may predict first-year college GPA, but not performance on the job later). Even when tests are not unfair in any of these senses, some argue that tests with adverse impact are socially unfair. "Merit" is not a simple matter that can be measured by a score, nor is merit always the predominant consideration in resource allocation. (Preference for children of alumni for college admissions illustrates the old saying "It's not what you know that matters it's who you know.")

Selection fairness models propose weighing social and economic values, and the value of diversity in the workplace or in schools, instead of or in addition to predictive validity of test scores in making decisions (Cole, 1981).

480

CHAPTER 16
Psychological
Tests and
Discrimination
in Education
and
Employment

Nature–Nurture Revisited

As part of President Lyndon Johnson's Great Society antipoverty program in the 1960s, funding was provided for compensatory and preschool programs, including Head Start. These programs were to provide needed intellectual stimulation for "culturally deprived" children in the hope that academic achievement and intelligence scores would increase. Evaluations of preschool educational programs showed mixed results. Some IQ change could be demonstrated in the short run, but the change in IQ scores was not lasting (but see Berrueta-Clements et al., 1984).

Arthur Jensen (1969, 2000; Rushton and Jensen, 2005) argued vigorously that groups of people differed in built-in, inherited types of intelligence (see also Herrnstein and Murray, 1994). He and others (Rushton and Jensen, 2005) said those differences needed to be taken into account in designing educational programs. Jensen's work took the heredity versus environment IQ controversy out of the academy and put it squarely in the political arena. Rushton and Jensen (2005) continue to press the same argument today with a great deal of documentation from the worldwide literature on racial and ethnic differences in test performance. The public discussion of racial differences in IQ scores was and is painful and divisive (Sternberg, 2005).

Declaring Intelligence Tests "Illegal"

In 1969, the San Francisco–based Association of Black Psychologists (See Elliott, 1987) called for an attack on IQ tests. The association claimed that tests improperly classified black children, placed them in inferior special education classes, and had deleterious effects on their psychological development (Williams, 1970). The not-so-hidden agenda was to have intelligence tests formally declared biased by the courts, in effect to have intelligence tests declared "illegal."

The disproportionate placement of minority children in classes for the Educable Mentally Retarded (EMR) provided the opportunity to mount a legal attack on testing (Bersoff, 1980). African American professional organizations and civil rights groups recruited children and families, including a black youth named Larry P., to bring a suit in their names. In this type of litigation, the real parties are often advocacy groups who seek to implement a political or social agenda through lawsuits brought in the name of individuals who are aggrieved. Larry P. was an unskilled, unemployed young man who was moved in and out of EMR classes throughout his school career. He finally left without graduating from high school. The principal defendant was Wilson Riles, a distinguished black educator who was superintendent of public instruction in California (*Larry P. v. Riles*, 1974, 1981).

New federal legislation favored mainstreaming of children with disabilities into standard classrooms as much as possible. The federal regulations (see section on administrative law in Chapter 1) for implementing the statutes required that if tests were used, they should not be racially biased. The plaintiffs in *Larry P.* sought an injunction barring the use of intelligence tests to place children in EMR classes, claiming the tests were racially biased. More African American than white students were placed in special classes as a result of the use of IQ tests.

Distinguished psychologists on both sides brought the heredity and environment controversy into the courtroom during an eight-month *bench trial* (a trial in front of a judge with no jury). The key issue was whether group differences in average scores were a function of *socioeconomic factors* (preparation for reading and for school, other

BOX 16.3

Testing for Court Purposes

The psychologists hired by the plaintiffs in *Larry P. v. Riles* (1972) retested Larry using nonstandard test procedures. Tested in this way, Larry had an IQ of 94, higher than he had ever obtained before. Several other plaintiffs who had histories of repeated school failure and placement in educable mentally retarded (EMR) classes also had higher scores when similarly tested. Test results based on nonstandard methods were used to argue that tests were unfairly classifying the plaintiffs as mentally retarded.

Many psychologists would not accept the plaintiff's argument. After completing a standard administration of an IQ test, psychologists sometimes go back and administer items in a different way to obtain more information about an individual's functioning and potential. However, this informal retesting is not used in computing an IQ score. Scores obtained using nonstandard procedures can't be compared with scores obtained using standard procedures. The norms used to interpret scores are based on standard administration.

child-rearing practices, parental attitudes toward school, and so on) or of *racial-cultural factors* (e.g., language used in the test and experience with concepts tested by test items). The court had the authority to act to correct racial discrimination that violated constitutional or statutory rights, and to prohibit the use of racially discriminatory tests. The court had no authority to correct general social ills stemming from socioeconomic causes. Consequently, the defendant state department of education claimed that racial differences in scores were related to socioeconomic and not racial factors. They carefully finessed evidence pointing to genetically based racial differences in intelligence test scores (Elliott, 1987). They claimed the tests were valid for special education placement (Lambert, 1981). The plaintiffs denounced IQ tests as racially and culturally biased. Federal judge Robert Peckham's decision in *Larry P.* agreed and in effect banned the use of IQ tests for purposes of placement in California EMR classes (*Larry P. v. Riles*, 1974; *Larry P. v. Riles*, 1981, p. 989).

Declaring Tests Legal

Elliott (1987) believes that as a result of the *Larry P.* trial, psychologists reappraised the relationship between intelligence test scores and achievement. The field came to a greater consensus about what constituted intelligence and about the validity of intelligence tests. Psychologists' defense of their tools came into play in a second case similar to *Larry P.* which was heard eight years later.

In Illinois, as in California, a disproportionate number of African American children were placed in EMR classes on the basis of test scores. A group called Parents in Action on Special Education (PASE) challenged the practice in a legal action initially brought as part of a larger school desegregation suit in Chicago (*PASE v. Hannon*, 1980). The *PASE* trial was almost a reprise of the *Larry P.* trial. It even had many of the same expert witnesses.

After hearing what he characterized as unconvincing and tangential testimony from experts, federal judge John F. Grady decided to review the WISC-R and the Stanford Binet IQ tests on an item-by-item basis himself. He concluded that the tests

482

CHAPTER 16
Psychological
Tests and
Discrimination
in Education
and
Employment

were not racially or culturally biased. His conclusion is consistent with those derived from psychometric studies of test-item bias (Gottfredson, 2000, 2005; Hunter and Schmidt, 2000; Jensen, 2000). On this basis, he ruled that the tests were valid for the purpose for which they were used, placement in EMR classes. Thus, one federal court said the tests were racially biased and a second court said they were not.

Despite Judge Grady's ruling, Chicago schools agreed to stop using standard IQ tests as part of a settlement with plaintiffs.

What Did the Lawsuits Accomplish?

The use of standardized intelligence tests was limited in many jurisdictions as a result of the lawsuits. School systems and psychologists adapted to the legal rules. Psychologists in California and in Chicago schools, banned from using standard IQ tests, employed achievement tests or adaptive behavior scales instead to determine who needed special education services. Some children who might have been classified EMR in the past were now either mainstreamed or classified as *learning disabled* (Elliott, 1987). We don't know whether the changes led to a better education for children. Some parents were pleased with the services provided in special education classes and would have preferred that their children stay in the program. Others felt their children were better off in mainstreamed classes.

The lawsuits did not resolve the questions of what intelligence tests measure and whether they are biased. In this instance, the attempt to settle an important set of inter-related scientific, educational, and sociopolitical issues through the adversarial legal system was not very satisfying to anyone.

⊠ College Admission and Affirmative Action

Test scores affect admissions to college, professional, and graduate schools. Should tests have as much influence as they do? The disagreements are not only about the validity of the tests, but also about what values should be promoted through policies affecting admission to selective schools. We are distributing a scarce resource when we decide on admission to selective schools, especially when public resources are involved.

The question of how much weight institutions of higher education should give tests in admission decisions became bound up in the question of affirmative action. In

---

BOX 16.4

Affirmative Action and Tests in Elementary School

In Buffalo, New York, a white student successfully challenged the race-conscious criteria used for admission to the city's elite high school, City Honors. Subsequent to her challenge, the admissions process emphasized test scores. The number of minority students admitted to City Honors declined from 52 to 40 percent and in another desirable city school from 57 to 34 percent (Heaney, 1998; Editorial, 1998). Many suits similar to the one in Buffalo challenged the use of race-conscious pupil assignment policies in public schools (See *Ho v. San Francisco Unified School District,* 1997). Schools committed to maintaining racial integration are trying to develop race-neutral criteria that would help maintain racial integration in schools and in programs. (See D. I. Levine, 2000, 2003; and section below.)

the 1960s and 1970s, universities and colleges became committed to affirmative action. **Affirmative action** refers to a policy of actively seeking to increase the percentage of minority students in the student body. Some schools vigorously recruited minority applicants and used different admission standards, often with lower test cutoff scores, for minority students.

Most postsecondary institutions admit almost everyone who applies with designated credentials—usually graduation from high school with the appropriate courses and a minimally acceptable grade point average. Affirmative action at the higher education level primarily affected students applying to the 20 percent of universities and colleges that are highly selective and to graduate and professional schools most of which are quite selective in admissions. With affirmative action, the racial composition and the distribution of test scores of the entering class in graduate and professional schools is probably different from what it would have been without race-conscious admission procedures.

Affirmative action programs use models of **selection fairness** (see Box 16.2), which attach importance to considerations and values other than "merit" defined only by the highest grades and test scores. In *University of California Regents v. Bakke* (1978), the U.S. Supreme Court accepted a selection fairness model (although they didn't use that term) for admission policies. At the same time, the Court limited the use of race as a factor in admission decisions.

The University of California, Davis Medical School had rejected a white applicant named Allan Bakke. The same year, the university admitted 16 minority students in a special program. Some of those students had lower grade point averages, Medical College Admission Test (MCAT) scores, and interview ratings than Bakke. Bakke sued the university, arguing that he was harmed because admission by a racial classification was improper. The case reached the U.S. Supreme Court in 1978 (*University of California Regents v. Bakke*).

A deeply split Court said that racial classification as used by the Davis medical school was improper. However, a majority agreed with Justice Lewis Powell's opinion that the university's goal of attaining a diverse student body was an acceptable reason for selecting some individuals by different criteria than others. He said that race could be one element in the mix of criteria used to select students, but it couldn't be the only or the primary factor. This ruling was to be influential in cases brought later.

In his partial dissent in *Bakke,* Justice Thurgood Marshall set forth the moral premises for affirmative action:

> It is because of a legacy of unequal treatment that we now must permit institutions of this society to give consideration to race in making decisions about who will hold the positions of influence, affluence and prestige in America.
>
> For far too long the doors to those positions have been shut to Negroes. If we are ever to become a fully integrated society, one in which the color of a person's skin will not determine the opportunities available to him or her, we must be willing to take steps to open those doors. I do not believe that anyone can truly look into America's past and still find that a remedy for the effects of the past is impermissible.

Opponents of affirmative action also appealed to fairness values. They argued that affirmative action based on race is unfair to majority members who have not themselves discriminated against minorities, and have only benefited from racial discrimination by others indirectly. It is also unfair to members of other minorities who themselves might have been subject to discrimination (e.g., Chinese Americans, who as a group attain higher than average scores on IQ and achievement tests). Opponents

484

CHAPTER 16
Psychological
Tests and
Discrimination
in Education
and
Employment

of affirmative action believed that changing the rules for race-related reasons is simply wrong, regardless of which race benefits. They valued a system of **just deserts**—one where each person receives what he or she earned regardless of color or background.

Others made more pragmatic objections to affirmative action. They valued efficiency, arguing that schooling is a scarce resource and that tests assist in using the resource efficiently. The validity of testing (see Rushton and Jensen, 2005; Sternberg, 2005) is central to these arguments. Test validity is not central to the arguments for affirmative action. Proponents assert that diversifying schools and workplaces would be good for the schools and workplaces, would be good for the country, and would result in a fairer allocation of social resources overall.

Reaction to Affirmative Action

Affirmative action resulted in an impressive increase in the number of African American students in colleges and in the professions. The percent of African American college students rose from 4.9 percent in 1955 to 11.3 percent in 1990. From 1970 to 2001, the percent of African Americans ages 25–29 having four years or more of college rose from 4.6 percent to 16.1 percent (Infoplease, 2004). Comparable progress is shown in the percent of African Americans in various professions (Richey, 2003). (See Table 16.1.)

Affirmative action programs proved politically unpopular. In California, Proposition 209, barring the use of racial or gender preferences in admission standards to California colleges and universities, and in other contexts as well, was passed by **referendum** (direct vote by citizens of the state rather than by vote of the legislature) in 1996 (Bearak, 1997). Affirmative action was ended in Florida in 1999 by Governor Jeb Bush's executive order. In 1996, federal courts ruled in favor of a white woman who alleged that the University of Texas' race-conscious admission practices violated equal protection (*Hopwood v. Texas*, 1996). *Hopwood* was a circuit court decision so it affected admission policies throughout its jurisdiction (Texas, Louisiana, and Mississippi).

The effects of the court decisions and legislative change were immediately apparent. Only 14 of the 792 students admitted to the prestigious University of California, Berkeley, law school for the fall of 1997 were African American, and none of those accepted the university's offer (Bearak, 1997). Similarly, the number of African Americans applying to the University of Texas law school dropped sharply. The effects on other college and graduate programs varied. Minority student admissions didn't fall as drastically in some graduate programs as in others (News & Comment, 1997).

To promote diversity while avoiding the direct use of race, Texas, California, and Florida each opted for different versions of a "percent" plan. The publicly supported

Table 16.1

African Americans in Professions 1978 and 2003 (%)

Profession	1978	2003
Lawyers and judges	1.2	5.1
Physicians	2.0	5.6
Dentists	2.3	4.1
Engineers	1.1	5.5
College and university professors	2.6	6.1

colleges and universities agreed to admit the top percent (from 4 percent in California to 20 percent in Florida) of each high school's graduating class without respect to test scores. The percent plan does not apply to private colleges and universities. While avoiding race-conscious selection, the percent plans have not succeeded fully in creating racially and ethnically diverse campuses (see discussion of percent plans below).

Affirmative Action and the U.S. Supreme Court

State supported universities throughout the country had widely varying admission practices involving race and federal appellate courts in different circuits had ruled differently on the constitutionality of some of the procedures. For example, the Ninth Circuit in the Far West had said that diversity was a compelling interest, and the Fifth Circuit in the South had said it was not. The U.S. Supreme Court stepped in to resolve the contradictory judicial rulings. The Court accepted for review two cases challenging the admission practices of the University of Michigan's Law School and its undergraduate College of Literature, Science and Arts (LSA). Test scores were in the background of these cases. Special consideration for African American applicants would not be necessary were it not for the discrepancy in mean test scores between African Americans and whites (Rushton and Jensen, 2005).

Barbara Grutter, a white Michigan resident, had a 3.8 GPA and a 161 LSAT. Her credentials were not strong enough for automatic admission to the highly competitive Michigan Law School. She was placed on a wait list, but she was not admitted. She sued, claiming the law school used race as a predominant factor in admissions decisions in violation of the Equal Protection Clause of the Fourteenth Amendment. Applicants with no better or even poorer credentials than hers who were African American, Latino, or Native American had a significantly better chance of admission than she did (*Grutter v. Bollinger*, 2003).

Jennifer Gratz (*Gratz v. Bollinger*, 2003) and Patrick Hamacher, both white, were denied early admission to LSA and were eventually rejected. Like Grutter, they claimed their applications were treated less favorably than those of members of the underrepresented minority groups targeted for affirmative action.

Under the legal analyses used with equal protection claims under the Fourteenth Amendment, race could be employed in the admission decision if the university put forth a recognized "compelling interest" that would be enhanced by some use of race, and if the use of race was "narrowly tailored" (see D. Levine, 2003). Both the law school admissions and the LSA undergraduate admissions offices justified the use of race in selecting students for admission by asserting that attaining a diverse student body was a compelling state (educational) interest.

Selection by race alone would not be "narrowly tailored" to achieve the university's objective of having a diverse campus. If admissions practices followed the precedent in *Bakke,* the determination as to whether a student would contribute to campus diversity had to be made on an individual basis. The Michigan law school claimed that in its admission practices, it was seeking a "mix of students with varying backgrounds and experiences who will respect and learn from each other." The Supreme Court approved the law school's admissions practices in *Grutter. The Court* accepted the desire for diversity as a compelling interest because the effect of a diverse student body went beyond the immediate effects on the campus. The Court majority noted society's

486

CHAPTER 16
Psychological
Tests and
Discrimination
in Education
and
Employment

interest in diversity as well. The majority opinion looked at practices in business and the military that pointed up the need to have leaders from diverse backgrounds.

Race as a "Plus" Factor

In *Grutter*, the University of Michigan Law School argued that it was "seeking a mix of students with varying backgrounds and experiences who will respect and learn from each other." The Law School noted that it reviewed each applicant's file, and although race was used as an intangible "plus" factor, it was not the defining feature of the successful application. Statistical models introduced by expert witnesses showed that if grades and test scores alone were used as admission standards, relatively few students from underrepresented minority groups would make it through the process. By looking at other characteristics and experiences that in the law school's view would make for a successful law student and a student who would contribute to diversity, the law school was able to increase the number of students it admitted from underrepresented minority groups so that minority students of each group made up a "critical mass."

The Court found that the law school's aim to achieve a critical mass was not the same as having a quota (i.e., admit a fixed number of members of minorities no matter what), which was prohibited. The majority opinion cited statistics showing that the number of African American, Latino, and Native American students in any entering law school class (those who actually accepted the offer to come to Michigan) varied from 13.5 percent to 20.1 percent. The Court majority concluded that the variation in numbers of minority students in the *entering* classes did not support a claim that the Michigan Law School was using a quota.

By a 5–4 vote the Court rejected Ms. Grutter's claim, thus approving the law school's admission procedure. In other words, affirmative action admissions, carried out with individual determinations and using race as a "plus," as the majority said the law school was doing, were acceptable practices. However, the Court's ambivalence about using race for admissions was manifest in its pointed statement that the use of race should cease after 25 years.

Statistics and Discrimination

The dissenters in *Grutter*, led by Chief Justice William Rehnquist, challenged the compelling interest argument. They cited studies that did not find evidence of the benefits claimed to flow from a diverse student body. Justice Clarence Thomas made a heartfelt plea that affirmative action programs were stigmatizing, contributing negatively to the campus environment. The chief justice also engaged in a statistical analysis of admissions data (those students the law school accepted in contrast to data on the composition of the students who actually came to the Michigan law school to study). He showed that there was a correlation between the number of minority applicants admitted and the number in the applicant pool. When African Americans were 9.7 percent of the applicant pool, 9.4 percent of the admissions that year were African American. When 7.5 percent of the applicant pool was African American, 7.3 percent of the admitted class was African American. From this correlation, the chief justice inferred impermissible race-based practices on the part of the law school. He wrote, "The tight correlation between the percentage of applicants and admittees of a given race, therefore, must result from careful race based planning by the Law School." He went on to say, "Indeed the ostensibly flexible nature of the Law School's admissions program . . . appears to be in practice, a carefully managed program designed to ensure proportionate representation of applicants from selected minority groups."

In contrast to his rejection of a similar argument with respect to the imposition of the death penalty (see the *McCleskey* case in Chapter 8), Chief Justice Rehnquist was willing to infer an institutional pattern of discrimination by race from the statistical data in the law school admissions context. Chief Justice Rehnquist did not require that applicants such as Ms. Grutter demonstrate that prejudicial and discriminatory action took place in the treatment of their individual applications to law school. He did not explain the difference in treatment of the data in the two situations.

Race = +20 Points Is Invalid

The Supreme Court came to a different conclusion in the cases of Michigan undergraduate applicants Gratz and Hamacher (*Gratz v. Bollinger,* 2003). The LSA used a point system based on a weighted total of high school GPA, standardized test scores, the quality of the high school the applicant attended, the strength of the high school curriculum, in-state residency, alumni relationship, a personal essay, and personal achievement or leadership. An applicant was entitled to 20 points based solely on membership in a designated underrepresented racial or ethnic minority group. The assignment of 20 points for underrepresented minority status when a total score of between 100 and 150 generally resulted in admission enhanced the opportunity for members of the favored minorities to win admission and disadvantaged other applicants. The Court said the university engaged in no individual determination to ensure that the successful applicant would have the requisite characteristics to contribute to campus diversity. The Court said that the LSA procedure impermissibly weighted race in a mechanical way and did not narrowly focus on applicant characteristics that would contribute to diversity of educational experience. The Court sent the university back to the drawing board to devise a system that would produce diversity without being unduly race conscious. Michigan modified the admissions procedure for LSA quickly after the decision (D. Levine, 2003). The change came too late to affect Gratz's and Hamacher's applications.

Law School Admissions

Is affirmative action truly helpful? Affirmative action is controversial among whites and members of other races who feel excluded from opportunities, and among some beneficiaries of affirmative action who feel they are stigmatized as undeserving no matter what their accomplishments. Sander (2004) examined the long-range effects of affirmative action admissions in law school.

With desegregation and affirmative action, law schools have become more open to African American enrollment than they were a few decades ago. Sander notes that in 2001, about 3,400 African Americans were enrolled in accredited law schools. The percent of first-year African American law students (7.7 percent) was just a little short of the percent of African Americans among college graduates in 2001. In 1964, African Americans were only 1.3 percent of total law school enrollment, and many of those students attended the few historically black law schools. It was the success of affirmative action programs in increasing the number of African American students in law schools that prompted Sander to study other criteria of success than sheer number of students enrolled.

Sander (2004) had access to systematic data gathered by the Law School Admissions Council covering the period from 1991 through 1997. The data, covering 27,000

488

CHAPTER 16
Psychological
Tests and
Discrimination
in Education
and
Employment

law students from 90 percent of the nation's law schools, tracked their progress from admission to passing the bar exam and their income as lawyers two or three years after graduation. The data set included LSAT scores, undergraduate GPA, law school GPA, whether the graduate passed the bar examination required for state licensing as an attorney, and earnings as lawyers. Sander also examined the data by a prestige ranking of law schools they attended.

First, he concluded that the black–white gap in admissions credentials (defined as LSAT score and undergraduate GPA) appeared at all levels of prestige of law schools. Second, nearly half of black students, having poorer admissions credentials than white students, also had first-year law school GPAs that placed them in the lowest decile of the grade distribution. Race, however, had no predictive value for first-year grades when one controlled for LSAT score and undergraduate GPA. Independent of race, those with stronger admissions credentials had better first-year law school grades. Independent of race, those with stronger admissions credentials also tended to complete law school within five years at higher rates. Blacks tend to have poorer admissions credentials at the schools that admitted them, and their attrition rates were higher. However, more than half of those with even the poorest credentials did graduate after five years, and more than 80 percent of those with middling credentials graduated within five years (Sander, 2004, Table 6.7). The discrepancies persisted when graduates take the state bar examination. Fewer black law graduates pass the bar examination on their first try compared to all accredited law school graduates (61 percent versus 88 percent). The bar pass rate for blacks through five attempts is 77.6 percent, compared to 95 percent of all graduates passing after five tries. Again, independent of race, credentials on admission and law school GPA were good predictors of passing the bar examination. Law school GPA also predicted earnings as a second-year associate in a law firm.

Sander (2004) believes that African Americans are harmed by preferential admissions policies. He notes that because some African Americans receive preferences, they enter law school with poorer credentials than their fellow students and do less well on average than white counterparts entering that school with higher credentials. He hypothesizes that many African American students, noticing they do less well, tend to fall behind and lose confidence, and may actually learn less than they would in a school where their credentials were more competitive.

Sander argues that color-blind law school admissions would achieve the aims of affirmative action in the long run. Without color-conscious preferential admissions policies, Sander hypothesizes, students would be admitted into schools where their admissions credentials would make them more competitive with their peers. Placed in such law schools, on average, African American students would perform better, feel more confident, graduate at higher rates, and pass the bar at higher rates. Getting better grades, Sander believes, would cause their earnings to be higher because high-paying, grade-conscious law firms would be more willing to hire them (Sander, 2004). If Sander is correct, overall more African American law students would do well, and more African American lawyers would be licensed to practice than under present affirmative action programs.

Sander's argument is premised on a belief that law schools would admit students based on their academic credentials without regard to race. His argument assumes there would be no "back sliding" into racially discriminatory practices that would close opportunities to African American students as in the past. Under Sander's proposal, the number of African American students enrolled in the most elite law schools would certainly decline. Sander does not believe that matters very much, if the overall number of African American lawyers goes up.

Other scholars sharply dispute Sander's "mismatch" hypothesis. They believe that without affirmative action, the decline in number of African Americans who become lawyers would be much greater than Sander predicts (Ayers and Brooks, 2005; Chambers et al., 2005). Other critics of Sander believe that the graduates of the most elite schools have more opportunities. Moreover, those graduating from elite schools after having been admitted under affirmative action considerations by and large have notable careers (Bok and Bowen, 1998; Wilkins, 2005). In Sander's data, the prestige of the law school from which a student graduated predicted earnings of lawyers in practice independently of other factors. If affirmative action admission policies are continued, given their approval by the U.S. Supreme Court, are there methods for supporting those students admitted through the programs so that they will achieve more strongly in law school and have greater success on the bar examination?

⊠ Non–Racially Based Solutions to Maintaining Diversity in Education

Educators generally are committed to the principle that a diverse campus is better educationally and better for society. Many institutions and employers want a diverse workforce and look to schools to provide it by educating a diverse student body. Leaders in the military and in business say it is necessary in today's world to have a diverse leadership, as the *Grutter* Court noted. However, from *Bakke* forward, it has been clear that simply giving preference in admissions on the basis of race alone would be a violation of equal protection. It is a considerable challenge to social scientists to develop admission formulas that are not directly racially based, but that will select more minority students than would be admitted using standard criteria of tests and GPA. The task is not easy. If the constitutionally acceptable proxy measure is not strongly correlated with race, it will not accomplish the task very well of selectively admitting minority students.

San Francisco's "diversity index." The legal challenges posed to the student assignment process in San Francisco's public schools illustrate the difficulties of maintaining racial and ethnic diversity within the confines set by federal and state law. In 1983, the San Francisco school district settled a federal class action suit brought by the San Francisco Branch of the NAACP by agreeing to impose racial caps on the number of students assigned to the schools in the system from nine different racial or ethnic groups. In a class action lawsuit filed ten years later, however, Chinese American students successfully challenged that student assignment plan. They argued that the court-approved plan of racial quotas discriminated against them in admissions to many schools, including the system's most elite high schools, and in assigning students to neighborhood elementary schools. Chinese Americans are the largest racial or ethnic group in the San Francisco schools, so the quotas hurt them more than any other group. They won their suit (*S.F. NAACP v. S.F. Unified School District*, 1999; D. Levine, 2000). The school district agreed in 1999 that it would no longer assign any student to any school or program on the basis of the student's race or ethnicity. The San Francisco Unified School District, recognizing the city was racially segregated by residence, nonetheless wanted to maintain a diverse school system.

Given the constraints of the court decision and California state law, which flatly prohibited any use of race in assignment decisions, San Francisco educational authorities

490

CHAPTER 16
Psychological
Tests and
Discrimination
in Education
and
Employment

developed an elaborate new system for student assignment (see D. Levine, 2003). The plan is complex. All students are eligible to attend a school anywhere in San Francisco, but those with siblings in a school are given preference for that school. Students needing special education or English language instruction can choose from among the schools with appropriate facilities.

All other students are assigned based on a combination of their choice and, in schools with a limited number of places, a "diversity index." If there are places in the school the student chooses, the student is admitted. The diversity index affects admission decisions for about 40 percent of students. If there are fewer seats in a school than applicants, a central computer calculates a diversity index based on students already assigned to the grade in the school. The new applicant is evaluated based on how that applicant contributes to the mathematical diversity index for a particular grade. Six factors enter into assessing the individual student's diversity value. The six factors are "socioeconomic status, academic achievement status, mother's educational background, language status, academic performance index, and home language" (D. Levine, 2003, pp. 529–530). The applicant contributing most to the diversity index of the grade is given preference to one who would contribute less.

The complex plan assigns students without reference to race and therefore meets all legal requirements. This plan has generated controversy because it is confusing to many parents who blame the index when their children do not get into favored schools. Nor has use of the diversity index reversed "severe resegregation" (D. Levine, 2003, p. 535). The program operates by parent choice. Although schools are diverse when measured by the index, when the pool of applicants to a particular school is not racially diverse, using the index for student assignment doesn't help to create racial diversity. If the goal is to maintain fully racially integrated schools, this plan, which avoids race-conscious school assignments, has not accomplished it. In contrast, the school system in Seattle, Washington, uses race as a tiebreaker in allocating positions in high schools (*Parents Involved v. Seattle School District No. 1*, 2005). (Unlike schools in California, schools in the State of Washington are not forbidden under state law from using race in student assignments.) Social scientists may yet devise some other race-neutral index that would better accomplish racial integration. New methods may become necessary because the U.S. Supreme Court has agreed to review the legality of Seattle's race-based assignment plan in 2007. (cert. Granted, 2006)

Percent plans. In higher education, some states have adopted a "percent plan" in which the top percent of the graduates of each of the state's high schools are guaranteed admission to an undergraduate campus within that state's university system. The purpose of the plan is to help make the university or college look more like the overall community, and to incorporate sufficient diversity in the student body to enrich campus discussion, learning, and student development.

If students were distributed proportionately by race in all high schools in a state, the percent plan wouldn't accomplish its purpose of increasing the enrollment of minority students. Such a plan's success depends on the fact that due to socioeconomic factors, secondary schools are heavily segregated by race and ethnicity (see Levine, Perkins, and Perkins, 2005). Thus, accepting a percent from each school into the higher education system should result in an increased number of minority students on campus, and the percent plan would not be overtly racially conscious. Some argue the percent plan is simply a return to older methods of accepting students into college based on grades and class standing.

Horn and Flores (2003) conducted an extensive evaluation of percent plans as they operated in Florida, Texas, and California. While we will summarize overall results, Horn and Flores point out that although the plans are all called *percent plans*, they differ a good deal from each other. In general, for a student to be eligible, the student has to be in the top rank (20 percent, 10 percent, and 4 percent, respectively) in his or her high school (computed differently in the three states) and has to complete the state's requisite college preparatory course of study. Percent plans are affected by differences in rates of completion of high school by race or ethnic group. In Texas, California, and Florida, in 2000, high school completion rates for whites and blacks differed between 15 and 20 percent. A similar discrepancy is recorded for Latinos in the three states, except that the difference in high school completion rate between whites and Latinos in Florida is smaller (8 percent).

The demographics of each state are changing. The percent of whites in each of the three states has been declining, the percent of Latinos has been increasing, and the percent of African Americans has remained fairly constant. The changing demographics means that the targets for a campus that reflects the overall community will also change. This may complicate the problem of devising an appropriate scheme for selecting students when everyone can't be admitted, especially to the most elite campuses in each state's university system.

Critics who emphasize merit based on tests are unhappy with this system, because the selected upper percent in different schools may represent very different levels of test performance. For example, in a troubled school with many low performing students, the top ten percent might consist of everyone who got at least 75 percent of the test questions right. In a highly successful school in wealthy neighborhood, a third of the students might score 80 and above on the same test and the top 10 percent might consist of those who scored 94 and above. A student from this school with a score of 92 could lose his or her university place to students from the other school with a score of 75. The method seems unfair to those who believe that test scores are sufficient to define merit.

There are also unplanned "filters" that determine who actually gets to college. Not everyone who is eligible (i.e., completes high school with requisite courses) will choose to apply. Whites and Asians apply in greater numbers compared to their representation in the population than African Americans or Latinos. Thus, the racial composition of the applicant pool will overrepresent whites and Asians and underrepresent African Americans and Latinos. The composition of the applicant pool may also reflect prospective student attitudes and beliefs about how members of minority groups are accepted on the campuses, about the encouragement to apply, and about resources such as financial support that might be available. Youth in predominantly white schools may be more likely to receive encouragement and information about college application from school guidance counselors, parents and relatives than youth in predominantly minority schools because fewer parents are college graduates.

As a result of all these factors, the students who are admitted under percent plans are likely to be those who would have been admitted without the percent plan. There may be little net gain in minority representation, especially in the highly selective campuses within each state university system. Horn and Flores (2003) believe that campuses should put into place better recruitment efforts, should make financial aid information more readily available to applicants and to accepted students, and should have retention plans on campus to assist those who might otherwise drop out without adequate support.

492

CHAPTER 16
Psychological
Tests and
Discrimination
in Education
and
Employment

These complex social dynamics suggest that plans to enhance campus or school diversity that do not take into account the complexity of the social context will fail to fully meet their goals. The legal solution alone is not enough.

Tests, Gender, and National Merit Scholarships

There is an extensive literature showing that tests of academic skills and knowledge have disparate impact (see Box 16.2) on gender groups (Henrie et al., 1997). Boys do better than girls, especially in math (see Table 16.2). Since tests taken in high school are used to award some important college scholarships, boys got more of the money, in addition to having more competitive-appearing application credentials.

In 1989, a federal district court (*Sharif by Salahuddin v. N.Y. State Education Department*, 1989) reviewed the New York State Education Department's policy of awarding Regents and Empire scholarships on the basis of SAT scores (presently called *SAT-I*). High school girls score lower than high school boys on the SAT. As a result, although 53 percent of the students taking the SATs were girls, girls received only 43 percent of the Regents scholarships and 28 percent of the Empire scholarships.

The court noted that the legislature meant the scholarships to reward performance in high school, not to support students who were predicted to get good first-year grades in college, the validation criterion for the SAT. The SAT wasn't validated as a measure of high school performance; in fact, girls performed as well or better than boys in high school as measured by grades. On this basis, the court rejected the sole use of the SAT for purpose of awarding the scholarships (*Sharif by Salahuddin v. N.Y. State Education Department*, 1989).

Change the test. The Preliminary Scholastic Assessment Test (PSAT) is used to determine whether students become semifinalists for the prestigious National Merit Scholarship Program (for all practical purposes, scores on the PSAT and the SAT are so highly correlated that they are equivalent tests). A large number of younger students other than juniors eligible for the scholarship awards take the PSAT for practice. The College Board which constructs, distributes and scores the tests earns a great deal of money from testing. The College Board encourages a two-step process: PSAT, and then SAT. In 2004, about 14 million high school juniors took the PSAT (Burdman, 2005). As high school juniors, their standing on the PSAT qualifies them to become National Merit Scholarship finalists.

The tests were developed and administered by the Educational Testing Service (ETS), which receives federal funds. The American Civil Liberties Union, working with an advocacy organization called FairTest, filed a complaint against the ETS under Title VI with the Department of Education, Office of Civil Rights. The complaint alleged that the PSAT and SAT tests had an adverse impact on girls and were culturally biased against them (see Box 16.2; ACLU, 1998). Boys scored higher than girls on both

Table 16.2

Average SAT Scores for College-Bound High School Seniors (2001–2002)

	Verbal Score	Mathematics Score
Males	507	534
Females	502	500

National Center for Educational Statistics (October 2002).

the verbal and mathematics sections. On the SAT, boys scored an average of 1,049, and females an average of 1,005 (Burdman, 2005). The gender difference is most important at the high end of the scale. In 2002, 2.8 percent of boys scored above 750 on the SAT Math, while only 1.1 percent of girls scored that high. More girls (758,737) than boys (660,270) took the SAT. If National Merit Scholarships were granted on the basis of very high test scores, nearly three times as many boys than girls would be awarded the scholarships, even though more girls than boys were headed to college. The gender gap in test scores resulted in the acceptance of about 40 percent of girls and 60 percent of boys as National Merit Scholarship semifinalists, a credential highly valued by college admissions officers (FairTest, 1999a). Colleges are often ranked by the number of National Merit Scholarship finalists and semifinalists they attract (Burdman, 2005).

The criterion used to establish the predictive validity (see Box 16.2) of the PSAT was first-year grades in college. The test was differentially valid for that purpose for boys and girls. Though girls obtain lower PSAT scores and lower SAT scores, girls get higher GPAs than boys in college; the test, therefore, underpredicted girls' performance (Dean, 1997).

The U.S. Department of Education worked out a settlement with ETS and the College Board, which sponsored the tests. ETS and the College Board were motivated to come to a resolution because they would lose federal funds if they were found to be discriminating. They agreed to modify the test to include a writing-skills section. More than 1.2 million high school students took the new test. Girls did slightly better than boys on the new writing skills section, but they still did slightly less well on the regular verbal section (mean raw scores: boys 48.9, girls 48.7) and more poorly on the math section of the tests (mean raw scores: boys 50.9, girls 47.6). Use of total scores would not wipe out the gender discrepancy. By 1999, with the new test, girls received 45 percent of college tuition awards. However, 56 percent of those who took the test were girls. Girls had better high school grades than boys. If it were not for the tests, the majority of scholarships would have gone to girls (FairTest Examiner, 1999b).

Girls, who on average have lower SAT scores than boys, have higher first-year college grades than boys. That means the SAT underpredicts the performance of girls. FairTest claims that the use of SAT scores to determine admissions and scholarships potentially denies girls equal educational opportunity (FairTest, 1999b). It is difficult to come by consistent data on the outcomes of the tests and the demographics of who won the National Merit Scholarships. The College Board tends to guard the data, claiming the awards are based on strictly on merit (Burdman, 2005).

Is there gender bias in tests? Researchers have tried to determine what the difference in test scores means. A strong body of work established what appears to be a biologically based male superiority on spatial reasoning tests (see Rushton and Jensen, 2005, for a review of some of these studies). Henrie et al. (1997) created a test of geographic knowledge with four subscales. Responding to items in one subscale required spatial reasoning (e.g., reading elevations on a map); responding to items in the other subscales did not. Men consistently obtained better scores on all four subtests. The hypothesis that the gender difference on the geography test was related only to a difference in spatial reasoning skills could not be supported.

Nelson, Aron, and Poole (1999) gave the geography test to students who were taking geography classes. There were gender-related differences in the test scores, but there were no significant differences in the course grades earned by men and women, despite initial differences on the knowledge of geography test. The test underpredicted female performance. If the geography test was used to select prizewinners, prizes would have gone to more men who did less well than predicted and would have excluded many successful women.

494

CHAPTER 16
Psychological
Tests and
Discrimination
in Education
and
Employment

In sum, if grades are used as criterion measures, nationally normed, standardized, multiple-choice tests appear to be biased against females. But if tests are really biased against females, we can't clearly say how. Of course, a critic might say that grades or graders are biased against males. Logically, it is not necessarily the standardized tests that are at fault.

The gender gap is well-known. A gender gap appears in many computerized multiple choice tests including the GRE, the MCAT, and the GMAT. On the LSAT, women tend to bunch in the middle of the distribution, while men more often get scores in the highest and lowest deciles of the distribution (Guyot, 2002). To some extent, it is due to the content of items. For example, early in the history of the SAT, girls scored higher than boys on the verbal portion of the SAT. To even things out, the SAT added questions about business, sports, and politics. No similar content bias is apparent in the math section of the test. However, multiple-choice and timed tests tend to favor boys. The gender gap disappears when other types of questions are used. Girls do better with short-answer tests, "constructed responses," and essays. Boys are more likely to be risk takers than girls and to guess on tests. Educated guesses are likely to be correct. Girls tend to respond only when they are sure of the answers. The timed nature of the test works against the problem-solving style that many girls use—work out a problem completely, consider more than one possible answer, and check answers. Though they are using desirable problem-solving approaches, these students may be penalized on timed tests. Untimed administrations of tests show much less of a difference between males and females than timed tests (FairTest, n.d.).

Using tests that favor males over females to assign scholarships affects which disciplines as well as which people get money. Women and men tend to enter different fields; fewer females enter the physical sciences, engineering, and mathematics. More women study humanities and social sciences, and enter the helping professions. When more scholarships are assigned to men, society is inadvertently making a decision about the relative social value of different fields of study. This problem too may diminish as gender differences in career choices become less pronounced.

We are not sure whether the problem primarily affects American students. In Britain, students take uniform achievement tests but are not given aptitude tests like the SAT and GRE. There, women are outperforming men on tests and in the universities. More women than men are graduating. Women are acquiring better credentials than men, and are entering graduate and professional schools and the professions in record numbers. Some critics express concern about the "feminizing" of the professions, and suggest that in the foreseeable future, it may be necessary to engage in affirmative action to ensure that males are sufficiently represented in certain fields (Hinsliff, 2004).

Achievement Tests, Minimum Competence Tests, and "High-Stakes" Testing

The achievement test is the primary method used to evaluate individual children's progress and to evaluate schools. Achievement tests have largely escaped the criticism leveled at intelligence tests. The content of achievement tests is facially related to what is taught in school. Most communities and parents want to be confident their children are learning what they are being taught. Achievement test scores may also be used to gauge the effectiveness of innovative educational methods. Our political will to correct inequities between schools or even to experiment with educational programs will be affected if test scores fail to rise with innovation (Campbell, 1974). The failure to improve achievement test scores or low-achievement test scores may be used as arguments for drastic reform of the public school system, for privatization of public education and its multibillion dollar budget, and for giving parents vouchers to pay for private and religious schools.

Types of Tests

Achievement tests are standardized and normed nationally. The average score of children in different grades is computed. Schools and individual students are rated as scoring below, at, or above the average. By definition, 50 percent of students should score below average on this type of test.

Minimum competence tests required by state law allegedly avoid the problem of 50 percent falling below average. Minimum competence tests purport to examine basic skills in reading, writing, and arithmetic. State educational authorities specify the test items that, if passed, signify competence. There is no "average" score. Schools may be judged by the number of students who meet the arbitrarily set minimum passing score for each grade level.

Tests are adopted by legislatures without careful pretesting to see that the testing program required by law actually accomplishes its ends. Critics of minimum competency testing argued that, contrary to the legislatures' intent, the minimum quickly turned into the goal to be achieved. The minimum competency standard resulted in "dumbing down" schooling, they said.

Minimum competency tests have now been replaced with "high-stakes" testing (Amrein and Berliner, 2002). Acting under state education laws, commissions or state boards of education set educational standards in various subject matters and then write tests reflecting accomplishment in those areas. In theory, the local curriculum then reflects the content of the state educational standards. The state then sets a "passing score"—for example, 70 percent correct. There is no validation of the passing score against some other criterion measure of accomplishment. Items may be "easier" or "harder." The pass score is often set by committees of educators and laypeople. Sometimes members of the committees may be motivated to set passing scores higher or lower by political agendas. They may wish to avoid holding back too many students, or wish to declare the latest untested innovation a success. The committee-set scores are never validated against any empirical criterion. In effect, they represent very fallible human judgment. We have no clear understanding of what it means educationally to say that a student "passed" a high-stakes test.

Testing is characterized as *high-stakes* because so much may hinge on student performance on the test—high school graduation, promotion from grade to grade, reputation of a school, teacher and administrator compensation, renewal of teacher or principal contracts, financial reward from state to local schools, punishment of local schools and school districts for failure to meet standards, and public embarrassment and ridicule when schools "fail." Under the federal No Child Left Behind Act, schools that fail to improve under high-stakes testing face a variety of sanctions.

Testing programs are also "high-stakes" for test constructors and firms that supervise testing. Nevada, a relatively small state, signed a $13.35 million contract for three years with a not-for-profit firm to provide a variety of services in overseeing tests used to determine school standings under the federal No Child Left Behind Act (Associated Press, 2004). Leading educational publishers are entering the market created by the federal No Child Left Behind Act by helping teachers to prepare for high-stakes testing (PR Newswire, 2004). It is not too far-fetched to speculate that commercial interests will

496

CHAPTER 16
Psychological
Tests and
Discrimination
in Education
and
Employment

begin shaping common curricula in different states to make the marketing of such test preparation materials more efficient. These developments may be thought of as an unanticipated consequence of having high-stakes testing written into law.

The Heisenberg Uncertainty Principle: Social Science Version

Donald T. Campbell once stated a social science hypothesis: whenever a resource allocation depends on an arbitrary, quantitative index, one of two (or both) possibilities will emerge. One possibility is that the index itself (for our purposes, the test score) might be corrupted, and the second is that the process (teaching) is corrupted to produce the index. Amrein and Berliner (2002) speak of this as the *social science version of the Heisenberg uncertainty principle* in physics, to the effect that measuring a phenomenon will affect it.

Cheating is a method of "corrupting the index." There are many documented cases of cheating on school achievement tests. It is not only children who cheat. Teachers or principals give students advance notice about the content of the tests, tests get stolen and their content distributed to potential test takers, and wrong answers may be "corrected." In one school, a "whistleblower" accused a supervisor of encouraging teachers to score statewide tests leniently, so that more borderline students would pass the test. The whistleblower was subject to administrative harassment (Winerip, 2006b). Cheating may violate state laws and subject the violator to criminal prosecution, or they violate regulations and subject the teacher or principal to administrative discipline.

Schools and individual students may also "massage" the rules to raise their grades without cheating outright. The College Board, which owns the SAT, expressed some concern because, based on a psychologist's or doctor's note stating the student had a disability, almost 10 percent of students in highly selective New England private high schools were given extra time to take the test. None of the students in ten inner-city high schools in Los Angeles requested or received the accommodation (Weiss, 2000). Taking extra time may improve the test score, but may also reduce the validity of the test score in predicting academic performance. For example, giving students extra time on the LSAT to accommodate for handicaps produced higher scores, but the students underperformed in class in the first year compared to predictions from the LSAT scores obtained under nonstandard testing conditions (Thornton et al., 2000).

John Cannell found that most school districts reported their students scored above national averages for standardized achievement tests, a mathematical impossibility sometimes called the "Lake Woebegon effect" (named for Garrison Keillor's claim that in Lake Woebegon, his mythical community in Minnesota, all the children are above average). In theory, high-stakes testing avoids the Lake Woebegon effect because there is no "average" score. Cannell attributed the Lake Woebegon effect in standard testing to test construction and marketing methods that artificially inflated scores as well as to outright cheating or manipulation (Cannell, 2006; Hartocollis, 1999). Cannell (2006) found the same practices in effect twenty years after he published his first highly regarded exposé.

The process is corrupted when educational decisions are made to improve test scores rather than to increase learning and when procedures are used that arbitrarily inflate scores. An example of corrupting the process is found in New York City schools. New York pays special attention to test scores in fourth and in eighth grades. One New York City school had many more third graders (220) than fourth graders (180). Students who did poorly on tests in the third grade were held back. The better students advanced, and thus fourth-grade test scores that counted were better than if all students in the school who should have been in the fourth grade took the test (Winerip, 2003).

Some observers claim poorer students are being "pushed out" of high schools because they will fail state tests and affect the school's standing as measured by the percentage of students passing state tests. They are not classified as dropouts but are counted in categories that conceal the dropout rate, another variable used to measure school performance (Lewin and Medina, 2003).

Under the No Child Left Behind Act, schools are supposed to report test scores separately for children with disabilities. Schools apparently evade the requirements by excluding students from taking the tests, by not reporting at all, or by concealing the dropout rate (Schemo, 2004). Cannell (2006) described a number of other methods of cheating in use in schools that emphasize testing. Some states use either all or as many as half the questions in a test year after year so teachers can drill students on those test questions. Test preparation materials often have questions in them that also appear on the tests themselves (Cannell, 2006).

Many school districts have their own accountability systems and publish ratings of schools. School ratings made under federal guidelines may be different than the systems that states use; federal and state ratings of individual schools may differ as a consequence. For example, Governor Jeb Bush had announced that two-thirds of Florida's 3,100 schools were high performing. However, under federal standards, 75 percent of the schools were rated as low performing. One federal standard asks schools to report what percent of students took annual standard tests. The standard for compliance is 95 percent. Many schools had failed to meet that standard affecting their rank. The seemingly arbitrary difference in rank is confusing to parents who may not appreciate the nuances of the rating systems (Dillon, 2004).

The percent of students in a school taking a test is an important issue. Amrein and Berliner (2002) showed that there is a highly significant correlation between the proportion of students in a school taking a high-stakes test and the average scores on the test. The lower the percent of students taking the test, the higher the average test score for the school. If schools can encourage their better students and discourage their less capable students from taking the high-stakes test, the school's average score will be higher than if all students took the test.

The focus on test scores is especially disturbing because it is unclear what the tests actually tell us about learning and performance, especially if scores are elevated by a classroom emphasis on test-taking techniques rather than on subject mastery (Thornton et al., 2000). Cannell claims that West Virginia didn't change its test for eight years. Teachers simply drilled students on the test items that would appear on the test year after year. Scores showed great improvement but can anyone claim that learning improved as well?

Emphasizing testing may turn students off to school. Webb (1990) cites an incident in which a group of California high school students were so fed up with constant drilling on tests and pep talks about how important it was to do well that the students deliberately "blew" the test. Parents' and teachers' groups sometimes protest the emphasis on tests. Scarsdale, New York, is a very well to-do-community where children generally score well on tests. On one occasion, parents organized carpools to take their children out of school for the test, and then brought them back again to finish the school day. One hundred ninety-five of 290 eighth graders didn't take the test (Fitzgerald, 2001). Teachers protested against the fourth- and eighth-grade testing program in use in New York State, claiming the testing program was causing harm to students (Simon, 2001). Goodnough (2001) reported that veteran teachers who can

498

CHAPTER 16
Psychological
Tests and
Discrimination
in Education
and
Employment

request changes in their classroom assignments were opting out of those grades where the testing load was heavy. Some school districts began school earlier, reducing the summer break in order to get an earlier start on preparing for tests (Steinberg, 2002a). Children as young as preschoolers are also facing more standardized testing (Steinberg, 2002b).

Effect of High-Stakes Testing on Learning

If high-stakes testing results in intensive training in how to take the state's test, then scores on that test may go up—but does that represent useful education? Amrein and Berliner (2000) tested learning in 18 states that have legally required high-stakes testing by examining how well students in those states did on other indices of student learning, academic achievement and academic accomplishment. They had access to data on the American College Testing program (ACT); the SAT; the National Assessment of Educational Progress (NAEP), a standard test administered nationally; and Advanced Placement (AP) examination scores. Amrein and Berliner tested the following hypothesis about learning: "If high-stakes testing of students really induces teachers to upgrade curricula and instruction or leads students to study harder or better, then scores should also increase on other independent assessments" (p. 21).

Any nonexperimental study without random assignment of students to conditions creates difficulties in interpreting the results. Amrein and Berliner (2002) used a quasi-experimental time series design to examine changes in test scores on other tests year by year before and after the introduction of high-stakes testing. First, examining the ACT data, two-thirds of states that used high school graduation examinations as the high-stakes test showed *decreases* in ACT performance after the tests were introduced compared to before. Similarly, 56 percent of states that used the high-stakes graduation exams showed small decreases in SAT performance after the introduction of the high-stakes test. Moreover, participation in the SAT examinations fell in 61 percent of the high-stakes states. Amrein and Berliner found a lack of impact on the NAEP math tests: "High-stakes testing policies did not usually improve the performance of students on the grade 4 NAEP math tests" (p. 52). They came to a similar conclusion about the grade 8 NAEP math tests and about the results of the NAEP reading tests—that performance on other measures was not consistently improved by high-stakes testing. Cannell (2006) reported similar findings that students could "read" on Tennessee or Texas or California tests but not on national tests.

Berliner et al. demonstrated that gains on the NAEP reading tests shown in some states were correlated with a decrease in the percent of students taking the test. In other words, if some students were excluded from taking the tests, the average score for those who did take the test was higher. Amrein and Berliner say, "These exclusionary policies were probably the reason for the apparent increases in achievement in several states" (p. 53). They conclude, "Both the uncertainty associated with high-stakes testing data, and the questionable validity of high-stakes tests as indicators of the domains they are intended to reflect suggest this is a failed policy initiative" (p. 54). (See Cannell, 2006, for similar results in different school systems.)

Measuring the effects of instruction and establishing accountability are desirable to improve education. However, the American Psychological Association (2001) and the American Education Research Association (2000) both caution strongly against relying on the results of a single test for high-stakes decisions. Both statements also caution against unintended consequences of high-stakes testing.

The reliance on a single test score was pressed by politicians and enacted through legislation. Educational funds have been diverted to publishers and consulting firms to promote training on tests. The training may constitute an educational distortion. The purpose of education is not simply to raise test scores, although proponents of high-stakes testing point to raised test scores and increasing numbers of students who meet the passing cutoff. Amrein and Berliner (2002) assert, "The proper goal of school learning is transfer of learning, that is the application or use of what is learned in one domain or context to that of another domain or context. . . . School instruction that can be characterized as training is ordinarily a narrow form of learning, where transfer of learning is measured on tasks that are highly similar to those used in the training" (p. 13). (See Cannell, 2006, for further examples.) High-stakes testing programs and the law itself make no provision for assessing the transfer of learning, and may inadvertently impede achieving broader educational goals. The hasty and thoughtless legislative adoption of measures based on what might be faulty assumptions (e.g., educational failure is the consequence of lazy teachers who are inadequately managed) has not demonstrably improved education.

Tests and Employment

The use of tests for job selection came under attack with the passage of Title VII of the Civil Rights Act of 1964 (see Box 16.5). Title VII was designed to protect workers against discriminatory practices by employers. As we can see from *Griggs v. Duke Power Company* 1971; see below), in the not-too-distant past, employment discrimination was open and severe. Later, psychological tests became part of the problem.

Disparate Impact and Business Necessity

In *Griggs v. Duke Power Company* (1971), the first challenge to the discriminatory use of employment tests to reach the Supreme Court, the important question presented was whether evidence of discriminatory impact without overt discriminatory actions (disparate treatment) was sufficient to bring a suit under Title VII of the Civil Rights Act.

Before 1965, the Duke Power Company had openly discriminated racially in its hiring practices. After Title VII, the company added two new requirements for all job positions except laborer. Individuals had to have a high school education, and had to achieve a satisfactory score on two professionally standardized tests used in personnel selection—the Wonderlic Personnel Test (of general intelligence) and the Bennett Mechanical Comprehension Test. Neither test had been validated against a standard of

---

BOX 16.5

Title VII of the Civil Rights Act of 1964
The act states, in part,

Sec. 703(a) It shall be an unlawful employment practice for an employer . . . (2) to limit, segregate, or classify his employees or applicants for employment in any way which would deprive or tend to deprive any individual of employment opportunities or otherwise adversely affect his status as an employee, because of such individual's race, color, religion, sex, or national origin.

(h) . . . it shall not be an unlawful employment practice for an employer . . . to give and to act upon the results of any professionally developed ability test provided that such test, its administration or action upon the results is not designed, intended or used to discriminate because of race, color, religion, sex or national origin.

500

CHAPTER 16
Psychological
Tests and
Discrimination
in Education
and
Employment

BOX 16.6

The Four-fifths Rule

When is disparate impact due to tests legally significant? The Equal Employment Opportunity Guidelines use a 4/5ths, or an 80 percent rule. A test has an apparent adverse impact if the proportion of *minority* applicants selected by the test is less than 80 percent of the proportion of *majority* applicants selected by the test, assuming no differential validity. For example, if a test score selects 10 percent of majority applicants, it has a disparate impact if it selects less than 8 percent of minority applicants.

actual performance within the company. Six percent of African Americans applicants passed the two tests, compared with 58 percent of the whites.

The U.S. Supreme Court ruled that it is not the employer's discriminatory *intent* that mattered. The discriminatory (disparate) *impact* of a test on the minority population triggered Title VII's protection. The opinion said,

> The Act proscribes not only overt discrimination but also practices that are fair in form, but discriminatory in operation. The touchstone is business necessity. If an employment practice which operates to exclude Negroes cannot be shown to be related to job performance, the practice is prohibited.

In other words, once a test was shown to have a **disparate impact** (to affect opportunities for employment for different groups differently), the employer had to prove a business necessity for using the test. The Court cited guidelines promulgated by the Equal Employment Opportunity Commission (EEOC), the government agency responsible for enforcing Title VII. The guidelines required that employers have data showing that a test is significantly correlated with job performance (29 CFR Sec. 1607/4(c)).

In *Albemarle Paper Co. v. Moody* (1975), a case involving another company that had openly discriminated against African Americans in the past, the U.S. Supreme Court considered how an employer could validate a test to show business necessity. Citing the American Psychological Association professional standards for test validation (1974), the *Albemarle* opinion set high standards for establishing that the use of tests was indeed a "business necessity."

Backing Off: Discriminatory Intent and Lower Standards of Validation

Griggs and *Albemarle* were Title VII cases (statutory). In a subsequent case, *Washington v. Davis* (1976), testing was challenged as a violation of the Due Process Clause of the Fifth Amendment to the Constitution. The case involved an employment test used by the District of Columbia police department, which had a disparate impact on African American applicants. Congress had said that Title VII did not apply to the District of Columbia, and for technical legal reasons the Fifth Amendment was used as the constitutional basis for the challenge, rather than the Fourteenth Amendment.

The U.S. Supreme Court ruled that a *constitutionally* based challenge, unlike a Title VII case, required a finding of *discriminatory intent* by the employer. If the selection procedure was neutral on its face, and served a permissible government end, disparate impact alone was not enough to require a remedy. The Court upheld the use of the police selection test, which it said was neutral on its face and served a legitimate government end of ensuring that police candidates had adequate verbal communication skills.

The U.S. Supreme Court's decision in *Washington v. Davis* watered down validation standards. Quoting the APA Standards for Educational and Psychological Tests (APA, AERA, and NCME, 1974), the Court recognized three types of validity—criterion validity, construct validity, and content validity. The Court accepted *content validity* (items are obviously related to the skills or knowledge being assessed; see Box 16.2) as a distinct method of validation. In doing so, it relieved employers of the necessity of showing that tests actually predicted job related performance measures. The test in the District of Columbia did predict performance in the training academy. That decision opened the door to validate tests against training criteria as well as job performance criteria.

In *Wards Cove Packing Co. v. Atonio* (1989), the U.S. Supreme Court made it even more difficult for plaintiffs to bring a job discrimination case. In response to this case, and a few other restrictive interpretations of Title VII, Congress eased the requirements for proof of job discrimination somewhat in the 1991 amendments to the Civil Rights Act. Even so, it is still not simple for plaintiffs to bring a successful suit. Courts are now deciding employment cases on the basis of highly technical evidence. Expert witnesses play important roles in these cases because of the complexities of evaluating appropriate comparison groups and establishing the validity of different selection procedures (Schwartz and Goodman, 1992). Over time, the courts made it more difficult to bring civil rights suits generally (see *Alexander v. Sandoval,* 2001) and easier for employers to defend the suits. Moreover, employers became more sophisticated in their use of tests, reducing the likelihood of a suit (Shoben, 2004). There are probably fewer suits brought on these grounds than in years past.

Professional Licensing

Licensing examinations, whose purposes are to protect "the public's health, welfare, safety and morals," are standardized instruments like other cognitive tests. Their use also has a disparate impact on minorities. For example, Dorsey (1983) studied the performance of minority candidates on licensing examinations in cosmetology in Missouri and in Illinois. All the candidates had already met education and training requirements. Nonetheless, minority candidates failed the test more often than white candidates. The workers who failed didn't leave the field. They tended to work in neighborhood shops operating out of homes rather than in better-paying shops, which offered more services at higher prices. Dorsey concluded that licensing requirements limited the upward mobility of unsuccessful candidates. There was no evidence the unlicensed cosmetologists were less competent or that they harmed consumers more often than licensed practitioners.

Court challenges brought against licensing examinations have failed. A plaintiff would have to demonstrate discriminatory intent under constitutional standards before a state would be forbidden to use a licensing examination (Herbsleb, Sales, and Overcast, 1985).

Hogan (1983) argues that professional licensing does little to improve the quality of professional services. Moreover, licensing with its implied sanctions does not protect the public very well (Carroll and Gaston, 1983); very few licensed practitioners are subject to professional discipline. Since licensing examinations have a disparate impact on minorities and do not meet the objective of protecting the public, Hogan suggests that alternative means for fulfilling the objectives of licensing might be explored.

502

CHAPTER 16
Psychological
Tests and
Discrimination
in Education
and
Employment

⊠ Tests Defended

As a result of lawsuits and controversy, many employers stopped using tests for selection purposes, relying on interviews or other less objective selection devices instead. Schmidt and Hunter (1981) claim that there has been a strong social cost in productivity as a result. They argue that the relationship between test scores and measures of productivity on the job is linear and highly significant statistically, if not perfect (see also Rushton and Jensen, 2005). Selecting personnel from the top of the test score range and going on down toward the bottom is an effective way of selecting productive workers. They claim that employer training costs increased, employer training program dropout rates increased, and output of goods and services became less efficient when test use was dropped.

Rushton and Jensen (2005) reviewed a mass of evidence for the theory that tests are biased and unfair to some minorities. They reviewed psychometric evidence that showed "similar patterns of internal item-consistency and predictive validity for all groups" (p. 241). In other words, the tests worked in about the same way in white and African American populations. There was no psychometric evidence of bias. The tests predicted performance for both groups equally well. If items on tests have different meanings for members of different racial groups, the pattern of item intercorrelations would be expected to be different in the two groups. They are not (Rushton and Jensen, 2005, pp. 242–243).

A central psychometric concept of intelligence is the *g*, or general intelligence, factor. Rushton and Jenson (2005) hypothesize that "*g*" is in large measure an inherited quality. It is this proposition that makes their work so socially controversial. The statistical methods of deriving *g* produce the same results in samples of whites and African Americans. Jensen and Rushton (2005) assert that the degree to which a test measures *g* is the degree to which the test score correlates with "scholastic and workplace performance" (p. 245). The results are the same if one uses supervisors' ratings as a criterion, as in the *Albemarle* case, or other indices of actual job performance as the criterion. General ability tests show just about the same size of validity coefficients across a wide range of jobs, from mechanic to insurance broker. The same tests predict success in training and predict performance on the job (Schmidt and Hunter, 1981; Cole, 1981).

Critics of tests note that while the validity coefficients for minority and majority groups are similar, they are not very high. Selection using test scores may produce less error than other methods but will still produce both false negatives (people who are predicted to do well on the job, but who don't) and false positives (people who are predicted to do poorly, but who would do well on the job). Mean differences between racial groups do not apply to all individuals. The distributions of scores overlap. Many African Americans exceed the white mean score and many whites fall below the African American mean (Rushton and Jensen, 2005). Social and legal rules should be written to permit the fullest development of each individual. However, if we use tests for selection or to allocate educational resources, in the foreseeable future, we will produce disparities in disparate opportunity for members of different racial groups. All groups may not appear proportionately to numbers in the population in all educational and occupational settings. To minimize apparent discrimination, Rushton and Jensen (2005) suggest that test makers emphasize face validity so that the items on tests used for selection appear to reflect job functions more closely.

To the critics, the validity of tests is not the central issue, nor efficiency the central value. The problem is one of being clear on the nature of racial differences in test scores and working to create "opportunities for growth and advancement" (Sternberg, 2005, p. 300). Moreover, critics also believe that the hereditarian position on group differences in intelligence (i.e., that intelligence is genetically inherited) is far from established and that it is socially divisive and destructive.

It is difficult to carry out this discussion in dispassionate terms. Gottfredson (2005b) writes that she has been subject to professional scorn and attacks by those who fervently disagree with the inherited nature of racial differences in intelligence she had written about. The arguments will continue because those who are opposed to the hereditarian view of racial differences in intelligence question whether the evidence is as firmly established as proponents assert.

However, the argument is less likely to go on through the courts. The U.S. Supreme Court handed down a sweeping decision in *Alexander v. Sandoval* (2001) that makes it very difficult to bring the type of lawsuits that challenged the use of tests under the 1964 Civil Rights Act. Individuals can still bring an action to vindicate individual rights, but they must prove intentional discrimination against them to prevail. Under this decision, actions based on evidence of disparate impact can be brought only by some agency of government. The decision means that many of the types of lawsuits discussed in this chapter will no longer be able to be brought in private suits under federal civil rights law. The cases may now be of historical interest as a case study in the interaction between law and psychology.

The *Sandoval* decision is an interpretation of sections of the Civil Rights Act, and is not a constitutionally based interpretation. That means that Congress could, if it chose, amend the civil rights law to permit the suits. Suits may still be brought in state courts on the basis of state law, but the decision underscores the dynamic and ever-changing nature of the fields of law and psychology.

Does Affirmative Action Affect Minorities Adversely?

While many people strongly believe in the necessity of affirmative action, few embrace it enthusiastically. It is a good example of "problem creation through problem solution." Affirmative action has opened the ranks of the middle class to many capable people, and has benefited the nation by giving gifted individuals the opportunity to realize their talents. However, it has also produced negative effects, including adverse psychological effects on some of those it benefits. In his opinion in *Grutter,* Supreme Court Justice Clarence Thomas, the second African American Supreme Court justice, remarked on the problem:

> The majority of blacks are admitted to the Law School because of discrimination [law school's admission policy favoring blacks], and because of this policy all are tarred as undeserving. This problem of stigma does not depend on determinacy as to whether those stigmatized are actually the "beneficiaries" of racial discrimination. When blacks take positions in the highest places of government, industry, or academia, it is an open question today whether their skin color played a part in their advancement. The question itself is the stigma—because either racial discrimination did play a role, in which case the person may be deemed "otherwise unqualified," or it did not, in which case asking the question itself unfairly marks those blacks who would succeed without discrimination. (*Grutter v. Bollinger,* 2003)

Steele (1997) discussed a number of psychological factors that might relate to poorer performance on tests and in school among African American students. These factors

504

CHAPTER 16
Psychological
Tests and
Discrimination
in Education
and
Employment

may also be relevant to understanding special stresses faced by African Americans in integrated educational settings in addition to those discussed by Justice Thomas. Rates of college completion and GPA on graduation among African Americans are somewhat lower than the average for all students (Steele, 1997). The result is what Steele calls *stereotype threat*. When "one is at risk of confirming a negative stereotype about one's group," Steele writes, "or of being seen or treated stereotypically, [it] causes emotional distress and pressure" (Steele, 1997, p. 618). The sense of racial vulnerability and ensuing anxiety may affect the willingness to strive, and thus affect performance. Stereotype threat is triggered by the "mere recognition that a negative group stereotype could apply to oneself in a given situation" (Steele, 1997, p. 617).

Affirmative action, by feeding into majority stereotypes about the competence of African American students, could be fueling stereotype threat. At the same time, by integrating work places at higher levels, affirmative action has done a great deal to compensate for discrimination and disadvantage, to begin to shift stereotypes, and as the U.S. Supreme Court recognized in *Grutter*, to provide the nation with the human capital it vitally needs.

The public policy implications of racial differences in mean test scores in education and in employment are far from obvious (Sternberg, 2005; Nisbett, 2005). We have made some progress using social science tools to support litigation and to influence legislation in moving toward an open society. The next generation of social action may well occur on other fronts, but social science tools and data will continue to be relevant.

Summary

Standardized psychological tests are one of the most important accomplishments of psychology as a science. The tests play central roles in the lives of many people. In recent years, the tests have come under legal scrutiny for social fairness. Because agencies of government frequently use tests to make resource allocation decisions (assignment to schools or to special classes, prizes awarded, and so on), tests have been challenged in lawsuits. They have also been challenged on ideological grounds. Some of the challenges succeeded in the courts, and others have not. In the 1960s, Congress passed laws making possible discrimination challenges to tests used by many employers. Initially these legal challenges succeeded, but with time the practices that were accepted as legitimizing tests (business necessity) became less strict. Nonetheless, the challenge to tests in the legal forum has required psychologists to articulate more carefully the basis for their practices.

The challenges to tests went hand in hand with affirmative action programs. Often when tests were not the exclusive basis for selection and other criteria aimed at increasing diverse representation were also used, many more minority members were able to enter school and college programs. When tests were weighted more heavily in the selection process, the number of minority members entering some graduate and professional schools declined. Observers asked whether affirmative action programs had some negative effects on those who apparently benefited from preferences.

Tests have also been challenged as having a gender bias. One result of the challenge was to modify the PSAT to try to equalize the rate at which males and females were awarded National Merit Scholarships.

Tests of competence and academic achievement have generated less social controversy then tests of general ability and aptitude. In an effort to improve education, federal guidelines and state laws have mandated increasing numbers of testing programs. These efforts to improve education by improving accountability through testing seem to be simplistic.

Although the adversarial process in a courtroom has distinct limits for settling scientific questions, it has forced social scientists to be explicit about their premises in a public forum.

This is an area in which the interplay between scientific considerations and public policy has been important. Psychologists have been educated to the fact that issues of test bias that were formerly academic in nature do have real impact on people's lives. The use of tests in many contexts can be defended, but we are also faced with other issues of fairness. Public policy problems related to opportunity cannot be dismissed or solved merely by noting that tests are technically sound.

Discussion Questions

1. In several different chapters in this book, we have noted that clinical judgments are on the average less accurate than statistically based judgments. How does this bear on the arguments about the fairness of using tests versus other criteria for admissions and employment decisions?
2. How might people's behavior be affected by the stress of "stereotype threat"? How could you test your hypothesis? Can you think of any measures that would reduce stereotype threat?
3. How can anyone measure the long-term benefits and burdens of using affirmative action in professional schools such as law and medicine?
4. Psychologists have long debated the construct of "intelligence" and how it is or isn't related to what "intelligence" tests measure. Do you think there is one general characteristic that we can call intelligence and that contributes to many more specific abilities? What kind of empirical findings would support your position? Weaken it?
5. Imagine you are asked to develop a set of requirements prospective X-ray technicians must meet to get a state license. What would you do? What if the measures you selected were known to have a disparate impact on some groups?
6. Imagine that you are asked to design a method of assigning students to public schools which does not use race as a criterion because of legal limitations, but which will achieve racial diversity. What would you do?

Key Terms

achievement tests	differential validity	minimum competence tests
affirmative action	disparate impact	nature/nurture
bias	diversity index	norm
Binet and Simon	face validity	prediction fairness
California Proposition 209	fairness	predictive validity
comparison group	Francis Galton	preschool programs
construct validity	general intelligence	referendum
content validity	intelligence	selection fairness
corrupting the index	just deserts	standard administration
corrupting the process	*Larry P. v. Riles*	tracking
criterion validity	merit	validity coefficients

CHAPTER **17**

Law, Ethics, and the Regulation of the Professions

The work of helping professionals, researchers, and teachers is regulated. **Regulation** means that rules are prescribed by a competent agency to direct, control, limit, or prohibit actions of those subject to its authority. Regulation is intended to redress the imbalance in power and knowledge between professionals and those who may be dependent on their ministration.

Professions seek to be self-regulating. Members of professions contend that others without their advanced education, special knowledge, and special skills cannot oversee their work. Therefore, they argue that members of the public do not have the knowledge to evaluate the services they receive from professionals. For example, patients have to trust the doctor who orders blood tests to select the right tests, to evaluate them, and to explain the results accurately. Patients or clients can't do these tasks for themselves. Because of the imbalance, society gives clients an enforceable right to insist that professionals act for their welfare.

There are three ways of regulating professionals in the United States: (1) state licensing, (2) professional ethical codes, and (3) malpractice suits. The state uses its power to pass laws authorizing a state agency to issue **licenses,** to set standards for licensees, and to enforce the standards by exacting penalties. **Professional associations** establish ethical codes to protect the public welfare by setting and publishing educational and practice standards for members. The codes are enforced through the professional association's moral authority and through social sanctions (e.g., expulsion from membership). Standards of practice are also enforced legally through malpractice suits brought by aggrieved clients against practitioners who fail in their **duty** to care for the client. All forms of professional regulation occur in an elaborate social context. The interests of the professions, their clients, insurance companies, legislatures, and the public interact to affect what the laws and procedures mean in practice.

In this chapter, we will look at the different mechanisms for ensuring competent and responsible professional mental health care. We will go on to discuss litigation arising from adults' assertions that, in the course of therapy, they remembered long-repressed incidents of childhood abuse. This is an area where lack of professional consensus about underlying scientific and ethical questions has led to both painful disagreements and new programs of research. We will review and discuss

- legal regulation.
- definitions of professional misconduct.
- disciplinary procedures and penalties.
- ethical codes and their principles, procedures, and penalties for violation.
- malpractice suits based on sex with psychotherapy clients.
- malpractice suits based on recovered memory therapy.

508

CHAPTER 17
Law, Ethics,
and the
Regulation of
the Professions

Government Regulation: Licensing and Certification

Legal regulation is based on the state's **police power** to set rules regarding health and safety and to enforce them through penalties for violations. The U.S. Supreme Court reviewed a case in which a physician's license had been suspended for six months because he had been convicted of a crime unrelated to the practice of his profession. In upholding the suspension, the Court said,

> It is elemental that a state has broad power to establish and enforce standards of conduct within its borders relative to the health of everyone there. It is a vital part of the state's police power. The state's discretion in that field extends naturally to the regulation of all professions concerned with health. (*Barsky v. Board of Regents,* 1954, p. 449)

States regulate the professions through licensing or **certification** laws that establish qualifications for obtaining a professional title and set standards of practice (see Box 17.1). Psychology is a regulated profession in all the states, as is social work (see http://kspope.com/licensing/index.php for information about licensing laws in each state and in Canada; for social work, see http://www.aswb.org).

While the purpose of licensing or certification is to protect the public, the policy also creates an exclusive "guild," restricting entry into the field. Membership has advantages for the professional who succeeds in gaining entry. Confidential communications between most licensed professionals and their clients are **legally privileged** (largely protected against compelled disclosure in a legal action). Insurance companies usually will not pay an unlicensed practitioner for services. Licensed members of the profession may have a social and economic interest in keeping membership limited. For example, most Ph.D. (doctor of philosophy) or Psy.D. (doctor of psychology) psychologists wish to retain the doctorate as the minimum educational credential for independent practice in psychology (DeLeon, 2000), although there is no research to support the proposition that master's-level psychologists provide inferior services or couldn't practice independently (Sleek, 1996). There are also many social workers in independent practice with an M.S.W. degree (masters of social work), who are licensed separately under different standards.

BOX 17.1

Licensing and Certification

A licensing law restricts the use of a professional title and the legislatively defined practice to members of the licensed professions. The laws establish qualifications for becoming a licensed member of a profession and grant some professions a virtual monopoly over certain areas of practice. Thus, only physicians may engage in surgery, and only lawyers can represent others in court.

State certification laws may include a definition of practice, but do not restrict the practice to certified practitioners. Certification laws restrict the use of a title only. For example, in a state where mental health titles are certified, anyone can call him- or herself a therapist and practice therapy, but he or she may not call him- or herself a psychologist or social worker if that title is certified.

Oversight and Discipline

509

Government
Regulation:
Licensing and
Certification

Licensing laws ensure that titled practitioners are qualified by virtue of education and experience to provide a professional service. When they have grievances against a licensed professional, clients can complain to the state agency that supervises that type of professional. Thus, the state exercises indirect supervision of practice through its ability to grant and take away licenses and to otherwise discipline practitioners for misconduct.

Professional misconduct. State licensing laws and regulations define **professional misconduct.** Unprofessional conduct includes such acts as exploiting a client for financial gain; fee splitting (sharing a fee with someone who has not performed services); conduct evidencing "moral unfitness"; and breaching confidentiality without prior consent of the patient or client. A complaint of professional misconduct is processed by a designated state agency or licensing board (see Box 17.2 for a generic description of processing a complaint; see Box 17.3 for sample decisions and penalties).

A stressful process. Resources allocated for investigation and adjudication of complaints are limited, and their resolution can take a long time. In New York State, for example, about half the complaints were still unsettled two years after their initiation. The process is stressful for everyone involved. Licensed practitioners charged with an offense face a threat to reputation and livelihood. They must undergo an intrusive investigation, and may have to bear the cost of legal counsel even if the accusations are ultimately dismissed. Some claim the legal standards for unprofessional conduct are too vague, the decisions arbitrary, and the disciplinary boards overly harsh.

Other critics claim that too few complaints are registered. They believe the process makes it difficult for clients to complain. It takes intelligence and persistence to find out how to file a complaint, and it is often difficult to prove the charge. The complainant,

---

BOX 17.2

Disciplinary Proceedings

Disciplinary procedures are similar in all the states. Each state must provide due process. Anyone may initiate a complaint of misconduct that the state must investigate. If the initial investigator finds "substantial evidence" of misconduct, the complaint is reviewed again by one or more state licensing board members. If warranted, the reviewers prepare written charges specifying the misconduct.

If the violation is minor (e.g., professional advertising or a record-keeping error), it may be resolved by an administrative warning that is kept confidential, and is not evidence of guilt. If the violation is serious, the accused is entitled to an adversary hearing before a panel appointed by the state board. The accused can be represented by an attorney, can cross-examine witnesses, can produce evidence and witnesses, and can subpoena witnesses. Rules of evidence are informal. After the hearing, the panel issues a finding of fact, stating the evidence pointing to a violation (guilt) or innocence on each charge, and a recommendation for a penalty. State laws usually provide for several levels of appeal within the agency; when these are exhausted, and the professional has lost, the professional can bring an action in a state court.

510

CHAPTER 17
Law, Ethics,
and the
Regulation of
the Professions

BOX 17.3

Sample Decisions and Penalties for Professional Misconduct

Breached confidentiality without consent	Censure, reprimand, $1,000 fine
Failed to maintain records of therapy and evaluation	2 years probation, $1,500 fine
Verbally abused patient; multiple relationships with patient; signed billing for services not rendered; exercised undue influence on patient to drop accusations of professional misconduct; sexual relationship with two supervisees	Revocation of license; $15,000 fine
Conviction for criminal possession of marijuana	1 year probation; $1,000 fine
Conviction for Medicaid fraud	2 years probation; $2,500 fine
Neither admitted nor denied charges of referring two patients to a palm reader and aiding and abetting the unlicensed practice of psychology.	Must successfully pass oral licensing examination and two educational courses, after which the charges will be withdrawn
Traveled to Las Vegas with client; gave client massage in hotel room; invited client to and engaged with client in nude hot tubbing at psychologist's home; bartered therapy for nude massage; shifted focus of therapy from client's presenting problem to his interest in extraterrestrial encounters	License revoked; costs of $9,205
Gross negligence in failing to accurately use and interpret two psychological tests that led to using an inappropriate therapy technique that led to patient harm	Five years probation

New York Board of Regents and the California Board of Psychology.

who already feels victimized, may have embarrassing details of his or her psychological life exposed in the hearing. The defense may claim the complaint is a product of the patient's psychopathology. For example, a common defense in complaints of sexual misconduct by the licensed professional is that the complainant suffers from a "borderline personality disorder" (Gutheil, 1989; Pope and Bouhoutsos, 1986). *Borderline personality disorder* is "a pervasive pattern of instability of interpersonal relationships, self-image, and affects, and marked impulsivity that begins by early adulthood and is present in a variety of contexts" (*DSM-IV-TR*; American Psychiatric Association, 2000, p. 685). Finally, critics of the licensing system claim that it is not able to control unethical practitioners who can continue practicing without the professional title even if their license is revoked (see Boxes 17.3 and 17.4).

New Sources of Complaints

Medical insurance and managed care. Insurance companies may reimburse psychologists for treating specified diagnoses only. The practitioner may be tempted to make a diagnosis not on clinical grounds, but on the basis of requirements for reimbursement (Kutchins and Kirk, 1997). Insurance companies may prosecute mental health providers who make false or fraudulent claims for insurance (Foxhall, 2000). If

> ## BOX 17.4
>
> ### Toothless Watchdogs?
>
> A psychologist in Idaho had his license suspended for ethical violations, including carrying on personal relationships with patients and misusing his influence over his patients. His license was suspended for three years, and he was required to take college courses in psychotherapy. However, he continued his practice. He took down his psychologist sign, and advertised in the Yellow Pages as a "counselor." He was ineligible to do evaluations for state agencies and courts, and insurers who didn't cover unlicensed practitioners wouldn't reimburse his patients. However, his practice was unchanged otherwise (Barenti, 1997).

convictions follow, the licensing board will probably institute an action to discipline the licensed professional.

Forensic practices and custody disputes. In order to augment their incomes free of the demands of **managed care,** some mental health providers with minimal specialty training may take on forensic work. (Managed care is a system of oversight of insurance claims and also of setting professional fees for defined services.) Their inexperience with forensic work may put them at greater risk of being the subject of an ethical or licensing complaint, especially in custody disputes.

An expert witness testifying in court usually has **immunity from suit** (i.e., he or she can't be sued successfully) stemming from the court testimony. However, a licensing board is not a court. State courts in Washington permitted the state's psychology examining board to discipline a psychologist based upon complaints stemming from his testimony in custody disputes (*Deatherage v. State of Washington Examining Board of Psychology*, 1997). The board concluded that the psychologist had committed misconduct in his court testimony in three custody disputes. The board and the courts deemed his failure to qualify statements, his mischaracterization of statements, his failure to verify information, and his interpretation of test data adequate grounds for a ten-year revocation of his professional license. Decisions such as *Deatherage* may allow unsuccessful parties in bitter cases, such as divorce and custody disputes, to punish opposing experts by filing licensing complaints.

Some argue that the potential for a disciplinary action will cause practitioners to become suitably cautious in their examinations and in what they are willing to assert in court. However, others believe it is important that experts feel free to present unpopular and controversial findings that might contribute to just outcome (see Box 17.5).

The Meadow case (see Box 17.5) concerned a criminal trial in which theoretically the adversarial system could offer defendants some protection against experts who made errors or speculated beyond their expertise. In custody disputes there is often, though not always, only one expert hired at the court's request. Custody disputes are often highly contentious. They are subject to frustrations and delays, and the custody evaluator's opinion may be decisive in influencing the judge (Eaton, 2004). The process itself may add to the emotional intensity of the custody dispute and the resulting desire to punish a successful opponent.

There do not seem to be recognized standards for who can be a custody evaluator, nor are there standard procedures for the evaluation. Ethical codes and their enforcement mechanisms may provide a form of regulatory control (Eaton, 2004). Seven to 10 percent of the ethics complaints made to the APA involve custody evaluations.

512

CHAPTER 17
Law, Ethics,
and the
Regulation of
the Professions

BOX 17.5

Legal Case in Point

Sir Roy Meadow, a pediatrician internationally renowned for his work with Munchausen syndrome by proxy (in which a mother harms her child or falsifies medical information to gain medical attention for the child) and with child abuse, was disciplined by the Fitness to Practice Panel in London because of his testimony in a murder trial. The panel found that he misused statistics to assert that the deaths of two children in the same family could not have been accidental. The panel said that he hadn't sufficiently checked the accuracy of his use of the statistics before testifying as an expert. The panel felt his errors were so egregious that his "name should be erased from the Medical Register." In effect, he lost his license to practice (General Medical Council, 2005).

Sir Roy appealed. Mr. Justice Collins ruled that the GMC's punishment was unduly harsh: "He made one mistake, which was to misunderstand and misinterpret the statistics . . . but that does not justify a finding of serious professional misconduct." Mr. Justice Collins noted that since the ruling, pediatricians had become unwilling to testify in child abuse cases. He said, "There can be no doubt that the administration of justice has been seriously damaged by the decision of the FPP in this case. . . . What is of fundamental importance is that a witness can be assured that if he gives his evidence honestly and in good faith, he will not be involved in any proceedings brought against him seeking to penalize him."

The GMC has been given leave to appeal Justice Collins's decision to Britain's highest court, the House of Lords. The Council is defending not just their specific decision, but their right to be the ultimate regulators of medical ethics. "Such immunity [from disciplinary action for testimony] would place doctors, and other professionals, beyond the reach of their regulator when writing reports for the courts or giving evidence" (Feeman, 2006).

The American Psychological Association Ethical Code

Most professional associations have **ethical codes.** The American Psychological Association (APA) first adopted an ethical code in 1953. Members were asked to submit "critical incidents" that, in their view, exemplified unethical practices. The submissions were reviewed and classified by an APA Committee on Ethics. The committee analyzed the concrete examples of what members thought were unethical actions to articulate the underlying ethical principles (Faden and Beauchamp, 1986). The APA revises the code periodically, the most recent taking effect in 2003. To reflect social and technological change, the new code extends the coverage of the ethics code to psychologists' professional activities using the Internet, e-mail, telephone, or other electronic transmissions (Introduction, 2002 Code; Principle 4.10(c)) See http://www.apa.ogr/ethics for the full text of the code of ethics and commentary on it). The National Association of Social Work has a code of ethics for its members, last revised in 1999. It is similar in its values and principles to the APA code of ethics (see http://www.socialworkers.org for the full text of the code of ethics).

The APA's code of ethics reflects areas of broad consensus among members and areas of compromise. Consumer protection is balanced with protecting the integrity of the profession and the interests of practitioners. Many of the ethical principles are stated in broad language to allow for different points of view within the organization and to allow for flexibility in application. The 2002 code emphasizes that the standards should allow for professional judgment and "guard against a set of rigid rules that might be quickly outmoded" (Introduction). Principle 2.04 says, "Psychologists' work is based on established scientific and professional knowledge of the discipline." The phrase *established scientific knowledge* might mean that psychologists should use only "empirically verified" methods. However, the phrase *professional knowledge of the discipline* allows for reliance on clinical experience. In this way, one ethical principle accommodates both those who believe that all clinical work, all forensic work, and all public statements should have a firm basis in underlying quantitative research, and those who believe that decisions can and must be made on the basis of experience and the clinical, theoretical, and qualitative research literature.

Underlying Ethical Principles

Right–duty relationship. Ethical principles are implemented through acts in a relationship. Psychologists and clients have a right–duty relationship. **Rights** are "powerful assertions of claims that demand respect and status" (Faden and Beauchamp, 1986, p. 6). Once a right is recognized, it entails "the imposition of a duty on others either not to interfere or to provide something" (p. 7). The right–duty relationship, to be meaningful, must be enforceable.

The ethical code specifies how psychologists should relate to clients, to students, to other professionals, or to the general public within the right–duty relationship. Two key principles underlie many of the specific provisions: autonomy and beneficence.

Client autonomy. The ethical code establishes respect for client autonomy as a key principle. Principle E of the 2002 Ethical Code states, "Psychologists respect the dignity and worth of all people and the rights of individuals to privacy, confidentiality, and self-determination." **Autonomy** refers to personal rule of self, based on free and informed choices (Faden and Beauchamp, 1986). Psychologists must struggle with the problem of dealing ethically with people whose capacity for autonomy is limited, for example, people whose competence to make decisions may be impaired and children who are not legally qualified to make their own decisions.

Beneficence. A second central principle is beneficence (Principle A, 2002 Code). **Beneficence** means that the professional has a fiduciary duty to protect the client's welfare. A **fiduciary duty** refers to a formal relationship in which one person relies upon and trusts another. The person who is relied on may not take selfish advantage of this trust. Professionals are obliged to work to benefit their clients, to remove or prevent harm to them, and to do no intentional harm (Principle A, 2002 Code, regarding **nonmaleficence** (first do no harm). Beneficence underlies much of the ethical code and is the value basis for the tort of malpractice (see Chapter 3).

When a client or patient does not want to accept treatment or counsel that the professional feels is necessary, the principle of beneficence may clash with the principle of client autonomy. However, the professional cannot undertake whatever intervention he or she thinks is warranted. The professional must obtain the client's **informed consent** (Principle 3.10, 2002 Code) or, if the client is legally incapable of giving consent, to seek assent and obtain permission from one authorized by law to give the consent (Principle 3.10(b), 2002 Code), respecting the value of autonomy. Professionals wrestle with questions of how much to press a client to accept unwanted help, and whether and when involuntary treatment is justified.

514

CHAPTER 17
Law, Ethics,
and the
Regulation of
the Professions

Enforcement of Ethical Standards

The code of ethics is enforced through a standing Ethics Committee (2002 Ethics Code, Introduction; see Rules and Procedures, 2001). It can be enforced only against APA members. The APA has no jurisdiction over nonmembers. The same is true for the NASW social work code of ethics.

Complaints against members are submitted in writing by members, nonmembers, or the committee itself (e.g., it learns of an action against a member by a state licensing board). The process of receiving and adjudicating complaints is similar to the process used by licensing boards (Ethics Committee, 2001; see also Koocher and Keith-Spiegel, 1998). After a final action is taken, for some offenses, the Board of Directors may notify state licensing boards or others concerned with a psychologist's professional activities (Introduction, 2002 Code). These latter groups may also initiate state disciplinary action based on that notification.

In 2003, the Ethics Committee received 274 inquiries, and 61 completed complaint forms. This was the lowest number of complaints since 1993. Only 0.07 percent of the membership was subject to a complaint. The average time to process cases closed during 2003 was 11.3 months from opening the case to final action by the committee. As a result of the investigations, in 2003, only 6 of the more than 150,000 APA members were terminated from membership. Two were terminated for sexual misconduct, 2 for insurance and fee problems, 1 because of a dual relationship, and 1 because therapy was terminated inappropriately. In addition, 7 were reprimanded or censured (American Psychological Association, 2003; 2005). In 2004, only 2 were terminated from membership. A comparable social work ethics committee received a similarly low number of complaints against its members.

New Ethical Problems

Therapy and Research on the Internet

One entrepreneurial psychologist likes to travel; he sees an e-mail, telephone, and Internet practice as advantageous because it can be maintained from anywhere (Psychotherapy Finances Online, 1997). He provides "online" therapy for a fee. He offers "free consultations." If he and the client agree that the therapy would be helpful, he obtains a signed "informed consent" agreement from the client before beginning treatment. He charges a dollar a minute. He gets payment in advance, refunding the unused portion to the client. His malpractice insurance covers him for online as well as telephone therapy.

What ethical guidelines are appropriate for this type of treatment? In what state must the psychologist be licensed: his home state, where the patient resides, or where he is located when he responds on line or by telephone? These questions are becoming more urgent. Internet therapy in different forms has spread with amazing rapidity (Rabasca, 2000). About 3 percent of psychologists now provide services using Internet "chat rooms" (Williams, 2000). The new APA Ethics Code (2002) applies to work conducted at a distance as well as to face-to-face encounters.

Research on the Internet also presents a new ethical problem. Are Internet communications and interchanges in "chat rooms" legitimate sources of data for psychological researchers? Studies of chat rooms do not involve informed consent, nor are participants aware they may be observed. On the other hand, they do not have an expectation of privacy. So far, **institutional review boards (IRBs)** that approve research proposals for ethical propriety have not seen Internet research as presenting ethical problems. More careful reviews may be in order (see Azar, 2000). What rules should be followed to protect against what sort of harm?

Participation in National Security–Related Interrogations

Widespread reports of alleged torture and other stressful **interrogation** techniques employed in the Abu Ghraib prison in Iraq, and at the holding center at Guantánamo Bay, Cuba, have shocked many Americans and others around the world. Reports that interrogation teams consulted with psychologists, psychiatrists, and other behavioral scientists to devise new methods or to monitor interrogations raise ethical issues (Mayer, 2005). In February 2005, the APA Board of Directors requested the APA's Presidential Task Force on Psychological Ethics and National Security to provide ethical guidelines for psychologists involved in these activities. The task force issued its report in June 2005.

The report asserted that psychologists are bound by the APA Code of Ethics whenever they serve by "virtue of their training, experience and expertise as psychologists." However, it is "consistent with the APA Ethics Code for psychologists to serve in consultative roles to interrogation and information-gathering processes for national security-related purposes." The task force reviewed the applicability of the code to this new activity.

The task force concluded it would be a violation of ethical obligations for psychologists to "engage in, direct, support, facilitate, or offer training in torture or other cruel, inhuman, or degrading treatment." If psychologists witness such activities, they have an ethical obligation to report these to appropriate authorities. The report does not define *torture*. If psychologists "serve in the role of supporting an interrogation," they should not use health-related information to the individual's detriment. Psychologists should be sensitive to the possible inconsistencies in serving as a "health care provider" and as a "consultant to an interrogation."

The report did not bar participation in such national security-related activities, but cautioned that psychologists in those roles needed to be alert to ethical dilemmas and should consult with other psychologists to clarify what they can do while remaining within ethical boundaries. There seems to be no specific ethical bar to participating in coercive activities that fall short of physical torture, although engaging in "other cruel, inhuman, or degrading treatment" may violate the ethical duty to respect client autonomy. Prisoners are not "clients" but, the ethical code requires respect for human autonomy, dignity and welfare. The ethical code would apply on the basis of those general principles.

The American Psychiatric Association adopted a policy forbidding psychiatrists to be part of interrogation teams. As a result the Pentagon said they would try to use only psychologists and not psychiatrists to help devise interrogation strategies (Lewis, 2006).

These are new ethical problems for which the Ethical Code and its principles can only provide guidelines, but not definitive answers in every situation. The task force did not review specific instances of alleged violations because it had no investigative or adjudicatory role.

◁ Malpractice Suits

Claims of harm due to violations of **professional standards of care** can be brought as **malpractice suits** for money damages through state courts (see the section on the

516

CHAPTER 17
Law, Ethics,
and the
Regulation of
the Professions

Tarasoff case in Chapter 3, and the section on medical malpractice in Chapter 5). In theory, fear of being sued will motivate professionals to maintain standards.

Successful malpractice suits against clinical psychologists and clinical social workers are rare compared to suits brought against medical practitioners. Over a 15-year period from 1990 through March 2005, the National Practitioners Data Bank listed only 915 successful suits against clinical psychologists. In the same time period, there were 199,373 successful claims against physicians. Less than 1 percent of malpractice lawsuit payments were made against clinical psychologists. The same source listed 181 suits against clinical social workers. Malpractice suits against psychologists and social workers are difficult to win, in part, because the broad range of competing theories and therapies makes it difficult to establish that a particular treatment was negligent. As the field adopts empirically verified treatment and detailed treatment manuals and guidelines for various forms of practice (e.g., custody evaluations and forensic practice), it may be easier to prove malpractice; a breach of a recognized standard of care can be made clear. Even if a breach of the standard of care is demonstrated, however, it will still be difficult for a plaintiff to prove that the harm, usually increased symptoms of emotional or behavioral problems, was "caused" by the psychotherapist's incompetent words or actions.

One index of the infrequency of successful suits is that the price of malpractice insurance for clinical psychologists has been declining at the same time as physicians have found their premiums going up. Depending on coverage, insurance premiums may cost less than $2,000 a year. Many insurance policies have begun limiting or even excluding coverage for sexual misconduct as another way to keep down losses. The insurer recommended by the APA limited recovery for claims of sexual misconduct to a total of $25,000. Before this change in coverage, Pope (1991) reported that 53 percent of the losses borne by the malpractice insurance company recommended by the APA involved sexual misconduct cases.

Sexual relationships with clients or patients are prohibited by the ethical codes of psychology, social work, psychiatry, nursing, and medicine. Engaging in sexual activities with a client is a cause of action for a malpractice suit as well as for a licensing and an ethical complaint. Several states have made it a crime to have sex with a client or patient.

In the past, a few therapists argued that a sexual relationship could be therapeutic for the client. Today, no ethical therapist would subscribe to that position. Having a sexual relationship with a client is a breach of the therapist's fiduciary duty to put the client's interests first. Such a relationship is often psychologically harmful to the client. In addition, sexual activities between therapists and patients affect the public perception of the integrity of the mental health profession.

The problem of sexual relationships between therapists and clients seems less important today than it did a few years ago. More recent surveys (Borys and Pope, 1989) show that fewer therapists admit to having had a sexual relationship with a client than was true a few years ago. Because the problem appears to have diminished in psychology, we will simply note the issues here (Koocher and Keith-Spiegel, 1998; Pope and Bouhoutsos, 1986).

The Hippocratic Oath

The prohibition on sexual relations with patients goes back to the Hippocratic Oath, which was first pronounced by the famous Greek physician Hippocrates in the fifth century B.C.:

I swear by Apollo the physician and by Aesculapius [Greek and later Roman god of medicine] to keep the following oath: I will prescribe for the good of my patients and never do harm to anyone. In every house where I come I will enter only for the good of my patients, keeping myself from all intentional ill-doing and all seduction, and especially from the pleasures of love with women or men, be they free or slaves.

Sexual relationships after the termination of treatment. Until 1992, the American Psychological Association had no explicit position on the ethics of a therapist having sex with a former client after the treatment relationship ended. In the past, therapists and clients who found themselves sexually attracted sometimes agreed to stop therapy, and then began a sexual relationship. In the 1992 and 2002 revisions of the ethical code, the APA prohibited sexual contact with former clients for two years after cessation of therapy (Principle 10.06, 2002 Code). Several states have adopted laws limiting **post-therapeutic sexual contact** (Koocher and Keith-Spiegel, 1998).

The issue is controversial (see Box 17.6). On the one hand, the choice to engage in a sexual relationship with the therapist after therapy may not really be free of the

---

BOX 17.6

A Legal Case in Point: No Substitute for Moral and Ethical Judgment

North Carolina is one of several states that incorporated the APA code of ethics into their definitions of professional misconduct. In these states, a violation of an ethical standard may result in a disciplinary action by a state licensing board.

In 1993, the North Carolina Psychology Board learned that a psychologist practicing in their state had been disciplined in Virginia because he had had sexual relationships with two former clients in the 1980s. Both relationships began about six months after the termination of treatment. The North Carolina Psychology Board held a hearing into the allegations and subsequently suspended the psychologist's license for 30 days, required that he practice only under supervision for five years, and ordered him to undergo therapy and evaluation with a psychologist other than his supervisor.

The psychologist appealed the licensing board ruling in the courts (*Elliott v. North Carolina Psychology Board*, 1997). He argued that the disciplinary action was unjustified because his sexual relationships with former clients occurred before 1992, at a time when the APA ethical code was silent on the issue of sexual relationships with clients after treatment has ended.

The North Carolina Court of Appeals upheld the disciplinary action. The Court said, "The code is intended as a floor for ethical conduct, a minimum set of standards with which psychologists must comply. It is not intended ... to provide a ceiling for ethical conduct above which any behavior short of illegal activity is accepted." The Court went on to say,

> How unfortunate when professional codes of conduct are used literally to define acceptable behavior. Even without a set of exact rules and regulations, surely the most educated amongst us are expected to understand values such as honesty, integrity and honor. Professional codes of conduct set minimal standards, and are no substitute for moral and ethical judgment. (*Elliott v. North Carolina Psychology Board*, 1997, 5)

518

CHAPTER 17
Law, Ethics,
and the
Regulation of
the Professions

potentially coercive effects of the **transference** (displacement of feelings toward important persons in the past onto the therapist). On the other hand, the rule disrespects a client's autonomy. After all, one goal of therapy is to enhance client autonomy. Adverse consequences of post-termination sexual relationships have not been documented.

Boundary violations. Plaintiffs undertake malpractice suits to receive monetary compensation for harms they have suffered caused by the therapist's negligence. Few therapists can afford to pay large damage awards; their insurance companies pay. However, insurance carriers now will not pay or will pay only limited damages for harms resulting from therapists' sexual transgressions. Because insurance companies won't pay, it is in the plaintiff's financial interest not to allege sexual transgressions, but to claim instead that minor boundary violations indicate a pattern of negligent treatment.

Boundary violations, like many forms of therapeutic negligence, can be difficult to prove. Entering into a business relationship with a present psychotherapy client would be a relatively clear cut violation; the therapist who did this would be confusing his own interests with those of the client. Such activities may make a therapist vulnerable should a malpractice suit or an ethics or licensing violation complaint be brought by the client. But the definition of a **boundary violation** is vague and context dependent. Therapists in different schools may view boundary violations differently. For example, Williams (1997) described a malpractice case in which a psychoanalytically trained psychotherapist–expert witness faulted a behavior therapist for standard cognitive behavioral practices including "assigning homework tasks to patients," "for hiring present and former patients into psychoeducational programs," and for standard sex therapy practices including "performing a sexological examination, and prescribing sensate focus instructions [that the client learn to focus on sensations during sexual experiences] in a case of sexual dysfunction" (p. 12, Internet version of Williams, 1997). Psychoanalysis proscribes any self disclosure by the therapist. Some therapies allow selective self-disclosure as a therapeutic tool—but inappropriate or excessive self-disclosure may sometimes be seen as a boundary violation.

Social context complicates the problem. Psychologists are urged to maintain professional boundaries by not socializing with clients. However, a lone psychologist in a small rural community may not be able to avoid social relationships with clients. Stringent efforts to avoid potential boundary violations in order to avoid suits may introduce an undesirable inflexibility into practice that might be harmful to some clients (Williams, 1997).

Memory Recovery or False Memories? A Source of Malpractice Suits

In this section, we will look at malpractice actions in relation to the recovered memory controversy. The controversy illustrates dramatically the development of new legal theories establishing grounds for negligence in relation to new professional practices. Knowledge that some clients have successfully pursued malpractice suits based on claims of induced false memories may have motivated some therapists to change their practices.

Memories of childhood abuse, recovered or induced? Patients or clients sometimes claim to recover previously forgotten or repressed memories of childhood sexual abuse during therapy. Some therapists have developed techniques, called **memory recovery** work, to help patients remember disturbing past events. Methods for recovering memories include hypnosis, age regression, guided imagery, dream interpretation, giving free rein to imagination, the use of family photos as memory cues, instructions to work at remembering and to keep journals, and interpreting physical symptoms as evidence of memories of abuse. Therapists who use these memory recovery techniques have higher proportions of clients who report recovering memories than those who don't use such techniques (Poole et al., 1995; Schwabe-Daniels, 1997). "Memory-focused" clinicians, those who make a great deal of use of memory recovery techniques, reported a higher percentage of their clients remembering abuse when the clients had initially denied it than did clinicians who used memory recovery techniques to a lesser degree. Sometimes the recovered memories are plausible, but some patients have reported bizarre or highly unlikely memories, such as memories stemming from the first year or two of life.

Dissociation and repressed memory. The controversy about recovered memories centers, in part, on the psychological processes that can account for the claim that memories can be unconscious, can affect the person's life and feelings, and can be recovered with no distortion after a long period of time. **Repression,** a central concept in psychoanalytic theory, refers to the expulsion of an idea, a feeling, or a memory from conscious awareness to avoid psychological pain. Repression can refer to the psychological processes of preventing the ideas, feelings, or memories from becoming conscious in the first place, or to the exclusion from awareness of something once experienced consciously. In psychoanalytic theory, repressed feelings or memories may be expressed in some form in symptoms.

Repression is difficult to demonstrate in the laboratory. Some believe that the concept of dissociation provides a better and potentially more scientific explanation of certain phenomena attributed to repression. **Disassociation,** a disruption in the usually integrated functions of consciousness, memory, identity, or perception of the environment, is one of the mechanisms some people use to cope with distress. The feeling of seeing oneself calmly from far away during an accident and an inability to remember what happened during one phase of the accident later although one never lost consciousness are examples of common dissociative responses. Dissociative symptoms may include repression of or amnesia for memories of past traumas (*DSM-IV-TR;* American Psychiatric Association, 2000, p. 519).

Bass and Davis (1988) proposed that a variety of disorders, including **dissociative identity disorder (DID, or multiple personality disorder),** bulimia, anxiety, and depression, could be "caused" by forgotten episodes of repeated sexual molestation in the distant past. The victims "dissociated" during the abuse. These experiences became the foundation for separate identities to form or for other symptoms. Most therapists following this theory use hypnosis and other memory recovery techniques to help the patient remember and verbalize childhood sexual abuse. The goal is to make conscious and reintegrate the person's memories and experience of self (see Box 17.7 for a discussion of dissociative identity disorder).

Controversy. As more cases of memory recovery and DID were reported, some clinicians and researchers began to challenge their validity. They asked how it was possible for therapists to assert that suddenly recovered memories of long-past events were accurate without corroborative evidence. An increasing number of women reported remembering fantastic forms of abuse involving satanic rituals, multiple murders, forced cannibalism, torture, and sexual abuse going back to the first year of life. There was no verification of the existence of the cultlike abuse networks reported by some recovered memory patients. Critics asserted that many, if not all, of these patients were actually reporting false memories and exhibiting therapy-induced symptoms. The

520

CHAPTER 17
Law, Ethics,
and the
Regulation of
the Professions

BOX 17.7

Multiple Personality Disorder (Dissociative Identity Disorder): A Diagnostic Fad?

In the past, multiple personality disorder was diagnosed rarely. The book, *The Three Faces of Eve* by psychiatrists Corbett Thigpen and Hervey Cleckly, and a subsequent movie based on the book made multiple personality familiar to the public, but few mental health professionals actually saw such cases. A few years later, *Sibyl*, another best-selling book and a TV movie based on the book, popularized multiple personality disorder. Mental health professionals reported a virtual epidemic of multiple personality disorders. Whereas Eve had 3 alter egos, and Sibyl 16, it was not unusual for clients to report many more personalities. The media picked up the phenomenon; multiple personality disorder guests exhibited their alter egos on command on popular TV shows and in movies. The diagnosis entered the *DSM-III* in 1980 as a dissociative identity disorder. A clinical treatment literature grew, and eventually a subspecialty developed with its own professional association, the International Society for the Study of Dissociation. Meanwhile, skeptics were raising questions about the accuracy of *The Three Faces of Eve* and *Sibyl* and about the validity of the multiple personality diagnosis in general. The premise for several successful suits against therapists was that multiple personality disorders or dissociative disorders were produced by the therapy, with adverse consequences for the patient (Acocella, 1998).

memory-enhancing techniques used in **memory-focused therapy** encouraged creative fantasizing and selective reinforcement by the therapists led some patients to experience and interpret their constructed memories as real past events. Similarly, critics believed that therapists using hypnosis, emotional arousal, group pressure, and psychoactive medications in a deliberate attempt to find alter egos and recover memories of trauma instead could be inducing the phenomena in suggestible and needy patients. The critics noted that individuals diagnosed with the disorder have very high scores on measures of hypnotizability, which is related to dissociative capacity (*DSM-IV-TR*; American Psychiatric Association, 2000).

In support of their position, critics cited the literature on memory, eyewitness testimony (see Chapter 6), and accuracy of memories of child witnesses, which indicates that memory in general is selective, constructive, and vulnerable to suggestion and context. They pointed also to literature on false confessions, trance induction, and brainwashing, and to experiments inducing false memories, as evidence that memory can be manipulated (see Porter, Yuille, and Lehman, 1999).

Clinicians and researchers who believed that abuse is often an important factor in psychopathology and that memories of abuse could be repressed in self-protection defended the claims of patients who recovered memories. The fact that memory recovery techniques and a memory focus lead more therapy clients to say they have recovered long-forgotten memories doesn't necessarily mean that the memories are false. It may simply mean that the techniques are successful. They were supported by some feminists who said that criticism of recovered memories was part of a broader pattern of dismissing women and children's complaints of sexual victimization. They noted that Freud had interpreted reports of sexual abuse by his female patients as fantasies, whereas now many believe the patients may have been describing real events. In their view, critics of repressed memory were encouraging denial of the prevalence of sexual abuse and, once again, blaming the victim.

Proponents of repressed memory pointed to cases in which memories of abuse were suddenly recovered, spontaneously as well as in therapy, and the abuse was later corroborated by other sources (Freyd, 1996). In other cases, evidence of extreme childhood sexual abuse of patients diagnosed with DID was found, although the patients themselves did not remember the abuse (see Lewis et al., 1997). As for DID, proponents argued that dissociative symptoms and selective amnesia for traumatic experiences have been recognized by clinicians and studied for over 100 years.

The controversy heated up with media attention, sensational malpractice suits and some criminal prosecutions as well. In a court of law, the key question was the one that none of the experts could legitimately claim to answer: how to tell whether the particular memory that was the basis of the suit was true or false.

Suits against parents. Some therapy patients who recovered memories of childhood abuse brought civil suits for money damages against their parents, alleging the parents had sexually abused them years earlier. Because the alleged abuse took place in the childhood home, if the defendant lost, damages would sometimes be covered by homeowner's liability insurance. Thus, there was a financial as well as an emotional motive for a suit.

Ordinarily, suits for damages for events that took place a long time ago would be barred by the **statute of limitations** (e.g., a suit must be brought within a few years, set by statute, from the time of the injury). Women's advocates, seeking legal reform to obtain justice for women who allegedly were sexually abused many years earlier, succeeded in influencing some states to change the statute of limitations for these claims. The change allowed a suit to go forward from the time the injury was discovered, not when it occurred.

Changing a statute of limitations causes its own legal problems, however. For example, Marion Stogner was indicted under a 1993 California statute for an offense allegedly committed 22 years earlier, when the statute of limitations under then-existing law was three years. By a 5–4 vote, the U.S. Supreme Court (*Stogner v. California*, 2003) held the 1993 law could not be used to prosecute Stogner because it violated the constitutional prohibition against **ex post facto laws** (making something a crime that was not a crime at the time the act was committed). Justice Stephen Breyer, writing for the majority, mentioned recovered memory and the false memory syndrome as problems in prosecuting cases when the crime allegedly was committed many years earlier (p. 564). Justice Anthony Kennedy, writing for the dissent in support of the validity of the California law, cited the Child Sex Abuse Accommodation Syndrome accounting for why children may delay in reporting sex abuse, and noted that child sexual abuse may cause lifetime emotional damage (p. 576).

Courts in states where the legislatures allowed an extension of the statute of limitations in civil cases were still faced with the evidentiary problems of determining whether the claimed recovered memory was sufficiently reliable or sufficiently verifiable to be the basis for extending the statute of limitations in the particular case being heard. They also had to consider the possibility that the patient had remembered the abuse all along but claimed to have discovered it in treatment in order to get around the statute of limitations.

Some of the patients who recovered memories were successful in suits against their parents and were awarded damages. In addition, some claimed worker's compensation for symptoms related to repressed memories, and others made claims for compensation

522

CHAPTER 17
Law, Ethics,
and the
Regulation of
the Professions

BOX 17.8

A Summary of the Clinical and Laboratory Study of False Memory and Recovered Memory

The false memory debate stimulated an outpouring of research on the question of whether false memories could be induced, whether "forgotten" memories could be restored without distortion, and whether we can identify the difference between false memories and true memories. Gleaves et al. (2004) provided a thorough and balanced review of the large body of research. The problems of memory have been studied by clinical means, including reports of specific cases. The patients made claims of recovered memories of sexual abuse while in therapy. There were also reports from those who claimed they were falsely accused by another, and from those who formerly claimed recovered memories of abuse and later recanted or retracted those memories. One problem is that reports of recovered memories rarely can be independently verified. Another is that the credibility of the source of the information can't be readily verified.

Gleaves et al. (2004) reviewed experiments in which investigators attempted to induce false memories in the laboratory. The experimenters used varied methods: determining if misinformation given to a participant is incorporated into memory when tested later; using hypnotically induced pseudomemories; imagining events to see if the imagined events are mixed together with experienced events in later recall; learning a story with a schema to see if events that are false, plausible, but consistent with the schema were incorporated into memory when tested later; and learning a list of words readily associated with a target word (e.g., *orchard, tree,* and *blossoms*), but not including the target word (*apple*). (The target word was often recalled falsely as if it had been on the list.)

The laboratory experiments show that some persons can be induced to report remembering things that did not occur. These experiments, while usually well done from a research design viewpoint, lack "ecological validity" (i.e., applicability to psychotherapy or to real experiences of sexual abuse). Nonetheless, the research is consistent enough to show that some memories are not necessarily accurate and that some false memories can be induced in some people.

Gleaves et al. examined whether memories that were apparently blocked can be recovered accurately at a later time. For a recovered memory to be believed, "(a) There must be corroborating evidence that the event in question was actually experienced by the person, (b) At some later time it must be found that the event in question cannot be recalled, and (c) After the period of inaccessibility, it must be found that the event can be successfully recalled" (Gleaves et al., 2004, 11). Gleaves et al. reviewed clinical evidence, anecdotes, and reports in legal cases. There is consistent evidence that forgetting of traumatic experience followed some time later by recovery of the memory of the traumatic experience is a real phenomenon.

There is also some laboratory evidence for blocked memories later recovered. The "tip of the tongue" experience is one example. Retroactive interference caused by memorizing two lists successively can result in some forgetting of the first list, but the original list can quickly be relearned showing some retention in memory despite the apparent loss. Recall of words on the first list can be enhanced by using recognition rather than recall showing some retention in memory. Hypnotically induced amnesia can be undone by a prearranged signal in the posthypnotic condition. In still other studies, participants are encouraged to "forget" material. This method frequently resulted in intrusive thoughts; the material the person tried to forget had an effect on thought and emotions.

(continued)

BOX 17.8

523

Malpractice
Suits

Gleaves et al. concluded that both false memories and recovered memories are real phenomena. Experimental research supports memory blocking and recovery of blocked memories. However, questions of internal and external validity abound when considering this laboratory research. A major problem is distinguishing between false and recovered memories. The issue arises in court cases involving recovered memories. The lack of research evidence on point poses challenges for experts testifying on both sides of the question.

through crime victim compensation funds (Legal Corner, *FMSF Newsletter*, 1999a). Recovered memories also provided the basis for criminal actions against a parent.

Malpractice suits against therapists. Other therapy patients who were exposed to memory recovery techniques came to believe the memories were false. Some sued their therapists for malpractice. They claimed that the therapist had impeded their recovery and caused them psychological harm by inducing false memories, and by using his or her influence to alienate them from their families or their children. An organization called the False Memory Syndrome Foundation (FMSF) played a role in generating and winning these lawsuits.

The False Memory Syndrome Foundation (FMSF): An Advocacy Organization

FMSF was founded by Pamela Freyd and her husband Peter as a support and advocacy group for parents who, like themselves, had their family lives disrupted by legal and personal conflict stemming from memories recovered in therapy. The organization grew quickly and now has chapters in many states.

Both academics, the Freyds put together a highly distinguished scientific advisory board for the FMSF. The FMSF provided support for parents, publicized the problem of the recovery of false memories, contributed to the development of legal strategies, and aided or consulted in writing briefs in malpractice suits brought against therapists for inducing false memories of sexual abuse. Some of the juries awarded the plaintiffs in these cases hundreds of thousands of dollars in damages, and a few made awards of millions of dollars. The *False Memory Syndrome Foundation Newsletter* (2004) listed eight suits in six states (two pairs of successful suits were in the same state) in which former patients or clients had been awarded $1 million or more in suits against therapists who had used therapies that resulted in false memories of abuse and had worsened their mental states, or had impaired their recoveries from the conditions for which they had sought help originally. Large awards also occurred in cases that settled without a trial.

In the suits, some patients diagnosed with DID alleged that the diagnosis and treatment were negligent and resulted in severe emotional damage. Some were able to demonstrate that their psychological conditions deteriorated under the treatments intended to bring out alter egos. Their therapists accepted the deterioration on the theory that the patient had to get worse in order to get better. These cases frequently involved a battle of the experts on both sides of the false memory or recovered memory issue. Some therapists lost their licenses as a result of the complaints (Legal Corner, *FMSF Newsletter*, 1999c). The FMSF has tried, unsuccessfully so far, to introduce

524

CHAPTER 17
Law, Ethics,
and the
Regulation of
the Professions

legislation barring therapists from using memory recovery techniques or inquiring about sexual abuse in the past unless the client raises the issues first.

The *Ramona* Case: Malpractice Suits by Third-Party Plaintiffs[1]

Ordinarily, people who are not in a direct treatment relationship with a professional do not have legal standing to sue the professional for damages. In the *Ramona* **case,** a parent was allowed to bring a suit for compensation for harms done to him by the therapist treating his child. The case encapsulates the problems associated with recovered memory therapy. The facts in the *Ramona* case are similar to those in other recovered memory cases and differ only in that a third party not in treatment recovered damages.

Diagnosis and treatment. Holly Ramona entered therapy at age 19, complaining of bulimia and depression. Her therapist told her that most patients with her symptoms had histories of sexual abuse. After a visit home, Holly said she thought her father looked at her in a sexual way. Later, she reported a brief flashback of her father's hand on her stomach when she was five or six. More flashbacks followed. She produced sexual associations in therapy. She nearly panicked during a gynecological exam. Her symptoms worsened.

The therapist recommended a **sodium amytal** ("truth serum") interview to determine whether Holly had real memories of sexual abuse. A psychiatrist admitted Holly to a hospital and administered the sodium amytal interview. During the interview, Holly said that her father raped her. The therapist and psychiatrist assured Holly that she couldn't tell lies under the influence of the sodium amytal. (Other experts vigorously disagreed and so testified in the malpractice trial.) Later, Holly reported other memories of incestuous abuse and of being forced by her father to orally copulate a dog. She had never revealed these episodes before, and claimed she had forgotten them.

Confrontation as healing. After the sodium amytal interview, Holly and the therapist were convinced the memories were of actual abuse. The therapist either agreed or suggested that it would be therapeutic for Holly to confront her father, Gary Ramona, and ask him to apologize and to get help for himself.

Gary Ramona was a successful, self-made executive in a major California winery. Estranged from his wife and warned to stay out of his daughter's treatment, he was shocked to learn that Holly had been hospitalized. When he arrived at the therapist's office for the meeting Holly had requested, he found his wife was also there. Holly accused Gary of raping her. During the meeting, the therapist aggressively told Gary about Holly's "memories" and encouraged Holly to provide more details. Although Gary Ramona denied ever having molested his daughter, the therapist told him that the sodium amytal interview provided the proof. His daughter, her therapist, and his estranged wife kept after him to confess. They refused to listen to his denials.

Following the confrontation, Mrs. Ramona, who had been pursuing a divorce, confided in some friends. They spread the word that Gary Ramona had committed incest. In addition to the social damage to his reputation, he lost his position as an executive at the winery.

---

[1]The material in this section is based largely on Johnston (1997) and Ewing and McCann, 2006, Chapter 14.

The malpractice suit. Holly decided to sue her father for damages emerging from the alleged incestuous relationship. Gary then sued the therapist, the psychiatrist, and the hospital for malpractice. Under the standard interpretation of the law, the therapist and the psychiatrist had no duty of care to Gary because he was not their patient. However, because the therapist had included him in the interview and had confronted him, the trial judge ruled that the suit could proceed. The trial, fully covered by the media, became a forum for judging the validity of recovered memories.

Battle of the experts. The suit began in November 1991 and ended almost two and a half years later. Gary spent hundreds of thousands of dollars on lawyers and on expert witnesses. He hired Park Dietz, the psychiatrist who had testified in the John Hinckley and Jeffrey Dahmer trials, and in the filicide trials of Andrea Yates and Deanna Laney (see Chapter 7); he also hired Elizabeth Loftus, a leading psychological expert on memory. They testified about the unreliability of recovered memories and said that Holly's memories could have been induced. Forensic witnesses for the defense testified to the validity of recovered memories and recovered memory techniques.

The verdict. Under California law, the civil verdict did not have to be unanimous. The jury decided by a 9 to 3 vote that the memories were more likely false than not, and that the defendants' treatment of Holly was negligent. If the defendants had not implanted the memories, they reinforced them. The defendants were also responsible for the confrontation between Holly and Gary that led to his losses. The jury awarded Gary $500,000 in damages, considerably less than he had asked. Nonetheless, someone who wasn't a patient had recovered damages from therapists (and their insurance companies) for their malpractice in inducing false memories. Since then, appellate-level courts in several states have found that the public interest would be served by holding therapists accountable to others who were foreseeably subject to injury because of the therapists' negligence. However, courts in other states have not upheld third-party suits (see Legal Corner, *FMSF Newsletter,* 1999a, for a listing of cases on both sides of the issue).

Postscript. Holly Ramona's lawsuit against Gary Ramona was eventually dismissed because many of her alleged memories emerged after the sodium amytal interview. Under California law, memories recovered after use of hypnotic drugs were not considered reliable and, thus, not admissible. Holly Ramona went on to graduate work as a marriage and family counselor. She hoped to counsel victims of sexual abuse. Gary Ramona was well on his way to rebuilding his career in the wine business.

Effects of Malpractice Suits

Effects on research. The controversy about recovered memory highlighted theoretical divisions within the profession of psychology. As a result, researchers have been developing new theories and experiments to try to develop a fuller understanding of memory (Freyd, 1996; Loftus and Ketcham, 1994). Some have been investigating important problems that would not have entered professional discourse in quite the same way had the issues not been introduced in lawsuits.

Effects on practice. After the successful lawsuits were brought against therapists, professional organizations and insurers cautioned therapists about potential liabilities of

526

CHAPTER 17
Law, Ethics,
and the
Regulation of
the Professions

BOX 17.9

The American Psychological Association's Inconclusive Stand

In an attempt to resolve the controversy (or at least to allow it to continue in a more professional tone), the APA established a working group to review the literature on memories of childhood abuse. In effect, the group agreed to disagree and called for continuing research. The following paragraphs are taken from the group's final report.

Where Do We Stand?

Inspection of the reviews and commentaries in this report indicates that we are in agreement concerning a number of key points. Indeed, we agree on the following:

1. Controversies regarding adult recollections should not be allowed to obscure the fact that child sexual abuse is a complex and pervasive problem in America that has historically gone unacknowledged.
2. Most people who were sexually abused as children remember all or part of what happened to them.
3. It is possible for memories of abuse that have been forgotten for a long time to be remembered.
4. It is also possible to construct convincing pseudomemories for events that never occurred.
5. There are gaps in our knowledge about the processes that lead to accurate and inaccurate recollections of childhood abuse.

APA Working Group (1998, 933).

using memory recovery techniques. One insurance company refused to provide insurance for therapists who used hypnotherapy to assist in the recovery of repressed memories.

Davis, Loftus, and Follette (2001) recommended that therapists add warnings about the dangers and limits of recovered memory therapy to the information they give clients when obtaining informed consent for treatment. They recommend that clients be informed of the

> (1) risk of no benefit, (2) the risks of foregone benefits [that one might receive from other treatment], (3) the risk of developing false memories, (4) the risk of recovery of false memories through use of specific therapeutic activities, (5) the enhanced risk of memory recovery procedures to specific patient categories [suggestible persons, those high on the DID scale, those low on self-confidence, and so on], (6) the risk of harm through the process of recovered memory therapy, (7) the risk of other potentially iatrogenic disorders, particularly Multiple Personality Disorders (MPD), and (8) the risk of harm resulting from recovery of traumatic memories (both true and false).

The *FMSF Newsletter* (Freyd, 2000) noted a marked decline in the number of requests they received from estranged parents, and a declining number of lawsuits. Some therapists may well have changed therapy practices. If this is the case, then we are seeing a "regulatory" effect of malpractice lawsuits on professional practice.

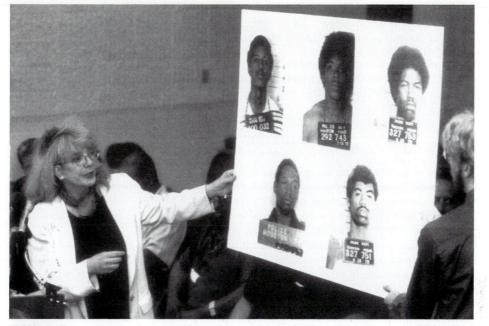

FIGURE 17.1

Elizabeth F. Loftus

Professor Loftus is a leading researcher on memory and eyewitness testimony. She has testified on numerous occasions, and has been subject to personal attack by extremists who believe she has been undermining the credibility of victims of abuse. Professor Loftus was accused of ethical violations, but the American Psychological Association found no basis for pursuing the complaints. Professor Loftus was later elected to the prestigious National Academy of Science, which recognizes only the most distinguished scientists in all fields of science.

Summary

Professions are regulated because the imbalance in knowledge and power between professionals and their clients makes the public vulnerable. The professionals are subject to state licensing or to certification requirements, and to disciplinary action by licensing boards for professional misconduct. The subjects of complaints are granted a hearing with due process rights before they can be disciplined. In addition, professional organizations also adopt professional codes of ethics as a means of self-regulation. These are enforceable within the membership. Finally, professionals who owe a fiduciary duty to their clients may be subject to malpractice suits for breach of those duties. In theory, the threat of malpractice suits encourages more careful and more ethical practice.

The ethical codes of the mental health professions uniformly condemn sexual relationships with clients or patients. The ban is based on a violation of an ancient ethical duty to act in the patient's interest and not to use one's position of power to exploit patients. Sexual misconduct used to account for over 50 percent of malpractice suits brought against therapists. In recent years, insurance companies have either excluded damages due to sexual relationships from insurance coverage or have limited them. Publicity, the number of disciplinary actions and suits, and the change in insurance practices may have decreased complaints of sexual relationships and increased complaints of "boundary violations."

528

CHAPTER 17
Law, Ethics,
and the
Regulation of
the Professions

In recent years, patients have sued for malpractice on the grounds that their therapists induced false memories of past sexual abuse, including bizarre abuse. Parents or other relatives of patients who were allegedly harmed by the therapists' actions in inducing false memories have sometimes been allowed to sue for damages. These lawsuits may have influenced practice by making therapists more cautious about using memory recovery techniques. The issue of induced or false memories versus real memories recovered in therapy is controversial, and has provided new directions for research.

Discussion Questions

1. Critics of the professions complain that it is difficult for a client to stop an incompetent or unethical professional from hurting others. Do you think this is true? Can you think of any way to improve the complaint systems?

2. Do you think other professionals, such as lawyers, should be required to avoid sexual relationships with clients, just as psychologists are? Why?

3. What principles could you refer to in considering whether or not it was appropriate for a therapist to touch a client? Do you think a pat on the hand by a middle-aged therapist would have the same meaning to an elderly client with impaired vision and hearing, a 20-year-old client, and a 5-year-old client? How could you ethically test a hypothesis about touching and age differences?

4. What, if any, ethical problems do you foresee arising from Internet therapy? Research conducted using online subjects? Plan an Internet experiment. What ethical issues should you consider in your proposed study?

5. Therapist defendants in false memory suits were accused of implanting memories of abuse that never occurred. Can you think of an ethical experiment to test whether an emotion-laden memory could be deliberately implanted?

Key Terms

beneficence
boundary violations
certification
disciplinary proceedings
dissociation
dissociative identity disorder
    (DID, or multiple person-
    ality disorder)
duty
ethical codes
ex post facto law
false memories
False Memory Syndrome
    Foundation (FMSF)

fiduciary duty
immunity from suit
informed consent
interrogation
institutional review
    boards (IRBs)
licenses
malpractice suits
managed care
memory-focused therapy
memory recovery
nonmaleficence
police power

posttherapeutic sexual
    contact
professional associations
professional misconduct
professional standards of
    care
Ramona case
repression
rights
sodium amytal
statute of limitations
transference

Glossary of Legal Terms

Abuse of discretion—excessive or improper use of authority. Appellate courts may overturn a ruling by a lower court judge on the grounds that the judge abused his or her discretion. However, a judge's rulings must be almost completely without foundation in the record to meet this standard.

Activist courts—courts that interpret the law or constitution in ways that modify, expand, or create new principles in order to accommodate social and historical change.

Adjournment in contemplation of dismissal—postponement of a proceeding with charges against a defendant or respondent to be dismissed completely if he or she does not get into further legal trouble within some specified period of time.

Adjudication—a trial or hearing to make a judgment (*adjudicate, v.*).

Adjudicative competence—competence to stand trial on a criminal charge.

Adjudicative facts—See **social facts.**

Administrative law—branch of law governing regulations promulgated by legislatively authorized administrative agencies. These regulations define how laws are to be implemented (e.g., social security disability determinations; environmental quality; food and drug standards, etc.).

Adversarial model or system—model or system of law characterized by opposing parties who contend against each other to try to win a judgment favorable to themselves. In this system, the judge acts as independent referee in contrast to the inquisitorial system in Europe in which the judge has a more active role.

Affirmative action—Methods for actively recruiting and selecting persons for employment or for schools to help ensure that candidates from groups formerly subject to legal discrimination (e.g. women, racial minorities) receive consideration.

Affirmative defense—an assertion made during a plea, which, if true, constitutes a defense against the charge. The person asserting an affirmative defense has the burden of proof. Insanity is an example of an affirmative defense.

Aggravating—characteristics or circumstances of a crime or wrong, which, if true, increase the perpetrator's level of guilt.

Amendment—change, including additions.

American Law Institute standard—standard for insanity including both a cognitive and a volitional prong proposed in 1962 by the American Law Institute (ALI), a quasi-official group of lawyers.

Amicus curiae **briefs**—briefs submitted by a person or a group who are not parties to the case but who would like to inform the court of their ideas or knowledge about the issues being argued. *Amicus curiae* means 'friend of the court.'

Appellant—someone bringing an appeal to a court (see **respondent**).

Arraignment—initial hearing in a criminal proceeding in which the judge informs the suspect of the charges and of his or her rights. The suspect enters a preliminary plea and the judge then decides whether to detain the defendant while he or she awaits trial, release him or her on his own recognizance, or release him or her on bail.

Assistance of counsel—The Sixth Amendment right to assistance of an attorney at every stage in a criminal proceeding from arraignment through trial and sentencing.

Autonomy—personal rule of self, based on free and informed choices.

Bail—the release of someone charged with an offense in return for a guarantee that he or she will remain within the court's jurisdiction and return at the appointed time for hearings and for trial; also a sum of money left with the court by a defendant, which will be forfeited if he or she does not respond to court orders to appear.

Battery—intentionally touching another without the person's consent.

Bench trial—either a civil or criminal trial held before a judge who hears the evidence and decides the case.

Beneficence—quality of acting to benefit another. A professional is ethically and legally obligated to act toward clients with beneficence.

Bifurcated trial—a two-phase trial, one phase to determine guilt, the other to determine punishment; used in death penalty cases, and some civil cases, to separate determination of liability or guilt from the determination of damages or punishment. Also called **split trial.**

Bill of Rights—First ten amendments to U.S. Constitution adopted in 1791.

Binding precedent—a legal decision or interpretation by a higher court that all the lower courts under its jurisdiction must follow.

Brief—a written document filed with a court summarizing the issues in the case and making arguments about relevant facts and interpretations of statutes and previous cases. Each side files a brief.

Burden of proof—rule governing which side in a dispute must prove the elements of its case. Generally, the party bringing the case to court, the prosecution or plaintiff, is the party that must shoulder the burden of proof. For example, because a criminal defendant is innocent until proven guilty, the prosecution generally has the burden to prove all the elements of its case in criminal trials.

Capital (crimes, offenses, cases)—potentially punishable by execution.

Casebooks—textbooks that teach a field of law through the presentation and discussion of court cases and related material.

Case law—the body of interpretations of previous cases giving meaning to provisions of specific statutes.

Cause of action—the event entitling a party to seek a judicial remedy by bringing a civil suit.

Certification—right to use a professional title granted by a state to those who meet legislatively established standards of training and practice. Certification laws may include a definition of practice, but do not restrict the practice to certified practitioners.

Challenge for cause—challenge to a potential juror's impartiality during jury selection to request the person be disqualified from serving on a particular jury; see **Peremptory challenge.**

Charge—the instructions the judge gives to the jury just before the deliberations begin.

Civil law—the branch of law governing disputes between private parties. Civil law governs disputes involving family law, administrative regulations, contracts, torts, and so on.

Class action suit—a suit in which a small group of people make a complaint on behalf of a larger group who can claim the same wrongs. A judge can certify plaintiffs as a class when the same set of facts and the same considerations of law affect them all.

Clear and convincing evidence—a standard of proof used in some civil cases (e.g., termination of parental rights; involuntary hospitalization); a standard weaker than beyond a reasonable doubt but stronger than preponderance of evidence.

Cognitive capacity—standard for deciding whether accused possesses sufficient knowledge of right and wrong to be held legally responsible for his or her actions.

Cognitive prong—the element of an insanity standard involving knowledge, understanding, or appreciation that an unlawful act was wrong. See also **volitional prong.**

Common law—the principles, found in case reports and law treatises, that courts have developed over the years to resolve cases.

Compelling state interest—a reason offered by the government that a court deems sufficiently important to justify legislation limiting a constitutionally protected right.

Competence—the absence of incapacitating disabilities and the possession of those characteristics that make a person "legally fit" to participate in a legal process. A competent person is someone with sufficient mental capacity to understand the information, to weigh good and bad consequences of different actions, and to make and express a choice.

Compulsory process—a procedure to compel someone to appear in court; a legally enforceable subpoena to require a witness to appear in court.

Conclusory testimony—testimony making a judgment about the guilt or responsibility of the defendant or respondent.

Confidentiality—an agreement not to disclose communications made in confidence. In a professional relationship, confidentiality is enforced by a civil suit, as an ethical issue, or as a violation of professional standards.

Confrontation clause—clause in the Sixth Amendment to the Constitution providing for the right of criminal defendants to confront witnesses against them.

Consortium—the companionship and services of a family member.

Corroborative evidence/testimony—evidence affirming, supplementing, or strengthening evidence already given.

Courts of last resort—a court from which no further appeal is possible, typically the highest appellate court in a state or the U.S. Supreme Court in the federal system.

Crime—an action defined in the state or federal criminal code that is punishable by imprisonment. Crimes victimize individuals and, in doing so, harm society.

Criminal action—an action in which the state, as representative of the people, is the party bringing charges against the defendant.

Custody—guarding, controlling, and maintaining a person or an object. Whoever has custody of a child has the right to make all decisions about the child.

Damages—court-awarded compensation to a plaintiff who has suffered harm or loss because of the defendant's failure to fulfill a duty.

Dangerous—likely to be physically violent toward others or him- or herself in the future.

***Daubert* standard**—a legal guideline for judges reviewing the scientific basis for expert testimony to decide admissibility—"good science".

Death-qualified jury—a jury selected in a capital case after potential jurors unwilling to impose the death penalty have been eliminated from consideration.

Defendant—the person against whom a charge is brought in criminal and some types of civil cases.

Deliberate indifference—a mental state (mens rea) implying the defendant disregarded any consequence of the criminal act, and the act was not impulsive.

Demeanor—a person's appearance and behavior.

Disparate impact—affecting opportunities or resources available to one group more than another.

Double-jeopardy—a provision of the Fifth Amendment to the U.S. Constitution specifying that a person found not guilty of a crime cannot be tried a second time for the same crime.

Due diligence—requisite attentiveness, activity, and care. For example, the state cannot terminate parental rights until it has tried with due diligence to reunite the family.

Due process—following all procedures required by laws; also fundamental fairness (see **procedural** and **substantive due process**).

***Durham* rule**—a standard for deciding when the accused lacks criminal capacity—act is a product of mental disease or defect.

Duty of care—the obligation to meet professional standards of practice when engaging in diagnosis or treatment. Professionals accept a duty to care for anyone to whom they agree to provide services.

Dynamite charge—the charge to continue deliberations given to a jury that has declared itself hung. In the charge, the judge attempts to "blast" the deliberations open again by asking those in the minority position to be sure that their beliefs are reasonable.

Elder abuse—the neglect, mistreatment, emotional and physical abuse, and financial exploitation of an elderly person.

Emancipated minor—a minor given adult status by a court prior to the age of majority under conditions established by state law, for example, upon marriage, when in the armed forces, or when living apart from one's parents with parental consent, and managing one's own financial affairs. An emancipated minor has many but not all of the rights of an adult (e.g., laws restricting drinking age still apply).

Enumerated powers—the specific areas in which Congress is authorized to legislate, which are listed in Article II, Sec. 8 of the Constitution. Specific prohibitions on congressional legislative powers are listed in Article II, Sec. 9.

Equity—justice based on fairness, involving court-ordered changes in circumstances or practices (an order to do something, or to cease doing something) but not money damages.

Ethical code—a standard promulgated by a professional association that its members are obligated to follow. Codes are explicitly linked to moral principles and are intended to protect the public welfare.

Executive power—the power to carry out or enforce laws.

Executor—a person named in a will to carry out (execute) the terms of the will.

Ex parte—involving only one of the parties to a dispute, with only one of the parties present.

Expert testimony—court testimony by someone a trial judge accepts as an expert because of person's experience or education; experts may express opinions.

Family preservation—a policy under law for social services to try to keep families together by interventions before removing a child, to make efforts to help the family, and to return the child to the parent as soon as feasible (family reunification) if a child is removed from a home. Judges are charged with reviewing child protection cases to see the policies are carried out.

Felony—a serious crime that can be punished by a prison sentence of more than one year.

Fiduciary duty—duty of care owed by the more powerful person in a formal (e.g., professional–client) relationship to the person who relies on and trusts in him or her. The person who is relied on may not "take selfish advantage of this trust . . ." Professionals are obliged to work to benefit another, to remove or prevent harm, and to do no intentional harm (principle of **nonmaleficence**).

Finder of fact—the person or entity responsible for deciding what really happened in a legal controversy; this may be a jury, a judge, or an administrative body.

For cause—for reasons the law recognizes as valid or important.

Forensic—suitable for use in a court of law.

Founded—in child protection investigations, a case is founded if investigators discover sufficient evidence (usually "some credible evidence") of maltreatment to support a determination for the record; substantiated; indicated. (The terminology differs in different states.)

Frye **standard**—a legal guideline for judges reviewing admissibility of expert testimony based on science; is the approach commonly used and accepted in the field?

Geographic jurisdiction—a specific area—state, county, region, etc.—where a court has the authority to act.

Grand jury—a jury of inquiry. In criminal proceedings, the grand jury represents the community at the **indictment** (formally charging a person with a crime) stage of a criminal proceeding, particularly in **felony** cases (more serious crimes).

Grant *certiorari*—to agree to hear a case at an appellate level. The appeals court asks the court below to forward a certified record of the case for its consideration (also see **writ of** *certiorari*).

Guardian ad litem—guardian appointed by a court to represent the interests usually of a minor but for the particular case only.

Guilt phase—the first phase of a bifurcated trial held in capital cases, during which the jury decides whether or not the defendant is guilty of a capital offense.

Habeas corpus **petition**—a petition to require an official to bring a party, often a prisoner, before a court and show that he or she was being held in accordance with law. The right to submit a *habeas corpus* petition is a protection against arbitrary detention.

Harassment—repeated use of words, gestures, and actions to intentionally annoy, alarm, threaten, or verbally abuse another person.

Hearsay—statements made to a witness out of court, not under oath, and not subject to cross-examination concerning a matter of which the witness has no direct personal knowledge, but introduced by the witness during testimony as proof of an allegation contained in the hearsay statement.

Hostile environment sexual harassment—ongoing sex-related verbal or physical conduct that is unwelcome or offensive. "Discriminatory intimidation, ridicule, and insult" that is "sufficiently severe or pervasive to alter the conditions of employment and create an abusive working environment" (*Meritor Savings Bank v. Vinson*, 1986).

Immunity from suit (for reporting in good faith)—the exemption of mandated reporters from tort liability for a good faith report of suspicion of child maltreatment. Parents who are reported cannot *successfully* sue mandated reporters for libel or damages even if the suspicion of abuse was unfounded by CPS.

Impartial—not favoring either party at the outset.

Impeach—to dispute, contradict, or disparage testimony.

Indicated—in child protection investigations, a case is indicated if investigators discover sufficient evidence (usually "some credible evidence") of maltreatment to support a determination for the record; substantiated; founded.

Indictment—formal charge of a criminal offense.

Informed consent—consent given knowingly, voluntarily, and intelligently after receiving information to what the person is agreeing.

Inquisitorial system—system of justice in use in much of Europe: judge or panel of judges takes the lead in developing the case at trial; contrast adversarial system.

In re—"regarding;" a term in the title of a case usually regarding a juvenile.

Insane—lacking the mental capacity to be held criminally responsible.

Insane delusion—an idea that has no basis, however slight, in fact and is not removable by presenting refuting information.

Institutional reform suits—suits brought by plaintiffs alleging unconstitutional treatment by institutions or agencies, or a violation of statutory standards of institutional care.

Institutional review boards (IRB)—committees set up by institutions (e.g., hospitals, universities, corporations) to review research proposals for ethical propriety.

Involuntary admission (to a psychiatric hospital)—admission without the patient's consent (usually on the grounds that the person is mentally ill and dangerous to self or others).

Irresistible impulse—see **volitional prong.**

Jails—pretrial holding centers.

Judgment proof—a defendant or respondent in a civil case is judgment proof if he or she has no seizable assets, so that there is nothing for the plaintiff to collect to compensate for harms done to him or her.

Judicial bypass—a proceedure allowing a minor to obtain a court's permission to have an abortion without first notifying or obtaining her parent's consent.

Judicial power—the power to say what law applies and what the law means in specific circumstances.

Judicial transfer—see **transfer laws.**

Judicial waiver (juvenile offenders)—a decision by the judge before whom a juvenile defendant appears to transfer the case from juvenile to adult court (or the reverse).

Jurisdiction—the legal right to exercise authority. Courts have jurisdiction over assigned subject matter (e.g., traffic courts, family court, surrogates court, civil court). They also have geographic jurisdiction (jurisdiction within a certain geographic area).

Jurisprudence—the philosophy or science of law.

Jurists—legal scholars, or persons who know the law as a result of study.

Jury nullification—the voiding or cancellation of a law by a jury when it renders a verdict inconsistent with that law but consonant with its own sense of justice.

Legally actionable—of a nature or severity to provide grounds for a lawsuit.

Legal realism—school of jurisprudence willing to examine empirical evidence as a basis for understanding law.

Legislative facts—see **social authority evidence.**

Legislative offense exclusions (juvenile offenders)—laws specifying that anyone charged with certain specified offenses may be tried as an adult, including those young enough to be considered juveniles otherwise.

Legislative power—the power to make laws.

Legislative waiver (juvenile offenders)—legislation transferring jurisdiction over youth considered or formerly considered juveniles from juvenile to adult court.

Liability—a legal obligation or responsibility (e.g., to be indebted; responsible for compensating for damages, etc.).

Liberty interests—basic elements of the rights guaranteed by the U.S. Constitution, especially the Bill of Rights, and the Thirteenth (no involuntary servitude), Fourteenth (due process, equal protection), and Fifteenth (voting rights) Amendments as interpreted by the courts.

License—permission to engage in a legislatively defined profession and use the professional title granted by states exclusively to those who meet legislatively established qualifications and follow set standards of practice. Licensing laws grant some professions a virtual monopoly over the practice (e.g., surgeons).

Lineup—a police procedure in which a crime victim or other eyewitness views a group of potential suspects (simultaneously or one by one), which may or may not include the actual suspect, and is asked if the perpetrator is among them.

Malice aforethought—willful and "wanton disregard for human life."

Malpractice suit—a suit brought by an aggrieved client against a professional practitioner in which the client alleges that he or she has been injured by the professional's failure in his or her duty to care for the client.

Mandated reporters—professionals required by law to report suspected child maltreatment.

Mediation—a method of resolving disputes by having a neutral third party work with the two contending parties to help them negotiate a settlement; an alternative to litigation.

Mens rea—"a guilty mind; a guilty or wrongful purpose; a criminal intent. Guilty knowledge and willfulness" (*Black's,* 8th Ed.).

Minor—a young person under a legislatively established age presumed to lack sufficient emotional and cognitive maturity to give consent, enter into contracts, or make other legal decisions.

Miranda **rights**—accused person's right to be informed of various rights, such as the right to an attorney, right to remain silent, etc.

Misdemeanor—a lesser crime; usually punishable by less than one year in prison.

Mitigating—characteristics or circumstances of a crime or wrong or of its perpetrator which, if true, lessen the perpetrator's level of guilt or degree of punishment.

the M'Naghten rule—the standard of insanity established by fifteen English judges in the case of political assassin Daniel M'Naghten. The court ruled that a defendant could plead insanity if, at the time of the commission of the act, he or she "was laboring under such a defect of reason, from disease of the mind, as not to know the nature and quality of the act he was doing; or if he did know it, that he did not know he was doing what was wrong."

Money damages—monetary compensation awarded by a jury to the successful plaintiff in a tort or malpractice suit after hearing evidence about the losses and expenses incurred by the plaintiff because of the injury, including the costs of medical care, lost wages, and, when appropriate, pain and suffering. See also **punitive damages.**

Neglect—children receiving physical care, medical care, or supervision falling sufficiently below standard to warrant intervention by the child protection system.

Negligence—a person's failure to do something he or she should have done, or not to do something he or she should have done that results in harm to another.

Non compos mentis—without power of mind; mentally deranged.

Nonmaleficence—the ethical principle of doing no intentional harm.

Objective standard—a standard courts refer to in making judgments about a person's perceptions and behavior. The objective view of a situation is often defined as the way a hypothetical reasonable (normal, rational) adult would see it. The objective standard can be used alone or with a **subjective** standard. The subjective standard is how the particular person actually in the situation at issue viewed it.

On point—legal jargon signifying statement is precisely on target for an issue.

Order of protection—in cases of domestic violence, a court order forbidding a person from engaging in threatening behavior. Orders of protection can direct an alleged abuser to stop abusive conduct, to leave or stay away from the family home, or to do (e.g., pay the rent) or refrain from doing anything else the judge specifies (e.g., stop following the victim around). The order may require supervised or restricted visitation with children. The order is functionally like an arrest warrant if the party named violates its terms. Also called a **restraining order.**

Own recognizance—releasing a defendant on his or her own promise to return to court as ordered without requiring financial or other sureties.

Parens patriae ('parent of nation') **powers**—state powers deriving from the conception of the state as a higher parent, responsible for the welfare of all its citizens. Provision of hospital care or welfare payments are examples of exercise of states' *parens patriae* power.

Parties with standing—the people who are directly involved in a legal case or controversy and have a stake in its outcome (What business is it of yours?); the complainant(s) and respondent(s) or defendant(s) in a civil case.

Pattern jury instructions—see **standard pattern jury instructions.**

Penalty phase—in death penalty cases, a second trial with the same jurors held after a person is convicted of a capital offense to decide whether or not execution is appropriate.

Peremptory challenge—a challenge to a juror for any reason. Parties are granted a certain number of challenges to jurors that can be made for any reason by attorneys on either side during jury selection.

Permanency planning—in child protection, planning to ensure that maltreated children who have been removed from their parent's home will be reunited with their family or placed in a permanent adoptive home within a reasonable period of time.

Petition on behalf of the child—a legal instrument asking a court to assume jurisdiction over a child or some aspect of a child's life because of the child's unlawful or improper behavior or because the child is in need of care.

Photographic identification—a police procedure in which a crime victim or other eyewitness views photographs of potential suspects and is asked if the perpetrator is among them.

Plaintiff—the aggrieved party who initiates a civil case.

Plea bargain—an agreement between a defendant in a criminal trial and the state whereby the state agrees to reduce the original charge and charge the defendant with a lesser crime or to request a lesser sentence if the defendant will agree to plead guilty.

Police power—the legitimate power of the state to make and enforce laws designed to protect the health and safety of the population. Criminal laws are an exercise of state's police power.

Policy—the general course, methods, or principles adopted by a government or legislature to guide its development of legislation or management of public affairs.

Prejudicial evidence—evidence likely to inflame juror feeling against a defendant.

Preponderance of the evidence—the standard of proof in most civil cases. Sometimes defined as the greater weight of the evidence. (See **standard of proof.**)

Presumption—a fact necessary for a legal claim may be proven as a proxy for another fact more difficult to prove (e.g., proof that a person is of a certain age is accepted as proof of competency). A presumption may be challenged and rebutted by other evidence.

Preventive detention—detention of someone, not for something he or she did, but for something he or she might do in the future (because of a prediction of future dangerousness).

Primary caretaker doctrine—the presumption that, other things being equal, the interests of young children are best served by awarding custody to the parent who has been their primary caretaker.

Privilege against self-incrimination—the right of a person charged with a criminal offense to refuse to testify against him- or herself (guaranteed by the Fifth Amendment).

Privileged communications—statements made within a protected relationship that the law exempts from forced disclosure in any legal forum. Protected relationships are those specified by statute and include those between a professional (doctor, lawyer, therapist) and a client that are believed to be dependent on confidentiality. The decision to allow or not allow the professional to disclose the communication is the client's. The extent of the protection against forced disclosure of privileged communications is decided by state legislatures.

Probate court—a special civil court having power to validate wills and administer estates. Called **surrogate court** in some states.

Probative—contributing to proof of a "fact" at issue in the trial. To be admitted, evidence has to meet two criteria: It has to help prove a fact at issue (**probative value**) and the probative value has to outweigh any prejudicial or misleading effects the information might have.

Procedural due process—following the law, following all the procedures established by law to ensure liberty and fairness.

Product rule—an expansive, psychiatrist-friendly standard for insanity promulgated by the New Hampshire legislature in 1869: A person is not guilty by reason of insanity if the criminal act was the *product* of a mental disease or defect.

Professional misconduct—conduct falling below ethically prescribed standards of professional behavior, as defined in a state licensing or certification statute.

Professional standard of care—usually defined by what a practitioner of equal training practicing in a particular community would do.

Proportionality—the principle applied to sentencing and punishment that the severity of punishment should be related to the seriousness of the crime and the degree to which the crime was intended (the punishment should fit the crime).

Pro se—for him- or herself; on his or her own behalf; representing oneself in court without retaining a lawyer.

Prosecutorial waiver—the decision by a prosecutor, authorized by the legislature, to prosecute a juvenile in adult instead of juvenile court or the reverse. In about a dozen states where the legislatures have authorized that certain crimes committed by juveniles can be treated as adult offenses, the prosecutor can choose whether to prosecute initially in adult criminal court or in juvenile court. Judges in states with prosecutorial waiver still have the power to waive in either direction after a hearing. (See also **reverse waiver**.)

Proximate cause—the immediate cause. In malpractice cases, the plaintiff must prove that the professional's action or inaction was the proximate cause of his or her injury, meaning that, had the professional acted differently, the injury would not have occurred.

Psychological injury—emotional damage resulting from an injury such as sexual harassment or defamation.

Punitive damages—monetary damages over and beyond compensation for other losses awarded in a suit by a judge or jury when it is found that an injury or wrong was inflicted intentionally or maliciously or resulted from a reckless disregard for the plaintiff's health or safety. Punitive damages punish a culpable defendant and set an example that, in theory, will deter others from similar conduct.

Quid pro quo **sexual harassment**—attempts to buy or extort sexual compliance by implicit or direct threats or promises of job-related consequences (e.g., sleep with me and I can make things easy for you).

Ratified—approved. The Constitution was ratified when it was approved by vote of the state legislatures.

Reasonable person standard—acts are viewed from the viewpoint of an average, normal person; an objective standard; applies to evaluation of what constitutes reasonable care in a negligence lawsuit.

Reasonable suspicion—a suspicion for which one has a reason; more than a hunch or conjecture.

Rebuttable presumption—a presumption is a fact, which if proven, allows an inference to another fact (e.g., (1) witness is an adult and (2) therefore competent to testify). A rebuttable presumption is one that can be challenged (e.g., the witness is an adult, but is severely mentally retarded, and therefore not competent to testify).

Recidivism—the repetition of additional offenses after serving a sentence, or during or after assignment to a treatment program or while serving probation.

Referendum—a direct vote by citizens on an issue (as opposed to a vote by their legislative representatives).

Regulation—rule prescribed by a competent agency to direct, control, limit or prohibit actions of those subject to its authority. When regulations are promulgated according to administrative law procedures, they have the force of law.

Remand—send back. When an appellate court overturns a lower court ruling because it finds that the lower court erred on a point of law, the appellate court may send the case back to lower court for reconsideration in light of the corrected interpretation.

Respondent—the party against whom a case is brought in some civil suits, or the party responding in an appeal from a previous decision.

Restraining order—see **order of protection**.

Reverse waiver—the decision by a criminal court judge to transfer a case involving a juvenile offender to juvenile court. Reverse waivers occur in states where the legislature requires that juveniles who commit specified crimes appear initially in adult criminal court. (See also **prosecutorial waiver**.)

Right of confrontation—the Sixth Amendment right to face and to cross-examine witnesses against him or her.

Rights—"powerful assertions of claims that demand respect and status . . . ." (Faden and Beauchamp, 1986, p. 6). Once a right is asserted, it entails "the imposition of a duty on others either not to interfere or to provide something" (p. 7).

Sequestered—separated or isolated. Juries, particularly those hearing sensational trials, are sometimes housed in hotels for the course of the trial so they will not be prejudiced by publicity and discussion surrounding the case.

Settled law—a legal issue resolved by previous definitive court decisions.

Sexual harassment—behaviors intended to manipulate or upset a person because of his or her sex.

Show up—a police procedure in which a crime victim or other eyewitness views a single suspect and is asked if he or she is the perpetrator.

Social authority evidence—general social science findings used by courts in deciding questions of law or policy. Also called **legislative facts.**

Social facts—factual matters relevant to issues in contention in a trial. The most familiar use of social scientists and other professionals in court is to testify about social facts. Also called **adjudicative facts.**

Social framework evidence/testimony—testimony by social scientists that provides juries or judges with general information that may help them evaluate and understand evidence about the specific facts of the case.

Some credible evidence—in child protection cases, the standard of strength of evidence needed for Child Protection workers to consider a report of suspected maltreatment substantiated or founded (states differ in the standards they use).

Sovereignty—absolute power to govern a state.

Split trial—see **bifurcated trial.**

Standard of proof—the standard indicating how strongly prosecutors or plaintiffs must prove their case for the fact finder to bring in a verdict in their favor. The standard of proof in criminal trials is "beyond a reasonable doubt." In most civil trials, the usual standard is "a (clear) preponderance of evidence." When more important interests are at stake, the stronger "clear and convincing evidence" standard is used (e.g., termination of parental rights; involuntary hospitalization).

Standard pattern jury instructions—verbatim instructions on trial issues found in a book used by judges to formulate charges to juries. The instructions have been approved by appellate courts in previous cases.

Standing—people who have standing in a case are part of the controversy and have a stake in its outcome (standing in a legal case, parties with standing).

Stare decisis—'abide by decided cases.' A legal principle requiring courts to try to follow case law or common-law precedents or principles when new questions of interpretation involving similar cases arise (see also **settled law**).

Status offense—legal violation by minor doing some act that would not be considered illegal if an adult did it, but is a violation of the juvenile code because it indicates that the minor is beyond parental control.

Status quo—the state of things now.

Statute of limitations—a law specifying that a criminal charge must be made or a civil suit brought within a specified period of time after the alleged crime or cause of action occurred, or, sometimes, after the injury was discovered (e.g., a suit must be brought within six years of the injury).

Statutory law—laws created by an act of a legislature.

Statutory rape—sexual relations with a person under the age of consent set by state law. Sex with an underaged partner is rape under the law even if the girl or boy says she or he wants relations and acts seductively.

Strict constructionist—courts that interpret laws or constitution narrowly, staying close to the original or literal meaning of the text.

Subjective standard—see **objective standard.**

Subject matter jurisdiction—subjects about which courts have the authority to act (e.g., cases over $75,000 in value; felonies; family offenses; traffic court; review of administrative decision, etc.).

Substantial obstacle/undue burden—standard for deciding whether a provision in a state law regulating a woman's right to obtain an abortion unduly interferes with the exercise of that right.

Substantiated—term used in some states to mean that a child protection case was investigated, and there was sufficient credible evidence to support a determination of child maltreatment. See also **founded** or **indicated.**

Substantive due process—laws and procedures that create, define, and regulate basic rights. Based on values inherent in the subject matter of a case.

Summary judgment—a pretrial motion asking for judgment on the law, assuming the parties agree on the facts. Either plaintiff or defendant may ask for summary judgment.

Surrogate court—see **probate court.**

Tarasoff **duty**—duty of a mental health professional to take appropriate action including warning a third party when a patient or client threatens harm to an identifiable other.

Tender years doctrine—the presumption that, other things being equal, the mother is the best custodian of small children.

Testamentary capacity—competence to make a will.

Testator—the person making the will.

Tort—a wrong. Tort cases are cases in which a plaintiff seeks money to compensate for an alleged injury caused by another's negligence or recklessness or other breach of duty.

Transfer laws—laws governing transfer of youth otherwise eligible for processing as a delinquent in juvenile court to or from adult criminal court.

Trial court—a court in which evidence in a legal case is first heard, and that decides matters of fact (what happened).

Ultimate issue—the essential and final question the trier of fact must decide, e.g., Is the defendant guilty of theft? Was the doctor negligent?

Uniform or Model Legislation—legislative guides or language prepared by scholarly organizations such as the American Law Institute and recommended to all state legislatures for adoption.

Unfounded—in child protection investigations, a case is "unfounded" or considered unsubstantiated if investigators fail to discover sufficient evidence of maltreatment.

U.S. Supreme Court—the highest court in the land, established in Article III of the Constitution.

Venire—a group or panel of prospective jurors assembled in a large room where they await a call for service on a trial (from Latin 'to come or appear').

Voir dire—the questioning of randomly selected prospective jurors by judge and lawyers so that both sides can determine their suitability to serve on that particular trial (from French, 'to speak the truth').

Volitional prong—the element of insanity standards involving inability to control one's behavior (e.g., a criminal action that resulted from an "irresistible impulse"). See also **cognitive prong.**

Voluntary—done without the undue influence of others, on the basis of adequate knowledge of the relevant facts, by someone able to reasonably foresee and weigh the consequences of different courses of action.

Ward—a person, usually a minor or incompetent person, placed by a court under the care of a guardian.

"Wild beast" standard—an early legal standard for insanity based on Roman law and reaffirmed in England in 1723: where a person is totally deprived of his understanding and memory, and does not know what he is doing, no more than an infant, than a brute or a wild beast.

Writ of *certiorari*—an order issued by the U.S. Supreme Court agreeing to hear an appeal. The Court directs the court below to certify the record of the case and submit it for review (also see **grant** *certiorari*).

References

Abbate, C. M. (1997). Finding solutions that work: Towards an integrated response to domestic violence. Summary and recommendations from the public hearing on "Strengthening the criminal justice response to domestic violence in New York City" chaired by State Senator Catherine M. Abbate, December 1996.

Abelson, R. (2001, June 10). Men are claiming harassment by men. *New York Times,* Business sec.

Abortion issue in Ohio case: National desk. (1998, October 14). *New York Times.*

Abplanalp, J. M. (1985). Premenstrual syndrome. *Behavioral Sciences and the Law,* 3, 103.

Abrams, D. (2004). Being more frugal with the death penalty. *Abrams Report.* http://msnbc.msn.com/id/3969370.

Ackerman, D. (2005, March 21). John DeLorean, Car man of the future. *Forbes.com.* http://www.forbes.com.

Ackerman, M. J., & Ackerman, M. C. (1997). Custody evaluation practices: A survey of experienced professionals (revisited). *Professional Psychology: Research and Practice,* 28(2), 137–145.

ACLU. (1998, January 27). Gap narrows in PSAT scores. *American Civil Liberties Union Freedom Network News.* http://www.aclu.org/news/w012798d.html.

Acocella, J. (1998, Apr. 6). The politics of hysteria. *New Yorker,* 74(7), 64–79.

Adams, S. F., Mahowald, M. B., & Gallagher, J. (2003). Refusal of treatment during pregnancy. *Clinics in Perinatology,* 30(1), 127–140.

Addington v. Texas, 441 U.S. 418 (1979).

Adler, N. E., David, H. P., Major, B. N., Roth, S. H., Russo, N. F., & Wyatt, G. E. (1990). Psychological responses after abortion. *Science,* 248, 41–44.

Adler, N. E., & Dolcini, P. (1986). Psychological issues in abortion for adolescents. In G. Melton (Ed.), *Adolescent abortion: Psychological and legal issues,* pp. 74–95. Lincoln: University of Nebraska Press.

Administration on Children and Families. (2004). Children's Bureau national adoption and foster care statistics. http://www.acf.hhs.gov/programs/cb/dis/afcars/publications/dlinkafcas.htm.

Administration on Children, Youth and Families. (2002). Child maltreatment, 2002. Washington, DC: Author. http://www.acf.hhs.gov/programs/cb/publications/cmreports.htm.

Administration on Children, Youth and Families, Children's Bureau. (2003). *The AFCARS Report, as of March 2003.* Washington, DC: Author.

Administrative Office of the U.S. Courts. (1999). *Annual report of the director.* Washington, DC: Author.

Ahn, N. (1994). Teenage childbearing and high school completion: Accounting for individual heterogeneity. *Family Planning Perspectives,* 26, 17–21.

Ake v. Oklahoma, 470 U.S. 68 (1985).

Akron v. Akron Center for Reproductive Health, 462 U.S. 416 (1983).

Alan Guttmacher Institute. (2004). Substance abuse during pregnancy. *State Policies in Brief.* http://www.guttmacher.org.

Alan Guttmacher Institute. (2004, August). Parental involvement in minors' abortions. *State Policy Briefs.* http://www.guttmacher.org/statecenter/spibs/spib_PIMA.pdf.

Albanesiu, C. (2004, October 19). Critics not pleased by change on domestic-violence data. *National Journal Group.*

Albemarle Paper Co. v. Moody, 422 U.S. 405 (1975).

Alexander v. Sandoval, 532 U.S. 275 (2001).

Allen v. United States, 164 U.S. 492 (1896).

Allen, M., Mabry, E., & McKelton, D-M. (1998). Impact of juror attitudes about the death penalty on juror evaluations of guilt and punishment: A meta-analysis. *Law and Human Behavior,* 22, 715–731.

Almeida, R., & Durkin, T. (1999). The cultural context model: Therapy for couples with domestic violence. *Journal of Marital and Family Therapy,* 25(3), 313–324.

Altman-Palm, N., & Tremblay, C. H. (1998). The effects of parental involvement laws and the AIDS epidemic on the pregnancy and abortion rates of minors. *Social Science Quarterly,* 79, 846–862.

Amato, P. R., & Gilbreth, J. G. (1999). Nonresident fathers and children's well-being: A meta-analysis. *Journal of Divorce,* 6(3), 55–69.

Amaya, M., & Burlingame, W. V. (1990). Judicial review of psychiatric admissions: The clinical impact on child and adolescent inpatients. In D. B. Wexler (Ed.), *Therapeutic jurisprudence,* pp. 281–291. Durham, NC: Carolina Academic Press.

Ambuel, B., & Rappaport, J. (1992). Developmental trends in adolescents' psychological and legal competence to consent to abortion. *Law and Human Behavior,* 16, 129–154.

Amerein, A. L., & Berliner, D. C. (2002, March 28). High-stakes testing, uncertainty, and student learning. *Education Policy Analysis Archives,* 10(18). Retrieved September 3, 2004, from http://epaa.asu.edu/epaa/v10n18/.

American Academy of Child and Adolescent Psychiatry, American Psychological Association, National Association of Social Workers, Inc., Virginia Chapter of the National Association of Social Workers, Inc., and Virginia Psychological Association. (1994). Brief of amici curiae in support of appellee. *Bottoms v. Bottoms,* Supreme Court of Virginia.

American Bar Association. (1983). *Recommendations on the insanity defense.* Washington, DC: Author.

American Bar Association. (1989). *American Bar Association criminal justice mental health standards.* Washington, DC: Author.

American Bar Association. (1995, Summer). Special issue on domestic violence. *Family Law Quarterly, 29(2).*

American Bar Association. (2004). Brief amicus curiae of the American Bar Association in support of the respondent. Submitted in *Roper v. Simmons* in the Supreme Court of the United States.

American Education Research Association. (2000). AERA position statement concerning high-stakes testing in pre-k–12 education. http://www.aera.net/bout/policy/stakes.htm.

American Law Institute (ALI). (2000). *Principles of the law of family dissolution: Analysis and recommendations.* Newark, NJ: Author.

American Medical Association. (2001). Diagnostic and treatment guidelines on domestic violence. http://www.ama-assn.org/ama/pub/category/3458.html.

American Psychiatric Association. (1983). American Psychiatric Association statement on the insanity defense. *American Journal of Psychiatry, 140,* 681–688.

American Psychiatric Association. (1987). *Diagnostic and statistical manual of mental disorders.* 3rd ed. Washington, DC: Author.

American Psychiatric Association. (1994). *Diagnostic and statistical manual of mental disorders.* 4th ed. Washington, DC: Author.

American Psychiatric Association. (2000). *Diagnostic and statistical manual of mental disorders (DSM IV-TR).* Washington, DC: Author.

American Psychological Association. (1987). In the Supreme Court of the United States. *Lockhart v. McCree.* Amicus curiae brief of the American Psychological Association. *American Psychologist, 42,* 69–68.

American Psychological Association. (1988). Brief for amicus curiae American Psychological Association in support of the respondent in neither party in *Price Waterhouse v. Ann. B. Hopkins,* 490 U.S. 228 (1989). Washington, DC: Author.

American Psychological Association. (1992). Ethical principles of psychologists and code of conduct. *American Psychologist, 47,* 1597–1628.

American Psychological Association. (1993). Brief for amicus curiae American Psychological Association in support of neither party in *Harris v. Forklift Systems,* 510 U.S. 17 (1993). Washington, DC: Author.

American Psychological Association. (1994). Guidelines for child custody evaluations in divorce proceedings. *American Psychologist, 49,* 677–680.

American Psychological Association. (2001). Appropriate use of high-stakes testing in our nation's schools. http://www. apa.org/pubinfo/testing html.

American Psychological Association. (2002). Brief for amicus curiae, American Psychological Association in *Sell v. United States* 539 U.S. 166 (2003).

American Psychological Association. (2003). Report of the Ethics Committee, 2003. *American Psychologist,* 59(5), 434–441.

American Psychological Association. (2005). The impact of abortion on women: What does psychological research say? APA Briefing Paper. Washington, DC: Author.

American Psychological Association. (2005). Report of the American Psychological Association Presidential Task Force on psychological ethics and national security. June 2005. http://www.apa.org/releases/PENSTaskForceReportFinal.pdf.

American Psychological Association. (2005). Report of the Ethics Committee, 2004. *American Psychologist,* 60(5), 523–528.

American Psychological Association. (2006). Index of APA amicus briefs by issue. http://www.apa.org/psyclaw/issues.html.

American Psychological Association, American Educational Research Association, & National Council on Measurement in Education. (1974). *Standards for educational and psychological tests.* Washington, DC: Author.

American Psychological Association—Committee on Ethical Guidelines for Forensic Psychologists. (1991). Specialty guidelines for forensic psychologists. *Law and Human Behavior, 15,* 655–665.

American Psychological Association—Committee on Professional Practice and Standards, APA Board of Professional Affairs. (1999). Guidelines for psychological evaluations in child protection matters. *American Psychologist, 54,* 586–593.

American Psychological Association Ethics Committee. (1997). APA statement on services by telephone, teleconferencing and Internet. http://www.apa.org/ethics/stmnt01.html.

American Psychological Association Ethics Committee. (2001). Rules and procedures. http://www.APA.org/ethics/rules.html.

American Psychological Association Working Group on Investigation of Memories of Childhood Abuse. (1998). *Psychology, Public Policy, and Law, 4,* 931–1078.

American Psychological Association Working Group on Investigation of Memories of Childhood Abuse. (1998). *Final conclusions of the American Psychological Association working group on investigation of memories of childhood abuse. Psychology, Public Policy, and Law, 4,* 933–940.

American Psychology–Law Society. (1996). Executive summary: The MacArthur violence risk assessment study. *American Psychology Law Society News,* 16(3), 1–3.

Anderson, C. (2004, September 14). Jury rejects idiot defense in sex assault. *San Francisco Daily Journal,* 2.

Anderson, E. M. (1996). The effect of mandatory reporting legislation on the teaching environment: A survey of New York State teachers. Unpublished doctoral dissertation. State University of New York at Buffalo.

Anderson, E. M., & Levine, M. (1999). Concern about allegations of child sexual abuse against teachers and the teaching environment. *Child Abuse & Neglect,* 23, 833–843.

Anderson, J. (2005, July 7). Study says malpractice payouts aren't rising. *New York Times,* C–1, C–7.

Apodaca v. Oregon, 406 U.S. 404 (1972).

Appelbaum, P. S., & Grisso, T. (1995a). The MacArthur treatment competence study I: Mental illness and competence to consent to treatment. *Law and Human Behavior,* 19(2),105–126.

Appelbaum, P. S., & Grisso, T. (1995b). The MacArthur treatment competence study III: Abilities of patients to consent to psychiatric and medical treatments. *Law and Human Behavior,* 19, 149–174.

Appelbaum, P. S., & Rosenbaum, A. (1989). *Tarasoff* and the researcher: Does the duty to protect apply in the research setting? *American Psychologist,* 44, 885–894.

Apprendi v. New Jersey 530 U.S. 466 (2000).

Archer, J. (2000). Sex differences in aggression between heterosexual partners: A meta-analytic review. *Psychological Bulletin,* 126(5), 651–680.

Aries, P. (1962). *Centuries of childhood.* New York: Knopf.

Armstrong, M. (2000, March 12). *Pryor v. Pryor. E!Online News.* http://eonline.com/News/Items/0,16143,00.html.

Aron, L. Y., & Olson, K. K. (1997, March). *Efforts by child welfare agencies to address domestic violence: The experiences of five communities.* Washington, DC: Urban Institute.

Arthur, R. (2004). Young offenders: Children in need of protection. *Law & Policy,* 26 (3/4), 309–327.

Associated Press. (2003a, March 2). Justice department opposes suspect's bid for two juries. *Buffalo News,* A–13.

Associated Press. (2003b). N.Y. education chief tosses test scores. http://www.cnn.com/2003/EDUCATION/06/25/math.test.ap.

Associated Press. (2004a, September 26). Boy, 7, charged in arson that killed retiree. *Buffalo News,* A–11.

Associated Press. (2004b, September 19). Costly errors prompt change in Nevada test contractor. *Las Vegas Review Journal,* http://www.lvrj.com.

Associated Press. (2005a, May 2). Huntsman snubs federal "No Child" requirements.

Associated Press. (2005b, February 17). Sex offender sued for slow home sales. *New York Times,* A–19.

Association of the Bar of the City of New York (2003). *Choosing between batterers education program models: Recommendations to the New York City Domestic Violence Criminal and Family Courts: A report of the Domestic Violence Committee.* New York: Author.

Association of Family and Conciliation Courts. (n.d.). *Model standards of practice for child custody evaluation.* Madison, WI: Author.

Atkins v. Commonwealth, 2006 WL 1550010.

Atkins v. Virginia, 536 U.S. 304 (2002).

Aubrey, M. (1987). Evaluation of competence to stand trial: Frequency of repeated referrals. *Journal of Psychiatry & Law,* 15, 425–431.

Aubrey, M. (1988). Characteristics of competence referral defendants and nonreferred criminal defendants. *Journal of Psychiatry & Law,* 16, 233–245.

Aubrey, M. R. (1989). A content analysis of jurors' deliberations in response to a simulated child sex abuse trial. Unpublished doctoral dissertation, State University of New York at Buffalo.

Auer, H. (2003, April 15). State ends loophole for young killers. *Buffalo News,* B–1.

Auerbach, J. S. (1976). *Unequal justice. Lawyers and social change in modern America.* New York: Oxford University Press.

Ayres I., & Brooks, R. (2005). Does affirmative action reduce the number of black lawyers? *Stanford Law Review,* 57, 1807–1854.

Azar, B. (2000). Online experiments: Ethically fair or foul? *Monitor on Psychology,* 31, 50–52.

Azar, S. T., & Benjet, C. L. (1994). A cognitive perspective on ethnicity, race, and termination of parental rights. *Law and Human Behavior,* 18, 249–268.

Azur, B. (1997). When research is swept under the rug. *APA Monitor,* 28(8), 1.

Babcock, J. C., Green, C. E., and Robie, C. (2004). Does batterers' treatment work? A meta-analytic review of domestic violence treatment. *Clinical Psychology Review,* 23(8), 1023–1053.

Bachrach, C. A., Stolley, K. S., & London, K. A. (1992). Relinquishment of premarital births: Evidence from national survey data. *Family Planning Perspectives,* 24, 27–32.

Baime, D. S. (2001). *Report to the Supreme Court.* Systemic Proportionality Review Project. 2000–2001 Term. Trenton: Supreme Court of New Jersey.

Baldus, D. C., Pulaski, C., & Woodworth, G. (1983). Comparative review of death sentences: An empirical study of the Georgia experience. *Journal of Criminal Law and Criminology,* 74(3), 661–753.

Baldus, D. C., Woodworth, G., & Pulaski, C. A. (1985). Monitoring and evaluating contemporary death sentencing systems: Lessons from Georgia. *University of California at Davis Law Review,* 18, 1375–1407.

Ballew v. Georgia, 435 U.S. 223 (1978).

Barber v. State, 592 So. 2d 330 (Fla. App. 2 Dist. 1992).

Barefoot v. Estelle, 463 U.S 880 (1983).

Barenti, M. (1997, Sept. 20). Psychologist with suspended license still seeing patients. *Post Register.* http://www .idahonews.com/92097/A_SECTIO/7372.htm.

Barnes, D. W., & Conley, J. M. (1986). *Statistical evidence in litigation: Methodology, procedure, and practice.* Boston: Little, Brown.

Barnes v. Costle, 561 F.2d 983 (D.C. Cir. 1977).

Barrett, D., & William, H. (2004, July 16). Climbie murder: Police to face misconduct charges. *Press Association Limited, Home News.*

Barrett, G. V., & Morris, S. B. (1993). The American Psychological Association's amicus curiae brief in *Price Waterhouse v. Hopkins. Law and Human Behavior,* 17, 201–215.

Barsky v. Board of Regents, 347 U.S. 442 (1954).

Bartollas, C., & Miller, S. J. (1998). *Juvenile justice in America.* 2nd ed. Upper Saddle River, NJ: Prentice Hall.

Bass, E., & Davis, L. (1988). *The courage to heal.* New York: Harper & Row.

Bathurst, K., Gottfried, A. W., & Gottfried, A. E. (1997). Normative data for the MMPI–2 in child custody litigation. *Psychological Assessment,* 9(3), 205–211.

Batson v. Kentucky, 476 U.S. 79 (1986).

Bauserman, R. (2002). Child adjustment in joint-custody versus sole-custody arrangements: A meta-analytic review. *Journal of Family Psychology,* 16(1), 91–102.

Baxtrom v. Herald, 383 U.S. 107 (1966).

Bazemore, G. (1998). Crime victims and restorative justice in juvenile courts. Judges as obstacle or leader? *Western Criminology Review,* 1(1). http://wcr.sonoma .edu/v1n1/bazemore.html.

Bearak, B. (1997, July 27). Questions of race run deep for foe of preferences. *New York Times,* A–1, A–19–20.

Bearman, P. S. , & Bruckner, H. (2000). *Promise to the future: Virginity pledges as they affect transition to first intercourse.* New York: Institute for Social and Economic Theory and Research, Columbia University.

Beaulie, M., & Messner, S. F. (1999). Race, gender, and outcomes in first degree murder cases. *Journal of Poverty: Innovations on Social, Political, and Economic Inequalities,* 3(1), 47–68.

Beck, C. J. A., & Sales, B. D. (2000). A critical reappraisal of divorce mediation research and policy. *Psychology, Public Policy, and Law,* 6 (4), 989–1056.

Beck, J. C. (1985a). The psychotherapist and the violent patient: Recent case law. In J. C. Beck (Ed.), *The potentially violent patient and the Tarasoff decision in psychiatric practice,* pp. 9–34. Washington, DC: American Psychiatric Press.

Beck, J. C. (1985b). A clinical survey of the Tarasoff experience. In J. C. Beck (Ed.), *The potentially violent patient and the Tarasoff decision in psychiatric practice,* pp. 59–81. Washington, DC: American Psychiatric Press.

Beckman, M. (2004, July 30). Crime, culpability and the adolescent brain. *Science,* 305, 596–599.

Bell, R. B. (1990). Testimony and statement. Hearing before the Committee on the Judiciary, House of Representatives, One Hundred First Congress, second session, on H. Con. Res. 172. Serial No. 81. Washington, DC: Government Printing Office.

Bell v. Thompson, 545 (U.S.).—(2005).

Bellotti v. Baird (I), 428 U.S. 132 (1976).

Bellotti v. Baird (II), 443 U.S. 622 (1979).

Benjamin, G., Andrew, H., & Gollam, J. K. (2003). Context of custody litigation. In G. Benjamin, H. Andrew, and J. K. Gollam (Ed.), *Family evaluation and custody litigation: Reducing risks of ethical infraction and malpractice,* pp. 11–16. Washington, DC: American Psychological Association.

Bennet, L., & Williams. O. (2001). *In brief: Controversies and recent studies of batterer intervention program effectiveness.* Applied Researach Forum. National Electronic Network on Violence Against Women. Washington, DC: National Resource Center on Domestic Violence.

Bennett v. Jeffreys, 40 N.Y. 2d 543 (1976).

Benson, M. L., & Fox, G. L. L. (2004). *When violence hits home: How economics and neighborhood play a role.* National Institute of Justice, Research in Brief 205004. Washington, DC: U.S. Department of Justice, Office of Justice Programs.

Bentele, U., & Bowers, W. J. (2002). How jurors decide on death: Guilt is overwhelming; aggravation requires death; and mitigation is no excuse. *Brooklyn Law Review,* 66, 1011-1080.

Berlin, F. S., Malin, H. M., & Dean, S. (1991). Effects of statutes requiring psychiatrists to report suspected sexual abuse of children. *American Journal of Psychiatry,* 148, 449–453.

Berliner, L. (1998). The use of expert testimony in child sexual abuse cases. In S. J. Ceci and H. Helmbrook (Eds.), *Expert witnesses in child abuse cases,* pp. 11–27. Washington, DC: American Psychological Association.

Berlow, A. (2002, August). Deadly decisions. http://www .americnradioworks.org/features/ deadlydecisions/index.html.

Berrueta-Clements, J. R., Schweinhart, L. J., Barnett, W. S., Epstein, A. S., & Weikart, D. P. (1984). *Changed lives: The effects of the Perry preschool program on youths through age 19.* Ypsilanti, MI: High/Scope Press.

Bersoff, D. N. (1980). Regarding psychologists testily: Legal regulation of psychological assessment in the schools. *Maryland Law Review,* 39, 27–120.

Bersoff, D. N. (1981). Testing and the law. *American Psychologist,* 36, 1047–1956.

Bersoff, D. N. (1987). Social science data and the Supreme Court: Lockhart as a case in point. *American Psychologist,* 42, 52–58.

Bersoff, D. N., & Ogden, D. W. (1987). In the Supreme Court of the United States: *Lockhart v. McCree. American Psychologist,* 42, 59–68.

Besharov, D. J. (1988). The need to narrow the ground for state intervention. In D. J. Besharov (Ed.), *Protecting children from abuse and neglect*, pp. 47–90. Springfield, IL: Charles C. Thomas.

Biklen, D. D. (1999). *Adoption of children in state foster care*. Hartford, CT: Connecticut State Law Revision Commission. http://www.cga.state.ct.us/lrc/Adoption/FosterCareReport.htm#Benefits.

Binet, A., & Simon, T. (1905). Upon the necessity of establishing a scientific diagnosis of inferior states of intelligence. In W. Dennis (Ed.) (1948), *Readings in the history of psychology*, pp. 407–411. New York: Appleton-Century-Crofts.

Binet, A., & Simon, T. (1905, 1908). The development of the Binet-Simon scale, 1905–1908. In W. Dennis (Ed.) (1948), *Readings in the history of psychology*, pp. 412–424. New York: Appleton-Century-Crofts.

Bingham, C., & Gansler, L. L. (2002). *Class action: The story of Lois Jensen and the landmark case that changed sexual harassment law*. New York: Doubleday.

Birnbaum, J. (1989). Report finds both good and bad initial results of Wisconsin's mandatory arrest law. *Women's Advocate*, 10(2), 3.

Black, H. C. (2004). *Black's Law Dictionary*. Abridged 8th ed. St. Paul, MN: West.

Blair v. Blair, 154 Vt. 201, 575 A.2d 191 (1990).

Blanck, P. D., & Berven, H. M. (1999). Evidence of disability after *Daubert*. *Psychology, Public Policy, and Law*, 5, 16–40.

Block, C. R. (2003a). Assessing risk factors for intimate partner homicide. *National Institute of Justice Journal*, 150, 5–8. Washington, DC: U.S. Department of Justice, Office of Justice Programs.

Block, C. R. (2003b). How can practitioners help an abused woman lower her risk of death? In Intimate Partner Homicide, *National Institute of Justice Journal*, 250. Washington, DC: National Institute of Justice.

Block, C. R., & Skogan, W. G. (2002). Do collective efficacy and community capacity make a difference "behind closed doors"? Report to the National Institute of Justice, December 2001. NCJRS document number 194711. Washington, DC: NCJRS.

Bloom, B. L., Asher, S. J., & White, S. W. (1978). Marital disruption as a stressor: A review and analysis. *Psychological Bulletin*, 85, 867–894.

Blum, R. W., Resnick, M. D., & Stark, T. (1990). Factors associated with the use of court bypass by minors to obtain abortion. *Family Planning Perspectives*, 22, 158–160.

Blumenthal, J.A. (1998). The reasonable woman standard: A meta-analytic review of gender differences in perceptions of sexual harassment. *Law and Human Behavior*, 22(1), 33–58.

Board of Education v. Rowley, 458 U.S. 176 (1982).

Bogess, S., & Bradner, C. (2000). Trends in adolescent males' abortion attitudes 1988–1995: Difference by race and ethnicity. *Family Planning Perspectives*, 32(3), 118–123.

Bograd, M. (1999). Strengthening domestic violence theories: Intersections of race, class, sexual orientation, and gender. *Journal of Marital and Family Therapy*, 25(3), 275–289.

Bogus, C. T. (2001). *Why lawsuits are good for America: Discipline and democracy, big business, and the common law (critical America)*. New York: New York University Press.

Bok, D., & Bowen, W. G. (1998). *The shape of the rivers: Long-term consequences of considering race in college and university admissions*. Princeton, NJ: Princeton University Press.

Bolling, I. M. (2003). *Adoption trends in 2003: Infant abandonment and Safe Haven legislation. 2003 Edition of the Report on Trends in the State Courts.* Washington, DC: National Center for State Courts.

Bonnie, R. J. (1983). The moral basis of the insanity defense. *American Bar Association Journal*, 69, 194–197.

Bonnie, R. J. (1990a). Dilemmas in administering the death penalty: Conscientious abstention, professional ethics, and the needs of the legal system. *Law and Human Behavior*, 14, 67–90.

Bonnie, R. J. (1990b). Grounds for professional abstention in capital cases: A reply to Brodsky. *Law and Human Behavior*, 14, 99–102.

Bonnie, R. J. (1992). The competence of criminal defendants: A theoretical formulation. *Behavioral Sciences and the Law*, 10, 291–316.

Bonnie, R. J. (1993). The competence of criminal defendants: Beyond *Dusky* and *Drope*. *Miami Law Review*, 47, 539–601.

Boring, E. G. (1957). *A history of experimental psychology*. 2nd ed. New York: Appleton-Century-Crofts.

Bornstein, B. H. (1999). The ecological validity of jury simulations: Is the jury still out? *Law and Human Behavior*, 23, 75–91.

Bornstein, B. H., & Rajki, M. (1994). Extra-legal factors and product liability: The influence of mock jurors' demographic characteristics and intuitions about the cause of an injury. *Behavioral Science and the Law*, 12, 127–147.

Borum. R., & Fulero, S. M. (1999). Errata: Empirical research on the insanity defense and attempted reforms: Evidence toward informed policy. *Law and Human Behavior*, 23(3), 375–394.

Borum R., & Reddy, M. (2001). Assessing violence risk in *Tarasoff* situations: A fact-based model of inquiry. *Behavioral Sciences & the Law*, 19(3), 375–385.

Borys, D., & Pope, K. S. (1989). Dual relationships between therapist and client: A national study of psychologists, psychiatry, and social workers. *Professional Psychology: Research and Practice*, 20, 283–293.

Bottoms v. Bottoms, 249 Va. 410, 457 S.E. 2d 1021 (1995).

Bottoms, B. L., & Goodman, G. S. (1989, April). The credibility of child victims of sexual assault. Paper presented at the Annual Meeting of the Eastern Psychological Association, Boston.

Bow, J. N., & Quinnell, F. A. (2001). Psychologists' current practices and procedures in child custody evaluations: five years after American Psychological Association guidelines. *Professional Psychology, Research, and Practice, 32*(3), 361–368.

Boy Scouts of America, National Capitol Area Council v. Pool, 809A.2d 1192 (2002).

Boylan, R. (n.d.). Open letter to the community about government harassment. http://www.ufonetwork.com/boylan/harassment/openletter.html.

Brace, C. L. (1880). *The dangerous classes of New York and twenty years' work among them.* 3rd ed. New York: Wynkoop & Hallenbeck.

Brady v. Hopper, 570 F. Supp. 1333 (District of Colorado, 1983).

Brady v. United States, 397 U.S. 742 (1970).

Brainerd, C. J., Reyna, V. F., & Poole, D. A. (2000). Fuzzy-trace theory and false memory: Memory in the courtroom. In D. F. Bjorklund (Ed.), *False memory creation.* Hillsdale, NJ: Erlbaum.

Braithwaite, J., & Mugford, S. (1994). Conditions of successful reintegration ceremonies: Dealing with juvenile offenders. *British Journal of Criminology, 34,* 139–171.

Brakel, S. J., Parry, J., & Weiner, B. A. (1985). *The mentally disabled and the law.* 3rd ed. Chicago: American Bar Foundation.

Braver, S. L., Ellman, I. M., & Fabricius, W. (2003). Relocation of children after divorce and children's best interests: new evidence and legal considerations. *Journal of Family Psychology, 17*(2), 206–219.

Bricklin, B. (1984). *Bricklin Perceptual Scales.* Furlong, PA: Village.

British Psychological Society. (2002). Ethical guidelines on forensic psychology 2002. http://www.bps.org.uk.

Brodsky, S. L. (1990). Professional ethics and professional morality in the assessment of competence for execution. *Law and Human Behavior, 14,* 91–97.

Brody, J. E. (1998, August 15). Researchers unravel the motives of stalkers. *New York Times,* F–1.

Brooks, A. D. (1974). *Law, psychiatry and the mental health system.* Boston: Little, Brown.

Brosig, C. L., & Kalichman, S. C. (1992). Clinicians' reporting of suspected child abuse: A review of the empirical literature. *Clinical Psychology Review, 12,* 155–168.

Brown v. Allen, 344 U.S. 443, 550 (1953).

Brown v. Board of Education, 347 U.S. 483, (1954).

Brown v. Board of Education of Topeka, 349 U.S. 294 (1955).

Brown, C. (2003, February 2). Pushing "Penny's Law" Family of slain woman won't rest until state changes sentencing rules for juveniles. *Buffalo News,* H–1.

Browne, A. (1990). Testimony and statement. In United States Senate, Committee on the Judiciary (1990). Hearing before the committee on the judiciary, U.S. Senate, One Hundred and First Congress, second session, on legislation to reduce the growing problem of violent

crime against women, part 2. (Serial No. J–101–80). Washington, DC: Government Printing Office.

Browne, A., & Finkelhor, D. (1986). Impact of child sexual abuse: A review of the research. *Psychological Bulletin, 99,* 66–77.

Bruck, M., & Ceci, S. J. (1995). Amicus brief for the case of State of *New Jersey v. Margaret Kelly Michaels* presented by Committee of Concerned Social Scientists. *Psychology, Public Policy, and Law, 1,* 272–322.

Bruck, R. (2003). The statutory definition of status offenders across the 50 states. *Southern Juvenile Defender Center.* http://www.childwelfare.net/SJDC/statusoffenders.html.

Brummer, C. E. (2002). Extended juvenile jurisdiction: The bets of both worlds. *Arkansas Law Review, 54,* 777–822.

Buck v. Bell, 274 U.S. 200 (1927).

Buckley, S. (2001, November 11). Human weeds. *St. Petersburg Times.*

Buel, S. (1990). Testimony and statement. In U.S. Senate, Committee on the Judiciary (1990). Hearing before the Committee on the Judiciary, U.S. Senate, One Hundred First Congress, second session, on legislation to reduce the growing problem of violent crime against women, part 2. Serial No. J–101–80. Washington, DC: Government Printing Office.

Burchfiel, N. (2005, January 19). Norma McCorvey (Roe) laments "holocaust of abortion." *CNSNews.com,* 2005.

Burdman, P. (2005, Spring). Scholarship sweepstakes: National merit program offers millions in scholarship dollars without regard to financial need. *National Crosstalk.* http://www.highereducation.org/crosstalk/ct205/news0205-scholarship.shtml.

Bureau of Justice Statistics. (1999, July). Mental health treatment of inmates and probationers. Bureau of Justice Statistics Special Report, NCJ 174463. Washington, DC: Author.

Bureau of Justice Statistics (2003). Key facts at a glance. http://www.ojp.usdoj.gov/bjs.

Burgess, D., & Borgida, E. (1997). Sexual harassment: An experimental test of sex-role spillover theory. *Personality and Social Psychology Bulletin, 23,* 63–75.

Burgess, D., and Borgida, E. (1999). Who women are, who women should be: Descriptive and prescriptive gender stereotyping in sex discrimination. *Psychology, Public Policy and Law, 5*(3), 665–692.

Burlington Northern v. White, 548 U.S.—(2006).

Burlington Industries v. Ellerth, 524 U.S. 742 (1998).

Burns, B. J., Costello, E. J., Erkanli, A., Tweed, D. L., Farmer, E. M. Z., & Angold, A. (1997). Insurance coverage and mental health service use by adolescents with serious emotional disturbance. *Journal of Child and Family Studies, 6*(1), 89–111.

Bush v. Gore, 531 U.S. 98 (2000).

Butts, J. A. (1996). *Offenders in juvenile court.* Washington, DC: Office of Juvenile Justice and Delinquency Prevention.

Butts, J., Hoffman, D., & Buck, J. (1999, October). Teen courts in the United States: A profile of current programs. OJJDP Fact Sheet #118. Washington, DC: Office of Juvenile Justice and Delinquency Prevention.

Buzawa, E. S., & Austin, T. (1998, July). Determining police response to domestic violence victims. In *Legal interventions in family violence: research findings and policy implications, a project of the American Bar Association's Criminal Justice Section, Commission on Domestic Violence, Center on Children and the Law, and Commission on Legal Problems of the Elderly*, 58. Presented to the National Institute of Justice. NCJ 171666. Washington, DC: National Institute of Justice.

Buzawa, E. S., & Buzawa, C. G. (2003). *Domestic violence: The criminal justice response.* 3rd ed. Thousand Oaks, CA: Sage.

Buzawa, E. S., & Hotaling, G., (2000). *The police response to domestic violence calls for assistance in three Massachusetts towns: Final report.* Washington, DC: National Institute of Justice.

Buzawa, E., & Hotaling, G. (2001). *An examination of assaults within the jurisdiction of Orange district court: Final Report.* Washington, DC: National Institute of Justice.

Caetano, R., Field, C. A., Ramisetty-Mikler, S., & McGrath, C. (2005). The 5-year course of intimate partner violence among white, black and Hispanic couples in the United States. *Journal of Interpersonal Violence,* 20(9), 1039–1057.

Caldwell, R. A., Bogat, G. A., & Davidson, W. S. II (1988). The assessment of child abuse potential and the prevention of child abuse and neglect: A policy analysis. *American Journal of Community Psychology,* 16, 608–624.

Caliber Associates. (2004). *Evaluation of CASA representation: Final report.* Fairfax, VA: Author.

Camara, W. J., & Merenda, P. F. (2000). Using personality tests in preemployment screening: Issues raised in *Soroka v. Dayton Hudson Corporation. Psychology, Public Policy, and Law,* 6(4), 1164–1186.

Cameron, P., & Cameron, K. (1997). Did the APA misrepresent the scientific literature to courts in support of homosexual custody? *Journal of Psychology,* 13, 313–332.

Campbell, D. T. (1974). Assessing the impact of social change. Paper presented at the Dartmouth/OECD Conference, Hanover, New Hampshire.

Campbell, J. C., Webster, D., Koziol-Mclain, J, Block, C. R., Campbell, D., Curry M. A., Gary, F., McFarlane, J., Sachs, C. Sharps, P. Ulrich, Y., & Wilt, S. S. (2003). Assessing risk factors for intimate partner homicide. In Intimate partner homicide, *National Institute of Justice Journal,* 250. Washington DC: National Institute of Justice.

Campbell, R. (1998). The community response to rape: Victim's experiences with the legal, medical and mental health systems. *American Journal of Community Psychology,* 26, 355–379.

Canedy, D. (2002, November 18). After conviction of boy, prosecutor switches sides. *New York Times,* A–14.

Cannell, J. J. (2006). Lake Woebegon, twenty years later. *Third Education Group Review,* 2(1).

Cardozo, B. N. (1921). *The nature of the judicial process.* New Haven, CT: Yale University Press.

Carlson, M. (1990, July 9). Abortion's hardest cases. *Time,* 22–26.

Carroll, S. L., & Gaston, R. J. (1983). Occupational licensing and the quality of service. *Law and Human Behavior,* 7, 139–146.

Carter, C. A., Bottoms, B. L., & Levine, M. (1996). Linguistic and socioemotional influences on the accuracy of children's reports. *Law and Human Behavior,* 20, 335–358.

Cartoof, V. G., & Klerman, L. V. (1986). Parental consent for abortion: Impact of the Massachusetts law. *American Journal of Public Health,* 76, 397–400.

Catalano, S. M. (2004, September). *Criminal victimization, 2003.* Bureau of Justice Statistics, National Crime Victimization Survey, NCJ 205455. Washington, DC: U.S. Department of Justice.

Cattell, J. McK. (1890). Mental tests and measurements. *Mind,* 15, 373–380.

"Oddfather" ends insanity ruse. (2003, April 7). *CBS News.* http://www.cbsnews.com/stories/2003/04/07/national/main548132.shtml.

Ceci, C. J., & Bruck, M. (1995). *Jeopardy in the courtroom.* Washington, DC: American Psychological Association.

Ceci, S. J., & Bruck, M. (1993). Suggestibility of the child witness: A historical review and synthesis. *Psychological Bulletin,* 113, 403–439.

Ceci, S. J., & Friedman, R. D. (2000). The suggestibility of children: Scientific research and legal implications. *Cornell Law Review,* 86, 33–108.

Center for Disease Control (CDC). (1997a). Special focus: Surveillance for reproductive health. *Morbidity and Mortality Weekly Report,* 46, 1–98.

Center for Disease Control (CDC). (1997b). Abortion surveillance: Preliminary data—United States, 1994. *Morbidity and Mortality Weekly Report,* 45, 1123–1127.

Centers for Disease Control (CDC). (2003). Teen birthrate continues to decline: African-Americans show sharpest drop. http://www.cdc gov/od/oc/media/pressrel/fs031217.htm.

Centers for Disease Control (CDC). (2004, November 26). *Morbidity and Mortality Weekly Report,* 53 (SS9).

Cervantes, N. N., & Cervantes, J. M. (1993). A Multicultural perspective in the treatment of domestic violence. In. M. Hansen & M. Harway (Eds.), *Battering and family therapy: A feminist perspective,* pp. 156–174. Newbury Park CA: Sage.

Chambers, D. L., Clydesdale, T. T., Kidder, W. C., & Lempert, R. O. (2005). The real impact of eliminating affirmative action in American law schools: An empirical critique of Richard Sander's study. *Stanford Law Review,* 57, 1855–1898.

Champion, D. J. (1998). *The juvenile justice system: Delinquency, processing and the law.* 2nd ed. Upper Saddle River, NJ: Prentice Hall.

Chang, J., Berg, C. J., Saltzman, L. E., & Herndon, J. (2005). Homicide: A leading cause of injury deaths among pregnant and postpartum women in the United States, 1991–1999. *American Journal of Public Health,* 95(3), 471–477.

Chavez, F. T. (1999). Black and white subjects' attitudes on the mandatory reporting of child abuse and neglect cases in the therapeutic context. Unpublished doctoral dissertation, State University of New York at Buffalo.

Child Welfare League (2002, September). Child welfare workforce. *Research Roundup.* http://www.cwla.org.

Childers, A. T. (1936). Some notes on sex mores among Negro children. *American Journal of Orthopsychiatry,* 6, 442–448.

Cirincione, C., & Jacobs, C. (1999). Identifying insanity acquittals: Is it any easier? *Law and Human Behavior,* 23, 487–497.

Clark v. Arizona 126 S. Ct. 2709 (2006).

Clark v. Arizona, No. 05–5966. Brief for the United States as Amicus Curiae (2006) at 13, 2006 WestLaw 542415.

Clary, F. (1982). Minor women obtaining abortions: A study of parental notification in a metropolitan area. *American Journal of Public Health,* 72, 283–285.

Clement, M. (1996). *Juvenile justice: Law and process.* New York: Butterworth-Heineman.

Clinton v. Jones, 520 U.S. 681 (1997).

CNN (1999, February 25). John King to die for black man's dragging death. http://www.cnn.pocom/US/9902/25/dragging.death.03.

Coalition for Prisoners' Rights Newsletter. (1998, July). http://www.sonic.net/~doretk/Issues/98–12%20WIN/kentuckyracialjustice.html.

Cohen, T. H., & Smith, S. K. (2004). *Civil trial cases and verdicts in large counties, 2001.* Bureau of Justice Statistics Bulletin. NCJ 202803. Washington, DC: Bureau of Justice Statistics.

Coker, D. (2001). Crime control and feminist law reform in domestic law: A critical review. *Buffalo Criminal Law Review,* 4, 801860.

Coker v. Georgia, 433 U.S. 584 (1977).

Cole, C. B., & Loftus, E. F. (1987). The memory of children. In S. J. Ceci, M. P. Toglia, & D. F. Ross (Eds.), *Children's eyewitness memory,* pp. 178–208. New York: Springer-Verlag.

Cole, N. S. (1981). Bias in testing. *American Psychologist,* 36, 1067–1077.

Coleman, S. (1999). *Mentally ill criminals and the insanity defense. A report to the Minnesota Legislature.* St. Paul, MN: Center for Applied Research and Policy Analysis, Metropolitan State University.

Colgrove v. Battin, 413 U.S. 149 (1973).

Commission on Domestic Violence Fatalities. (1997, October). *Report to the Governor, October 1997.* New York State Office for the Prevention of Domestic Violence. http://www.opdv.state.ny.us/publications.

Commonwealth v. LeFave, 430 Mass. 169, 714 N.E. 2d 805 (1999).

Compaan, C., Doueck, H. J., & Levine, M. (1997). Mandated reporter satisfaction with child protection: More good news for workers? *Journal of Interpersonal Violence,* 12, 847–857.

Compart, A. (1996, November 11). The war on harassment. *Air Force Times.*

Conner, K. R., Cerulli, C., & Caine, E. D. (2002). Threatened and attempted suicide by partner-violent male respondents petitioned to family violence court. *Violence and Victims,* 17(2), 115–124.

Conrad, C. S. (2001, March). "Death-qualification" leads to biased juries: Capital punishment views impact jury selection—statistical data included. *USA Today Magazine.*

Consumer Advisory Board v. Glover, 151 F.R.D. 496 (D. Me., 1993).

Cook, S. L. (2000, November 20). Measurement issues. Presentation, National Institute of Justice Gender Symmetry Workshop, Arlington Virginia.

Cooper, D. K. (1997). Juveniles' understanding of trial-related information: Are they competent defendants? *Behavioral Sciences & the Law,* 15, 167–180.

Cooper, V. G., & Zapf, P. A. (2003). Predictor variables in competency to stand trial decisions. *Law and Human Behavior,* 27(4), 423–436.

Corrado, R. R., Vincent, G. M., Hart, S. D., & Cohen, I. M. (2004). Predictive validity of the psychopathy checklist: Youth Version for general and violent recidivism. *Behavioral Sciences & the Law,* 22(1), 5–22.

Corwin, D. L., Berliner, L., Goodman, G., Goodwin, J., & White, S. (1987). Child sexual abuse and custody disputes: No easy answers. *Journal of Interpersonal Violence,* 2, 91–105.

Costanzo, M. (1997). *Just revenge: Costs and consequences of the death penalty.* New York: St. Martin's.

Costello, J. C. (2002). Why have hearings for kids if you're not going to listen? A therapeutic jurisprudence approach to mental disablity proceedings for minors. 71 *U. Cincinnati Law Review* 19.

Costello, J. C. (2003). "The trouble is they're growing. The trouble is they're grown." Therapeutic jurisprudence and adolescents' participation in mental health care decisions. 29 *Ohio N. U. L. Rev.* 607.

Cozzarelli, C., Sumer, N., & Major, B. (1998). Mental models of attachment and coping with abortion. *Journal of Personality and Social Psychology,* 74, 453–467.

Coy v. Iowa, 487 U.S. 1012 (1988).

Crafts, L. W., Schneirla, T. C., Robinson, E. E., & Gilbert, R. W. (1938). *Recent experiments in psychology.* New York: McGraw-Hill.

Craig, C., & Herbert, D. (1997). The state of children: An examination of government-run foster care. National Center of Policy Analysis. http://www.ncpa.org/studies/s210/s210.html.

Crawford v. Washington, 541 U.S. 36 (2004).

Crombbag, H. F. M. (2003). Adversarial or inquisitorial: Do we have a choice? In P. J. Van Koppen and S. D. Penord (Eds), *Adversarial versus inquisitorial justice: Psychological perspectives on criminal justice systems*, 21–26. New York: Kluwer Academic/Plenum.

Crosby, C. A., Britner, P. A., Jodl, K. M., & Portwood, S. G. (1995). The juvenile death penalty and the Eighth Amendment: An empirical investigation of societal consensus and proportionality. *Law and Human Behavior, 19*, 245–261.

Crosby-Currie, C.A. (1996). Children's involvement in contested custody cases: Practices and experiences of legal and mental health professionals. *Law and Human Behavior, 20*(3), 289–312.

Crowley, M. J., O'Callaghan, G., & Ball, P. J. (1994). The juridical impact of psychological expert testimony in a simulated child sexual abuse trial. *Law and Human Behavior, 18*(1), 89–105.

Culhane, S. E., Hosch, H. M., & Weaver, W. G. (2004). Crime victims serving as jurors: Is there bias present? *Law and Human Behavior, 28*(6), 649–659.

Cummien, A. J. (1985). Pathological gambling as an insanity defense. *Behavioral Sciences and the Law, 3*, 85.

Curry, T. R., Lee, G., & Rodriguez, S. F. (2004). Does victim gender increase sentence severity? Further explorations of gender dynamics and sentencing outcomes. *Crime & Delinquency, 50*(3), 319–343.

Cutler, B. L., & Penrod, S. D. (1995). *Mistaken identification: The eyewitness, psychology and the law.* Cambridge: Cambridge University Press.

Cutler, B. L., Penrod, S. D., & Dexter, H. R. (1989). The eyewitness, the expert psychologist, and the jury. *Law & Human Behavior, 13*, 311–332.

Dahir, V. B., Richardson, J. T., Ginsburg, G. P., Gatowski, S. I., Dobbin, S. A., & Merlino, M. L. (2005). Judicial application of *Daubert* on psychological syndrome and profile evidence: A research note. *Psychology, Public Policy, and Law, 11*(1), 62–82.

Dann, B. M., & Hans, V. P. (2004). Recent evaluative research on jury trial innovations. *Court Review, 41*(1), 12–19.

Dao, J. (2004, October 8). New federal rules gather data about battered women. *New York Times.* http://www.nytimes.com/2004/10/08/politics/08shelter.

Daubert v. Merrell Dow Pharmaceuticals, Inc., 509 U.S. 579 (1993).

David, H. P. (1972). Abortion in psychological perspective. *American Journal of Orthopsychiatry, 42*, 61–68.

Davidson, H. A. (1995, Summer). Child abuse and domestic violence: Legal connections and controversies. *Family Law Quarterly, 29*(2), 357–373.

Davis, D., Loftus, E., & Follette, W. C. (2001). Commentary: How, when and whether to use informed consent for recovered memory therapy. *Journal of the American Academy of Psychiatry and Law, 29*, 148–159.

Davis v. Monroe County Board of Education, 526 U.S. 629 (1999).

Davis, K. C. (1960). *Administrative law and government.* St. Paul, MN: West.

Davis, P. (2004, November 25). Is Hinckley ready for society? *MSNBC News*, Newsweek Society.

Davis, R. C., Smith, B. E., & Nickles, L. (1998, July). Prosecuting domestic violence cases with reluctant victims: assessing two novel approaches in Milwaukee. In *Legal interventions in family violence: research findings and policy implications, a project of the American Bar Association's Criminal Justice Section, Commission on Domestic Violence, Center on Children and the Law, and Commission on Legal Problems of the Elderly,* 71–72. Presented to the National Institute of Justice. NCJ 171666. Washington, DC: National Institute of Justice.

Davis, R.C., Smith, B. E., & Taylor, B. (2003). Increasing the proportion of domestic violence arrests that are prosecuted: A natural experiment in Milwaukee. *Criminology & Public Policy, 2*(2), 263–282.

Deatherage v. Examining Board of Psychology, 134 Wn.2d 131, 948 P.2d 828 (1997).

Death Penalty Focus of California. (n.d.). The cost of the death penalty in California. http://www.worldpolicy.org/globablrights/dp/dp-cost.html.

Death Penalty Information Center. (2004). Home page. http://www.deathpenaltyinfo.org.

Death Penalty Information Center. (2005). Future dangerousness predictions wrong 95% of the time: New study on capital trials exposes widespread unreliable testimony. http://www.deathpenaltyinfo.org/article.php?scid=1&did=944.

De Atley, R. K. (2006). Courts: The judge didn't believe witness that Kelly was retarded. He killed three in the 1980s. Inland Southern California, April 3, *http://www.pe.com/localnews/inland/stories/PE_News_Local_P_kelly_04.d8bb670.html.*

Deaux, K., & Emsweiler, T. (1974). Explanations of successful performance on sex-linked tasks: What is skill for the male is luck for the female. *Journal of Personality and Social Psychology, 29*, 80–85.

Dedman, B. (1998, August 8). Secret Service challenges assassin stereotypes. *New York Times,* New York Edition, sec. 1, 20.

DeFrances, C. J. (2002, May). Prosecutors in state courts, 2001. Bureau of Justice Statistics Bulletin. NCJ 193441. Washington, DC: Bureau of Justice Statistics.

DeFrances, C. J., Storm, K. J., & Bureau of Justice Statistics Statisticians. (1997, March). *National survey of prosecutors, 1994: 7 prosecuted in state criminal courts.* National Criminal Justice Publication 164265. Washington, DC: U.S. Department of Justice Office of Justice Programs and Office of Juvenile Justice and Delinquency Prevention.

Delaware v. Prowse, 440 U.S. 648 (1979).

DeLeon, P. H. (2000). The science-practice synergy. *Monitor on Psychology, 31*, 5.

Dershowitz, A. M. (1994). *The advocate's devil.* New York: Warner.

Devine, D. J., Clayton, L. D., Dunford, B. B., Seying, R., & Pryce, J. (2001). Jury decision making: 45 years of empirical research on deliberating groups. *Psychology, Public Policy, and Law, 7*(3), 622–727.

Devlin, P. (1966). *Trial by jury.* London: Stevens and Son.

D.H. v. J.H, 418 N.E. 2d 286 (Ind. App., 1981).

Diamond, S. S. (1993). Instructing on death: Psychologists, juries, and judges. *American Psychologist, 48,* 423–434.

Dillon, S. (2004, September 5). Good schools or bad? Ratings baffle parents. *New York Times.* http://www.nytimes.com/2004/09/05/education/05school.html.

District of Columbia v. B.J.R., 332 A.2d 58 (1975).

Dixon v. United States, 548 —(2006).

Doan, B. (1997). Death penalty, policy, statistics and public opinion. *Focus on Law Studies, 12*(2), 3.

Documents. (1989). A measured response: Koop on abortion. *Family Planning Perspectives, 21,* 31–32.

Documents. (1990). More on Koop's study of abortion. *Family Planning Perspectives, 22,* 36–39.

Doe v. Bolton, 410 U.S. 179 (1973).

Dokecki, P. R. (2004). *The clergy sexual abuse crisis. Reform and renewal in the Catholic community.* Washington, DC: Georgetown University Press.

Donovan, P. (1983). Judging teenagers: How minors fare when they seek court-authorized abortions. *Family Planning Perspectives, 15,* 259–267.

Doris, J. (Ed.). (1991). *The suggestibility of children's recollections.* Washington, DC: American Psychological Association.

Dorsey, S. (1983). Occupational licensing and minorities. *Law and Human Behavior, 7,* 171–181.

Doueck, H. J., Bronson, D. E., & Levine, M. (1992). Evaluating risk assessment implementation in child protection: Issues for consideration. *Child Abuse and Neglect, 16*(5), 637–646.

Doueck, H. J., Levine, M., & Bronson, D. E. (1990). *Final report of the Child at Risk Field System: Findings from Ontario County.* Buffalo, NY: Research Center for Children and Youth.

Drake, B., & Zuravin, S. (1998). Bias in child maltreatment reporting: Revisiting the myth of classlessness. *American Journal of Orthopsychiatry, 68,* 295–304.

Drizin, S., & Leo, R. A. (2004). The problem of false confessions in the post-DNA world. *North Carolina Law Review, 82*(3), 891–1007.

Drope v. Missouri, 420 U.S. 162 (1975).

Dugan, L. (2002). *Domestic violence legislation: Exploring its impact on domestic violence an the likelihood that police are informed and arrest, final report.* NCJRS, award no. 97-WT-VX-004, document no. 196853. Washington, DC: NCJRS.

Dugan, L., Nagin, D. S., & Rosenfeld, R. (2003). Do domestic violence services save lives? *National Institute of Justice Journal, 250* (special issue on intimate partner homicide), 16–43.

Duggan, L. M. III, Aubrey, M., Doherty, E., Isquith, P., Levine, M., & Scheiner, J. (1989). The credibility of children as witnesses in a simulated child sex abuse trial. In S. J. Ceci, D. F. Ross, & M. P. Toglia (Eds.), *Perspectives on children's testimony,* pp. 71–99. New York: Springer-Verlag.

Duncan v. Louisiana, 391 U.S. 145 (1968).

Duncan, A. D., & Hively, W. (1998, March 6). Sexual harassment: A functional analysis of plaintiffs and defendants. Paper presented at the American Psychology and Law Society Conference, Los Angeles California.

Duncan, G. J., & Hoffman, S. D. (1990). Teenage welfare receipt and subsequent dependence among black adolescent mothers. *Family Planning Perspectives, 22,* 16–20.

Dunford, F. W. (2000). The San Diego Navy Experiment: An assessment of interventions for men who assault their wives. *Journal of Consulting and Clinical Psychology, 68,* 468–476.

Dunn v. Johnson, 162 F.3d 302 (5th Cir., 1998), cert. denied, 526 U.S. 1092 (1999).

Du Pont's competency to stand trial for murder in dispute. (1996, September 22). *New York Times,* A–33.

Duren v. Missouri, 439 U.S. 357 (1979).

Durham v. United States, 214 F.2d 862 (D.C. Cir., 1954).

Dusky v. United States, 362 U.S. 402 (1960).

Dutton, D. G. (1988). *The domestic assault of women.* Newton, MA: Allyn & Bacon.

Dutton, M. A. (1998, July). Impact of evidence concerning battering and its effects in criminal trials involving battered women. In *Legal interventions in family violence: Research findings and policy implications, a project of the American Bar Association's Criminal Justice Section, Commission on Domestic Violence, Center on Children and the Law, and Commission on Legal Problems of the Elderly,* 66–67. Presented to the National Institute of Justice. NCJ 171666. Washington, DC: National Institute of Justice.

Eaton, L. (2004, May 23). For arbiters in custody battles, wide power and little scrutiny. *New York Times.* http://www.nytimes.com.

Eaton, L. (2004, August 8). Divorced parents move, and custody gets trickier. *New York Times* on the Web, New York region. http://www.nytimes.com.

Eaton, L., & Kaufman, L. (2005, April 26). In problem-solving courts, judges turn therapist. *New York Times,* A–1, A–20.

Eckenrode, J., Powers, J., Doris, J., Mansch, J., & Balgi, N. (1988). Substantiation of child abuse and neglect reports. *Journal of Consulting and Clinical Psychology, 56,* 9–16.

Edelson, J. L. (1996). The overlap between child maltreatment and woman abuse. National Resource Center on Domestic Violence. http://www.vaw.umn.edu.

Edelson, J. L. (1997). Problems with children's witnessing of domestic violence. National Resource Center on Domestic Violence. http://www.vaw.umn. edu.

Edelson, J. L. (1998a). Focus: Adult violence and its impact on children. In *Family Violence: Emerging pro-*

grams, pp. 74–75. Reno, NV: National Council of Juvenile and Family Court Judges.

Edelson, J. L. (1998b): Focus: Men who batter as parents. In *Family violence: Emerging programs,* pp. 150–151. Reno, NV: National Council of Juvenile and Family Court Judges.

Edelson, J. L. (1999a). Children's witnessing of adult domestic violence. *Journal of Interpersonal Violence,* 14, 839–870.

Edelson, J. L. (1999b). The overlap between child maltreatment and woman battering. *Violence against Women,* 5, 134–154.

Edelson, J. L. (2001). Studying the co-occurrence of child maltreatment and domestic violence in families. In S. A. Graham-Berman and J. L. Edelson (Eds.), *Domestic violence in the lives of children: The future of research, intervention and social policy,* pp. 91–110. Washington, DC: American Psychological Association.

Edelson, J. L., Eisikovits, Z., & Guttmann, E. (1985). Men who batter women. *Journal of Family Issues,* 6(2), 229–247.

Edens, J. F., Buffington-Vollum, J. K., Keilen, A., Roskamp, P., & Anthony, C. (2005). Predictions of future dangerousness in capital murder trials: Is it time to "disinvent the wheel"? *Law and Human Behavior,* 29(1), 55–86.

Editorial. (1990, August 30). A 10-year-old's nightmares and a weakness in the law. Must boy retell horrible events in courtroom? *Buffalo News,* B-2.

Editorial. (1998, September 8). New rules must still blend merit, diversity. *Buffalo News,* B-2.

Edmond, G., & Mercer, D. (2004). *Daubert* and the exclusionary ethos: The convergence of corporate and judicial attitudes toward the admissiblity of expert evidence in tort litigation. *Law & Policy,* 26(2), 231–257.

Edmonson v. Leesville Concrete Co., 500 U.S. 614 (1991).

Edwards v. Edwards, 205 Neb. 255, 287 N.W.2d 420 (1980).

Edwards, L. P. (1987). The relationship of family and juvenile courts in child abuse cases. *Santa Clara Law Review,* 27, 201–270.

Ehrensaft, N. K. (2003). Intergenerational transmission of partner violence. *Journal of Consulting and Clinical Psychology,* 71, 741–753.

Ehrlich, J. S. (2003). Grounded in the reality of their lives: Listening to teens who make the abortion decision without involving their parents. *Berkeley Women's Law Journal,* 18, 61–180.

Eigen, J. P. (1999). Lesion of the will: Medical resolve and criminal responsibility in Victorian insanity trials. *Law & Society Review,* 33, 425–459.

Eisenstadt v. Baird, 405 U.S. 438 (1972).

Elam-Evans, L. D., Strauss, L. T., Herndon, J., Parker, W. Y., Whitehead, S., & Berg, C. J. (2002, November 28). *Abortion surveillance—United States,* 1999. 15(SS09), 1–28.

Ellerbe v. Hooks, 416 A.2d 512 (Pa., 1980).

Ellison v. Brady, 924 F.2d. 872 (9th Cir., 1991).

Elliott v. North Carolina Psychology Board, 348 N.C. 230, 498 S.E.2d 616 (1998).

Elliott, R. (1987). *Litigating intelligence: IQ tests, special education and social science in the courtroom.* Dover, MA: Auburn House.

Elliott, R. (1991). Social science data and the APA: The Lockhart brief as a case in point. *Law and Human Behavior,* 15, 59–76.

Ellman, I. M., Kurtz, P. M., Scott, E. S., Weithorn, L. A., & Bix, B. H. (2004). *Family law, cases, text, problems.* 4th ed. Newark, NJ: LexisNexis.

Ellsworth, P. C. (1991). To tell what we know or wait for Godot? *Law and Human Behavior,* 15, 77–90.

Elwork, A., Sales, B. D., & Alfini, J. J. (1977). Juridic decisions: In ignorance of the law or in light of it? *Law and Human Behavior,* 1, 163–189.

Emery, R. E. (2005). Parental alienation syndrome: Proponents bear the burden of proof. *Family Court Review,* 43(1), 8–13.

Emery, R. E., Laumann-Billings, L., Waldron, M., Sbarra, D. A., & Dillon, P. (2001). Child custody mediation and litigation: Custody, contact, and co-parenting 12 years after initial dispute resolution. *Journal of Consulting and Clinical Psychology,* 69, 323–332.

Emery, R. E., Matthews, S. G., & Wyer, M. M. (1991). Child custody mediation and litigation: Further evidence on the differing views of mothers and fathers. *Journal of Consulting and Clinical Psychology,* 59(3), 410–418.

English, D. J. (1998). The extent and consequences of child maltreatment. *Future of Children,* 8, 39–53.

English, D. J., Marshall, D. B., Brummel, S., & Orme, M. (1999). Characteristics of repeated referrals to child protective services in Washington State. *Child Maltreatment,* 4, 297–307.

Ennis, B. J., & Litwack, T. R. (1974). Psychiatry and the presumption of expertise: Flipping coins in the courtroom. *California Law Review,* 62, 693–752.

Epstein, D. (1999). Rethinking the roles of prosecutors, judges, and the court system. 11 *Journal of Law & Feminism,* 3. http://cyber.law.harvard.edu/vaw00/epstein.html.

Erikson, E. H. (1968). Identity, youth, and crisis. New York: Norton.

Ethics Committee of the American Psychological Association. (1992, October). Rules and procedures. *American Psychologist,* 47, 1612–1628.

Ethics Committee of the American Psychological Association. (1997). Report of the Ethics Committee, 1996. *American Psychologist,* 52, 897–905.

Evans, D. L., Foa, E. B., Gur, R. E., Hendin, H., O'Brien, C. P., Seligman, M. E. P., & Walsh, B. T. (Eds.). (2005). *Treating and preventing adolescent mental health disorders: What we know and what we don't know. A research agenda for improving the mental health of our youth.* New York: Oxford University Press.

Everson, M. D. (1997). Understanding bizarre, improbable, and fantastic elements in children's account of abuse. *Child Maltreatment, 2*, 134–149.

Ewing, C. P. (1987). *Battered women who kill.* Lexington, MA: Lexington Books.

Ewing, C. P. (1990a). *When children kill: The dynamics of juvenile homicide.* Lexington, MA: Lexington Books.

Ewing, C. P. (1990b). Psychological self-defense: A proposed justification for battered women who kill. *Law and Human Behavior, 14*(6), 579–594.

Ewing, C. P., & McCann, J. T. (2006). *Minds on trial: Great cases in law and psychology.* New York: Oxford University Press.

Faden, R. R., & Beauchamp, T. L. (1986). *A history and theory of informed consent.* New York: Oxford University Press.

Fagan, J. (1996). The comparative advantage of juvenile versus criminal court sanctions on recidivism among adolescent felony offenders. *Law and Policy, 18*, 77–114.

Faigman, D. L. (1989). To have and have not: Assessing the value of social science to the law as science and policy. *Emory Law Journal, 38*, 1005–1095.

Faigman, D. L. (1991). "Normative constitutional fact-finding": Exploring the empirical component of constitutional interpretation. *University of Pennsylvania Law Review, 139*, 541–615.

Faigman, D. L. (2004). *Laboratory of justice: The Supreme Court's 200-year struggle to integrate science and the law.* New York: Times Books.

Faigman, D. L., Kaye, D. H., Saks, M. J., & Sanders, J. (2005). *Modern scientific evidence: The law and science of expert testimony.* 2005–2006 ed. Eagan, MN: Thomson/West.

Faigman D. L., & Wright, A. J. (1997). The battered woman syndrome in the age of science. *Arizona Law Review, 39*(1), 67–115.

FairTest. (1999). PSAT Gap and National Merit Winners. http://fairtest.org/pr/psatchrt.htm.

FairTest. (n.d.). Gender bias in college admission tests. http://www.fairtest.org/facts/genderbias.htm.

FairTest Examiner. (1999a, Spring).Gender bias victory wins millions for females but National Merit Test remains biased. http://www.fairtest.org/examarts/spring99/genderbiasvic.html.

FairTest Examiner. (1999b, Fall). SAT gender gap grows again. http://www.fairtest.org.

False Memory Syndrome Foundation. (2004). Settlements and awards exceeding $1 million in recovered memory malpractice suits. *FMS Foundation Newsletter, 13*(2), 9.

Family Planning Perspectives. (1990). 22, 36–39.

Fantuzzo, J. W., & Mohr, W. K. (1999). Prevalence and effects of child exposure to domestic violence: The Future of children. *Domestic Violence and Children, 9*, 21–32.

Faragher v. City of Boca Raton, 524 U.S. 775 (1998).

Farber, M. A. (1990, June). The tormenting of Hilary. *Vanity Fair,* 120–127, 193–204.

Faretta v. California, 422 U.S. 806 (1975).

Faux, M. (1988). *Roe v. Wade.* New York: Macmillan.

Feder, L., & Forde, D. R. (2000). *A test of the efficacy of court-mandated counseling for domestic violence offenders: The Broward experiment.* Washington, DC: National Institute of Justice.

Feeley, M. M., & Rubin, E. L. (1998). *Judicial policy making and the modern state: How the courts reformed America's prisons.* New York: Cambridge University Press.

Feeman, S. (2006, February 17). Sir Roy Meadow will not be struck off after winning appeal. *TimesOnline.* http://www.timesonline.co.uk.

Fein, R. A., & Vosskuil, B. (1998). *Protective intelligence and threat assessment investigations: A guide for state and local law enforcement officials.* Washington, DC: National Institute of Justice.

Feld, B. C. (1999). *Bad kids: Race and the transformation of the juvenile court.* New York: Oxford University Press.

Feldman, K. W. (1997). Evaluation of physical abuse. In M. E. Helfer, R. S. Kempe, & R. D. Krugman (Eds.), *The battered child,* 5th ed., pp. 175–220. Chicago: University of Chicago Press.

Feldman-Schorrig, S. (1995). Need for expansion of forensic psychiatrists' role in sexual harassment cases. *Bulletin of the American Academy of Psychiatry and the Law, 23*, 513–522.

Felner, R., and Terre, L. (1987). Child custody dispositions and children's adaptation following divorce. In L. Weithorn (Ed.), *Psychology and child custody determinations,* pp. 106–153. Lincoln: University of Nebraska Press.

Felson, R. B. (2002). *Violence and gender reexamined.* Washington, DC: American Psychological Association.

Felthous, A. R., & Kachigian, C. (2001). To warn and to control: Two distinct legal obligations or variations of a single duty to protect? *Behavioral Sciences and the Law, 19*(3),355–373.

Female offenders: An emerging crisis. (n.d.). Compiled from a report funded by the Office of Juvenile Justice and Delinquency Prevention http://www.juvenilejustice.com/female.html.

Fenster, J. (2004). The relationship between optimism about race relations, black awareness, and attitudes toward transracial adoption. *Journal of Ethnic and Cultural Diversity in Social Work, 13*(3), 45–67.

Fields, M. D. (1986). Spouse abuse as a factor in custody and visitation decisions. In R. E. Cohen, M. McCabe, & V. Weiss, (Eds.), *Child abuse and neglect,* pp. 147–168. Supreme Court of the State of New York, Appellate Division, First Department.

Finder, A. (1999, June 6). Jailed until proved not guilty: Man's 19-month confinement shows plight of those too poor to post bail. New York Times, Final, Section 1, p. 41.

Finder, A. (1999, June 6). *New York Times,* Metro sec.

Fine, G. A. (1999). John Brown's body: Elites, heroic embodiment, and the legitimation of political violence. *Social Problems,* 46, 225–249.

Finer, L. B., & Henshaw, S. K. (2006). Disparities in rates of unintended pregnancy in the United States, 1994 and 2001. *Perspectives on Sexual and Reproductive Health,* 38(2), 90–96.

Finkel, N. J. (1988). *Insanity on trial.* New York: Plenum.

Finkel, N. J. (1990). De facto departures from insanity instructions: Towards the remaking of common law. *Law and Human Behavior,* 14, 105–122.

Finkel, N. J. (1991). The insanity defense: A comparison of verdict schemas. *Law and Human Behavior,* 15, 533–556.

Finkel, N. J., & Duff, M. A. (1989). The insanity defense: Giving jurors a third option. *Forensic Reports,* 2, 235–263.

Finkel, N. J., & Handel, S. F. (1988). How jurors construe insanity. *Law and Human Behavior,* 13, 41–59.

Finkelhor, D. (2004, December 1). E-mail communication based on NCANDS reports.

Finkelhor, D., & Browne, A. (1985). The traumatic impact of child sexual abuse. *American Journal of Orthopsychiatry,* 55, 530–541.

Finley, L. M. (2004). The hidden victims of tort reform: Women, children and the elderly. Emory Law Journal, 53, 1263–1313.

Finn, P., & Colson, S. (1998, July). Civil protection orders, current court practice and enforcement. In *Legal interventions in family violence: Research findings and policy implications, a project of the American Bar Association's Criminal Justice Section, Commission on Domestic Violence, Center on Children and the Law, and Commission on Legal Problems of the Elderly,* 43–46. Presented to the National Institute of Justice, NCJ 171666. Washington, DC: National Institute of Justice.

Finz, S. (2004, February 26). Judge denies two motions for Peterson. Defense sought sequestering as well as separate juries for trial and penalty. *San Francisco Chronicle.*

Firestone, D. (1999, April 11). Arkansas tempers a law on violence by children. *New York Times,* sec. 1, 20.

Fischer, K., Vidmar, N., & Ellis, R. (1993). The culture of battering and the role of mediation in domestic violence cases. *Southern Methodist University Law Review,* 46, 2117–2174.

Fischoff, B. (1975). Hindsight = / = foresight: The effect of outcome knowledge on judgment under uncertainty. *Journal of Experimental Psychology: Human Perception and Performance,* 1, 288–299.

Fisher, D. (2000, September 28). County lockups are bursting at the seams. *Seattle-Post Intelligencer.*

Fiske, S. T., Bersoff, D. N., Borgida, E., Deaux, K., & Heilman, M. E. (1993). What constitutes a scientific review? A majority retort to Barrett and Morris. *Law and Human Behavior,* 17, 217–233.

Fiske, S. T., & Taylor, S. E. (1984). *Social cognition.* New York: Random House.

Fitzgerald, J. (1999). "Junior" Gotti pleads guilty. http://www.abcnews.go.com/sections/us/DailyNews/gotti990–405.hmtl.

Fitzgerald, J. (2001, May 4). Eighth-graders boycott state science exam. *Buffalo News,* A-1.

Fitzgerald, L. F. (1993). Sexual harassment: Violence against women in the workplace. *American Psychologist,* 48(10), 1070–1076.

Fitzgerald, L. F. (2003). Sexual harassment and social justice: reflections on the distance yet to go. *American Psychologist,* 58(11), 915–924.

Fitzgerald, L. F., Buchanan, N. T., Collinsworth, L. L., Magley, V. J., & Ramos, A. M. (1999). Junk logic: The abuse defense in sexual harassment litigation. *Psychology, Public Policy, and Law,* 5(3), 730–759.

Fitzgerald, L. F., & Shullman, S. L. (1985, August). The development and validation of an objectively scored measure of sexual harassment. Paper presented at the annual meeting of the American Psychological Association, Los Angeles.

Fleeman, M. (1996, October 14). Whites outnumber blacks in Simpson pool. *Buffalo News,* A-3.

FMS Foundation. (2002). Nursery teachers regain reputations in England. *FMS Foundation Newsletter,* 11(5), 3.

FMS Foundation Newsletter. (1993). 2, 7.

Folks, H. (1902). *The care of destitute, neglected and delinquent children.* New York: Macmillan.

Foote, C., Levy, R. J., & Sander, F. E. A. (1985). *Cases and materials on family law.* 3rd ed. Boston: Little, Brown.

Ford v. Wainright, 106 S.Ct. 2595 (1986).

Ford, D. A., & Regoli, M. J. (1998, July). The Indianapolis domestic violence prosecution experiment. In *Legal interventions in family violence: Research findings and policy implications, a project of the American Bar Association's Criminal Justice Section, Commission on Domestic Violence, Center on Children and the Law, and Commission on Legal Problems of the Elderly,* 62–63. Presented to the National Institute of Justice. NCJ 171666. Washington, DC: National Institute of Justice.

Foretich v. Morgan, 351 F.3d 1198 (D.C. Cir., 2003).

Forst, B. (1983). Capital punishment and deterrence: Conflicting evidence. *Journal of Criminal Law and Criminology,* 74(3), 927–942.

Forsyth, W. (1875). History of trial by jury. 2nd ed. Prepared by James Appleton Morgan. Jersey City, NJ: Frederick D. Linn.

Foucha v. Louisiana, 504 U.S. 71 (1992).

Fox, J. A., & Zawitz, M. W. (2000, March). Homicide trends in the United States: 1998 update. U.S. Bureau of Justice Statistics Crime Data Brief. NCJ 179767. http://www.ojp.usdoj.gov/bjs/homicide/homtrnd.htm.

Fox, J. A., & Zawitz, M. W. (2004, November). Homicide trends in the United States: 2002 update. Bureau of Justice Statistics Crime Data Brief. NCJ 204885. Washington, DC: U.S. Department of Justice.

Fox, S. J. (1981). *Modern juvenile justice.* 2nd ed. St. Paul, MN: West.

Foxhall, K. (2000a). How to protect your practice from fraud and abuse charges. *Monitor on Psychology, 31,* 64–66.

Foxhall, K. (2000b). Suddenly a big impact on criminal justice. *Monitor on Psychology, 31,* 36–37.

Fray-Witzer, E. (1999). Twice abused: Same-sex domestic violence and the law. In B. Leventhal & S. E. Lundy (Eds.), *Same-sex violence: Strategies for change,* pp. 19–42. Thousand Oaks, CA: Sage.

Freedman, A. M. (2001). Commentary: The doctor's dilemma: A conflict of loyalties. *Psychiatric Times,* 18(1).

Freeman, M. B. (2003, October). Child protection in the 21st century: Privitization of child protective services: Getting the lion back in the cage? *Family Court Review,* 41, 449–456.

Freemon, F. R. (2001). The origin of the medical expert witness: The insanity of Edward Oxford Journal of Legal Medicine, 22(3), 349–373.

Freyd, J. J. (1996). *Betrayal trauma.* Cambridge, MA: Harvard University Press.

Freyd, P. (2000). Dear friends. *False Memory Syndrome Foundation Newsletter,* 9(1), 1.

Fried, C. S., & Reppucci, N. D. (in press). Youth violence: Correlates, interventions, and legal implications. In B. L. Bottoms, M. B. Kovera, & B. D. McAuliff (Eds.), *Children and the law: Social science and policy.* New York: Cambridge University Press.

Friederich, W. N. (1988). Behavior problems in sexually abused children. In G. E. Wyatt & G. J. Powell (Eds.), *Lasting effects of child sexual abuse,* pp. 171–191. Newbury Park, CA: Sage.

Friedman, L. M. (1985). *A history of American law.* 2nd ed. New York: Simon & Schuster.

Frye v. United States, 293 F.1013 (D.C. Cir., 1923).

Fryer, G. E., Poland, J. E., Bross, D. C., & Krugman, R. D. (1988). The child protective service worker: A profile of needs, attitudes, and utilization of professional resources. *Child Abuse & Neglect,* 12, 481–490.

Fuentes v. Shevin, 407 U.S. 67 (1972).

Fuhr, J. (1988). Mediation readiness. *Family and Conciliation Courts Review,* 27, 71–74.

Fukunaga, K. K., Pasewark, R. A., Hawkins, M., & Gudeman, H. (1981). Insanity pleas: Interexaminer agreement and concordance of psychiatric opinion and court verdict. *Law and Human Behavior,* 5, 325–328.

Fulero, S. M., & Finkel, N. J. (1991). Barring ultimate issue testimony: An insane rule? *Law and Human Behavior,* 15, 495–508.

Furman v. Georgia, 408 U.S. 238 (1972).

Furstenberg, F. F., Jr., Brooks-Gunn, J., & Morgan, S. P. (1987). *Adolescent mothers in later life.* New York: Cambridge University Press.

Furstenberg, F. F., Jr., Levine, J. A., & Brooks-Gunn, J. (1990). The children of teenage mothers: Patterns of childbearing in two generations. *Family Planning Perspectives,* 22, 54–61.

Gabora, N. J., Spanos, N. P., & Joab, A. (1993). The effects of complainant age and expert psychological testimony in a simulated child sexual abuse trial. *Law and Human Behavior,* 17, 103–119.

Gagliardi, G. J., Lovell, D., Peterson, P. D., & Jemelka, R. (2004). Forecasting recidivism in mentally ill offenders released from prison. *Law and Human Behavior,* 28(2), 133–155.

Galanter, M. (1974). Why the "haves" come out ahead: Speculations on the limits of legal change. *Law and Society Review,* 8, 95–151.

Galanter, M. (2004). The vanishing trial: An examination of trial and related matter in federal and state courts. *Journal of Empirical Legal Studies,* 1(3), 459–570.

Gambrill, E., & Shlonsky, A. (2000). Risk assessment in context. *Children and Youth Services Review,* 22(11–12), 813–837.

Garbarino, J., Guttman, E., & Seeley, J. W. (1988). *The psychologically battered child.* San Francisco: Jossey-Bass.

Garcia, L., Hurwitz, E. L., & Kraus, J. F. (2005). Acculturation and reported intimate partner violence among Latinas in Los Angeles. *Journal of Interpersonal Violence,* 20(8), 569–590.

Gardner, W., Scherer, D., & Tester, M. (1989). Asserting scientific authority: Cognitive development and adolescent legal rights. *American Psychologist,* 44, 885–894.

Garey, M. (1985). The cost of taking a life: Dollars and sense of the death penalty. *University of California Davis Law Review,* 18, 1221–1273.

Garofalo, R., Wolf, R. C., Wissow, L. S., Woods, E. R., & Goodman, E. (1999). Sexual orientation and risk of suicidal attempts among a representative sample of youth. *Archive of Pediatric and Adolescent Medicine,* 153(5). http://arhcpedl.ama-assn.org/issues/v153n5.

Garrett, P. M. (2004). Talking child protection. The police and social workers "working together." *Journal of Social Work,* 4(1), 77–97.

Garrow, D. J. (1994), *Liberty and sexuality: The right to privacy and the making of* Roe v. Wade. New York: MacMillan.

Garska v. McCoy, 278 S.E.2d 357 (W. Va., 1981).

Gebser v. Lago Vista Independent School District, 524 U.S. 274 (1998).

Geffner, R., & Pagelow, M. D. (1990). Mediation and child custody issues in abusive relationships. *Behavioral Sciences and the Law,* 8(2), 151–160.

Geffner, R., & Rosenbaum, A. (1990). Characteristics and treatment of batterers. *Behavioral Sciences and the Law,* 8(2), 131–140.

Geis, G. (1972). *Not the law's business.* Rockville, MD: NIMH Center for Studies of Crime and Delinquency.

Geis, G., & Meier, R. F. (1985). Abolition of the insanity plea in Idaho: A case study. In R. Moran (Ed.), *The annals of the American Academy of Political and Social Science,* pp. 72–86. Beverly Hills, CA: Sage.

Gelles, R. J. (1977). No place to go: The social dynamics of marital violence. In M. Roy (Ed.), *Battered women: A psychosociological study of domestic violence,* pp. 46–62. New York: Van Nostrand Reinhold.

Gelles, R. J. (1986). School-age parents and child abuse. In J. B. Lancaster & B. A. Hamburg (Eds.), *School-age pregnancy and parenthood: Biosocial dimensions,* pp. 347–377. New York: Aldine de Gruyter.

Gelles, R. J., Kinnevy, S., & Cohen, B. J. (2002). *The police as child protective service investigators: An evaluation of the transfer of responsibilty for child maltreatment investigations in four counties in Florida.* NCJ 189634. Washington, DC: NCJRS.

General Accounting Office. (1993). *Foster care: Services to prevent out-of-home placements are limited by funding barriers.* Washington, DC: General Accounting Office.

General Electric Co. v. Joiner, 522 U.S. 136 (1997).

General Medical Council. (2005, July 15). Recent press releases. London.

Georgia v. McCollum, 505 U.S. 42 (1992).

Georgia Department of Corrections. (2004). Special populations. http://www.dcor.state.ga.us/CORRINFO/ResearchReports/SpecialPopulations.html.

Gianni, J. (2003). Juvenile proceedings: Change the definiton of "child" to include 18-year-old individuals charged with status offenses. *Georgia State University Law Review,* 20, 56–60.

Gibbons, P., Mulryan, N., & O'Connor, A. (1997, May). Guilty but insane: The insanity defense in Ireland, 1850–1995. *British Journal of Psychiatry,* 170, 467–472.

Gilmore, P. (2003, December 30). Attorney General Opinion No. 2003–35. Issued to Phyllis Gilmore, executive director, Behavioral Sciences Regulatory Board, Topeka, Kansas.

Givelber, D. J., Bowers, W. J., & Blitch, C. L. (1984). *Tarasoff,* myth and reality: An empirical study of private law in action. *Wisconsin Law Review,* (2), 443–497.

Givelber, D. J., Bowers, W. J., & Blitch, C. L. (1985). The *Tarasoff* controversy: A summary of findings from an empirical study of legal, ethical and clinical issues. In J. C. Beck (Ed.), *The potentially violent patient and the Tarasoff decision in psychiatric practice,* pp. 35–57. Washington, DC: American Psychiatric Press.

Glaberson, W. (1999a, August 17). Ohio Supreme Court voids legal limits on damage suits. *New York Times,* A–10.

Glaberson, W. (1999b, July 16). State courts are sweeping away laws limiting legal limits on damage suits. *New York Times,* A–1.

Glaberson, W. (1999c, June 7). Some plaintiffs losing out in Texas' war on lawsuits. *New York Times,* A–1, 20.

Glassman, J. B. (1998). Preventing and managing board complaints: The downside risk of custody, mediation and assessment services: Implications for psychological practice. Professional *Psychology: Research and Practice,* 29(2), 115–120.

Gleaves, D. H., Smith, S. M., Butler, L. D., & Spiegel, D. (2004). False and recovered memories in the laboratory and clinic.: A review of experimental and clinical evidence. *Clinical Psychology: Science and Practice,* 11(1), 3–28.

Globe Newspaper Co. v. Superior Court, 457 U.S. 596 (1982).

Glod, M. (2005, August 6). Va. Killer is retarded, jury says: Execution set. *Washington Post.* http://www.washingtonpost.com.

Godinez v. Moran, 509 U.S. 389 (1993).

Godwin, T. M., Steinhart, D. J., & Fulton, B. A. (n.d.). *Peer justice and youth empowerment: An implementation guide for teen court programs.* Washington, DC: American Probation and Parole Association.

Goldberg, C. (1999, November 23). Spouse abuse crackdown, surprisingly, nets many women. *New York Times,* A1.

Goldberg, D. (1996, September 21). Du Pont competency at issue in hearing. *Washington Post,* A–13.

Golding, S. L., & Roesch, R. (1987). The assessment of criminal responsibility: An historical approach to a current controversy. In I. B. Weiner & A. K. Hess (Eds.). *Handbook of forensic psychology,* pp. 395–436. New York: John Wiley.

Goldkamp, J. S., Gottfredson, M. R., Jones, P. R., & Weiland, D. (1995). *Personal liberty and community safety: Pretrial release in criminal court.* New York: Plenum.

Goldkamp, J. S., Weiland, D., Collins, M., & White, M. (1998, July). The role of drug and alcohol abuse in domestic violence and its treatment: Dade County's domestic violence court experiment. In *Legal interventions in family violence: research findings and policy implications, a project of the American Bar Association's Criminal Justice Section, Commission on Domestic Violence, Center on Children and the Law, and Commission on Legal Problems of the Elderly,* 74–75. Presented to the National Institute of Justice. NCJ 171666. Washington, DC: National Institute of Justice.

Goldstein, A. S. (1967). *The insanity defense.* New Haven CT: Yale University Press.

Goldstein, J., Freud, A., & Solnit, A. J. (1973). *Beyond the best interests of the child.* New York: Free Press.

Goldstein, J., Solnit, A., Goldstein, S., & Freud, A. (1996). *The best interests of the child: The least detrimental alternative.* New York: Free Press.

Golombok, S., MacCallum, F., Goodman, E., & Rutter, M. (2002). Families with children conceived by donor insemination: a follow-up at age twelve. *Child Development,* 73, 952–968.

Gondolf, E. W. (1988). The effect of batterer counseling on shelter outcome. *Journal of Interpersonal Violence,* 3, 275–289.

Gondolf, E. W. (2002). Oral remark. Batterer Intervention: Where do we go from her? *Workshop Notes,* National Institute of Justice. http://www.usdoj.gov/nij/vawprog/battererintervention.html.

Gonzales v. Oregon, 126 S.Ct. 904 (2006).

Gonzalez v. Raich, 545 U.S. 1 (2005).

Goode, E. (2002, February 4). Group backs gays who seek to adopt a partner's child. *New York Times* on the Web, national.

Goodman, G. S. (1984). Children's testimony in historical perspective. *Journal of Social Issues,* 40, 9–31.

Goodman,. G. S., Quas, J. A., Bulkley, J., & Shapiro, C. (1999). Innnovations for child witnesses: A national survey. *Psychology, Public Policy and Law,* 5(2), 255–281.

Goodman, G. S., Aman, C., & Hirschman, J. (1987). Child sexual and physical abuse: Children's testimony. In S. J. Ceci, M. P. Toglia, & D. F. Ross (Eds.), *Children's eyewitness memory,* pp. 1–23. New York: Springer-Verlag.

Goodman, G. S., Bottoms, B. L., Herscovici, B. B., & Shaver, P. (1989). Determinants of the child victim's perceived credibility. In S. J. Ceci, D. F. Ross, & M. P. Toglia, (Eds.), *Perspectives on children's testimony,* pp. 1–22. New York: Springer-Verlag.

Goodman, G. S., Golding, J., & Haith, M. M. (1984). Jurors' reactions to child witnesses. *Journal of Social Issues,* 40, 139–156.

Goodman, G. S., Levine, M., & Melton, G. B. (1992). The best evidence produces the best law. *Law and Human Behavior,* 16, 244–251.

Goodman, G. S., Levine, M., Melton, G. B., & Ogden, D. W. (1991). Child witnesses and the confrontation clause. The American Psychological Association brief in *Maryland v. Craig. Law and Human Behavior,* 15, 13–29.

Goodman, G. S., Rudy, L., Bottoms, B. L., & Aman, C. (1990). Children's concerns and memory: Ecological issues in the study of children's eyewitness testimony. In R. Fivush & J. Hudson (Eds.), *Knowing and remembering in young children,* pp. 249–284. New York: Cambridge University Press.

Goodman, G. S., Taub, E. P., Jones, D. P. H., England, P., Port, L.K., Rudy, L., & Prado, L. (1992). Testifying in criminal court. *Monographs of the Society for Research in Child Development,* 57 (Serial No. 229), 1–142.

Goodman, G. S., Tobey, A. E., Batterman-Faunce, J. M., Orcutt, H., Thomas, S., Shapiro, C., & Sachsenmaier, T. (1998). Face-to-face confrontation: Effects of closed-circuit technology on children's eyewitness testimony and jurors' decisions. *Law and Human Behavior,* 22, 165–203.

Goodman-Delahunty, J. (1998). Approaches to gender and the law: Research and applications. *Law and Human Behavior,* 22(1), 129–144.

Goodman-Delahunty, J. (1999). Pragmatic support for the reasonable victim standard in hostile workplace environment cases. *Psychology, Public Policy and Law,* 5(3), 519–555.

Goodnough, A. (2001, June 14). High stakes of fourth-grade tests are driving off veteran teachers. *New York Times,* A–1.

Gordon, D. (1990). Testimony and statement. Hearing before the Committee on the Judiciary, House of Representatives, One Hundred First Congress, second session, on H. Con. Res. 172. (Serial No. 81). Washington, DC: U.S. Government Printing Office.

Gordon, D. (1998, July). Validity of "battered woman syndrome" in criminal cases involving battered women. In Legal interventions in family violence: Research findings and policy implications, a project of the American Bar Association's Criminal Justice Section, Commission on Domestic Violence, Center on Children and the Law, and Commission on Legal Problems of the Elderly, 64–65. Presented to the National Institute of Justice. NCJ 171666. Washington, DC: National Institute of Justice.

Gordon, L. (1988). *Heroes of their own lives: The politics and history of family violence: Boston 1880–1960.* New York: Viking.

Gorney, C. (1999, June 13). Teaching Johnny the appropriate way to flirt. *New York Times Magazine,* 45.

Gothard, S., Viglione, D. J., Jr., Meloy, J. R., & Sherman, M. (1995). Detection of malingering in competency to stand trial evaluations. *Law and Human Behavior,* 19, 493–505.

Gottfredson, D. M., & Snyder, H. N (2005, July). The mathematics of risk classification: Changing data into valid instruments for juvenile courts. National Center for Juvenile Justice Report. NCJ 209158. Washington, DC: Office of Juvenile Justice and Delinquency Prevention.

Gottfredson, L. S. (2005a). What if the hereditarian hypothesis is true? *Psychology, Public Policy, and Law,* 11(2), 311–319.

Gottfredson, L. M. (2005b). Suppressing intelligence research: Hurting those we intend to help. In R. H. Wright and N. A. Cummings (Eds.), *Destructive trends in mental health,* pp. 155–186. New York: Routledge.

Gottfredson, L. S. (2000). Skills gaps, not tests, make racial proportionality impossible. *Psychology, Public Policy and Law,* 6(1), 129–143.

Gould v. Gould, 116 Wis. 2d 493, 342 N.W. 2d 426 (1984).

Gournic, S. J. (1990). Professional standards and hindsight bias: Implications for determinations of negligence. Unpublished doctoral dissertation. State University of New York at Buffalo.

Gratz v. Bollinger, 539 U.S. 244 (2003).

Grearson, K. W. (2004). Proposed uniform child witness testimony act: An impermissible abridgment of criminal defendants' rights. 45 *Boston College Law Review,* 467–498.

Green, T. A. (1985). *Verdict according to conscience: Perspectives on the English criminal jury trial, 1200–1800.* Chicago: University of Chicago Press.

Greene, E. (1988). Judge's instructions on eyewitness testimony: Evaluation and revision. *Journal of Applied Social Psychology, 18,* 252–276.

Greene, E., & Loftus, E. F. (1998). Psycholegal research on jury damage awards. *Current Directions in Psychological Science, 7,* 50–54.

Greenfield, L. A., & Stephan, J. J. (1993). Capital punishment 1992. Bureau of Justice Statistics Bulletin. Washington, DC: Bureau of Justice Statistics.

Greenhouse, L. (1998a, June 27). Supreme Court spells out rules for finding sex harassment. *New York Times,* A-1.

Greenhouse, L. (1998b, June 28). Companies set to get tougher on harassment. *New York Times,* A-1.

Greenhouse, L. (1998c, June 30). Supreme court weaves legal principles from a tangle of litigation. *New York Times,* A-20.

Greenhouse, L. (1998d, June 30). School districts are given a shield in sex harassment. *New York Times,* A-1.

Greenhouse, L. (1999, May 24). The Supreme Court; the overview; sex harassment in class is ruled schools' liability. *New York Times,* A-1.

Greenhouse, L. (2000, Apr. 19). Justices force two new hearings on death row. *New York Times,* A-1.

Greenhouse, L. (2004, November 2). Justices mull rights of those seeking police protection. *New York Times.* http://www.nytimes.com/2004/11//02/politics.

Greenhouse, S. (2001, July 15). Federal suit accuses city of not acting on harassment complaints. *New York Times,* New York region.

Greenhouse, S. (2003, February 2). Immigrant sisters accuse bakery managers of sex harassment. *New York Times,* New York region.

Greenwood, G. L., Relf, M. V., Huang, B., Pollack, L. M., Canchola, J. A., & Catania, J. A. (2002). Battering victimization among a probability-based sample of men who have sex with men. *American Journal of Public Health, 92*(12), 1964–1969.

Gregg v. Georgia, 428 U.S. 153 (1976).

Griffin, P. (1999, September). Developing and administering accountability-based sanctions for juveniles. *JAIBG Bulletin.* Washington, DC: Office of Juvenile Justice and Delinquency Prevention.

Griffin-Carlson, M. S., & Schwanenflugel, P. J. (1998). Adolescent abortion and parental notification: Evidence for the importance of family functioning on the perceived quality of parental involvement in U.S. families. *Journal of Child Psychology & Psychiatry & Allied Disciplines, 39,* 543–553.

Griggs v. Duke Power Co., 401 U.S. 424 (1971).

Grilo, C. M., Becker, D. F., Fehon, D.C., Walker, M. L., Edell & McGlashan, T. H. (1998). Psychiatric morbidity differences in male and female adolescent inpatients with alcohol use. *Journal of Youth and Adolescence, 27*(1), 29–41.

Grisso, T. (1981). *Juveniles' waiver of rights: Legal and psychological competence.* New York: Plenum.

Grisso, T. (1991). A developmental history of the American Psychology–Law Society. *Law and Human Behavior, 15*(3), 213–232.

Grisso, T. (1992). Five-year research update (1986–1990): Evaluations for competence to stand trial. *Behavioral Sciences and the Law, 10*(3), 353–369.

Grisso, T. (1996). Society's retributive response to juvenile violence: A developmental perspective. *Law and Human Behavior, 20*(3), 229–248.

Grisso, T. (1997). The competence of adolescents as trial defendants. *Psychology, Public Policy and Law, 3,* 3–32.

Grisso, T., & Appelbaum, P. S. (1992). Is it unethical to offer predictions of future violence? *Law and Human Behavior, 16*(6), 621–634.

Grisso, T., Appelbaum, P. S., Mulvey, E. P., & Fletcher, K. (1995). The MacArthur treatment competence study II: Measures of abilities related to competence to consent to treatment. *Law and Human Behavior, 19*(1), 127–148.

Grisso, T., Cocozza, J., Steadman, H. J., Fisher, W., & Greer, A. (1994). The organization of pretrial forensic evaluation services: A national profile. *Law and Human Behavior, 18*(213), 377–394.

Grisso, T., & Saks, M. J. (1991). Psychology's influence on constitutional interpretation. *Law and Human Behavior, 15*(2), 205–211.

Grisso,T., Steinberg, L., Woolard, J., Cauffman, E., Scott, E., Graham, S., Lexeen, F., Reppucci, N. D., & Swartz, R. (2003). Juveniles' competence to stand trial: A comparison of adolescents' and adults' capacities as trial defendants. *Law and Human Behavior, 27*(4), 333–363.

Griswold v. Connecticut, 381 U.S. 479 (1965).

Gross, J. (2006, April 21). Learning to savor a full life, love life included. *New York Times,* A-1, A-17.

Gross, S. R. (1985). Empirical studies of race and death: The judicial evaluation of evidence of discrimination in capital sentencing. *University of California at Davis Law Review, 18,* 1275–1325.

Grove, W. M., & Meehl, P. E. (1996). Comparative efficiency of informal (subjective, impressionistic) and formal (mechanical, algorithmic) prediction procedures: The clinical–statistical controversy. *Psychology, Public Policy and the Law, 2*(2), 293–323.

Grutter v. Bollinger, 539 U.S. 306 (2003).

Guardianship of Shannon, 218 Cal. 490, 23 P.2d 1020 (1933).

Guevara, L., Spohn, C., & Herz, D. (2004). Race, legal representation and juvenile justice: Issues and concerns. *Crime & Delinquency, 50*(3), 344–371.

Gutek, B. A., & O'Connor, M. (1995). The empirical basis for the reasonable woman standard. *Journal of Social Issues, 51,* 151–166.

Gutek, B. A., O'Connor, M. A., Melancon, R., Stockdale, M. S., Geer, T. M. & Done, R. S. (1999). *Psychology, Public Policy, and Law, 5*(3), 596–629.

Gutheil, T. G. (1989). Borderline personality disorder, boundary violations, and patient–therapist sex: Medicolegal pitfalls. *American Journal of Psychiatry,* 146, 597–602.

Gutheil, T. G. (2001). Moral justification for *Tarasoff*-type warnings and breach of confidentiality; A clinician's perspective. *Behavioral Sciences and the Law,* 19(3), 345–353.

H. L. v. Matheson, 450 U.S. 398 (1981).

Hafemeister, T. L. (1992). Comparing law reviews for their amenability to articles addressing mental health issues: How to disseminate law-related social science research. *Law and Human Behavior,* 16, 219–231.

Hagen, M. A., & Castagna, N. (2001). The real numbers: psychological testing in custody evaluation. *Professional Psychology, Research, and Practice,* 32(3), 269–271.

Hamdan v. Rumsfeld, 548 U.S.—(2006).

Hamdi v. Rumsfeld, 542 U.S. 507 (2004).

Handler, J. F., & Zatz, J. (Eds.). (1982). *Neither angels nor thieves: Studies in deinstitutionalization of status offenders.* Washington, DC: National Academy Press.

Haney, C. (1993). Psychology and legal change: The impact of a decade. *Law and Human Behavior,* 17(4), 371–398.

Haney, C., & Lynch, M. (1997). Clarifying life and death matters: An analysis of instructional comprehension and penalty phase closing arguments. *Law and Human Behavior,* 21, 575–594.

Haney, W. (1981). Validity, vaudeville, and values. A short history of social concerns over standardized testing. *American Psychologist,* 36, 1021–1034.

Hanley, R. (1993, March 9). Juror's remarks bring a caution in Glen Ridge. *New York Times,* B-5.

Hanley, R. (1993, March 17). 4 are convicted in sexual abuse of New Jersey woman. *New York Times,* A-1, B-4.

Hanley, R. (1993, March 21). Prosecutors' tense moment at Glen Ridge assault trial. *New York Times,* A-40.

Hann, R. G., Meredith, C., Nuffield, J., & Svoboda. (2002). Court site study of adult unrepresented accused in the provincial criminal courts. Robert Hann and Associates Limited, and ARC Applied Research Consultants. Prepared for Department of Justice, Canada. Ottawa: Department of Justice.

Hannaford-Agor, P. L., Hans, V. P., Mott, N. L., & Munsterman, G. T. (2002). *Are hung juries a problem?* Washington, DC: National Center for State Courts, National Institute of Justice.

Hans, V. P. (1986). An analysis of public attitudes toward the insanity defense. *Criminology,* 4(2), 393–415.

Hans, V. P. (2000). *Business on trial: The civil jury and corporate responsibility.* New Haven, CT: Yale University Press.

Hans, V. P., & Lofquist, W. W. (1994). Perceptions of civil justice: The litigation crisis attitudes of civil jurors. *Behavioral Sciences & the Law,* 12(2), 181–196.

Hans, V. P., & Vidmar, N. (1985). *Judging the jury.* New York: Plenum.

Hansen, H., & Goldenberg, I. (1993). Conjoint therapy with violent couples: Some valid considerations. A Multicultural perspective in the treatment of domestic violence. In M. Hansen & M. Harway (Eds.), *Battering and family therapy: A feminist perspective,* pp. 82–92. Newbury Park CA: Sage.

Harbeck, K. M. (1997). *Gay and lesbian educators. Personal freedoms, public constraints.* Malden, MA: Amethyst Press.

Hardy, M. (2006, April 21). Lawyer asks high court to spare condemned client, *Richmond Times-Dispatch,* B3.

Harmon, R. B., Rosner, R., & Owens, H. (1998). Sex and violence in a forensic population of obsessional harassers. *Psychology, Public Policy and Law,* 4(1, 2), 236–249.

Harper, G., & Irvin, E. (1985). Alliance formation with parents: Limit setting and the effect of mandated reporting. *American Journal of Orthopsychiatry,* 55, 550–560.

Harrell, A. (1998, July). The impact of court-ordered treatment for domestic violence offenders. In *Legal interventions in family violence: research findings and policy implications, a project of the American Bar Association's Criminal Justice Section, Commission on Domestic Violence, Center on Children and the Law, and Commission on Legal Problems of the Elderly,* 73. Presented to the National Institute of Justice. NCJ 171666. Washington, DC: National Institute of Justice.

Harrell, A., & Smith, B. (1998, July). Effects of restraining orders on domestic violence victims. In *Legal interventions in family violence: research findings and policy implications, a project of the American Bar Association's Criminal Justice Section, Commission on Domestic Violence, Center on Children and the Law, and Commission on Legal Problems of the Elderly,* 49–51. Presented to the National Institute of Justice. NCJ 171666. Washington, DC: National Institute of Justice.

Harris v. Forklift Systems, 510 U.S. 17 (1993).

Harris v. McRae, 448 U.S. 297 (1980).

Harris, L. A. (1997). The ABA calls for a moratorium on the death penalty: The task ahead—reconciling justice with politics. *Focus on Law Studies,* 12(2), 4.

Harris, R. (2000, November 19). Author awaiting execution gets Nobel nod. *Buffalo News,* A-13.

Hart, B. J. (1992). Children of domestic violence: Risks and remedies. http://www.mincava.umn.edu/hart/risks&r.htm.

Hartigan v. Zbaraz, 484, U.S. 171 (1987).

Hartman-Stein, P. (1999). Legal competence, a consulting niche for geropsychologists. *National Psychologist,* 8(4).

Hartocollis, A. (1999, June 20). New math: No one is below average. *New York Times Week in Review,* 3.

Hastie, R., Penrose, S. D., & Pennington, N. (1983). *Inside the jury.* Cambridge, MA: Harvard University Press.

Hastie, R., Schkade, D., & Payne, J. (1998). A study of juror and jury judgments in civil cases: Deciding liability for punitive damages. *Law and Human Behavior,* 22(3), 287–314.

Haugaard, J. J. (1988). Judicial determination of children's competency to testify: Should it be abandoned? *Professional Psychology,* 19, 102–107.

Haugaard, J. J., & Reppucci, N. D. (1988). *The sexual abuse of children.* San Francisco: Jossey-Bass.

Haugaard, J. J., Reppucci, N. D., Laird, J., & Nauful, T. (1991). Children's definitions of the truth and their competency as witnesses in legal proceedings. *Law and Human Behavior,* 15(3), 253–271.

Hawkins, S. A., & Hastie, R. (1990). Hindsight: Biased judgments of past events after the outcomes are known. *Psychological Bulletin,* 107, 328–340.

Healey, K., Smith, C., & O'Sullivan, C. (1998). *Batterer intervention: Program approaches and criminal justice strategies.* Washington, DC: U.S. Department of Justice.

Healey, K. M., & Smith, C. (1998, July). Batterer programs: What criminal justice agencies need to know. *Research in Action.* NCJ 171683. Washington, DC: National Institute of Justice.

Healy, W. (1915). *The individual delinquent: A text-book of diagnosis and prognosis for all concerned in understanding offenders.* Boston: Little, Brown.

Heaney, J. (1998, August 31). Life after quotas. *Buffalo News,* A-1, A-4.

Hechler, D. (1988). *The battle and the backlash: The child sex abuse war.* Lexington, MA: Lexington Books.

Heilbrun, K. (1997). Prediction versus management models relevant to risk assessment: The importance of legal decision-making context. *Law and Human Behavior,* 21(4), 347–361.

Heilbrun, K., Leheney, C., Thomas, L., & Honeycutt, D. (1997). A national survey of U.S. statutes on juvenile transfer: Implications for policy and practice. *Behavioral Sciences & the Law,* 15(2), 125–149.

Heilbrun, K., Nezu, C. M., Keeney, M., Chung, S., & Wasserman, A. L. (1998). Sexual offending: Linking assessment, intervention, and decision making. *Psychology, Public Policy, and Law,* 4(1/2), 138–174.

Heinbecker, P. (1986). Two years' experience under Utah's mens rea insanity law. *Bulletin of the American Academy of Psychiatry and Law,* 14(2), 185–191.

Heinze, M. C., & Grisso, T. (1996). Review of instruments assessing parent competencies used in child custody evaluations. *Behavioral Sciences and the Law,* 14(3), 293–313.

Helland, E., & Tabarrok, A. (2002). Public versus private law enforcement: Evidence from bail jumping. http://mason.gmu.edu/~stabarro/Publicvprivate.pdf.

Henrie, R. L., Aron, R. H., Nelson, B. D., & Poole, D. A. (1997). Gender-related knowledge variations within geography. *Sex Roles,* 36, 605–623.

Henshaw, S. K. (1997). Teenage abortion and pregnancy statistics by state, 1992. *Family Planning Perspectives,* 29, 115–122.

Henshaw, S. K. & Silverman, J. (1988). The characteristics of prior contraceptive use of U.S. abortion patients. *Family Planning Perspectives,* 20(4), 158–168.

Henshaw, S. K., & Van Vort, J. (1989). Teenage abortion, birth and pregnancy statistics: An update. *Family Planning Perspectives,* 21, 85–88.

Herbsleb, J. D., Sales, B. D., & Overcast, T. D. (1985). Challenging licensure and certification. *American Psychologist,* 40, 1165–1178.

Herrnstein, R. J., & Murray, C. (1994). *The bell curve.* New York: Free Press.

Hetherington, E. M., Bridges, M., & Insabella, G. M. (1998). What matters? What does not? Five perspectives on the association between marital transitions and children's adjustment. *American Psychologist,* 53(2), 167–184.

Hill, A. (1998, March 19). A matter of definition. *New York Times,* A-21.

Hinsliff, G. (2004, August 15). So it's a woman's world. *The Observer.*

Ho v. San Francisco United School District, 965 F. Supp. 1316 (N.D. Cal. 1997)

Hobson v. Hansen, 269 F. Supp. 401 (D.D.C., 1967). appeal dismissed, 393 U.S. 801 (1968).

Hodgson v. Minnesota, 497 U.S. 417 (1990).

Hoffman, E. A. (2004). Selective sexual harassment: differential treatment of similar groups of women workers. *Law and Human Behavior,* 28(1), 29–45.

Hogan, D. B. (1983). The effectiveness of licensing: History, evidence, and recommendations. *Law and Human Behavior,* 7(2, 3), 117–138.

Hoge, S. K., Bonnie, R. J., Poythress, N., & Monahan, J. (1992). Attorney–client decision making in criminal cases: Client competence and participation as perceived by their attorneys. *Behavioral Sciences & the Law,* 10(3), 385–394.

Hoge, S. K., Bonnie, R. J., Poythress, N. Monahan, J., Eisenberg, M. & Feucht-Haviar, T. (1997). The MacArthur adjudicative competence study: Development and validation of a research instrument. *Law and Human Behavior,* 21(2), 141–180.

Holdsworth, W. S. (1931). *A history of English law.* Vol. I. Boston: Little, Brown.

Holmes, S. A. (April 16, 2000). Look who is questioning the death penalty. *New York Times Week in Review,* 3.

Holmes, T. H., & Rahe, R. H. (1967). The social readjustment rating scale. *Journal of Psychosomatic Research,* 11, 213–218.

Holt, V. L., Kernic, M. A., Lumley, T., Wolf, M. E., & Rivara, F. P. (2002). Civil protection orders and risk of subsequent police-reported violence. *JAMA,* 288 (5), 589–594.

Holtzworth-Munroe, A., Meehan, J. C., Herron, K., Rehman, U., & Stuart, G. L. (2000). Testing the Holtzworth-Munroe and Stuart (1994) batterer typology. *Journal of Consulting and Clinical Psychology,* 68(6), 1000–1019.

Holtzworth-Munroe, A., & Stuart, G. L. (1994). Typologies of male batterers: Three subtypes and the differences among them. *Psychological Bulletin,* 116(3), 476–497.

Hopkins, A. (2005). *Price Waterhouse v. Hopkins:* A Personal Account of a Sexual Discrimination Plaintiff. 22 *Hofstra Labor & Employment Law Journal* 357.

Hopwood v. Texas, 78 F.3d 932 (5th Cir. 1996).

Horn, W. F. (2004, May 13). State efforts to comply with federal child welfare reviews. Testimony to Subcommittee of Human Resources Committee on House Ways and Means. Federal Clearing House Congressional Testimony. http://www/jrsa/org/pubs/forum/archives/Mar92.html.

Horn, C. C., & Flores, S. M. (2003). *Percent plans in college admissions. A comparative analysis of three states' experiences.* Civil Rights Project. Cambridge, MA: Harvard University.

Horowitz, I. A. (1985). The effect of jury nullification instruction on verdicts and jury functioning in criminal trials. *Law and Human Behavior,* 9(1), 25–36.

Horowitz, I. A. (1988). Jury nullification: The impact of judicial instructions, arguments, and challenges on jury decision making. *Law and Human Behavior,* 12(4), 439–453.

Hotaling, G.T. & Buzawa, E. (2001, June). *An Analysis of Assaults in Rural Communities: Final Report.* Federal Grant #MA0095–400. Washington, DC: U.S. Department of Justice, Office of Community Oriented Policing Services.

Hoult, J. (2006). The evidentiary admissibility of parental alienation syndrome: Science, law and policy. *Children's Legal Rights Journal,* 29(1), p. 1–61.

House of Representatives. (1989). *The federal role in determining the medical and psychological impact of abortion on women.* Washington, DC: Author.

House of Representatives, Committee on the Judiciary, One Hundred First Congress, second session. (1990). Hearing on H. Con. Res. 172 (Serial No. 81). Washington, DC: Government Printing Office.

Hovey v. Superior Court, 28 Cal. 3d 1 (1980).

Howell, J. C. (1996). Juvenile transfers to the criminal justice system: State of the art. *Law & Policy,* 18(1, 2), 17–60.

Hoyt, S., & Scherer, D. G. (1998). Female juvenile delinquency: Misunderstood by the juvenile justice system, neglected by social science. *Law and Human Behavior,* 22(1), 81–107.

Hunter, J. E., & Schmidt, F. L. (2000). Racial and gender bias in ability and achievement tests: Resolving the apparent paradox. *Psychology, Public Policy and Law,* 6(1), 151–158.

Huntley, J.E. & Costanzo, M. (2003). Sexual harassment stories: Testing a story-mediated model of juror decision-making in civil litigation. *Law and Human Behavior,* 27(1), 29–52.

Hurley, D. (2005, April 19). Divorce rate: It's not as high as you think. *New York Times* online, Health section. http://www.nytimes.com.

Hyman, H. M., & Tarrant, C. M. (1975). Aspects of American trial jury history. In R. J. Simon (Ed.), *The jury system in America,* pp. 21–44. Beverly Hills, CA: Sage.

Iacono, W. G., & Lykken, D. T. (1997). The scientific status of research on polygraph techniques: The case against polygraph tests. In D. L. Faigman, D. H. Kaye, M. J. Saks, & J. Sanders (Eds.), *Modern scientific evidence: The law and science of expert testimony,* vol. 1, 582–618, 627–629, 631–633. 2005–2006 ed. Eagan, MN: Thomson/West.

Ibn-Tamas v. United States, 407 A.2d 626 (D.C. App., 1979).

Idaho v. Wright, 497 U.S. 805 (1990).

In re Gault, 387 U.S. 1 (1967).

In re Marriage of Burgess 13 Cal. 4th 25 (1996).

In re Marriage of LaMusga. 32 Cal. 4th 1072 (2004).

In re Walker, 282 N.C. 28, 191 S.E.2d 702 (1972).

In re Winship, 397 U.S. 358 (1970).

Infoplease (2004). Educational attainment by race and Hispanic origin: 1940–2001. http://www/infoplease/cp,/ipa/A0774057.html.

Insanity Defense Reform Act; Public Law 98–473. (1984).

Isquith, P. K. (1990). Attributions of responsibility to child sex abuse victims: The impact of jury instructions. Unpublished doctoral dissertation, State University of New York at Buffalo.

Isquith, P. K., Levine, M., &, Scheiner, J. (1993). Blaming the child: Attribution of responsibility to victims of child sexual abuse. In G. S. Goodman & B. L. Bottoms (Eds.), *Child victims, child witnesses,* pp. 203–228. New York: Guilford Press.

Jackson v. Indiana, 406 U.S. 715 (1972).

Jackson v. Commonwealth of Virginia, 266 Va. 423, 587 S.E.2d 532 (2003).

Jackson, S., Feder, L., Forde, D. R., Davis, R. C., Maxwell, C. D., & Taylor, B. G. (2003). Batterer intervention programs: Where do we go from here? NCJ 195079. Washington, DC: U.S. Department of Justice, National Institute of Justice.

Jacobson v. Massachusetts, 197 U.S. 11 (1905).

Jaffe, F. S., Lindheim, B. L., & Lee, P. R. (1981). *Abortion politics: Private morality and public policy.* New York: McGraw-Hill.

Jameson, B. J., Ehrenberg, M. F., Hunter, M. A. (1997). Psychologists' ratings of the best-interests-of-the-child custody and access criterion: A family systems assessment model. *Professional Psychology: Research and Practice,* 28(3), 253–263.

J.E.B. v. Alabama ex rel T.B., 511 U.S. 127 (1994).

Jensen, A. R. (1969). How much can we boost IQ and scholastic achievement? *Harvard Educational Review,* 39, 1–123.

Jensen, A. R. (2000). Testing: The dilemma of group differences. *Psychology, Public Policy and Law,* 6(1), 121–127.

Johnson v. Johnson 564 P.2d 71 (Alaska 1978).

Johnson v. California, 545 U.S. 162 (2005).

Johnson v. Louisiana, 406 U.S. 356 (1972).

Johnson, D. (2000, February 19). Illinois Governor hopes to fix a "broken" justice system. *New York Times*, A–7.

Johnson, M. K., & Foley, M. A. (1984). Differentiating fact from fantasy: The reliability of children's memory. *Journal of Social Issues, 40*, 33–50.

Johnson, M. K., & Robbennolt, J. K. (1998). Using social science to inform the law of intestacy: The case of unmarried committed partners. *Law & Human Behavior, 22*(5), 479–499.

Johnson, M. P. (1995). Patriarchal terrorism and common couple violence: two forms of violence against women. *Journal of Marriage and the Family, 57*, 283–294.

Johnson, M. P. (2000, November 20). Conflict and control. Presentation, National Institute of Justice Gender Symmetry Workshop, Arlington, Virginia.

Johnson, W. R. (2003, June 29). Don't downplay the risks of abortion. *Brownsville Herald*, 2003, E–3.

Johnston, J. H. (2003, October 6). Surfing the National Archive. *Legal Times*, 26.

Johnston, J. R. (1994). High-conflict divorce. *Future of Children, 4*(1), 165–182.

Johnston, M. (1997). *Spectral evidence: The* Ramona *case: Incest, memory, and truth on trial in Napa Valley.* Boston: Houghton Mifflin.

Joint Legislative Audit and Review Commission. (2001). Review of Virginia's system of capital punishment. Richmond: Virginia General Assembly.

Jones, B. J. (2000). *Role of Indian tribal courts in the justice system.* Native American Topic Specific Monograph, Washington, DC: Center on Child Abuse and Neglect.

Jones, L., & Finkelhor, D. (2001, January). The decline in child sexual abuse cases. *Juvenile Justice Bulletin.* Washington, DC: Office of Juvenile Justice and Delinquency Prevention.

Jones, R. (2000). Guardianship for coercively controlled battered women: breaking the control of the abuser. *Georgetown Law Journal* (4), 605–657.

Jones v. United States, 463 U.S. 354 (1983).

Joyce, T., & Kaestner, R. (2000). The impact of Mississippi's mandatory delay law on the timing of abortion. *Family Planning Perspectives, 32*(1), 4–13.

Joyce, T., Kaestner, R., & Colman, S. (2006). Changes in abortions and births and the Texas parental notification law. *New England Journal of Medicine, 354*(10), 1031–1038.

Justice for All. (2004). http://www.prodeathpenalty.com.

Juvenile Court Statistics. (2003, July). 1999 Report. http://ncjrs.org.html/ojjdp/201241/chap3b.html.

Kadish, S. H., & Paulsen, M. G. (1975). *Criminal law and its processes.* 3rd ed. Boston: Little, Brown.

Kadushin, A., & Martin, J. A. (1988). *Child welfare services.* 4th ed. New York: Macmillan.

Kalichman, S. C. (1991). Laws on reporting sexual abuse of children. *American Journal of Psychiatry, 148*, 1618–1619.

Kalichman, S. C. (1993). *Mandated reporting of suspected child abuse: Ethics, law & policy.* Washington, DC: American Psychological Association.

Kalichman, S. C. (1999). *Mandated reporting of suspected child abuse: ethics, law & policy.* 2nd ed. Washington, DC: American Psychological Association.

Kalichman, S. C., & Craig, M. E. (1991). Professional psychologists' decisions to report suspected child abuse: Clinician and situation influences. *Professional Psychology: Research and Practice, 22*, 84–89.

Kalven, H., & Zeisel, H. (1966). *The American jury.* Boston: Little, Brown.

Kamin, L. J. (1974). *The science and politics of IQ.* Potomac, MD: Erlbaum.

Kantaras v. Kantaras (2003). In the Circuit Court of the Sixth Judicial Circuit and for Pasco County, Florida. Case No. 985375CA.

Kantaras v. Kantaras 884 So.2d 155 (Fla. App., 2004).

Kansas v. Bethel, 275 Kan. 456 (2003).

Kansas v. Hendricks, 521 U.S. 346 (1997).

Kasian, M., Spanos, N. P., Terrance, C. A., & Peebles, S. (1993). Battered women who kill: Jury simulation and legal defense. *Law and Human Behavior, 17*(3), 289–312.

Kassin, S. (1997). The psychology of confession evidence. *American Psychologist, 52*, 221–233.

Kassin, S. M. (2005). On the psychology of confessions. Does innocence put innocents at risk? *American Psychologist, 60*(3), 215–228.

Kassin, S. M., Ellsworth, P. C., & Smith, V. L. (1989). The "general acceptance" of psychological research on eyewitness testimony: A survey of the experts. *American Psychologist, 44*, 1089–1098.

Kassin, S. M., Meissner, C. A., & Norwick, R. J. (2005). "I'd know a false confession if I saw one": A comparative study of college students and police investigators. *Law and Human Behavior, 29*(2), 211–227.

Kassin, S. M., Tubb, V. A., Hosch, H. M., & Memon, A. (2001). On the "general acceptance" of eyewitness testimony research. A new survey of the experts. *American Psychologist, 56*(5), 405–416.

Kassin, S. M., & Wrightsman, L. S. (1985). Confession evidence. In S. Kassin and L. Wrightsman (Eds.), *The psychology of evidence and trial procedure*, pp. 67–94. Beverly Hills, CA: Sage.

Kassin, S. M., & Wrightsman, L. S. (1988). *The American jury on trial: Psychological perspectives.* New York: Hemisphere.

Katkin, D. (1982). *The nature of criminal law.* Monterey, CA: Brooks/Cole.

Katkin, D., Bullington, B., & Levine, M. (1974). Above and beyond the best interests of the child. An inquiry into the relationship between social science and social action. *Law and Society Review, 8*, 669–687.

Kaufman, J., & Zigler, E. (1989). The intergenerational transmission of child abuse. In D. Cicchetti and V. Carlson (Eds.), *Child maltreatment*, pp. 129–150. Cambridge: Cambridge University Press.

Keenan, L. A. (1985). Domestic violence and custody litigation. *Hofstra Law Review, 13,* 407.

Keilitz, I. (1987). Researching and reforming the insanity defense. *Rutgers Law Review, 39*(2/3), 289–322.

Keilitz, S., with Guerrero, R., Jones, A. M., & Rubio, D. M. (2000). *Specialization of domestic violence case management in the courts: A national survey.* New York: National Center for State Courts.

Keilitz, S., Hannaford, P., & Efkeman, H. (1998, July). The effectiveness of civil protection orders. In *Legal interventions in family violence: Research findings and policy implications, a project of the American Bar Association's Criminal Justice Section, Commission on Domestic Violence, Center on Children and the Law, and Commission on Legal Problems of the Elderly,* 47–48. Presented to the National Institute of Justice. NCJ 171666. Washington, DC: National Institute of Justice.

Kelley, F. (1882, August). On some changes in the legal status of the child since *Blackstone. International Review,* 83–98. Reprinted in S. N. Katz (Ed.), *The legal rights of children.* New York: Arno Press.

Kelly, J., & Johnston, J. (2001). The alienated child: A reformulation of parental alienation syndrome. *Family Court Review, 39* (3), 249–267.

Kelly, J. B., & Lamb, M. E. (2003). Developmental issues in relocation cases involving young children: When, whether and how? *Journal of Family Psychology, 17*(2), 193–205.

Kelly-Dreiss, S. (1990). Testimony and statement. In U.S. Senate, Committee on the Judiciary (1990). Hearing before the Committee on the Judiciary, U.S. Senate, One Hundred First Congress, second session, on legislation to reduce the growing problem of violent crime against women, part 2. Serial No. J–101–80. Washington, DC: Government Printing Office.

Kempe, C. H., Silverman, F., Steele, B., Droegmueller, W., & Silver, H. (1962). The battered child syndrome. *Journal of the American Medical Association, 181,* 17–24.

Kent v. United States, 383 U.S. 541 (1966).

Kentucky Racial Justice Act, sec. 1, ch. 532, KRS, 1998.

Kerr, P. (1991, November 24). Mental hospital chains accused of much cheating on insurance. *New York Times,* A–1, 28.

Kerry, F. (2000, February 4). Details of visit raise claims that grandmother abused Elian. *Buffalo News,* A–3.

Kershaw, S. (2002, September 3). Digital photos give the police a new edge in abuse cases. *New York Times.* http://www.nytimes.com/2002/09/03/nyregion/03ABUS.

Keyes v. Denver School District No. 1, 413 U.S. 189 (1973).

Kirk, S. A., & Kutchins, H. (1992). *The selling of DSM: The rhetoric of science in psychiatry.* New York: Aldine de Gruyter.

Kirkland, K. (2003). A legal perspective on family psychology and family law: comment on the special issue. *Journal of Family Psychology, 17*(2), 263–266.

Kitzmann, K. M., & Emery, R. E. (1993). Procedural justice and parents satisfaction in a field study of child custody dispute resolution. *Law and Human Behavior,* 17(5), 553–568.

Klein, A. R. (1998, July). Re-abuse in a population of court-restrained male batterers: Why restraining orders don't work. In *Legal interventions in family violence: Research findings and policy implications, a project of the American Bar Association's Criminal Justice Section, Commission on Domestic Violence, Center on Children and the Law, and Commission on Legal Problems of the Elderly,* 52–53. Presented to the National Institute of Justice. NCJ 171666. Washington, DC: National Institute of Justice.

Kluger, R. (2004). *Simple justice: The history of* Brown v. Board of Education *and black America's struggle for equality.* Rev. and expanded ed. New York: Knopf.

Kolata, G. (1998, July 11). In implant case, science and the law have different agendas. *New York Times,* sec. A.

Koocher, G. P., & Keith-Spiegel, P. (1998). *Ethics in psychology. Professional standards and cases.* 2nd ed. Hillside, NJ: Erlbaum.

Koski, D. D. (2002). Jury decision making in rape trials: A review and empirical assessement. *Criminal Law Bulletin, 38*(1), 21–159.

Kotlowitz, A. (1999, March 8). A reporter at large: The unprotected. *New Yorker,* 42–53.

Kovera, M. B., & Cass, S. A. (2002). Compelled mental health examinations, liability decisions, and damage awards in sexual harassment cases: issues for jury research. *Psychology, Public Policy, and Law, 8*(1), 96–114.

Kovera, M. B., Gresham, A. W., Borgida, E., Gray, E., & Regan, P. C. (1997). Does expert psychological testimony inform or influence juror decision-making? A social cognitive analysis. *Journal of Applied Psychology, 82*(1), 178–191.

Kovera, M. B., & McAuliff, B. D. (2000a). The effects of peer review and evidence quality on judge evaluations of psychological science: Are judges effective gatekeepers? *Journal of Applied Psychology, 85*(4), 574–586.

Kovera, M. B., & McAuliff, B. D. (2000b, March). Attorneys' evaluations of psychological science: Does evidence quality matter. Paper presented at the biennial meeting of the American Psychology–Law Society, New Orleans.

Kovera, M. B., Russano, M. B., & McAuliff, B. D. (2002). Assessment of the commonsense psychology underlying Daubert: Legal decision makers' abilities to evaluate expert evidence in hostile work environment cases. *Psychology, Public Policy and Law, 8*(2), 180–200.

Kovnick, J. A., Applebaum, P. S., Hoge, S. K., & Leadbetter, R. A. (2003). *Psychiatric Services, 54*(9), 1247–1252.

Kozol, H., Boucher, R., & Garafalo, R. (1972). The diagnosis and treatment of dangerousness. *Crime and Delinquency, 18,* 371–392.

Krackow, E., & Lynn, S. J. (2003). Is there touch in the game of Twister? The effects of innocuous touch and suggestive questions on children's eyewitness memory. *Law and Human Behavior, 22*(6), 589–604.

Kraus, D. A., & Sales, B. D. (1999). The problem of "helpfulness" in applying *Daubert* to expert testimony: Child custody determinations in family law as an exemplar. *Psychology, Public Policy, and Law, 5*(1), 78–99.

Kraus, D. A., & Sales, B. D. (2000). Legal standards, expertise, and experts in the resolution of contested child custody cases. *Psychology, Pubic Policy and Law, 6*(4), 843–879.

Kraus, S. (1995, September 14). Grant struggles to fit in at Tufts. *Yaledailynews.com.*

Kressel, N. J., & Kressel, D. F. (2002). *Stack and sway: The new science of jury consulting.* Boulder, CO: Westview.

Kruh, I. P., & Brodsky, S. L (1997). Clinical evaluations for transfer of juveniles to criminal court: Current practices and future research. *Behavioral Sciences & the Law, 15,* 151–165.

Kumho Tire Co. v. Carmichael, 526 U.S. 137 (1999).

Kropp, P. R., & Hart, S. D. (2000). The Spousal Assault Risk Assessment (SARA) guide: reliability and validity in adult male offenders. *Law and Human Behavior, 24*(1), 101–118.

Kulik, C. T., Perry, E. L., & Pepper, M. B. (2003). Here comes the judge: The influence of judge personal characteristics on federal sexual harassment case outcomes. *Law and Human Behavior, 27*(1), 69–86.

Kutchins, H., & Kirk, S. A. (1997). *Making us crazy: DSM: The psychiatric bible and the creation of mental disorders.* New York: Free Press.

LaBine, S. J., & LaBine, G. (1996). Determinations of negligence and the hindsight bias. *Law and Human Behavior, 20,* 501–516.

Laing, L, (2001, June 21–22). Domestic Violence- Emerging Challenges. Paper presented at the 4th National Outlook Symposium on Crime in Australia, New Crimes or New Responses. Australian Institute of Criminology, Canberra.

Lake v. Arnold, 232 F.3d 360 (3d Cir 2000).

Lambert, N. (1981). Psychological evidence in *Larry P. v. Wilson Riles:* An evaluation by a witness for the defense. *American Psychologist, 36,* 937–952.

Landers v. Chrysler Corporation, 963 S.W. 2d 275 (Mo. Ct. App. 1997).

Larry P. v. Riles, 343 F. Supp. 1306 (N.D. Cal 1972), aff'd 502 F. 2d 963 (9th Cir. 1974).

Larry P. v. Riles, 495 F. Supp. 926 (N.D. Cal., 1979), aff'd on state law grounds 793 F. 2d 969 (9th Cir. 1981).

Lawrence v. Texas, 539 U.S. 558 (2003).

Lazoritz, S. (1990). Whatever happened to Mary Ellen? *Child Abuse and Neglect, 14,* 143–149.

Lebow, J. (2003). Integrative family therapy for disputes involving child custody and visitation. *Journal of Family Psychology, 17,* 181–192.

Lee, C. M., Beauregard, C. P. M., & Hunsley, J. (1998). Lawyers' opinions regarding child custody, mediation and assessment services: Implications for psychological practice. *Professional Psychology: Research and Practice, 29,*(2), 115–120.

Lefkowitz, B. (1997). *Our guys.* Berkeley: University of California Press.

Legal Corner. (1997). Outcomes of recent malpractice suits against therapists brought by former patients claiming negligent encouragement or implantation of false memories. *FMSF Newsletter, 6*(11), 7–9.

Legal Corner. (1999a). Courts deny crime victims and worker's compensation funds to "repressed memory" claimants. *FMSF Newsletter, 8*(2), 6.

Legal Corner. (1999b). Malpractice suits claiming suggestion of false memories. *FMSF Newsletter, 8*(4), 7–12.

Legal Corner. (1999c). Braun surrenders license in plea agreement. *FMSF Newsletter, 8*(8), 9.

Lehr v. Robertson, 463 U.S. 248 (1983).

Leichtman, M. D., & Ceci, S. J. (1995). The effects of stereotypes and suggestions on preschooler's reports. *Developmental Psychology, 31,* 568–578.

Leippe, M. R. (1995). The case for expert testimony about eyewitness memory. *Psychology, Public Policy and Law, 1*(4), 909–959.

Leippe, M. R., & Romanczyk, A. (1987). Children on the witness stand: A communication/persuasion analysis of jurors' reactions to child witnesses. In S. J. Ceci, M. P. Toglia, and D. F. Ross (Eds.), *Children's eyewitness memory,* pp. 155–177. New York: Springer-Verlag.

Leiter, M. T. (2001, October 31). PINS age change delayed by state. Study finds law to aid parents and children under age 18 burdensome to overtaxed system. *Putnam County News and Recorder, 1.*

Levesque, R. J. R. (2000). *Adolescents, sex and the law.* Washington, DC: American Psychological Association.

Levett, L. M., & Kovera, M. B. (2002). Judicial notebook: Psychologists battle over the general acceptance of eyewitness research. *Monitor on Psychology, 33*(11), 13.

Levi, E. H. (1949). *An introduction to legal reasoning.* Chicago: University of Chicago Press.

Levin, A (2000). Child witnesses of domestic violence: How should judges apply the best interests of the child standard in custody and visitation cases involving domestic violence. *UCLA L. Rev. 47,* 813–857.

Levine, D. I. (2000). The Chinese American challenge to court-mandated quotas in San Francisco's public school: Notes from a (partisan) participant–observer. *Harvard Black Letter Law Journal, 16,* 39–145.

Levine, D. I. (2003). Public school assignment methods after Grutter and Gratz: The view from San Francisco. *Hastings Constitutional Law Quarterly, 30*(40), 511–540.

Levine, D. I., Jung, D. J., Schoenbrod, D., & Macbeth, A. (2006). *Remedies: Public and private.* 4th ed. Eagan, MN: Thomson/West.

Levine, D. I., Slomanson, W. R., Wingate, C. K. , & Shapell, R. J. (2005). *Cases and materials on California civil procedure.* 2nd ed. St, Paul, MN: Thomson/West.

Levine, M. (1976). The academic achievement test: Its historical context and social functions. *American Psychologist, 31,* 228–238.

Levine, M. (1981). *The history and politics of community mental health.* New York: Oxford University Press.

Levine, M. (1985). The adversary process and social science in the courts: *Barefoot v. Estelle. Journal of Psychiatry and Law, 12,* 147–181.

Levine, M. (1986). The role of special master in institutional reform litigation: A case study. *Law & Policy, 8,* 275–321.

Levine, M. (1998). Do standards of proof affect decision making in child protection investigations? *Law and Human Behavior, 22*(3), 341–347.

Levine, M. (1999). "The legal culture must assimilate the scientific culture" and vice versa? *Law & Policy, 21*(1), 77–89.

Levine, M. (2000). The Family Group Conference in the New Zealand Children, Young Persons and Their Families Act of 1989: Review and evaluation. *Behavioral Sciences & the Law, 18*(4), 517–556.

Levine, M., & Battistoni, L. (1991). The corroboration requirement in child sex abuse cases. *Behavioral Sciences & the Law, 9*(1), 3–20.

Levine, M., & Doherty, E. (1991). The Fifth Amendment and therapeutic requirements to admit abuse. *Criminal Justice and Behavior, 18,* 98–112.

Levine, M., Doueck, H. J., Anderson, E. M., Chavez, F. T., Diesz, R. L., George, N. A., Sharma, A., Steinberg, K. L., & Wallach, L. (1995). *The impact of mandated reporting on the therapeutic process: Picking up the pieces.* Thousand Oaks, CA: Sage.

Levine, M., Doueck, H. J., Freeman, J. B., & Compaan, C. (1996, September 16–21). Children and Youth Services Review, 18, 693–711.

Levine, M., Doueck, H. J., Freeman, J. B., & Compaan, C. (1998). Rush to judgment? Child protective services and allegations of sex abuse. *American Journal of Orthopsychiatry, 68,* 101–107.

Levine, M., Farrell, M. P., & Perrotta, P. (1981). The impact of rules of jury deliberation on group developmental processes. In B. D. Sales (Ed.), *The trial process,* pp. 263–304. New York: Plenum.

Levine, M. & Howe, B. (1985). The penetration of social science into legal culture. *Law & Policy, 7,* 173–198.

Levine, M., & Levine, A. (1992). *Helping children: A social history.* New York: Oxford University Press.

Levine, M., & Perkins, D. V. (1997). *Principles of community psychology.* 2nd ed. New York: Oxford University Press.

Levine, M., Perkins, D. D., & Perkins, D. V. (2005). *Principles of community psychology: Perspectives and applications.* 3rd ed. New York: Oxford University Press.

Levine, M., & Singer, S. I. (1988). Delinquency, substance abuse and risk taking in middle class adolescents. *Behavioral Sciences and the Law, 6,* 1–16.

Lewin, T. (2001, July 11). Zero-tolerance policy is challenged. *New York Times.* http://www.nytimes.com/200/01/11/national/11DOME.html.

Lewin, T. (1998, March 22). Debate centers on definition of harassment. *New York Times,* A–1.

Lewin, T., & Medina. J. (2003, July 31). To cut failure rate, schools shed students. *New York Times,* A–1, A–22.

Lewis, C. C. (1980). A comparison of minors' and adults' pregnancy decisions. *American Journal of Orthopsychiatry, 50,* 446–453.

Lewis, C. C. (1981). How adolescents approach decisions: Changes over grades seven to twelve and policy implications. *Child Development, 52,* 538–544.

Lewis, C. C. (1987). Minors' competence to consent to abortion. *American Psychologist, 42,* 84–88.

Lewis, D. O., Yeager, C. A., Swica, Y., Pincus, J. H., & Lewis, M. (1997). Objective documentation of child abuse and dissociation in 12 murderers with dissociative identity disorder. *American Journal of Psychiatry, 154,* 1703–1710.

Lewis, N. A. (2002) Mental issue keeps grip on Sept. 11 case. The New York Times. Health, July 10, *http://query.nytimes.com/gst/fullpage .html?sec = health&res = 9B05E1D71430F933A2574.*

Lewis, N. A., (2006). Military alters the makeup of interrogation advisers. *New York Times,* Wednesday, June 7, A-20.

Lewis, O. D., Mallouh, C., & Webb, V. (1989). Child abuse, delinquency, and violent criminality. In D. Cicchetti & V. Carlson (Eds.), *Child maltreatment,* pp. 707–721. Cambridge: Cambridge University Press.

Libby, A. M., Cuellar, A., Snowden, L. R., & Orton, H. D. (2002). Substitution in a Medicaid mental health carve-out: Services and costs. *Journal of Health Care Finance, 28*(4), 11–23.

Lidz, C. W., Mulvey, E. P., Arnold, R. P., Bennett, N. S., & Kirsch, B. L. (1993). Coercive interactions in a psychiatric emergency room. *Behavioral Sciences and the Law, 11*(3), 269–280.

Lieberman, J. D., & Sales, B. D. (1997). What social science teaches us about the jury instruction process. *Psychology, Public Policy and the Law, 3*(4), 589–644.

Lillie and Reed v. Newcastle City Council (2002) High Court of Justice, Queen's Bench Division 2002 EWHC 1600 (QB); Case Nos: HQ9903605, HQ9903606.

Lind, E. A., Maccoun, R. J., Ebener, P. A., Felstiner, W. L. F., Hensler, D. R., Resnik, J., & Tyler, T. R. (1990). In the eye of the beholder: Tort litigants' evaluations of their experiences in the civil justice system. *Law & Society Review, 24,* 953–996.

Lindsay, R. C. L., & Bellinger, K. (1999). Alternatives to the sequential lineup: The importance of controlling the pictures. *Journal of Applied Psychology, 84*(3), 315–321.

Lindsay, R. C. L., Lea, J. A., Nosworthy, G. J., Fulford, J. A., Hecot, J., LeVan, V., & Seabrook, C. (1991). Biased lineups: Sequential presentation reduces the problem. *Journal of Applied Psychology, 70,* 556–564.

Lindsay, R. C. L., & Wells, G. L. (1985). Improving eyewitness identifications from lineups: Simultaneous versus sequential lineup presentation. *Journal of Applied Psychology, 70,* 556–564.

Linhorst, D. M., & Dirks-Linhorst, P. A. (1997). The impact of insanity acquitees on Missouri's public mental health system. *Law and Human Behavior, 21*(3), 327–338.

Link, B. G., & Stueve, A. (1994). Psychotic symptoms and the violent/illegal behavior of mental patients compared to community controls. In J. Monahan & H. J. Steadman (Eds.), *Violence and mental disorder: Developments in risk assessment,* pp. 137–159. Chicago: University of Chicago Press.

Linsalata, P., Durfee, D., & Harmon, B. (1996, March 10). Prosecution stung by jury consultants in Kevorkian trial. *Detroit News.* http://detnews.com/menu/stories/39287.htm.

Lippke, R. L. (2002). Crime reduction and the length of prison sentences. *Law & Policy, 24*(1), 17–35.

Lipovsky, J. A., Tidwell, R., Crisp, J., Kilpatrick, D. G., Saunders, B. E., & Dawson, V. L. (1992). Child witnesses in criminal court: Descriptive information from three southern states. *Law and Human Behavior, 16*(6), 635–650.

Liptak, A. (2003, May 30).Ohio case considers whether abuse victim can violate own protective order. *New York Times.* http://www.nytimes.com/2003/05/30/national/ABUS.html.

Liptak, A. (2002, April 14). Religion and Law. Insurance companies often dictate legal strategies used by dioceses. *New York Times,* A–24.

Liptak, A. (2004, September 15). Fewer death sentences being imposed in U.S. *New York Times,* A–14.

Lipton, J. P. (1999). The use and acceptance of social science evidence in business litigation after *Daubert. Psychology, Public Policy, and Law, 5*(1), 59–77.

Little, K. (2004, December). Family violence: an intervention model for dental professions. *Office of Victims of Crime (OVC) Bulletin.* Washington, DC: Office of Justice Programs.

Litwack, T. R. (1985). The prediction of violence. *Clinical Psychologist, 38,* 87–91.

Litwack, T. R. (2003). The competency of criminal defendants to refuse, for delusional reasons, a viable insanity defense recommended by counsel. *Behavioral Sciences & the Law, 21*(2), 135–156.

Litzelfelner, P. (2000). The effectiveness of CASAs in achieving positive outcomes for children. *Child Welfare, 79*(2), 179–193.

Liu, Z. (2004). Capital punishment and the deterrence hypothesis: Some new insights and empirical evidence. *Eastern Economic Journal, 30*(3), 237–258.

Lockett v. Ohio, 438 U.S. 586 (1978).

Lockhart v. McCree, 476 U.S. 162 (1986).

Loeb, L., & Schack, R. J. (1987). The uncertain status of the mental health professional's "duty to warn." *New York State Bar Journal, 59,* 32–35.

Lofton v. Secretary of the Florida Department of Children and Families, 358 F.3d 804 (11th Cir 2004) Cert denied, 543 U.S. 1081 (2005).

Loftus, E. F. (1979). *Eyewitness testimony.* Cambridge, MA: Harvard University Press.

Loftus, E. F., & Davies, G. M. (1984). Distortions in the memory of children. *Journal of Social Issues, 40,* 51–67.

Loftus, E. F., & Doyle, J. M. (1997). *Eyewitness testimony: Civil and criminal.* 3rd ed. Charlottesville, VA: Lexis Law.

Loftus, E. F., & Ketcham, K. (1994). *The myth of repressed memory.* New York: St. Martin's.

Lally, S. J. (2003). What tests are acceptable for use in forensic evaluations? A survey of experts. *Professional Psychology, Research and Practice, 34*(5), 491–498.

Lopez-Williams, A., Levine, M., Schlegel, A., Yagle, M., & Alexander, G. (under review). Gender and referral type differences in psychopathology, impairment, and treatment history among non-detained youth in the juvenile justice system.

Lowenfield v. Phelps, 484 U.S. 231 (1988).

Lubik, J. D., & Moran, J. R. (2003). Lethal elections: Gubernatorial politics and the timing of executions. *Journal of Law and Economics, 46,* 1–25.

Luepnitz, D. A. (1979). Which aspects of divorce affect children? *Family Coordinator, 28,* 79–86.

Luepnitz, D. A. (1982). *Child custody.* Lexington, MA: Lexington Books.

Luginbuhl, J. (1992). Comprehension of judges' instructions in the penalty phase of a capital trial: Focus on mitigating circumstances. *Law and Human Behavior, 16*(2), 203–218.

Luginbuhl, J. & Middendorf, K. (1988). Death penalty beliefs and jurors' responses to aggravating and mitigating circumstances in capital trials. *Law and Human Behavior, 12*(3), 263–281.

Luker, K. (1984). *Abortion and the politics of motherhood.* Berkeley: University of California Press.

Lundberg, S., & Plotnick, R. D. (1990). Effects of state welfare, abortion and family planning policies on premarital childbearing among white adolescents. *Family Planning Perspectives, 22,* 246–251.

Lymberis, M. T. (n.d.). Sexual misconduct in the practice of child and adolescent psychiatry. http://www.calpsych.com/lymberis/misconduct.htm.

Lyon, T. D. (2002). Expert testimony on the suggestibility of children. pp 378–411. In. B. L. Bottoms, M. B. Kovera, & B. D. McAuliff (Eds.), *Children, social science and the law.* New York: Cambridge University Press.

MacKinnon, C. A. (1979). Sexual harassment of working women. New Haven, CT: Yale University Press.

Maguire, K., & Pastore, A. L. (Eds.). (1998). *Sourcebook of criminal justice statistics 1997.* U.S. Department of Justice, Bureau of Justice Statistics. Washington, DC: Government Printing Office.

Maguire, K., & Pastore, A. L. (Eds.) (1999). *Sourcebook of criminal justice statistics*. U.S. Department of Justice, Bureau of Justice Statistics. Washington, DC: Government Printing Office.

Maher v. Roe, 432 U.S. 464 (1977).

Major, B., Mueller, P., & Hildebrandt, K. (1985). Attributions, expectations, and coping with abortion. *Journal of Personality and Social Psychology,* 48, 585–599.

Major, B., Richards, C., Cooper, M. L., Cozzarelli, C., & Zubek, J. (1998). Personal resilience, cognitive appraisals, and coping: An integrative model of adjustment to abortion. *Journal of Personality and Social Psychology,* 74, 735–752.

Malpass, R. M., & Kravitz, J. (1969). Recognition for faces of own and other race. *Journal of Personality and Social Psychology,* 13, 330–334.

Manegold, C. S. (1993, March 19). Glen Ridge verdict may be milestone for retarded. *New York Times,* B–16.

Manson v. Brathwaite, 432 U.S. 98 (1977).

Maracek, J. (1986). Consequences of adolescent childbearing and abortion. In G. Melton (Ed.), *Adolescent abortion: Psychological and legal issues,* pp. 96–115. Lincoln: University of Nebraska Press.

Marbury v. Madison, 1 Cranch 137 (1803).

Marnell, R. I., & Schwartz, S. R. (2004, August 27). The emancipation of children: Age of majority versus 21. *New York Law Journal,* 4.

Marsiglio, W. & Shehan, C. L. (1993). Adolescent males' abortion attitudes: Data from a national survey. *Family Planning Perspectives,* 25, 162–169.

Maryland v. Craig, 497 U.S. 836 (1990).

Mason, P. T., Jr. (1972). Child abuse and neglect. Part I: Historical overview, legal matrix and social perspectives. *North Carolina Law Review,* 50, 293–349.

Matarazzo, J. D. (1990). Psychological assessment versus psychological testing: Validation from Binet to the school, clinic, and courtroom. *American Psychologist,* 45, 999–1017.

Mathiesen, T. (1998). Selective incapacitation revisited. *Law and Human Behavior,* 22(4), 455–479.

Matter of Knowack, 158 N.Y. 482 (1899).

Matter of Marriage of Cabalquinto, 100 Wash.2d 325, 669 P.2d 886 (1983).

Matter of Nicole V., 71 N.Y.2d 112 (1987).

Matter of Reed v. Reed, 240 A.D. 2d 824 (1997).

Matter of Star Leslie W., 63 N.Y.2d 136 (1984).

Mayer, J. (2005, July 11–18). A reporter at large. The experiment. Is the military devising new methods of interrogation at Guantanomo? *New Yorker,* 60–71.

Maynard, R. A. (Ed.). (1996). *Kids having kids: A Robin Hood Foundation special report on the costs of adolescent childbearing.* New York: Robin Hood Foundation.

Mazur, R. & Aldrich, L. (2002). *What makes a domestic violence court work?* New York: Center for Court Innovation.

McAdams, J. (1997). Comment. In *The death penalty: A scholarly forum. Focus on Law Studies,* 12, 9.

McAuliff, B. D., & Kovera, M. B. (2002).The status of evidentiary and procedural innovations in child abuse proceedings. In B. L. Bottoms, M. B. Kovera, & B. D. McAuliff (Eds.), *Children, social science and the law,* ch. 16, 412–443. New York: Cambridge University Press.

McCartney, J. R., & Campbell, V. A. (1998). Confirmed abuse cases in public residential facilities for persons with mental retardation: A multi-state study. *Mental Retardation,* 36, 465–473.

McDonald v. McDonald, 608 N.Y.S.2d 477 (N.Y. App. Div. 1994).

McCleskey v. Kemp, 481 U.S. 279 (1987).

McCloskey, M., Egeth, H., & McKenna, J. (Eds.) (1986). The experimental psychologist in court: The ethics of expert testimony. *Law and Human Behavior,* 10, (1/2), 1–181.

McCormack, J. (1999, February 15). Coming two days shy of martyrdom: A college class frees a wrongfully convicted man. *Newsweek International.* http://www.newsweek.com/nw-srv/issue/07_99a/printed/int/us/na0807_1.html.

McCrea, R. C. (1910). *The humane movement: A descriptive survey.* New York: Columbia University Press.

McCurdy, K., & Daro, D. (1994). Current trends in child abuse reporting and fatalities: The results of the 1992 annual fifty state survey. Working paper no. 808. Chicago: National Committee for Prevention of Child Abuse.

McGarry, A. L., Curran, W. J., Lipsitt, P. D., Lelos, D., Schwitzgebel, R., Rosenberg, A. H., Balcanoff, E., Bender, F., Bendt, R., & Chayet, N. (1973). *Competence to stand trial and mental illness.* Washington, DC: Superintendent of Documents, Government Printing Office.

McGeehan, P. (2003, March 7). Two Wall Street firings said to be linked to harassment, *New York Times,* Business sec.

McGeehan, P. (2004, July 13). Morgan Stanley settles bias suit with $54 million. *New York Times,* Business sec.

McGinley, H., & Pasewark, R. A. (1989). National survey of the frequency and success of the insanity plea and alternate pleas. *Journal of Law and Psychiatry,* 17, 205–221.

McGough, L. (1998). A legal commentary: The impact of *Daubert* on 21st century child sexual abuse prosecutions. In S. J. Ceci and H. Helmbrook (Eds.), *Expert witnesses in child abuse cases,* pp. 265–281. Washington, DC: American Psychological Association.

McGough, L. S. (1994). *Child witnesses: Fragile voices in the American legal system.* New Haven, CT: Yale University Press.

McGraw, B., Farthing-Capowich, D., & Keilitz, I (1985). The "guilty but mentally ill" plea and verdict: Current state of knowledge. *Villanova Law Review,* 30, 117–191.

McHugh, M. C. (1993). Studying battered women and batterers: Feminist perspectives on methodology. In. M. Hansen & M. Harway (Eds.), *Battering and family therapy: A feminist perspective,* pp 69–71. Newbury Park, CA: Sage.

McKechnie, W. S. (1914). *Magna Carta: A commentary on the Great Charter of King John.* 2d ed. New York: Burt Franklin.

McKeiver v. Pennsylvania, 403 U.S. 528 (1971).

McKinnon, R., & Wallerstein, J. S. (1986). Joint custody and the preschool child. *Behavioral Science & Law,* 4, 169–183.

McKnight, C. (1992). *Life without* Roe: *Making predictions about illegal abortions.* Washington, DC: Horatio R. Storer Foundation.

McNeely, R. L., & Robinson-Simpson, G. R. (1987). The truth about domestic violence, a falsely framed issue. *Social Work,* 32(6), 485–490.

McNeely, R. L., & Robinson-Simpson, G. R. (1988). The truth about domestic violence revisited: A reply to Saunders. *Social Work,* 33(2), 184–188.

McNeese, C. A., & Jackson, S. (2004). Juvenile justice policy. Current trends and 21-st century issues. In A. R. Roberts (Ed.) (2004), *Juvenile justice sourcebook,* ch. 2, 41–68. New York: Oxford University Press.

Mecham, L. R. (2004). 2004 annual report of the director. http://www.uscourts.gov/judgususc/judbus.html.

Meehl, P. E. (1954). *Clinical versus statistical prediction: A theoretical analysis and review of the evidence.* Minneapolis: University of Minnesota Press.

Meehl, P. E., & Rosen, A. (1955). Antecedent probability and the efficiency of psychometric signs, patterns or cutting scores. *Psychological Bulletin,* 52, 194–216.

Meissner, C. A., & Brigham, J. C. (2001). Thirty years of investigating the own-race bias in memory for faces: A meta-analytic review. *Psychology, Public Policy, and Law,* 7(1), 3–35.

Menjoge, S. S. (2003). Testing the limits of anti-discrimination law: How employers' use of pre-employment psychological and personality tests can circumvent Title VII and the ADA. *North Carolina Law Review,* 82, 326–365.

Melton, G. B. (1981). Children's competency to testify. *Law and Human Behavior,* 5(1), 73–85.

Melton, G. B. (1983). Toward "personhood" for adolescents: Autonomy and privacy as values in public policy. *American Psychologist,* 38, 99–103.

Melton, G. B. (1984). Developmental psychology and the law: The state of the art. *Journal of Family Law,* 22, 445–482.

Melton, G. B. (Ed.). (1987a). *Reforming the law: Impact of child development research.* New York: Guilford.

Melton, G. B. (1987b). Legal regulation of adolescent abortion: Unintended effects. *American Psychologist,* 42, 79–83.

Melton, G. B. (1990). Law, science, and humanity: The normative foundation of social science in law. *Law and Human Behavior,* 14(4), 315–332.

Melton, G. B. (1994). Expert opinions: "not for cosmic understanding." In B. D. Sales and G. R. VandenBos (Eds.), *Psychology in litigation and legislation,* pp. 55–100. Washington, DC: American Psychological Association.

Melton, G. B., & Pliner, A. J. (1986). Adolescent abortion: A psycholegal analysis. In G. B. Melton (Ed.), *Adolescent abortion: Psychological and legal issues,* pp. 1–39. Lincoln: University of Nebraska Press.

Melton, G. B., & Russo, N. F. (1987). Adolescent abortion: Psychological perspectives on public policy. *American Psychologist,* 42, 69–72.

Melton, G. B., Weithorn, L. A., & Slobogin, C. (1985). *Community mental health centers and the courts: An evaluation of community-based forensic services.* Lincoln: University of Nebraska Press.

Menninger, K. (1928). Medicolegal proposals of the American Psychiatric Association. *Journal of Criminal Law, Criminology and Police Science,* 19, 367–373.

Mercy, J. A., & Saltzman, L. E., (1989). Fatal violence among spouses in the United States, 1976–1985. *American Journal of Public Health,* 79(5), 595–599.

Meritor Savings Bank v. Vinson, 477 U.S. 57 (1986).

Meyer v. Nebraska, 262 U.S. 390 (1923).

Miller-El v. Dretke, 545 U.S. 231 (2005).

Miller, C., Miller, H. L., Kenney, L., & Tasheff, J. (1999). Issues in balancing teenage clients' confidentiality and reporting statutory rape among Kansas Title X clinic staff. *Public Health Nursing,* 16(5), 329–336.

Miller, H. A., Amentia, A. E., & Conroy, M. A. (2005). Sexually violent predator evaluations: Empirical evidence, strategies for professionals, and research directions. *Law and Human Behavior,* 29(1), 29–54.

Miller, R. D. (2003). Hospitalization of criminal defendants for evaluation of competence to stand trial for restoration of competence: Clinical and legal issues. *Behavioral Sciences & the Law,* 21(3), 359–391.

Miller, R. K., Maier, G. J., Van Rybroek, G. J., & Weidemann, J. A. (1989). Treating patients "doing time": A forensic perspective. *Hospital and Community Psychiatry,* 40, 960–962.

Mills, L. G. (1999). Commentary: Killing her softly: Intimate abuse and the violence of state intervention. *Harvard Law Review,* 113, 550–612.

Minda, G. (1995). *Postmodern legal movements.* New York: New York University Press.

Miranda v. Arizona, 384 U.S. 436 (1966).

Missouri v. Simmons 944 S.W.2d 165, (1997).

Mnookin, R. H. (1975). Child-custody adjudication: Judicial functions in the face of indeterminacy. *Law and Contemporary Problems,* 3, 226–293.

Mnookin, R. H. (1985). *Bellotti v. Baird:* A hard case. In R. H. Mnookin (Ed.), *In the interest of children: Advocacy, law reform and public policy,* pp. 15–65. New York: W. H. Freeman.

Mnookin, R. H., & Weisberg, D. K. (2005). *Child, family and state: Problems and materials on children and the law.* 5th ed. Boston: Aspen.

Mocan, H. N., & Gittings, R. K. (2003). Getting off death row: Commuted sentences and the deterrent effect of capital punishment. *Journal of Law and Economics, 46,* 453–478.

Moenssens, A. A., Starrs, J. E., Henderson, C. E., & Inbau, F. (1995). *Scientific evidence in civil and criminal cases.* 4th ed. Westbury, NY: Foundation Press.

Mohr, J. C. (1978). *Abortion in America.* New York: Oxford University Press.

Monahan, J. (1976). The prevention of violence. In J. Monahan (Ed.), *Community mental health and the criminal justice system.* New York: Pergamon.

Monahan, J. (1981). *Predicting violent behavior: An assessment of clinical techniques.* Beverly Hills, CA: Sage.

Monahan, J. (1982). The prediction of violent behavior: Developments in psychology and law. In C. J. Scheirer & B. L. Hammonds (Eds.), *The Master Lecture Series,* vol. 2: *Psychology and the Law,* pp. 147–176. Washington, DC: American Psychological Association.

Monahan, J. (1984). The prediction of violent behavior: Toward a second generation of theory and policy. *American Journal of Psychiatry, 141,* 10–15.

Monahan, J. (1988). Risk assessment of violence among the mentally disordered: Generating useful knowledge. *International Journal of Law and Psychiatry, 11,* 249–257.

Monahan, J. (1992). Mental disorder and violent behavior: Perceptions and evidence. *American Psychologist, 47,* 511–521.

Monahan, J. (1993). Limiting therapist exposure to *Tarasoff* liability: Guidelines for risk containment. *American Psychologist,* 48, 242–250.

Monahan, J. (1997). The scientific status of research on clinical and actuarial predictions of violence. In D. L. Faigman, D. H. Kaye, M. J. Saks, & J. Sanders (Eds.) (2002), *Modern scientific evidence: The law and science of expert testimony,* pp. 300–318. St. Paul, MN: West.

Monahan, J., & Walker, L. (2006). *Social science in law: Cases and materials.* 6th ed. Westbury, NY: Foundation Press.

Monastersky, R. (1998, April 18). Courting reliable science. *Science News.*

Monsour, K. J., & Stewart, B. A. (1973). Abortion and sexual behavior in college women. *American Journal of Orthopsychiatry, 43,* 804–814.

Montoya, J. (1995). Lessons from *Akiki* and *Michaels* on shielding child witnesses. *Psychology, Public Policy and Law, 1*(2), 340–369.

Moran, G., Cutler, B. L., & De Lisa, A. (1994). Attitudes toward tort reform, scientific jury selection, and juror bias: Verdict inclination in criminal and civil trials. *Law and Psychology Review, 18,* 309–328.

Morris, M. (2006, January 10). PM sets out "respect" approach to tackle hooliganism. *Independent,* 2.

Morris, N., Bonnie, R., & Finer, J. J. (1986–1987). Should the insanity defense be abolished? An introduction to the debate. *Journal of Law and Health, 1,* 113–140.

Morris, N., & Miller, M. (1987, March 1–7). Predictions of dangerousness in the criminal law. *Research in Brief.* Washington, DC: National Institute of Justice.

Morrison, B. (1994, February 14). Children of circumstance. *New Yorker,* 48–60.

Morse, S. J. (1978). Crazy behavior, morals, and science: An analysis of mental health law. *Southern California Law Review, 51,* 527–654.

Morse, S. J. (1982). Failed explanations and criminal responsibility: Experts and the unconscious. *Virginia Law Review, 68,* 971–1084.

Morse, S. J. (1985). Excusing the crazy: The insanity defense reconsidered. *Southern California Law Review,* 58, 777–836.

Morse, S. J. (1986). *Psychology, determinism, and legal responsibility.* Nebraska Symposium on Motivation 1985. Lincoln: University of Nebraska Press.

Moye v. Moye, 627 P. 2d. 799 (Idaho, 1981).

Mueller, P., & Major, B. (1989). Self-blame, self-efficacy, and adjustment to abortion. *Journal of Personality and Social Psychology, 57,* 1059–1068.

Muensterberg, H. (1923). *On the witness stand.* New York: Clark Boardman. (Originally published in 1908 by Doubleday, Page).

Mulford, C. F., Reppucci, N. D., Mulvey, E. P., Woolard, J. L., & Portman, S. L. (2004). Legal issues affecting mentally disordered and developmentally delayed youth in the justice system. *International Journal of Forensic Mental Health, 3*(1), 3–22.

Muller v. Oregon, 208 U.S. 412 (1908).

Mulvey, E. P., & Lidz, C. W. (1984). Clinical considerations in the prediction of dangerousness in mental patients. *Clinical Psychology Review, 4,* 379–401.

Mulvey, E. P., & Lidz, C. W. (1993). Measuring patient violence in dangerousness research. *Law and Human Behavior, 17*(3), 277–288.

Mumley, D. L., Tillbrook, C. E., & Grisso, T. (2003). Five year research update (1996–2000): Evaluations for competence to stand trial (adjudicative competence). *Behavioral Sciences & the Law, 21*(1), 329–350.

Murphy, J. M. (1976). Psychiatric labeling in cross-cultural perspective. *Science, 191,* 1019–1028.

Murray, J. P., with assistance of H. T. Rubin (1983). *Status offenders. A sourcebook.* Boys Town, NE: Boys Town Center.

Myers, J. E. B. (1987). *Child witness law and practice.* New York: John Wiley.

Myers, J. E. B. (2004). *A history of child protection in America.* Sacramento, CA: Author.

Myers, J. E. B., Redlich, A. D., Goodman, G. S., Prizmich, L. P., & Imwinkelried, E. (1999). Jurors' perceptions of hearsay in child sexual abuse cases. *Psychology, Public Policy and Law, 5*(2), 388–419.

Myrdal, G. (1964). *An American dilemma.* Vol. 2: *The Negro social structure.* New York: McGraw-Hill.

Nabozny v. Podlesny 92 F.3d 446 (7th Cir 1996).

National Adoption Information Clearinghouse (NAIC). (2003). *About the federal child abuse prevention and treatment act.* Washington, DC: Author.

NAACP. (1999, November 21). N.A.A.C.P. seeks to limit use of college board tests. *New York Times,* A–39.

National Association of Court Management. (1997). *The courts' response to domestic violence.* NACM miniguide. Williamsburg, VA: Author.

National Association of School Psychologists. (2004). Position statement on sexual minority youth. http://www.nasponline.org/information/pospaper_glb.html.

National Campaign to Prevent Teen Pregnancy. (2004). Teen pregnancy prevention provisions in welfare reform legislation. http://www.teenpregnancy.org/about/pdf/wrkeypoints.pdf.

National Center for Education Statistics. (2002, October). Average SAT scores for college-bound high school seniors, 2001–2002.

National Center for Health Statistics. (2004). *Health U.S., 2004, with chart book on trends in health of Americans.* Hyattsville, MD: Author.

National Center for State Courts. (2005, Spring). The vanishing trial: Implications for bench and bar. *Civil Action, 4*(1).

National Center on Women and Family Law. (1990). Orders of protection backlash. *Women's Advocate,* 11(4), 3.

National Council of Juvenile and Family Court Judges. (1998). *Family violence: Emerging programs for battered mothers and their children.* Reno, NV: Author.

National Council of Juvenile and Family Court Judges Family Violence Department. (1999). *Effective Intervention in Domestic Violence and Child Maltreatment Cases: Guidelines for Policy and Practice.* Reno, NV: Author.

National GAINS Center for People with Co-occurring Disorder in the Justice System. (2003). *Surveys of mental health courts.* Delmar, NY: Author.

National Institute of Justice. (2004, November). Violence against women: Identifying risk factors. NIJ Research in Brief, NCJ 197019. Washington, DC: U.S. Department of Justice, Office of Justice Programs.

National Institute of Justice. (1999, October). The Impact of arrest on domestic violence: Results from five policy experiments. *National Institute of Justice Journal,* 27–28.

National Mental Health Association. (2004). *NMHA Policy Positions: In support of the insanity defense.* http://www.nmha.org/positions/ps18.cfm.

National Research Council. (1993). *Understanding child abuse and neglect.* Washington, DC: National Academy Press.

National Youth Court Center. (2005). Highlights from the National Youth Court Initiative 1994–2005. In *Session,* newsletter of the National Youth Court Center, 5(3).

Neely v. Newton, 149 F.3d 1074 (10th Cir 1998), cert. denied, 525 U.S. 1107 (1999).

Neil v. Biggers, 409 U.S. 188 (1972).

Nelson, B. D., Aron, R. H., & Poole, D. A. (1999). Underprediction of female performance from standardized knowledge tests: A further example from the Knowledge of Geography test. *Sex Roles,* 41, 529–540.

Nelson, B. J. (1984). *Making an issue of child abuse.* Chicago: University of Chicago Press.

Neumann, D. A. Houskamp, B. M., Pollock, V. E., & Briere, J. (1996). The long-term sequelae of childhood sexual abuse in women: A meta-analytic review. *Child Maltreatment,* 1, 6–16.

New Jersey Supreme Court Task Force. (1986). *Women in the courts: The second report.* Trenton, NJ: Administrative Office of the Courts.

New York City Task Force on Family Violence, co-chairs: Ruth W. Messinger and Ronnie M. Eldridge. (1993). *Behind closed doors: The city's response to family violence: Report of the task force on family violence.* New York: Author.

New York State Bar Association. (1988). Child abuse—a continuing tragedy in New York State. A Report of the New York State Bar Association Special Committee on Women in the Courts. New York Task Force on Women in the Courts. (1986–1987). *Fordham University Law Journal,* 15.

New York State Commission on Judicial Conduct. (2004). In the Matter of the Proceeding Pursuant to Section 44, sub-division 4, of the Judiciary Law in Relation to Patrick J. McGrath, a Judge of the County Court, Rensselaer County. http://www.scjc.state.ny.us/Determinations/M/mcgrath.htm.

News and Comment. (1997). Ban has mixed impact on Texas, California grad schools. *Science,* 277, 633–634.

Nicholls, T., & Petrila, J. (2005). Gender and psychopathy. Vols. 1 and 2. *Behavioral Sciences & the Law,* 23(6), 24(1).

Nicholson, R. A. (1999). Forensic assessment. In R. Roesch, S. D. Hart, and J. R. P. Ogloff (Eds.), *Psychology and law: The state of the discipline,* pp. 121–173. Perspectives in Law and Psychology, vol. 10. New York: Kluwer Academic/Plenum.

Nicholson, R. A., & McNulty, J. L. (1992). Outcome of hospitalization for defendants found incompetent to stand trial. Behavioral Sciences and the Law, 10(3), 371–383.

Nicholson, R. A., Robertson, H. C., Johnson, W. G., & Jensen, G. (1988). A comparison of instruments for assessing competence to stand trial. Law and Human Behavior, 12(3), 313–321.

Nicholson v. Scoppetta, 116 U.S. Fed. Appx. 313 (2nd Cir. 2004).

Niedermeier, K. E., Horowitz, I. A., & Kerr, N. L. (1999). Informing jurors of their nullification power: A route to a just verdict or judicial chaos? *Law and Human Behavior,* 23(3), 331–352.

Nieves, A. (1992, December 15). Sex-attack trial divides Glen Ridge. *New York Times,* B–1, B–7.

Nightingale, N. N. (1993). Juror reactions to child victim witnesses: Factors affecting trial outcome. *Law and Human Behavior,* 17(6), 679–694.

Nigro, G. N., Buckley, M. A., Hill, D. E., & Nelson, J. (1987). When juries "hear" children testify: The effects of age and speech style on jurors' perceptions of testimony. In S. J. Ceci, D. F. Ross, & M. P. Toglia (Eds.), *Perspectives on children's testimony,* pp. 57–70. New York: Springer-Verlag.

Nisbett, R. E. (2005). Heredity, environment, and race differences in IQ: A commentary on Rushton and Jensen (2005). *Psychology, Public Policy, and Law,* 11(2), 302–310.

Nohejl, C. A. (1992). Probative aspects of the medical evaluation for child sexual abuse. *Behavioral Sciences & the Law,* 10(4), 455–473.

Nohejl, C. A., Doueck, H. J., & Levine, M. (1992). Risk assessment implementation and legal liability in CPS practice. *Law & Policy,* 14(2), 185–208.

North Carolina, Using Medical Monitoring Device, Executes Killer. (2006, April 22). *New York Times,* A–11.

Note. (1963). Alternatives to 'Parental Right' in child custody disputes involving third parties. *Yale Law Journal,* 73, 151–170.

Nurcombe, B., & Partlett, D. F. (1994). *Child mental health and the law.* New York: Free Press.

Nuzum, M. (n.d.). Summary of state restorative justice legislation. http://www.stopviolence.com/restorative/rjleg-summary.htm.

O'Connell, P. E., & Straub, F. (1999, Spring). Why the jails didn't explode. *City Journal.*

O'Connor, M., Gutek, B. A., Stockdale, M., Geer, T. M., & Melancon, R. (2004). Explaining sexual harassment judgments: looking beyond gender of the rater. *Law and Human Behavior,* 28(1), 69–96.

Office of Program Policy Analysis and Government Accountability. (2000). Justification review. 72% of youth restored to competency are able to move to delinquency proceedings. *Florida Monitor.* http://www.oppaga.state.fl.us/reports/pdf/0.

Ogden, D. W. (1990). Brief for amicus curiae American Psychological Association in *Craig v. Maryland.* 89–478, October term, 1989.

Ogloff, J. R. (1998). The risk assessment enterprise: Selective incapacitation or increased predictive accuracy. *Law and Human Behavior,* 22(4), 453.

Ogloff, J. R. P. (1991). A comparison of insanity defense standards on juror decision making. *Law and Human Behavior,* 15(5), 509–532.

Ohio v. Lucas, 100 Ohio State 3d 1 (2003).

OJJDP. (1996). Balanced and Restorative Justice Program Summary. http://ncjrs.org/pdffiles/bal.pdf.

OJJDP. (2003a, June). Juveniles in court. *National Report Series Bulletin.*

OJJDP. (2003b, August 11). *Statistical Briefing Book.* http://ojjdp.ncjrs.org/ojstatbb/html/qa190.html.

Okamoto, S. K., & Chesney-Lind, M. (2004). Understanding the impact of trauma on female juvenile delinquency and gender-specifc practice. In A. R. Roberts (Ed.) (2004), *Juvenile justice sourcebook,* ch. 16, 381–393. New York: Oxford University Press.

Olasky, M. (1992). *Abortion rites: A social history of abortion in America.* Washington, DC: Regnery.

Olson, L. (1980). Social and psychological correlates of pregnancy resolution among adolescent women: A review. *American Journal of Orthopsychiatry,* 50, 432–445.

Oncale v. Sundowner Offshore Services, 523 U.S. 75 (1998).

O'Neill, M. L., Lidz, V., & Heilbrun, K. (2003). Adolescents with psychopathic characteristics in a substance abusing cohort: Treatment processes and outcomes. *Law and Human Behavior,* 27(3), 299–313.

O'Neill, W. L. (1967). *Divorce in the Progressive era.* New Haven, CT: Yale University Press.

Orloff, L. E. (1990). Statement. Hearing before the Committee on the Judiciary, House of Representatives, One Hundred First Congress, second session, on H. Con. Res. 172. (Serial No. 81). Washington, DC: Government Printing Office.

Osofsky, J. D., & Osofsky, H. J. (1972). The psychological reaction of patients to legalized abortion. *American Journal of Orthopsychiatry,* 42, 48–60.

O'Sullivan, C. (2002). Domestic violence, visitation and custody decisions in New York Family Courts, final report. NCJ 195792. Washington, DC: U.S. Department of Justice.

Otto, R. K. (1994). On the ability of mental health professionals to "predict dangerousness": A commentary on interpretations of the "dangerousness" literature. *Law and Psychology Review,* 18, 43–68.

Padro v. Visiting Nurses Service of New York, 276 A.D.2d 352, 714 N.Y.S.2d 438 (2000).

Painter v. Bannister, 258 Iowa 1390, 140 N.W.2d 152 (1966).

Palmer, S. E., Brown, R. A., & Barerra, M. E. (1992). Group treatment program for abusive husbands: Long term evaluation. *American Journal of Orthopsychiatry,* 62, 276–283.

Palmore v. Sidoti, 466 U.S. 429 (1984).

Parents Involved v. Seattle School District No. 1 126 S. Ct. 2351 (2006).

Parham v. J. R., 442 U.S. 584 (1979).

Parish, J. (1998, July). Trend analysis: Expert testimony on battering and its effects in criminal cases. In Legal interventions in family violence: Research findings and policy implications, a project of the American Bar Association's Criminal Justice Section, Commission on

Domestic Violence, Center on Children and the Law, and Commission on Legal Problems of the Elderly, 68–70. Presented to the National Institute of Justice. NCJ 171666. Washington, DC: National Institute of Justice.

Parker, C. (1999). How to win hearts and minds: Corporate compliance policies for sexual harassment. *Law & Policy,* 21(1), 21–48.

Parry, J. (1985). Incompetence, guardianship and restoration. In S. J. Brakel, J. Parry, and B. A. Weiner, (Eds.), *The mentally disabled and the law,* pp. 369–427. 3rd ed. Chicago: American Bar Foundation.

PASE v. Hannon, 506 F. Supp. 831 (N.D. Ill. 1980).

Pasewark, R. A. (1986). A review of research on the insanity defense. *Annals of the American Academy of Political and Social Science,* 484, 100–114.

Pasewark, R. A., & Seidenzahl, D. (1979). Opinions concerning the insanity plea and criminality among mental patients. *Bulletin of the American Academy of Psychiatry and Law,* 7(2), 199–202.

Patchel, C. H. (1996). Diverting status offenders: The effects of legislative change on case processing in two counties. Unpublished Ph.D. dissertation, Department of Sociology, State University at Buffalo.

Pate v. Robinson, 383 U.S. 375 (1966).

Payne v. Tennessee, 501 U.S. 808 (1991).

Pears, R. (2003, October 13). Welfare spending shows huge shift. *New York Times.* http://www.nytimes.com/2003/10/13/politics/13WELFARE.html.

Pearson, J. (1997). Divorce mediation and domestic violence. Center for Policy Research. NCJ 164658. Washington, DC: U.S. Department of Justice.

Pearson, J., & Thoennes, N. (1989). Divorce mediation: Reflections on a decade of research. In K. Kressel, D. G. Pruitt, and Associates (Eds.), *Mediation research: The process and effectiveness of third-party intervention,* pp. 9–30. San Francisco: Jossey-Bass.

Pearson, J., & Thoennes, N. (1990). Custody after divorce: Demographic and attitudinal patterns. *American Journal of Orthopsychiatry,* 60(2), 233–249.

Peddle, N., & Wang, C-T. (2001). Current trends in child abuse prevention, reporting and fatalities: The 1999 fifty state survey. Chicago: National Center on Child Abuse Prevention Research. http://www.preventchildabuse.org.

Pelman ex rel. Pelman v. McDonald's Corp., 396 F.Supp.2d 439 (S.D.N.Y. 2005).

Pennington, N., & Hastie, R. (1986). Evidence evaluation in complex decision making. *Journal of Personality and Social Psychology,* 51, 242–258.

Pennington, N., & Hastie, R. (1990). Practical implications of psychological research on juror and jury decision making. *Personality and Social Psychology Bulletin,* 16, 90–105.

Pennington, N., & Hastie, R. (1991). A cognitive theory of juror decision making: The story model. *Cardozo Law Review,* 13, 519–557.

Pennsylvania Discovery and Evidence Reporter. (2004, January 28). Evidence-expert opinion evidence: Lack of reliability sinks a false confession expert's testimony on police interrogations. *Pennsylvania Discovery and Evidence Reporter,* 10(11).

Pennsylvania State Police v. Suders, 542 U.S. 129 (2004).

Penrod, S., & Cutler, B. (1995). Witness confidence and witness accuracy: Assessing their forensic relation. *Psychology, Public Policy, and Law,* 1(4), 817–845.

Penry v. Lynaugh 492 U.S. 302 (1989).

People v. Andrew Goldstein, 810 N.Y.S.2d 100 (2005).

People v. Day, 2 Cal. App. 4th 405 (1993).

People v. Ferguson 670 N.Y.S. 2d 327 (App. Div. 1998).

People v. Johnson 95 N.Y.2d 368 (2000).

People v. Kriho, 996 P.2d 158 (Col. App. 1999)

People v. Lara, 432 P.2d 202 (Cal., 1967).

People v. Lee 96 N.Y.2d 157 (2001).

People v. McQuillan, 393 Michigan 511, 221 N.W.2d. 569 (1974).

People v. Moscat, 777 N.Y.S.2d 875 (2000).

People v. Poddar, 10 Cal.3d 750 (1974).

People v. Radcliffe, 764 N.Y.S.2d 773 (Supreme Court of New York, Bronx County, 2003).

People v. Valoree Jean Day, 2 Cal. App. 4th 405 (1993).

People v. Ventura, 801 N.Y.S.2d 241 (2005).

People v. White, 780 N.Y.S.2d 727 (2004).

Perlin, M. L. (1992). *Tarasoff* and the dilemma of the dangerous patent: New directions for the 1990's. *Law and Psychology Review,* 16, 29–63.

Perlin, M. L., & Dorfman, D. A. (1996). Is it more than "dodging lions and wastin' time"? Adequacy of counsel, questions of competence, and the judicial process in individual right to refuse treatment cases. *Psychology, Public Policy, and Law,* 2(1), 114–136.

Perry, E. L., Kulik, C. T., and Bourhis, A.C. (2004). The reasonable woman standard: Effects on sexual harassment court decisions. *Law and Human Behavior,* 28(1), 9–28.

Perry, N. W., McAuliff, B. D., Tam, P., Claycomb, L., Dostal, C., & Flanagan, C. (1995). When lawyers question children: Is justice served? *Law and Human Behavior,* 19, 609–629.

Petchesky, R. P. (1984). *Abortion and woman's choice.* New York: Longman.

Peters, D. P. (1987). The impact of naturally occurring stress on children's memory. In S. J. Ceci, M. P. Toglia, & D. F. Ross (Eds.), *Children's eyewitness memory,* pp. 122–141. New York: Springer-Verlag.

Petersen, M. (1999, July 15). Working mother regains custody of two children, *New York Times,* C10.

Peterson, J. (1926). *Early conceptions and tests of intelligence.* Yonkers, NY: World Book.

Pichler, S. (2005). *Pregnancy and childrearing among U.S. Teens.* Washington, DC: Planned Parenthood.

Pickerell, J. M., Jackson, R. B., & Newman, M. A. (2006). Changing perceptions of sexual harassment in the federal workforce 1987-1994. *Law & Policy,* 28(3), 368–394.

Pierce, C. S., & Brodsky, S. L. (2002). Trust and under-standing in the attorney-juvenile relationship. *Behavioral Science and the Law, 20* (1–2), 89–107.

Pierce v. Society of Sisters, 268 U.S. 510 (1925).

Pine Tree Legal Assistance. (2002). Indian Child Welfare Act update. *Wabanaki Legal News.* A newsletter of Pine Tree Legal Assistance. http://www.ptla.org/ptlasite/wabanaki/icwa.htm.

Planned Parenthood. (2001). The emotional effects of induced abortion. http://www.plannedparenthood.org/pp2/portal/files/medicalinfo/abortion/fact-01060.

Planned Parenthood of Missouri v. Danforth, 428 U.S. 52 (1976).

Planned Parenthood of SE Pa. v. Casey, 505 U.S 833 (1992).

Planned Parenthood v. Ashcroft, 462 U.S. 476 (1983).

Planned Parenthood admits "judge shopping" for teen abortions in Texas. (2002, March 24). *Houston Chronicle.*

Plessy v. Ferguson, 163 U.S. 537 (1896).

Poffenberger, A. T. (1942). *Principles of applied psychology.* New York: Appleton-Century.

Pollack. D. (2002). The capacity of a mentally retarded parent to consent to adoption. *Newsletter,* Center for Adoption Research, University of Massachusetts.

Pollard v. E.I. Du Pont De Neurours, Inc., 412 F.3d 657 (6th Cir 2005).

Pollard v. E.I. Du Pont De Neurours, Inc., 532 U.S. 843 (2001).

Poole, D. A., & Lamb, M. E. (1998). *Investigative interviews of children: A guide for helping professionals.* Washington, DC: American Psychological Association.

Poole, D. A., Lindsay, D. S., Memon, A., & Bull, R. (1995). Psychotherapy and recovery of memories of childhood sexual abuse: U.S. and British practitioners' opinions, practices and experiences. *Journal of Consulting and Clinical Psychology, 63,* 426–437.

Pope, K. S. (1991). Ethical and legal issues in clinical practice. In M. Hersen, A. E. Kazdin, & A. S. Bellack (Eds.), *The clinical psychology handbook,* pp. 115–127. 2nd ed. New York: Pergamon.

Pope, K. S., & Bouhoutsos, J. C. (1986). *Sexual intimacy between therapists and patients.* New York: Praeger.

Pope, L. M., Adler, N. E., & Tschann, J. M. (2001). Postabortion psychological adjustment: Are minors at increased risk? *Journal of Adolescent Health, 29*(1), 2–11.

Porter, S., Yuille, J. C., & Lehman, D. R. (1999). The nature of real, implanted, and fabricated memories for emotional childhood events: Implications for the recovered memory debate. *Law and Human Behavior, 23*(5), 517–538.

Poser, S., Bornstein, B. H., & McGorty, E. K. (2003). Measuring damages for lost enjoyment of life: The view from the bench and the jury box. *Law and Human Behavior, 27*(1), 53–68.

Posner, R. (2003). *Law, pragmatism and democracy.* Cambridge, MA: Harvard University Press.

Pottick, K. J., McAlpine, D. D., & Andelman, R. B. (2000). Changing patterns of psychiatric inpatient care for children and adolescents in general hospitals, 1988–1995. *American Journal of Psychiatry, 157*(8), 1267–1273.

Pound, R. (1906). The causes of popular dissatisfaction with the administration of justice. *American Law Review, 40,* 729–749.

Pound, R. (1908). Mechanical jurisprudence. *Columbia Law Review, 8,* 605–623.

Pound, R. (1910). Law in books and law in action. *American Law Review, 44,* 12–36.

Powell, B., & Downey, D. B. (1997). Living in single parent households: An investigation of the same-sex hypothesis. *American Sociological Review, 62*(4), 521–539.

Powell, T. A., Holt, J. C., & Fondacaro, K. M. (1997). The prevalence of mental illness among inmates in a rural state. *Law and Human Behavior, 21*(4), 427–438.

Powers v. Ohio, 499 U.S. 400 (1991).

Poythress, N. G., Bonnie, R. J., Monahan, J., Otto, R., & Hoge, S. K. (2002). *Adjudicative competence. The MacArthur studies.* New York: Kluwer Academic/Plenum.

Poythress, N. J., Bonnie, R. J., Hoge, S. K., Monahan, J., & Oberlandes, L. B. (1994). Client abilities to assist counsel and make decisions in criminal cases. *Law and Human Behavior, 18*(4), 437–452.

Poythress, N. J., & Brodsky, S. L. (1992). In the wake of a negligent release lawsuit: An investigation of professional consequences and institutional impact on a state psychiatric hospital. *Law and Human Behavior, 16*(2), 155–174.

Poythress, N. J., Weiner, R., & Schumacher, J. E. (1992). Reframing the medical malpractice reform debate: Social science research implications for non-economic reform. *Law and Psychology Review, 16,* 65–112.

PR Newswire. (2004a, November 17). Unprecedented new study finds recruiting adoptive families a top barrier to finding permanent homes for children in foster care. *Washington Dateline.*

PR Newswire. (2004b, September 9). Holt releases middle school science curriculum for Indiana aligned to state science standards. http://80-web.lexis-nexis.com.gate.lib.buffalo.edu/universe/printdoc.

President's Commission on Mental Retardation. (1976). *The mentally retarded citizen and the law.* New York: Free Press.

Price Waterhouse v. Hopkins, 490 U.S. 228 (1989).

Prince v. Massachusetts, 321 U.S. 158 (1944).

Printz v. United States, 521 U.S. 898 (1997).

Protection and Advocacy, Inc.. (2001). *Report of an investigation into the death of Lisa Russell on August 7, 1998.* Oakland, CA: Protection and Advocacy, Inc., Investigations Unit.

Pruett, M. K., Ebling, R., & Insabella, G. (2004). Critical aspects of parenting plans for young children: Interjecting data into the debate about overnights. *Family Court Review*, 42(1), 39–59.

Pruett, M. K., & Hoganbruen, K. (1998). Joint custody and shared parenting: Research and interventions. *Child and Adolescent Psychiatric Clinics of North America*, 7, 273–294.

Pruett, M. K., Insabella, G. M., & Gustafson, K. (2005). The collaborative divorce project: a court-based intervention for separating parents with young children. *Family Court Review*, 43(1), 38–51.

Pruett, M. K., & Pruett, K. D. (1998). Fathers, divorce and their children. *Child and Adolescent Psychiatric Clinics of North America*, 7, 389–407.

Pruett, M. K., & Santangelo, C. (1999). Joint custody and empirical knowledge: The estranged bedfellows of divorce. In R. M. Galatzer-Levy and L. Kraus (Eds.), *The scientific basis of child custody decisions*, pp. 389–424. New York: John Wiley.

Psychological Society of Ireland. (2005). Criteria for the accreditation of academic postgraduate training courses in forensic psychology. http://www.psihq.le/DOCUMENTS/Forguidelines.pdf.

Psychotherapy Finances Online. (1995, November). Malpractice: New policy for psychologists takes aim at APA Insurance Trust. *Psychotherapy Finances*. http://199.190.86.8/psyfin/Nov95/malpract.html.

Psychotherapy Finances Online. (1997). Practice profile: On-line therapy provides access to self-pay patients. *Psychotherapy Finances*. http://www.psyfin.com/psyfin/Readers/RS0897C.html.

Puzzanchero, C., Stahl, A. L., Finnegan, T. A., Tierney, N., & Snyder, H. N. (2003, July). *Juvenile court statistics, 1999*. Washington, DC: National Center for Juvenile Justice. http://ncjrs.org.html/ojjdp/201241/chap3b.html.

Quas, J. (2005, March 5). Beyond the question "Are children suggestible?" New directions in child witness research. Paper presented at the conference of the American Psychology Law Society, La Jolla, CA.

Quas, J. A., Wallin, A., Papini, S., Lench, H., & Scullin, M. (2005). Suggestibility, social context, and memory for a novel experience in young children. *Journal of Experimental Child Psychology*, 91, 315–341.

Quindlen, A. (1992, December 13). 21 going on 6. *New York Times*, E–17.

Quinsey, V., Harris, G., Rice, M., & Cormier, C. (2005). *Violent offenders: Appraising and managing risk*. 2nd ed. Washington DC: American Psychological Association.

Rabasca, L. (2000). Self-help sites: A blessing or a bane? *Monitor on Psychology*, 31, 28–30.

Radelet, M. L., & Miller, K. S. (1992). The aftermath of *Ford v. Wainwright. Behavioral Sciences and the Law*, 10(3), 339–351.

Ramsland, K. (2004). Andrea Yates: Ill or evil? *Notorious murders/Women who kill*. Courttv.com.

Rand, D. C. (1997). The spectrum of parental alienation syndrome. Part I. *American Journal of Forensic Psychology*, 15 (3).

Rand, D. C., Rand, D., & Kopetski, L. (2005). The spectrum of parental alienation syndrome. Part III. *American Journal of Forensic Psychology*, 23(1), 15–43.

Rashid, F. N. (2004). Juvenile crime and punishment: Assessing the relationship between violent crime rates and punishment. http://wwwecon.stanford.edu/academics/Honors_Theses/Theses_2004.Rashid.pdf.

Raskin, D. C., Honts, C. R., & Kircher, J. C. (1997). The scientific status of research on polygraph techniques: The case for polygraph tests. In D. L. Faigman, D. H. Kaye, M. J. Saks, & J. Sanders (Eds.), *Modern scientific evidence: The law and science of expert testimony*, vol. 1, 565–582, 619–627, 629–631. 2005–2006 ed. Eagan, MN: Thomson/West.

Rattner, A. (1988). Convicted but innocent: Wrongful conviction and the criminal justice system. *Law and Human Behavior*, 12(3), 283–293.

Ravich, D. (1974). *The great school wars: New York City, 1805–1973*. New York: Basic Books.

Ray, I. (1962). *A treatise on the medical jurisprudence of insanity*. Cambridge, MA: Harvard University Press.

Realmuto, G. M., & Ruble, L. M. (1999). Sexual behaviors in autism: Problems of definition and management. *Journal of Autism and Developmental Disorders*, 29(2), 121–127.

Reaves, B. A. (1992). Pretrial release of felony defendants, 1990. Bureau of Justice Statistics Bulletin. NCJ 139560. Washington DC: Bureau of Justice Statistics.

Rebovich, D. J. (1996). Prosecution response to domestic violence: Results of a survey of a large jurisdictions. In E. S. Buzawa and C. G. Buzawa (Eds.), *Do arrests and restraining orders work?* pp. 176–191. Newbury Park, CA: Sage.

Redding, R. E. (1999). Reconstructing science through law. *Southern Illinois University Law Journal*, 23, 585–610.

Redding, R. E. (2001). Sociopolitical diversity in psychology: The case for pluralism. *American Psychologist*, 56(3), 205–215.

Redlich, A. D., Silverman, M., & Steiner, H. (2003). Preadudicative and adjudicative competence in juvenile and young adults. *Behavioral Sciences & the Law*, 21(3), 393–410.

Redlich, A. D., Steadman, H. J., Monahan, J. Petrila, J. & Griffin, P. A. (2005). The second generation of mental health courts. *Psychology, Public Policy, and Law*, 11(4), 527–538.

Reed, J. (1978). *From private vice to public virtue*. New York: Basic Books.

Reeves, R. (2004). Voluntary hospitalizations of adolescents. *Adolescent Psychiatry*, 28, 14.

Reisner, R. (1985). *Law and the mental health system*. St. Paul, MN: West.

Reissman, F. (1965). The "helper-therapy" principle. *Social Work*, 10, 27–32.

Rennison, C. M. (2003, February). Intimate partner violence, 1993–2001. Bureau of Justice Statistics: Crime Data Brief. NCJ 197838. Washington, DC: U.S. Department of Justice.

Rennison, C. M., & Welchans, S. (2000). *Intimate Partner Violence*. Bureau of Justice Statistics Special Report. Washington, DC: U.S. Department of Justice.

Renzetti, C. M. (1993). Violence in lesbian relationships. In M. Hansen & M. Harway (Eds.), *Battering and family therapy: A feminist perspective*, pp. 188–199. Newbury Park, CA: Sage.

Reppucci, N. D. (1999). Adolescent development and juvenile justice. *American Journal of Community Psychology*, 27, 307–326.

Resnick. P. J. (1997). Malingered psychosis. In R. Rogers (Ed.), *Clinical assessment of malingering and deception*, ch. 3, pp. 47–67. New York: Guilford.

Reuters. (2006). Italian court: Not a virgin? Sex crimes aren't as serious. http://www.cnn.com/2006/WORLD/europe/02/17/italy.abuse.reut/index.html.

Rex v. Arnold, 16 How. St. Tr. 695 (1724, England).

Richards, K. (1992). *Tender mercies: Inside the world of a child abuse investigator*. Chicago: Noble Press.

Richardson, K. H. (1983). *The Salem witchcraft trials*. Salem, MA: Essex Institute.

Richey, W. (2003, March 28). Affirmative action's evolution. *Christian Science Monitor*. http://www.christiansciencemonitor.com/2003/0328/p01s01-usju.html.

Richie, J., Alford, N. H., Jr., & Effland, R. W. (1982). *Decedents' estates and trusts: Cases and materials*. 6th ed. Mineola, NY: Foundation Press.

Riggins v. Nevada, 504 U.S 127 (1992).

Rimmer, S., & Bonner, R. (2000, August 23). New death penalty furor. *International Herald Tribune*, 1.

Ring v. Arizona, 536 U.S. 584 (2002).

Ringel, C. (1997). *Criminal victimization 1996: Changes 1995–96 with trends, 1993–1996*. National Crime Victimization Survey. NCJ–165812. Washington, DC: Bureau of Justice Statistics.

Riverside County v. McLaughlin, 500 U.S. 44 (1991).

Robbennolt, J. K., & Studebaker, C. A. (1999). Anchoring in the courtroom: The effects of caps on punitive damages. *Law and Human Behavior*, 23(3), 353–373.

Robbennolt, J. K., & Studebaker, C. A. (2003). News media reporting on civil litigation and its influence on civil justice decision making. *Law and Human Behavior*, 27(1), 5–27.

Roberts, A. R. (2004). Epilogue: National survey of offender treatment programs that work. In A. R. Roberts (Ed.) (2004), *Juvenile justice sourcebook*, ch. 21, 536–561. New York: Oxford University Press.

Roberts, C. F., & Golding, S. L. (1991). The social construction of criminal responsibility and insanity. *Law and Human Behavior*, 15(4), 349–376.

Roberts, C. F., Golding, S. L., & Fincham, F. D. (1987). Implicit theories of criminal responsibility: Decision making and the insanity defense. *Law and Human Behavior*, 11(3), 207–232.

Robinson, B. A. (2004). Post-abortion syndrome (a.k.a. PAS or PASS). http://www.religioustolerance.org/abo_post.htm.

Robinson, D. N. (1980). *Psychology and law*. New York: Oxford University Press.

Roe v. Wade, 410 U.S. 113 (1973).

Roesch, R., & Golding, S. L. (1980). *Competence to stand trial*. Urbana: University of Illinois Press.

Rogers, A. (1993). Coercion and "voluntary" admission: An examination of psychiatric patient views. *Behavioral Sciences and the Law*, 11(3), 259–267.

Rogers, J. (1997). Current status of clinical methods. In R. Rogers (Ed.), *Clinical assessment of malingering and deception*. New York: Guilford.

Rogers, J. L., Bloom, J. D., & Manson, S. M. (1984). Insanity defenses: Contested or conceded? *American Journal of Psychiatry*, 141, 885–888.

Rogers, J. L., Boruch,. R. F., Stoms, G. B., & DeMoya, D. (1991). Impact of the Minnesota parental notification law on abortion and birth. *American Journal of Public Health*, 81, 294–298.

Rogers, R. (Ed.). (1997). *Clinical assessment of malingering and deception*. 2nd ed. New York: Guilford Press.

Rogers, R., & Ewing, C. P. (1989). Ultimate opinion proscriptions: A cosmetic fix and a plea for empiricism. *Law and Human Behavior*, 13(4), 357–374.

Rogers, R., Jackson, R. L., Sewell, K. W., & Harrison, K. S. (2004). An examination of the ECST-R as a screen for feigned incompetency to stand trial. *Psychological Assessment*, 16(2), 139–145.

Rogers, R., Jackson, R. K., Sewell, K. W., Tillbrook, C. E., and Martin, M. S. (2003). Assessing dimensions of competency to stand trial: construct validation of the ECST-R. *Assessment*, 10(4), 344–351.

Roper v. Simmons, 543 U.S. 551 (2005).

Rose, M. R. (1999). The peremptory challenge accused of race or gender discrimination? Some data from one county. *Law and Human Behavior*, 23(6), 695–702.

Rosen, J. (1999, May 31). Score another for the behavior police. *New York Times*, A13.

Rosen, J. (2005, April 17). The unregulated offensive. *New York Times Magazine*, 42–49, 66, 128, 130.

Rosenbaum, A., & O'Leary, K. D. (1981). Children: The unintended victims of marital violence. *American Journal of Orthopsychiatry*, 51, 692–699.

Rosenberg, C. E. (1968). *The trial of the assassin Guiteau: Psychiatry and law in the gilded age*. Chicago: University of Chicago Press.

Rosenberg, M. S. (1987a). Children of battered women: The effects of witnessing violence on their social problem-solving abilities. *Behavior Therapist*, 10(4), 85–89.

Rosenberg, M. S. (1987b). New directions for research on the psychological maltreatment of children. *American Psychologist*, 42(2), 166–171.

Rosenthal, R. (1995). *State of New Jersey v. Margaret Kelly Michaels:* An overview. *Psychology, Public Policy and Law,* 1(2), 246–271.

Ross, D. F., Dunning, D., Toglia, M. P., & Ceci, S. J. (1989). Age stereotypes, communication modality, and mock jurors' perceptions of the child witness. In S. J. Ceci, D. F. Ross, & M. P. Toglia (Eds.), *Perspectives on children's testimony,* pp. 37–56. New York: Springer-Verlag.

Ross, D. F., Dunning, D., Toglia, M. P., & Ceci, S. J. (1990). The child in the eyes of the jury: Assessing mock jurors' perceptions of the child witness. *Law and Human Behavior,* 14(1), 5–23.

Ross, D. F., Miller, B. S., & Moran, P. B. (1987). The child in the eyes of the jury: Assessing mock jurors' perceptions of the child witness. In S. J. Ceci, M. P. Toglia, & D. F. Ross (Eds.), *Children's eyewitness memory,* pp. 142–154. New York: Springer-Verlag.

Ross, S. M. (1996). Risk of physical abuse to children of spouse abusing parents. *Child Abuse & Neglect,* 20, 589–595.

Rothman, D., & Casey, P. (1999, July). Therapeutic jurisprudence and the emergence of problem-solving courts. *National Institute of Justice Journal,* 12–19.

Rottman, S. (2006). California execution postponed indefinitely. http://abcnews.go.com/US/print?id = 1648069.

Rotundo, M., Nguyen, D., & Sackett, P. R. (2001). A meta-analytic review of gender differences in perceptions of sexual harassment. *Journal of Applied Psychology,* 86, 914–922.

Ruethling, G. (2006, February 8). Nebraska man sentenced for having sex with girl, 13. *New York Times,* A–11.

Rumsfeld v. Forum for Academic and Institutional Rights, Inc., 547 U.S. (2006).

Rushton, J. P., & Jensen, A. R. (2005). Thirty years of research on race differences in cognitive ability. *Psychology, Public Policy, and Law,* 11(2), 235–294.

Russo, N. F., & Dabul, A. J. (1997). The relationship of abortion to well-being: Do race and religion make a difference? *Professional Psychology, Research & Practice,* 28, 23–31.

Rust v. Sullivan, 500 U.S. 173 (1991).

Ryerson, E. (1978). *The best laid plans: American's Juvenile Court experiment.* New York: Hill & Wang.

Saccuzzo, D. P., Johnson, N. E., & Koen, W. J. (2003). *Mandatory custody mediation: Empirical evidence of increased risk for domestic violence victims and their children.* NCJ 195422. Washington, DC: U.S. Department of Justice.

Safran, C. (1976, November). What men do to women on the job. *Redbook,* 149.

Saks, M. J. (1992). Do we really know anything about the behavior of the tort litigation system—and why not? *University of Pennsylvania Law Review,* 140, 1147–1292.

Saks, M. J. & Marti, M. W. (1997). A meta-analysis of the effects of jury size. *Law and Human Behavior,* 21(5), 451–467.

Salekin, R. T., Yff, R. M. A., Neumann, C. S., Leistco, A. R., & and Zalot, A. A. (2002), Juvenile transfer to adult courts: A look at the prototypes for dangerousness, sophistication-maturity, and amenability to treatment through a legal lens. *Psychology, Public Policy and Law,* 8(4), 373–410.

Sales, B. D., Elwork, A., & Alfini, J. (1977). Improving jury instruction. In B. D. Sales (Ed.), *Perspectives in law and psychology,* vol. 1: *The criminal justice system,* pp. 23–90. New York: Plenum.

Sales, B. F., & Hafemeister, T. (1984). Empiricism and legal policy on the insanity defense. In J. Monahan & H. J. Steadman (Eds.), *Mentally disordered offenders: Perspectives from law and social science,* pp. 253–278. New York: Plenum.

Saltzman, A., & Proch, K. (1990). *Law in social work practice.* Chicago: Nelson, Hall.

Sander, R. H. (2004). A systemic analysis of affirmative action in American law schools. *Stanford Law Review,* 57, 367.

Sandler, R., & Schoenbrod, D. (2003). *Democracy by decree: What happens when courts run government.* New Haven, CT: Yale University Press.

Santelli, J. S., Morrow, B., Anderson, J. E., & Duberstein-Lindberg, L. (2006). *Perspectives on Sexual and Reproductive Health,* 38(2), 106–111.

S. F. NAACP v. S.F. Unified School District 59 F. Supp.2d 1021 (N.D. Cal., 1999).

Santilli, L. E., & Roberts, M. C. (1990). Custody decisions in Alabama before and after the abolition of the tender years doctrine. *Law and Human Behavior,* 14(2), 123–138.

Santosky v. Kramer, 455 U.S. 745 (1982).

Sarason, S. B., & Doris, J. (1969). *Psychological problems in mental deficiency.* 4th ed. New York: Harper & Row.

Sarason, S. B. (1978). The nature of problem solving in social action. *American Psychologist,* 33, 370–380.

Sas, L. (1991). *Reducing the system-induced trauma for child sexual abuse victims through court prepartion, assessment and follow up.* London, ON: Child Witness Project, London Family Court Clinic.

Saunders, D. G. (1988). Other "truths" about domestic violence: A reply to McNeely and Robinson-Simpson. *Social Work,* 33(2), 179–183.

Saunders, D. G. (1994). Child custody decisions in families experiencing woman abuse. *Social Work,* 39(1), 51–59.

Saunders, D. G. (1994). Posttraumatic stress symptom profiles of battered women: A comparison of survivors in two settings. *Violence & Victims,* 9(1), 31–44.

Savitsky, J. C., & Lindbolm, W. D. (1986). The impact of the guilty but mentally ill verdict on juror decisions: An empirical analysis. *Journal of Applied Social Psychology,* 16, 686–701.

Sawhill, I. V. (2000, Winter). Welfare reform and reducing teen pregnancy. *Public Interest.*

Saywitz, K., Goodman, G., Nicholas, G., & Moan, S. (1991). Children's memory of a physical examination involving genital touch: Implications for reports of child sexual abuse. *Journal of Consulting and Clinical Psychology, 5, 682–691.*

Scalia, A. (2002, May). God's justice and ours. *First Things,* 123, 17–21.

Schaaf, J. M., Alexander, K. W., Goodman, G. S., Ghetti, S., Edelstein, R. S., & Castelli, P. (2002). Children's eyewitness memory: True disclosures and false reports. In B. L. Bottoms, M. B. Kovera, & B. D. McAuliff (Eds.), *Children, social science and the law,* ch. 14, pp. 342–377. New York: Cambridge University Press.

Schacter, D. L. (1999). The seven sins of memory: Insights from psychology and cognitive neuroscience. *American Psychologist,* 54(3), 182–203.

Schaeffer, R. (2000, February 19). Who wants to be a contestant? *New York Times,* op-ed, A–29.

Schall v. Martin, 467 U.S. 253 (1984).

Schechter, S., & Edelson, J. L. (1994, June 8–10). In the best interest of women and children: A call for collaboration between child welfare and domestic violence constitutencies. Reprint of briefing paper prepared for the conference Domestic Violence and Child Welfare: Integrating Policy and Practice of Families, sponsored by the University of Iowa School of Social Work and the Johnson Foundation, Wingspread, Racine, WI. http://www.mincava.umn.edu.

Scheck, B., Neufeld, B., & Dwyer, J. (2000). *Actual innocence.* New York: Doubleday.

Scheidegger, K. (2003). Maryland study, when properly analyzed supports death penalty. Criminal Justice Legal Foundation. http://www.cjlf.org/deathpenalty/MdMoratoriaum.htm.

Schemo, D. J. (2004, August 30). School achievement reports often exclude the disabled. *New York Times,* A–10.

Schlegel, J. H. (1979). American legal realism and empirical social science: From the Yale experience. *Buffalo Law Review,* 28, 459–586.

Schlegel, J. H. (1980). American legal realism and empirical social science: The singular case of Underhill Moore. *Buffalo Law Review,* 29, 195–323.

Schmidt, F. L., & Hunter, J. E. (1981). Employment testing: Old theories and new research findings. *American Psychologist,* 36, 1128–1137.

Schmidt, J. D., & Sherman, L. W. (1996). Does arrest deter domestic violence? In E. S. Buzawa & C. G. Buzawa (Eds.), *Do arrests and restraining orders work?* pp. 43–53. Newbury Park, CA: Sage.

Schmidt, M. G., Reppucci, N. D., & Woodward, J. L. (2003). Effectiveness of participation as a defendant: The attorney-client relationship. *Behavioral Sciences and the Law,* 21(2), 175–198.

Schopp, R. F. (1996). Therapeutic jurisprudence and conflicts among values in mental health law. In D. B. Wexler & B. Winick (Eds.), *Law in a therapeutic key,* pp. 723–738. Durham, NC: Carolina Academic Press.

Schuller, R. A. (1992). The impact of battered woman syndrome evidence on jury decision processes. *Law and Human Behavior,* 16(6), 597–620.

Schuller, R. A., & Hastings, P. A. Trials of battered women who kill: The impact of alternative forms of expert evidence. *Law and Human Behavior,* 20(2), 167–188.

Schuller, R. A., & Vidmar, N. (1992). Battered woman syndrome evidence in the courtroom: A review of the literature. *Law and Human Behavior,* 16(3), 273–291.

Schulte, B. (2000, March 26). A teacher's worst nightmare—false charges. *Buffalo News,* A–10.

Schulz, V. (1998). Reconceptualizing sexual harassment. *Yale Law Journal,* 107, 1683–1805.

Schwabe-Daniels, K. (1997). Therapist suspicion of child sexual abuse histories in adult patients: Differences as a function of client report and therapist focus. Unpublished doctoral dissertation. State University of New York at Buffalo.

Schwartz, D. J., & Goodman, J. (1992). Expert testimony on decision processes in employment cases. *Law and Human Behavior,* 16(3), 337–353.

Schwartz, H. I., Vingiano, W., & Perez, C. B. (1990). Autonomy and the right to refuse treatment: Patients' attitudes after involuntary medication. In D. B. Wexler (Ed.), *Therapeutic jurisprudence,* pp. 189–200. Durham, NC: Carolina Academic Press.

Schwartz, L. L. (2003). A nightmare for King Solomon: The new reproductive technologies. *Journal of Family Psychology,* 17(2), 229–237.

Scott, E. S., Reppucci, N. D., & Woolard, J. L. (1995). Evaluating adolescent decision making in legal contexts. *Law and Human Behavior,* 19(3), 221–244.

Scullin, M. H., Peters, E., Williams, W. M., & Ceci, S. J. (2000). The role of IQ and education in predicting later labor market outcomes: Implications for affirmative action. *Psychology, Public Policy, and Law,* 6(1), 63–89.

Select Committee on Children, Youth and Families, House of Representatives (1990). *No place to call home: Discarded children in America.* Washington, DC: Government Printing Office.

Sell v. United States, 539 U. S. 166 (2003).

Sengupta, S. (1998a, June 8). A jury's difficult passage toward a verdict of death: Killer is condemned with ambivalence. *New York Times,* A–20.

Sengupta, S. (1998b, September 29). Defense seldom wins if suspect handles it. *New York Times,* A–25.

Sevcik, K. (2003, August 10). Has Stanley Williams left the gang? *New York Times Magazine,* sec. 6, 34–37.

Sgroi, S. M., Porter, F. S., & Blick, L. C. (1982) Validation of child sexual abuse. In S. M. Sgroi (Ed.), *Handbook of clinical intervention in child sexual abuse,* pp. 39–79. Lexington, MA: Lexington Books.

Shanker, T. (2004, December 8). Commanders are faulted on assaults at Academy. *New York Times,* Politics sec.

Shapiro, B. J. (1983). *Probability and certainty in seventeenth century England: A study of the relationships* between natural science, religion, history, law and literature. Princeton, NJ: Princeton University Press.

Shapiro, B. (2000, March 26). Capital offense. *New York Times Magazine*, 19–20.

Sharif by Salahuddin v. N. Y. State Education Department, 709 F. Supp. 365 (S.D.N.Y. 1989).

Shenon, P., & Lewis, N. A. (2002, March 28). France warns it opposes the death penalty in terror trial. *New York Times*.

Shepard, A. (1998). Child abuse charges in custody fights—Part I. *Law Guardian Reporter*, 14(3), 1–3.

Shiff, A. R., & Wexler, D. B. (1996, July–August). Teen court: A therapeutic jurisprudence perspective. *Criminal Law Bulletin*, 342–357.

Shoben, E. W. (2004). Disparate impact theory in employment discrimination: What's *Griggs* still good for? What not? *Brandeis Law Journal*, 42, 597–622.

Short, J. L. (2006). Creating peer sexual harassment: Mobilizing schools to throw books at themselves. *Law & Policy*, 28(1), 31–59.

Shuman, D. W. (1993). The psychology of deterrence in tort law. *University of Kansas Law Review*, 42, 115–168.

Shuman, D. W., Greenberg, S., Heilbrun, K., & Foote, W. E. (1998). An immodest proposal: Should treating mental health professionals be barred from testifying about their patients? *Behavioral Sciences and the Law*, 16(4), 509–523.

Shuman, D. W., Hamilton, J. A., & Daley, C. E. (1994). The health effects of jury service. *Law and Psychology Review*, 18, 267–307.

Shuman, D. W., & Sales, B. D. (1999). The impact of *Daubert* and its progeny on the admissibility of behavioral and social science evidence. *Psychology, Public Policy, and Law*, 5(1), 3–15.

Siecus Report. (2002, February-March). Teen pregnancy, birth and abortion. *Siecus Report*, 30(3).

Siegel, A. M., & Elwork, A. (1990). Treating incompetence to stand trial. *Law and Human Behavior*, 14(1), 57–65.

Silver, E., Cirincione, C., & Steadman, H. J. (1994). Demythologizing inaccurate perceptions of the insanity defense. *Law and Human Behavior*, 18(1), 63–70.

Silver, E., Mulvey, E. P., & Monahan, J. (1999). Assessing violence risk among Discharged psychiatric patients: Towards an ecological approach. *Law and Human Behavior*, 23(2), 237–255.

Silverman, J. G., Raj, A., Mucci, L. A., & Hathaway, J. E. (2001). Dating violence against adolescent girls and associated substance use, unhealthy weight control, sexual risk behavior, pregnancy, and suicidality. *Journal of the American Medical Association*, 286(5), 572–579.

Silverstein, H., Fishman, W., Francis, E., & Speitel, L. (2005). Easier said than done: Tennessee's efforts to implement mandated parental consent for abortion and the judicial waiver process. *Law and Policy*, 27(3), 399–428.

Simon, L. M. J. (1995). A therapeutic jurisprudence approach to the legal processing of domestic violence cases. *Psychology, Public Policy, and Law*, 1(1), 43–79.

Simon, P. (2001, May 24). Buffalo teachers want tests cut back. *Buffalo News*, B-1.

Singer, S. I. (1996a). *Recriminalizing delinquency: Violent juvenile crime and juvenile justice reform*. Cambridge: Cambridge University Press.

Singer, S. I. (1996b). Merging and emerging systems of juvenile and criminal justice. *Law & Policy*, 18(1,2), 1–15.

Singer, S. I. (1997). A critical assessment of teen courts as an emerging avenue of governmental control. Paper presented at the 1997 American Society of Criminology meetings, San Diego, CA.

Sjostedt, G., & Grann, M. (2002). Risk assessment: What is being predicted by actuarial prediction instruments. *International Journal of Forensic Mental Health*, 1(2) 179–183.

Skinner v. Oklahoma, 316 U.S. 535 (1942).

Skipper v. South Carolina, 476 U.S. 1 (1986).

Sleek, S. (1996, September). Members confront master's licensing. *APA Monitor*. http://www.apa.org/monitor/sep96/sppa.html.

Slobogin, C. (1985). The guilty but mentally ill verdict: An idea whose time should not have come. *George Washington Law Review*, 53, 494–527.

Slobogin, C. (1995). Therapeutic jurisprudence: Five dilemmas to ponder. *Psychology, Public Policy and the Law*, 1(1), 193–219.

Slobogin, C. (1999). The admissibility of behavioral science evidence in criminal trials: From primitivism to *Daubert*, to voice. *Psychology, Public Policy, and Law*, 5, 100–119.

Small, M. A. (1992). Policy review of child abuse and neglect reporting statutes. *Law & Policy*, 14(2), 129–152.

Small, M. A., & Tetreault, P. A. (1990). Social psychology, marital rape exemptions and privacy. *Behavioral Sciences and the Law*, 8(2), 141–150.

Smith, E. M. (1973). A follow-up study of women who request abortion. *American Journal of Orthopsychiatry*, 43, 574–585.

Smith, V. L., & Kassin, S. M. (1993). Effects of the dynamite charge on the deliberations of deadlocked mock juries. *Law and Human Behavior*, 17, 625–643.

Snyder, H. N. (1998, December). Juveniles arrests 1997. *Juvenile Justice Bulletin*.

Snyder, H. N. (2000, July). *Sexual assault of young children reported to law enforcement: Victim, incident, and offender characteristics*. National Center for Juvenile Justice. NCJ 182990. Washington, DC: National Center for Juvenile Justice.

Solotoff, L. (1998). Childhood sexual abuse, borderline personality disorder, and sexual compulsivity addiction: Is it a factor in sexual harassment cases? American Bar Association. http://www.bna.com/bnabooks/ababna/mr/98/RRSOLO.doc.

Sorin, M. D. (n.d.). *Out on bail.* National Institute of Justice Criminal File Study Guide. Washington, DC: U.S. Department of Justice, National Institute of Justice.

Sourcebook of criminal justice statistics. (2002). U.S. Department of Justice, Bureau of Justice Statistics. Washington, DC: Government Printing Office.

Sourcebook of criminal justice statistics. (2003). U.S. Department of Justice, Bureau of Justice Statistics. Washington, DC: Government Printing Office. http://www.albany.edu/sourcebook/pdf/t555.pdf.

Spain, S. E., Douglas, K. S., Poythress, N. G., & Epstein, M. (2004) The relationship betrween psychoathic features, violence and treatment outcome: The comparison of three youth measures of psychopathic features. *Behavioral Sciences & the Law,* 22(1), 85–102.

Special Report. (n.d.). Under siege: The Indian Child Welfare Act of 1978. http://www.liftingtheveil.org/icwa.htm.

Sparf v. United States, 156 U.S. 51 (1895).

Spiegel, A. (2005, January 3). The dictionary of disorder. How one man defined psychiatric care. *New Yorker,* 56–63.

Sporer, S. L., Penrod, S., Read, D., & Cutler, B. L. (1995). Choosing confidence and accuracy: A meta-analysis of the confidence-accuracy relations in eyewitness identification studies. *Psychological Bulletin,* 118, 315–327.

Stacey, J., & Biblarz, T. (2001). (How) does the sexual orientation of parents matter? American *Sociological Review,* 66(2), 159–183.

Stack v. Boyle, 342 U.S. 1 (1951).

Stagner v. California 539 U.S. 607 (2003).

Stanford v. Kentucky, 492 U.S. 361 (1989).

Stanley D. v. Deborah D., 467 A.2d 249 (N.H., 1983).

Stanley v. Illinois, 405 U.S. 645 (1972).

Stark, E. (1998, July). Mandatory arrest of batterers: A reply to its critics. In *Legal interventions in family violence: Research findings and policy implications, a project of the American Bar Association's Criminal Justice Section, Commission on Domestic Violence, Center on Children and the Law, and Commission on Legal Problems of the Elderly,* 57. Presented to the National Institute of Justice. NCJ 171666. Washington, DC: National Institute of Justice.

Stark, E. (1990). Testimony and statement. Hearing before the Committee on the Judiciary, House of Representatives, One Hundred First Congress, second session, on H. Con. Res. 172. (Serial No. 1). Washington, DC: Government Printing Office.

Stark, E. (2000, November 20). Oral Presentation and remarks. National Institute of Justice Workshop on Gender Symmetry. Arlington, Virginia.

State ex rel Williams v. Marsh, 626 S.W.2d 223 (Mo. 1982).

State Farm Mutual Automobile Insurance Co. v. Campbell, 538 U.S. 408 (2003).

State of Kansas v. Bethel 275 Kan. 456, 66 P.3d 840 (2003).

State of Louisiana v. Hypolite Foret, 628 So. 2d 1116 (1993).

State v. Margaret Kelly Michaels, 642 A.2d 1372 (N.J., 1994).

State v. Benoit, 126 N.H. 6, 490 A.2d 295 (1985).

State ex rel. Simmons v. Roper, 112 S.W.3d 397 (Mo. 2003).

State v. Halgren 137 Wash.3d 340, 971 P.2d 512 (1999).

State v. Kelley, 478 A.2d. 364 (N.J., 1984).

State v. Lockhart, 542 S.E.2d 443 (W. Va., 2000).

Steadman, H. J. (1985a). Empirical research on the insanity defense. In R. Moran (Ed.), *The annals of the American Academy of Political and Social Science,* pp. 58–71. Beverly Hills, CA: Sage.

Steadman, H. J. (1985b). Insanity defense research and treatment of insane acquittees. *Behavioral Science and the Law,* 3, 37–38.

Steadman, H. J., & Braff, J. (1983). Defendants not guilty by reason of insanity. In J. Monahan & H. J. Steadman (Eds.), *Mentally disordered defendants: Perspectives from law and social science.* New York: Plenum.

Steadman, H. J., Callahan, L. A., Robbins, P. C., & Morrissey, J. P. (1989). Maintenance of an insanity defense under Montana's "abolition" of the insanity defense. *American Journal of Psychiatry,* 16, 357–360.

Steadman, H. J., McGreevy, M. A., Morrissey, J. P., Callahan, L. A., Robbins, P. C., & Cirincione, C. (1993). *Before and after* Hinckley: *Evaluating insanity defense reform.* New York: Guilford Press.

Steadman, H. J., Monahan, J., Hartstone, E., Davis, S. K., & Robbins, P. C. (1982). Mentally disordered offenders: A national survey of patients and facilities. *Law and Human Behavior,* 6, 31–38.

Steadman, H. J., & Morrissey, J. P. (1986). The insanity defense: Problems and prospect for studying the impact of legal reform. *Annals of the American Academy of Political and Social Science,* 484, 115–126.

Steadman, H. J., Mulvey, E. P., Monahan, J., Robbins, P. C., Applebaum, P. S., Grisso, T., Roth, L. H., & Silver, E. (1998). Violence by people discharged from acute psychiatric inpatient facilities by others in the same neighborhoods. *Archives of General Psychiatry,* 55, 393–401.

Steadman, H. J., & Redlich, A. D. (2006). *Final report: An evaluation of the Bureau of Justice Assistance Mental Health Court Initiative.* NIJ 213136. Washington, DC: National Institute of Justice, Office of Justice Programs.

Steadman, H. J., Rosenstein, M. J., MacAskill, R. L., & Manderscheid, R. W. (1988). A profile of mentally disordered offenders admitted to inpatient psychiatric services in the United States. *Law and Human Behavior,* 12(1), 91–99.

Steadman, H. J., Silver, E., Monahan, J., Applebaum, P. S., Robbins, P. C., Mulvery, E. P., Grisso, T., Roth, L. H., & Banks, S. (2002). A classification tree approach to the development fo actuarial violence risk assessment tools. *Law & Human Behavior,* 24(1), 83–100.

Steblay, N. M. (1992). A meta-analytic review of the weapon focus effect. *Law and Human Behavior,* 16(4), 413–424.

Steblay, N. M. (1997). Social influence in eyewitness recall: A meta-analytic review of lineup instruction effects. *Law and Human Behavior,* 21(3), 257–297.

Steblay, N. M., Besirevic, J., Fulero, S. M., & Jiminez-Lorente, B. (1999). The effects of pretrial publicity on juror verdicts: A meta-analytic review. *Law and Human Behavior, 23*(2), 219–235.

Steblay, N., Dysart, J., Fulero, S., & Lindsay, R. C. L. (2001). Eyewitness accuracy rates in sequential and simultaneous lineup presentations: A meta-analytic comparison. *Law and Human Behavior, 25*(5), 359–373.

Steele, C. M. (1997). A threat in the air: How stereotypes shape intellectual identity and performance. *American Psychologist, 52,* 613–629.

Stefan, S. (1996). Race, competence testing, and disability law: A review of the MacArthur competence research. *Psychology, Public Policy, and Law, 2*(1), 31–44.

Stefan, S., & Winick, B. J. (2005) A dialogue on mental health courts. *Psychology, Public Policy, and Law, 11*(4), 507–526.

Steinberg, J. (2002a, August 18). Edgy about exams, schools cut the summer short. *New York Times,* A–21.

Steinberg, J. (2002b, December 4). For Head Start children, their turn at testing. *New York Times,* A–27.

Steinberg, K. S. (1994). In the service of two masters: Psychotherapists' struggle with child maltreatment mandatory reporting laws. Unpublished Ph.D. thesis, Department of Psychology, State University of New York at Buffalo.

Steinberg, K. S., Levine, M., & Doueck, H. J. (1998). Effects of legally mandated child-abuse reports on the therapeutic relationship: A survey of psychotherapists. *American Journal of Orthopsychiatry, 67,* 112–122.

Steinberg, L., & Cauffman, E. (1996). Maturity of judgment in adolescence: Psychosocial factors in adolescent decision making. *Law and Human Behavior, 20*(3), 249–27.

Sternberg, R. J. (2005). There are no public-policy implications: A reply to Rushton and Jensen (2005). *Psychology, Public Policy, and Law, 11*(2), 295–301.

Steinmetz, S. K. (1977). Use of physical violence between marital couples to resolve fights. In M. Roy (Ed.), *Battered women: A psychosociological study of domestic violence,* pp. 63–71. New York: Van Nostrand Reinhold.

Stephan, J., & Brien, P. (1994). Capital punishment, 1993. Bureau of Justice Statistics Bulletin. Washington, DC: U.S. Department of Justice.

Stevens, P., & Eide, M. (1990, July-August). The first chapter of children's rights. *American Heritage,* pp. 84–91.

Stockdale, M. S., Visio, M., and Batra, L. (1999). The sexual harassment of men: Evidence of a broader theory of sexual harassment and sex discrimination. *Psychology, Public Policy, and Law, 5*(3), 630–664.

Stockdale, M. S., O'Connor, M., Gutek, B. A., & Geer, T. (2002). The relationship between prior sexual abuse and reactions to sexual harassment: literature review and empirical study. *Psychology, Public Policy, and Law, 8*(1), 64–95.

Stone, A. A. (1976). The *Tarasoff* decisions: Suing psychotherapists to safeguard society. *Harvard Law Review, 90,* 358–378.

Stone Lantern Films. (1990). *Asylum.* Produced by Sarah Mondale and Sarah B. Patton. Princeton, NJ: Films for the Humanities and Sciences.

Stott, M. W. R., & Olczak, P. V. (1978). Relating personality characteristics to juvenile offense categories: Differences between status offenders and juvenile delinquents. *Journal of Clinical Psychology, 34,* 80–84.

Stout, D. (2005, January 5). Pentagon toughens policy on sexual assault. *New York Times,* Politics sec.

Strauder v. West Virginia, 100 U.S. 303 (1880).

Straus, M. A. (1994). *Beating the devil out of them: Corporal punishment in American families.* New York: Lexington Books.

Straus, M. A. (1999). The controversy over domestic violence by women: a methodological, theoretical, and sociology of science analysis. In X. Arriaga & S. Oskamp (Eds.), *Violence in intimate relationships,* pp. 17–44. Thousand Oaks, CA: Sage.

Straus, M. A. (2000, November 20). Oral presentation and remarks. National Institute of Justice Workshop on Gender Symmetry, Arlington, VA.

Straus, M. A., Gelles, R. J., & Steinmetz, S. (1980). *Behind closed doors.* New York: Doubleday, Anchor.

Straus, M. A., Hamby, S. L., Boney-McCoy, S., & Sugarman, D. B. (1996). The Revised Conflict Tactics Scales (CTS2). *Journal of Family Issues, 17*(3), 283–316.

Streib, V. L. (1988, March). Decline and fall of juvenile capital punishment: The beginning of the end of a scandalous American practice? Paper presented at the Mid-Year Conference of the American Psychology–Law Society, Miami Beach, Florida.

Strichartz, A. F., & Burton, R. V. (1990). Lies and truth: A study of the development of the concept. *Child Development, 61,* 211–220.

Strict bail conditions for Gotti. (1998, September 18). *New York Times,* A–23.

Strier, F. (1999). Whither trial consulting? Issues and projections. *Law and Human Behavior, 23*(1), 93–115.

Strom, K. J., Smith, S. K., & Snyder, H. N. (1998). *Juvenile felony defendants in criminal courts.* Bureau of Justice Statistics Special Report. Washington, DC: U.S. Department of Justice.

Studebaker, C. L., & Goodman-Delahunty, J. (Eds). (2002). Expert testimony in the courts: The influence of the Daubert, Joiner, and Kumho decisions. *Psychology, Public Policy, and Law, 8*(2–3–4), 139–372.

Summit, R. C. (1988). Hidden victims, hidden pain: Societal avoidance of child sexual abuse. In G. E. Wyatt & G. J. Johnson (Eds.), *Lasting effects of child sexual abuse,* pp. 39–60. Newbury Park, CA: Sage.

Swan, S. (2000a, November 20). Oral presentation and remarks. National Institute of Justice Workshop on Gender Symmetry, 2000. Arlington, VA.

Swan, S. (2000b, November 20). Women's use of violence. Presentation, National Institute of Justice Gender Symmetry Workshop, Arlington, VA.

Synder, H. N. (1998, December). Juvenile arrests 1997. *Juvenile Justice Bulletin.* Washington, DC: U.S.

Department of Justice, Office of Justice Programs, Office of Juvenile Justice and Delinquency Prevention.

Szasz, T. (1963). *Law, liberty and psychiatry.* New York: Macmillan.

Talwar, V., Lee, K., Bala, N,. & Lindsay, R. C. L. (2002). Children's conceptual knowledge of lying and its relation to their actual behaviors: Implications for court competency examinations. *Law and Human Behavior,* 26(4), 395–415.

Talwar, V., Lee, K., Bala, N., & Lindsay, R. C. L. (2004). Children's lie-telling to conceal a parent's transgression: Legal implications. *Law and Human Behavior,* 28(4), 411–438.

Tan, N. T. (1991). Implications of the divorce mediation assessment instrument for mediation practice. *Family and Conciliation Courts Review,* 29, 26–40.

Tarasoff v. Regents of the University of California, 108 Cal. Rptr. 878 (Ct. App. 1973); reversed and remanded, 13 Cal. 3d 177 (1974); modified, 17 Cal. 3d 425 (1976).

Task Force Presidential Advisory Group on Anticipated Advances in Science and Technology. (1976). The science court experiment. *Science,* 193, 653–656.

Tatara, T. (1995). *An analysis of state laws addressing elder abuse, neglect and exploitation.* Washington, DC: National Center on Elder Abuse.

Tate, D. C., Reppucci, N. D., & Mulvey, E. P. (1995). Violent juvenile delinquents: Treatment effectiveness and implications for future action. *American Psychologist,* 50, 777–781.

Tauteoli, K., Oldroyd, R., & Lewis, R. (1992). Child sexual abuse: statistics, trends and case outcomes. http://www.jrsa.org/pubs/forum/archives/Mar92.html.

Tavernise, S. (2004, November 26). Legal precedent doesn't let facts stand in the way. *New York Times.* http://www.nytimes.com/2004/11/26/nyregion/26decision.

Taylor, B. G., Davis, R. C., & Maxwell, C. D. (2001). The effects of a group batterer treatment program in Brooklyn. *Justice Quarterly,* 18, 170–201.

Taylor v. Louisiana, 419 U.S. 522 (1975).

Taylor v. Taintor, 83 U.S. 366 (1873).

Taylor v. Taylor, 508 A.2d 964 (Md., 1986).

Technical Working Group for Eyewitness Evidence. (1999). *Eyewitness evidence: A guide for law enforcement.* Washington, DC: National Institute of Justice. http://www.ncjrs.org/txtfiles1/nij/178240.txt.

Teplin, L. A. (1983). The criminalization of the mentally ill: Speculation in search of data. *Psychological Bulletin,* 94, 54–67.

Terman, L. M. (1916). *The measurement of intelligence.* Boston: Houghton Mifflin.

Terry, D. (1998a, April 12). Too sick to die? Jury will decide condemned man's fate. *New York Times,* A–14.

Terry, D. (1998b, May 15). Killer of 3 is mentally fit to be executed, a California jury finds. *New York Times,* A–16.

Tesler, Pauline H., Tesler, Sandmann & Fishman Law Offices, Mill Valley, CA. (2000, December). Collaborative law: A new paradigm for divorce lawyers. *Psychology, Public Policy, & Law,* 5(4) 967–1000.

Texas v. Johnson, 491 U.S. 397 (1989).

The National Council of Juvenile and Family Court Judges (2006). *Navigating Custody and Visitation Evaluations in Cases with Domestic Violence: a Judge's Guide.* FVD-11. Available free at fvdinfo@ncjfcj.org

Thibaut, J., & Walker, L. (1975). *Procedural justice: A psychological analysis.* Hillside, NJ: Erlbaum.

Thoennes, N., & Tjaden, P. G. (1990). The extent, nature and validity of sexual abuse allegations in custody/visitation disputes. Child Abuse and Neglect, 14, 151–163.

Thompson v. Oklahoma, 487 U.S. 815 (1988).

Thompson, G. (1999, April 18). Afraid of husbands and the law: Deportation risk grows for abused illegal residents. *New York Times,* Metro sec., 37.

Thornberry, T. P. (1994, December). Violent families and youth violence. Office of Juvenile Justice and Delinquency Prevention, Fact Sheet 21. Washington, DC: OJJDP.

Thornburgh v. American College of Obstreticians and Gynecologists, 476 U.S. 747 (1986).

Thornton, A. E., Reese, L. M., Pashley, P. J., & Dallessandro, S. P. (2000, May). Predictive validity of accommodated LSAT scores. Law School Admissions Council, Technical Report 01–01.

Tjaden, P., & Thoennes, N. (1998, November). Prevalence, incidence and consequences of violence against women: Findings from the National Violence Against Women survey. Research in Brief. National Institute of Justice Centers for Disease Control and Prevention. NCJ 172837. Washington, DC: National Institute of Justice.

Tobesman, R. T. (1990). Statement. Hearing before the Committee on the Judiciary, House of Representatives, One Hundred First Congress, second session, on H. Con. Res. 172. (Serial No. 81). Washington, DC: Government Printing Office.

Tolman, A. O. (2001). Clinical training and the duty to protect. *Behavioral Sciences and the Law,* 19(3), 387–404.

Tomkins, A. J., Steinman, M., Kenning. M. K., Mohamed, S., & Afrank, J. (1992). Children who witness woman battering. *Law & Policy,* 14, 169–184.

Toobin, J. (1998, February 9). The trouble with sex. *New Yorker,* 48–55.

Town of Castle Rock v. Gonzales, 125 S.Ct. 2796 (2005).

Trial of James Hadfield (K.B. 1800). In T. B. Howell, A complete collection of state trials, vol. 27 (1820), 1281 et seq.

Tribe, L. H. (1990). *Abortion: The clash of absolutes.* New York: Norton.

Troxel v. Granville, 530 U.S. 57 (2000).

Turner, D. (2001, January 23). Bush's abortion order buoys conservatives. *Buffalo News,* A–1, A–4.

Turner, W. P. (1990). Testimony and statement. Hearing before the Committee on the Judiciary, House of Representatives, One Hundred First Congress, second session, on H. Con. Res. 172. (Serial No. 81). Washington, DC: Government Printing Office.

Umbreit, M. S. (2000). *Family group conferencing: Implications for crime victims*. St. Paul: Center for Restorative Justice & Peacemaking, School of Social Work, University of Minnesota.

Umbriet, M. S., Coates, R. B., & Vos, V. (2002). *The impact of restorative justice conferencing: A review of 63 emopricial studies in 5 countries*. St. Paul: Center for Restorative Justice & Peacemaking, School of Social Work, University of Minnesota.

Underwager, R., & Wakefield, H. (1992). Poor psychology produces poor law. *Law and Human Behavior, 16*(2), 233–243.

United Nations. (1990). Convention on the Rights of the Child. GA Res. 44.25, UN1448 GAOR, 44th Sess. (Supp. No. 49 at 166), UN Doc. A/44/49; 28 ILM (1989), entered into force September 2, 1990.

U.S. Advisory Board on Child Abuse and Neglect. (1993). *Neighbors helping neighbors: A new national strategy for the protection of children*. Washington, DC: Administration for Children and Families.

U.S. Bureau of Criminal Justice Statistics. (1988). *Report to the nation on crime and Justice*. 2nd ed. NCJ–105506. Washington, DC: U.S. Department of Justice

U.S. Bureau of Criminal Justice Statistics. (1990a). *Jail inmates*. Washington, DC: U.S. Department of Justice.

U.S. Bureau of Criminal Justice Statistics. (1990b). *Census of local jails*. Washington, DC: U.S. Department of Justice.

U.S. Bureau of Criminal Justice Statistics. (1995, September). *Spouse murder defendants in large urban counties*. NCJ–156831. Washington, DC: U.S. Department of Justice.

U.S. Bureau of Criminal Justice Statistics. (1996, December). *Female victims of violent crimes*. NCJ–162602. Washington, DC: U.S. Department of Justice.

U.S. Bureau of Education. (1880). *Legal rights of children*. Washington, DC: Government Printing Office.

U.S. Bureau of the Census. (1993). *Statistical abstract of the United States*. Washington, DC: U.S. Department of Commerce.

U.S. Bureau of the Census. (1994). *Statistical abstract of the United States*. Washington, DC: U.S. Department of Commerce.

U.S. Bureau of the Census. (1997). *Statistical abstract of the United States*. Washington, DC: U.S. Department of Commerce.

U.S. Bureau of the Census. (1998a). Living arrangements of children under 18 years old: 1960 to present. Tables 156, 160. http://www.census.gov/population/sociodem/ms-la/tabch-1.txt.

U.S. Bureau of the Census. (1998b). Marital status and living arrangements: March 1998 (Update) Current population reports, Series P20–514. http://www.census.gov/prod/99pubs/p20-514u.pdf.

U.S. Children's Bureau, 1912–1972. (1974). *Children and youth: Social problems and social policy*. New York: Arno.

U.S. Commission on Civil Rights. (1978). *Battered women: Issues of public policy*. Washington, DC: Author.

U.S. Department of Health and Human Services, Administration for Children and Families, Children's Bureau. (2003). *Decision making in unsubstantiated child protective services cases.* Washington,. DC: Author.

U.S. Department of Justice. (n.d.). http://www.ncjrs.org/txtfiles1/nij/178240.txt.

U.S. Department of Justice, Bureau of Justice Statistics. (2005a). Homicide trends in the U.S.: Intimate homicide. http://www.ojp.usdoj.gov/bjs/homicide/intimates.htm.

U.S. Department of Justice, Bureau of Justice Statistics. (2005b). Family violence statistics. http://www.ojp.usdoj.gov/bjs/abstracat/fvs NCJ 207846.

U.S. Merit Systems Protection Board. (1981). *Sexual harassment in the work place—is it a problem?* Washington, DC: Author.

U.S. Merit Systems Protection Board. (1987). *Sexual harassment of federal workers: An update*. Washington, DC: Author.

U.S. Merit Systems Protection Board. (1995). *Sexual harassment in the federal workplace: Trends, progress, continuing challenges*. Washington, DC: Author.

U.S. Senate, Committee on the Judiciary. (1990). Hearing before the committee on the judiciary, US Senate, One Hundred First Congress, second session, on legislation to reduce the growing problem of violent crime against women, part 1 and 2. (Serial No. J–101–80). Washington, DC: Government Printing Office.

U.S. Supreme Court. (2005). http://www.supremecourtus.gov/about/about.html.

United States v. Bankston, 121 F.3d 1411 (11th Cir 1997).

United States v. Booker, 543 U.S. 220 (2005).

United States v. Brawner, 471 F.2d 969 (D.C. Cir. 1972).

United States v. Dougherty, 473 F. 2d 1113 (DC Cir. 1972).

United States v. Downing, 753 F.2d 1224 (3d Cir. 1985).

United States v. Egwaoje, 335 F.3d 579 (7th Cir. 2003).

United States v. Hall, 93 F.3d 1337 (7th Cir. 1996).

United States v. Hinckley, 525 F. Supp. 1342 (D.D.C. 1981).

United States v. Jackson, 390 U.S. 570 (1968).

United States v. Jones, 336 F.3d 245 (3d Cir. 2003).

United States v. Lester, 254 F. Supp. 2d 602 (E.D. Va. 2003).

United States v. Lopez, 514 U.S. 549 (1995).

United States v. Morrison, 529 U.S. 598 (2000).

United States v. Salerno, 481 U.S. 739 (1987).

United States v. Telfaire, 469 F.2d 552 (D.C. Cir. 1972).

United States v. Wade, 388 U.S. 218 (1967).

University of California Regents v. Bakke, 438 U.S. 265 (1978).

Upchurch, D. M., & McCarthy, J. (1989). Adolescen child-bearing and high school completion in the 1980s: Have things changed? *Family Planning Perspectives, 21,* 199–202.

Valmont v. Bane, 18 F.3d 992 (2d Cir. 1994).

Van De Kamp, J. (1986). *Report on the Kern County child abuse investigation.* Sacramento, CA: Office of the Attorney General.

Ventura, S. J., Clarke, S. C., & Mathews, T. J. (1996). Recent declines in teenage birth rates in the United States: Variations by state, 1990–1994. *Monthly Vital Statistics Report,* 45, Centers for Disease Control and Prevention, National Center for Health Statistics.

Verkaik, R. (2000, August 25). New law will force juries to give reasons for verdicts. *Independent,* 4(23), 1.

Vidmar, N. (1997). *Medical malpractice and the American jury.* Ann Arbor: University of Michigan Press.

Visher, C. A. (1987). Jury decision making: The importance of evidence. *Law and Human Behavior,* 11(1), 1–18.

Viteles, M. S. (1932). *Industrial psychology.* New York: Norton.

Wadlington, W. J. (1983). Consent to medical care for minors: The legal framework. In G. B. Melton, G. P. Koocher, & M. J. Saks (Eds.), *Children's competency to consent,* pp. 57–74. New York: Plenum.

Wagner, A. (2004, November 25). Hinckley denied trips. *Washington Times,* Metropolitan sec.

Walcott, D. M., Cerundolo, & Beck, J. C. (2001). Current analysis of the Tarasoff duty: An evolution towards the limitation of the duty to protect. *Behavioral Sciences and the Law,* 19(3), 325–343.

Waldfogel, J. (1998). *The future of child protection.* Cambridge, MA: Harvard University Press.

Waldo, C. R., Berdahl, J. L., and Fitzgerald, L. F. (1998). Are men sexually harassed? If so, by whom? *Law and Human Behavior,* 22(1), 59–80.

Walker, L., & Monahan, J. (1987). Social frameworks: A new use of social science in law. *Virginia Law Review,* 73, 559–598.

Walker, L. E. (1979). *The battered woman.* New York: Harper & Row.

Walker, L. E. (1984). *The battered woman syndrome.* New York: Springer.

Walker, L. E. (1999). Psychology and domestic violence around the world. *American Psychologist,* 54(1), 21–29.

Wallach, L. (1993). With confidence in their integrity: Informed consent, custody and child maltreatment. Unpublished preliminary thesis. State University of New York at Buffalo, Psychology Department.

Wallerstein, J. S., & Kelly, J. B. (1980). *Surviving the breakup: How children and parents cope with divorce.* New York: Basic Books.

Wards Cove Packing Co. v. Atonio, 490 U.S. 642 (1989).

Warner, G. (2000, April 14). Serving to protect: Courts make gains against abuse cases. *Buffalo News,* A-1, A-8.

Warren, J., Fitch, W., Dietz, P., & Rosenfeld, B. (1991). Criminal offense, psychiatric diagnosis, and psycho-legal opinion: An analysis of 894 pretrial referrals. *Bulletin of the American Academy of Psychiatry and the Law,* 19, 63–69.

Warren, J. I., Murrie, D. C., Chauhan, P., Dietz, P. E., & Morris, J. (2004). Opinion formation in evaluating insanity at the time of offense: An examination of 5175 pre-trial evaluations. *Behavioral Sciences & the Law,* 22(2), 171–186.

Warshak, R. A. (2001). Current controversies regarding Parental Alienation Syndrome. *American Journal of Forensic Psychology,* 19(3), 29–59.

Washington v. Davis, 426 U.S. 229 (1976).

Washington v. Davis, 547 U.S. 2006.

Washington v. Harper, 494 U.S. 210 (1990).

Washington v. United States, 390 F.2d 444 (D.C. Cir. 1967).

Watson, H., & Levine, M. (1989). Psychotherapy and mandated reporting of child abuse. *American Journal of Orthopsychiatry,* 59, 246–256.

Webb, R. A. (1990). Achievement tests and educational equality in the Little Rock schools. Unpublished paper, Department of Psychology, University of Arkansas at Little Rock.

Weberling, L. C., Forgays, D. K., Crain-Thooreson, C., & Hyman, I. (2003). Prenatal child abuse risk assessment: a preliminary validation. *Child Welfare,* 82(3), 319–334.

Webster v. Reproductive Health Services, 492 U.S. 490 (1989).

Webster, C. D. (1998). Comment on Thomas Mathiesen's selective incapacitation revisited. *Law and Human Behavior,* 22(4), 471–476.

Webster, C. D, Douglas, K. S., Eaves, D., & Hart, S. D. (1997). *The HCR–20 scheme: Assessing risk for violence.* Version 2. Burnaby, BC: Mental Health, Law, and Policy Institute, Simon Fraser University.

Webster's New International Dictionary of the English Language. (2003). 11th ed. Abridged. Springfield, MA: G. & C. Merriam.

Weeks v. Angelone 528 U.S. 225 (2000).

Weihe, V. R. (1998). *Understanding family violence.* Thousand Oaks, CA: Sage.

Weil, M., & Sanchez, E. (1983, March). The impact of the *Tarasoff* decision on clinical social work *practice. Social Services Review,* 112–124.

Weiner, B. A. (1985). Mental disability and the criminal law. In S. J. Brakel, J. Parry, & B. A. Weiner (Eds.), *The mentally disabled and the law.* 3rd ed., pp. 693–801. Chicago: American Bar Foundation.

Weinstein, B. (1996). The effects of reporting of suspected child abuse and maltreatment on the psychotherapy relationship. Unpublished doctoral dissertation, New School, New York, NY.

Weisgram v. Marley Co., 528 U.S. 440 (2000).

Weiss, K. R. (2000, January 9). Faking feared in extra SAT time granted rich whites. *Buffalo News,* A-5.

Weiss, P. (1998, May 3). Don't even think about it. *New York Times Magazine,* 43–81.

Weissman, E. (1999, January). No season of hope/ Adolescent defendants in adult courts. *NYS Psychologist,* 19–24.

Weisz, V., Lott, R. C., & Thai, N. D. (2002). A teen court evaluation with a therapeutic justice perspective. *Behavioral Sciences & the Law,* 20(4), 381–392.

Weisz, A. N., Tolman, R. M., & Saunders, D. G. (2000). Assessing the risk of severe domestic violence: The importance of survivors'predidctions. *Journal of Interpersonal Violence,* 15(1), 75–90.

Weithorn, L. A. (1984). Children's capacities in legal contexts. In N. D. Reppucci, L. A. Weithorn, E. P. Mulvey, & J. P. Monahan (Eds.), *Children, mental health and the law,* pp. 22–55. Beverly Hills, CA: Sage.

Weithorn, L. (1988). Mental hospitalization of troublesome youth: An analysis of sky-rocketing admission rates. *Stanford Law Review,* 40, 773–838.

Weithorn, L. A. (2001). Protecting children from exposure to domestic violence: the use and abuse of child maltreatment statutes. *Hastings Law Journal,* 53(1), 1–156.

Weithorn, L. A. (2005). Envisioning second-order change in America's response to troubled and troublesme youth. *Hofstra Law Review,* 33(4), 1305–1506.

Weithorn, L. A., & Campbell, S. B. (1982). The competency of children and adolescents to make informed treatment decisions. *Child Development,* 53, 1589–1598.

Weitzman, B. C. (1989). Pregnancy and childbirth: Risk factors for homelessness? *Family Planning Perspectives,* 21, 175–178.

Wellborn, O. G. (1991). Demeanor. *Cornell Law Review,* 76, 1075–1105.

Wells, G. L. (1986). Expert psychological testimony: Empirical and conceptual analyses of effects. *Law and Human Behavior,* 10(1/2), 83–95.

Wells, G. L. (1993). What do we know about eyewitness identification? *American Psychologist,* 48, 553–571.

Wells, G. L. (1997). The scientific status of research on eyewitness identification. In D. L. Faigman, D. H. Kaye, M. J. Saks, & J. Sanders, J. (Eds.), *Modern scientific evidence: The law and science of expert testimony,* vol. 1, pp. 452–479. St. Paul, MN: West.

Wells, G. L., Lindsay, R. C. L., & Ferguson, T. J. (1979). Accuracy, confidence, and juror perceptions in eyewitness identification. *Journal of Applied Psychology,* 64, 440–444.

Wells, G. L., & Olson, E. A. (2003). Eyewitness testimony. *Annual Review of Psychology,* 54, 277–295.

Wells, G. L., & Seelau, E. P. (1995). Eyewitness identification: Psychological research and legal policy on lineups. *Psychology, Public Policy, and Law,* 1(4), 765–791.

Wells, G. L., Small, M., Penrod, S., Malpass, R. S., Fulero, S. M., & Brimacombe, C. A. E. (1998). Eyewitness identification procedures: Recommendations for lineups and photospreads. *Law and Human Behavior,* 22(6), 603–647.

Wells, G. L., Turtle, J. W., & Luus, C. A. E. (1989). The perceived credibility of child eyewitnesses: What happens when they use their own words? In S. J. Ceci, D. F. Ross, & M. P. Toglia (Eds.), *Perspectives on children's testimony,* pp. 23–36. New York: Springer-Verlag.

Wertheimer, A. (2003). *Consent to sexual relations.* New York: Cambridge University Press.

Westbrook v. Arizona, 384 U.S. 150 (1966).

Wexler, D. B. (1990). *Therapeutic jurisprudence: The law as a therapeutic agent.* Durham, NC: Carolina Academic Press.

Wexler, D. B. (1995). Reflections on the scope of therapeutic jurisprudence. *Psychology, Public Policy, and Law,* 1(1), 220–236.

Wexler, D. B., & Winick, B. J. (1991). *Essays in therapeutic jurisprudence.* Durham, NC: Carolina Academic Press.

Wexler, D. B., & Winick, B. J. (1996a). Introduction. In D. B. Wexler and B. J. Winick (Eds.), *Law in a therapeutic key,* xvii–xx. Durham, NC: Carolina Academic Press.

Wexler, D. B., & Winick, B. J. (Eds.). (1996b). *Law in a therapeutic key: Developments in therapeutic jurisprudence.* Durham, NC: Carolina Academic Press.

Wexler, R. (1990). *Wounded innocents. The real victims in the war against child abuse.* Buffalo, NY: Prometheus.

Whipple, G. M. (1909). The observer as reporter: A survey of the "psychology of testimony." *Psychological Bulletin,* 6, 153–170.

Whipple, G. M. (1918). The obtaining of information: Psychology of observation and report. *Psychological Bulletin,* 15, 217–248.

Whitcomb, D., Shapiro, E. R., & Stellwagen, L. D. (1985). *When the victim is a child: Issues for judges and prosecutors.* Washington, DC: National Institute of Justice.

White, T. M. (2003). An evaluation of the impact of the Adoption and Safe Families Act of 1997 on permanency related out comes in six United States states. Unpublished Ph.D. dissertaion, University of Pennsylvania, School of Social Work.

White, W. S. (1991). *The death penalty in the nineties.* Ann Arbor: University of Michigan Press.

Widom, C. S. (1992, October). The cycle of violence. National Institute of Justice Research in Brief. Washington, DC: National Institute of Justice.

Wiener, R., Pritchard, C., & Weston, M. (1995). Comprehensibility of approved jury instructions in capital murder cases. *Journal of Applied Psychology,* 80, 455–467.

Wiener, R. L., & Gutek, B.A. (1999). Advances in sexual harassment research, theory and policy. *Psychology, Public Policy and Law,* 5(3), 507–518.

Wiener, R. L., Hurt, R. E., Russell, B., Mannen, K., & Gasper, C. (1997). Perceptions of sexual harassment: The effects of gender, legal standard, and ambivalent sexism. *Law and Human Behavior,* 21(1), 71–93.

Wiener, R. L., Watts, B. A., Goldkamp, K. H., & Gasper, C. (1995). Social analytic investigation of hostile workplace environments: A test of the reasonable woman standard. *Law and Human Behavior,* 19(3), 263–281.

Wiener, R. L., Winter, R., Rogers, M., & Arnot, L. (2004). The effects of prior workplace behaviour on subsequent sexual harassment judgments. *Law and Human Behavior*, 28(1), 47–68.

Wieter v. Settle, 193 F. Supp. 318 (W.D. Mo. 1961).

Wigmore, J. H. (1909). Professor Muensterberg and the psychology of testimony. *Illinois Law Review*, 3(7), 399–445.

Wikipedia. (2006). Zacarias Moussaoui. http://enwikipedia.org/wiki/Zacarias_Moussaoui.

Wilgoren, J. (2002, February 9). Divorce court proceeds in a lawyer-free zone. *New York Times* on the Web.

Wilgoren, J. (2005, August 30). Rape charge follows marriage to a 14-year old. *New York Times*, A-1, A-16.

Wilkins, D. B. (2005). A systematic response to systemic disadvantage: A response to Sander. *Stanford Law Review*, 57, 1915–1961.

Williams v. Florida, 399 U.S. 78 (1970).

Williams v. Williams, 104 Ill. App. 3d 16, 432 N.E.2d 375 (1982).

Williams, K. (1981). Few convictions in rape cases: Empirical evidence concerning some alternative explanations. *Journal of Criminal Justice*, 9, 29–39.

Williams, K. R. & Houghton, A. B. (2004). Assessing the risk of domestic violence reoffending: A validation study. *Law and Human Behavior*, 28(4), 437–455.

Williams, M. H. (1992). Exploitation and inference: Mapping the damage from therapist–patient sexual involvement. *American Psychologist*, 47, 412–421.

Williams, M. H. (1995). How useful are clinical reports concerning the consequences of therapist–patient sexual involvement? *American Journal of Psychotherapy*, 49, 237–243.

Williams, M. H. (1997). Boundary violations: Do some contended standards of care fail to encompass commonplace procedures of humanistic, behavioral and eclectic psychotherapies? *Psychotherapy*, 34, 238–249.

Williams, R. L. (1970). Black pride, academic relevance and individual achievement. *Counseling Psychologist*, 2, 18–22.

Williams, S. (2000). How is telehealth being incorporated in psychology practice? *Monitor on Psychology*, 31, 15.

Williams, W. M. (2000). Perspectives on intelligence testing, affirmative action, and educational policy. *Psychology, Public Policy, and Law*, 6(1), 5–19.

Winerip, M. (2003, April 2). An embedded reporter in the trenches of P.S. 48. *New York Times*, A-17.

Winerip, M. (2006b, May 17). Odd math for 'Best High Schools" list. *New York Times*, A-21.

Winerip, M. (2006a, February 8). In Bronx, a possible case of high school cheating, but not by students. *New York Times*, A-19.

Winick, B. J. (1985). Restructuring competence to stand trial. *UCLA Law Review*, 32, 921–985.

Winick, B. J. (1992). Competence to be executed: A therapeutic jurisprudence perspective. *Behavioral Sciences and the Law*, 10, 317–337.

Winick, B. J. (1995). Ambiguities in the legal meaning and significance of mental illness. *Psychology, Public Policy and the Law*, 1, 534–611.

Winick, B. J. (1996). Foreword: A summary of the MacArthur treatment competence study and an introduction to the special theme. *Psychology, Public Policy, and Law*, 2(1), 3–17.

Winick, B. J. (1997). The jurisprudence of therapeutic jurisprudence. *Psychology, Public Policy and the Law*, 3(1), 184–206.

Winslow, S. (2004). Charter schools . . . leaving children behind? *Augusta Free Press Online*. http://www.augustafreepress.com/stories/ storyReader@25341.

Wise, T. P. (1978). Where the public peril begins: A survey of psychotherapists to determine the effects of *Tarasoff*. *Stanford Law Review*, 31, 165–190.

Witherspoon v. Illinois, 391 U.S. 510 (1968).

Witt, P. H. (2003). Transfer of juveniles to adult court. The case of H. H. *Psychology, Public Policy, and Law*, 9(3/4), 361–380.

Wohl, A., & Kaufman, B. (1985). *Silent screams and hidden cries*. New York.

Women's Rights Law Reporter. (1986). *State v. Kelly:* Amicus briefs. Issue 9, 245–257.

Woodward, C. V. (1966). *The strange career of Jim Crow*. New York: Oxford University Press.

Wright, D. B., Boyd, C. E., & Tredoux, C. G. (2001). A field study of own-race bias in South Africa and England. *Psychology, Public Policy, and Law*, 7(1), 119–133.

Wright, R. H., & Cummings, N. A. (2005). *Destructive trends in mental health*. New York: Routledge.

Wulczyn, F. H., & Hislop, K. B. (2002). Topic #3 Adoption dynamics. The impact of the Adoption and Safe Families Act. Chapin Hall Issue Papers on Foster Care and Adoption.

Wuori v. Zitnay, Docket N. 75–80-P (D. Me. July 14 1978).

Yates v. Texas, Tex. App. Lexis 81 (January 6, 2005).

Yellin, E. (2000, April 20). For Tennessee, first execution in 40 years. *New York Times*, A-12.

Yerkes, R. M. (1921). Psychological examining in the United States Army. In W. Dennis (Ed.) (1948), *Readings in the history of psychology*, pp. 528–540. New York: Appleton-Century-Crofts.

Yoshihama, M., Hammock, A. C., & Horrocks, J. (2006). Intimate partner violence, welfare receipt, and health status of low-income African American women: A lifetime analysis. *American Journal of Community Psychology*, 37(1/2), 95–109.

Youngberg v. Romeo, 457 U.S. 307 (1982).

Zabin, L. S., Hirsch, M. B., & Emerson, M. R. (1989). When urban adolescents choose abortion: Effects on education, psychological status and subsequent pregnancy. *Family Planning Perspectives*, 21, 248–255.

Zaibert, L. A. (1997). Intentionality and blame: A study on the foundations of culpability. Unpublished doctoral dissertation, Department of Philosophy, State University of New York at Buffalo.

Zapf, P. A., & Viljoen, J. L. (2003). Issues and considerations regarding the use of assezsment instrumtents in the evaluation of competency to stand trial. *Behavioral Sciences and the Law*, 21(3), 351–367.

Zarazua, J. (2005, January 8). Inmate's execution halted. Questions about his mental capacity cause a second delay. *San Antonio Express-News*, 1B.

Zernike, K. (2005, July 19). Executed man may be cleared in new inquiry. *New York Times*, A-1, A-17.

Zernike, K. (2006, April 19). Study fuels a growing debate over changing police lineups. *New York Times*, A1, A-17.

Zimmerman, P. R. (2005). Estimates of the deterrent effect of alternatifve execution methods in the United States: 1978–2000. Working Paper Series. http://papers.ssrn .com/so13/papers.cfm?abstract_id = 355783.

Zimring, F. E. (1993). Research on the death penalty: On the liberating virtues of irrelevance. *Law & Society Review*, 27, 9–17.

Zimring, F. E. (1998). *American youth violence*. New York: Oxford University Press.

Zimring, F. E. (2005). *American juvenile justice*. New York: Oxford University Press.

Zimring, F. E., & Laurence, M. (n.d.). Death penalty. Crime File Study Guide, NCJ97219. Washington, DC: National Institute of Justice.

Zorza, J. (1998). Must we stop arresting batterers?: Analysis and policy implications of new police domestic violence studies. (1998, July). In *Legal interventions in family violence: Research findings and policy implications, a project of the American Bar Association's Criminal Justice Section, Commission on Domestic Violence, Center on Children and the Law, and Commission on Legal Problems of the Elderly*, 55–56. Presented to the National Institute of Justice. NCJ 171666. Washington, DC: National Institute of Justice.

Zuger, A. (1998, July 28). A fistful of hostility is discovered among women. *New York Times*, F-1.

Zusman, J., and Simon, J. (1983). Differences in repeated psychiatric examinations of litigants in a law suit. *American Journal of Psychiatry*, 140, 1300–1304.

Name Index

Subject Index

Divorce *continued*
effects on children of, 383–385
IPV and, 369–372
Dixon v. United States, 373
DNA tests, 161, 163, 221, 244–246
Domestic violence, 344–345
Doonesbury, 168
Double jeopardy, 13, 126, 532
Draco, 187
Drope v. Missouri, 91
Drug treatment and competence, 111
Due diligence, 308–309, 532
Due process, 10, 18–19, 22, 34, 101
child abuse and, 294
definition, 532
incompetency and, 109–110
Due process rights, 252
Duncan v. Louisiana, 131
Dunn v. Johnson, 103
Duren v. Missouri, 228
Durham rule, 192, 193–194, 532
Dusky v. U.S., 89, 94
Duty of care, 507, 525, 532
Dying with their rights on, 113
Dynamic variables, 59
Dynamite charge, 143, 532

Ecological validity, 46, 173, 321
Edmonson v. Leesville Concrete Co., 151
Educable Mentally Retarded (EMR), 480
Education
achievement tests/minimum
competence tests/high-stakes
tests, 494–499
college admission and psychological
testing, 482
law school admissions and
psychological testing, 485,
487–489
maintaining diversity in, 489–494
No Child Left Behind Act and, 5,
477–478, 495–496, 497
percent plans and, 490–492
psychological testing in schools and,
478
Educational progress, 477
Educational Testing Service (ETS),
492–493
Edwards v. Edwards, 118
*Effective Intervention in Domestic Vio-
lence and Child Maltreatment Cases:
Guidelines for Policy and Practice*, 368
Eighth Amendment, 219, 240, 242, 244
Eisenstadt v. Baird, 423
Elder abuse, 109, 532
Elizabethan Poor Laws of 1601, 285
Ellerbe v. Hooks, 391
*Elliot v. North Carolina Psychology
Board*, 517
Ellison v. Brady, 458
Emancipated minor, 107, 532
Emotional abuse, 301–302
Employment
disparate impact of tests on, 478
psychological testing and, 499–501
Encoding, 167–168
Enumerated powers, 3, 532

Epistemological approach to death
penalty, 236–237
Equal Employment Opportunity
Commission (EEOC), 446, 500
Equity, 532
Error rate of predictions, 56
Estimator variables, 165
Ethical code, 512–515, 532
Ethics. *see also* Values
American Psychological Association
(APA) and, 48
child custody and, 405–408
and competence to be executed, 106
jury consultation and, 150–151
medical insurance/managed health
care and, 510–511
relative inaccuracy of predictions and,
63
Evaluation of legally relevant capacities,
95–96
Evidence
acceptable/unacceptable, 138–141
hearsay, 328–329
rule of, 140–141
strength of, 133–134
Ex parte, 406, 533
Ex post facto laws, 521
Excessive corporal punishment, 294
Execution, 104–106. *see also* Death
penalty
Executive power, 7, 532
Executor, 107, 533
Experimenter effects, 181
Expert panels, 43
Expert testimony, 40, 533
abuse of discretion standard and,
42–43
competency and, 110
consensus in the field and, 173–175
criteria for admissibility of, 16
*Daubert v. Merrell Dow
Pharmaceuticals* and, 336–338
ecological validity and, 173
effect of, 177–178
on eyewitness accuracy, 166
as harmful to jurors, 174, 176
immunity from suit and, 511
insanity defense and, 203–211
jurors and, 174, 176
and presentation of research findings
in court, 176–179
External validity, 46
Eyewitness testimony
accuracy and, 169, 172–173
blind lineups and, 179–181
confidence of, 172–173
consensus in the field and, 173–175
death penalty reforms and, 244
ecological validity and, 173
exclusion of, 165–166
and expert testimony as harmful to
jurors, 174, 176
inaccurate reconstruction of events
and, 164–165
and initial assessment of confidence,
182
lineups and, 170–172

and lowering perceived situational
demand, 181
and presentation of expert testimony
findings in court, 176–179
research paradigms and, 169–170
research-based reforms of, 179
support of, 166–169
unreliability of single eyewitness, 165
and use of distractors, 181

Face validity, 96
Fact-finders, 130, 138
Failure to appear (FTA), 72
Fair Employment Practice Agencies
(FEPAs), 465–466
Fairness, 479, 483–484
False confessions, 161–163
False identification, 171, 179–181
False memory, 522–523
False Memory syndrome Foundation
(FMSF), 523–525, 526
False negative error, 57
False positive error, 57
Family conferencing, 34
Family court, 292, 303–304
Family Group Conference (FGC), 278–280
Family preservation policy, 290, 310, 533
Family reunification policy, 310
Family Violence Program (FVP), 357
Family-interaction models of IPV, 345
Faragher v. City of Boca Raton, 464
Faretta v. California, 102–103, 411–412
Federal Trade Commission, 8
Federalism, 3–7
Federal/state judicial systems, 12–15
Felony, 6, 198, 533
Females and delinquency, 254–255
Feminist models of IPV, 345
Ferguson, Colin, 103–104
Fiduciary duty, 533
Fifth Amendment, 91, 126
File drawer studies, 171
Filicide, 206–207
Finder of fact, 13, 533
First-degree murder, 188
Flag burning, 20
For cause, 533
Ford v. Wainwright, 104, 106
Forensic practice, 33, 208–209, 533
Foster care, 289–290, 309
Foucha v. Louisiana, 200–201, 205
Founded child abuse cases, 288, 294,
533, 540
Fourteenth Amendment, 422, 485
Friend of the court. *see Amicus curiae*
briefs
Frye standard, 533
Frye v. United States, 40–41
Fuentes v. Shevin, 10
Fugitive rates (FR), 72
Functional magnetic resonance imaging
(fMRI), 166
Furman, Georgia, 21
Furman v. Georgia, 219–220, 228

Garska v. McCoy, 386–387
Gault, In re, 252, 257–258, 269

Predictor variables, 56
Prejudicial evidence, 537
Prejudicial testimony, 138
Preliminary Scholastic Assessment Test (PSAT), 492–493
Preponderance of the evidence, 18, 295, 303, 537
Prescriptive stereotypes, 452
Presumption, 537
Pretrial hearings, 45–46
Pretrial holding centers, 69
Pretrial publicity, 139–140
Prevalence, 345, 450
Preventive detention, 537
Price Waterhouse v. Hopkins, 451–453
Primary caretaker doctrine, 386–387, 537
Primary caretakers, 381, 387
Prince v. Massachusetts, 398
Printz v. United States, 6
Privacy right, 425–426
    psychological propositions/liberty and, 426–427
    psychological testing and, 478
    sexual harassment and, 463
Privilege against self-incrimination, 537
Privileged communications, 537
Privileged disclosure, 295
Pro se, 102, 411–412, 538
Pro-arrest policies, 358–359
Probability
    dangerous label (accuracy) and, 56
    of future outcomes, 53
Probate court, 107, 537
Probative testimony, 138, 538
Probative value, 40
Procedural due process, 10–11, 538
Procedural justice
    fairness perception of, 136
    and jury as small group, 136–138
    zealous advocacy and, 135–136
Process schizophrenia, 209
Product rule, 192, 538
Product test, 213
Professional associations, 507
Professional misconduct, 509–510, 538
Professional standards of care, 515–516, 538
    therapists and, 77
Proportionality, 219, 228, 538
Prosecution, IPV and, 360–361
Prosecutorial waiver, 538
Proximate cause, 538
Psychiatric hospitalization, 116–117
Psychodynamic psychotherapy, 366
Psychological injury, 453–458, 538
Psychological testing
    achievement tests/high-stakes testing, 494–499
    college admission/affirmative action and, 482–485
    disparate impact of tests, 478
    employment and, 499–501
    historical roots of, 474–478
    in defense of, 502–504
    in educational settings, 478–480
    intelligence tests as "illegal", 480–481
    intelligence tests as "legal, 481–482

and maintaining diversity in education, 489–494
U.S. Supreme Court/affirmative action and, 485–489
Psychology, *see also Tarasoff v. Regents of the University of California. see also* Social science
    adjudicative fact provision and, 35
    and age and competence, 106–107
    amicus curiae briefs and, 38–40, 47–49
    competence to be executed, 104–106
    effect of legal system on, 45–46
    ethical standards/ codes and, 47
    findings as evidence in legal proceedings, 40–44
    impact on law, 31–34
    insanity defense and, 188
    interrogation methods and, 162–163
    and law (post-WWII), 32–33
    legislator informants/lobbyists and, 37
    mental health recommendations, 95
    objectivity/values and, 47–49
    social framework provision and, 36–37
    Szasz, Thomas and, 108–109
    therapeutic jurisprudence and, 34
Psychometrics, 55–56
Psychosis, 204–207, 212–213, 439. *see also* Insanity defense
Psychotherapeutic models of IPV, 345
Psychotherapy and child abuse cases, 307
Psychotropic drugs and competency, 111
Punitive damages, 153, 538
    medical malpractice and, 155

Quid pro quo sexual harassment, 450, 465–466, 538

Racial Justice Act of 1998, 230–231
Racial profiling, 63–64, 397
Ramona case, 524–525
Rape. *see* Sexual relationships consent
Ratification, 3, 538
Rearrest rates (RR), 72–73
Reasonable care, 464
Reasonable person standard, 458, 538
Reasonable suspicion, 538
Reasonable victim standard, 459
Reasonable woman standard, 458–461
Rebuttable presumption, 370, 538–539
Receiver operating curve (ROC), 59
Recidivism, 539
    Family Group Conference (FGC) and, 280
    insanity defense and, 203
    juvenile court and, 251, 254–255
Recklessness, 188
Reconstruction of events, 164
Recovered memory, 522–526
Recriminalization of delinquency
    adolescent immaturity and, 262–266
    historical roots of, 259–260
    juvenile convictions and, 266–267
    reduction via recriminalization, 268–269
    transfer laws and, 260–262, 267–268

Referendum, 484, 539
Regulation, 539
    definition, 507
    government, 508–512
Rehabilitation, 222–223, 266
Relative inaccuracy of predictions of dangerousness, 63
Release on one's own recognizance, 70–72, 536
Reliability, 96
    eyewitness experts and, 175–176
    mental illness diagnosis and, 208
    of single eyewitness, 165
Religion. *see also* Bible
    child custody and, 398
    death penalty and, 223–224, 227
    and dropping IPV charges, 360
    jurisprudence and, 29
    pregnancy choices and, 437
Relocation and child custody, 398–400
Remand, 41
On remand, 536
Repeat players, 135
Representation of oneself, 102–103
Repressed memory, 46, 519
Research
    abortion cases and, 429–431, 438
    child witnesses and, 336–338
    and discipline of psychology, 45–46
    divorce and, 383–384
    effects of malpractice suits on, 525
    eyewitness accuracy and, 169
    false confessions and, 164
    on gay parents, 394–395
    policy change and, 64
Research paradigms, 169
Respondent, 16, 539
Restorative justice theory, 275
Restraining order, 536. *see also* Orders of protection
Retest reliability, 96
Retribution, 223–224
Reversals, 20
Reverse waiver, 539
Rex v. Arnold, 190
Riggins v. Nevada, 100–101, 112
Right of confrontation, 127, 539
Right to jury trial, 130
Right to privacy, 422–424
Right-duty relationship, 513
Rights, 539
Ring v. Arizona, 237–238
Risk assessment, 52, 54, 59–64
    child abuse and, 298
    death penalty and, 226
    IPV and, 351
Risk management, 61–63, 307
    court appearance and, 72
Roe v. Wade, 9, 20
    instigation of, 423–424
    limitations of privacy right and, 425–426
    prior to, 421–422
Romper Room, 421–422
Roper v. Simmons, 49, 244, 264
Rule of thumb, 343
Rumsfeld v. Forum, 5
Rust v. Sullivan, 9